TOWARDS A RATIONAL
PHILOSOPHICAL ANTHROPOLOGY

About the author: Joseph Agassi, M.Sc., physics, Hebrew University of Jerusalem, Ph.D., logic and scientific method, University of London, formerly assistant and leading disciple of Sir Karl Popper, has taught in London, Hong Kong, the U.S., and his native Israel; he lectured extensively in many countries; has up to 200 publications in the learned press and a few books; now holds a dual appointment in Boston University and Tel-Aviv University. He is a corresponding member of the International Academy for the Philosophy of Science.

THE VAN LEER JERUSALEM FOUNDATION SERIES

TOWARDS A RATIONAL
PHILOSOPHICAL ANTHROPOLOGY

by

JOSEPH AGASSI

MARTINUS NIJHOFF / THE HAGUE / 1977

ISBN 90 247 2003 6

SET IN ISRAEL BY ISRATYPESET, JERUSALEM

PRINTED IN THE NETHERLANDS

Preface

The thesis of the present volume is critical and dual. (1) Present day philosophy of man and sciences of man suffer from the Greek mistaken polarization of everything human into nature and convention which is (allegedly) good and evil, which is (allegedly) truth and falsity, which is (allegedly) rationality and irrationality, to wit, the polarization of all fields of inquiry, the natural and social sciences, as well as ethics and all technology, whether natural or social, into the totally positive and the totally negative. (2) Almost all philosophy and sciences of man share the erroneous work ethic which is the myth of man's evil nature — the myth of the beast in man, the doctrine of original sin. To mediate or to compromise between the first view of human nature as good with the second view of it as evil, sociologists have devised a modified utilitarianism with deferred gratification so-called, and the theory of the evil of artificial competition (capitalist and socialist alike) and of keeping up with the Joneses. Now, the mediation is not necessary. For, the polarization makes for abstract errors which are simplistic views of rationality, such as reductionism and positivism of all sorts, as well as for concrete errors, such as the disposition to condemn repeatedly those human weaknesses which are inevitable, namely man's inability to be perfectly rational, avoid all error, etc., thus setting man against himself as all too wicked. Be it as it may, I propose that the Greek dichotomy between nature and convention was powerful stuff that offered a challenging extremist framework for the philosophy and the sciences of man, yet one which has outlived its usefulness; in the distant past it was challenging but in the recent past it became increasingly a hindrance: it helped suppress or confuse efforts to develop an alternative to it or challenging scientific theories that do not fall well within its confines. Strangely, it is now possible to argue that a more moderate framework than the Greek polarization of everthing into nature and convention may be by far the more challenging one. A more moderate framework will enable us to develop both a better philosophy and a better science of man – to develop a better image of man. Only if we dispose of the Greek dichotomy will the road be cleared for a more moderate yet more rational picture of man as only partly rational, hopefully more at peace with himself, his partial rationality, and his partial democracy; as partly rational, but progressing – both in his education and in his ability to resolve conflicts. In brief, the chief aim of the present study is to attack the no longer so very important yet still too prevalent all-or-nothing attitude in philosophy and to offer some rudiments of an outline of a substitute to it in the theory that takes certain un-polarized human qualities as central, such as the limited (but) human dignity, suffering, understanding, and struggle.

The following five chapters evolved out of three lectures delivered (in Hebrew) at the Van Leer Jerusalem Foundation in May 1971, and one lecture delivered at the Boston Colloquium for the Philosophy of Science, Boston University, in October 1972. The first chapter is an expansion of the first lecture delivered in Jerusalem; the second chapter is an expansion of the Boston lecture and more so of points raised in the ensuing discussion; the third chapter expands the second Jerusalem lecture; the fourth and fifth chapters, the last Jerusalem lecture. I do not know why this has happened, or how the neat and orderly ascent exhibited in the table of contents – much too orderly, to my taste – has come into being. Perhaps I just repressed the obvious until it hit me in the face.

My gratitude is, first and foremost, to Dr. Yehuda Elkana of the Hebrew University of Jerusalem, director of the Van Leer Jerusalem Foundation; he invited me to deliver the lectures, took generous care of all the technicalities involved, and invited me to submit the final version plus notes (of which more in the introduction) for publication. I am deeply indebted, also, to admirable Miriam Balaban, editor of the same Foundation for her help in day to day matters, as well as for her patience and constant encouragement. And I am indebted to the Van Leer Jerusalem Foundation and to Esther Shashar, now executive editor of the Foundation for the technical assistance which went into the production of this work. Also, my gratitude to Professor Robert S. Cohen of Boston University, Chairman of the Boston Colloquium for the Philosophy of Science, who advised me on the final composition of this work. My gratitude, also, to Professors Edward Davenport and John Wettersten who read the penultimate version and made valuable comments. The indices were prepared by Charles M. Sawyer, Eva Alkon Katz and myself. I much appreciate their help.

Of all the people from whose conversations and exchange I have profited, I hope, in the writing of this work, I can only mention the few with whom I had lengthy exchanges which I feel have left a broad and deep impression on me. These are Judith Buber Agassi, Robert S. Cohen, Shmuel Ettinger, Ernest Gellner, Edward Goodman, Daniel Greenberg, Berek Gross, Ian C. Jarvie, Kurt Klappholz, and J.O. Wisdom. I cannot adequately acknowledge my debt to them.

Any debt to the giants of our tradition cannot, of course, be expressed except in an intellectual history. I have tried to do some justice in the present work to our intellectual history, but I am all too aware of my deficiency in this respect. I hope, however, that the pervasive influence of Spinoza, Marx, Freud, and Russell will be noted by the connoisseurs; but the most immediate and direct influence on me is, of course, that of my teacher, Sir Karl Popper, whose methodology as well as social philosophy I take as points of departure.

Herzliah, Israel, Summer 1974
Sudsbury, Mass., U.S.A., Winter 1975

TABLE OF CONTENTS

Introduction: Against the Elitism of Excessive Scholarship

Many studies, especially those of ambitious nature, suffer from excessive annotation and documentation. They exhibit too much scholarship. The social function of such exhibition is to intimidate and thus discourage the uninitiate from publishing, especially ambitious works.[1] Here I wish to discuss this function, explain my displeasure with it, and help the ambitious reader to beat the system by offering a quick and easy method of simulating the scholarly stance.

The annotation and documentation of this volume seem to me quite redundant, and certainly suffering from excess. I have undertaken it at the insistence of Dr. Elkana, who has invited me to give the lectures on which this work is based and to submit the work for publication. I therefore feel that, first of all, I owe it to the reader to explain my conduct, since I do not wish to place the responsibility for my actions anywhere else than with me.

This is not the first time that I publish a heavily documented and annotated text, and, as before, I do it with mixed feelings. The purpose of documentation and annotation is to aid the specialist reader who wishes to pursue a point further than the intended reader. For the latter, parsimony may be essential: a reader flooded with references will not easily know which to pursue. Sometimes, indeed, a crucial debt is expressed in a reference hidden in a mass of scholarly ones. The concealed purpose of heavy documentation and annotation is not so much, in my opinion, to help or confuse the judicious reader (specialists do not generally need help and they see through the confusions when they want to) as to browbeat the less judicious one. This observation is a bit unkind, perhaps, since it is the "lay" reader who usually asks for documentation. That is to say, because readers are less independently minded than they might profitably be, they wish to be challenged as little as possible, and they can achieve that by putting a premium on challenge — such as high level of scholarship. Quite a few papers are rejected, let me observe, though admittedly stimulating, on the ground that they are "not sufficiently well documented". All I have gained from having published extensive documentations and annotations is that my calling these grapes of scholarship sour is ascribed by popular gossip not to any inability to attain them but to some regrettable anarchistic strain in my character.

I acknowledge that heavy documentation and annotation has some limited merit: it imposes discipline on its author, it affords him the opportunity to spend enjoyable time in a library, perhaps it makes him check and eliminate some of his worst errors, perhaps also express his personality in the peculiar medium of references and notes (which few have thus far exploited). But the wood gets all too often lost for the trees, the average reader gets bullied, the average student and scholar get intimidated. In such cases, though not always, in my deep sympathy for their unnecessary suffering, I consider excessive footnoting an evil.

The evil, to repeat, is that of intimidation. This may be located either in the act of the intimidator or in the weakness of the intimidated. It seems more reasonable — though it is not — rather to block the act of intimidation than to eliminate the weakness, the disposition to be intimidated. For, it is claimed, eliminating the weakness would require an arduous process of reeducation and self-education. And so, in the interests of the intimidated, intimidators are allegedly blocked by the existing elaborate machinery of refereeing and reviewing all scholarly and scientific publications which is supposed to eliminate all sorts of undesirable developments. This blocking acts as a sort of censorship. Censorship is usually very counterproductive. Thus, as I observe, censors in fact encourage rather than discourage intimidation: censorship does not prevent authors from intimidating their readers, but rather it enables editors to intimidate authors and even force authors to intimidate their readers. But my opposition to censorship is more of a matter of principle: it is wrong for anyone other than the author, journal editor, or publisher, to take their responsibility for their part in the publication. It is an excellent rule that the only persons who should be responsible for publication of anything whatsoever are those specifiable by the law of the land (I restrict myself here to the laws of democracies[2]) to be responsible for what they actually do. If anyone, in particular, feels like publishing an intimidating essay or tract, he should surely be free to do so. And we should be free to torpedo the attempt at intimidation — by exposing his techniques as sham.

It is all too easy to appear much more of a scholar than one is, provided one is not awed by scholarship. A drop of scholarship about the history of scholarship is the best remedy against the malady of excessive respect for scholarship. From time immemorial, the scholar was one who primarily read. If he had to write, he was often gratified by expressing himself in a brief marginal note in the book he read. Since the malady of excessive awe to scholars was prevalent amongst scribes, marginal notes often got interpolated. This led scholars to make their notes obviously scholarly, their notes often consisting of documentation or of a mere scholarly hint, such as, "compare this text with . . ." The commentaries — Hellenistic and medieval — which started as one man's documentations and annotations of another man's book, soon developed independently, especially when more than one author was so treated, and notes appeared as strings of scholarly pearls. Naturally, first came the pearls, then the technique of stringing them, especially when the printing press came and made publication a major decision. Stringing was the hardest, for it all too often betrayed inevitable lacunae in scholarship; authors delayed publication — they still do — until they could consult a few more authors on this or that subtopic, or until they died and their colleagues, executors, or heirs made for them the decision to publish or not to publish. This is what I.C. Jarvie has christened as thoroughness mentality. This mentality suited well times of veneration of the written word, especially when it came in fits and starts, when commentaries were meant to restore the original word and its sanctity. Even today there are still writers, good, bad, and indifferent, who dare not express themselves, or do not wish to, except by presenting such strings of scholarship, and who hesitate to publish the strings unless they appear with no gap and bear testimonies to their authors' omniscience. Other writers prefer to write their own smooth text and add a string of pearls to support them as marginal notes, much in the style emulated here. Texts without scholarship, I am repeatedly told, and emphatically so, are dismissed out of hand. All counterexamples to this are declared special cases — and with much justice: scholarship or no scholarship, any volume not dismissed out of hand is, *eo ipso,* a special case.

There is one simple method of deception, among many, which I have found regularly practiced by some of the best scholars around; I do not know why. When they say something that they cannot document they surround it by things they can heavily document. I usually

find out what they wish to say by finding the most heavily documented pages of their books and reading the undocumented sentences
in these very pages. I do not know why this method of deception is
practiced, except that the author who uses it may feel that he is doing
something wrong which he should conceal. The something wrong here
would be an unsupported claim; the code by which it is wrong is
inductivism, the code which perpetuates the archaic thoroughness
mentality.

Inductivism, more precisely, is two conflicting codes. One says, to
be any good a theory must emerge from facts through a long process
of hard study. The other says, a good theory may come first but it
should be supported by facts all the same, as if it emerged from them.
These two ways of seeing inductivism are what causes the trouble. One
who gives up the first and endorses the second can easily comply by
the inductive standard. The father of modern inductivism, Sir Francis
Bacon, already noted this and fumed against it: he said that those who
first speculate and then look for support usually distort the facts to fit
their views. I am unimpressed: we all distort facts to some extent, and
those of us who are sufficiently flexible often prefer to alter their
views, contrary to Bacon's observation that people never do. He was
clever but too suspicious; partly because he was no scholar and had no
experience of the joy of liberation from mistakes.[3]

For my part, I suggest, if ever you decide to write, that you write
first and read afterwards; you will find it much easier and much more
enjoyable. Abandon entirely the old mode of the commentator, and
when you write, make your writing your central activity, not your
reading. Let your imagination run wild and serve you as a source of
information. Read after you write, in order to check what you wrote.
Reading may then show you in error. You can then correct your manuscript either by erasing the error and replacing it with its better alternative, or keep the error there as a step in the development of the
views that you present to your reader. When it is of interest, I recommend retaining the old error (as an error, of course) and adding the
correction. One way or another this will give you ample opportunity
to document and annotate too, if you wish. And do not worry if not
every page is documented, or else annotate without any documentation. For my part, I recommend giving the notes something of an
artistic coherence, a peculiar style and a leitmotif or two. But this goes
above and beyond the standard requirement. (I still recommend it,
though: it is much fun.)

I have aired these suggestions with various scholars. Some were
shocked, like government lawyers who were shown a new and huge

loophole in the income-tax laws.[4] Others said: you can do it, do it! — meaning, not many are as clever as you in finding and utilizing the loophole, thank God. They are thus still concerned with limiting the number of writers. Let me, therefore, discuss why.

There is, no doubt, a horror in face of the flood of publications. Philosophers like Polanyi[5] and Popper[6] agree on one point: something ought to be done here. They fear, of course, trite publications; but the fear of significant ones is much more widespread. Coming to think of it, the two fears amount to the same. In the wake of Michael Polanyi, indeed, Thomas S. Kuhn[7] has propagated the vulgar doctrine of the paradigm which says that all members of the scientific clan must emulate one paradigm, or else chaos will reign. (That is to say, even a significant work is of no avail in the state of chaos.)[8] This claim is both untrue and pernicious, and I wish to expose the fears underlying the fear of much significant work being published. One fear is, obviously, that diverse significant writers will disagree, thus forcing the little man to make up his own mind as to whom to follow. The other fear is that he will not even have the time to read all of them. So the fear is that of being left out in the cold. It is, in brief, a herd philosophy. For, no one says, I wish all eligible bachelors except 100 or so were somehow ineligible so I could properly choose a spouse; but they do say, as Kuhn recommends, I wish there were very few competing leaders. And this is the true cause of much intimidation that goes on under the guise of the demand for excessive scholarship.[9]

The restrictive character which extensive documentation and annotation and empirical checking often have, is not only a matter of restrictive intentions. The lack of consideration for the reader alone may make the annotation messy and expressive of an author's unpleasant self-centeredness. The author may then quote an authority in order to show his independence of it, in a sort of priority claim. Claims for priority go well with intense scholarship for many reasons which are so transparent that one might wonder how scholars with so much learning and insight miss the point; trying to impress the reader favorably, they achieve the opposite.

I recommend, in opposition to this, that authors consciously develop an atmosphere which they find congenial and which emanates from their notes and compensates the reader for his effort, by pleasing him. In particular I recommend that the references be made not only to a narrow compass of scholarly work. Accordingly, I have referred to science fiction. Social scientists have now begun using literature as a quarry for scholarly exercises; but they use only fossilized material, which has otherwise ceased to be living literature.

Let me explain the ideology behind science fiction and how I intend to use it.

A convenient starting point may well be Lord Snow's celebrated *The Two Cultures*. It may be remembered that he noticed in the very beginning of his lecture that social scientists may be in between the two cultures, between the artists and the scientists. But he felt they rather split into the two groups. In that lecture, and more so in its follow-up (they are published together), the two cultures are characterized by two qualities: tools and politics. The tools are divided into software and hardware; the politics into reactionary and progressive. The software are books and pictures and fantasy; they belong, says Snow, to the reactionaries; the hardware are experiments and field-work and mathematics and such; they belong, says Snow, to the progressives. All this is so pitifully Baconian — inductivist, and old-fashioned at that — that all one needs to do is draw the readers' attention to it.[10]

Snow himself notes in his second lecture, that his thesis really boils down to the claim that scientists are temperamentally progressive and that artists are not. He notes that Dostoevsky was a reactionary, though a humane and wise one: he really does not wish to put down the artists when he says that they are temperamentally reactionary. Now Snow also notices the existence of some progressive writers, whether novelists or poets; he does not in the least feel that this refutes his thesis — on the contrary, it only shows that artists can fight their temperament quite successfully, or perhaps even change it.

Snow's position puzzles me. It may indeed be the case that artists, especially novelists and poets, are reactionaries; perhaps the existence of an odd progressive writer is indeed neither here nor there. But by Snow's own light, the progressivist literature about science, as well as science fiction literature, should spell both progressivism and the hope for a better future.[11] It is the irony of history that the most reactionary and rearguard among the leading science fiction writers, Robert Heinlein, has endorsed Snow's view in order to conclude that science fiction is the only progressive and the only avant-garde literature today.[12] This indicates that we should try to state what is progressive in science fiction literature (it is almost never avant-garde, of course).

The most widespread aspiration (utopian or not)[13] of progressive science fiction writers is to get rid of the common man: he is banished, discouraged, killed, or he improves.[14] The common man today is forced to play robot, as many a stag or a cock is forced to play eunuch; and we do not need to robotize humans any longer. Science fiction, be it art, popular art, or mere trash, is moved, to a large extent, by a dream, a dream of a free man who follows no leader and needs no servant.[15] Such a man does not fear excessive creativity, and he does not feel obligated to take notice of every worthwhile creation either. Progressive science fiction rests on the maxim, live and let live; or rather, expand and let others expand: expansion is joy, learning is exploration, is adventure.

The need for drudgery is gone. The work ethic is still with us.[16] It makes us feel guilty if we are not on top of things, up-to-date, *au courant*. And to keep on top of things we have to work so hard that we resent those who add to the stock of things to be on top of. Work ethic is understandably misanthropic and illiberal: it opposes the idea of letting others expand at their own pace, at their own risk.

The incredulous reader may ask, how the work ethic causes preventing others from expanding. The answer is involved. First, if you expand I have more work to learn what you have achieved, and so you better expand slowly or I will be unable to catch up with the explosion of knowledge. Second, work ethic leads to the inductivist theory that learning is the process of hard work and slow expansion: your exploration, then, is not a knowledge-expansion, since it is adventurous; it is fun, but also it is the neglect of your duty to spend long tiring hours on the bench, at the microscope and in the library.

Thus inductivism and work ethic cooperate,[17] and their corollary is that you should write tedious notes rather than an adventure of ideas. I find this corollary objectionable and harmful. Let those who wish to write tedious notes, or not so tedious notes, do as they please; and let the adventurous minds do as they please too. For my part, I like intellectual adventure more than scholarly annotation. And I wish to point out that adventure is tolerated by free spirits and is opposed to in the name of scholarship by the timid. It is not enough to live in a world where human robots are redundant: we have also to combat the imposition of the thoroughness mentality which perpetuates the ethos of the human robot.[18]

The reader may, then, consider it paradoxical that the notes in this volume are a concession to the ethos which they combat. Be it so. The first two chapters include an attempt to expose the work ethic as the outcome of the inductivist fear of error, a fear that sounds like the basis of true science, and that, true to itself, presents man as a robot operated on by threats. In the third chapter I expose this fear as rooted in mythology, the mythology which polarizes truth and error, reality and appearance, nature and culture. In the last two chapters I expound the idea of a free adjustable man who freely interacts with his society. I thus expose the conflict between the individual and society as a mythological polarization: not that the conflict does not exist, but that it cannot be the cornerstone of the philosophy of the social sciences as it hitherto was. Man is by nature, many would agree as a matter of course, a self-liberating social animal, a problem-solver and a conflict-resolver. Yet the self-same people who accept this as a matter of course also contradict it as a matter of course, at times by declaring that naturally man is born free, and at times by declaring that naturally man is born into society and so is irrevocably limited by it. This should be better noted: the theories that man is born free, or born into society, are parts of one myth, and one that conflicts with the view that man is, and should be, self-liberating.[18]

My deepest concern, then, is in self-liberation. And I wish to make the following the most central pragmatic corollary of my study. Regrettably, people who could succeed in this process but fail due to failure of their nerve, have the urge to discourage others — perhaps in order to prove the generality of the failure of nerve. People with any aspiration whatever, need to hear others' responses; they should, however, take care not to consult discouraging pedants. Moreover, we can alter institutionally the response pattern of such people and make them seek redemption by encouraging others. The world will be a much better place to live in if today's systematic discouragement for its own sake — in the world of learning or in the artistic world or anywhere else — will be curbed.[19]

Notes

1. The study of the function of excessive scholarship in the form of exegesis and pedantry can be found in the first chapter, on decidophobia, of Walter Kaufmann's delightful *Without Guilt and Justice, From Decidophobia to Autonomy*, Wyden, New York, 1973, where the annotation and references are presented in a particularly elegant and greatly commendable method.

2. It is no doubt the law of land that certain publications need documentation. Quite generally, and without entering any legal technicalities, in some countries the publication of information harmful to others — whether individuals or parties — must be accompanied by evidence of a certain sort. The law does not demand the evidence to be conclusive, but the testing of it to be of certain kinds and the results of the test sufficiently supportive by certain well-set criteria.

    When I discuss the alleged need for support, I do not discuss matters covered by such laws. Rather, I discuss the fact that scientists and scholars can always publish information that they cannot support as mere conjectures. Yet the inductive code which many scientists endorse forbids the publishing of conjectures, especially on informative matters. And I am arguing against them.

3. Bacon's view that publicly committed intellectuals cannot change their views was confirmed by the bitter struggle the phlogistonists put against the anti-phlogistonists and refuted by the acceptance of the refutation of Newtonian optics in 1818. Even Laplace gracefully gave way though Davy reports it cost him dearly and changed his character.

The idea that the revolution in optics refuted Bacon belongs to William Whewell who responded to Sir John Herschel's dogmatic adherence to Baconianism. Yet a Baconian view of the revolution in optics was soon modified in a convincing manner, and the modified version was soon made popular, and vulgarized, I think, by S.P. Langley, Florian Cajori, Dampier-Whetham, Max Planck, and Thomas S. Kuhn. The neo-Baconian view is this: the publicly committed intellectuals do not change their views; they simply die out and leave the field to younger, less prejudiced minds. To this Martin Buber answered (*Israel and the World*, "Prejudices of Youth", p. 42) that young people's opinions are less well-founded than those of older people and so are more likely to be prejudices — in Bacon's own sense (though Buber does not discuss the nature of prejudice; which is a pity).

All this is discussed at some length in my *Towards An Historiography of Science, History and Theory,* Beiheft 2, 1963, facsimile reprint Wesleyan University Press, Middletown, Conn., 1967, sections 1 and 12 in particular, and my "Revolutions in Science, Occasional or Permanent?" *Organon,* Vol. 3, 1966, pp. 47–61. See also my "Science in Flux: Footnotes to Popper", in R.S. Cohen and M.W. Wartofsky, eds., *Boston Studies in the Philosophy of Science,* Reidel and Humanities, Dordrecht and New York, 1968, pp. 293–323, reprinted in my *Science in Flux,* Reidel, Dordrecht, 1975; my "Continuity and Discontinuity in the History of Science", *J. Hist. Ideas,* Vol. 34, 1973, pp. 609–626, especially section 1, The Radicalist View of Science and Its History; and my "Sir John Herschel's Philosophy of Success", in Russel McCormmach, ed., *Historical Studies in the Physical Sciences*, Vol. 1, University of Pennsylvania Press, 1969, pp. 1–36.

4. There are further, and very specialized, functions of a detailed annotation. The most delicate operation for the annotation of an avant-garde text is that of dispensing with the kind of pig-headed objections to the ideas an author develops which only high-powered and erudite scholars can have and usually do have. Such notes enable their author to display erudition and competence equal to theirs, so as to show they need not be ashamed to learn something from him in case he has something new to say. Thus, he can dispel the difficulties which only learned readers can have by discussing highly critically and in an erudite fashion some of their sacred cows — but this is effective only if the author can slaughter the cow in one single sure hit or blow or slash; he better check this with pig-headed scholars, and not lose his patience while doing so (easier said than done). Finally, in his notes an author can correlate earlier and later parts of his study, thereby not only offering further connections, but also an anticipation and thus a quick entry to his world of ideas and its ways, particularly by the impatient pig-headed scholar.

All this is considering the possibility of winning the pig-headed high-powered reader. Now this is not easily describable by any given rules since the pig-headed

high-powered reader is at times the doorman of the scientific elite club who has
his own ideas about whom to approve of and why. Yet, just because he is the
doorman, winning him may open many doors. I am speaking from personal experience, and all I can add is that these doormen can be real bastards who would just
as easily close a door in your face because they compete, or think they compete,
with you in some quite extra-intellectual domain. Also, these pig-headed high-
powered bastards often read only notes and then blame the author for what they
think he says in his text — especially when they have their own reasons, as
mentioned. Now whenever a work is ambitious, especially ambitious in its very
scholarship, it may well invite hostility for the very extra-intellectual quality of
being too ambitious. — Note, here, that excessive scholarship is treated by the
scholarly doorman as extra-scholarly; and quite rightly. — And when someone
picks on you concerning a very subtle scholarly point, there will be no more than
a handful of people the world over who will be willing and able to pronounce on
such a point when it does not involve them in a quarrel, and perhaps none when it
does. Hence annotation may, indeed, be a risky business. The best is to outlive
these bastards (easier said than done) and see their private empires crumble or
taken over by who knows whom.

5. Michael Polanyi, *Logic of Liberty*, London, 1951, recommends academic freedom, quite unqualified, including, p. 33, the freedom "to teach one's subject in
the light of one's own opinion". This freedom he denies quite explicitly in his
Knowing and Being, University of Chicago Press, Chicago and London, 1969, p. 94,
and recommends in addition censorship in the learned press, p. 93. He himself
feels that all this can be misused, pp. 94–5. See also note 8 to this introduction.
   A similar argument is used by Leszek Kolakowsky in defence of censorship at
large, in his *Essays on Catholic Philosophy*, Warsaw, 1955, which I have been
unable to see. Leopold Labedz quotes the salient passage on p. 73 of his "Leszek
Kolakowsky: or, Ethics and Communism", *Soviet Survey*, No. 23, January–March
1958, pp. 71–8:

   "Just as every American gangster can practice his profession *ad lib.*, if only he
   has enough money to pay the judges and police, so every intellectual gangster
   can bamboozle his readers if only he has enough money to publish his products ... In the socialist countries the scientist and philosopher must be responsible to the reader, and there is no freedom to cheat the people with the
   output of the morbid minds of any street charlatan ..."

   The sad fact is that in his *Logic of Liberty* and other early works Polanyi
indefatigably argued against planned science, saying science must be free and for
this it needs a free society. Now, it turns out, he thinks science should be planned,
though by its own leadership rather than the leadership of the community at
large. And for this, indeed, society at large needs to be democratic indeed. Kolakowsky does not ask, what happens when the leadership is in error, whom is it
responsible to? Polanyi says, in his *Personal Knowledge* and elsewhere, that the
acceptance of the authority of the leadership of science is voluntary. This is

seemingly liberal, except that, by definition, it makes the dissenters outsiders until and unless they win, and so it is liberal, if at all, only in a free society.

6. Sir Karl Popper goes a step further than Polanyi. He requires that the censorship be not only voluntary but also self-imposed. He wants the restrictions internalized, and by means of the Hippocratic oath, which he recommends that every scientist take (this recommendation was made by a few authors after Hiroshima). And so he writes on p. 52 of his "The Moral Responsibility of the Scientist", *Encounter*, Vol. 32, No. 3, March 1967, pp. 52–7, that "the establishment of high standards to judge our work by, and the duty to constantly raise these standards by hard work, are indispensable". Popper opposes censorship but requires that we accept the maxim *sagesse oblige* akin to *noblesse oblige*. Now what *noblesse* should *oblige* may be controversial, but less than what *sagesse* should. In particular, whether *sagesse*, just as much as whether *noblesse*, is an excuse for snobbism, standoffishness, elitism, or not, is surely debatable. I, for one, find the scientific elitism the worst kind, and find Popper's exhortation a force pushing in that direction, no less objectionable than Polanyi's. See also Popper's "Autobiography", sections 10 and 12, in P.A. Schilpp, *The Philosophy of Karl Popper*, La Salle, Ill., 1974.

7. Thomas S. Kuhn, "The Function of Dogma in Scientific Research", in A.C. Crombie, ed., *Scientific Change*, London, 1963, pp. 347–369, and 386–395.
See in particular, on pp. 392–3 his use of Polanyi's idea of tacit knowledge to justify his avoidance of terms like "intellectual framework", "conceptual model", "basic assumptions" and "methodological rules"; he identifies his "finger-exercise" or "practice-problem-solving" or even "paradigm" with Polanyi's "tacit knowledge". See also next note.

8. The view that diversity leads to anarchy is the most gripping of conservative ideas, especially in politics, especially in Communist countries. See my "Methodological Individualism", *British J. Soc.*, Vol. 11, 1960, pp. 244–270, reprinted in John O'Neill, *Modes of Individualism and Collectivism*, Heinemann, London, 1973. See also my "Institutional Individualism", in the same journal, Vol. 26, 1975, pp. 144–155.
Polanyi explicitly warns against diversity: "The continued pursuit of science would break down" he pronounces, *Knowing and Being*, University of Chicago Press, Chicago and London, 1969, p. 80, "if scientists came widely to disagree about the nature of things."
The same holds for Thomas S. Kuhn, of course, who expresses the need for dogmatism in the essay cited in the previous note and in his contributions to I. Lakatos and A. Musgrave, eds., *Criticism and the Growth of Knowledge*, Cambridge, 1971. See also my review of that volume, "Tristram Shandy, Pierre Menard and all that", in *Inquiry*, Vol. 14, 1971, pp. 152–164, where I discuss in detail the censorship within science. I should add here that the popularity of the views of Kuhn reflects the herd-like character of the world of learning, much in

confirmation of his view. See Kaufmann on decidophobia, mentioned in note 1 above.

I wish to express my agreement with Paul Feyerabend's analysis of the anti-diversity dogmatism of Polanyi and Kuhn, which he labels fancily as Kuhn's principle of tenacity. His analysis is sociological and he views all this as a variant of the vastly popular method of brainwashing. See Paul Feyerabend, "Science, Freedom, and the Good Life", *Philosophical Forum*, Vol. 1, No. 2, Winter 1968, pp. 127–135.

An example, and a notable and detailed one is Robert Cogan, reporting on the fact that he could not get a novel work on music theory published, in his remarkable paper, "Teaching Music Theory: The Conservatory", in *J. Music Theory*, Vol. 18, No. 1, Spring 1974, pp. 59–73, p. 71:

> "It is axiomatic that human beings and institutions ... are often conservative ... yet ... we have found agreement and support ... The most backward force on the theoretical teaching scene, however, is publishing. What is taught, and how, is all too often determined by publishers and editors. Inordinate power to control the availability of ideas is theirs. Their decisions have long rendered unavailable to faculty and students ... Their habitual preference has been for second-rate dilution over the authentic theoretical, pedagogical masterpiece ... In the land of academic freedom the publishing industry has acted as an invisible, unaccountable censor. Decisions are made on the basis of mass marketing, as well as out of vested interests ..."

Let me add three points. First, the censorship phenomenon in university teaching: my studies corroborate Cogan's: both inside and outside information agree on this point. Second, the market mechanism: it does not work in publishing due to an almost total lack of competition: there is almost no free entry since the market is a giant (publishing privately, which is relatively easy, must fail, since authors cannot distribute; publishers decide not to distribute books they publish thus killing them, etc. — very much like in the movie industry). Third, there is the vested interest of the ignorant professor who wishes to remain on top and so resist radical change (see my "Revolutions in Science, Occasional or Permanent?" mentioned in note 3 above). But the major reactionary force is the fear of the flood of publications as expressed by Polanyi and Popper and quoted in notes 5 and 6 above. See also my *Functions of Intellectual Rubbish*, forthcoming.

9. The solution to the problem of the flood of publication seems to be in the opposite direction, as Willard F. Libby says in his "Man's Place in the Physical Universe", in John R. Platt, ed., *New Views of the Nature of Man, The Monday Lectures*, 1965, University of Chicago Press, Chicago and London, 1965, pp. 1–15, pp. 11ff.:

> "In particular, the language barrier must go down, and we must be able to publish in a matter of days instead of months, and these publications must be available to all — in a kind of scientific newspaper. We get a glimpse of how this can be managed if we think of the rapid copying machines and the effect they have on our handling of information."

Indeed, he says, putting a television to a microfilm reading machine would already do this, and it is only a matter of cost. I think it is not even a matter of cost. Consider the fact that in the seventeenth to twentieth centuries publishing a paper or a book was a matter of months at most, whereas nowadays it is a year at least for learned works — I had a paper delayed in *Mind* for four years! — and to extrapolate this, given the increase in publication pressure, is mind-boggling. The pressure can be relieved (a) by the building of a central storage of microfilms with a telecommunication system connecting it to all university and public libraries, plus (b) the rule that any material entered to the central storage's catalogue is a proper learned publication.

Clifton Burke, *Printing It,* Ballantine Books, New York, 1972, describes the exuberance of overpublication, mainly by student bodies of all sorts and other poor institutions during the political ferment in San Francisco, and the breakthroughs it brought with it in reconsideration of printing and publishing techniques. It is almost as if to show that the very problem of overpublication in the academic press, coming from quarters and people with nothing much to say, is hardly worth considering: when something has got to be said it will be said. But, of course, this is facile and eroneous. With all the printing progress about, I find much important material circulating among publishers and taking years to be printed and years more to gain attention. The remedy then, seems to me that offered by Daniel A. Greenberg: publish just about everything!

10.   A note on Snow and his erstwhile critics. There is little doubt and there is nothing in what is said here to deny that most of Snow's opponents thus far, and F.R. Leavis (*Two Cultures?*, 1962), in particular, only confirm Snow in his view of the spokesmen of the artistic and of cultural establishments as plainly romantic and reactionary. See Ernest Gellner, *The Devil and Modern Philosophy*, Routledge, London, 1974, p. 21. See also M. Polanyi, *Knowing and Being*, University of Chicago Press, Chicago and London, 1969, p. 40.

It might also be noted that the two cultures were described in detail in science fiction of all sorts, from H.G. Wells' *Time Machine* and *Shape of Things to Come* to Asimov's *Caves of Steel* and *The Naked Sun.*

See also my "Beyond Rationalism and Romanticism: Transcending the Two Cultures", to be published in the *Proceedings of the Haifa 1974 Symposium on Ethics in the Age of Pervasive Technology.*

11.   Reformist philosophy of social science has a few expressions. See, however, Isaac Asimov "Social Science Fiction", in R. Breknor, ed., *Modern Science Fiction, its Meaning and its Future*, New York, 1953, pp. 157–176, p. 192:
"I am saying this: it is useless to attempt to solve the tremendous problems of our times by adopting one of only two attitudes. Either to resist change, any change, and hold savagely to the status quo, or to advocate change, a certain change, and no other change. Neither of these views is flexible. Both are static. The result of a collision of such views is almost always disastrous.
I say there must be a third group, one which realizes that there cannot be a

status quo forever, but which also realizes that the exact nature of the change which will best suit the currently changing social and economic forces may not be guessed at very far in advance.

Franklin Delano Roosevelt's New Deal represented such a third group. He broke with the brute capitalism of the twenties, yet did not accept a doctrinaire socialism. Roosevelt frankly and unashamedly experimented. He stated in one of his fireside chats that he liked to try *something*. If it worked, fine; if not, he tried something else.

I cannot help but wonder if a maturely developed sense of social experimentation may not some day bear as much fruit for society as physical experimentation has done for science.

Certainly, there is a good deal of this notion in science fiction. Its authors, as a matter of course, present their readers with new societies, with possible futures and consequences. It is social experimentation on paper; social guesses plucked out of air."

12. For Robert A. Heinlein's vulgar version of Snow's *Two Cultures* see Basil Davenport et al., *The Science Fiction Novel, Imagination and Social Criticism*, Advent, Chicago, 1959, 1969. Heinlein's essay is called "Science Fiction: its Nature, Faults, and Virtues" (pp. 17–63). His conclusion is remarkable (pp. 61–2).

". . . all science fiction prepares young people. . . leads in the direction of mental health, of adaptability . . . preaches the need for freedom of the mind and the desirability of knowledge. . . . We can expect it slowly to increase in amount and in quality . . . as directed primarily at the superior young person and secondarily at his thoughtful elder . . . serious and mature literature . . .

. . . I do expect to see some decrease in the neurotic and psychotic fiction now being palmed off as "serious literature". . . . In the meantime, to the extent that science fiction influences its readers towards greater knowledge, more independence of thought, and wider intellectual horizons, it serves its prime function."

13. For the utopian character of science fiction see, for example Isaac Asimov, "The Magic Society", *Boston University Graduate Journal,* Vol. 15, No. 9, Winter 1966–7, pp. 9–14. See also Section XXIV below. Chad Walsh, *From Utopia to Nightmare,* Harper & Row, New York and Evanston, 1962, p. 164, notices, very astutely, I think, that most utopias are ruled by élites whereas most anti-utopias are not utterly hopeless just because of a "saving remnant" which is an inverted élite, and that thus, both kinds are antidemocratic. (He adds, p. 172, less astutely, I think, that most utopians are radicalist, whereas most anti-utopians are conservative.) I think most utopians and most anti-utopians are radicalists and progressivists. Of the leading writers, only H.G. Wells was both utopian and anti-utopian, both radicalist and conservative. See also Mark R. Hillegas, *The Future as a Nightmare, H.G. Wells and the Anti-Utopians,* Oxford University Press, New York, 1967. My only doubts about this astute observation is that it is easy to classify any aspirations described literarily in diverse philosophical manners.

To take one example, K.R. Popper identifies all utopianism — radicalist or conservative – as historicist (see his *The Open Society and its Enemies*, Routledge, London, 1945, and many later editions, including Princeton University Press and Harper Torchbooks, and his "Utopia and Violence", reprinted in his *Conjectures and Refutations*, Routledge and Basic Books, London and New York, 1963, 1965). This was contested by Fred Polak (who, however, refrains from naming Popper), in his *The Image of the Future*, translated and abridged by Elise Boulding, Jossey-Bass Inc., San Francisco, Washington, 1973, p. 161. His claim is that the English are Utopians, the Germans are not. It is not a serious argument, yet it is thought-provoking. For my part I cannot see B.F. Skinner's utopian *Walden II* as historicist.

To take another example, on p. 248 Polak describes how the Mannheim-type "unattached intelligentsia" was attracted to totalitarian doctrines of the most brutal kind through frustration and "fatalistic self-contempt" which he ascribes not to deterministic futurism or historicism, but to a loss of an "image of the future." He views them as "drifting intelligentsia" and complains that "intellectuals no longer constitute an élite . . . They too become swallowed up by the masses." I shudder to read such sentiments and such a polarization in a book that professes so much humanism. Even Polak's contempt for universities (p. 249) is apalling though his strictures be just.

To take a third and last example, it is easy to take any rosey science fiction as utopian, just as it is easy to take the philosophy of a writer of bedroom farces to be expressed in his writings. It is a fact, recorded in an excellent paper, Jean Chesneaux "Jules Verne's Image of the United States," in Peter Brooks, ed., *The Child's Part*, Beacon Press, Boston, 1972, pp. 111–127, that Jules Verne systematically described the U.S. as a liberal technological utopia. I seriously doubt that he meant this rather than used it as a handy ploy. Of course, even ploys betray some idea or another, but things cannot always be taken at face value when fiction is concerned. Similarly, some of the most violent inconsistencies, e.g., between Nietzschean and Marxian views, can make for superb fiction, e.g., some of Jack London's.

14. The topic of the destruction of the common man is quite complex. First of all, it should not be confused with catastrophism, ancient or modern, biblical – as divine punishment – or Greek – due to blind fate; nor is it to be confused with mass-murder crime melodrama (usually science fiction by default); nor is it a matter of artistic quality or its absence. But, perhaps the greatest difficulty is to distinguish between utopian and science fiction mass destruction, and between descriptions and prescriptions concerning it.

Let us notice, first, that science fiction is full of stories of the destruction of the common man, at times malevolently at times benevolently (as in Kurt Vonnegut, *Piano Player*, where people suffer from the realization of the redundancy and pointlessness of their lives and are allowed luxurious suicide). I confess that on the whole I think this fact has not drawn the attention it deserves. Even Kingsley Amis' perceptive *New Maps of Hell*, which is a survey of science fiction, does not refer to it.

There is a detailed study of H.G. Wells's story of destruction of our civilization prior to the rise of utopia in Mark R. Hillegas, *The Future as a Nightmare, H.G. Wells and the Anti-Utopians,* Oxford University Press, New York, 1967, Chapter IV, especially p. 63. I confess I find Hillegas too glib on this crucial point. I am also puzzled that works on George Bernard Shaw do not take sufficient notice of his *Back to Methuselah,* final act, where all defective people are "discouraged" and consequently drop dead. In any case, clearly, Wells and Shaw did put the topic on the map. (Of course, not in all Wells's utopias is the elimination of the common man done by liquidation. In *Men like Gods,* eugenics, birth control, and, more than anything else, intensive education, makes every human uncommon. Shaw, too, held similar ideas; see his *Pygmalion* for an example.)

The case of utopianism is not much different. The place of the common man in a utopian society is of much concern to George Kateb in his *Utopia and Its Enemies,* Schocken, New York, 1963, see especially Chapter 5 "Against Guaranteed Abundance" and Chapter 7 "Character in Utopia." In a utopian exaggeration, geration, Kateb suggests, we are apt to encapsule the common man and do him injustice, even knowingly turn him into a robot. The *locus classicus,* I suppose, is G.B. Shaw's preface to his *Major Barbara* where he accuses the revolutionaries of wanting every charwoman to be a princess.

The question is, will a utopian recommend the act of mass destruction so as to achieve his dream? In a famous passage in Plato's *Republic* such an act is actually recommended and, says Popper (*Open Society,* Chapter 9), in all sincerity. Popper's critics say, this is only a thought experiment. Can such disagreements be examined rationally? Obviously, it is hard to respond to critics who declare what is likeable in Plato, Plato's own but what is not likeable the mere flying of a kite, especially since what we like is variable and so not always what is likeable. Yet Plato himself may have stuck to the dialogue form not only on account of its attractive qualities but also on account of these ambiguities. Come to think of it, the ambiguity is shared by almost all utopians who traditionally present their blueprints as parts of some fantasy or another.

This makes it hard to demarcate utopia from science fiction. In rare cases we can say the piece of fiction is not expressive of the author's own views, either because he is a better story teller than a social philosopher or because he can alter his blueprints from story to story or because he advisedly puts his utopia in the very distant future. This would resolve the contradiction between Shaw's *Major Barbara* and his *Back to Methuselah* mentioned in this note. It also allows for Isaac Asimov's experimentalism, note 11 above, and his utopianism, note 13 above. It will also show that Popper's critics have a point when declaring Plato's *Republic* fantasy, yet one which only strengthens Popper's complaints: Plato, he says, was intent on weakening his readers' critical disposition towards his views. Quite generally, the gratification from science fiction derives from an image of society which solves our problems without going into all these things that make readers so impatient when attempting to solve the same problems here and now, and utopianism may be of the same sort, i.e., political self-deception.

This applies to some works, both utopian and science fiction, very well, for example Fred Hoyle's *October the First Is Too Late,* where mass destruction is the result of wickedness, yet also the unexpected gateway to a future utopia. This is substantially the same idea as that of Kant — see next note — who expressed both respect for the common man and the premonition of a catastrophe. It applies less to Plato's *Republic,* and even less to the philosophy of Nietzsche, all of Walter Kaufmann's arguments to the contrary notwithstanding (*Nietzsche: Philosopher, Psychologist, Antichrist,* Princeton University Press, Princeton, N.J., 1950; revised edition paperback, Meridian Books, New York, 1956). In spite of all modifications due to Kaufmann's discussion and to his and others' findings about forgeries, a general idea remains in Nietzsche's writings and is so understood by diverse readers. As George Santayana puts it in his *The German Mind: Philosophical Diagnosis,* Thos-Crowell, New York, 1968, p. 131, "A lover of the beautiful must wish almost all his neighbours out of the way . . . contagious misery spoiled one's joy, freedom, and courage. Disease should not be nursed but cauterised; the world must be made clean. Now there is a sort of love of mankind, a jealous love of what man might be, in this much decried maxim of unmercifulness. Nietzsche rebelled . . . His heart was tender enough, but his imagination was impatient." This is the same sentiment as that which Popper describes as utopian canvas cleaning. (See his *The Open Society and Its Enemies,* Routledge, 1945, and later editions, Chapter 9.)

Yet I must say that it is one thing to envisage a possible future utopia and quite another thing to demand the reduction of the number of the members of the species or of the elimination of certain specimens. We must admit the possibility of a dream which is neither declared a necessary distant future nor used as license for brutality of any sort.

15. For social castration in animal society see note 121 to Section X below. Perhaps the recurrent theme in science fiction of the vanishing of the human robot is the greatest utopian quality of science fiction, save perhaps the brotherhood of mankind, i.e., the dream of the elimination of prejudices against aliens, against others' religions, etc. It is hard to say, because, obviously, from the viewpoint of enlightenment these two dreams are one. The reason that the abolition of the human robot, however, is a great relief but the abolition of prejudice is a mere convenience is that we are torn between respect for the humanity of the human robot and contempt for his voluntary debasing of it. The conflict, of course, is ancient and runs deep. It is, incidentally, quite intriguing that the contrast between Socrates' respect for workers and slaves and Plato's contempt for them is the earliest sign of transformation from Plato's Socratic dialogues to his Platonic ones; the ambivalence is shown in the fairly early *Meno*, where the slave is called boy, yet he knows Pythagoras's theorem and gives a proof of a special case of it. Attitudes to simple people, thus, are the best clues to the Socratic problem.

The best known expression of the ambivalence is Kant's (in the Prussian Academy's edition of his *Works*, Vol. 20, p. 44, quoted in translation by Frederick P. van de Pitte in his *Kant as Philosophical Anthropologist*, Nijhoff, The Hague, 1971, p. 13):

"There was a time when I believed that all this [pursuit of knowledge] constituted the real worth of mankind, and I despised the rabble who know nothing.
Rousseau set me right. This dazzling advantage vanished; I am learning to
honor men, and I would regard myself as of much less use than the common
laborer if I did not believe that this speculation can give value to everything
else to restore the rights of mankind."

Now Kant put the emphasis on the common man and had at once to face the
question of his education — the education of mankind, in fact. For, there are two
stages in education: first, to make man act in enlightened self-interest rather than
confused one, and second, through enlightened self-interest to disinterested respect for the moral law. It is the first stage which Kant finds most bothersome: and
he says of the education of mankind — meaning the first stage — that it will be
wholesome but harsh and severe, and in its process will bring about almost
destruction to the whole human race (van de Pitte, *op. cit.*, p. 105). See also J.
Passmore, *The Perfectability of Man*, Scribner, New York, 1970, pp. 217—20.

It is no accident, then, that the vanishing of the human robot is so often his
cruel elimination. Yet, for my part, I think that in our post-Marxian post-Freudian
age it is ever so easy to get rid of the human robot by democratizing him — by
attacking the work ethic, by decentralizing power, and by democratizing educational institutions, productive and service organizations, research, the arts, etc.

The science-fiction thesis that we can do without the common man, that we
can have a society with exceptional people only, has been questioned, of course.
(See, e.g., Ernst Mayr, "Biological Man and the Year 2000", *Daedalus*, Vol. 96, No.
3, pp. 832—6.) But I wish to stress that I am not speaking here of creatively
outstanding men, but of morally outstanding ones, namely the autonomous or
independent; therefore, the question Mayr debates is not relevant to my point,
though it is to science fiction. The question is, is every morally outstanding man
also intellectually outstanding? Science fiction answers affirmatively all too often,
of course.

This science fiction view has support from known facts. For, in our own
society the autonomous are so few, that they doubtless stand out as very intelligent, even though not all the very intelligent are autonomous. Yet, doubtlessly,
when autonomy will be the rule, this will have to be reexamined.

I am speaking empirically. Though many teachers look for bright-eyed students, their experiences are not pooled, and all we know is that grades, on the
whole, are random. But taking able teachers, we will break from the pattern. We
will find that most able teachers go after native talent, and that lack of courage
renders native talent impotent and teachers' investment waste. It seems to me
that, looking at cruel facts, we can easily conclude that investing in brave students
is more promising, especially if we help them train for autonomy.

16. When speaking of "the" work ethic I refer to a popular myth. There is no
unique attitude towards work even within a narrow compass of a fairly monolithic
group such as the early Reformation thinkers, let alone all twentieth century
positivists and other academics. For more details see *Humanitas*, Vol. 7, No. 2,
Fall 1971, especially Dennis H. Wrong, "The Meaning of Work in Western Culture".

Nevertheless, I report that most academics I have met believe that hard work is good for the soul and that output is a linear, or at least a monotonously increasing, function of input of effort alone. When pressed they admit that the factor is a function of the individual talent and favorable circumstances. This admission alone suffices to refute their theory, but they prefer not to think. For my part, I found in my adolescence that without entertainment, especially music, my own productivity reduces drastically, so I preferred to increase my productivity by seeking entertainment rather than working hard. More generally, the rational thing to do is to decide beforehand, and check empirically the decision, what portion of one's work-time should be alloted to preparation of conditions congenial to work, and what portion to work proper. It is my observation that most of my colleagues are highly inefficient, due to the lack of such planning. Indeed, some of them spend most of their time cleaning their desks in the hope of having them clear enough one day so as to be able to do their work. Others work hard in spite of having a very messy desk. In both cases we see the work ethic at work, together, I suppose, with a high degree of ambivalence.

For further details of the correlation between inductivism and work ethic see my "Unity and Diversity in Science", referred to in note 8 to Section I below, especially the notes.

17. I am not insensitive to the fact that Bacon saw in his inductivism an application of the work ethic of his day. I discuss this in my doctoral dissertation (University of London, 1956, unpublished).

18. There is little doubt that much of science fiction expresses this struggle, much of it describes it, much of it warns against the ill consequences of failure. I discuss some of this in Section XXIV below.

There is hardly any need to remind the reader that science fiction, good, bad, and indifferent, hardly ever employs Einsteinian relativity — it usually is Newtonian — regularly describes telepathy and telekinesis and even takes recourse to straight occultism, and regularly permits the instantaneous transfer (jump) of whole chunks of matter over unlimited distances. It really hardly relates to science, but explores the impact of technology on society, be it utopian or social experimental. Thus, much fiction is not considered science fiction because it is merely scientifically oriented rather than expresses the concerns and results of technology. But there is a literature which is chiefly concerned with science and its place in our culture and in our civilization, good and bad, optimistic, pessimistic, and wavering. I wish to mention one such writer, Aldous Huxley, who has lived as much in the world of science and its concerns as any modern man did. Huxley shows scientific concerns, for example, for the ecologic disasters caused by science, even in a non-science work of fiction, such as *Point Counterpoint,* whereas Snow, when writing on atomic bomb men, for example, offers normal, non-science concerns and activities (*The New Men* and *Corridors of Power*).

Huxley suffered from two closely related dichotomies which are paramount in all his writings and in diverse forms: nature versus art and nature versus convention. The chief expression of the nature versus art dichotomy is the idea that purely natural man is an ape and purely artificial man is a machine. Natural man leaves the world as it is and neglects it, artifact-making man vanquishes nature and so himself. As to nature versus convention, it again polarizes the ape from the robot. The primary expression here is in the feeling that emotions are neither natural sensations nor manipulated sensations. Huxley feared promiscuity as much as he was fascinated by it. Was natural man monogamous or promiscuous? Is monogamy natural or conventional? These questions tortured him and expressed themselves in his works. Are novels natural or artificial? This question, too, drove him insane. (Already Plato equated the nature-convention and nature-art dichotomies, and conceded that art is inferior to nature which at best it imitates.)

There was a time when Huxley looked for a solution to his question in the work ethic, or rather in a special version of the work ethic becoming an ancient Roman and a modern Briton. But he seems to have given it up — it simply fizzled out after expressing itself only in his minor novels and essays (especially "comfort"), perhaps symptomatic of his period of excessive mental strain.

The only solution he could offer to this question was taking mind-affecting drugs, which are, curiously, both very primitive and, he erroneously assumed, highly sophisticated. In other words, what Huxley was really after was peace of mind, and what he thought had robbed him of his peace of mind was the nature-art and the nature-convention dichotomies, i.e. the nature-culture dichotomy. The drug-culture, then, seemed to him as offering peace of mind by offering a way which transcends the dichotomy. This is the thesis of his *Doors of Perception* and later similar works, ending up with his last book, which is his *Island*. The latter is a positive novel coming after a long series of negative novels. The former is an essay on intuition as broadened by drugs. He also has an essay on vision endorsing a most dubious theory of vision which transcends the art-nature dichotomy in that it artificially creates conditions in which an artefact — eyeglasses — is rendered redundant.

No matter what I think of Huxley's merit as an artist, and no matter what I think of his views on diverse matters, I cannot but admire his concern with scientific questions and philosophic questions about science and about man.

19. A final note to the future compiler of notes and references. There are ever so many scholars who will always be able to tell you how many important references you have missed. To try and check all the references they suggest is to start developing into a scholar: it is a full-time job. It is not surprising that the learned scholar is unable to discriminate: he is too busy compiling references to have time to think or learn to think. He even holds the opinion that having sufficiently many references at your fingertip is the best form of scholarly thinking, whereas it is often nothing but scholarly cataloguing and mere associations of ideas.

Chapter One

Man as Machine

The point of this chapter can be put as follows: The theory that man is a machine (of any sort whatever) may be viewed in two very different ways, the extremist and objectionable, and the more moderate which may be true. Man is a machine may mean, man is merely a machine; that is to say, qualities peculiar to humanity, such as thought and morality, have no roots in human nature; and so morality, freedom, dignity and nobility, thinking, thoughtfulness, and rationality — all these are mere illusions. Man is a machine may, however, mean, not man is just a machine, but man is a very special kind of machine which, by its specific virtues, can suffer, can show dignity and nobility, etc.[1] Whereas to say that man is merely a machine seems objectionable, to say that man is a machine may be to say the truth — recent developments may show us we know much too little about machines to finally decide that this is or is not the case: we had better speak only tentatively on these matters.[2] Now, most people understand the view that man is a machine to mean that he is only a machine and so his suffering, thinking, etc., are all illusions.[3] And most people so understand this because of the ancient doctrine which divides the world into reality and appearance,[4] truth and illusion, and nothing in between — a view which I reject.[5]

Reduction, traditionally, was meant to perform two tasks which were identified in ancient Greek metaphysics — the task of explaining and the task of eliminating. Assuming that reality explains appearances and so appearances are mere illusion, makes explaining the same as explaining-away, i.e. eliminating. This identification is an error we must dispose of.

Notes

1. John Passmore, *The Perfectability of Man*, Scribner, New York, 1970, p. 281:
"By treating men as machines, whose perfection is to be equated with technical
perfection, it (i.e., modern industrial civilization) helps to destroy sympathy,
compassion, kindliness." An intriguing discussion of "man as machine" and "man
is a mere machine" can be found in the appendix to J. Lederberg, "Orthobiosis:
The Perfection of Man", in Arne Tiselius and Sam Nilsson, eds., *The Place of
Value in a World of Facts, Proceedings of the 14th Nobel Symposium, Stockholm,
September 15–20, 1969,* Wiley Interscience Division, New York, London, Sydney; Almquist & Wiksell, Stockholm, 1970, pp. 29–58, where "mere" is objected
to and contrasted with "highly complex . . . intelligent . . ." etc. On the whole the
appendix uses a positivistic argument: a problem soluble "in principle" may be in
fact insoluble by any computer the size of the visible universe! I find this argument forceful against positivism but not otherwise, and the idea of "highly complex" too vague; see below. The statement "matter thinks" usually sounds to
philosophers to mean, that thinking is nothing but certain clicks in a computer or
a brain, certain physical processes. Alternatively they would take it to be a mis-
statement, the application of a mental predicate to a physcial noun and hence a
misapplication (a category mistake) and hence a meaningless pseudo-statement.
This dichotomy is exactly what W. V. Quine denies in his essay "The Scope and
Language of Science", reprinted in his *The Ways of Paradox and Other Essays,*
New York, 1966; see especially the two concluding paragraphs (p. 232).
      (This is not to endorse Quine's ontology, but to warn those quick to declare a
statement a pseudo-statement without worrying about the system and rules of
formation in which it makes sense – in truth or in mere allegation. As to my
reasons for not endorsing Quine's ontology see my "What is A Law of Nature?"
referred to in note 8 to Section I below, where I explain why I think ontology
cannot rest on logic alone but must rest on a given metaphysics.)
      The question of meaning of such statements already worried the Vienna Circle,
especially R. Carnap, who at times considered "this stone thinks about Vienna"
meaningless but later was ready to view it as false.
      See also Richard Taylor, "How to Bury the Mind-Body Problem" *American
Philosophical Quarterly*, Vol. 6, 1969, pp. 136–143. Taylor tries to refute the
thesis that matter cannot think, and he declares that this thesis is the ground for
the problem, and he combats it. He thus short-circuits the theory of substance
altogether, yet it was this theory that gave rise to the problem. So far I fully agree
with him. But he goes further and pokes fun at the modern parlance about the
mental and physical states which replaces the classical parlance about minds and
bodies. And he is quite right to oppose this but he misses his own target. Those
who speak of states insist that mental states are mere reflections of physical states.
Why not the other way around? Because at heart they are still believers in the
substance theory and are proper materialists, but they talk in a new and positivistic language. The neutral language, if it were at all possible, should be phenomenological, and so, at the very least should make mental states not mere

parallels to things, but states of things *tout court*. Here Taylor is in a stronger position than he notices.

2. Not only do we need more physics to judge whether a thinking machine is possible: we may need more mathematics as well. See J. von Neumann, *The Computer and the Brain*, Yale Paperbound, New Haven and London, 1958, Introduction: "I suspect that a deeper mathematical study of the nervous system . . . will affect our understanding of the aspects of mathematics itself that are involved. In fact, it may alter the way in which we look on mathematics and logics proper. I will try to explain the reason for this belief later." The explanation, incidentally, comes at the end of the volume, where von Neumann shows the profound difference between a computer's system of self-correction and that of the living nervous system.

It is a known fact that von Neumann himself could compute in a way that others could imitate only with the aid of computing machines. It is a moving fact that in this volume he played down his own unique forte and emphasizes the superiority of the most ordinary qualities of most ordinary thinkers over the computer's and his own dazzling performances.

If we take von Neumann's view that automatic computing is inferior to mathematical reasoning seriously, we shall not wonder any longer at the presence of idiot savants, and we may consider them akin to what professional musicians call derisively gypsy violinists (with no insult to gypsies intended). Now this means that possibly everyone is a potential idiot savant: with all the merit and advantage of ordinary teaching – of arithmetic, music, etc. – it causes (much less harm than traditionally, but) still a lot of harm, and such that can, perhaps, be further reduced by further experimentation, especially with more cooperation and less pressure, overt or (worse) covert. See also notes 83 to Section VIII, 105–7 to Section X, and 89 to Section XX.

3. The idea of a human robot is very widespread in science fiction; its ancestry surely is the Frankenstein monster and before that the medieval and Renaissance magician's homunculus and incubus and succubus and Golem. But whereas all those are revolting pretenders who make us wonder if we are not pretenders as well, the human robot is a source of consolation, and is better than human and the pride of mankind. Of course, being better than man, the robot is offering a new and subtler danger, but (Karel Čapek's *R.U.R.* notwithstanding) we do not fear him the way we fear Frankenstein's monster: we fear him like we may fear imprisonment in the Garden of Eden. See Bruce Mazlish, "The Fourth Discontinuity", *Technology and Culture,* Vol. 8, No. 1, Winter 1967. Isaac Asimov's *I, Robot* is the best expression of just this fear.

Speaking quite phenomenologically, the difference between the magical human substitute and the scientific human substitute is the same as the difference between supernatural beings and super-intelligent bug-eyed aliens: it brings to the fore our ambivalences one way or another (we are against magic, but; or, we are for science, but). The similarity between all four is the hidden – right or wrong but ever present — idea that men are not mere robots, and that we belong to the species the way we belong to a family. Can you fancy a robot with a family life? Descartes was asked, can clocks reproduce? Samuel Butler's answer is, yes (*Erewhon*). See below end of Section VI and note 33 there. But can they have friends? All science fiction students of robotics have trouble here.

The writers of science fiction play with ideas and feelings they have inherited from the Enlightenment and the Romantics. The Enlightenment is excellently described by Heinrich Heine, *Religion and Philosophy in Germany,* beginning of Part III, in a story about a machine built by an Englishman which perfectly emulates a human being; the mechanical man pestered his maker with the request, give me a soul! and the maker could not comply. In Mary Shelly's novel, as Mazlish notes, the atmosphere is very different. The monster is repulsive, yet he wants love, he needs a soul; but his maker is heartless. This is the kind of stuff that science fiction feeds on: science fiction not only excites the imagination and airs ambivalences; it also adumbrates widespread metaphyscial doctrines. It also adumbrates moral problems and theories in connection with metaphysics, of course. It is, of course, a semi-escapist literature, both airing and allaying our metaphysical anxieties.

4. The dichotomy between reality and appearance makes anthropology partic- ularly difficult, and Kant was the philosopher who felt this difficulty first. Apparently man is evil, of course. But if he really is good, then appearances are misleading and should be ignored, and there is no problem left. Kant wanted to endorse the view of the Enlightenment of the essential goodness of man, but in order to avoid this trouble of having to consider evil as mere phenomena he also postulated an essential evil in man; but if there is an essential evil, a real evil, then it is eternal and uneliminable. The evil is but the fact of imperfection in man, he suggested in his effort to wriggle out of it. But this did not help: Kant was saddled with a real evil which is uneliminable. He therefore added the hypothesis that once the good in man becomes apparent it will prevail, and he added that before that, most of mankind may be destroyed. All this was still to no avail, of course. The difficulty cannot be resolved within the polarizations of real-apparent, good- evil, etc. See, for all this, Frederick van de Pitte, *Kant as Philosophical Anthro- pologist*, Nijhoff, the Hague, 1971.

5. For the details of the criticism of the dichotomy between appearance and reality, see my "Sensationalism", *Mind,* Vol. 75, 1966, pp. 1—24 (reprinted in my *Science in Flux*, Reidel, Dordrecht and Boston, 1975), especially the conclusion.

I POSITIVISM IS TO BE REJECTED OUT OF HAND

Philosophical anthropology is the question, what is man,[6] and the different answers to it, as well as the debate about them. It is sup- posed to offer a general view of man, an overview, a metaphysical foundation for the various sciences of man. True to the title of this work, I shall discuss some preliminaries hoping to dispose of obstacles which stand in the way of this inquiry developing in a manner congenial to rational philosophy.

The first and foremost obstacle is so-called positivism, whether traditional or modern. Positivism is hostile to all metaphysical undertakings and to all metaphysical overviews, whether of man or of the inanimate nature.[7] In my younger days I invested much energy in arguing against positivism, and in extolling metaphysics as an unavoidable and desirable set of regulative principles for science — principles dialectically interacting with science. I do not withdraw what I said then; now I consider it rather trivial.[8] The challenge of the anti-metaphysical viewpoint is not enough of a challenge for young philosophers, so I do not advise others to imitate me. Nevertheless, anti-metaphysics is not the bottom of the barrel, since it draws inspiration from the even worse folly of foolish metaphysicians. I shall mention an example later on.

As a matter of fact, we do have metaphysical ideas which influence our studies of man. Some of these ideas are indigenous to the social sciences, others are borrowed from other fields. To illustrate the triviality of all this, I shall bring an amusing example. Sometimes one and the same scientific problem is attacked with the aid of different metaphysical ideas, borrowed from different fields; this leads to amusing contrasts. Darwin's theory of plasticity has led thinkers in the neo-Darwinian era to suggest that those species of animals which are equipped with fewer innate release mechanisms (I.R.M.) have higher adaptive abilities, and so are better fitted for survival.[9] This is counter-intuitive, since it means that species of animals which at birth need more intense and prolonged nursing survive better than species of animals which are born with their mature capacities available at once.[10] Such species, we are told, are not very pliable and so they are slow to adapt and hence poor at surviving in changing conditions. They need long periods of mutation to make any adaptive progress. So much for one approach. On the basis of logic and information theory and the like, Noam Chomsky developed a different approach. He has arrived at the opposite view of man as born with a tremendous and most complex innate system, indeed with a whole linguistic capacity.[11] So man's linguistic capacity is a crucial substitute for his lack of I.R.M.s, and becomes, for Chomsky, something at least partially like an I.R.M. itself. I do not wish to argue the pros and cons of these two views. They seem to clash, and they are obviously both too elusive to be put to empirical tests and crucial experiments. They are thus unscientific, yet they embrace scientific views: in short, they are metaphysical. It is hard to see what we can do with them — except, of course, put them to work against each other. Kant would have been delighted, then, as he thought the only role a metaphysics can play is to combat another metaphysics, resulting in a stand-off. Yet, this view of the barrenness of metaphysics, he admitted, did not quench his passionate interest in the subject. Today we may more easily ignore both the injuction against metaphysics and the passion for metaphysics, and merely ask a question — one possibly rich with metaphysical implications, but nevertheless empirical: is man equipped with few innate release mechanisms or with many? How do I.R.M.s affect an animal's capacity to survival?

A moment's thought will suggest that I have poorly presented the problem at hand. The innate release mechanisms the biologists speak of are complete. A simple example is the newborn child's innate ability to find the nipple when it is offered by his mother which then develops into complex and evolving patterns of behavior.[12] This example is contrasted with the spider's innate ability to perform the amazingly complex operation he uses in order to catch a fly with no mother around anywhere. The mechanisms in both the human and the spider are innate and present at birth. The innate release mechanism Chomsky speaks about, if we can call it that, is not the ability to do something — to find a nipple, to build a spiderweb, or to compute on command the coefficients to a certain Bessel function; rather Chomsky speaks of the infant's ability to learn to do something; not the facility with language, but the ability to acquire it (which means using it correctly in ways never used before); not the ability to act in accord with an inbuilt program, but the ability to. . .[13] I do not quite know how to complete this sentence. To complete it is one of the tasks facing any future rational philosophical anthropology. I shall discuss this later. Let me only observe here that though Chomsky does offer us a metaphysical theory of language, one might claim that as yet he does not embed it in a general theory of man (at least not explicitly so). This, of course, is no critique of Chomsky, who has enough opposition on his hands already.

It is perhaps a strange fact, so strange that one might even tend to deny that it is a fact at all, but perusal in the literature will show it to be so: positivism leads us to ignore the fact that man alone is a speaking animal. Classical positivists minimized this fact, as do some of Chomsky's opponents. The reason is obvious: man shares with other animals many aspects of language, including that of communication, and as far as these aspects are concerned the difference between human and other animal languages is entirely a matter of degree.[14] The aspect of language usually attributed to man alone is conceptual, and concepts are too elusive for most positivists. It is no accident that Chomsky's review of Skinner's work on language is a classic.[15] Whatever else we may say about the debate — which is still open and continuing — Skinner's positivism led him to view language as identical with verbal behavior, his intention being to eliminate conceptual language from language, and this was the target of Chomsky's attack. It is Skinner's execution of his positivist program that Chomsky devastated so dramatically. But this is not to say that Chomsky solved any problem; he merely opened the way to developing linguistics and psycholinguistics along his own metaphysical lines, one of the many possible programs employing the view that language is not merely behavioral but also conceptual.

So much for positivism: we have interesting questions to discuss and we do not need the positivist's permission to do so, especially since, his protestations to the contrary notwithstanding, he has his own metaphysics and is thus, if not inconsistent, at least a party to the dispute. As I have said, positivism is not the worst philosophy — metaphysical confusions which allegedly justify the positivist's strongly felt need to combat metaphysics are easy to come by. This is particularly so in the matter at hand, namely the question of reduction in philosophical anthropology. Some writers on philosophical anthropology reduce all philosophy, or even all philosophy and all science, indeed all human activity and thought and all their objects, to philosophical anthropology. This is sometimes justified by the flimsy (since question begging) argument that the proper study of man is man, sometimes by the similarly flimsy argument that since all knowledge we have is human knowledge it is properly subsumed under the study of human knowledge, which is a part of the study of man, i.e. philosophical anthropology. I do not wish to quarrel with Feuerbach's famous remark that even when man looks at the starry heaven he sees in it a reflection of himself; I merely think it is preposterous to conclude from this that astronomy is but the study of a reflection of man; I do not see that astronomy is a part of anthropology because the astronomer is human; to say that astronomy willy-nilly reflects some of man's qualities, his strengths and limitations, is true; but to say that therefore it has nothing to do with the heavenly bodies is somewhat extravagant; it has to do chiefly with the heavenly bodies even though it incidentally reflects the astronomer[16] and at times even studies him carefully, e.g. when discovering or determining his personal equation so-called.

   Whereas some philosophers foolishly reduce all study to anthropology, others reduce anthropology to rational theology. They may
use the flimsy argument that since man is made in the image of God,
the study of man is part and parcel of the study of God. Or they may
use the following argument: in the final analysis we find that everything is in the bosom of God; the quest for certainty must lead us to
the final analysis; hence all philosophy and all learning must rest on
the definition of God as its only solid foundation.
   This last argument seems to me still the best argument in the line of
certainty. In the kingdom of certitude Spinoza still is the champion. [17]
In the kingdom of certitude the most cogent idea is still the idea that
all knowledge is (rational or natural) theology. But we have come a
long way since Spinoza: we should sympathize with those twentieth-
century thinkers who, in their very quest for certainty, utilize fragments of his better ideas, whether philosophers and scientists who
uphold the verification principle or activists who swear by the principle of real involvement as utter commitment (*engagement*); but
sympathy need not lead to rational debate: we do not argue rationally
(i.e. in a give and take fashion) with a relic or a fossil from whom we
expect no new ideas or criticisms (unless we are proselytizers).

Notes to Section I

6. Philosophical anthropology centers round the question, what is man. I do not
mean to imply that every field is definable by a question. Philosophy of mind, for
example, does not, and abstract algebra centers round a few questions and these
change in time.
   Philosophical anthropology is these days an increasingly popular subject of
university curriculum — usually under the title "philosophy of man" in parallel to
"philosophy of mind" or "philosophy of nature" etc. The new field is often
introduced on the false claim that Marxism has offered a new philosophical
anthropology; that Marxian philosophical anthropology has remained fresh and
has not fared as badly as Marxian economics and political theory; and that
Marxian philosophical anthropology has to offer fresh and important insights into
contemporary troubling practical issues.

7. That positivism is the hostility to all unanswerable questions, as such, is perhaps the great discovery in Wittgenstein's *Tractatus logico-Philosophicus*, London,
1922 — though of course, this fact is not created but only observed by Wittgenstein, and succinctly formulated: the puzzle, i.e., unanswerable question, he said,
does not exist. We can find it, indeed, in older writings, from Bacon's and Descartes to date. In his inaugural lecture, *The Scope of Anthropology*, London,
1967, Claude Lévi-Strauss says (p. 38), "in a semantic system, chastity is

related to 'the answer without a question' as incest is related to 'the question without an answer' ". Bacon, we remember, speaks of metaphysics as the rape of Nature, as forcing Her into a preconceived mold, and as putting Her in chains. By contrast he speaks of induction as showing attention to Her smallest whim, as that humility which brings Her to show Her secrets; serve Her so as to conquer Her. It did not occur to me, until I read the passage of Lévi-Strauss here quoted, how deep the sexual symbolism runs in Bacon, though his cabbalistic ancestry is one I have discussed a few times on various occasions. For Bacon see my "Unity and Diversity in Science", referred to in the next note, especially notes 12, 17, and 24; also note 11. For Lévi-Strauss, see Section XI below.

8. I am alluding here to my essay, "The Nature of Scientific Problems and Their Roots in Metaphysics", in M. Bunge, ed., *The Critical Approach: Essays in Honor of Karl Popper,* London and New York, 1964, pp. 182–211; see also my "What is a Natural Law?", *Studium Generale,* Vol. 24, 1971, pp. 1051–1056, and my "Unity and Diversity in Science", in R. S. Cohen and M. W. Wartofsky, eds., *Boston Studies in the Philosophy of Science,* Vol. 4, Reidel, Dordrecht, and Humanities, New York, 1969, pp. 465–522 (all three papers are reprinted in my *Science in Flux,* Boston Studies in the Philosophy of Science, Vol. 26, Reidel, Dordrecht and Boston, 1975), where I attacked positivism in order to prepare the ground for the presentation of my own views of metaphysics as sets of regulative ideas for science – a view propounded here too. See also my book – in collaboration with Aaron Agassi – *The Continuing Revolution, A History of Physics from the Greeks to Einstein,* McGraw-Hill, New York, 1968, and my *Faraday as a Natural Philosopher*, University of Chicago Press, Chicago and London, 1971.

9. For an excellent presentation of the I.R.M. theory see Robert J. Richards, "The Innate and the Learned: The Evolution of Konrad Lorenz's Theory of Instinct", *Phil. Soc. Sci.,* Vol. 4, 1974, pp. 111–133; p. 113 presents the key concept: "Within his theory of instinct the I.R.M. has the status of a theoretical entity, postulated to explain the innate readiness of an animal to respond . . .". Sir Gavin R. de Beer in his *Embryos and Ancestors,* Oxford, revised edition, 1951, makes the same point. Birds able to learn a lot are worth breeding carefully – evolutionarily speaking. So, birds which hatch very immature and remain dependent for long turn out cleverer than birds able to cater for themselves almost from birth. (See also next note.)

It is very far from my intention to endorse the views here reported. It is quite possible that infants are not so much in need of care as we assume, that a penalty for excessive infant care is the atrophy of certain instincts. This seems to be the view of a few researchers. See the correspondence column of *Science,* Vol. 177, 22 September, 1972, pp. 1057ff., for the latest on the topic, and note that the participants suppress their own speculations in an inductivist mood. Nevertheless, clearly, some animals, in particular humans, die if born and at once neglected, others do not (and there are even stranger cases, where the presence of adults is dangerous to the newborn). And so, clearly, there is a kernel of truth to these views, but I am not clear myself how to go about it.

See Géza Róheim, *The Origins and Function of Culture,* New York, 1943, pp. 17ff. for the history of these views. See René A. Spitz, *No and Yes, on the Genesis of Human Communication,* New York, 1957, Chapter 5, pp. 23ff., for a succinct restatement of the thesis that animals with more accomplished inborn mechanisms (precocial) are less adaptable than those with less accomplished ones (altricial), and references there. The *locus classicus* is, perhaps, Lorenz's paper, "The Comparative Method of Studying Innate Behavior Patterns", *Sympos. Soc. Exp. Biol.,* Vol. 4, 1950. The central difficulty inherent in this kind of study is, of course, the absence of a scale of comparison of either degrees of innateness or degrees of adaptability; that is to say, we have no rule telling us that for every two cases, one is more or equal or less than the other; not even for any given specifiable circumstances. Nevertheless, we can compare some extreme cases, and this may do for a beginning of a heuristic discussion. See, however, note 13 below.

Spitz encounters the difficulty in the very beginning of his discussion where he can see some aspects of humans which are more innately determined than those of other mammals, some less.

Spitz's is the most elaborate attempt to combine Lorenz with Freud, or rather to adjust Freud to Lorenz. Yet he is too apologetic and his deviations from Freud are not clearly marked. (Compare his theory of dreams with Freud's.) Also he does not touch upon sensitive topics, such as homosexuality. For, here Lorenz's theory of release mechanisms bears interesting results which do tend to conflict with Freud's views (see note 12 to Chapter 2, Section VI, below). A sensitive topic which Róheim raises is the fact that man alone has a period of latency (which Freud wanted to ascribe to some racial memory explicable by a selection mechanism, but could not). See also notes 14, 21, 22 to Section VI below.

Still, there is no doubt that Spitz is ingenious in his attempt to start with the theory of the newborn's tendency to move its head from left to right and back is the source of the use of this movement as a sign of refusal. The theory, incidentally, already occurs in rudiments in Darwin, *Notebooks of Man,* etc., p. 37; Howard E. Gruber, *Darwin on Man, A Psychological Study of Scientific Creativity Together with Darwin's Early and Unpublished Notebooks,* transcribed and annotated by Paul H. Barrett, Foreword by Jean Piaget, Dutton, New York, 1974, p. 337.

10. The point was first made by Sir Gavin de Beer, I suppose in his *Embryology and Evolution,* Oxford, 1930, p. 91: "paedomorphosis means plasticity, i.e., evolution, while gerontomorphosis means the opposite."

This passage is quoted in Géza Róheim, *Psychoanalysis and Anthropology, Culture Personality, and the Unconscious,* New York, 1950, 1968, Chapter 10, on the unity of mankind, p. 422. This work may be the best history to date of the study of the question, is man's slow maturation process an evolutionary advantage. Though very informative, it is highly unreliable (see, for example, the references to Sir Solly Zuckerman and compare them with the original). Róheim is especially informative about the influence Freud had, especially through his theories of infant sexuality and of the id, on both anthropology and ethology (see esp. pp.

411–12, 420–1). This is little known and particularly interesting in view of the fact that Lorenz never acknowledged Freud's influence of him – first for obvious political reasons, I suppose, and second because as an inductivist and a critic of Freud's associationism and death-wish theory he could not see him as his teacher. See also below, notes to Section VI.

The matter of the possibility of death caused by the merest death wish or despair, is complicated by the medical prejudice that the autonomous nervous system is, indeed, autonomous (i.e. not subject to volition, much less to decisions). This has been noted by Anne E. Caldwell, *The Origins of Psychopharmacology: From CPZ to LSD*, Charles C. Thomas, Springfield, Ill., 1970, p. 50. See also p. 163: "According to Cannon, 'death would result as a consequence of the state of shock produced by continuous outpouring of adrenalin' says Richter, who concluded that a phenomenon of sudden death 'occurs in man, rats, and many other animals as a result of hopelessness; it seems to involve overactivity primarily of the parasympathetic system'." Richter found that "after elimination of hopelessness the rats do not die" even when the change is chemically induced. References are given to W.B. Cannon, " 'Voodoo' Death" *Amer. Anthrop.*, Vol. 44, 1942, pp. 169–181, reprinted, *Psychosom. Med.*, Vol. 19, 1957, pp.|182–190, and to C.P. Richter "On the Phenomenon of Sudden Death in Animals and Man", *Psychosom. Med.*, Vol. 19, 1957, pp. 191–198.

Now both despair and the activity of the autonomous system have strong relevance to drug addiction. Medical men define addiction, as distinct from, say, mere habit, as that habitual consumption whose stoppage causes withdrawal symptoms; and withdrawal symptoms are, of course, of the autonomous nervous system. This is all cock-and-bull. The same drug can, but need not, be addictive – e.g. alcohol and opium. And even when addictive, it can be cured – by hope. Yet the hope is often masked by palliatives, though these soon become addictive – e.g. heroin and methadone. Also, in despair one can be addicted to behavior patterns involving no special chemicals – e.g. food and gambling. All this is to no avail and arguing with medical people and with drug rehabilitation people on these lines only makes them blow their cool.

It is hard to know what makes people boasting of scientific attitudes to lose their tempers when facing refuting evidence. Nor is it easy to see how else they can prevent people from drawing their attention to the evidence. At times they might declare the witness unreliable, but Cannon's paper is not easily dismissable. The fact that it was noted only after it ceased to threaten mechanistic prejudices, however, may give us a clue: mechanists want to keep at least the autonomous system mechanistic. But this is an error: without the distinction between the voluntary and the involuntary the very idea of involuntary action is impossible. And so, it is advisable to assume volition in our explanations even on the hypothesis that finally it should be explained by hypotheses which do not assume volition. This is also Boyle's principle of toleration. See note 25 to Section II.

11. The Chomskian literature is vast; I suppose Noam Chomsky's *Cartesian Linguistics*, New York, 1966, is still his best manifesto, unless it is his shorter

version of the same, namely, *Language and Mind*, New York, 1968. An excellent bibliography on linguistics can be found in the English version of Adam Schaff, *Language and Cognition*, edited by Robert S. Cohen, based on a translation by Olgierd Wojtasiewicz, McGraw-Hill, New York, 1973.

12. The view that a child has an innate mechanism for searching the nipple is quite generally accepted, less on empirical grounds − it is not clear how it can be tested − than on the ground of its excellent fit with the spirit (i.e. meta-physical presuppositions) of feedback theories, of ethology, of psycholinguistics, of reflex theory, of almost all theories except the very oldest associationistic models. The author who makes most of it is René Spitz in his already mentioned *No and Yes* (with no as the primordial headshake of the infant who is looking for the nipple). The only possibly dissenting voice I have found is that of John Bowlby, the disciple of Melanie Klein. As a reviewer of his *Attachment*, London and New York, 1969, in *Times Literary Supplement* (reprinted in *Psychiatry and Social Science Review*, Vol. 4, No. 7, 1970) puts it,

> "It is doubtful whether anyone who reads this book will ever again be able to maintain that the human infant's dependence on his mother derives solely from its need for her breast . . . he will have to recognize that mother-infant relationship is an enormously subtle interaction, in which the infant's smiling, crying, clinging, gasping, babbling, listening − and the mother's responsiveness to these messages − play as important a part in attaching infants . . . and mothers . . ."

13. The theory that diverse authors from Sir Gavin de Beer to René Spitz seem to be groping towards is the idea that the less programmed is the more able to learn. Now this formulation is obviously erroneous, as a stone is least programmed yet also least able to learn. The ideal is, roughly, that an animal should have maximal program capacity but minimum program. This formulation is better but also highly questionable since it is based on the distinction between hardware and software; in the computer world this distinction has recently been almost entirely ended and at least is in need for a redefinition. The idea that constants are replaced by parameters is objectionable on similar grounds. And so we are still groping, yet we understand the idea. Piaget uses extensively the idea of progress by replacing constants with parameters plus know-how for operating with them; for this he has to idealize learning and ignore the differences between different human cultures. (See my review of Theodore Mischel, ed., *Cognitive Development and Epistemology*, in *Phil. Soc. Sci.*, Vol. 2, 1972, pp. 367−8.) The view that replacing constants with parameters is fetalization may explain why dyslexics are often both seemingly retarded and obviously gifted, on the assumption that they are further fetalized than the average and so more evolved. See Yehuda Fried, "Dyslexia and Organization of Space", *Acta Paedopsychiatria*, Vol. 35, 1968, pp. 79−85, where Piaget's view is applied to dyslexia and the view is empirically argued that dyslexics have to construct what other children are able to see intuitively. If so, we may assume that parents' inability to cope with dyslexics may cause systematic misunderstandings and fear, thus leading to autism and related

phenomena. This will explain the high incidence of high intelligence in those cases too: it is largely a misunderstanding rooted in a false view parents and teachers have concerning learning, talent, ability, etc. We should have more misunderstandings and problems explained this way if it is true that often dyslexia and hyperkinesis go together.

14. "The range of what has seemed to be human has been progressively reduced as lower organisms have come to be better understood". B. F. Skinner, "The Experimental Analysis of Behavior", *Contingencies of Reinforcement,* Appleton-Century-Crofts, New York, 1969. The passage is also quoted by Bernard Elevitch, "The Scientist as Political Oracle," *Modern Occasions,* Winter 1972, pp. 120–125, p. 120. See also below, Section VIII, and notes.

15. Chomsky's review of B. F. Skinner's *Verbal Behavior,* New York, 1957, is in *Language,* Vol. 35, 1959, pp. 26–58. Reprinted as Chapter 21 of J. A. Fodor and J. Katz, eds., *The Structure of Language: Readings in the Philosophy of Language,* Englewoods Cliffs, N.J., 1964. It "marks in a sense the new era in linguistic methodology" says Y. Bar-Hillel, in his *Aspects of Language,* Jerusalem, 1970, p. 177. I wonder.

Chomsky's attitude towards the idea of uncovering the essential universal in the specific is discussed in various works mentioned in note 20 to Chapter 2 of his *Language and Mind,* New York, 1968: see p. 40 and p. 55 there. On this, at least, Skinner and Chomsky are in full agreement, as noticed by Gilbert Ryle in his splendid criticism of Chomsky quoted below, note 48 to Section VII.

16. One can view astronomy as part of anthropology; one can view the two as irrelevant to each other; and one can have different views. Clearly, Feuerbach thought astronomy can teach anthropology something because it is so very different from it. In the beginning of *The Essence of Christianity*, he says:

"Man becomes self-conscious in terms of his object: the consciousness of the object is the self-consciousness of man. Man is comprehended in terms of his object: his nature is revealed to you by means of it. The object is man's revealed essence, his true, objective *I*. And this holds true not only of mental but of sensible objects. Even those objects furthest removed from man are revelations of human nature, because, and insofar as, they are objects for man. Even the moon, the sun, and the stars call to man, know thyself! That he sees them, and sees them in the way that he sees them, serves as an indication of his own nature. The animal is affected by the light which is necessary to his life-needs. Man is affected by the indifferent light of the remotest stars. Only man has pure, disinterested satisfactions and feelings – man alone celebrates theoretical festivals of sight. The eye which gazes upon the starry heavens sees that useless and harmless light, which has nothing in common with the earth and its needs, manifested in it its own nature and origin. The eye is of a heavenly nature. Therefore, it is by means of the eye that man rises beyond the earth; therefore, theory begins with the contemplation of the heavens. The first philosophers were astronomers. The sky reminds man that his nature is not only to act, but to contemplate as well."

I have quoted Feuerbach's famous passage long enough to give the reader the evidence that Feuerbach said neither anything outrageous nor anything profound. Indeed he was just rhapsodizing on the theme of the conclusion of Kant's *Critique of Practical Reason* on the assumption, I presume, that it was familiar enough to his reader. Whereas Kant spoke of two things that moved him, the starry heaven above him and the moral law within him, Feuerbach tried to relate the two. Yet even this is hardly a novelty. "Aristotle . . . held that the origins of man's knowledge of the divine were twofold" says Gilbert Murray (*Four Stages of Greek Religion,* Columbia University Press, New York, 1912, p. 116, referring to Aristotle, fr. 12ff.),

"the phenomena of the sky and the phenomena of the human soul. It is very much what Kant found two thousand years later. The spectacle of the vast and ordered movements of the heavenly bodies are compared by him in a famous fragment with the marching forth of Homer's armies before Troy. Behind such various order and strength there must surely be a conscious mind . . .."

How exasperating all this must be to the modern reader: Aristotle, Kant, Feuerbach, God the architect, God in the image of man — a lot of learning and excitement over centuries, and for very little results. There is no doubt that Feuerbach's claim that God is in man's image is neither disproof nor even an irreligious sentiment. "The Orphic carried to the grave on his golden scroll the same boast" tells us Murray (*op. cit.,* p. 128). "First, I am the child of Earth and of the starry Heaven; then, later, 'I too am become God'. " In other words, ecstasy encompasses all emotions and enables one to sympathize with all and so see interconnection anywhere one likes (pp. 125, 130). It is hard to believe that the most exalted remarks of Kant and Feuerbach go no further than ancient magic, but I think it is time to counter the Marxist (Engels is the greater culprit) enthusiasm over Feuerbach's philosophy of religion and the deathblow it allegedly dealt to all religion as such, namely as superstition. I suppose the only thing to do is to treat religion anthropologically with no pretense at a refutation.

17. See my "Unity and Diversity in Science", note 8 above. The place of Spinoza is discussed in the notes there and in notes 6 and 7 to Chapter 2 below.

The link between certitude, the topic of this section, and reductionism, the topic of the next one, is the widespread doctrine that certainty = science and science = reductionism, and so certainty = reductionism, even though the speculative nature of all reductionism, materialist or Spinozist (parallelist), is so very obvious.

This widespread doctrine is ascribed by Emile Durkheim to Saint-Simon and Comte. See his *Socialism and Saint-Simon,* Antioch Press, 1958, i.e., *Socialism,* Colliers, New York, 1962, edited with an introduction by Alvin W. Gouldner, from the edition originally edited with a preface by Marcel Mauss, Chapter 6, "The Doctrine of Saint-Simon: The Foundation of Positivism", pp. 127–146, especially pp. 136–7.

II REDUCTIONISM IS AN ATTRACTIVE METAPHYSICS

Leaving, then, both anti-metaphysics and the quest for certainty which leads to metaphysics of doubtful value, our removing of obstacles will become a bit more tedious before it regains interest. When we approach philosophical anthropology, then, as the metaphysics of the study of man, we may perhaps be allowed a few paragraphs in order to clarify both the existing terminology and a minor awkwardness which it involves.

The word "metaphysics" may mean the first principles of physics, or the first principles of any other field of interest, as expressed, for example, in Kant's term "the metaphysics of morals". Nowadays, instead of Kant's term we use the term "meta-ethics". Likewise we employ Bernard Shaw's "meta-biology" and Freud's "meta-psychology".[18] And so, instead of philosophical anthropology we might, perhaps, be tempted to speak of meta-anthropology, or meta-sociology, or of meta-something-or-other. Those who answered the question what is Man, by: Man is a spiritual being, developed the idea of the spiritual sciences; those who said man is essentially a political animal or a social animal, spoke of the social sciences; those for whom man is a complex system manifesting complex behavior patterns, spoke of the behavioral sciences.[19] Clearly, there are great differences of opinion here between diverse thinkers. They may prefer not to come out in the open and clash in a rational debate; and in order to gratify them on this matter we may create different faculties or departments for the spiritual sciences or humanities, for the social sciences, and for the behavioral sciences. This will, indeed, prevent the open clash of opinion. We may thus conceal the differences of opinion, but not resolve the differences of opinion; on the contrary, we thus make them inherent to the situation. When one thinker says psychology is a part of the social sciences, and another says, sociology is a part and parcel of (social) psychology, there is genuine disagreement, all pretense to the contrary notwithstanding. When the conflict of opinions is disguised by new departmental administrative arrangement — by creating the subject "social psychology" in the psychology department, for example — the metaphysical conflict turns unintentionally into a sort of departmental competition or empire building; but at root it still is a genuine metaphysical disagreement.

The regrettable fact about positivism is thus, that it does not banish metaphysics, and metaphysical conflicts, as it claims to be doing, but rather it suppresses the conflicts and forces them into an underground existence. The situation is here that of making metaphysics into a victim-less crime, so-called, and thus very similar to the sociologically very familiar cases of banishment of prostitution, gambling, and the use of drugs: making them illegal does not banish them in the least but makes it impossible to control them, and so, innocuous as they surely are, they become associated with genuinely antisocial patterns of behavior. And so, even on the assumption that metaphysics is a drug and the prostitution of learning — and some metaphysics certainly is such — even on these assumptions it should not be banished but allowed to come into the open and criticized openly on points where criticism is fair. In particular, it is very important not to condemn departmental empire building but invite ambitious expansionists to express openly their reasons for their expansionism, their views of the significance and insignificance of theirs and others' departments and subdepartments.

No doubt, such a policy would quickly give rise to clearer state-ments of existing metaphysical disagreement. Or shall we say, in our own case, meta-anthropological disagreement? We can say "meta-anthropological" only if we use it as a blanket term for all the sciences of man, generalizing as well as historical — not as a blanket term covering social anthropology alone. But perhaps in order to avoid confusing meta-anthropology in the broad sense of all social sciences and in the narrow sense of social anthropology we had better stick to the label "philosophical anthropology" [20] to designate the broader set. Thus, if we wish to identify the sciences of man with social anthro-pology we can do so by asserting the identification of philosophical anthropological" only if we use it as a blanket term for all the sciences cation as we choose. Or, still better, some will assert it and some will deny it, and then will hopefully engage in a metaphysical controversy.

My recommendation, then, is to retain a terminology neutral to the disagreement: to designate the general theory of the sciences of man, whether psychologically, sociologically, or spiritually orientated, we shall use the term "philosophical anthropology"; and for more restricted theories and the debates over them, we shall retain the terms "meta-anthropology", "meta-sociology", "meta-psychology", etc.

This resolves the use of the term "metaphysics", then, and splits metaphysics into meta-physics, meta-biology, meta-psychology, meta-anthropology, and philosophical anthropology — the latter containing both meta-psychology and meta-anthropology, etc. Finally, what we get when we combine all these meta-studies together, perhaps along with rational theology, is often known as metaphysics on a grand scale, or grand-scale metaphysics. [21] As to the term "metaphysical", it can be likewise split. But I recommend that we do not split it as there is hardly any need for this as yet.

Undoubtedly, the most positivistic theory of philosophical anthropology claims that all the sciences of man are reducible to psychology, that is to say, to laws of observable conduct of individual people. Most adherents of psychological reductionism also hope to reduce psychology to physics.[22] Some waive that. Freud once said that in the last resort there are only two sciences, physics and psychology.[23] Of course, this includes a meta-biology which says all biology is physics — a version of Darwinian mechanism.[24] But when in a more philosophical mood Freud tended to see even psychology as physics: he tried to reduce all psychology to two basic drives which man shares with other animals, hunger and the sex drive, hoping that biology would reduce these drives to physics, so that when the reduction of biology is complete, psychology will fall into the lap of physics like a ripe fruit.[25] Indeed, Freud is one of the contributors to the development and increased popularity of the concept of homeostasis which is now so familiar to students of cybernetics and/or the theory of servomechanisms.[26] We should note in passing the positivistic character of the Freudian meta-psychology, including its avoidance of anything specifically human. Admittedly, suppression, repression, projection, sublimation, symbolism, etc., are, for Freud, unintentionally perhaps, specifically human. Freudian psychology, then, hardly conforms to Freudian meta-psychology. This may be a criticism of Freud — but I do not know how fair it is. For he did notice the discrepancy, and hoped it would be cleared off. Also, as he got older he became more critical of his own positivism.

Much the same criticisms can be directed at Watson's behavioristic meta-psychology. It has been said of it, and with justice, that it is not even a program for the reduction of psychology to physics, since the central motives it ascribes to us, of fright, fight, and love, being motives, cannot be parts of physics. Yet they are not specifically human, and so may be viewed, via a proper meta-biology, as reducible all the same. Of course, whether a tenable meta-biology of that kind can be constructed, is questionable. Positivists, however, take such a possibility for granted, and so Watson is not peculiar on this point.

It is hard for the philosophical anthropologist to resist discussing such questions as, can we reduce man to animal or even to machine — yet I wish here to offer a way of resisting discussion of reductionism altogether and see how far it gets us.

The temptation of reductionism is all too clear. This question is, what is man? Take the best known answer to this, one of Aristotle's answers: Man is a rational animal. What is an animal? It makes all the difference to our view of man, whether we view animals as automata, as homeostatic systems, or as something else. The matter – the answer to the first question – is not thereby fully decided, to be sure, but a long distance towards a decision already has been covered by the answer to the second question. To take the most famous example: Descartes, we may remember, viewed all animals as automata, except man. This doctrine itself created strong reaction against Descartes, which we need not discuss here. Descartes' view was important, no matter how strong the reaction, and how historically important the two variants on Cartesianism which it brought about – that which sees man as a machine, and that which denies that any animal is a machine. Certainly the mechanistic part of Cartesianism was important, not only his mechanistic animal physiology, including his new idea of nerves as signal-conveyers; his non-mechanistic psychology was important too. Descartes' very distinction between man and other creatures was of great significance, because it raised with increased force the question, what in man is rational and what in man is mechanical? And it was Descartes who suggested, as a general criterion, that whatsoever man shares with any other animal is not rational but purely mechanical. Thus, not only pain and pleasure, but even signals and memory are mechanical. And thus Descartes was the inventor of memory banks, the foreshadowing and the adumbration of the view we hold today, according to which my library, even the public library around the corner, is an extension of my memory as long as, and to the extent that, I am able to go there and dig up some information. Similarly, Descartes foreshadowed the idea of racial memory which gained significance first in biology and then in psychology.

I shall return to all this later on. I mention it here in order to show how important even meta-biology is, in this case Descartes' mechanistic meta-biology, to the student of philosophical anthropology. It is therefore not surprising that even today students of this field are tempted to go back to metaphysics-on-a-grand-scale à la Descartes and Spinoza, to create a rational theology, a meta-physics, a meta-biology, and a philosophical anthropology, and try to unify them in a complete *Weltanschauung*, in a total world picture. I do not object to this: it is, on the contrary, a most exciting venture. Yet I recommend that we also try, from time to time, to resist sliding into meta-biology or into meta-physics, not to mention theology.[27] For, otherwise, we shall perhaps never come to the point. No doubt, the choice is hard to make. If we do slide to meta-physics and meta-biology, hoping to settle the question, what is Animal, before coming to the question, what is Rational, we may, in doing so, be postponing indefinitely our philosophical anthropological studies, our study of Man as Rational Animal. Yet if we skip the question, what is Animal, and go straight to what is Rational we shall not know what kind of rationality an animal, any animal, possesses. [28] One of the central problems of meta-biology and of philosophical anthropology still is, can biology be reduced to physics? And how can we know this without some idea of physics or at least meta-physics? How can we know if the Rational is or is not the Spiritual without finding our whether or not matter can think? [29]

I would endorse the historical hypothesis, advanced by Erwin Schrödinger in his *Nature and the Greeks* and his *Science and Humanism:* [30] interest in physical things stems often enough from the fact that we possess physical bodies. Already in antiquity reductionism fascinated quite a few philosophers, with anthropologies as diverse as those of Pythagoras and of Democritus. Moreover, historically, the very idea of reductionism was not satisfactory enough to prevent the sliding from philosophical anthropology to meta-physics. Let me, then, try at once to suggest an approach to reduction which will help us avoid discussing it, that is, an approach that will help us avoid sliding from philosophical anthropology to meta-physics; in that connection I shall, however, have to say something about scientific method. And so I may end up skidding in one direction in order to avoid sliding into another. But let me try anyhow, and attempt to keep my methodological digression brief: it will be profitable, I hope, as I intend to use its conclusions throughout this work.

Notes to Section II

18. The term "meta-biology" is presented in the end of Shaw's preface to his *Back to Methuselah*. The term "meta-psychology" occurs in Freud's works and occupies a literature of its own. See Ernest Jones, *The Life and Work of Sigmund Freud*, Basic Books, New York, 1961, index, Art. "meta-psychology". Shaw's term "meta-biology" may be replaced by Marjorie Grene's "philosophical biology" (*Approaches to a Philosophical Biology*, Basic Books, New York and London, 1968). It is perhaps also possible to view the term "philosophical psychology" which appears in so many a philosophy syllabus, a competitor to Freud's "meta-psychology".

19. An exasperating fact is that both terms "metaphysics" and "science" cause so much debate and misunderstanding that seem purely verbal but in fact mostly center round tacit prestige claims. The use of "metaphysics" as having more to do with physics than theology is very much in line with the use of the term to cover the theories of the *physiologoi* (= the physicists) of Aristotle's *Metaphysics,* Book

Alpha, from Thales to Democritus, as well as the use of Descartes, Boyle, and Kant. Nevertheless it irks English-speaking philosophers, especially those not swept by the positivistic linguistic fashions. They feel — I report an observation — that this is a new attempt to rob them of the legitimacy of what they are doing, which is as often as not rational theology within some framework of grand-scale-metaphysics or another.

The displeasure in certain German-speaking circles is very similar, except that there the term denoting legitimacy is not "metaphysics" but "spiritual science", or even "historical science" and "dogmatic science". Of course, the major label is the first, and the one incorporated in a title of a grand work by Wilhelm Dielthey (*Einleitung in die Geisteswissenschaften*, 1883), no doubt under the influence of, and echoing, Hegel's *The Science of Logic*. This may explain the insistence on the historical claim — true but irrelevant — that the label is a translation of Mill's term — it is traditional English, really — "moral science", meaning social science. See Hayek's "Scientism and the Study of Society", *Economica*, 1942, reprinted in his *The Counter Revolution of Science,* Free Press of Glencoe, 1955, p. 209, note 19 and in John O'Neill, *Modes of Individualism and Collectivism,* Heinemann, London, 1973, p. 27 n. Also Heinz Mans, "Simmel in German Sociology", in Kurt H. Wolff, ed., *Georg Simmel, 1858–1918, A Collection of Essays With Translations and a Bibliography,* Ohio University Press, Colombus, Ohio, 1959, p. 181. Also K. R. Popper, *Conjectures and Refutations,* London and New York, 1963, p. 368 n.

Georg Simmel introduced the term "philosophical sociology" to express the view that philosophical anthropology equals meta-sociology, or as a synonym to "meta-sociology", or to denote sociology proper. Finally, he was unable to decide whether the unity of the social sciences is in a metaphysical presupposition, as he often said, or of method, as he said, e.g., in Kurt H. Wolff, *op. cit.*, p. 312:

"... In its relation to the existing [human] sciences, sociology is therefore a new method, an instrument of investigation, a new way of getting at the subject matter of all those sciences. It thus presents a parallel to induction [in the physical sciences] ... But induction is no more a special science — much less an all-embracing one — than sociology ..."

Yet he managed to remain stimulating and interesting though somewhat disappointing at times.

Georg Simmel's metaphysical idea of sociology has been developed carefully and in quite some detail by Nicholas J. Spykman, in his *The Social Theory of Georg Simmel,* New York, 1965. What is most conspicuous in this book is the clear and systematic use of the word "metaphysics" in the proper traditional sense — evidently thanks to Simmel or to Kant and his immense influence on Simmel.

Spykman notices, mainly, the fact that sociologism is a metaphysics which renders sociology the queen, the embracing framework or the foundation, of all social sciences. He presents Simmel's view as sociologism, but tries to distinguish sociology as a science from the sociology of sociologism. I daresay this could be done by viewing today's sociology as a science and the sociology of the future as the regulative idea and thus the metaphysics of sociologism. But to accept this one must reject Simmel's lamentable relativism, his major break with Kant.

See Kurt H. Wolff, *op. cit.*, p. 193 for Simmel's anti-positivism, p. 188 for Durkheim's hostility for Simmel, and p. 216 for the hostility which Spykman himself drew.

With no hostility to Spykman I wish to say that Simmel did not quite endorse sociologism since he refused to reduce individuals to society. See Section XX below and note 79 there.

I must admit, though, that Simmel was not always half as clear as one might expect. He operates with a Kantian dualism of form and content that at times means nonreduction of individuals, sometimes not. See Rudolf H. Weingartner, "Form and Content in Simmel's Philosophy of Life" and F. H. Tenbruck, "Formal Sociology", both in Kurt H. Wolff, *op. cit.*, especially pp. 55, 84, and 88, and compare p. 140. See also pp. 110–113 there, about the ambiguity of Simmel's concept of form. See also Matthew Lipman, "Some Aspects of Simmel's Conception of the Individual" in the same volume which shows that at times but only at times content and form apply to the individual as much as to society.

20. The term "philosophical anthropology" was first introduced by A. G. Baumgarten in his *Metaphysica* and was sanctified by Kant. It meant then quite a different thing, namely empirical sociology or empirical social anthropology or, more accurately, at least in Kant's work, empirical sciences of man. What Kant has or would have labelled philosophical anthropology in our sense is, I presume, "the metaphysical foundations of morals", or "the metaphysical foundations of anthropology". See Frederick van de Pitte, *Kant as Philosophical Anthropologist*, Nijhoff, the Hague, 1971, p. 3.

Van de Pitte presents Kant's philosophical anthropology as the center of Kant's philosophical activity. He is puzzled, however, by Kant's excessive acknowledgement to Hume (p. 42), as are many commentators who see links between Kant's critical and precritical work. Russell, indeed, altogether denies Kant's debt to Hume, or even that Kant ever woke up from his dogmatic slumber. Yet I think Kant's own introduction to his *Anthropology* offers a better view; wanting to erect an empirical science of man he wanted to emulate Newton. Hume did so but failed. Kant tried the same after correcting Newton's view of the empirical method itself. See Lewis White Beck, *Studies in the Philosophy of Kant*, Bobs-Merrill, Indianapolis, 1965, pp. 10–11 and comments on this in van de Pitte, *op. cit.*, pp. 47, 70ff.

For the origins of the modern term "philosophical anthropology" as used here with Max Scheler and Helmuth Plessner, and its meaning as the principle of a synthesis of all sciences dealing with Man, see H. Wien, "Trends in Philosophical Anthropology and Cultural Anthropology in Postwar Germany", *Philosophy of Science*, Vol. 24, No. 1, 1957. See also Habermas's definition, quoted in note 11 to Section XXI below.

Paul Kurtz in his "Human Nature and Values: Comments on Polin" (in Paul Kurtz, ed., *Language and Human Nature, A French-American Philosophers' Dialogue*, St. Louis, 1971), p. 121, reads the title "philosophical psychology", so common amongst English-speaking philosophers of the so-called analytic persuasion, to be synonymous with "philosophical anthropology" except that "it is far less ambitious". It is, of course, psychologism, i.e., the identification of philosophical anthropology with meta-psychology. What counts as ambitions and what not, however, is a different matter. Bacon says, be humble and do small chores, and Nature will reward you and yield Her secrets to you. When it comes to humility, Bacon bragged, he was the very best.

21. The need for the distinction drawn here between grand-scale metaphysics and metaphysics in the narrow sense was felt already in the eighteenth century, when Christian Wolff introduced the term general metaphysics (*metaphysica generalis*, as opposed to *metaphysica specialis*).

22. The literature on reduction is swelling. I wish to refer to some clear and helpful texts. John Kemeny's *A Philosopher Looks at Science*, Princeton, 1959, is one. Kenneth F. Schaffner, "Approaches to Reduction", *Philosophy of Science*, Vol. 34, 1967, pp. 137–147 is another, more technical but very useful. Herbert Feigl's *The "Mental" and the "Physical", an Essay and a Postscript*, Minneapolis, 1967, has an extensive bibliography. For my criticism of that essay, in line with what is presented here, see my review of *Minnesota Studies in the Philosophy of Science*, Vol. II, in *Mind*, Vol. 68, 1959, pp. 275–277. See also note 2 to Chapter 2 below.

It is a sophisticated contradiction inherent in positivism that it declares reductionism both meaningless and true.

A valiant attempt to get over this inherent contradiction is that of A. M. Turing, "Computing Machinery and Intelligence", *Mind*, Vol. 54, 1950, reprinted in Alan Ross Anderson, ed., *Minds and Machines*, Prentice Hall, Englewood Cliffs, N.J., 1964. See the ensuing discussion there, especially by Keith Gunderson, and the bibliography.

Turing declares the question, do machines have minds, meaningless and replaces it with another. This technique is standard at least since Carnap treated it as standard. Now suppose it is all right to replace a meaningless question with a significant and meaningful one, and suppose the replacement is open to criticism which, when accepted as valid leads to new attempts at better replacement. Surely, in that case the allegedly meaningless question thus treated stands out as somewhat more significant than the truly meaningless question, is the number two green? Indeed it becomes a regulative idea, namely metaphysical in Kant's sense.

Turing's substitute question is, roughly, are there tasks performable by humans and not performable by machines? And Turing guesses that all tasks still not performable by machines today will be in the not so distant future. But one such task, I think, is described in the previous paragraph: present a series of substitutions to a baffling question, each of which is empirically examinable, and each of which is a better grasp of the original question than its predecessor.

(See also the two concluding sections of W. Sluckin, *Minds and Machine*, Revised Edition, Penguin, London and Baltimore, 1960: "The Metaphysics of Cybernetics" and "The Impact of Cybernetics upon Psychology".)

The author of this anti-Turing thesis, seems to be Norbert Wiener, who defends it in his admirable *God and Golem Inc.*, *Comments on certain Points where Cybernetics Impinges on Religion*, MIT Press, Cambridge, Mass., 1964, by claiming that robots only handle well-put questions, but questions are usually not well-put.

In his presidential address to the American Philosophical Association, Western Division, 1973, "Logic, Computers, and Men" (*Proceedings and Addresses of the American Philosophical Association*, Vol. 46, 1972–3, APA, Hamilton College, Clinton, New York, 1973, pp. 39–57), Arthur W. Banks advocates Turing's thesis: "A finite deterministic automation can perform all natural human functions". The proof is the same as that of Borges' "Library of Babylon": Given a finite but large enough library with all possible finite but large letter combinations, and that library will of necessity include all the books we have. And so Banks can and does end his address with a "QED": who says that *ars combinatorica* is a dead dream of Renaissance metaphysicians?

Reductionism is a metaphysics presented by positivists as a methodology or epistemology. In line with this, positivists prefer to talk of primary concepts rather than of the traditional metaphysical primary entities or substances. The difference between primary concepts and primary entities is presented as a matter of logical precision alone — between words and things. Yet there is no possible correspondence between alleged primary entities and alleged primary concepts akin to the alleged correspondence between facts and allegedly true statements. For example, the Democritean atom is primary, yet the concept of a Democritean atom is not: the concepts of divisibility and termination together (with negation) help to define it. See also note 55 to Section IV below.

In Peter F. Strawson's *Individuals* (Oxford, 1959) the concept of the individual person is presented as primary, meaning, of course, that an individual person is a primary entity in the metaphysical sense. See my criticism of this confusion in my review of *Minnesota Studies,* Vol. II, mentioned early in this note. See also A. J. Ayer, *The Concept of a Person and Other Essays,* London and New York, 1963, Macmillan & St. Martin Press pp. 85–92, which deals with the confusion.

23. See S. Freud, *New Introductory Lectures on Psychoanologies*, Lecture 35: A Weltanschauung?: "For sociology, too, dealing as it does with the behavior of people in society cannot be anything but applied psychology. Strictly speaking, there are only two sciences, psychology, pure and applied, and natural science."

Lévi-Strauss echoes Freud's reductionism: "ne relève pas des sciences sociales, mais de la biologie et de la psychologie", he says, I do not remember where, and he applies this dictum to totemism; see his *Totemism,* translated by Rodney Needham, Beacon Press, Boston, 1970, p. 57, where it is declared "no longer a cultural phenomenon . . . it belongs to psychology and biology, not to anthropology". See, however, note 27 to this section for a different view of Lévi-Strauss.

24. This is neither to endorse Darwin's mechanism nor to admit that it had any measure of success, but merely to refer to the well-known historical fact. More about Darwinism in the next chapter.

25. The interpretation of Freud as a Darwinian reductionist suggests that he had the idea of the primariness of physiological drives (food, sex, and other) fairly early in the day. This may be criticized by the historical claim that Freud was initially very reluctant to ascribe to the sex-drive the importance he did ascribe to it after a long internal struggle. But this claim is false, as Frank Cioffi forcefully argues in his "Wollheim on Freud" in *Inquiry,* Vol. 15, 1972, pp. 171–186. And so, it was indeed the young Freud who insisted on stepwise reductionism. The middle Freud had the pseudoscientific pseudomechanistic theory of the cathexis or mental energy. The late Freud tended to leave reductionism to itself and wondered how basic is man's death wish.

The importance of the idea of stepwise reductionism was, indeed, very great for the young Freud who violated the crude accepted mechanism of "no psychosis without neurosis" (i.e., no mental damage without physical damage to the nervous system – usually the central nervous system) in favor of a seemingly more mentalistic view of psychopathology. And so he felt his mechanism was vindicated by his – alleged – reduction of all psychopathology to basic drives and their satisfaction or otherwise, which he rightly felt, I assume, had to be dealt with anyway by mechanistically inclined biologists. Later in life, when he felt the scientific character of his theories was beyond reasonable doubt, the problem of mechanism worried him much less.

The program of stepwise reduction was first advanced by Robert Boyle in the Proëmial Essay to his *Certain Physiological Essays* of 1661. When he reduced the spring of the air to the spring of the air atoms he was violating Cartesian physics. But this, he said, should not annoy even an orthodox Cartesian, since, when the Cartesian will succeed in the attempt – which they must undertake anyway – to reduce the spring of a steel spring to a Cartesian mechanism, they will thereby also have reduced Boyle's theory that way. The logic of Boyle's reasoning and that of the one I ascribe to Freud are identical. I have discussed it at length in my doctoral dissertation (London, 1956, unpublished) as Boyle's principle of methodological tolerance.

26. The *locus classicus* is J. C. Flugel's "The Death Instinct, Homeostasis and Allied Concepts" of 1949, reprinted in his *Studies in Feeling and Desire*, London, 1955. The detailed, and not very convincing, discussion is to be found in Nigel Walker, "Freud and Homeostasis" in the *Brit. J. Phil. Sci.*, Vol. 7, 1956, p. 61:

"Freud's use of the concept of homeostasis, in the hypothesis that the 'nervous system is an apparatus having the function of abolishing stimuli', is of great interest, not only because it represents the pessimistic core of his materialism but also because it appears to anticipate by a quarter of a century the notions of cybernetics. Although it is usually overlooked in psychoanalysts' expositions of psychoanalysis, it is the unifying concept that links together the wish-fulfilment explanation of dreams, the defence-mechanisms of the ego and the repetition compulsion. It also led Freud by a fallacious argument, to the notion of the death-instinct.

Dreams, according to Freud, were the efforts of the sleeping 'psychic apparatus' to cancel or compensate for stimuli which threatened to awake it. If the thirsty sleeper did not dream of drinking his thirst would awaken him: therefore he dreams of drinking. Later, Freud explained the various 'defence mechanisms' by which the ego defends itself against the demands of the instincts (repression, sublimation, etc.) as the efforts of the central nervous system to escape these internal stimuli: being unable to escape by flight, as it would from external stimuli, it has resort to these means of abolishing, or at least reducing their impact. This was twenty years before W. B. Cannon invented the word 'homeostasis': but the notion is clearly developed in Freud's mind."

(Freud's work is of 1915 or 1900 at the earliest and W. B. Cannon's, *The Wisdom of the Body*, of 1932.)

Walker is quite in error: Cannon's merit is more than in a mere introduction of a term. Homeostasis is certainly a nineteenth century idea, clearly expounded by Claude Bernard for example. As Flugel shows, it was repeatedly applied to biology and psychology already in the nineteenth century (if not from time immemorial, as Ralf Dahrendorf suggests, *Essays in the Theory of Society*, Stanford University Press, Stanford, 1968, pp. 113, 116–7; see also Otto Mayr, *The Origins of Feedback Control*, M.I.T. Press, Cambridge, 1970). So neither Freud nor Cannon were beginners. And Cannon's coinage of a new word is really neither here nor there.

(Incidentally, I do not know why authorities and encyclopedias of diverse sorts give the birthdate of the word "homeostasis" as 1932 when Cannon's book refers to earlier uses of the term, in his 1929 "Organization for Physiological Homeostasis".)

(The technique of praising thinkers for verbal innovations is the result of certain problems insoluble for inductivists. See my *Towards an Historiography of Science*, mentioned in note 10 to section I, above, especially section III and notes 42, 43.)

The novelty of Cannon's work is in its physiological comprehensiveness. It began with the effect of shock on the reduction of blood pressure below the critical level (in WWI), a typically homeostatic problem; it developed into a fully fledged homeostatic physiology. Admittedly, Cannon mentions fear and pain, and at times even speaks of society as a homeostat. These, however, are mere asides in his otherwise purely physiological and purely homeostatic classic book. Freud's homeostats, by a great contradistinction, are purely psychological (though in the hope that one day they will be physiologically explained).

This soon became license, and made reductionism a mere pious embellishment. Rod Stagner, *Psychology of Industrial Conflict*, New York & London, 1956, for example, treats biological needs and ideological values on equal footing while admitting, incidentally, that in a sense they are on "different levels". This is a joke.

The contrast between Cannon and Freud can best be observed in the attempt to apply Cannon's view straight to psychology — by J. M. Fletcher in his "The Wisdom of the Mind", *Sigma X: Quart.*, Vol. 26, 1938, pp. 6–16, and "Homeostasis as an Explanatory Principle in Psychology", *Psych. Rev.*, Vol. 49, 1942, pp.

80–87. (See also H. H. Toch and A. H. Hastorf, "Homeostasis in Psychology", *Psychiatry*, Vol. 18, 1955, pp. 81–92.) This is also the place to notice, in passing, that Thomas S. Szasz began his departure from Freud by noticing that thermodynamics, information theory, and cybernetics have rendered Freud's mechanistic view of man obsolete even from the physical viewpoint, let alone the psychological one. See further notes 51ff. to Section III below.

27. "I regard anthropology as the principle of all research", says Claude Lévi-Strauss (*The Savage Mind*, Chicago University Press, 1966, p. 248), and he makes it clear that he means all research, not only all social research: he quotes (note, p. 248) the logician E. W. Beth (*The Foundations of Mathematics*, Amsterdam, 1949, p. 151), to say "Logic and logistics are empirical sciences belonging to ethnography rather than psychology". This is an extreme form of anthropologism.

In the same place where Lévi-Strauss declared his anthropologism, he ascribes to Sartre the view that "defines man in terms of dialectic and dialectic in terms of history". (I do not pretend, as Lévi-Strauss does, to understand this. But I understand and agree with his following statement (p. 256): "Sartre is certainly not the only contemporary philosopher to have valued history above other human sciences and formed an almost mystical conception of it.") It is therefore attractive but difficult to speak of historism as akin to anthropologism, sociologism, mechanism, etc. See my "Methodological Individualism", referred to in note 8 to Introduction, note 11 there.

28. The sentiment expressed here is very much the same as expressed by Marjorie Grene in her essay on philosophical anthropology in Raymond Klibansky's *Contemporary Philosophy, A Survey*, Florence, 1969, pp. 215–20, p. 217:

"Now, while it is true that philosophical tasks are conceptual, not empirical, and while philosphers cannot and should not run on the heels of every advance in science, it is nevertheless the case that there are advances in science, and crises in science, whose relevance to philosophy is patent."

29. The view that philosophical anthropology is impossible without a philosophy of nature is expressed in Marjorie Grene's *Approaches to a Philosophical Biology*, Basic Books, New York and London, 1968, pp. 65–6, and ascribed to Helmuth Plessner; see his *Die Stufen des Organischen und der Mensch*, Berlin, 1928, 1965.

30. Erwin Schrödinger, *Nature and the Greeks*, Cambridge University Press, 1954; see also *Science and Humanism*, Cambridge University Press, 1951.

III EXPLANATION IS NOT ELIMINATION

Science aims at satisfactory explanation. Satisfactory explanation is very different from explaining away or from eliminational explanation, as I shall now call it. Let me first give an example. When Freud explains premonition as dreams and fantasies which come true, he does not wish to offer a satisfactory explanation of the phenomenon of foreknowledge.[31] Indeed he denies that foreknowledge exists. He explains it away by satisfactorily explaining the appearance of foreknowledge, by satisfactorily explaining why people seem to observe foreknowledge, whether their own, their neighbors', or their saints': They ignore refuted premonition, express wishful thinking (benign or destructive, even self-destructive!), etc. Freud explains away all such claims for foreknowledge, because he feels the "phenomena" are only apparent. Now, since the word "phenomenon" means appearance, it sounds odd to speak of an apparent phenomenon[32] which is explained by being eliminated, as I have just done, in contradistinction to a real phenomenon which is satisfactorily explained. It is like speaking of the distinction between realistic or true fiction and fictitious or escapist fiction. I cannot discuss this point here. I have elsewhere discussed and rejected the ancient dichotomy between appearance and reality — in favor of grading our view of nature into levels of reality.[33] Briefly, let me say here, if there are degrees of appearance, then we can say that to Freud the appearance of foreknowledge is very dreamlike, of a very high degree of appearance.

In a way, as Popper has already indicated, all explanation is elimination — in the sense that a satisfactory explanation alters the very appearances it comes to explain, meaning that new theories create new appearances. Thus, when Newton explained Galileo's finding that gravitational acceleration is constant, he indeed replaced it with the claim that terrestrial gravitation under ordinary circumstances is almost or practically or apparently constant.[34] It is important, for present purposes, to notice the difference between Newton's explanation of Galileo's law and Freud's explanation of premonition. Freud's explanation, but not Newton's, practically does away with that which was to be explained. Newton modifies what he explains only slightly; but Freud modifies it so drastically that it ceases altogether to be what it was initially claimed to be, namely, what brought it to our attention in the first place. That which was to be explained in Freud's case, but not in Newton's case, got entirely lost after the explanation. Freud explained *claims* to foreknowledge, not foreknowledge; Newton explained the [local] *fact* of constant gravitational acceleration.[35]

The point deserves further elaboration by illustration. The classical example of a reduction is that of chemistry to physics, which has allegedly been satisfactorily effected. The reduction of the phenomenon of acids, for example, to a theory of acidity, enables us to speak of sweet acids as well as of sour or acidic acids (as J. A. Paris observed regarding the upheavals in chemistry that he had witnessed early in the nineteenth century). [36] Thus, something has been eliminated from chemistry (the "tautology" that all acids are sour) when it was reduced to physics. The reduction of chemistry to physics in general also enriches chemistry quite a bit, and makes chemistry include all sorts of interatomic and intramolecular actions, not originally intended to count as chemistry, including adhesion, cohesion, crystallography, allotropy, colloidal chemistry, and even the properties of ionic hydrogen and ionic oxygen, and perhaps even phenomena not strictly chemical such as the behavior of solutions, etc. Yet, on the whole, the very reduction of chemistry to physics, far from eliminating it, entrenches it as the domain of specifiable physical phenomena, namely those of interatomic actions, or atomic interactions, including perhaps atomic as well as molecular forces. The exact specification is still unclear and fluid, as the reduction is in fact not quite complete; but it more or less covers older specifications; chemistry is preserved with but marginal changes.

The greatest critic of Darwinism was Samuel Butler. [37] His criticism was this: Darwinian meta-biology aims at reducing biology to physics not by explaining living systems but by explaining them away. For, suppose that what characterizes a living system is that it evolves into diverse species by ecological interaction with its environment; then, surely, machines, which evolve symbiotically with man, are living things. Hence, what is living and what not becomes very different indeed from what it looked previously; the differentiation of the living from the nonliving begins to look arbitrary and pointless; life is explained, if at all, not satisfactorily but by elimination. A Darwinian may try to accept this criticism but emasculate it: he may say, this is correct, and this is as it should be; indeed life has to be explained not satisfactorily but away. [38] Perhaps life is no more of a phenomenon than foreknowledge, he might say. I shall dismiss this move by saying, we have more repeatable experience of life than of foreknowledge. If we had repeatable experiences of foreknowledge we would not like Freud's derisive elimination of it. It is undesirable to eliminate repeatable phenomena.

All this does not close the Darwin-Butler debate. Nor was it intended to. The debate was merely used to illustrate the difference between satisfactory elimination and satisfactory explanation. Whether one agrees with Butler or not, one must concede that he has introduced here an intuitive criterion which works fairly well and which may cause some trouble to some reductionists. This is quite a merit.

Let us employ Butler's criterion a bit longer to make this clear. Take the mechanistic biologist, the one whose meta-biology is the reduction of all physiology to physics. Ask a mechanist to explain, say, sexual intercourse, and he will center on glandular secretions, mechanochemistry, and chemical trigger actions, and such. Ask him, then, what characterizes, say, the peak of the sex act, the orgasm; he will not be able to say much more than that it is a certain glandular activity, accompanied by a massive disturbance of the whole system, a massive discharge of energy, etc. [39] Let that be so. Will the mechanist admit other massive disturbances and discharges of energy as cases of orgasm — say a mass demonstration, panic, a battle, or a huge thunderstorm? If he will, he may find himself in company with certain so-called primitive cosmologists, who have been studied with great curiosity by all sorts of social anthropologists. He will have, then, to readjust his view about primitive cosmology. Now, right or wrong, this need for a readjustment, for admitting as valid a hitherto unacceptable primitive view, and the fact that this need for readjustment is a result of an attempt at a reduction of one biological phenomenon to mechanochemistry — all this, to the best of my knowledge, is quite new: yet it is merely an application of Butler's criterion; an attempt to illustrate its very generality: unwittingly reductionism all too often tends to be eliminational. [40]

There is little doubt that we can trace in history both kinds of reductionism, explanatory and eliminational. The explanatory reductionist, the one who hopes to explain, says: matter thinks; the eliminatory reductionist, the one who hopes to eliminate, says: man does not think but merely responds in a complex manner determined by the complex and delicate apparatus which is in his skull. The strange fact is that seemingly the two reductionist approaches are so remote in tendency, yet it seems so easy to slide from the one to the other. Such facts, we remember, fascinated Immanuel Kant. The second part of his third Critique, his Critique of Judgment, which is an essay, "Critique of Teleological Judgment", is largely devoted to the question, can biology and psychology be reduced to physics. In a footnote there — why is it that so often the best passages in classical works are marginal? — Kant says that when exercising reductionism "at one time a lifeless matter, or again a lifeless God, at another, a living matter, or else a living God, have been tried." And, of course, he rejects all alternatives as metaphysical or uncritical. [41]

Kant's observation would not have been so exciting and perspicacious if it were not the case that most reductionism was of one kind — eliminational. Most reductionists, that is, tried to postulate lifeless matter, to use Kant's term. For it was his keen observation that the existing asymmetry between the two kinds of reductionism is a mere accident. Now the asymmetry still exists. I feel that the eliminational reductionists have gained both much popularity and much criticism. And I feel that, to retain Kant's view of the philosophical symmetry between the two, we should stress the less common form of reductionism, and discuss it critically.

In line with this, I shall now cite two modern observers who try not to explain away but to explain; and who try to postulate not dead matter but a living matter and a living God, to use Kant's idiom. Let me present, then, with all due respect and admiration, the failure of Ronald D. Laing, who tried to avoid explaining man away by postulating the living God, and of Arthur Koestler, who tried the same with living matter.

Laing thinks that a normal person identifies himself with his own body, whereas a schizophrenic views his own body with great detachment. This accommodates Federn's theory of schizophrenia as the lack of bodily feeling, and thus the failure to distinguish one's body as a self from one's environment. It also presents great spiritual leaders, however, whether Socrates or the Buddha, as schizophrenics. Which has an enormous appeal to some schizophrenics, and arouses enormous hostility in others, particularly those who practice psychotherapy. Laing says at the beginning of his *The Divided Self*, that among those who view man as a machine, the philosopher may be thought perfectly normal, but others will be rightly classed as schizophrenic. This, says Laing, is somewhat arbitrary; it should therefore be explained away rather than explained satisfactorily.[42]

Here we have a theory of schizophrenia which favors this condition and decidedly does not eliminate it. Rather, explaining the condition in a certain manner it readjusts the delineation so as to include Socrates and Descartes; for, each of them viewed his own body a part of their environment, the way a driver views his car a part of his environment rather than an extension of his body. (This, incidentally, is not quite true of all drivers, and so throws suspicion on Federn's and Laing's views of schizophrenia.) And so we have a new problem: does Laing admire all schizophrenics or only some?[43] He seems to have to say all, since he explains away the difference between Socrates and Ophelia. This has some merit, to be sure, since Don Quixote, though he is as mad as Ophelia, is a man of stature not unlike Socrates; but, alas! he is exceptional. Since this fact is denied by Laing's theory, this theory seems to me, at least, quite unacceptable as it is: it explains away schizophrenia as a suffering and the schizophrenic as a patient in need of help! Likewise, Laing does not say whether normal men are mere machines, and whether schizophrenics are all divine beings within the machine.[44] It seems that Laing explains away the suffering of schizophrenics and the humanity of others.

Here we have, then, an example of a gifted and concerned thinker, who goes deep and so is in need of better principles than he has. A fact some heartless psychiatrists view with quite unprofessional *Schadenfreude*.

Arthur Koestler, in his celebrated *The Ghost in the Machine*, chafes at Skinner for dehumanizing man, for explaining man away by his presentation of man as a mere stimulus-response mechanism, much like a rat or a pigeon. Yet he is engaged in a very similar act of dehumanization, of explaining man away as merely a complex piece of machinery. Koestler's own view is expressed in Appendix I to that volume, as well as in his favorable references to Bertalanffy,[45] and his discussion of homeostasis. He makes it amply clear that his view is nothing short of the view of man as a homeostatic machine.[46] Only, he thinks with Bertalanffy and other General Systems theorists that man is a complex homeostat; he is not just a large collection of feedback mechanisms. When it is stable, a large collection of feedback mechanisms becomes a new entity – a feedback mechanism of a given degree of complexity. The degrees of complexity, we are further told, are arranged in a hierarchy. The place man occupies in the hierarchy, then, is what delineates man from other animals, and animals from mere automata. Koestler, then, is a reductionist of sorts, but one who insists on not explaining away the reduced entity. He therefore claims to be an antireductionist, and I shall not quarrel with him on this last point since I agree that normally reductionists are eliminationists whereas he tries to avoid eliminating life. Rather, I feel, his theory is untenable in its very effort to be noneliminational.

The obvious question to ask anyone who follows the track of General Systems theory is, where does he think purpose, or goal-directedness, or teleology, enters the picture? One need not be either a Spinoza or a Kant to realize that this is the central question.[47] Koestler has at least one chapter devoted to it (Chapter XI). It starts with the condemnation of the official – mechanistic – view of purposelessness in biology, as based on the claim that if there were purpose in Nature it would have to come from God. No, says Koestler: purpose comes from the individual, it is implicit in Nature. This is what Kant saw as a materialistic reductionism, *par excellence*, which he called the finality of nature, tried out with dead matter and dead God, living matter and living God.

This can be well illustrated by the Butlerian mode of arguments developed above. Suppose Koestler is right; assume that stable complex feedback systems — those which somehow retain their complexity — are indeed purposeful; clearly, this does not make a simple guided missile a purposeful being — it is a mere simple feedback mechanism; but what should we say about a sophisticated missile, such as an interplanetary one?[48] And will Koestler view a jumbo jet plane or a stable social organization as purposeful? Koestler himself knows that the individual can shift control to his inbuilt automatic pilot (p. 206) whenever he acts absentmindedly — that is to say when he is immersed in thoughts while performing an easy and simple task, such as dishwashing. But at that point Koestler shifts his discussion to consciousness and he fails to pursue the discussion which gave rise to his points.[49] For, here he should ask, what is the difference between an automatic pilot and a pilot with a purpose, and answer the question so as to enable us to apply his theory to that case. If one may translate this difference between a purposeful pilot and an automatic pilot into General Systems theory, one may perhaps ascribe to Koestler the (unintentional) advocacy of the view that the more complex and stable organism is the more purposeful.[50] This will make Koestler wonder where to place the dinosaur in his hierarchy. It will also force Koestler to view great computers as living systems, perhaps — unless he will say they are unstable or poorly organized.[51] Yet undoubtedly this will make Koestler appear a collectivist who views the social ends above and beyond the individual ends. It is clear from the general tone of the book that Koestler notices this, and very reluctantly. Indeed, he does see animal populations as superindividuals, but his political views, clearly, oppose it.[52] In brief, Koestler has not tried to differentiate the purposeful from the purposeless complex, and so, contrary to his claim, he either failed to reduce purpose to complexity, or he has reduced and explained away all purpose as mere chimera.[53]

Notes to Section III

31. Sigmund Freud, *The Interpretation of Dreams*, standard edition of *Complete Works*, Volume V, 1953 and many reprints, see Index, Art. "Premonitory Dreams".

For example, p. 621,

"And the value of dreams for giving us knowledge of the future? There is of course no question of that . . . Nevertheless the ancient belief . . . is not wholly devoid of truth . . . But this future, which the dreamer pictures as the present, has been molded by his . . . wish . . ."

Appendix A is about a case of premonitory dream, the crucial point being (p. 623),

"... On seeing him she felt convinced that she had dreamt the night before of having this very meeting at that precise spot ..."

The conclusion is (p. 625),

"Thus the creation of a dream after the event ... is ... a form of censoring ..."

In brief, Freud's views were traditional hard-line rationalistic — "there is of course no question" — yet he explains the prevalence of superstitions not as optical illusions of sorts (Bacon) or national (Hegel) or class (Marx) centered bias, but as neuroses.

See also Freud's *Dreams and Telepathy,* 1922, standard edition of *Complete Works,* Vol. XVIII, pp. 197–220, where Freud tries to remain open-minded. This is not to say that his mind was at ease as it would be, had he said only, thus far we have no data on it but we may; and we shall treat them as they come up. Rather, he was both alarmed and fascinated by the idea. See his *New Introductory Lectures,* Lecture 30, Dreams and Occultism, third paragraph from end, p. 54 of Vol. XXII of the standard edition.

"... I too felt a dread of a threat against our scientific *Weltanschauung,* which, I feared, was bound to give place to spiritualism or mysticism if portions of occultism were proved true. Today I think otherwise."

The editors also refer to his posthumous "Psychoanalysis and Telepathy", 1941, standard edition, Vol. XVIII, pp. 177–81. In this work Freud begins with an allusion to Adler and Jung (p. 177, note) adding,

"scarcely, then, do we feel ourselves safe from these enemies [!], when another peril has arisen. And this time it is something tremendous, something elemental, which threatens not us alone but our enemies, perhaps, still more."

What a projection of hostility as well as of a conflict!

32. The word "epiphenomenalism" indicates a deviation from the dichotomy appearance-reality, and in the same way in which Husserl's "essence of phenomena" does; for if phenomena can be epiphenomena or essences of phenomena, then there may be the essence of an epiphenomenon and epi-essence-of-a-phenomenon, etc. *ad lib.* But what the epithet "epiphenomenon" may mean within the distinction reality-appearance, here is an appearance that is clearly no reality. I doubt that this clear meaning is the historically correct one, however. Rather, epiphenomenalism means, since mental phenomena are no more than phenomena, they can safely be explained away.

"Banished mind from the universe" is Butler's expression. "Not only mind, but life of any sort, was banished from the universe;" adds Shaw (preface to R. A. Wilson, *The Miraculous Birth of Language*, Philosophical Library, New York, 1948, p. 14), and "and Materialism went stark raving mad."

33. See my "Sensationalism", mentioned in note 5 to Section I above.

34. See Sir Karl Popper, *Objective Knowledge: An Evolutionary Approach*, Oxford, 1972, Chapter 5, "The Aims of Science" (first published in 1957).

35. The distinction between explaining and explaining away is nowhere so crucial as in psychiatry. Claims for systematic foreknowledge, to use our present example, when they come from an unexpected source, will at once be viewed as a sign of some psychopathology. As Ronald Laing says in his *The Divided Self*, Tavistock Publications, London, 1960; Pelican, London, 1965, Chapter 1, p. 22; cf. Chapter 4, p. 70, mechanistic views expressed by disturbed people are signs of schizophrenia. So are solipsistic views, as J. O. Wisdom notes; see his *The Unconscious Origin of Berkeley's Philosophy*, Hogarth Press, London, 1953; see Index, Art. Hallucination. Even the concern with such theories is a sign of emotional disturbance. The reason for this is, of course, that whereas philosophers wish to explain human phenomena, including emotional and intellectual interactions, (borderline) psychotics wish to explain them away. I do not mean to say that every act of explaining away is (borderline) psychotic, however: I am merely speaking here of the motivation of some disturbed minds, which is to explain away human interaction in a vain effort to resolve conflicting tendencies to seek and yet to reject interaction (out of "natural" desires plus fears). This theory of the psychotic's motivation may be true or false; my point here is that even in order to assert it, already, we need the distinction between explaining and explaining away; otherwise, in asserting it we would simply confuse philosophers and psychotics, the philosopher's quest for knowledge with the psychotic's desire to escape a conflict, curiosity with escape. No doubt the two — curiosity and escape — may be linked in diverse ways (malignant or benign); but we need not confuse them.

In a similar way social anthropologists, even when they are relativists and do not wish to contradict claims of primitive people for magical power, nonetheless explain away such claims, or at least refuse to explain them as true. This point was forcefully made by Ernest Gellner. See his "The New Idealism" in I. Lakatos and A. Musgrave, eds., *Problems in the Philosophy of Science*, Amsterdam, 1968, pp. 377–406, 426–32; reprinted in his *Cause and Meaning in the Social Sciences*, Routledge, London and Boston, 1973, pp. 50–77, esp. p. 69.

36. J. A. Paris, *The Life of Sir Humphry Davy*, Colburn and Bentley, London, 1831, p. 172 and note.

"Instead of possessing that ponderosity which we should have expected in a body otherwise metallic, it [the new alkaline metal] is so light as not only to swim upon the surface of water, but even upon that of naphtha, by far the lightest liquid in nature. Davy, however, very justly argues, that low specific gravity does not offer a sufficient reason for degrading this body from the rank of a metal; for amongst those which constitute the class, there are remarkable differences with respect to this quality, that platina is nearly four times as heavy as tellurium. In the philosophical division of bodies into classes, the analogy between the greater number of properties must always be the foundation of arrangement.

The propriety, and even the necessity of such a compact become daily more apparent, as our knowledge of bodies extends. If we were to degrade a substance from its class, in consequence of the absence of some one quality which enters into its more perfect examples, we should soon find ourselves involved in paradoxes. — What idea, for instance, could we form of an acid — its sourness? — Prussic Acid — Arsenious Acid, are not sour. — Its tendency to combine with an alkaline or earthy base? — If so, sugar is an acid, for it combines with lime. I remember a chemist having been exposed to much ridicule from speaking of a *sweet* acid — Why not?"

In a brief aside about science I. Lakatos speaks in his "Proofs and Refutations, IV", *Brit. J. Phil. Sci.*, Vol. 14, 1963—4, pp. 296—342, p. 322, of the fact that glass is a (supercooled) fluid, saying it is "concept-stretching". Clearly, the mechanism of stretching differs in science and mathematics.

37. The *locus classicus* for Butler's critique of Darwin is, of course, his *Erewhon*. There have been quite a few complaints about the neglect of this great thinker, and so I shall leave the topic now, merely expressing my regret that the complaints are still valid.

The Darwin-Butler controversy is still awaiting a judicious examination. Meanwhile see Phyllis Greenacre, *The Quest for the Father: A Study of the Darwin-Butler Controversy as a Contribution to the Understanding of the Creative Individual,* International Universities Press, New York, 1963. Howard E. Gruber, *Darwin the Man, A Psychological Study of Scientific Creativity,* Dutton, New York, 1974, p. 44, note, comments on this volume, saying, "The new material in our book . . . may lead some psychoanalysts to reconsider some of their interpretations".

There may be an adumbration of Butler's idea in earlier works — I am unconvinced.

"... philosophy has the honor of laying before us, with modest pride, her contribution towards the subject: that life is a Permanent Possibility of Sensation. Truly a fine result! A man may very well love beef, or hunting, or a woman, but surely, surely, not a Permanent Possibility of Sensation. . ."
says Robert Louis Stevenson, in his essay, "Aes Triplex", sixth paragraph. See his *Essays,* selected and edited with an introduction and notes by William Lyon Phelps, Scribners, New York, 1892, 1906, 1909, p. 48.

It is not clear whether Stevenson rightly complains that philosophy explains life away or erroneously denies the possibility that (love of) life ever be properly explained. But in any case all this is much too vague, and we should beware of reading too much into a vague and highly suggestive text, even though, of course, some may indeed be inspired by such a text and many more may enjoy reading it.

38. The view that life should be explained away is ascribed by Sir Karl Popper to La Mettrie, N. W. Pirie, and A. M. Turing — to La Mettrie without justice and to Turing with justice. (Pirie talks meaninglessly about "The Meaninglessness of the Terms Life and Living".) See Popper's "Of Clouds and Clocks" notes 38 and 39 and reference, there, as well as the text to these notes; republished in Popper's *Objective Knowledge, An Evolutionary Approach*, Oxford, 1972, pp. 224—5.

Popper argues against the view that life is indistinguishible from non-life by asserting that art and technology and their rules did not exist prior to the existence of life. I find this argument question-begging.

39. The similarity between sex and violence, in man and generally in animal, is not new; see note 26 to Section VI below. I am anxious to stress, lest I be misunderstood, that I do not reject the theory of orgasm as a total discharge akin to a storm. I only deny that saying so supports mechanism. As to the theory itself, it is an interesting one which, for example, demands a reinterpretation of reported cases of men ejaculating during a psychotic collapse or in the heat of the battle, since this theory suggests that such events need not be sexual at all, but part of a total discharge derivative of a nonsexual effort. I have observed a thirteen-year-old meningitis patient die and stiffen with an erection and I cannot easily imagine that this was anything related specifically to sex in any way.

What all this indicates to me is not only that orgasm is different from a storm, but even that there is a sexual orgasm, to be distinguished from an orgasm due to different excitements; by a mechanistic distinction between these, if mechanism is to be held in the face of such facts. Needless to say, there is nothing so subtle in the mechanistic literature as yet.

Now, of course, the hypothesis that orgasm is a total discharge may be false, and I wonder whether it is at all testable, especially in view of the facts that on the one hand sexual discharge need not be orgasmic and on the other hand orgasm need not be sexual even when it includes a sexual discharge. At best we may imagine a physical measure of a total discharge, say physical exhaustion, and a psychological expression of orgasm, say as reported by the subject. This would make the hypothesis barely testable, and only after further specification of the mental side of a total discharge of unusual kinds. For this, at the very least, most of the current sexological studies should be taken as a point of departure but treated with much suspicion.

40. The latest authoritative expression of the traditional confusion between eliminational and explanatory reduction is C. G. Hempel, "Reduction: Ontological and Linguistic Facets", in S. Morgenbesser, P. Suppes, and M. White, eds., *Philosophy, Science, and Method: Essays in Honor of Ernest Nagel*, New York, 1969, and see also Marshall Spector's review of this in *Metaphilosophy*, Vol. 2, 1971, pp. 254ff.

An expression of the distinction between eliminational and explanatory reduction, can be found in John Hospers, "What is Explanation", first published in *J. Phil.*, 1946; revised version in Antony Flew, ed., *Essays in Conceptual Analysis,* McMillan, London, St. Martin's Press, New York, 1956, pp. 94–119; reprinted in Joel Feinberg, ed., *Reason and Responsibility, Readings in Some Basic Problems of Philosophy*, Dickens Publ. Co., Belmont, Calif., 1965, pp. 180–191, in the final section, section 9. Also, Mario Bunge, *Method, Model and Matter,* Reidel, Dordrecht and Boston, 1973, p. 61:

"Explanation does not involve ontological reduction: the peculiarities of a whole that are not present in its components are not wiped out upon being explained as an outcome of the integration of its parts. Hence naive reductionism is false. In particular, it is not true that an organism is nothing but an aggregate of macromolecules . . ."

Bunge continues, p. 62, to present organisms as emergent multilevel systems. On this I have no fixed views. Note, also, that Bunge boldly concludes from this that "vitalism is not dead" (pp. 44, 65). A similar view of Claude Lévi-Strauss is quoted in note 50 below.

Bunge's view, need I say, is a minority view. The current majority view is expressed, for example, in K. R. Popper's *Objective Knowledge,* Clarendon Press, Oxford, 1972, pp. 290–1, where reduction and explanation are identified, e.g. of chemistry to physics, and the hope is expressed that biology will not be successfully reduced. But this raises the question, what is the criterion for a successful scientific explanation, and here it seems, not refutability but knowledge proper guides Popper's discussion. For, even if biology cannot be truly a part of physics, what in Popper's system prevents the advancement of biology by offering false and refutable physical explanations of all known biology? And does he not imply that the physics with which we explain chemistry today is satisfactory because obviously it is true? If so, then he deviates here from his philosophy as he expounds it everywhere elsc, i.e., as a theory of science as conjectural.

41. The important footnote is to Kant's *Critique of Judgment,* §72.

The proposal to append a speculation to some solid empirical research first appears in Robert Boyle, Proëmial Essay, *Certain Physiological Essays,* 1661, reprinted in part as preface to Peter Shaw's popular edition of Boyle's philosophical works. The practice became standard in the 18th century. Newton emulated it in his own idiosyncratic way in his *Opticks, Queries,* and in his *Principia,* 3rd ed., *Scholium Generale.* When it became standard to state one's speculation in a final footnote, I cannot say. Of course, at times an important idea comes in a note, final or not, simply because it is a loose end.

42. R. D. Laing, *The Divided Self,* Tavistock Publications, London, 1960, Pelican, 1965.

Laing's thesis, as put in his *The Politics of Experience,* London and New York, 1967, p. 83 (see also p. 70) is, "There is no such 'condition' as 'schizophrenia', but the label is a social fact and the social fact is a *political event.*" He thus not only defends the so-called schizophrenic, which is what Thomas S. Szasz does too (*The Myth of Mental Illness,* Hoeber, Secker and Warburg, New York and London, 1961); he goes further than Szasz in condemning the normal: "What we call normal is a product of repression" (p. 11, see also p. 41). "True sanity entails . . . the dissolution of the normal ego, that false self competently adjusted . . . through this death a rebirth, and the eventual reestablishment of a new kind of ego-functioning . . ." (p. 101). See note 24 to Section VI below.

Laing's insight into the so-called adjusted living-dead has a long tradition going back to Kierkegaard, John Donne, and yonder. His idea of holy madness is ancient. Yet he is in error about adjustment. First, the normal living-dead is adjusted but not well-adjusted, because not further adjustable. As Shaw says in *Fanny's First Play*, members of the middle class are only well-adjusted as long as they stay put, whereas both aristocrats and workers are more pliable. Second, the schizophrenic is one who cannot contain his being abnormal, who is as unadjusted in a normal society as a member of it would be in an abnormal one.

Indeed, Laing himself faces this when he explains who gets labelled schizophrenic: "The experience and behavior that gets labelled schizophrenic is *a special strategy that a person invents in order to live in an unlivable situation*" (p. 79, italics in the original). Here the similarity and difference between Laing and Szasz are striking, where Laing is the more compassionate and Szasz the more reasonable: Laing protests that society is an accomplice and even a source of incentive in the terrible act of relinquishing one's responsibility whereas Szasz demands that this act be never recognized. My sympathy goes to both of them, but I really think they both pay little attention to prevention which seems to lie in the hope that we may train people to adjust with little pain to diverse societies without compromising their moral or other principles. There is a moment at which one decides to get sick, said Charcot, and both Laing and Szasz study the meaning of that moment. I think, however, it is not the decision to become schizophrenic, but the theory of what it is to be one, the diagnosis, not the case history, that matters here. There is the widespread theory, very clearly expressed in the muddled and very objectionable, Th. Freeman, J. L. Cameron, and A. McGhie, *Chronic Schizophrenia,* Preface by Anna Freud, Foreword by T. Ferguson Rodger, Tavistock Publications, London, 1958, Chapter 6, Confusion of Identity, pp. 52–60: sanity equals identity, i.e. clear, secure identity. This theory is first, false, and second, a great concession which Laing unnecessarily makes to the Establishment.

There is no doubt that certain individuals can function normally, if at all, only without identity; yet the only way their psychiatrists try to help them, is by imposing identities on them. If what Laing says is that we should not force them to accept an identity, he is quite right. But he says more. He agrees with the view that the normal, socially stable person, must have ontological security, and yet he rejects stability. But it is so obvious that the heroes he speaks of as examples of socially unstable, from Socrates down, were eminently sane. And so the argument that insanity is good as exemplified by Socrates breaks down: Socrates was with no secure identity, yet sane. The same holds for Shakespeare, at least according to Borges, who imagines that Shakespeare suffered from his lack of identity and found some consolation in the theatre.

This is not to say that one has to be a man of genius to be sane yet with no identity. Indeed, many actors are obviously with "weak personalities" to their loss in this or that way but to the benefit of their art. Similarly, many rather undistinguished intellectuals are "absent-minded professors", especially professors of philosophy, who find personal salvation in the most helpful friendly involvement in young people's disturbing intellectual difficulties. Thus, Shakespeare and Socrates are rare in outstanding achievement but certainly not so rare examples of sane selflessness.

See for example Laing's *Politics of Experience*, p. 96, for a discussion of ego-loss as benign, as madness, but "to be mad is not necessarily to be ill". I should like to think that there is only a verbal difference, not a disagreement here, that Laing does not think we need an identity. But I read him to say the journey into the psychotic experience, when not ill, helps us develop a newer and better identity, whereas I say we do not need an identity or we can operate with alternative ones and so feel detached from any sense of identity and have no ontological security. I think Laing feels that the journey into inner space is important and frightening due to a temporary loss of this security. If so, I think there is a clear disagreement: we can feel insecure but not afraid, whereas he thinks it is quite frightening and must terminate "in a new kind of ego-functioning" (p. 101).

It is hard to say how much Laing holds an exaggerated thesis and how much he holds a reasonable thesis put in exaggerated wording. When he says "madness need not be all breakdown. It may also be a breakthrough" he not only is saying the obvious, he implicitly concedes that often madness is, alas, rather a breakdown than a breakthrough. Yet his message in the very end of his *The Politics of Experience* ("The Bird of Paradise"), his most famous aphorism, is, "If I could turn you on, if I could drive you out of your wretched mind, if I could tell you, I would let you know" goes much further, both in assuming that (since normal) I am wretched, and that if I go crazy I'd be better off. (Should we say, I'd have a breakthrough rather than a breakdown, or should we say Laing is searching for that madness which is all breakthrough and no breakdown?)

Nelson N. Foote, "Identification as the Basis for a Theory of Motivation", *Am. Soc. Rev.*, Vol. 16, No. 1, 1951, pp. 14–21, p. 18: "Establishment of one's identity to oneself is as important in interaction as to establish it for the other".

This is a prescriptive overtone pasted on a descriptive statement. I grant, on the whole, the truth of the description. It is, nonetheless, a cruel fact that identity is so obligatory and even final. As to finality, when a person needs a change of identity badly, for example, if he has dangerous traits (alcoholic, gambling, etc.) his nearest and closest are impatient with his change, viewing it as a deviation — since it is still easier for themselves to see him as unchanged. As to obligatory nature, some schizophrenics who can be cured only without searching for identity, are molested, for their own good, by psychiatrists who erroneously try to force them into a mold and help them build an identity for themselves (Corbett Thigben and Harvey M. Cleckley, *The Three Faces of Eve*, Kingsport, Tenn., 1957).

The fact that some people may do better without identity is adumbrated in a strange book, Robert Jay Lifton, *Boundaries, Psychological Man In Revolution*, Random House, New York, 1967, 1968, 1969. On p. 45 Lifton presents what he calls "the Protean revolutionary style":

"One patient of mine . . . referred to himself as 'wearing a number of masks' which he could put on or take off. He asked the question, 'is there, or should there be, one face which should be authentic?' . . ."

p. 46: ". . . Saul Bellow . . . In *The Adventures of Augie March* . . . we meet a picaresque hero with an impressive talent for adapting himself to divergent social worlds. . . .

"... I think it is because of Protean traits ... that Sartre strikes us as such an embodiment of twentieth-century man ... Sartre ... refers to human consciousness as 'a sheer activity transcending towards objects', and 'a great emptiness, a wind blowing towards objects' . . ."

I do not myself accept this characterization of Sartre, and I find the quoted passage but a histrionic restatement of an idea of Franz Brentano, yet one which is worth noticing. Whereas, since Descartes, mind (as a substance) was equated with consciousness, Brentano approached the mind (not metaphysically but empirically) declaring as a fact that consciousness is transitive, i.e. that we cannot be conscious except of something, of an object of consciousness. There was a long way from this to the total demolition of the self (as a substance), already suggested (on purely epistemological grounds) by Hume over a century earlier, but this is, I think, the beginning of the end. Once the self is gone, the (Freudian) super-ego cum ego, or the (classical) character, is gone as well.

To return to Lifton, commenting on Sartre's autobiography, *The Words* (p. 48), he says,

"Now here we see a fundamental breakdown in the boundaries of mentorship and authority ... [it] has enormous consequences throughout the world . . ."

And further (p. 58),

"... Protean man retains some of this Utopian imagery [of Science], but he finds it increasingly undermined by massive disillusionment. More and more he calls forth the other side of the God-devil polarity generally applied to science . . . This kind of profound ambivalence . . ."

Finally, p. 63

"the whole stability-change issue badly needs general psychological reevaluation, especially in regard to the kinds of significant change that can take place within a person while much else remains constant . . ."

which is true, yet misses the chance to attack the "stability-change issue" as just another polarity – due to an inexplicable pro-Mao sentiment (pp. 67ff.), culminating with an odd panegyric on Mao's *existential absolute, an insistence upon all-or-none confrontation with death"*, which is a mixture of fanaticism and cheap existentialism.

Lifton does contrast the Maoist man with the Protean man (pp. 90–91), but he hopes that the Cultural Revolution is a stage which accelerates the rise of the Chinese Protean man (pp. 91–92), which is old-fashioned drab historicism, even though he declares him "a despot" (p. 111), and concludes (last sentence) with a denunciation of historicism.

One of the very few places where I have found the accepted theory of identity questioned is in Edna M. O'Hern's review of Adam Curle, *Mystics and Militants: A Study of Awareness, Identity, and Social Action*, Tavistock Publications, London, 1972, in *Contemporary Sociology*, Vol. 3, No. 1, January 1974, p. 31:

"Perhaps this book is more valuable for the questions it suggests than for those

it answers. If it is true that high belonging-identity combined with low awareness is the chief correlate of support of oppressive systems, is this necessarily always and everywhere true ...? ... is it possible for individuals to live a rich and meaningful life without significant belonging-identity?"
It must be stated categorically: yes. We know of many individuals who did very well without it, whose life's quality developed only after they preferred to have no belonging-identity at all.

Change of identity is advocated in Lewis M. Killian and Sanford Bloomberg, "Rebirth in a Therapeutic Community: A Case Study", *Psychiatry*, Vol. 38, 1975, pp. 39–54, especially p. 53.

See also D. Holbrook's review of Laing's works, "R. D. Laing and the Death Circuit", *Encounter,* August 1968 and *Psychiatry and Social Science Review,* Vol. 3, April 1969, as well as my "Philosophy as Literature: the Case of Borges" in *Mind,* Vol. 39, 1970, pp. 117–135. See also S. Halleck, *Psychiatry and Dilemmas of Crime: A Study of Causes, Punishment and Treatment,* Harper, New York, 1967, and T. Szasz, L. H. Rogler and A. B. Hollingshead, *Trapped: Families and Schizophrenia.*

The theory of identity is confused, and the easiest, perhaps is to clear its history, beginning with ambiguities, confusions, and distortions in Freud himself. Freud's theory presents the ego as mere space-time-causality coordinator. This is extremely clear, but Freud added that the clear division between the id, ego, and super-ego exists or shows only in cases of conflict. That is to say, the ego has to coordinate rationally between the id, which gives us our drives, and its opponent the super-ego which gives us both constraints on our drives and an added motive, the ego-ideal which is one's self-image. The identity theory is the view that the ego includes also a clear idea of the self-image or else it is sick. And, contrary to repeated claims that psychosis is a severe neurosis Freud said also that psychosis is damage to the ego-meaning, to the coordination; but once we have the self-image in the ego, there is plenty of room for maneuver.

All this led to two related developments. Adler declared that the division of the mind is an error — this is a minor point — and that a person's style and character are important, though often rooted in a false theory of the person's continuity. And, finally, he declared a person's social position and view of it as very important. All this influenced Freudians, especially Karen Horney and Erik Erikson, but this influence is ignored by the Freudian Establishment, which endorses these ideas as if they were more or less Freud's own. See H. L. and R. R. Ansbacher, eds., *The Individual Psychology of Alfred Adler,* Basic Books, New York, 1956, Harper Torch, 1964, 1967, p. 16; also their introduction to their edition of A. Adler, *Superiority and Social Interest,* 3rd revised edition, Viking Press, New York, 1964.

Meanwhile Paul Federn developed the Freudian concept, trying hard not to damage the sense of continuity, to minimize the differences between Freud and himself. See, for a conspicuous example, his 1949 Topeca lectures (after the Master died); Paul Federn, *Ego Psychology and the Psychoses,* edited with Introduction by Edoardo Weiss, Imago Publication, London, 1953, pp. 210–260; p. 212:

"Although Freud's theory of the ego and the id is well formulated, it is not that theory but the familiar phenomenon of the *ego feeling* that proves the existence of the ego. The ego is not merely . . . There is in every individual the ego unit which remains the same . . . The ego feeling enables the individual to distinguish between the ego as subject and the whole outer world, and also between the ego as object and all representations of object."

The editor adds a note "In handwriting at this point is, Martin Buber *Das Ich und das Du*", referring to Buber's *Ich und Du*. Yet on the whole, Federn's theory was psychologistic (following Freud's remark on the body-ego, speaking of the boundary of the body); it was not sociological and completely ignored the social niche of the person: the sociological component was introduced by Karen Horney (quoted below, note 44 to Section XXIII) via Freud's idea of the ego-ideal, i.e. the self-image, and by Erik Erikson via the idea of identity as social identity, making the Freudian theory of sanity conservative: to be sane is to accept one's social place.

Identity became very popular, especially with its adaptation to existentialism. See Rollo May, "The Emergence of Existential Psychology" in Rollo May, ed., *Existential Psychology*, Random House, New York, 1961, 1967, pp. 11–51, especially pp. 45–7. In that essay, as elsewhere, the "ego" and "non-ego" are identified with the "being" and "non-being" of the Existentialists. Existentialism looks anti-Establishment since it brands the conformists living-dead; Erikson's theory is Establishment; their combination looks like having the cake and eating it too. For the general theory of combining both conservative and radicalist theories of society see Section XI and notes. For the fact that this combination is puritanical if not older see note 74 to Section XXV below.

43. See *Inquiry*, Vol. 15, Nos. 1–2, Summer 1972, issue on mental health, especially James M. Glass, "Schizophrenia and Perception: A Critique of the Liberal Theory of Externality", pp. 114–145, and Ronald B. de Sousa, "The Politics of Mental Illness" (review of Szasz' *The Manufacture of Madness*), pp. 187–202, and references there. See also Y. Fried and J. Agassi, *Paranoia, Boston Studies*, Reidel, 1976.

44. A note on the so-called problem of other minds.

The problem, is man a machine, is the same as, does man have a mind. Somehow – schizophrenically, I think – this is also identified with the so-called problem of other minds, which is, how do I know that people other than myself possess minds? This is the problem of Bishop Berkeley. He said, first, what exists is what is perceived; second, people exist. It looks as if he contradicted himself: after all (according to his theory of vision), we do not see people. At most we can allow that I exist, as I directly perceive myself (!). From then on, says Berkeley, we go by analogy. Ergo, I do not know, I only guess (by induction), that others exist too. Can there be a way for me to know for sure that others exist? Clearly, if not, then (induction by) analogy is not allowed since it permits the existence of all sorts of unperceived (unknown) entities.

For Hume, by contrast, neither my mind nor other minds exist in the sense of being a substance. They exist in a more common sense, which he thinks he explains without reference to substance (but does not). In the common sense, says Hume (*Treatise,* Book II), not only I exist, but also I perceive the existence of others, directly, through a sense known as sympathy. So, for Hume, minds do not exist, yet the problem of other minds is easily solved.

Hence the problem of other minds has nothing much to do with our problem, is man a machine. I need not discuss it at all.

The claim that the philosophical problem of other minds is a pseudo-problem can be found in Marjorie Grene, *Approaches to a Philosophical Biology*, Basic Books, New York and London, 1968, p. 107: "For persons are persons, *by definition,* only insofar as they take a stand . . . to be capable of putting myself in the place of others". See also her pp. 162ff., 189ff. The book does not refer to Martin Buber, though it seemingly often alludes to him.

45. Bertalanffy's General Systems theory is declared ridiculously general and vague in Ida R. Hoos, *System Analysis in Public Policy. A Critique*, University of California Press, Berkeley, 1972. For my part I will not pretend to be familiar with it beyond the ideas expressed and discussed in the present work.

46. Koestler shows more sophistication and up-to-date knowledge than reviewers and critics credit him with. Thus he rejects reinforcement altogether in favor of feedback. See also text to note 96 to Section IX below for Skinner's comment on Koestler.

See Norbert Wiener, *The Human Use of Human Beings, Cybernetics and Society*, Houghton Mifflin, Boston, 1950, Doubleday, New York, 1955, p. 26, towards end of Chapter 1:

"If I pick up my cigar, I do not will to move any specific muscles. Indeed, in many cases, I do not know what those muscles are. What I do is to turn into action a certain feedback mechanism; namely a reflex in which the amount by which I have yet failed to pick up the cigar is turned into a new and increased order to the lagging muscles, whichever they may be. In this same way, a fairly uniform voluntary command will enable the same task to be performed from widely varying initial positions . . ."

47. R. Polin, "The Sense of the Human", in P. Kurtz, ed., *Language and Human Nature, A French-American Philosopher's Dialogue*, St. Louis, 1971, pp. 87–112, pp. 87–8, notes Kant's enormous impact here:

"When it comes to determining the sense of man, practical philosophy since Kant has been increasingly faced with a new difficulty . . . the Kantian effect to postulate a metaphysics based on ethics instead of deducing, in accordance with tradition, an ethic based on metaphysics. Man is thought of more and more . . . as an . . . acting freedom, and less and less as a nature . . .

". . . [We] recognize in man a nature whose main characteristic is . . . his freedom . . ."

See also Ian C. Jarvie, "Is Technology Unnatural?" *The Listener*, Thursday,

March 9, 1967, Vol. 57, No. 1980, pp. 322–324 and 333, last sentences:
"If we do build robot women, perhaps there will be a public demand for them to be clearly marked. They are, after all, not the real thing. How long such an invidious new caste system could last is anybody's guess. Far more sensible to jettison the false philosophy on which it is based."

48. K. M. Sayre, *Consciousness: A Philosophic Study of Minds and Machines*, New York, 1969, claims (p. 169) that "consciousness is a form of information processing; in particular a patterned response on a part of an organism's information-processing system to stimulation of its sensory receptors." He offers a model there, a model "bound to appear deficient in many respects if taken as a description", which it is not intended to be: the model "indicates in broad outlines some of the processes" etc. – necessary but not sufficient conditions. It is then not surprising that the author can conclude that machines may be conscious, free agents, etc.: any model of consciousness, if realizable, enables us to build a conscious machine. This conclusion, in accord with Butler's criticism but perhaps not taking sufficient account of it, belongs, I suppose, to Norbert Wiener. See note 22 to Section II and note 46 above.

49. This is not to reject the thesis which Koestler advocates, namely, that consciousness is an attribute of complex systems of certain degree of complexity rather than of goal-directedness. E. Ray John, "Switchboard vs. Statistical Theories of Learning and Memory", *Science,* 8 September 1972, Vol. 177, No. 4052, pp. 850–864, says, on p. 862, that his statistical theory "is also descriptive of the subjective experience of remembering"; he can, he says, "define" i.e. explain "the memory content of consciousness in an animal . . ." His speculation which he claims so much for relates to data that the "subjective experience, 'remembering', is the concomitant of the release of the electric wave-shape representing a specific memory." The speculation says,
"subjective experience in man should be attributed to the temporal patterns of coherence in the enormous populations of neurons which make up our brains . . . The continuity and stability of content of human consciousness . . . arise from invariant features of the patterned fluctuations in coherent statistical ensembles."
If this be the case, then we can construct conscious computers which, however, will not have goals of their own. But I cannot see a computer having any emotion, consciousness or any other.

50. An opposition to reductionism as eliminational can be found in S. H. Bartley's paper, "Psychology as a Biological Science", in J. R. Royce, *Toward Unification in Psychology, The First Banff Conference on Theoretical Psychology,* University of Toronto Press, 1970, pp. 185–209. On p. 190, he claims that "reductionism [is] to be avoided . . . whatever set of facts is actually required to solve a psychological problem is psychology" which is excellent, except that a solution is usually a theory, seldom a fact. Anyway, he goes on,

"Reductionism, the pitfall of today's novice and yesterday's veteran, is not to be read into my suggestions. Reductionism is to be excluded in all cases. You are to be reminded that each level of description and organization has its own existence and no level is to be either reduced to another one or in any way to be taken as identical to it. A is *always* A, B is *always* B. Some sort of relation may be spoken of, but one can never be transmuted into the other."

This impressive quote means, I think, we can try to explain A by B, perhaps even succeed all the way; but we do not thereby explain away one domain by the other. For, Bartley does seem to recommend psychology as biological – not, however as mere biology. See also *op. cit.*, p. 212.

The conditions here specified at so great a detail against explaining away by reduction are succinctly stated by Claude Lévi-Strauss in the conclusion of his *The Savage Mind*, Chicago University Press, 1966, p. 247:

"The reductions I am envisaging are thus legitimate, or indeed possible, only if two conditions are satisfied. First, the phenomena subjected to reduction must not be impoverished ... Secondly, one must be ready to accept, as a consequence of each reduction, the total overturning of any preconceived idea concerning the level, whichever it may be, one is striving to attain ... And when we do finally succeed in understanding life as a function of inert matter, it will be discovered that the latter has properties very different from those previously attributed to it ... Scientific explanation consists not in moving from the complex to the simplex but in the replacement of a less intelligible complexity by one which is more so."

51. The term "mechanists" is disliked by materialists, observes George Bernard Shaw (preface to R. A. Wilson, *The Miraculous Birth of Language*, Philosophical Library, New York, 1948, p. 14), "for a machine, like Paley's watch, is a product of purpose and design; and this the ultra-Darwinian would not tolerate at any price." On the same page Shaw declares that "Darwin . . . was never a Darwinian."

In his *The Study of Man*, The Lindsay Memorial Lectures, 1958, Chicago, 1959, pp. 47–56, Michael Polanyi discusses at length the thesis that since machines operate to specifications, technology is not reducible to physical science. To say that man is a machine, he says, is true, since we may patent inventions which operate to the same specifications to which animal organs operate. Yet, he concludes, this is not the reduction of physiology to physical science. But, in addition, man is higher than mere machines or other animals: "Animals may be lovable, but man alone can command respect" (p. 59): he possesses language, art, science. These are creatures of "cultural standards" such as the respect for the truth which enables one to stand up against the society which has taught him these standards (pp. 61–2). Polanyi follows this idea to the conclusion that men have minds above and beyond their mental capacities (p. 65). I confess I find the logic of the sequence of arguments here somewhat puzzling.

R. O. Kapp presents this or a similar view – life is control, is ordering, is purposefulness, which can be found both in living systems and in their extensions into machineries. This can be found in his discussion note in the *Brit. J. Phil. Sci.*,

Vol. 8, 1957, pp. 159—60. The hostility with which it was met in Kapp's lifetime is as puzzling, or as capricious, as the popularity it enjoyed after his death, when it was repeated, without reference to him, by distinguished people, some of whom had known him personally.

Similar views were expressed by T. S. Szasz in a brief and scholarly note, "Men and Machines", *Brit. J. Phil. Sci.*, Vol. 8, 1958, pp. 310—17. In retrospect it is fascinating to note that Szasz' realization of the unorthodox and far-reaching characteristics of the second law of thermodynamics lead him to reconsider mechanism in general and Freud's in particular. Of course, he was also greatly influenced by the liberal tradition, as well as by the liberal reading of R. D. Laing.

See also Marjorie Grene, "Aristotle and Modern Biology", *J. Hist. Ideas*, Vol. 33, 1972, pp. 394—424, which mentions organizational and information theoretical attempts at reducing biology to physics. Its bibliography is interesting though it does lack some references which one might hope to see there. See also note 53 below.

52. For all these points see, A. Koestler, *The Ghost in the Machine*, e.g., pp. 53—55, 308, 329.

It should be noted that Jacob von Uexküll, the father of the biological approach which preceded General Systems, did draw the conclusion that cities and societies are superindividuals with lives of their own, and did use this to support his very conservative political views. Indeed, in an obvious sense superindividuals exist as homeostats of sorts; yet they have no consciousness and no purpose. See my "Methodological Individualism", referred to in note 8 to the Introduction.

Now all this is hardly surprising. Indeed, it was noted in passing in a by now famous passage in Karl Marx's *Grundrisse* (trans. with a foreword by Martin Nicholaus, Vintage Books, Random House, New York, 1973, p. 693) in which Marx distinguishes a mere tool from a machine "which possesses skill and strength in the place of the worker, is itself a virtuoso, with a soul of its own in the mechanical law acting through it; and it consumes coal . . ." But Marx did nothing with this and omitted it from the final version where only the brutal competition between worker and machine is discussed (*Kapital*, Chapter 15). Marx could not apply his economic theory to a fully automated plant under capitalism, though it fits exquisitely his theory of socialism.

And here lies the moral of the story: viewing man and machines alike comes easy; taking care of the implications of this very point in a consistent manner is what is so difficult. And confusing an easy task with a difficult one is the source of so much philosophical trouble. See my "Positive Evidence in Science and Technology", *Philosophy of Science*, Vol. 37, 1970, pp. 261—270, reprinted in my *Science in Flux*, Reidel, Dordrecht and Boston, 1975.

53. Jacob Bronowski, *The Identity of Man*, 1965, paper edition, Garden City, New York, 1966, claims in the final section, "Man is a machine by birth but a self by experience". Does the machine have experience and does experience render it a self? In section 6 of part I Bronowski says "Even a machine can become unique . . . a machine acquires an individuality, as I do." A self, however, is an active sort of individuality. Can then a machine be active? The question hinges on the sense of action — that of a free agent — and so on the sense of freedom — not subject to law in all respects. This links with individuality and experience by the thesis, section 2 of part I, man's "procedures for getting experience cannot all be formalized." To the extent that this is true of machines as well, adds Bronowski, it is so because "a machine is not a natural object, it is a human artifact." This is also the chief thesis of Norbert Wiener's classic *God and Golem Inc., A Comment on Certain Points Where Cybernetics Impinges on Religion*, MIT Press, Cambridge, Mass., 1964.

Popper views man as a problem-solver and thus as a non-machine. Admittedly, machines too can solve problems, but only to complete programming. Hence, man — indeed any animal — is an unprogrammed problem-solver. To this the standard reply is, we can have random programming. This, replies Popper, is like random writing of books. It can be done, but then who will decide which few of the very many random books make sense and which few of those are interesting? The same idea is much elaborated by the great writer Jorge Luis Borges in diverse essays and stories. (Interest, of course, is purposeful.)

IV IN PRAISE OF METHODOLOGICAL PLURALISM

If discussions about reduction and elimination may on occasion be reasonable, then a reductionism should not aim at elimination as a matter of course. If the reduction of chemistry to physics, for example, does not eliminate chemistry, then perhaps the reduction of social anthropology to physics likewise need not eliminate social anthropology. If so, then we may try to do meta-anthropology or, more generally, philosophical anthropology, for a while, without sliding into meta-physics.

All this is far from being conclusive. We know too little physics and too little meta-physics to know how much force such arguments may sustain in the face of the progress of the sciences. This is, indeed, why, in our ignorance, we do not stick to one method or another, we do not require ourselves to start only with physics or only with psychology or social anthropology, only with empirical findings on the smallest scale, or only with grand-scale metaphysics proper. We try in all directions, including that direction of philosophical anthropology which avoids the question, can anthropology be reduced to physics, namely, is man a machine?

There is here an observation, a factual observation, made and explained by a hypothesis. To repeat: we try all directions because we are ignorant and so have no preferred direction. This hypothesis opposes practically everything written in the field of methodology. Most philosophers who write on scientific method recommend one or another set of different rules; and most of them also observe — erroneously I think — that only one of the different sets of rules is properly applied. The ones who are metaphysically inclined recommend starting from first principles as the solid foundation, and since they really mean first principles they raise the questions of reduction right away. Those who are opposed to speculative or metaphysical thinking, often insist on sticking to minute facts. By which they mean very concrete and very tangible facts. In this manner many of them discover reductionism by insisting that concepts, thoughts, even happiness and sufferings, dignity and noble acts, are not in the least tangible.[54] Personally, I am not an expert on the tangible. Emile Durkheim endorsed both positivism and collectivism; in order to reconcile both of these attitudes of his he declared he could observe societies as concrete units, a feat which already amused F. A. von Hayek.[55] If we dispense with tangible certainty we can, in any case, have both methodologies, the a priorist and the empiricist, not as rightful claimants for supremacy, but as two of many possible sets of rules of methods of unknown fruitfulness.

For my part, I am a trifle biased against the extreme empiricist method, both on account of its pathological tangibilism or concretism, and on account of its finding merit in disorder; and so I think it is of extremely narrow applicability.[56] When in a metaphysical mood I always look for guiding principles, for regulative ideas of all sorts, and when in a skeptical mood I advocate pluralism and let the better party win.

This kind of Darwinian skepticism is not new with me. It was advocated by Peirce, Mach, Boltzmann, Freud, and quite a few others.[57] It became the cornerstone of the philosophy of Sir Karl Popper who was my Ph.D. thesis adviser. Yet in the work where he advocated this Darwinism, his classic *Logik der Forschung*, he demanded that science should ruthlessly attempt the invention and subsequent exclusion of as many ideas as possible (quite at variance with Darwinism proper), so that the fittest, which survive, should also be as fit as possible. Accordingly, he recommended starting only with the most vulnerable ideas available, with those ideas which are in principle the most easily refutable. In such a system, obviously, there is no need for first principles of any kind, reductionist or nonreductionist.[58]

Suppose science is satisfactory explanation, and suppose we look for satisfactory explanations, testing them, and the like. Why, then, can we not confine our discourse to science? Why at all go to the study of its first principles? In one place Popper explicitly joins Heisenberg's program of eliminating metaphysics from science. To be more precise, Popper decidedly gives metaphysics its right of existence, and he also admits that an individual can scarcely avoid holding some metaphysical view or other; he confesses himself to be a believer in realism, the simplicity of nature, etc. Yet just where he makes this confession, he makes it clear that he will not allow metaphysics into science and keeps at least his own metaphysical views strictly private. [59]

Whereas Popper's view of metaphysics in his *Logik der Forschung* of 1935 is clearly tinged with old-fashioned positivism, his view of metaphysics in his *The Open Society and Its Enemies*, which he wrote during World War II, is very unclear, if not inconsistent, seemingly ranging from admiration for Plato's theory of ideas to a violent positivist attack on Whitehead's endorsement of metaphysics. Against Whitehead he uses, as if the strongest kind of argument, the argument that metaphysics does not, and presumably cannot, progress. This as an argument is invalid and as a contention untrue. The significance of Popper's *Open Society* is that it introduces a new philosophical anthropology — objectionable, but interesting. It describes Man as suffering under the strain of civilization. According to Popper's theory we live in times of transition, where there is a conflict between Man's collectivist natural tendencies and his civil tendencies which are individualistic in their moral character. [60] Nowadays, after the views of Konrad Lorenz and his followers, as well as Lévi-Strauss' paradoxical ideas, have won popularity, this theory is fairly commonplace; yet at the time it was quite a novelty. Also, Popper's *Open Society* is distinguished for its pragmatic toleration of theoretical reductionism and/or determinism: as long as on the commonsense level the positivist admits the duality of man as mind and matter, and as long as the positivist is willing to act as a responsible agent, his metaphysical convictions to the contrary are harmless. We may notice here a very clever twist: the traditional positivist ends up a reductionist; so Popper, with the same positivistic-pragmatist mode of argumentation, brings commonsense to an almost Cartesian dualism of sorts.

I say "of sorts", because Popper says he is a Cartesian dualist, [61] but I cannot see how. Descartes started with metaphysics on a grand scale, with a theory of substance. [62] A substance is a final reality, or should I say a primary reality. Hence it cannot change. Proof: if it can change, its change has to be explained, and the explanation will pertain to a final reality which is not the substance whose change is explained; which is absurd. Q.E.D. Likewise, substances cannot interact. Proof: if they did they would be alterable; also the interaction would have to be explained, etc. Q.E.D. Now, for Descartes the mind is a substance;

with the added bonus that, unalterable, the mind is immortal; and with the added headache that mind and body cannot interact. The problem what to do with this headache is the classical mind-body problem. Take away the theory of substance, and you have no mind-body problem left. There are other pertinent problems here. In particular, even without a substance doctrine proper, we can ask, can there be a mindless body or a bodyless mind? And if we are body and mind, how do the two interact? All this is as remote from Descartes as a substanceless philosophy from a substance philosophy. We still ask, however, is man a machine? To this Popper says, no. He thinks this makes him a Cartesian. But here he is in plain error. The argument for his no, he claims, is methodological. I have tried to show that he is in plain error here as well: whether a machine or not, man is a moral being; this is as much as we can conclude from the methodological argument. As to whether man is or is not a (moral) machine, it is still an open question.

Perhaps we can claim more on methodological grounds. Whether man is a machine or not may be interesting for various reasons, depending on how the debate on this question develops. But the question, what is man, can be treated more immediately with the aim of developing viable research programs for the human sciences, even without developing a fully fledged substance theory and without developing a metaphysics on a grand scale. We may even develop research without any elaborate research program, or with programs limited to this or that extent. [63] And some of them, then, may leave open the question: in the last resort, is man a machine or not?

We may take man as a thinking moral entity strictly on the commonsense level, as a given fact to be examined and taken into account while we examine varieties of human facts. Had Popper been more consistent in his hostility to metaphysics, he would oppose not only the positivist's reductionist metaphysics, but its opposite as well. It is doubtless not very consistent for one who expressly wishes to eliminate metaphysics to end up advocating a metaphysics. Even if the positivist's reductionism, when replacing common sense, does away with responsibility, even if we therefore need commonsense dualism, this dualism is phenomenological, not metaphysical, much less Cartesian. [64]

The doctrine of substance, to conclude, is not commonsense, nor is it incidental to classical metaphysics. Rather, it is what gave metaphysical activity its rationale — from the days of Thales to the days of Kant. Kant's critical philosophy, his Copernican Revolution, was to shift philosophy from the doctrine of substance to the doctrine of man. He thus created both extremes. On the one hand he offered us a (critical) metaphysics which in future may claim a scientific status. On the other hand he held the view that for every (objectivist) meta-physical theory which you may invent I can invent an alternative which is equally convincing. The subtlety which Kant in his genius plunged into is still not sufficiently mastered. This was the last throw of classical philosophy, anyway. And now it is perhaps too old-fash-ioned for anyone to invest too much effort to clear up – even if it were at all possible.

Let me begin here with a dual thesis instead of the classical views. First, there may be degrees of reality instead of merely appearances and realities. For example, the hierarchies of scientific theories each explanatory of its predecessor may exhibit levels of depth or of prox-imity to reality as explained in Popper's classic paper "Three Views Concerning Human Knowledge." [65] Second, that in the history of science we see that fields of enquiry are delineated and given their unity by pertaining to given sets – sometimes competing sets – of first principles. I have argued this historical thesis to my satisfaction as far as the physical sciences are concerned in my paper "The Nature of Scientific [I should have said, Physical] Problems and Their Roots in Metaphysics" and in *The Continuing Revolution.* [66] I think the same historical thesis holds in the human sciences and hence my choice of topic for the present volume. These two theses – one concerning a hierarchy of scientific theories, and one regarding a series, perhaps a hierarchy, of meta-theories – require some coordination between them, and no one has tried to do this as yet. Moreover, clearly, the very tentativeness of the first principles of physics (meta-physics) makes it tough to discuss the first principles of the sciences of man (philosophical anthropology) – since obviously the two may be inter-related. We see, then, that the whole situation is in turmoil. To this turmoil, I think, a pluralist approach may very well be most suit-able, at least more suitable than the prevalent, rather rigid, formal ones. Also, the turmoil has one benefit to offer.

The chief trouble with metaphysical studies thus far, I contend, is that they were made as matters of faith, as some sort of substitute for religion. There were those who believed man was really an automaton, there were those who believed man was really made in the image of God. What I suggest here, in line with my previous studies, is that faith is a strictly private matter; and that metaphysical systems or sets of first principles may be presented and considered as competing sys-tems, each having its pros and cons and that these can be objectively explored.

Notes to Section IV

54. It was George Bernard Shaw who observed, and Jorge Luis Borges who repeated emphatically, that the flatness of positivism makes the positivist's world real hell: when any suffering becomes even mildly intense it becomes quite tangible, and so the world in which it occurs. It was W. Somerset Maugham who said, so many philosophers discuss toothache, one might think no suffering is greater than that. See Shaw's *Man and Superman*, Borges' "A Note on (toward) Bernard Shaw", Maugham's *The Summing Up*, London and New York, 1938, LXVIII (p. 262). See also my "Philosophy as Literature: The Case of Borges", *Mind*, Vol. 39, 1970, pp. 287–94, and my "The Future of Berkeley's Instrumentalism", *Studi. Intl. Filos.*, Vol. vii, Fall 1975, pp. 167–178.

55. Auguste Comte, in spite of his hierarchy of sciences, declared (*Cours, IV*, p. 258) in a famous statement that social fact "is certainly much better known and more immediately accessible" than individual facts, quoted by F. A. Hayek, who attacks this as "sheer illusion", in *Individualism and Economic Order*, University of Chicago Press and Routledge, Chicago and London, 1948, "The Facts of the Social Sciences", p. 62, reprinted from *Ethics*, Vol. 56, pp. 1–13.

See also F. A. Hayek, *The Counter Revolution of Science, Studies on the Abuse of Reason*, Free Press of Glencoe, 1955, paper edition, 1964, part 1, Chapter VI, p. 54 and notes. Paradoxically, he says, the anxiety to avoid subjectivity leads the collectivists to the possibility "to confine themselves to 'objective facts' " and thus become all the more subjectivists by misplacing concreteness. The literature on social facts is enormous, confusing social facts, social institutions, sociological concepts (which are, perhaps, not definable by psychological ones alone), sociologism (the view that institutions are not outcomes of psychological interactions between individuals), collectivism (sociologism plus the assertion that collectives have interests or lives of their own), and the inductivist-collectivist claim that social institutions are directly observable. It is this last point which I am here stressing, and shall therefore take first.

Of course, positivists need not be inductivists but can be fictionalists of all sorts, including conventionalists, instrumentalists, pragmatists, etc. But whatever view a positivist has, he claims that either he can see institutions, or he can deduce by induction that they exist, or both; alternatively, he is no collectivist. Now comes the crucial point: the inductivist who believes he can conclude the existence of social entities from observations but not observe them directly seems (and I think correctly) to be implying that he is a reductionist. This, indeed, is the origin of reductionism or individualism of method. (See my "Methodological Individualism", referred to in note 8 to the Introduction.) Let me also make again, *à propos* of this, another observation. This is also the methodological excuse the positivists have for holding a reductionist metaphysics, though it is only good for a reductionism within the social sciences, not all round, as they take for granted that it is. The fictionalist who says he cannot ever see social entities declares them to be fictions. Hence, the positivist collectivist, be he an inductivist or an instrumentalist, must declare some social entities to be observable.

It is quite amazing how much confusion abounds here. The latest clarification is not good enough, though by far the best. It is Steven Lukes, *Emile Durkheim, His Life and Work, A Historical and Critical Study,* Allen Laine, the Penguin Press, London, 1973, p. 9, notes 39 and 40, in the section on Durkheim's concept of social facts. *"Fait"*, comments Lukes, "has a somewhat different meaning from 'fact', signifying 'that which exists or occurs or is real' rather than 'that which is the case.' Nonetheless, we will, for simplicity, use the term 'social fact'." That is to say, *'fait'* signifies not fact but thing. This leads us to the next note, dealing with Durkheim's use of 'things (*choses*)', which Lukes says quite correctly, has "at least four senses, viz. (1) phenomena with characteristics independent of the observer; (2) phenomena whose characteristics can only be ascertained by empirical investigation (that is, as opposed to a prior reasoning or intuition); (3) phenomena which can only be studied through 'external' observation – that is by means of indicators, such as legal codes, statistics, etc. . . ."

I shall not analyze this passage since I have already proven that a positivist collectivist must admit that some social entities are observable. (And no one denies Durkheim was both a collectivist and a positivist.) I have proven in an earlier note (note 22 to Secion II above) that a reducible concept is not the same as a reducible entity (a point, I suppose, made in this dispute by J. W. N. Watkins *à propos* the shift in the debate from social institutions to societal facts. See his "The Principle of Methodological Individualism", *Brit. J. Phil. Sci.,* Vol. 3, 1952–3). Clearly, a concept is not a law (which is a statement, though a concept can be "implicitly defined" by a law), and a law governs institutions but is seldom an institution (except when the institution in question is the law). That sociologism is not the same as collectivism I have discussed elsewhere (the above-mentioned "Methodological Individualism" and "Institutional Individualism") and, in a new way in the present study, Section XX, where psychology and sociology are both described as irreducible. Social facts, it is said, involve social institutions, and their descriptions involve social concepts. Even if this were true it would be no invitation to confuse observed facts, institutions, and concepts. But it is false, and counterexamples abound.

56. Extreme empiricism is the endorsement of "the authority of experience" (to use the words of the second, 1663, Royal Charter of the Royal Society of London). Now when the authority of experience is challenged by instances of errors of experience the domain of authoritative experience is narrowed to "pure experience", but what is "pure experience" likewise tends to be repeatedly narrowed and rendered increasingly elusive. (See my "Sensationalism", *Mind,* Vol. 75, 1966, pp. 1–24, reprinted in my *Science in Flux*, 1975.)

The reason, however, that it is possible for an extreme empiricist to continue his studies is that he narrows his concept of experience only when under attack; in his scientific work he may be very imaginative indeed.

Now, no doubt, one form of what Walter Kaufmann (*Without Guilt and Justice,* New York, 1973) calls decidophobia is what he calls microscopism, and one form of microscopism may be an extreme version of extreme empiricism; this, however, should not prove the cowardice of empiricism, since microscopists can turn their mind to any microscopic venture, mathematical, scientific — theoretical or experimental — literary, or anything else. All one can say is that the inductivist mythology rationalizes microscopist scientists in telling them, as Bacon already did, that microscopic behavior is fabulously rewarding in the end.

57. A recent recommendation for pluralism in the sciences of man can be found in S. Koch "Epilogue", in S. Koch, ed., *Psychology: A Study of A Science,* Vol. 3, McGraw-Hill, New York, 1959, and repeated in William W. Rozeboom, "The Art of Metascience, or, What Should A Psychological Theory be?", in Joseph R. Royce, ed., *Toward Unification in Psychology, The First Banff Conference on Theoretical Psychology,* University of Toronto Press, Toronto, 1970, pp. 55–163, p. 74. For a fairly comprehensive recommendation and discussion of pluralism, see Helmut F. Spinner, *Pluralismus als Erkentnismodell,* Suhrkamp, Frankfurt, 1974.

58. The full expression of Popper's intellectual Darwinism can be found in his *Objective Knowledge, An Evolutionary Approach,* Clarendon Press, Oxford, 1972; though it already clearly appears in his *Logik der Forschung* of 1935. The difference between Popper's and others' version of this intellectual Darwinism is discussed in my "The Novelty of Popper's Philosophy of Science", *Intl. Phil. Quart.,* Vol. 8, 1968, pp. 442–463 (reprinted in my *Science in Flux,* Reidel, Dordrecht and Boston, 1975). My criticism of it appears in my "Postscript: On the futility of Fighting Philistines", a review of Popper's *Objective Knowledge, An Evolutionary Approach,* in *Philosophia,* Vol. 4, 1974, pp. 163–201.

59. See previous note.
    The idea that metaphysical realism, and metaphysical interpretations of scientific theories, are unavoidable but private and unscientific, was first, to my knowledge, advanced by Sir A. S. Eddington. (I have discussed it in my essay "The Novelty of Popper's Philosophy of Science"; see previous note.) Eddington, however, has concluded from this that scientific theories have no real claims, i.e. are meaningless formulas, i.e. sheer conventional modes of representation. Popper's own theory in his *Logik der Forschung* is expressly anti-conventionalist, and his falsificationism is, doubtless, in some sense realistic, though not realistic enough to expressly endorse the correspondence theory of truth. Yet even after Popper endorsed that theory he still speaks of realism above and beyond that of scientific theories, yet still as a private metaphysics. I have discussed Popper's realism in my review of *Objective Knowledge*; see previous note. See also next note.

60. The reference to times of transition is in the opening of Popper's *Open Society*; I do not know how much he thinks the strain of civilization is transitory. His faith in the classic work ethic makes one assume that he does, his anti-essentialism that he does not. For the strain of civilization see below, Section XXIII, Culture is No Burden, and notes, especially note 41.

61. Sir Karl Popper's last word on the mind-body problem seems to be included in his *Of Clouds and Clocks, An Approach to the Problem of Rationality and the Freedom of Man*, the Arthur Holly Compton Memorial Lecture, 1965, Washington University, St. Louis, Mo. 1966, reprinted as Chapter 6 of his *Objective Knowledge* (see note 58). Clouds and clocks are statistically governed systems and causally governed ones, and freedom is constrained if we are clocks, but we are not. A problem which Popper calls Compton's problem is, how do improbable events such as public meetings or lectures take place at all? Since, clearly, these much depend on announcements, namely on the communicable meaning of announcements. Popper translates this problem into, how can abstract meanings operate as means of physical control of bodies (of individual participants in the meetings) (p. 15)? This is solved by the very claim (p. 22) that contents and meanings do have the ability to control, that "their power of influencing us is part and parcel of these contents and meanings". They can control because they have the power to control. Back to Molière!

This, adds Popper, entails a solution to the problem which Popper identifies as the classical mind-body problem or Descartes' problem. That problem, he declares (p. 16), may be formulated as follows: how can such things as states of mind — volitions, feelings, expectations — influence or control the physical movements of our limbs?" And *vice versa*. In a footnote (43) Popper refers not to Descartes but to himself and to Compton, claiming that the former is less Cartesian than the latter, adding a positive high-handed verdict: "I have no sympathy with the Cartesian talk of a mental *substance* or a thinking *substance* — no more than with his material *substance* or extended *substance*." The reference is to Popper's own *Conjectures and Refutations* where Greek metaphysics is praised sky-high. This is very sad.

Though what Popper calls Descartes' problem is not that of Descartes, it still is an important problem. Popper claims to have solved it, but I cannot see that he has. See also next note.

62. I do not mean to rescue Descartes' grand metaphysics or theory of substance: these indeed are too old-fashioned. I only wish to insist that once we give up Descartes' old-fashioned foundations, and so his problem — Descartes' or *the* body-mind problem — disappears (and gives rise to new ones, of course).

I think that, likewise, Cartesian doubt must also go, as Polanyi insists in his *Personal Knowledge, Towards a Post-Critical Philosophy*, Chicago University Press, Chicago, 1958, Chapter 9, "Critique of Doubt", pp. 269–298, though I do not think this justifies Polanyi's rejection of all total doubt, Cartesian as well as skeptic. See my "Sociologism in the Philosophy of Science", *Metaphilosophy*, Vol. 3, 1972, pp. 103–122, and the end of my "Changing Our Background Knowledge", *Synthèse*, Vol. 19, 1968–9, pp. 453–464.

The old-fashioned character of Descartes' doubt has not, to my knowledge, been sufficiently noticed. It seems to me that to view his — and Bacon's — radicalism as an offshot of the ancient polarization of nature and convention is somewhat new. See K. R. Popper's "On the Sources of Our Knowledge and

Ignorance", in his *Conjectures and Refutations,* Routledge & Basic Books, 1962, 1963, where Popper presents the idea of the expurgated mind of Bacon and Descartes as a variant of ancient doctrines. As to the polarization between nature and convention, Popper accepts all of it, except that he denies that convention is always totally arbitrary, as explained in Chapter III below. This is a very important qualification, but not a sufficient one. See my "Modified Conventionalism is More Comprehensive than Modified Essentialism", in P. A. Schilpp, ed., *The Philosophy of Karl Popper,* Open Court, La Salle, Ill., 1974, pp. 693—6, and Popper's comments on it. See also my "Modified Conventionalism" in my *Science in Flux*, Reidel, Dordrecht and Boston, 1975.

The ancient character of Descartes' doubt can be shown, perhaps, also in the detail of his reasoning. His celebrated proof (his *Cogito erasus*), I doubt, therefore I think, therefore I am, is a formal presentation of Plato's *Apology*: Socrates is ignorant yet wise, because he is conscious of his ignorance and so he knows himself (i.e. his limits) whereas the artisans who know their art are ignorant of their general ignorance and so not wise. Here take wisdom = knowledge = certainty, namely folly = ignorance = doxa or opinion or doubtfulness; and Descartes' proof holds. These equations may not perhaps be ones which Socrates would accept; they are certainly ones Plato advocated, and the differentiation between Plato and Socrates, as well as the Socratic Problem, came much later.

Descartes' *Cogito* is discussed in Chapter 5 of Jaakko Hintikka, *Knowledge and the Known,* Reidel, Dordrecht and Boston, 1974. Hintikka does not refer to the Apology, but only to St. Thomas and to St. Augustin.

63. Norwood Russell Hanson, *Patterns of Discovery*, Cambridge University Press, 1958, paper edition, 1965, Chapter IV, "Theories", begins with endorsing as partial both the inductive method of generalization from observed facts (induction by enumeration) and the hypothetico-deductive method (of testing). The inductive view is, indeed, false, since induction by enumeration is rare yet the inductive view claims universality. Yet the hypothetico-deductive method is defective too. First (p. 70), we begin with data to explain, not with hypotheses. Second, the hypothetico-deductivist says, the next step is just to get hold of a hypothesis, yet in actual historical processes hypotheses were conceived in series which have elements in common, such as the series of hypotheses generated by Kepler, Galileo, and others — the rest of the volume is devoted to the others. The series may contain hypotheses which soon get refuted, but this is another matter.

It is regrettable that Hanson only illustrated his view but did not say much in general. In the final page (158) he says, "Intelligibility is the goal of physics, the fulfillment of natural philosophy; for natural philosophy is philosophy of matter, a continual conceptual struggle to fit each new observation of phenomena into a pattern of explanation. Often the pattern precedes the recognition of the phenomenon . . ." His essay "Is there a Logic of Discovery?" in H. Feigl and G. Maxwell, eds., *Current Issues in the Philosophy of Science,* Holt, Rinehart, and Winston, New York, 1961, pp. 20—35, is clearer on this, but his examples are sketchier.

64. This is not meant to express any endorsement of common sense. There are myriads of conflicting commonsense views of man. Let me mention one conflict which I find most intriguing: the case of self-sacrifice. Machiavelli said (*The Prince*, Chapter 17) that people are thankless, fickle, and cowardly, who will sacrifice everything — including their own lives and those of their sons — for the sake of the powerful prince who has no need for them; but will rebel when the prince needs their help. Sounds familiar; yet equally familiar is C. P. Snow's remark (*Variety of Men*, London and New York, 1967, pp. 149—151, chapter on Churchill) that nothing attracts the multitude more than the promise (Churchill's) of nothing except blood, sweat, and tears. Evidently, our immediate tendency is to agree with both. This illustrates Claude Lévi-Strauss' view: myths come in polarized pairs; we accept both poles but apply them in varying mixtures to different cases; myths, thus, think for us. And so common sense is just a system of myths accepted by a community. And the acceptance of opposite polar views obviously indicates that both views are mistaken; yet they are both intriguing and will not be easily ignored: we feel we do need a substitute, an alternative view — a new philosophy of man. Perhaps Marx offers a third view — of man as enslaved throughout history and so as treacherous; but towards the socialist revolution, in utter despair, he becomes noble again (as he was in prehistory). If so, then, unlike Machiavelli and Snow, Marx is terribly unconvincing uncommonsense, for, the defense of Marx's (Spinozist) doctrine on this issue of self-sacrifice is through the classic (Spinozist) doctrine of enlightened self-interest. And this sounds strange. Bertrand Russell, *Mysticism and Logic*, Allen and Unwin, London, 1910, 1966, Ch. 1. The Elements of Ethics, §33, refutes egoism by the Argument from self-sacrifice, saying it condemns it and is thus "sufficiently contrary to plain fact." He then, §34, refutes the eighteenth-century variant of it. The idea, sacrifice yourself in your own interest — not risk your life, but jump into the flames, for your own good — does, no doubt, astonish us in its inconsistency. It is hardly conceivable that Marx was insensible to this criticism. Yet he was a bit cavalier about it: only in an early manuscript he refers to it, and briefly. He says, in a true Spinozist spirit, if a man sacrifices himself, he does so out of an inner necessity of sorts. See Robert C. Tucker, *Philosophy and Myth in Karl Marx*, second edition, Cambridge University Press, 1972, p. 16, where the passage is quoted from *German Ideology*, MEGA, Vol. V, p. 227.

65. K. R. Popper, "Three Views Concerning Human Knowledge", now in *Conjectures and Refutations* London, 1962, 1963. See also his "The Aims of Science", now in his *Objective Knowledge*, Oxford, 1972.

66. See reference in note 8 to Section I above.

In these works I present the view of metaphysical foundations of science as a historical thesis, not as a methodological thesis. The former also uses this historical fact to explain, to a large extent, the existing coordination and cooperation between scientists. That is to say, I assert that, within the realistic tradition, most science seeks to find the nature of things, and that, within the metaphysical tradition, the general answers to questions about the nature of things are meta-physical, and that, within the skeptical tradition, any metaphysics can be over-thrown.

The thesis discussed here — social variables and their ranges belong to universal philosophical anthropology — is, I think, what is most obviously missing in both the Weberian tradition and the Durkheimian functionalist one. This is, indeed, what makes both so fragmentary, especially in view of the relativism of the functionalists and of Weber himself. The reason is quite obvious. The collectivist or functionalist theories offered no clear idea about the individual's alleged mode of integration in his society in general. The classical individualistic tradition offered a fully fledged theory of the variables — they are the ranges of human motives, passions, or what have you. Yet this range has proven to be too narrow. The Weberian model, however, allowed practically any type we could imagine.

Modern theorists of recent times naturally seek the universal in the range of variables, even if not sufficiently systematically. Now I shall not discuss here the obvious, the field of linguistics, which did strive, especially with Jakobson's phonetics, for this. Let me rather discuss social anthropology. Beginnings can be found in theories explaining a supposedly fairly universal transition of systems of totemism and exogamy from matrilineal to patrilineal societies by the existence of a fairly narrow range of reasonable possible alternatives.

This, I think, is the strong allure of Lévi-Strauss even to those who feel that he takes much liberty with his material. Let me quote the end paragraph of his "The Bear and the Barber", *J. Roy. Anth. Inst.,* Vol. 93, 1963, pp. 1–11, reprinted in William A. Lessa and Evon Z. Vogt, eds., *Readings in Comparative Religion, A Comparative Approach,* 2nd edition, Harper and Row, New York, 1965:

"Lastly, by analyzing a specific example, I have attempted to validate a methodological approach which I have been trying to follow in France and which Dr. Leach is following in England. According to this approach societies are not made up of floatsome and jetsome of history, but of variables; thus, widely different institutions can be reduced to transformations of the same basic figure, and the whole of human history may be looked upon merely as a set of attempts to organize differently the same means, but always to answer the same questions."

Yet I reject the idea that the method here advocated rejects the floatsome and jetsome of history by reducing them. I think that this method applies not only structurally but also to groups of possible solutions to scientific problems — such as Jarvie's analysis of the extant theories of cargo cults in Chapter 3 of his *The Revolution in Anthropology.* I think Lévi-Strauss will admit this point upon re-flection, since he insists, even in the lines preceding the above-quoted passage, "that the 'truth value' is an unavoidable dimension of structural method. No common analysis of religion can be given by a believer and a non-believer." I need not say how salutary I consider this realism. See references cited in note 70 to Section V.

See my *Towards an Historiography of Science*, final section.

V IN PRAISE OF IDLE SPECULATION

Popper still has weapons against metaphysics in his arsenal. He has an objection to the present study, as he taboos all "what is . . . ?" questions. Philosophical anthropology, we remember, asks, what is man. In my opinion Popper's attack is valid only regarding what is quite marginal to metaphysics. I have no difficulty in sticking to any metaphysics (which asks, what is matter, or what is man) while endorsing both his attack on the quest for certitude (as well as on any of its modern surrogates), and his attack on essential definitions which indeed are answers to "what is . . . ?" questions. For, not all answers to "what is . . . ?" questions are essential definitions. (For example, "man is essentially a machine" is definitely not an essential definition by any standard.) I shall not enter all this here, except to notice in favor of Popper that many philosophers indeed still yearn for certainty and hope to achieve it by essential definitions, and that essential definitions may indeed be childish. I cannot avoid the temptation of offering in capsule form a piece of Heidegger's so-called philosophy, from two of his essays on *What is Metaphysics?* – one on, "What is Truth?" and one on, "What is Freedom?" Truth he defines as essentially the acceptance of facts as they are, of not tampering with reality; truth, he says, is the let-be of the what-is. Likewise, he defines freedom as essentially the recognition of necessity, which is Hegel's famous definition; in Heidegger's words, freedom is the let-be of the what-is. He then concludes: truth equals freedom. Very profound.

This illustrates my earlier contention that however bad positivism is, there is always a worse metaphysics to which it deserves to be applied. Popper opposes all what is . . . questions as invitations for essential definitions. His anti-essentialism has recently been declared as a point shared with Wittgenstein and so it is now publicly renowned. [67] Let me say, then, in opposition to all the rational philosophers, and in spite of the embarrasing practices of all sorts of essentialists, that we do ask what is . . . questions all the time, that we thereby clumsily invite speculations on first principles, and that though too much speculation – as much human activity anywhere – leads to naught, at times we hit on interesting speculations. [68] I am well aware of the fact that most rationalist philosophers and most scientists will not approve of this. Indeed, they will not approve of my Darwinian approach throughout this discussion, which suggests studies along diverse lines, including diverse sorts of idle speculations, in the hope that at times something worthwhile may come of it. But against all this I shall bluntly say the following. Arguments from human folly,

if ever valid, should lead to the conclusion that all we ever did is
wrong, perhaps even that the race should commit suicide. For example, democracy was often rejected on the true ground that many
follies were committed under its banner. Together with metaphysics
and democracy, I repeat, any human activity, including science, can be
rejected on the ground that much folly was committed in its name.
And, of course, by the same token we may reject the argument that
metaphysics is evil since much folly was committed in its name, since
much folly was committed in the name of this argument; it is, thus,
obviously invalid, as it leads to its own invalidation.

Here we come to the deepest and most popular root of positivist
anthropology, which was invented by Sir Francis Bacon. Man is a lazy
creature: being lazy he is unwilling to study and is always willing to
speculate rather than study; his laziness thus leads to ignorance and to
metaphysics. Hence for his own salvation man must be made to work
hard and he must be taught to avoid idle speculations. Man does not
like to revise his opinions. He prefers to believe firmly in any given
speculation which answers all questions with ease and resists assaults
and demands for revision.[69] The second element, concerning man's
reluctance to alter his view, is more sophisticated and intriguing than
the first, concerning man's laziness. Bacon only explains the reluctance
psychologically. No teacher wants to confess error since he fears losing
(intellectual) power over his disciples. Recently this point was taken
up again. E. E. Evans-Pritchard has hinted or suggested — and many of
his disciples have argued — that we are all trapped within the conceptual systems of thought in which we are.[70] Popper denies that all
systems are traps — he thinks we can be critical in some instances —
but he notes too that some systems are traps.[71] He calls these traps
reinforced dogmas and claims that their main characteristic is the fact
that they include devices which turn criticism into confirmations.
Such devices, of course, can be built into any system of the science or
metaphysics of man, but not to physics proper or meta-physics
proper. There are simpler devices, however, which will neutralize any
criticism, and which can be built into any system, whether sociological
or physical. This is the method of adding to the terminology of a
system minor *ad hoc* adjustments, which rebound the criticism with
minimum effort. Sir Francis Bacon condemned this technique as that
of frivolous distinctions and exhorted his readers not to become lazy
and dogmatic by succumbing to its allure. The great conventionalist
philosophers, Poincaré and Duhem, frankly advocated its application
up to a point. Popper, again, spoke against it; in tune with changing
times, what Bacon called a frivolous distinction Popper called the

conventionalist twist. More significantly, Popper did not rely on Baconian exhortation (which unfortunately, he still took resort to), but on social institutions and conventions, against the application of the conventionalist twist. People, said Popper, are reluctant to alter their views; social circumstances, however, may bring the change anyway. This is quite in tune with the twentieth-century ethos.

Perhaps this ethos is responsible for the fact that traditionally it was the first element, man's laziness, of Bacon's philosophical anthropology, which was emphasized much more than its second element, man's dogmatism. For, Bacon and his followers were concerned with physics much more than with man (though Bacon, at least, felt that the final concern of man is man himself). The immense effort which the physical sciences require may have something to do with the popularity amongst scientists of the view that man is lazy, the so-called Protestant ethic. It is, however, but a modern version of the old doctrine of original sin. It is still common to most scientists and all positivists; it is the one item of sophisticated modern philosophy which is not beyond the reach of even elementary and high school teachers all over the western world, as well as in this country, especially science teachers.[72] And they all believe it and preach it and practice it the best they can, with old math and new, old physics and new, doing untold damage. But I anticipate myself.

It may sound strange or inconsistent that positivism should have, of all things, a moralistic foundation, a stern Protestant view of the nature of man; but I think it is so. Whether consistent or not, positivism is frightfully attractive in combining the misanthropic work ethic,[73] including the narrow-minded idea that we should not waste ourselves in idle and conceited speculation, with the idea that science is strict demonstration and hence the opposite of speculation; that science is actually the hard work of the study of minute facts and of their very careful explanation with the aid of vigorous logic and mathematics.[74] This is a combination of anti-intellectualism now with intellectualism in principle, justified by a stern moralistic view of man and offered with stern moralizing, with the requirement to dedicate oneself humbly to a small scientific task which requires hard work. Perhaps I should be a bit fairer: for positivists, enlightenment (=science) = freedom: ignorance (=metaphysics) = slavery. Hence, for the positivist, the fight against ignorance is a moral struggle for freedom, for the transcendence of the self, for efforts to become more like gods, to defeat mortality, and so on. These are flawed arguments, perhaps, but they do help us see our positivist forerunners in the better light which they deserve.

And so I have reached the conclusion of this chapter. There is the strong tendency to exclude as metaphysical all what is . . . questions, including the question, "what is man?" This tendency is positivistic, the tendency to send the person asking this kind of question to perform serious, detailed, empirical, scientific tasks; to work in the spirit of humility. Likewise there is the positivistic tendency to ignore elusive entities such as conceptual thinking and such as suffering. The verbalization of these tendencies into injunctions, 'do not ascribe to man concepts or sufferings', may lead us to an attempt to justify this, by saying that man is inherently not different from other animals, all animals being inherently homeostatic mechanisms. Or the verbalization may be in terms of physicalism: those words are unscientific which physicists do not use. That is to say, the positivist both combats philosophical anthropology and may offer a reductionist philosophical anthropology. Now, clearly, such philosophical anthropology is a challenge — a challenge to reduce man to machine — and thus a task, and even a difficult task, a challenge to work hard, and thus (by the positivistic standard) both moral and scientific.

The only question which remains is, what remains of ethics if man is a mere machine? I do not know, but clearly in the heyday of positivism and/or mechanism the view of man as machine was meant to make us more moral, not less. A story which illustrates this was told by Leonhard Euler to a German princess in favor of Christian Wolff, a philosopher with whom Euler generally had little or no sympathy. Wolff, says Euler,[75] was expelled from Prussia by King Frederick because he defended the Prussian soldiers against flogging, on the ground that they were mere automata who meant no wrong and so should be spared. The expulsion, incidentally, indicates that the king was unable to rebut the philosopher. This, incidentally, was characteristic of him, for he was enlightened in thought and divorced all thought from action — as much as he could, of course. For he could not always keep them separate: at one point he had to link thought and action and expel a thinker from his court, much though he liked to adorn it with celebrities.

Popper's response to the whole story is obvious: the king could say, if the soldiers are mere automata, then I may flog them to my heart's content, or as means of making them obey me. This is consistent with the major line of Popper's philosophic criticism. For Wolff, soldiers were automata and so faultless; but they were still human and so deserving not to be flogged when faultless. Hence, for Wolff mechanism led to the conclusion that no punishment was ever just! For Popper the same premise led to the conclusion that any distinction between the just and the unjust is arbitrary. To avoid being flogged the soldiers must be considered human from the first, he says. And to this I agree. And, he adds, we cannot, then, view them as machines of any kind whatsoever. Here I cannot agree. This may be so — but I contend that the question whether it is so is still wide open.

My point in the present chapter was: we do observe that men are thinking and suffering beings, even though we still do not know whether they are or can be machines. For, if one day we conclude that morality can never apply to machines then we shall be able to conclude that men cannot be machines — and conversely. All traditional philosophical anthropology, I contend, with the sole exception of that of Kant, overlooked this point to some extent or another. This, rather obvious, point of scientific methodology seems to be at the root of the discussion. It is unsatisfactory to explain away the observed specific human qualities: Perhaps man is a machine, but if so then he is a machine of a very special kind, a thinking and a suffering machine, and hence a moral machine. If such a machine is not possible, then, obviously man is not a machine. One way or another, we cannot overlook or explain away man's observed moral peculiarities.

Let me now, in conclusion of this chapter, repeat this point in a more traditional philosophical cast. Since mechanistic reductionism is positivistic and clearly anti-religious, let me begin my recasting by reminding the reader of the physico-theological proof of the existence of God.

The physico-theological proof of the existence of God has many versions. Crudely, the believer says, when you see a written page you do not assume the possible, though highly improbable hypothesis that an inkwell was spilled on a piece of paper, and the blot came out in the shape you see it; rather, someone exists who is the author of this page. The page is nature, and God is its author.

The irreligious or atheist or skeptic or agnostic may reply, if he wishes, that events are indeed not the improbable occurence of a set of possibilities out of all a priori possibilities; rather, given the existence of laws of nature most given events are probable. For example, given Newtonian mechanics and yesterday's sunrise, today's or tomorrow's sunrise become a virtual certainty, whereas without laws every sunrise is equally improbable and the fact that for so many thousands of years the sun rose so faithfully becomes nothing short of a miracle. Given the laws of nature in general, then, life on earth may be explained, too, as a probable phenomenon. If so, then the laws should be viewed as the laws of physics, and life as one form of the material world, not as a miracle but as a scientific fact.

It is, psychologically, an amusing observation that science should satisfy our need for security in a rational way, that physics is expected to reassure us that the sun will, indeed, rise tomorrow. It is also amusing that physics fails somewhat at this task: not only does physical theory tell us that the sun will certainly go out one day — it tells us also that it will possibly explode tomorrow as a supernova. But let us ignore all small likelihoods. Let us consider only the probable, and trust the laws of nature.

The trust in the laws of nature may be viewed as a trust in a deity of sorts. Indeed, this is Spinoza's central tenet: God equals Nature. Those who took the physico-theological proof seriously were greatly attracted by Spinoza's philosophy; for example, Kant. It is customary to say that Kant has killed all the proofs of the existence of God, whereas in fact he stressed that he only found them incomplete but not worthless — especially not the physico-theological proof. Philosophers of the religious establishment remained quite disenchanted.

This only shows that the philosophers of the religious establishment have missed the point. They claimed, we remember, that an ink blot in the shape of a written page is less likely than that the page was written by an intelligent author. [76] Now this is so in the very presence of the laws of nature as we know them. Of course, when we talk of a page literally, we have no difficulty speaking of human authors; and we have no written pages which we cannot ascribe to human authors quite convincingly. But we have the pages of the history of the world, of life on earth, of the genetic code, etc. If we are utter reductionists then we deny the existence of laws other than physical. Does physics make the genetic code likely? Or human intelligence?

The answer is clear: for a reductionist, one way or another, the pecularity of life is in its very complexity. This is so widely accepted that even authors like B. F. Skinner, [77] who try hard to put aside their reductionist biases, insist on equating life with complexity — i.e., high improbability. There is little doubt that reductionists are fully aware of the weakness of this point: they are trying to meet it squarely. They have two complimentary research programs, which together may enable reductionists to face the genetic code and human intelligence and all that as something other than a most improbable miracle. The one program is the hope of proving the stability of biological and of bioenergetic systems. Its adherents wish to show that, given life on earth as we know it, it is most likely that the situation will remain more or less as it is: nucleic acids naturally reproduce themselves, enzymes naturally decompose and recompose organic matter, skins keep animal bodies intact since they naturally retain their elasticity and strength, etc., etc. This is the program of biophysics. The other program is to look at earth as a speck in the cosmos: however unlikely a life-supporting planet is, given vast enough a galaxy, and we have quite a few of those, and given enough time, life must appear in one or another of them. This program is really only in its diapers.

How do we measure stability and improbability? Answer: by the use of the laws of nature. Now suppose this is true. Let us return to our metaphor of the written page. Is it, perhaps, written by the laws of nature alone? In the vast expanses of all the known galaxies, not to mention those beyond our present horizon, there surely are uncountable space-time regions of the size occupied by the minute entity called *homo sapiens*. And in those there must be ever so many myriads of entities of the shape of a page or a slate with some sort of markings on them. And, need one say, this page, book, or even library, improbable as it surely is, is not so odd when placed among all of them. There is the story of all those monkeys typing away at random on all those typewriters, so as to produce at random one reasonable page. It is a foolish story; a mere teaser; it should be replaced by its variant just mentioned that a reasonable page may be an ink blot which is rare but not surprising among the myriads of ink blots in the universe. This variant is the foundation of much of current researches, except that the ink blot which the researchers speak of is made not of ink but of nucleic acids and the reasonable reading of them as the genetic code.

This is not to say that reductionism is false, not even that the reductionist attempt to render intelligible our improbable earth is an error. For all I know reductionism is true, and we are merely an improbable element in an immense population. [78] Yet this very statement is a serious modification of reductionism as it is traditionally understood, and in the following way.

Traditionally, reductionists were determinists — they tried to explain even mental events by the strictest laws of physics. Meanwhile statistical laws entered physics too. And the main questions of statistics are, what population do we study, how do we identify it, what qualities are distributed over the population and by what distribution law. When we identify all throws of one given die as a population, or of all unbiased dice, or of all dice ever made by man, we do something which looks reasonable, both from the statistical and from the commonsense viewpoint. But when we mix playing cards and dice together with, say, vital statistics, then it all ceases to make sense. The reason for this is that we think populations proper have certain qualities in common (which Popper calls propensities). [79]

What utter reductionists overlook, then, is that matter has the propensity to come to life. Is this propensity describable by the laws of physics? If not, reductionism is false; if yes, physics is today much too limited. This last point was repeatedly made by Erwin Schrödinger. [80] Now, a reductionist may object: if reductionism is true, then life is explicable by physics, and so needs no special mention. But this objection hides the confusion between explaining and explaining away. Physics is supposed to explain all sorts of phenomena which are repeatedly mentioned, like that of the starry heavens. Suppose physics explains – or will explain – both the appearance of the starry heavens and of life. Surely, then, life will have a status not inferior to that of the solar system or the Milky Way! Hence, even for reductionists life must be as separate an entity as the nebulae or the phenomena peculiar to plasma physics.

Now let us suppose that life is an extra-physical property; or, on the contrary, let us suppose that one quality of physical matter is that it can come to life. Either way we have established the obvious fact that life is here to be taken account of. Will taking account of it amount to the explanation of my authorship of this page by the laws of physics? If yes, then ideal physics contains in it the theory of the propensity of matter to develop the ability to think. If not, the ability comes to the world from the outside. But one way or another, surely it exists in this world. The anti-religious move of the reductionist is either useless or beside the point. For, it may reduce thinking to the laws of nature; but that makes the laws even more wonderful and so, to the religious, a still stronger evidence of the finger of God. The error of reductionism, thus, is the confusion of the explanation of thinking with explaining it away.

As to answering the question, parenthetically, does the existence of thinking, of the laws of nature, of nature, does any existence whatsoever indicate the existence of a God? I have no idea. If anyone can speculate on it and come up with interesting ideas, I shall be most interested. [81]

Notes to Section V

67. The history of the ascription of anti-essentialism to Wittgenstein is curious. First, the terminology is, from the start, Popperian (the traditional term is "realism", not "essentialism"). Second, obviously there is justice to the ascription in the very trivial sense that Wittgenstein as a positivist opposed all philosophical theses, essentialism included. Hence, the very ascription of anti-essentialism without the ascription of anti-nominalism is the claim that Wittgenstein was not as

much of a positivist as he claimed to have been. The origin of the ascription is
Paul Feyerabend's celebrated and doubly anthologized review of Wittgenstein's
Philosophical Investigations. In his conclusion Feyerabend claims that Wittgen-
stein was an anti-essentialist and his view was not so new and not so revolutionary.

Curiously, Popper's anti-essentialism, his methodological nominalism, is in a
sense more positivistic: he is also an anti-nominalist. In a sense, of course, he is
less of a positivist, in that he allows for the possible existence of essences, which
to a Wittgensteinian positivist seems meaningless (see, e.g. Richard Hare's contribution to M. Bunge's *The Critical Approach*, London and New York, 1964).
Indeed, Popper seems to be an essentialist in his views of World 3, though not so
when he rejects "talk about substance" (see notes 61 and 62 to Section IV above).

68. For more details see my essay "The Logic of Questions and Metaphysics",
Philosophical Forum Vol. 5, 1974, pp. 529–556; reprinted in my *Science in
Flux*, Reidel, Dordrecht and Boston, 1975, and "Who Needs Aristotle?", in R. S.
Cohen and M. W. Wartofsky, *Boston Studies in the Philosophy of Science*, forth-
coming.

Popper himself has raised the difficulty concerning "what is?" questions that
he himself has asked, namely, what is science? what is life?

Of course, it is not an essentialist definition that he is after. But he does have
an idea about science and about life and he wants a better idea of them.

Popper has repeatedly stated that he merely proposed a convention, so that his
view is not criticizable by historical examination. I found this an error: he himself
regularly uses historical arguments. See my "The Logic of Scientific Inquiry",
Synthèse, Vol. 26, 1974, pp. 478–814.

Moreover, a criterion can be a touchstone or a defining characteristic. E.g. of a
touchstone of gold and the specific gravity of gold the former may operate better
but it is the latter that we really consider significant. And Popper offers a specific
gravity of science, not a touchstone of it. Moreover, his definition of science was,
at first, refutability and later progress towards the truth. It may well be that his
latter criterion, though it be no repudiation of the former, still makes it a mere
touchstone!

As to what is life? Popper says it is problem solving (P. A. Schilpp, ed., *The
Philosophy of Karl Popper,* Open Court, LaSalle, Ill., 1974, pp. 142–3), where
problem solving includes adjustability. What he does with the relatively unadjustable spider as compared with the relatively adjustable pup, how he handles prob-
lem-solving unadjustable computers, etc., I do not know.

In the same work, p. 110, section 30, "Debates with Schrodinger", he says of
Schrödinger, "And the very fact that he raised the question *What is Life?* in that
marvellous book of his, gave me the courage to raise it again for myself (although
I tried to avoid the *what-is?* form of the question)". He did not, and on p. 143 he
answers the *what-is?* question by a statement about the essence of life (rightly
putting the word essence in quotes to disclaim finality and/or verbality).

69. For Bacon's doctrine and its roots in the cabbalistic and hermetic tradition of his day see my "Unity and Diversity in Science" mentioned in note 8 to Section I. See also my "The Origins of the Royal Society", *Organon*, Vol. 8, 1970, pp. 117–135.

70   The literature on Evans-Pritchard's ideas is swelling. For a critical debate see Robert Borger and Frank Cioffi, eds., *Explanation in the Behavioral Sciences*, Cambridge University Press, 1970, the debate between Jarvie and Winch. See also I. C. Jarvie and J. Agassi, "The Rationality of Magic", *Brit. J. Soc.*, Vol. 18, 1967, pp. 55–74, reprinted in B. Wilson, ed., *Rationality*, Oxford, 1970, pp. 172–193, and "Magic and Rationality Again", in *Brit. J. Soc.*, Vol. 24, 1973, pp. 236–245. See also these two authors and Tom Settle, "The Grounds of Reason", *Philosophy*, Vol. 45, 1970, pp. 54–50. See also Tom Settle, I. C. Jarvie, and Joseph Agassi, "Towards a Theory of Openness to Criticism", *Phil. Soc. Sci.,* Vol. 4, 1974, pp. 83–90. See also my "Was Wittgenstein Really Necessary?", forthcoming, and also my "Rationality and the *Tu Quoque* Argument", *Inquiry*, Vol. 16, 1973, pp. 395–406.

71.   See K. R. Popper, *Conjectures and Refutations*, London and New York, 1962, 1963, p. 49; see also Y. Fried and J. Agassi, *Paranoia,* 1976, for the application of this idea to psychopathology.

72.   See, for example, Carl Rogers, "Facilitation of Significant Learning", in Laurence Siegel, ed., *Instruction, Some Contemporary Viewpoints*, Chandler Pblg. Co., San Francisco, 1967. Teachers behave, he says, as if the truth were known; which it is not. I have chosen Rogers because he is a prestigious observer of the contemporary scene. But the literature on the horrors of schools is too long to summarize or even list here. Let me only mention the autobiographies of Einstein, Russell, and Popper, as a token.

The fact that scholars are supposed to have certain opinions is so deeply embedded in our tradition that it goes unchallenged. At the very least a scholar is supposed to alter his view in the face of evidence, or lose his status of scholar. Thus Barrington Moore Jr. says (*Reflections on the Causes of Human Misery and Upon Certain Proposals to Eliminate them*, Beacon Press, Boston, 1972, p. 95), "a scholar's role is not that of an advocate such as, for example, a trial lawyer. If a defense lawyer is suddenly surprised by a piece of evidence or an argument turned up by the prosecution, he is never supposed to say, 'My, I had never thought of that! It's a good point and my client must be guilty.' On the other hand, that is exactly what an intellectually honest scholar is supposed to do under such circum-stances . . . [Otherwise] he is *ipso facto* unable to fulfill the role of scientist or scholar." This is a factual claim in flagrant violation of the facts, both legal and scientific. On the scientific side we have, e.g. Einstein's report of the general judgment of Lorentz as a great scholar and scientist, his upholding of rejected scientific views notwithstanding. But, of course, the very idea that we can control our beliefs or opinions is highly questionable, and was already denied both by Robert Boyle in his *Occasional Reflections*, Section 4, Discussion XI, and by

Spinoza in his *Tractatus*, Chapter 20. See Albert Einstein, *Ideas and Opinions*, Crown Publishers, New York, 1954. "H. A. Lorentz's Work on the Cause of International Cooperation", pp. 70–72, p. 71:

". . . The marvellous thing about the effect of his personality was this: independent and stubborn natures, such as are particularly common among men of learning, do not readily bow to another's will and for the most part accept his leadership grudgingly. But when Lorentz is in the presidential chair, an atmosphere of happy cooperation is invariably created, however much those present may differ in their aims and habits of thought."

Also, *op. cit.*, "Address at the Grave of H. A. Lorentz", p. 73 ". . . Everyone followed him gladly, for they felt that he never set out to dominate but only to serve . . ." Also, *op. cit.*, "H. A. Lorentz, Creator and Personality", pp. 73–6, p. 76, ". . . Never did he give the impression of domineering, always of serving and helping . . . Only in my later years was I able to appreciate fully this half-skeptical, half-humble attitude."

73. For those who think that the work ethic is a thing of the past I should mention the empirical research of Harold L. Wilensky which led him to the conclusion to the contrary (*Harvard University Program on Technology and Society, 1964–1972, A Final Review*, Cambridge, Mass., 1972, p. 141):

"The nineteenth-century secular religion of work may be attenuated in the affluent society, but work itself remains central in two senses. First, considering all hours worked – . . . there is no sign that the trained population is suffering a marked decreased willingness to log these hours. Second, the primordial meaning and function of work . . . social contact . . . mainstream of the community life. Employment remains symbolic of a place among the living."

And those who think that at least sophisticated intellectuals are free of this superstition may see its latest expression in Popper's autobiography, in Paul A. Schillp, ed., *The Philosophy of Sir Karl Popper*, La Salle, Ill., 1974, *passim*. Also Walter Kaufmann's delightful *Without Guilt and Justice*, New York, 1973, p. 226, "most professors are imbibed by *Weber's Fallacy*" he says,

"Max Weber, the greatest sociologist of our century, not only wrote about protestant ethic but also perpetuated it in his immensely influencial lecture, 'Scholarship as a Profession'."

Kaufmann continues with the beautiful slogan (p. 227), "scholarship is the opiate of the intellectual." See also note 64 above on Lord Snow's observation that people may love promises of nothing but blood, sweat, and tears. Indeed, the work ethic is regularly diluted with its opposite pole, namely with utilitarianism – again in accord with Lévi-Strauss.

74. Bertrand Russell hoped that adding logic and mathematical rigor to philosophy would render it more respectable. It is an interesting fact that Russell was a positivist of sorts and an adherent to Protestant ethic. He changed his views on both philosophy and ethics. It is impossible to do justice to the interesting development of Russell's views in anything short of a monograph. It is worth noticing, however, that in the end of his brief autobiography in P. A. Schilpp, ed., *The Philosophy of Bertrand Russell*, Evanston, 1944, Harper, New York, 1963, "My Mental Development", pp. 1—20, he found (p. 20) "much satisfaction" that his requirement was accepted and led to cooperation and he considers this the "extention" of rationality to philosophy.

75.   Leonhard Euler, *Letters to A German Princess*, Letter 84.

76.   "Most modern scientists" says Richard Albert Wilson (*The Miraculous Birth of Language*, New York, 1948, p. 100) so very aptly,

> "continue to speak of the material world of mechanical forces as the real and permanent world, and of man with all his mental faculties and moral purposes as an extrinsic chance-comer and would-be usurper, that by some kind of 'biological accident', as Mr. Santayana puts it, has got upon the surface of a physical world of mechanical forces that have no intrinsic connection with the higher part of his own life, his mental and moral aims. This pseudo-scientific view appears in various ways in much of the representative poetry and fiction of the last seventy-five years, as well as in science and philosophy."

As an example very much to the contrary he cites Shaw's *Man and Superman*.

See also my "On the Limits of Scientific Explanation: Hampel and Evans-Pritchard" in *Philosophical Forum,* Vol. 1, 1968, pp. 171—183.

77.   Skinner's views will be discussed in detail in Sections VIII and IX below. Here I only wish to refer to the well-known fact that at times Skinner sides with mechanism, at times suspends judgment on a very strong and general principle — i.e. inductivism or operationalism. See Skinner's *Cumulative Record*, Appleton, New York, 1959, and his "The Machine that is Man", *Psychology Today*, April 1969, pp. 20—25 and pp. 60—63. See also the well-known paper by R. A. Boak and M. S. Halliday, "The Skinnerian Analysis of Behavior", in R. Borger and F. Cioffi, eds., *Explanation in the Behavioral Sciences*, Cambridge University Press and McMillan of Canada, Cambridge and Toronto, 1970, pp. 345—374 and 381—6, as well as my (uncomplimentary) review of it, "Listening in the Lull", *Phil. Soc. Sci.,* Vol. 2, 1972, pp. 319—332, pp. 327—9. See also Karl Schick, "Operants", *J. Expt. Anal. Behavior,* Vol. 15, 1971, pp. 413—23.

There is no doubt that Skinner always tried to be open-minded (though I think he failed). See, for example, B. F. Skinner, "Behaviorism at Fifty", *Science*, Vol. 140, May 31, 1963, pp. 951—8, p. 953; reprinted in T. W. Wann, ed., *Behaviorism and Phenomenology; Contrasting Bases for Modern Psychology*, Chicago, 1963.

> "Behaviorists have from time to time examined the problem of privacy, and some of them have excluded sensations, images, thought-process, and so on, from their deliberations. When they have done so not because such things do not exist but because they are out of reach of their methods, the charge is justified that they have neglected the facts of consciousness . . . An adequate science of behavior must consider events taking place within the skin of the organism . . . The skin is not that important as a boundary."

Yet the skin is most important; see note 2 to Section XXI below. Skinner concludes: "No entity or process which has any explanatory force is to be rejected on the ground that it is subjective or mental."

Rather, he concludes, such mentalistic explanations should be viewed as "way stations". For the origins of this methodological tolerance see note 25 to Section II above.

78. B. Russell in *Human Knowledge, Its Scope and Limits*, London and New York, 1948 and many later editions, part I, Chapter IV, Biological Evolution, notices the rarity of life, views life as systemic, yet is fully and explicitly reductionist. See pp. 32, 36, and 47 there. Let me stress that any argument from rarity makes it virtually certain, by virtue of Bernoulli's theorem, that given enough space and time and we are all reproduced somewhere.

79. The literature on Popper's theory of propensity is enormous. For Popper's own works on the topic see bibliography in P. A. Schilpp, *The Philosophy of Karl Popper*, Open Court, La Salle, Ill., 1974. See also Tom Settle, "Induction and Probability Unfused" and Patrick Suppes "Popper's Analysis of Probability in Quantum Mechanics" in that volume.

80. E. Schrödinger, *Mind and Matter*, Cambridge, 1958, pp. 44–7. See also "On the Peculiarity of the Scientific World-View" and "The Spirit of Science" reprinted in his *What is Life and Other Essays*, Doubleday Anchor, New York, 1956.

81. My claim that the anti-religious move of the reductionist will make the laws ever more wonderful should not deter the anti-religious reductionist, of course. Whether wonderful laws are testimonies for the greatness of God is a different matter. It was Psalm 19 which was supposed to say so, and a line of mystical thinkers, call them cabbalists or Pythagoreans or light-mystics, from Giovanni Pico de la Mirandola to Galileo, insisted on this point. See my "On Explaining the Trial of Galileo", *Organon*, Vol. 8, 1971, pp. 138–166. The argument played a significant role in the famous Newton-Leibniz debate. See A. Koyré, *From a Closed World to the Infinite Universe*, John Hopkins Press, Baltimore and London, 1956, 1968, 1970 and my review of it, "Koyré on the History of Cosmology", in the *Brit. J. Phil. Sci.*, Vol. 9, 1958, pp. 234–245. Though natural religion or physico-theology left science when Laplace told Napoleon he did not need it, no doubt thinkers such as Oersted (the author of *The Soul in Nature*), Einstein, and others still felt moved by it. Yet, their natural religion was so very remote from traditional religion that traditional religion has now very little to gain from physico-theology. See also my "Can Religion Go Beyond Reason?", *Zygon*, Vol. 4, 1969, pp. 128–168 (reprinted in my *Science in Flux*, Reidel, Dordrecht and Boston, 1975).

Chapter Two

Man as Animal

The extremist rejection of all that is distinctly human on the ground that man is a mere machine is parallel to the extremist rejection of all that is distinctly human on the ground that man is a mere animal. In conformity with my anti-all-or-nothing attitude, I reject both of these views. Methodologically the discussion of the view that man is a mere animal parallels the view that man is a mere machine. Both are metaphysical; both suffer historically from being masked as parts of the positivist − anti-metaphysical − view of science. Both, consequently, suffer from the confusion of a program (to explain) with its execution, and hence the confusion between successful explanation and facile explanation away. Also, historically, both confusions are protected by moralizing − against metaphysics and for hard scientific labors. The confusions, when seen as psychopathological confusions, differ significantly in the case of mechanism, which is psychotic, from the case of biologism, which is neurotic.[1] Further, and still historically, whereas mechanism is not deeply linked with the development of the physical sciences, biologism, being Darwinian, is deeply involved with the growth of both biology and psychology.

Logically, mechanism and biologism are independent: one may endorse both, or endorse only one of them and reject the other, or *vice versa*, or reject both. In historical fact, however, the endorsement of mechanism plus the rejection of biologism was unthinkable. And, of course, the reason for this was the reductive hierarchy, the so-called hierarchy of sciences, with sociology reducible to psychology, to physiology, to biochemistry, to chemistry, to physics, to mechanics.[2] Therefore, no one ever entertained the view that man is merely mechanical but not merely animal, or that man is a merely mechanical animal but his dog is a nonmechanical animal: the scale of reduction excludes such possibilities quite *a priori*.

That we take the scale of reduction for granted, however, does not make it true. Why do we accept it? There is almost no literature on this question, except for remarks in Plato and Aristotle, and the scale itself, which was articulated a century or two after it was accepted: the first to publish it explicitly was Auguste Comte, who was a positivist and who pretended that we accept it for a methodological rather than a metaphysical reason. Yet he betrayed at least one additional reason — moral — when he put ethics on the top of the scale:[3] though we reduce man to his atoms, he seems to imply, we rate molecules more valuable than atoms, protein more valuable than other molecules, and we rate successively higher hardware machinery, dogs, men, and societies. Now Comte never stated this. Indeed my own statement raises a problem: are sophisticated machines inferior to isolated protein molecules? General Systems theory, at least, ought to tell us: the more complex stable organization should be the more valuable, it seems; but how this should apply is not clear, nor even whether the scale is one-dimensional as a scale should be. (The levels of organization and/or stability, as well as of complexity, are here involved, and, as a point of mathematical truth, two or three scales cannot be collapsed into one.[4])

Nor was the moral attitude which may be implicit in the Comtean scale clear enough. Traditional moralists have enjoined man to starve his animal nature while nourishing his divine nature.[5] They scarcely noticed that they ascribed all man's objectionable traits to his animal nature — including, of course, such distinct human characteristics as chitchat, gossip, and slander, as well as domineering, lust for power, and malevolence. In the Age of Reason the animal in man was officially liberated but only after a thorough sublimation: Spinoza, who rehabilitated Nature by identifying it with God also was the apostle of liberalism and magnanimity who declared the pleasure of learning — i.e. scientific research — the greatest of all pleasures and the only one to bring peace of mind and thus true happiness.[6] Spinoza was the undeclared leader of the Age of Reason (undeclared since he was a heretic and a Jew), whose ideas thus became more profoundly influential than they would be were they aired critically.[7] And so, throughout the Age of Reason, man was ascribed animal drives on the one hand, and his high aspirations were given fuller vent than ever on the other.[8] The creed was that these two are not incompatible with each other, nor does either conflict with man's (and animal's) mechanical nature. Naturally, then, the animal drives were posited without much examination, and the aspirations rather than the drives gained the focus of attention.[9]

Until Darwin and Freud opened a new era. [10]

Notes

1. For the demarcation between psychosis and neurosis see Y. Fried and J. Agassi, *Paranoia, Boston Studies*, Vol. 50, 1976, final chapter. It will be clear then that the cases discussed here can be easily generalized; it will likewise be clear that the psychopathology associated with mechanism is more intellectual than that of biologism. This is explicable by the fact that biologism is primitive whereas mechanism is sophisticated. Indeed, when primitives compare the animate with the inanimate they reduce machines, or even stones, to animals, not the other way round. The question why animism and magic are more primitive than mechanism is a very difficult one, but certainly has to do with the meaning which magic projects onto things. Mechanism, when it reacts to magic, declares the world meaningless, i.e. indifferent to human meanings. Indeed mechanism tends to explain away even animal emotion, thinking, etc. See my "On the Limits of Scientific Explanation: Hempel and Evans-Pritchard", in *Philosophical Forum*, Vol. 1, 1969, pp. 171–183, as well as Jarvie and Agassi, "The Rationality of Magic", mentioned above, note 70 to Section V.

2. A brief and beautiful exposition in one paragraph of Comte's hierarchy is to be found in E. E. Evans-Pritchard, *The Comparative Method in Social Anthropology*, Athlone Press, University of London, 1963, pp. 25–26. The paucity of clear expositions of this hierarchy is discussed in my "Unity and Diversity in Science" mentioned in note 8 to Section I.

The hierarchy of the sciences is discussed by H. Putnam and R. Oppenheim, in their "Unity of Science as a Working Hypothesis", in H. Feigl, M. Scriven, and G. Maxwell, eds., *Minnesota Studies in the Philosophy of Science*, Vol. 2, University of Minnesota Press, Minneapolis, 1958, pp. 3–36.

Why is the hierarchy Comte's? Is it merely because he gave it a clearer and sharper expression than his many predecessors? I do not think so. I think he answered a great need, namely that of offering a method and a justification of it, the method being historicism and its justification being naturalistic – in the sense of K.R. Popper, *The Poverty of Historicism*, Routledge, London, 1957. Nevertheless, the great articulation has something to do with the fact that the hierarchy is named after Comte. For, in his naturalistic historicism he followed Saint-Simon, who was not that articulate.

I think here I merely restate the view of the matter to be found in Emil Durkheim, *Socialism*, edited with introduction by Alvin Gouldner, from the edition originally edited, and with a preface, by Marcel Mauss, Colliers, New York, 1958; see especially p. 143. No doubt, Kant already gave a full support to historicism – see note 1 to Chapter 3 below – yet the doctrine is typically nineteenth century.

For the importance of the Comtean hierarchy, see Helmut F. Spinner, "Science without Reduction, A Criticism of Reductionism with Special Reference to Hummel and Opp's 'Sociology without Sociology' " *Inquiry*, Vol. 16, 1973, pp. 16–94, a spirited and well-documented attack on reductionism with an extensive bibliography, offering fallibilist theoretical pluralism as an alternative. The author notices that reductionism restricts the application of theories from one field to another to cases where the applied theory is more fundamental (e.g. applying physics to biology is permitted but not vice versa), and he recommends just this kind of forbidden moves. Indeed, the history of science is full of such forbidden moves as noticed by Jean Piaget in his "Méthodologie des Relations Interdisciplinaires", in *Archives de l'Institut International des Sciences Théoriques*, Vol. 18, De la Méthode, Méthodologies Particulières et Méthodologie en Général, Office International de Librairie, Bruxelles, 1972, pp. 85–94. See p. 85: "Summary: The future of experimental sciences seems to depend on the development of interdisciplinary relations. The frontier of experimental science remains artificial as it is bound to what is observable, and progress of research means going further to reach necessary coordination. One should proceed differently in sciences which can, or cannot, be ordered in a hierarchy, and also in relations between sciences of facts and defective theories."

Piaget endorses in that essay (p. 88) the criticism of neo-Darwinism by Lucien C. M. J. Cuénot in his *Inventions et Finalité en Biologie*, Flammarion, Paris, 1941.

3. Putting ethics on top of the hierarchy of the sciences is not Auguste Comte's invention. One can find an explicit statement of it both in Sir Francis Bacon's *Advancement of Learning* and in Spinoza's *Ethics*, as well as in many intermediary writers. Of course, the idea itself is ancient and was transmitted to the moderns in many channels, chiefly hermetic and cabbalistic. See notes to my "Unity and Diversity in Science", mentioned in note 8 to Section I.

4. I am alluding to Hilbert's completeness theorem. If we wish to order all points of the plane in one line then we lose Archimedes' axiom, that is to say we acquire the corollary that there exist pairs of finite magnitudes one infinitely bigger than the other. If a scale implies Archimedes' axiom, then, it follows, two scales cannot collapse into one. Of course, whole fields of inquiry, such as intelligence tests, collapse a few magnitudes – between six and ninety or so – into one, by a technique of weighted significance. This, in itself, may be intuitively quite acceptable. Thus, we can say, the degree of attractiveness of a potential bride is made up from a given percentage of her beauty, plus another given percentage of her intelligence, of her dowry, etc. But this is not collapsing many scales into one: it is the hypothesis that various factors contribute, in given weights, to a potential bride's degree of desirability, or of a student's potential ability, i.e. intelligence. The question can be raised, then, will she be more desirable or less if her beauty was one peg down and her dowry one thousand dollars up. The answer is given, of course, by the weights. The economists answer this question with indifference curves which, indeed, do not offer a complete ordering in all cases, and are not at

all easy to put in the above formula but which takes care of the fact that weights vary with magnitude: a dowry increase of a thousand dollars may mean a lot or very little depending on the size of the dowry to be increased. With intelligence tests mathematics has not gone as far as with economics. See my "The Twisting of the I.Q. Test", *Philosophical Forum*, Vol. 3, 1972, pp. 260–272.

The idea of progress has been ever so often criticized as unilineal or unidirectional, namely as a scale. I do not wish to deny that it may be very worthwhile to attempt to characterize life, but not before giving up Comte's idea of the hierarchy of the sciences: there must be many dimensions to science as well as to life.

It may comfort some readers to know that even in mathematics, where the ancient and modern dreams of unification — by a hierarchy, of course — have played a significant role comparable to none, even there all attempts at a unification have failed. Today an increasing number of philosophers of mathematics are willing to consider the possibility that mathematical problems diversify.

5. The idea, starve the animal in you, feed the divine in you, is traditionally associated with Christian ethics, Christian metaphysics, etc. The *locus classicus,* I think, should remain Heinrich Heine, *Religion and Philosophy in Germany* and Bertrand Russell, *Marriage and Morals,* even though, undoubtedly, more learned works exist. Since Ahad Ha'am and Martin Buber defined Judaism as more realistic a religion than Christianity, anti-ascetic, monastic-within-the-world, etc., and since in modern Judaism their view has much currency, let me say this. First, Judaism had both ascetic and anti-ascetic trends ever since the beginning and to this very day. Second, the debate about asceticism is a red herring, since the ascetic ideal, east and west, is not the sacrifice but the overcoming of desire. The first question is, should we welcome desire? Only if we answer it in the negative do we have, as the second question, how much realism requires that we should reluctantly yield to it. Thus, it matters less that in his legal works Maimonides recommends frugality as close to asceticism as he thinks is reasonable; what matters more is that philosophically he identifies the flesh with the devil. Thus in his *Guide for the Perplexed,* Part III, Chapter VIII, he says, "Man's shortcomings and sins are all due to his body's matter and not its form; while all his merits are exclusively due to his form", and so on and so forth. And so, he implies, even the most sophisticated evil act, planned with as much forethought as conceivable, has nothing to do with the spirit and is "exclusively" due to the flesh!

The two yes-or-no-questions, is man divine in part, and is man good, are both central to philosophical anthropology of all ages throughout western — and even oriental — thought. Strangely enough, the predominant answer is, man is divine in part and he is (due to his non-divine or animal part) downright evil. The radicalist anti-traditional, anti-religious, enlightened, or rationalist, view is that man is wholly animal, yet (naturally) good. The argument for man's goodness goes thus: from the assumption that matter is not good it does not follow that it is evil; it can be indifferent. Indeed, the material world, i.e. the world as a whole, is actually morally indifferent. All there is, then, is just facts, devoid of all motive power. And reason, whose task is to comprehend or copy reality, is thus likewise quite indifferent. What, then, activates us? Nothing but our animal drives. But these drives are, themselves, a part of the natural world, and so indifferent. And so there is no need to endorse or to resist these drives. Therefore, we reason that we may let our animal drives drive us. The most famous saying on all this is David Hume's (*Treatise*, Book II, Part III, Section III): "Reason is, and ought only to be, the slave of the passions." (This sounds like the fallacy of concluding a norm from a fact; it certainly is not: it is amoralism. See also Section IX below, especially note 108, for a criticism of this amoralism of Hume.) Clearly, Hume's saying expresses the doctrine of the natural goodness of man, a utilitarian and a materialistic variant of (the Spinozist variant of) Plato's version of Socratic eudaimony.

The long and the short of it is that traditional western religions oppose autonomy and distrust man, whereas enlightenment preaches autonomy. All the rest — and the content of the previous paragraph — is just frills and post-hoc ratiocinations. There is no difficulty at all in viewing man as neither good nor evil, yet endowed with appetites and dispositions both animal and spiritual. Even man's spiritual appetites can be both good and evil, as Kant argued when establishing to his satisfaction that nothing is unconditionally good (or evil) except good (or ill) will.

The idea that man has spiritual appetites in a nonreligious sense can be found in K. R. Popper, *The Open Society and Its Enemies*, London and New York, 1945, etc., where he tries to translate Socrates' injunction, "care for your soul!" to the language accepted to members of the Vienna Circle (Vol. I, Chapter 10, note 45). The idea that the question of autonomy is logically prior to all philosophy of man is both there and in Walter Kaufmann's *Without Guilt and Justice*, New York, 1973. As Kaufmann argues, the doctrine of enlightened self-interest did not bring about the desired autonomism, and its translation to puritanic or protestant or work ethic (deferred gratification) has rendered it impotent. So, man's alleged natural goodness finally turned out to be a preacher's ploy just as man's alleged natural evil used to be.

6. Spinoza's ethics is clearly meant to be a variant of Socratic eudaimony. Perhaps it is a variant of views of Maimonides who insisted (in a famous passage, commentaries on *Mishnah, Sanhedrin*, 10, introduction, which outraged his contemporaries) that the reward of virtue is virtue itself and so the promise of reward in the world to come, though meant to be fulfilled, is as irrelevant as the peanuts the schoolmaster offers children who read their lesson well. The saying "the reward of virtue is virtue" is Talmudic, but may be read in different ways, as cryptic sayings always can. Nonetheless, the fact that it does avail itself of a eudaimonic reading is itself quite interesting. We tend to forget that Socrates' own final argument for his eudaimonism was the existence of a just desert in afterlife. It is curious that some Jewish thinkers were more realistic eudaimonists than Socrates, already in the Middle Ages if not in Talmudic times. See my "Conventions of Knowledge in Talmudic Law", in *J. Jewish Studies*, Vol. 25, Feb. 1974, pp. 16–34, also published in Bernard S. Jackson, ed., *Studies in Jewish Legal History: In Honor of David Daube*, Jewish Chronicle Publ., London, 1974.

The idea that the reward of virtue is virtue itself is the same as that peace of mind is priceless — one which even Hume endorsed in a pinch; see previous note and note 108 to Section IX below. This is but a variant of an extremely wide-spread view that worship is a great delight. In natural religion worship equals learning. The idea, worship equals learning equals the greatest pleasure, is known in Spinoza's phrase, the intellectual love of God. It can be found in Maimonides' *Guide for the Perplexed,* part III, Chapter LI, where reference is made to a sexual metaphor in Psalm XCI, 14, plus commentary where the sexual aspect is stressed. Of course, this is commonplace in the cabbalistic literature, but it is interesting to see how prevalent it really is.

7. See R. Colie, "Spinoza and the Early English Deists", *J. Hist. Ideas,* Vol. 20, January 1959, pp. 23—46 and his *Light and Enlightenment,* Cambridge University Press, 1957; see also P. Vernière, *Spinoza et la Pensée Française avant la Révolution,* 2 vols., Presses Universitaires, Paris, 1954.

8. An exception of sorts is Kant who viewed all emotions and all passions as morally irrational and so as obstacles to overcome. He viewed man's social passion — his desire to excel, to influence, control, and have power over others — as both irrational and yet the cause for competition which urges man to overcome his irrationality quite unwittingly (see Frederick P. van de Pitte, *Kant As Philosophical Anthropologist,* Nijhoff, The Hague, 1971, p. 25.) Here is Kant's supreme deviation from the more purist — Spinozist — version of the enlightenment which saw the pursuit of knowledge a sufficiently strong selfish sentiment for the development of rationality to the full. Now, clearly, for Kant himself the pursuit of knowledge sufficed, but while his philosophy centered on it he had contempt for the common man (see quotation, note 15 to the Introduction). Hence he was speaking here for the common man, in a passage which, though reminiscent of Adam Smith and, before him, Herman Mandeville, is for the first time applied to the highest pursuit — of knowledge — as unintended, and thus is pregnant with thoughts of Hegel (the cunning of reason), of Nietzsche (the will to power), and of more irresponsible people; Kant ends up recommending education which is "wholesome, but harsh and severe" (van de Pitte, *op. cit.,* pp. 27, 105) as the means by which the common man is either destroyed or learns to abide by the lofty destiny of the human race. Harsh liberalism is a dangerous doctrine.

9. Isaac Asimov, *The Human Brain,* Boston, 1963, summed this up very simply. "Yet the division between 'rational man' and 'irrational brute' cannot be maintained . . . The difference . . . is [of degree] ."
"Does the fact that behavior can be modified even in simple animals wipe out the distinction between man and other creatures? Of course it doesn't. That the gap . . . exists is obvious and incontrovertible. The only question is whether the gap exists by virtue of man's exclusive possession of reason."
The question with which the second quoted paragraph begins has already been answered with equal finality in the first! And Asimov simply returns to it with

examples of animal reasoning and memory. He concludes, surprisingly only to those who fail to notice this, that, indeed,

"One thing is sure. Reason alone does not explain the gulf that lies between man and other animals."

But notice that "Reason" is used, throughout his discussion, in the sense of the behaviorist or other kinds of reductionists. Thus, the opening idea of no-qualitative difference (in reason) leads to qualitative difference (elsewhere).

10. To be more precise, it was the rise of Romanticism, and more precisely, the underground influence of romantic thinkers on rationalistic ones. The whole study of underground movements in science is fascinating and I cannot discuss it here. Hegel's influence on Darwin, inasmuch as it exists, has been discussed by E. Cassirer, *Problem of Knowledge, Philosophy, Science, and History since Hegel*, translated by W. H. Woglom and C. W. Hendel, Yale University Press, New Haven, Conn., 1950; Owsei Temkin has discussed underground influences of this kind more systematically and thoroughly. See Owsei Temkin, "The Historiography of Ideas in Medicine", in Edwin Clarke, ed., *Modern Methods in the History of Medicine,* Athlone Press, University of London, 1971, pp. 1–21 and references there. (See also my books mentioned in note 8 to Section I above.)

The Romantics attacked radicalist philosophical anthropology in two directions: first, they introduced a new component, the necessity of tradition; second they blew up an existing component — man's brute or animal nature (which is a mixture of good and evil). They also tried to combine the two in a sort of rubbishy pretentious pseudo-reductionism. Be it as it may, it was this worst pseudo-rationalism that attracted Feuerbach; and his making it more rationalistic was epoch-making.

I do not think it has ever been noticed that the contemporary efforts in developing animal psychology for the specific purpose of applying it to the philosophy of man — particularly that of Konrad Lorenz — owes so much to Ludwig Feuerbach, even though the ideas of Feuerbach were absorbed into the culture with modifications which were later further modified in the opposite direction so as to resemble their original form as if they were pieces of plastic with memory. But see, for example, Henri Lefebvre's "Reply to Professor Roderick Chisolm and Comments", in Paul Kurtz, ed., *Language and Human Nature, A French-American Philosophers' Dialogue*, St. Louis, 1971, pp. 155–163, p. 160:

"For Feuerbach 'human nature' is defined on an almost biological plane, as the general or generic essence of the species: perception, desire, enjoyment. In relation to this essence lost in the course of history, alienation is defined."

This, I submit, is the essence of Lorenz's philosophical anthropology. As Lefebvre himself notices, we receive Feuerbach via Marx; his passage here quoted follows thus:

"It is easy to show that Marx used Feuerbach against Hegel and Hegelian dialectics against Feuerbach's anthropology . . ."

"Although it is superseded, put back in its place, the anthropology of Feuerbach does not become ideology pure and simple in Marx . . . It still has a meaning ... without going as far as the idea of total revolution, originated by the working-class ... this anthropology stands out as a landmark: humanism, that is, concern with "the human being", sensitive, sensorial, sensual."

In other words, when rectifying Marxism of its errors we get back to Feuerbach. Somehow, however, the passage I have quoted is too lengthy: it is apologetic for Marx. It is admittedly still true of Marx, whose Feuerbachian attempt to rationalize Romanticism into a version of humanism shines through his errors – political or moral. Unfortunately, this does not seem true of Lorenz who likes sensitivity in measure, when exhibited by man or by dog. For Marx, see Robert C. Tucker, *Philosophy and Myth in Karl Marx*, Cambridge University Press, 1972. For Lorenz, see below, next Section, notes 21, 24, 26–31. See also his *Man Meets Dog*, Methuen, London, 1954, Penguin, 1964, especially Chapter 8, "Choosing a Dog".

VI   MAN-AS-ANIMAL IS NOT THE ANIMAL-IN-MAN

The fact that there is an animal in man is incontestable. The view that man is an animal and nothing else is a metaphysical view, in conflict with Jewish, Christian, and other metaphysics, such as Cartesian metaphysics, all of which endow man, but not other animals, with the Image of God. All this, I would have thought, is obvious enough. Yet it is obfuscated by those who intentionally regard views of man as animal as a mere focusing on the animal in man.[11] Thus, when Freud says all man's drives are originally the sex drive, he reduces all drives to animal drives;[12] yet Konrad Lorenz, in a kind of indulgence to the great man, declares this to be nothing but an exaggeration of the importance of sex, which exaggeration comes naturally to one whose gaze is fixed for many years on one thing.[13]

Now there is no doubt that this view of Freud, meant to be benign, makes an ass out of him. Freud was as familiar as any normal human being with the existence of many a motive which in appearance or on the face of it is not sexual and hardly related to sex. What he said is that though in appearance it is not sex, in reality, and in particular in origin, it is. Of course, Freud also went into the details of the mechanisms of apparently nonsexual motives in attempts to expose them as sexual in essence. That is to say, his view of reality did alter his view of appearance. This is hard to express as long as we insist on two and only two levels, appearance and reality. It becomes easier if we admit levels of appearances: for then we can say, and even in truth, that Freud's view of reality made him deepen our ordinary view of things: as the quip "your id is showing" illustrates (where id stands for some sexual interest or another), our very superficial view today is less superficial than it was before Freud, thanks to his view of the depths which stand behind the appearances.[14] This very interaction between views of reality and the enrichment of appearances is lost once we kindly dismiss Freud's view that all motives are in reality the sex drive. Freud was mistaken, I suppose, but he surely does not deserve to be dismissed offhand.

I must hurry along, but I cannot leave this point unexplained. [15] Quite generally we all feel the difference between the respectful disagreement we may have with people who we consider knowledgeable and intelligent, with whom we would readily engage in debate, and the disrespectful disagreement we have with people whom we consider presumptive, ignorant, or fanatic, and with whom we will not have a debate for any intellectual purpose. Now often it is people of the first kind that we respect enough to overlook their errors, especially after they have died, thus placing them unwittingly in the second category. Usually we merely quote their views which we do not think mistaken, and pretend that their mistakes do not exist, but when the mistakes are not well tucked in, we unwittingly treat them disrespectfully by our very dismissal of them. The history of metaphysical ideas is one where this cannot be done, and so we usually feel inclined to pretend that this history does not exist or at least does not count. It is time to alter this habit. Thus, let us notice, Freud's attempt to reduce everything to sex was wild and ingenious and defective. Because of it the world is a better place to live in. Back to man as animal.

The animal-in-man, or, more contemptuously, the beast-in-man, meant not so much cruelty and stupidity, as we may read it today; rather, it meant sex. Until recently apes used to kidnap beautiful blondes not only in fiction but also in some biology texts. [16] Love was lofty; making love base. Bertrand Russell has said that in adolescence he would not correlate his excitement over a love poem and his attraction to the maid's buttocks. [17] When Freud made the correlation, he still insisted that in appearance the love poem need not be the expression of plain sex drive, only in reality it is. To put it in his jargon, the id, the racial memory, the purely animal, the unconscious (not to be confused with the subconscious), is where the pure sex drive dwells. The ego, the super-ego, even the emotions repressed by the super-ego into the subconscious or the fore-conscious (which is the area between the subconscious and the conscious, so-to-speak, the threshold of consciousness), all this is far from being pure sex. All this subtlety was lost on people scandalized by Freud and frightened by him as by the ape who — or is it which? — kidnapped the blonde. [18] Thus, when we speak of the animal-in-man we can see primeval energy working in a civilized setting, yet when we speak of man-as-mere-animal, we see civilized man as reducible to, or as explicable as, essentially an animal.

There is a simple objection to this presentation of mine, which well deserves notice. The proponent of the objection will declare frivolous the distinction between the animal-in-man and man-as-animal. When we see man-as-animal, as if he were an animal, we deliberately ignore the non-animal residue or the non-animal essence in man. Now, if man happens to be nothing but an animal, the residue will be empty or null, and man-as-animal will turn out to be seen as an animal and as man at once; otherwise, the residue will be non-empty and what we will see when looking at man-as-animal will not be man as such but the animal-in-man and only the animal in man.

There is great merit in this argument. Indeed, though I do reject the argument, I see no mistake in any of the steps employed in it; indeed, each step is nothing but a demonstrable truth. The reader can convince himself of this by the ancient normal test of logical truth: he can put the word "computer" instead of "animal" in the previous paragraph or "computer" instead of "animal" plus "animal" instead of "man", and so forth. What I reject, however, is the claim that these logical truths invalidate the distinction between viewing man as animal and viewing the animal in man. This I can disprove: the argument applies to seeing man as he is, rather than attempts to view him this way or that, attempts rooted in our shortcomings. Let me elaborate.

We do not know whether man is a mere animal or not, whether his rationality, such as it is, is an animal quality or extra-animal quality inexplicable by reference to his animal nature alone. When we look at man-as-animal we try to see him as we usually see him but in an effort to comprehend what we see as manifestations of an animal nature. It is, in other words, an exercise; an exercise which usually fails either because of our lack of intelligence or because we go against nature — we do not know why. The exercise is not merely to mark those facts which look animal, and not merely those which can be explained as animal, but also to mark, clearly, those which do look as definitely not animal and to wrestle with them in an effort to render them animal; to explain them as animal.

And so, though the objection contains only true statements, indeed truisms, it does not hold as an objection to our distinction between looking at man-as-animal and looking at the animal-in-man, because the objection applies to the discussion of the case of seeing correctly all along, not to the discussion of any case of looking; to the finished product, not to the efforts which may or may not lead to it one day.

This has some far-reaching consequences. The view [19] of man-as-animal is like the view of man-as-machine — not an explanation but a mere program; and the argument confuses the program with the finished product. Now, when a program is confused with the finished product, we may fool ourselves and think that certain appearances have been explained when they have not been explained. And we may, in these cases, fool ourselves and think that these same appearances are in no need of explanation as they are explained away; as mere chimera. We may, finally, alternate between these two forms of self-deception concerning the same appearances. Each of these three tactics deserves notice.

The vacillation between two and only two (or any other fixed number of) theories each of which is unsatisfactory is one of the commonest modes of intellectual behavior. Methodologically speaking, it amounts to a dogmatism, the dogma being that which is shared by the two alternatives (i.e., their disjunction). Psychologically, the vacillation is a fixation, probably a neurotic one, on the dogma at hand. Culturally, it is the inherent mode of mythical thinking which will be discussed in some detail in the next chapter. The first of our two alternatives, the idea that some program for explanation has been executed, leads one at once to pseudo-science of the kind discussed already by William Whewell over a century ago and sufficiently elaborated upon by my teacher Sir Karl Popper. The second of our two alternatives, that of explaining away, has been discussed in the previous chapter. There is one point to add to that discussion: the psychological components of viewing man as machine and of explaining away his apparently mechanical aspects is the syndrome of schizophrenia as discussed by R. D. Laing; the psychological component of the same regarding man-as-animal is quite different.

I wish to dwell upon this point. Though it is psychologically very interesting, it is not the psychological interest that I am after here. Rather, I wish to dwell on the psychology of centering on man-as-animal for different purposes. I wish to bring out as clearly as I can the difference between the program of reducing man to machine and that of reducing man to animal — regardless of whether we can further reduce animals to machines. And I wish to bring out the flavor of this difference, the difference in psychological overtones. Also, I wish to bring out the difference between the contemplation of the animal-in-man, which is not peculiar or necessarily challenging, and the contemplation of man-as-animal which is a peculiar and challenging program. And I wish to bring out the difference between the program, the attempt to explain man as animal, and its successful execution.

Considering the animal-in-man, then, one may contemplate such a typically animal function as food intake. One may resent this as a fetter and dream of freedom from it, whether by the intervention of divine providence or by the application of future technology. By contrast to this, one may muse about food intake fondly, and relive some experiences of it which are memorable, say, after some ravishing hunger, or with terrific company, or in the most exquisite eating place. One may even contemplate food intake religiously or in a vitalist fashion, and muse about the inability of the condemned to death to consume his last meal, and view food intake and the craving for food as participation in the cycle of life, as an umbilical cord of sorts, as a part of what makes life on earth as a living and pulsating whole, and participants in it, man and other animals, "brethren in pain." [20]

Considering man-as-animal, on the other hand, we look at things differently. At first glance we tend to ignore all the frills, and view food intake mainly as the calming down of an enormously powerful drive. This immediately puts the ability of a given individual to provide for himself, indeed the whole person who contemplates the matter, as a subject of contemplation: am I economically self-sufficient? How does this contemplation feel? Now we do not have as yet a general answer to the second question, but I observe some specific answers to it — cases of how this contemplation feels. A nature-boy like Konrad Lorenz can face nature and take care of himself, right in the middle of the wilderness; he knows this fact and he feels an inner glow when noticing it; he is proud to be a nature-boy. A city boy and a Jew-boy like Sigmund Freud will be lost in the wilderness; contemplating this fact he will be filled with anxiety and irritated helplessness; he will at once notice this and be filled with shame and guilt and further anxiety and further irritation. He will wish to change the subject but will feel obliged to go on — regardless of the torment or enjoying the torment, and wondering which of these two options regarding torment is true. Thus we have a full-blown neurosis on our hands — one which surfaces by a simple intellectual exercise. [21]

It is not clear to me whether it was Freud, Kafka, Erik Erikson, or someone else, who noticed that anxieties, neuroses, and psychoses, whatever their source, may express themselves as, and be triggered by, general philosophic questions. [22] Here is one that seems common among modern intellectuals.

The insecurity which is intensified by contemplating one's own economic insufficiency outside society may easily spill over to the feeling that one only clings to one's society out of helplessness, not out of approval. Society, that is, may well be corrupt, and my staying in it a weakness. Moreover, this conclusion can be shared by one who feels fairly secure in the bosom of nature: why does he not follow his bent and relinquish society? [23]

The question, should I go to the wilderness, is thus enhanced by the view of man-as-animal. For, as an animal man exhibits a culture that may very well be a symptom of sickness, or at least redundant, or inexplicable, or at the very least, to be explained away. All thinkers who view man as animal show the curious concern for the future of mankind that betrays doubt as to the value of human culture. [24] Here both Freud and Lorenz, victim and hunter, share the same question. Can we destroy culture without destroying mankind? If so, is it advisable? Is culture and civilization a movement away from true human nature?

Is Rousseau right after all? The anxiety is the fear that Rousseau is right, and so something terrible is going to happen to all of us. It is no wonder that our vacillating about whether man is mere animal in the sense that we may one day explain him as animal or in the sense that in his folly he deviates from his animal nature and covets disaster, that this vacillation may whip up neuroses and even mass-hysteria — in the form, at present, of the ecological movement. [25]

The view of culture as neurosis — Freud's view — does not conflict with Lorenz's and others' generalization and simplification of objective conflict situations. A conflict, says Lorenz, is not a deep and complicated psychological subtlety, but simply a signal which may be read in quite opposite manners. Is my neighbor's present gesture of baring his teeth a smile or a snarl? [26] The same, then, may hold for culture. Is our culture and civilization an expression of man's rationality or is our city but an anthill? We speak of culture as an achievement, but possibly culture is but a sickness, or a mirage, or a mere varnish. Konrad Lorenz clearly tries to explain culture away by explaining animal psychology by reference to mere instincts, [27] or rather to mere innate release mechanisms, and by explaining man as mere animal. Does he then approve or disapprove of culture? I shall now explain his ambivalence.

Lorenz is very able in employing a technique which can be found already in Darwin, but which he uses to his own purposes frequently, and which goes like this. Assume that it is possible to reduce human qualities such as love and friendship and the like to simple biological mechanisms; we thereby justify our reference to such human qualities; hence we can use anthropomorphic language describing animal behavior, including fears and friendship (but not cruelty!). [28] He thus manages to humanize animals both by anthropomorphism and by explaining away what he dislikes and explaining what he likes. [29] He can do the same with society, [30] and it makes him uneasy.

Lorenz's theories have been, and still are, subject to detailed criti-

cism. This is not the place to dwell on them.[31] His general theory
assumes ritualization as a major hereditary development, and this
looks like the inheritance of acquired characteristics, i.e., Lamarckism.[32] Whether this is so or not, I cannot say. That he by and large
manages in his books to put man and beast on a par is a fact, thus
making some of his readers happy, some nervous; I suppose it makes
them all a bit happy and a bit nervous. But are his geese happy or
nervous when they contemplate the possibility of putting geese and
other beasts on a par? I do not know how to put this kind of question
to them.

Of course, nobody can ask geese any abstract question. But most
people agree that this is a cheap way of arguing against the view that
man is but an animal. This may indeed be so. When Descartes said that
animals are machines, people objected that machines cannot reproduce. Well, as Samuel Butler has argued[33] — very cogently, one must
admit — machines can reproduce themselves. And today machines do
produce machines in certain fully automated factories. And so, the
argument from reproduction — clocks cannot reproduce — is invalid.
Is the argument from abstract thinking — geese do not comprehend
human language — not likewise invalid? However abstract and complex a question we may have, there may be a future computer which
can answer it whereas my clock cannot; yet that computer is nevertheless but a distant relative of my clock. Now, can we substitute men
and geese for computers and clocks in the previous sentence? Darwin
says that we are distant relatives of geese and so, clearly, what is good
for computers and clocks, is good for men and geese: some machines
can think, and some animals can too.[34] Except that Darwin's view
already rests on the view of man as but an animal, and, of course,
whereas no one as yet contests that clocks and computers are of·the
same ilk, the claim of Darwin and his followers that men and geese,
not to say animals and machines, are of the same ilk, is hotly contested. How strong was the case of Darwin is hard to say; but how
strong is now the neo-Darwinian case?

Notes to Section VI

11. H. Stuart Hughes, *Consciousness and Society,* New York, 1958, p. 125,
quotes Egon Friedell to say "Is, then, Freud a metaphysician? Yes, but he does
not know it." *Kulturgeschichte der Neuzeit,* Munich, 1931, translated by Charles
Francis Atkinson, *A Cultural History of the Modern Age,* New York, 1939,
Volume III, p. 479. The metaphysics was in part a variant of the Enlightenment
view (see note 5 above), in part an extension of Darwinism. This latter aspect of

Freud's metaphysics, his Darwinism, has been unequivocally stated in the penulti-mate page of John C. Greene, *The Death of Adam: Evolution and its Impact on Western Thought*, Iowa State University Press, Ames, 1959, Mentor, New York, 1961; see also note 14 below.

12. Freud's theory that all drives are originally for food and for sex are eminent-ly rooted in biologism, and more specifically in a mistaken animal psychology. It is no surprise, then, that the best and strongest criticisms of his ideas come from ethology. In retrospect the criticisms also throw new light on these theories, and explain much of the force of Freud's doctrines.

In retrospect it is even difficult to sympathize with Freud's mistakes, but only due to the profound change of the intellectual background to the discussion. Thus, when Freud noted the presence of an attraction between any two humans, and excluding some cannibalistic instinct, he could see in this nothing but sex, and so he concluded that we are all latent homosexuals. Now some animals are herd animals and so latent homosexuals, some are loners and so are not. But what shall we do with monogamous herd animals, social animals, as certain birds certainly are (comparing clucking women to clucking flocks of geese is a case in point)? Also, Freud never noted the attraction of humans to dog or horse, or else he would have branded it sexual too! Perhaps he could view this as symbiosis, and reduce all symbiosis not to sex drive but to food drive. If so, then the symbioses of shepherds with sheep or with dog are so different from each other and Freud-ianism is just too crude to differentiate them. And men's attraction to each other may, then, be declared more symbiotic or food-oriented than sexual. Of course, to the extent that males and females of the species can be confused by members of the same species, a Lorenzian view of ambiguous stimuli, though insufficient (see note 26 below) explains better than Freud the prevalence of homosexuality in all-male preserves, such as jails, barracks, and Moslem stag parties.

The discussion on whether to reduce male attraction to male society to sex or to food vanishes with Freud's theory of the libido which reduces both sex drives and hunger to the happiness principle. To say all desires are reducible to the happiness principle sounds tautologous but is not, since there may be the opposite principle, thanatos or the death wish. Lorenz severely attacked Freud, saying animals have no death wish. He does not argue this point, however. Why primitive people can successfully wish to die, as reported by many anthropologists, but not modern men, is a fascinating problem. If the report is true, then Lorenz is in error. Anyone who was rejected by his peers and felt physically sick, I suspect, will here side with Freud as against Lorenz. Freud, indeed, was amply rejected. Indeed, more than he experienced rejection he craved it. See note 38 to Section XIII below. Lorenz, by contrast, always toed the line, even when the line ended up with a crook rather than a hook. See notes 119 to Section X and 61 to Section XIX below on Hegel's views of all desire as self-destructive.

13. Konrad Lorenz, introduction to the 1965, Chicago edition of Charles Darwin's classic *The Expression of Emotions in Animals and Man* (1870). In the

introduction Lorenz dismisses offhand all general principles, metabiological and metapsychological, in a postivist-inductivist mood. He also praises there Darwin's metabiological principles, in an inductivist mood of success worship. I am not referring to this passage in order to debate its thesis but in order to illustrate a popular prejudice which has consequences that I wish to discuss.

Let me mention that Jones' life of Freud is a mixture of candid exposition and silly cover-ups of parts of the great and well-known shifts in Freud's metaphysics from mechanism to a kind of dualism. But I cannot enter this enormous topic here. See also notes 15, 32 and 43 below.

14. It is, no doubt, a development only partly due to Freud, that made us see the prevalence of the sexual interest more clearly than our predecessors. Not only psychologists, but also biologists, started noticing the fact, and so also writers of the period. I was particularly impressed with Edmond Rostand's *Cyrano* which, in 1897, presents as an ideal love without sex, an ideal possible to endorse and live by only through an ingenious and lucky mixture of self-deception and resourceful-ness — both poured in quantities. Freud viewed the exercise of resourcefulness as a sublimation, as the diversion of (sexual) energies into new outlets. Sartre is more perceptive in saying that the very activity of the resourceful person is his means of self-deception. No doubt the culture which makes one hate sex also makes one approve of hard work and resourcefulness. This, in particular, is true of Freud himself. And so, the similarity between Freud and Rostand goes further than what light Freud's theory can shed on Rostand's story! See also note on p. 13 of David Bakan, *Sigmund Freud and the Jewish Mystical Tradition*, Van Nostrand, Prince-ton, Toronto, New York, London, 1958.

But let us move to Freud's place in biology. That he was a Darwinian is fairly obvious (see note 25 to Section II above and notes 32 to Section VI, 43, 48, and 52 to Section VIII below). The following quotation from W. P. Pycroft, *The Courtship of Animals*, Hutchison, London, 1913, p. 162, seems remarkable:

"Though not commonly realized, and though denied by some, the sexual in-stincts are the dominant factors in the animal world. Even Man himself, the Lord of Creation, knowing good and evil, cannot escape their overmastering rule. [Those who wish to escape their rule] they are suffering from a dis-ease . . . a "Disharmony" as Metschinikoff calls it, a disease which blinds their perception of the motive power . . . For these same despised instincts are the sacred fires of our being . . . all that makes us human, love, ambition and life itself . . ."

The other example is the famous work of Sir Solly Zuckerman, *The Social Life of Monkeys and Apes,* London and New York, 1932, end of Chapter 17, "The Development of Social and Sexual Responses", p. 290.

"In describing our present knowledge of the socio-sexual development of apes and monkeys, this chapter has also revealed how scanty this knowledge is compared with the established data concerning similar developments in lower mammals . . . in many ways monkeys and apes run parallel to human beings in their sexual development."

Here comes a reference to Freud's *Three Contributions to a Theory of Sex*. The earlier studies of lower mammals referred to, are also from the twenties. The earliest study of sexuality in the monkey is of K. S. Lashley and J. B. Watson, 1913 — *J. Anim. Behav.*, Vol. 3, pp. 114–139. It concerns infant sexuality and Oedipal relations. See also Gerrit S. Miller, "Some Elements of Sexual Behavior in Primates, and their Possible Influence on the Beginnings of Human Social Development", *J. Mammalogy*, Vol. 9, 1928, pp. 273–293; H. C. Bingham, "Sex Development in Apes" *Comp. Psych. Monographs*, Baltimore, Vol. 5, 1928, pp. 1–161; Robert and Ada Yerkes, *The Great Apes. A Study of Anthropoid Life*, Yale University Press, New Haven, Conn., 1929.

Zuckerman's work contains an enlightening historical introduction and a rich bibliography of over 400 items, including a few from the psychoanalytic press (concerning the sex life of primates). Yet it contains one reference to Freud, no. 116A, namely one of the very last items added. The author tells us in his preface that the volume came out due to the surprising interest in a lecture he gave in 1929 on the subject. His historical introduction indicates that inasmuch as his initial interest was kindled by existing works, these too, e.g. Malinowski's and G. S. Miller's critique of Malinowski's, were influenced by Freud. (Also E. H. Howard and R. Griffault.) The fact that Malinowski's response to Freud was highly hostile could conceal this at the time, but today we consider a strong response, whether positive or negative (due to the influence of Einstein and Popper, I venture to guess), to be a sign of strong influence. It is interesting that Zuckerman, though not directly familiar with Freud, it seems, does somehow report it, as well as observations regarding both infantile sexuality and Oedipal relations. I suppose this shows that already in the twenties Freud exerted much anonymous influence.

But we should not exaggerate the importance of the influence of animal psychology on our sexual liberation. Indeed, until quite recently only the avant-garde dared study the field freely. See Sir Julian Huxley's complaint in his *The Uniqueness of Man*, London, 1941, p. 191:

"Animal courtship is an unfashionable topic among biologists at present; and I do not exaggerate when I say that it is one on which both ignorance and prejudice prevail."

And so it should not be surprising to find out that Freud had a major influence even on the work of Konrad Lorenz in the thirties.

The importance of Freud's theory of aggression for the development of Lorenz's theory is stressed in some places, for example, Wolf Lepenies and Helmut Nolte, eds., *Kritik der Anthropologie*, Munich, 1971, third essay, "Über gesellschaftstheoretische Implikationen des Aggressionsbegriffs", especially pp. 105, 113, 118, 119, 122, 126, 132. Later studies on Lorenz in German abound and follow suit.

15. This whole matter of our need to learn to admire great ideas even when they are false is explained at length in my *Towards an Historiography of Science*, first seven sections, and my "Science in Flux: Footnotes to Popper", both mentioned in note 3 to the Introduction above.

I think there is still some need to vindicate metaphysical disagreements. I learned from Popper to make light of the disagreement between Freud and Adler: both see, in appearance, the presence of both the sex drive and the craving for peer approval; but whereas the one reduces the latter to the former, the other does the opposite. I now find the disagreement extremely interesting, and I think the history of the Freudian shift towards Adlerianism well worth a serious study. See also W. W. Bartley, III, "Theories of Demarcation Between Science and Metaphysics", in I. Lakatos and A. Musgrave, eds. *Problems in the Philosophy of Science, Proceedings of the International Colloquium in the Philosophy of Science, 1965*, Vol. 3, North Holland, Amsterdam, 1968, pp. 40–64, especially pp. 47 and 58. I have expressed my deep regret at the irrelevant *ad hominem* response of Popper to Bartley's excellent challenge – which can be found in the same volume, pp. 88–102 – in my "Tristram Shandy, Pierre Menard, and All That", *Inquiry*, Vol. 14, 1971, pp. 152–164, and in my "Postscript: On the Futility of Fighting Philistines", *Philosophia*, Vol. 4, 1974, pp. 163–201.

See also note 13 above and notes 19 and 43 below.

16. The story of the superstitious attitude to apes as expressed even by biologists is due to Robert and Ada Yerkes, *The Great Apes. A Study of Anthropoid Life*, Yale University Press, New Haven, Conn., 1929. The complementary superstition is, of course, the view of different kinds of humans as apes; see Loren Eisley, *Darwin's Century, Evolution and the Men who Discovered it*, Doubleday, New York, 1958, Chapter X, Section 11.

Darwin himself was of the opinion that certain monkeys are attracted to women. See his Notebook on Man, Mind and Materialism, pp. 137–8; see also p. 106; published in Howard E. Gruber, *Darwin on Man, A Psychological Study of Scientific Creativity, Together with Darwin's Early and Unpublished Notebooks*, transcribed and annotated by Paul H. Barrett, foreword by Jean Piaget, Dutton, New York, 1974, pp. 292 and 286.

17. Bertrand Russell, *Marriage and Morals*, London, 1929, pp. 79–80. This is the book in which Russell managed to rid himself for good of Protestant ethic, so-called. It is psychologistic rather than reformist in tendency; nevertheless it is already superseded in many ways. Yet I think it deserves to remain a classic. It is regrettable that sociologists have hardly any good word for this pioneer sociologist; they are even ignorant of the fact that he is the discoverer of the evils of modern suburban life (*op. cit.* and *The Conquest of Happiness*).

18. It was Bertrand Russell who observed that people failed to notice the most important corollary to Freud's theory, which is that childhood is miserable, merely because they were so busy combatting it. See Bertrand Russell, *On Education Especially in Early Childhood, i.e. Education and the Good Life*, Allen and Unwin, Boni and Liveright, London and New York, 1925, pp. 44ff., 126, 171, 192–5, 197–8, 210; also his *Education and the Social Order, i.e. Education and the Modern World*, Allen and Unwin, W. W. Norton, London and New York,

1932, p. 135, reprinted in R. E. Egner and L. E. Denonn, eds., *The Basic Writings of Bertrand Russell, 1903–1959,* Simon and Schuster, New York, 1967, p. 431; also his *The Scientific Outlook,* 1931, 1959, Norton Library, New York, p. 182.

19. I wish to make it clear that the view which generates an explanatory program is true or false, a metaphysics which contradicts a competing metaphysics perhaps. Not knowing which of the competitors is true, we may pursue both. Popper thinks (*Open Society,* last chapter) that they are not statements but interpretations or points of view. His idea strangely accords with R. G. Collingwood's *Essay on Metaphysics,* where Collingwood is driven to the view that metaphysics is inarticulable, and for similar methodological reasons (of positivism plus critical attitude, which together paint one into a corner).

It seems to me that Protestant ethic made Popper far too indignant of people, say Freud and Adler, who confused their interpretations (which generated programs for explanations) with explanations proper. It seems to me that the over-reaction led him to hostility, which is plainly regrettable. It is amazing to find no written notice by Popper to the great contributions to humanity made by these two individuals. He is surprisingly harsh to them. See also note 15 above.

20. The view of animals as "our brethren in pain" is from Darwin's notebooks, see reference in note 36 to Section VII below. It is clearly an expression of a deeply religious sentiment. Now, some twentieth-century philosophical anthropologists have argued from man's religious faculties, especially yearning, that some theological tenets are true. Darwin himself was observed (*The Descent of Man,* London, 1871, pp. 95–6) that dogs' feelings towards their masters are inherently religious. But Freud has argued, in his *The Future of an Illusion,* that the religious faculties are rooted elsewhere. At the same time Jack London found them in dogs and other animals. He describes yearnings very forcefully in his "Call of the Wild" and elsewhere, and taboo in *Jerry of the Islands* and elsewhere. The same idea can be found in Kafka's animal short stories. The fact that religious sentiments exist, whether in fairly low animals or in anti-religious philosophers of the highest degree of sophistication is significant; but its import is far from clear. See also Robert Louis Stevenson's "The Man Who Was God".

21. Konrad Lorenz, *Man Meets Dog* (Penguin, 1964), Introduction, says, since cats are independent they are not domesticated but wild. The enormous premium placed on economic autonomy by Lorenz may well explain why Freud's enormous influence on Lorenz has thus far been overlooked. Admittedly Lorenz gave false scent by openly criticizing Freud and by openly accepting views of others whom he calls his masters. And, indeed, this is almost proper, for it behooves one to have many masters and to criticize them openly; except that Lorenz also has criticisms to those whom he calls his masters yet he suppresses them; and he should call Freud his master as well, yet he does not. The main reason why all this was not noticed is a change in wind: Freud writes with the sensitivity of a civilized and cultured person torn between criticizing and cherishing his civilization, and Lorenz tries to exude the

112 MAN AS ANIMAL

wholesomeness of a nature boy; Nazi or liberal, he feels he is in control. I shall come to Lorenz's own anxiety about this wholesomeness soon. This discussion should illustrate the fact that the flavor of a writer need not be the best indicator of the import of his message. And, in particular, the neurotic flavor of Freud, or the wholesome nature of Lorenz, whould not mislead us to judge them one way or another.

22. For Erik Erikson see his introduction to G. B. Blaine and C. C. McArthur, *Emotional Problems of the Student*, Appleton-Century-Croft, New York, 1961, 1971. For Kafka see below, notes 65–6 to Section XV. On Freud's view of education as essential to neurosis there is a literature. I am particularly impressed with his idea — first note of final section of *Civilization and its Discontent* — that everyone is made to think "everyone else fulfills those ethical demands" that he fails to. I do not mean to say that anxieties and neuroses are themselves misconceptions but that they involve misconceptions. This even Freud has noticed when he saw neuroses as intellectual blind spots.

The most enlightening point in Geza Róheim's *Psychoanalysis and Anthropology*, New York, 1950, 1968, is the thesis, on p. 412, which he ascribes to Freud (quite generously, I suppose): *neurosis is an archaism*. Here archaism is meant as a regression in general, of an individual to his own childhood, or to a more primitive social context. Indeed, after quoting Freud about neurosis as a childhood regression he completes the restatement of his thesis by saying "Neurosis is a . . . duplication of exaggeration of the process that made us human." Further (p. 413), he says "regression is a universal emotion", including here, however, "wistful yearnings for the glories of childhood, ritual representations of rebirth, and our dreams" as regressions. I do find it a bit hard to take these as regressions, or regressions as neuroses, or regressions as archaisms, or even "wistful yearnings etc." as archaisms; they are archaisms, I think, only when they become fixations. Freud himself explains in many of his works that childhood patterns, even when fairly fixated, become neuroses only if fixated again (not jettisoned) during adolescence. For further discussion and references see Y. Fried and J. Agassi, *Paranoia, Boston Studies*, Vol. 50, Reidel, Dordrecht and Boston, 1976.

23. The question, "why do I stay?" is more forcefully felt by intellectuals who can migrate. Noam Chomsky, one of the leaders of the intellectuals' movement against the Vietnam war and other ills started his campaign in the *New York Review of Books* with calling America Fascist and confessing to the feeling of doing wrong by staying there, rather than, say, accepting an appointment in Oxford, England. He suggested that he could only partly expiate for his weakness by starting, all too late, to protest against his society's ills.

24. Lorenz always concludes his studies by the homily that we be good Christians. Can he not analyze Christianity with the aid of his learning theory?

All due respect to Lorenz's specific discoveries and his ideas of I.R.M. and imprinting should not obscure the fact that his writings are pretentious and merely parasitic on ideas of bolder thinkers of wider scope, such as Freud.

There is little doubt that some of the present-day ethology came from ideas which were in the air in political thinking — if thinking is not too complimentary a word — of the day. It was reflected also in the literature and the literary criticism of the day. Thus D. H. Lawrence said, "what ails me is the absolute frustration of my primeval societal instinct ... I think societal instinct much deeper than sex instinct — and societal repression much more devastating ... I am weary even of my individuality, and simply nauseated by other people's." (Quoted in Irving Howe's *Decline of the New*, New York, 1970, p. 28.) Regrettably, this critique of Freud and other classical individualistic thinkers was meant as a support of collectivism and irrationalism all the way. Valid criticism is often well used by intellectuals who are irrationalists, i.e. who oppose criticism.

It is worth mentioning that Freud repeatedly expressed the view — quite eighteenth century — that civilization and culture are mere degeneration, means of social oppression, expression of prejudice — which he viewed as neuroses. He also repeatedly expressed the view that the eighteenth-century ideal society is impossible and so branded himself conservative. See *The Future of an Illusion*, originally published in 1927, and comments by H. Stuart Hughes, *Consciousness and Society*, New York, 1958, pp. 136ff. See also Hughes' perceptive remark, p. 145, that *Totem and Taboo* is a parable like Rousseau's *Social Contract* — only, as Malinowski observes, with savages, who are no longer noble but rather maladjusted and middle-class, as signatories to the contract.

For Freud's radicalism see Stanley Rothman and Phillip Isenberg, "Freud and Jewish Marginality", *Encounter*, December 1974, Vol. 43, No. 6, pp. 46–54 and references there. Yet the major radicalist element in Freudian theory and practice is simply that they "presuppose an ideal of sanity, from which the patient has departed and to which he is to be brought back ..." Bertrand Russell, *Skeptical Essays*, Allen and Unwin, London, 1928, 1934, Chapter IV, p. 49.

It was this "ideal of sanity" which is ideally enlightened self-interest that Malthus and Darwin have shattered. For, whereas the eighteenth-century thinkers optimistically saw harmony of interest everywhere, even in the most ruthless competition provided it is enlightened, the nineteenth century saw bitter irresolvable conflicts in the struggle for survival. The development of social Darwinism, even of Fascist versions of it, though not Darwinian, has some undeniable inner logic. Yet, of course, the discovery of family planning proved to many that the application of Darwinism to humans is a special case. This line of thought has an inner logic of its own, which made Karl Marx admire Darwin, since Marx saw social life as a series of struggles for survival coming to an end due to progress. Similarly Kropotkin says, *Mutual Aid, A Factor of Evolution*, with a foreword by H. L. Beales, Penguin, London 1939, Chapter III, third paragraph, p. 75, "and we have had of late quite a school of writers who, taking possession of Darwin's terminology rather than his leading ideas, made of it an argument in favour of Hobbes' view upon primitive man, and even succeeded in giving them a scientific appearance." Similarly Emile Durkheim, *The Division of Labor in Society*, translated by George Simpson, Free Press and McMillan, Glencoe and London, 1933, 1964, pp. 196–7, declares hedonism mock-Darwinian: "Thus, we find altruism from the beginning of humanity and in a truly intemperate form. For these privations that the savage imposes upon himself in obedience to religious tradition, the abnegation with which he sacrifices his life when society demands . . . is not all this altruism?"

Here the Darwinian origin of functionalist collectivism shows. And these doctrines can both be used for humane and for inhuman ends, just as Darwinism is used by Durkheim to defend religion and by Freud to declare it a mere illusion.

25. For the ecological movement's nature mysticism and culture-as-disease theses, see John Passmore, "Removing the Rubbish, Reflections on the Ecological Craze", *Encounter*, April 1974, Vol. 42, pp. 11–24, and references there. See also his *Man's Responsibility for Nature*, Duckworth, Scribner's, London, New York, 1974.

26. The idea of objective ambiguity go to Lorenz's predecessors, Pavlov and Henry Eliot Howard, who says in his *An Introduction to the Study of Bird Behavior*, Cambridge University Press, 1929, p. 72:

"First let us remember that both sexes behave in extravagant fashion not only when excited sexually but when they attack an intruder or are concerned about their young."

Nevertheless, I think it was Lorenz who applied this idea systematically and also explained Freudian neuroses that way, all the way. Of course, assuming, in accord with note 22 above, that the theory is that neurosis is regressive or "archaic" and also that it is rooted in an objective conflict situation, makes it doubly primitive. Its being a fixation may then, perhaps, be claimed to be a mere sign of its primitive nature.

I do not wish to endorse Lorenz's Pavlovian theory of conflict as the ambivalence created by ambiguous signals. It is a marvellous theory and I think we should try it first in every case (just as the electrician checks the fuse box first). But I think it is obvious that (by and large) only acculturated animals suffer from what Walter Kaufmann has christened decidophobia (in his marvellous *Without Guilt and Justice*, New York, 1973), and that neurosis proper is decidedly decidophobic.

I propose therefore to distinguish the emotional conflicts rooted in ambivalences rooted in ambiguities as Lorenzian, and to declare them un-neurotic except for cases where the subject is positively attracted to, or invites, Lorenzian conflicts. Consequently, Pavlov's allegedly neurotic dogs (and likewise Joseph Wolpe's neurotic cats) should be considered non-neurotic. It is, nonetheless, a fact that genuinely neurotic — decidophobic — dogs have been observed (and they clearly emulate their human companions).

27. The translation of the title of Lorenz's book, known in English as *On Aggression* is, "On the So-Called Evil", i.e. on the preferability of explaining evil away. (It was the book's subtitle which gave rise to the English title, it being, roughly,

"On the natural history of aggression".) The mistranslation, I think, is no accident but the result of an attempt to conceal the fact that Lorenz preaches amoralism at least in the sense that there is no room in his views for moral responsibility.

An incredible example is Edmund Leach's review of K. Lorenz and R. Ardrey (reprinted in M. F. Ashley Montagu, *Man and Aggression*, Oxford University Press, Oxford, London, New York, 1968, pp. 65–73), where he praises the one and scolds the other (p. 65): "Lorenz, on the other hand, is concerned to show that animal aggression is only a 'so-called evil' and that its adaptive consequences are advantageous or at least neutral." I do not know when last so much twisting was done by the mere switch, in a descriptive phrase, from the definite article to the indefinite article. Konrad Lorenz can explain away the moral side of everything. In his "The Enmity between Generations and its Probable Ethological Causes", *Nobel Symposium 14, The Place of Value in the World of Facts*, Arne Tiselius and Sam Nilsson, eds., Almqvist and Wiksell, Stockholm, John Wiley and Sons, New York, London and Sydney, 1970, pp. 385–458, as well as in the end of his Nobel Lecture, *Science,* Vol. 185, 19 July 1974, pp. 229–234, he argues that survival is enhanced by the tensions between the old conservatives and the young radicals, and that hence neither is "good" or "bad" except that "excesses as well as deficiency of any such function cause illness", and so is bad, where excess may go either this way or that way, or both ways together (thereby turning tensions into schisms).

This doctrine is infantile, of course; yet, were it true, we should not conclude that survival requires that some be radical, some conservative; at most we could conclude that survival is enhanced if some argue, as the devil's advocates or sincerely, but well, for this side and against the other, and some argue the other way around. It is clear that Lorenz has not heard of the devil's advocate, though I think he will say in 1940 he was one (see next note and note 30 below).

28. It is amusing to notice that the idea justifying the Darwin-Lorenz technique of anthropomorphizing animals, namely that men are animals plain and simple, also justifies anthropomorphizing machines, on the theory that men are machines. This, of course, is Butler's argument: mechanism and animism come dangerously close to each other. The way Lorenz explains cruelty (*On Aggression*) is often too flimsy for words. He says a cat plays with a mouse for exercise, and so is not cruel. Proof: when he has had enough exercises he stops torturing the mouse. I suppose the same held even for Nazi human torturers though as a result of their German training they often were more thorough than cats and so tired not so quickly. (See his *On Aggression,* Chapter 6, 13th and 14th paragraph, and Chapter 13, 12th and 13th paragraphs from the end of the chapter.)

The worst thing about Lorenz is his definition of aggression as the hostility shown by an animal towards any member of its own species. Example, an animal's defence of its territory against an intruder. It is, of course, a matter of little difference to us whether we call aggressor the intruder fish, or the fish who is nesting and who is intruded upon. But take the German Nation's need for elbow room and the resistance of certain European nations to its expansion, and you find both aggressor and defendant engaged in the natural act of aggression which is common to man, fish, and fowl. See also note 30 below.

29. Lorenz's anthropomorphism has a great asset of liberating and of permitting him to try to observe new phenomena anthropomorphically from the start. This is in contrast with the older Cartesian program — both a gain and a loss, I should say in my standard pluralist mood — as expressed, for example, by C. Lloyd Morgan, *Life, Mind, and Spirit,* William and Norgate, London, 1926, 1929, pp. 60—61, end of Lecture.

"Some thirty years ago I accepted as a part of my policy in comparative psychology a rule which I may here restate. In no instance should we interpret an act as the outcome of a higher mental process if it can be adequately interpreted as the outcome of a process that stands lower in the psychological scale."

Quoted in Henry Eliot Howard, *An Introduction to the Study of Bird Behavior,* Cambridge University Press, 1929, p. 89. Howard tries to explain territoriality as a lower function, *à la* Watson's behaviorism, and decides (final paragraph) that it cannot be done.

"Morgan's Canon" as it is known, was presented, practically in the same wording, in his *Introduction to Comparative Psychology* (1894), Chapter 3. Also quoted by Howard E. Gruber, *Darwin on Man,* Dell, New York, 1974, p. 235.

The success of Konrad Lorenz is, obviously, that of scientific reactionary irrationalism, akin to that of D. H. Lawrence, T. S. Eliot, Michael Polanyi, and T. S. Kuhn. The failure of Lorenz's critics is, alas!, the symptom of the general low level of philosophizing these days, more precisely of philosophical criticism — largely due to the split of philosophy into the devil of positivism, on its blind idolization of science and blind hostility to metaphysics, and the deep blue sea of phenomenology and existentialism, and similar deep, dark metaphysics frankly hostile to science. (There are also the schools of Catholic and Marxist philosophers, but we need not bother about them here.)

One of the best in the generally poor anti-Lorenz literature is Alexander Alland Jr., *The Human Imperative,* Columbia University Press, New York and London, 1972, a decent critique of the Lorenz-Ardrey-Morris philosophy, stating that they reject all social science in favor of psychology, that they dangerously ignore the social aspect of social problems, e.g. they try to solve the problem of war by inventing war games, that they thereby are de facto defenders of the social status quo. In criticism he offers, for example, the observation that even the ability of a monkey to perform sexually reasonably well depends on his social conditions. I do endorse this criticism but think it is not really pushing the opponent to the corner nearly hard enough. See also notes 14 above and 31 below.

Lorenz is arbitrary in his explaining away evil but not goodness, cruelty but not kindness, cooperation but not hostility. He is thus quite arbitrary in ethics, in metaphysics and in science as well; he is also arbitrary in parallel lines which convert evil — what we normally view as evil — into virtue — by an evolutionary theory of sorts — the parallels being sheer paralogisms which explode once stated explicitly as in the above sentence. Indeed, the intelligent reader will require not that I argue against the views attributed to Lorenz in this paragraph, but that I establish my attribution itself. The references, incidentally, are easy to find, but the attribution is the result of some sophistication, e.g., of the noticing that whereas Lorenz calls intra-specific acts of hostility, aggression, regardless of the fact that in nature intra-specific hostilities are at times mutual, e.g. in competition over virgin female or territory, and at times one-sided, e.g. when one party intrudes into the territory and even the family nest of the other; he ignores the cooperation of members of a colony in favor of their hostility to intruders, and discusses their crowding partly as sheer self-defence, partly as anti-evolutionary; for, he observes, at times overcrowding results in starvation. The fact is that territorial isolation as well as the sharing of a territory in cooperation have their advantages and disadvantages, just as much as the lack of all territorial claims; yet Lorenz offers an impression that claims for territorial rights are on the whole evolutionary advantageous, and thus virtuous. I suggest that the interested reader examine these claims of mine by checking any work of Lorenz pertaining to the questions at hand, whether popular or not, scientific or not.

Reading Lorenz critically arouses admiration for his empirical findings and hypotheses, but it also causes astonishment at his poor logic and his singing to the gallery. Yet, when all is said and noted, there remains Lorenz the modern myth maker whose myth can be put in a simple Lévi-Straussian form (see section XI for explanation and discussion):

good : evil :: kindness : cruelty :: hostility : cooperation
do not explain > explain away

Lorenz harps on our tendency to view vegetarianism as morally commendable while adhering to our carnivorous habits — which fact, he says, leads us to a hypotheses, but it also causes astonishment at his poor logic and his singing to harps on our reluctance to see that we breed animals to suit our own needs and tastes. He offers us a way to accept ourselves as we are by accepting as a simple fact of nature what we usually consider as evil. Darwin already suggested that Nature is cruel, and that we must accept Her. But Darwin never condoned cruelty, even when evolutionarily favored, whereas Spencer should have but did not, and Lorenz plainly does. He suggests that doing away with hypocrisy and noticing a cruel streak in ourselves is superior, even though, indeed, while, we thereby condone our cruel streak. Lorenz regrets only the fact that due to the use of artefacts in acts of hostility, our killing becomes distant and impersonal and so it gets out of hand. Surely this claim, regrettable or not, is amply refuted to Lorenz's own satisfaction (yet he does not withdraw it) by all sorts of sadistic killing, such as the Nazi atrocities, and by all face to face mortal encounters, from that of Cain and Abel to that of the latest headlines. Here Lorenz tacitly endorses Freud's myth that our killing was the act that was the base of our humanity. Yet, whereas Freud spoke of the ensuing sense of guilt as human, not of the killing itself, Lorenz speaks of the evolution of man into a tool-making animal and thus into both human — because intelligent — and murderous — because he circumvented Nature's safeguard against murder. This sounds more scientific but it is just plainly refuted by the evidence: killing by the extended hand preceded killing by ballistic means, and ancient trepanations seem to indicate that murder is an ancient art (the extant ancient trepanated skulls are all too often cut on the left-hand side, presumably to repair damage to fractured skulls caused by right-handed enemies). And sticks and stones are tools common among animals, whether simian or avian, or even elephantine.

30. L. Eisenberg, "The *Human* Nature of Human Nature", *Science*, Vol. 176, 14 April 1972, pp. 123–8, expresses on p. 124 the view that Konrad Lorenz compared the civilization of humans to the domestication of animals as an expression of his Fascism, and he quotes, as evidence, a paper by Lorenz of 1940 (*Z. Angew. Psychol. Charakterkunde*, Vol. 59, 2), where Lorenz uses arguments of this sort in order to support the claim that "the racial idea as the basis of our state has already accomplished much in this respect", referring, at the very least, to the notorious Nuremberg laws which forbid intermarriage, and at worst to the worst in Nazi practices. All this is Eisenberg.

Eisenberg himself, however, stresses on the next page that the argumentation of Lorenz is not serious, and supports pseudoscientifically a priori social philosophical ideologies.

The question is, how serious are any of Lorenz's ideas? (We take his facts as more or less unproblematic.) No doubt, his theory of imprinting is important. (Perhaps in part it has the status of observed facts − not that observation reports are ever unchallengeable.) No doubt, his methodology and metaphysics are confused. What about the in-between material? I think it is mainly rubbish.

31. The most easily accessible review of Lorenz on aggression is the M. F. Ashley Montagu, ed., *Man and Agression,* Oxford University Press, 1968. Its main theme is that Lorenz and more so Robert Ardrey, make a false analogy from beast to man. I find this weak: all analogy is hypothesis and so perhaps false, but the critic has to argue that the hypothesis he is attempting to criticize is in conflict with some accepted or commendable claims. See also notes 14 and 29 above for more references.

32. For the view of Lorenz as a Lamarckian, expressed in K. R. Popper, *Objective Knowledge,* see note 47 to Section VII below.

Amusingly enough the inheritance of ritualized acts occurs not only in Lorenz but also in Freud, whether in the inheritance of the Oedipus, or even more generally. See E. Jones, *The Life and Work of Sigmund Freud*, Vol. I, Basic Books, 1953, Chapter on Personal Life 1890–1900, p. 347 (p. 221 of the Doubleday Anchor abridged edition).

33. The claim, now commonplace, that machines can reproduce themselves, is Butler's epoch-making argument in his "Darwin among the Machines" discussed earlier in Chapter I, which is presented at great length in his classical *Erewhon.* The reader may puzzle at the fact that whereas I use Butler's point as an argument unfavorable to reductionism in Chapter I, I use it as a favorable one here. But, indeed, the fact is that Butler removes one objection and replaces it with another by one stroke of genius: the claim that machines can reproduce themselves (say records in record factories) destroys the objection against Descartes and puts a stronger one against Darwin.

34. The parallel between clock:computer:: geese:men seems to me more than an accident. Rather, it is the anti-reductionist pro-reductionist argument applied to both cases. Thus, consider the following fictitious debate between A. M. Turing and R. O. Kapp:

Kapp: Machines cannot reproduce themselves utterly unaided.

Turing: We can specify conditions and machines for which this is possible.

Kapp: Your specifying makes reproduction not automatic.

Turing: From the moment of implementation — of life or of machine, either will continue unattended as long as conditions permit.

Kapp: And when conditions sufficiently alter, the machines stop.

Turing: And so with mankind.

Kapp: No; mankind may struggle for survival.

Turing: We can introduce random factors to machines so that they might do that.

Kapp: The random factor will be destructive rather than helpful.

Turing: Human experimentation is risky too.

Kapp: But men struggle seeking the more successful conditions for survival, whereas machines can only behave randomly.

Thus, all dualists are, in effect, vitalists as opposed to the mechanists who decide that experiments are but random events. The leading Darwinian idea, Butler and Shaw rightly insisted, is to reduce effort to random proliferations plus selection. This point is repeated by Jorge Luis Borges in many of his essays. For Popper's failed effort to reconcile his dualism with Darwinism see my review of his *Objective Knowledge* mentioned in note 58 to section IV above.

VII THE PHILOSOPHICAL WEAKNESS OF NEO-DARWINISM

There is a fundamental difference between the reduction of man to machine and to animals. We do not feel any serious difficulty on the side of physics when we talk of man as machine. Oh, physics has its problems galore, but none of them is directly resultant from the question, is man a machine, or even changes in the slightest by the choice of the one or the other answer to that question.

Not so in biology.[35] The thesis that man shares his descent with other animals is, in historical fact, what is known as the Darwinian revolution, and Darwin himself, as his notebooks testify, saw it thus and declares man and other animals to be "brethren in pain."[36] Of course, analytically, the thesis, man is a mere animal, is independent of the thesis, man descends from nonhuman animals. Yet to view that man is a descendant from an ape yet deny his sheer animality cannot be taken seriously today,[37] and the view that he is merely an animal but not a descendant of an ape is even less seriously entertained.[38] And so, in historical fact, the thesis that man is a mere animal is strongly tied to the theory of the origins of the species and the problems of the one are the problems of the other.

Much has been written about the allegedly scandalous fact that Mendelian genetics, allegedly so amply demonstrated by Mendel himself by empirical means, was overlooked and forgotten. Some writers have tried to absolve their predecessors by noting that at the time ever so many facts seemed to conflict with Mendel's theory. Others still, draw attention to the fact that Mendel said nothing about mutations and so, it seemed, he endorsed a pre-Darwinian theory of the immutability of the species.

There is a kernel of truth in each of these explanations. Mendel's facts could be remembered by his opponents and noted as problematic; this would have made them better scientists regardless of anything else. And Mendelism does seem most contrary to the facts. Historians and biologists alike say the facts of Mendelism are all too obvious, yet anyone who has even so much as glanced at the attempts to apply Mendelism to selective breeding, say of dairy cows, as well as to population studies, particularly relating to the fine grades of grayness of the human skin (which, incredibly, have aroused so much interest), cannot escape noticing that if Mendelism does apply to these cases, no one knows how it does: the situation is obviously messy: scores of "genes" have to interplay to create the intuitively obvious fine grades. This quite apart from the fact that the discovery of the nucleic acids and their reproductive functions, far from telling us what a "gene" is, raises the problem afresh and in a new and fascinating light.[39]

The real difficulty, however, is that these observations are generalizable to throw severe doubts on all the paleontological and psychological evidence amassed by Darwin himself (not the ecological evidence, though). The most obvious popular examples, such as the evolution of the horse's hoof — indeed all morphological evidence, and paleontological evidence naturally tends to be morphological — seems hardly related to Mendelian genetics.[40] When the genetic mechanism alters we can expect an alteration in the offspring. No doubt, alternations in offspring may also result from the environment, from the paucity of food which may alter the size of the species (compare Englishmen with New Zealanders) to the effects of specific chemicals in one's food (which may, like thalidomide, cause drastic changes, in laboratories as much as in nature). Whatever the changes, they are not gradual, cannot be expected to emerge gradually, except under very specific circumstances not yet studied. We have no theories of trends as yet.

Darwin considered both morphological and psychological changes acquired and then inherited. This will make him, in popular parlance, a Lamarckian. Darwin himself acknowledged similarity with Lamarck but strongly denounced Lamarck for some elements of his theory which were too speculative for his taste. [41]

An example which I find impressive is Darwin's idea that every psychological trait in man has its origins, however dim, in other animals. [42] The most specific human trait is, of course, language; and so it is a good test case. For Darwin language is rooted in speech, speech in music, music in mating calls. After this, Freudianism seems but a small step. [43] And it is no surprise, I think, that Freud, more than anyone next to Darwin, is the person behind the growth of contemporary animal psychology: Do other animals exhibit infant sexuality? Do infant animals exhibit aggression towards the adults with whom they sexually compete? Courtship and aggression were the central topics of animal psychology until social anthropologists stepped into the picture and found, apart from pecking orders and such psychological factors, also sociability [44] and even social classes. [45]

Darwin and his followers, then, made much of the idea that there is a trend connecting animal mating calls with speech, etc. The problem, how do trends develop, did not concern Darwin much. [46] He assumed that characteristics that have survival value survive and undergo modification: the idea of plasticity was for him an intuitive idea of innate propensities for developing trends, and selection eliminated some of these possibilities allowing others to develop. (The later idea of I.R.M. is a modern variant of it.) The genetic code theory puts all this in question, of course, in the following obvious way.

A modification of the genetic code is generally quite different from a modification of a characteristic. When we change one letter in a word we do not necessarily change its meaning slightly. Thus, although a cat is more similar to a leopard than to a bat its designation in English is not. It is hardly conceivable that a series of small changes in the genetic mechanism will cause small morphological changes the like of which paleontologists exhibit in defense of Darwin. [47]

And so the question, was Darwin a Lamarckian? has shifted to the historical background. But if he was, then so was Freud who followed him fairly closely; and we have no Freudian analogue to neo-Darwinism as yet! [48]

Diverse Darwinians and Freudians have struggled and are still struggling with these difficulties: how can we explain trends in small steps as results of mere discrete genetic mutations? The most obvious suggestion would be, perhaps the mutations are products of interactions of two sets of factors, inherited and environmental; perhaps the inherited changes are drastic, the environmental ones in small steps, and only the environmental ones are manifested. This is the metaphysical guiding idea behind works of Lloyd Morgan, Sir Charles Sherrington, Sir Julian Huxley, and Freud, of course, [49] as well as the contemporary school of Continental philosophical anthropology. That school stems, no doubt, from the work of Jakob von Uexküll, and he was a vitalist and a collectivist and a Kantian. Yet these philosophical anthropologists are all Darwinian-Freudian to this or that extent, knowingly or not, with proper acknowledgement or not. (Freud is often an unacknowledged, and even unnoticed influence, these days.) [50]

The guiding idea here is one already presented in the first chapter. It is the idea that the more evolved species acquire less specific and more plastic inner release mechanisms (I.R.M.), that the complete (adult) biological makeup of the animal is thus not merely its genetic background spelled out, but the outcome of the interaction of the genetic material with its environment. [51] The epitome of this evolution is man, we remember, whose fetus is allowed to stay half its incubation time or so outside the womb so as to interact strongly with the environment and make the most of his adaptive plasticity [52] (postnatal fetalization, this is called). [53]

There is strong common sense to this view, and a striking confirmation, in cloning, so-called: a fertilized frog's egg had its nucleus replaced by a nucleus from a cell of an unrelated frog. The ovum developed into a frog different from, yet with identical hereditary mechanism as, the unrelated frog (except for the hereditary mechanism biologists ascribe to the cytoplasm). [54] The nucleus extracted from the unrelated frog interacted with its environment, chiefly the cytoplasm of the ovum, and hey, presto! it grows! [55]

And yet, how does this explain trends such as the evolution of the horse's hoof, the ritualization of a signal of courtship or of aggression, the growth of the human speech capacity? We honestly do not know. Or rather, we do not know, and the more honest about it we are the better it is for us and our understanding of our predicaments. [56] And since the question, is man a mere animal, and what sort of mere animal he is, much hinges on the question, how and by what virtue he has evolved, we should note that we hardly know how to go about answering these questions.

Attempts to integrate man in the fabric of nature are very frustrating. What do we compare him with? Notice the amusing expression, to be found in a few eighteenth- and nineteenth-century works, "a rational being, e.g., man," as if we might as well choose another example.

Leibniz[57] had the theory of degrees of rationality. We can still see traces of his idea in the diverse textbooks and popular science books which tell us that a dog's waking life is akin to man's dreaming life. Leibniz thought even stones can think, however poorly, but no one took up this idea.[58] Now Leibniz's theory postulates the existence of superhuman intelligences − not angelic but corporeal. In the past this sounded remote: in the present it does not: we expect to meet corporeal supermen, in the shape of human mutants or in the shape of extraterrestrial intelligences.[59] In the year 1600 Giordano Bruno was burned at the stake officially because he believed in extraterrestrial intelligences; a century later Leibniz's suggestion that they exist still sounded quaint; in the years of lunar expedition even children believe in them as a matter of course.

And so, strangely, accepting Bruno and Leibniz we find it particularly important to try and integrate man's rationality into the fabric of nature. We start with what we have: the intelligence of other animals and of man-made machines. Let us now center on the intelligence of animals.

Unfortunately, we find again that our confusions about our Darwinian heritage are a serious obstacle. It is not that we have to agree or disagree with Darwin: we may well forget him if we can. But we cannot, and our second best is to decide how much we agree with him and how much not. For, Darwin had it here both ways and for good reasons; and much as in our ignorance we forget him, we readduce his ideas repeatedly. Darwin, on the one hand, viewed all changes as gradual, and denied that any human characteristic exists which has no root, however feeble, in the animal world. Species, however, were for him a totally different matter. Two groups of animals would be two different species if and only if there exists a gap between them. This is so even if the gap is largely due to accidental geographical separation. Indeed, this is speciation: one species developing two trends of characteristics with a gap, which, when wide enough, defines two species instead of one. The trend itself Darwin saw as the growth of acquired characteristics of survival value in the circumstances and which are in stages inherited.[60] The question is now, how does all this look with the rise of neo-Mendelism?

The greatest benefit of neo-Mendelism is that it enables us to offer theories about species with a common descent which can or cannot interbreed, as the case may be. Such characteristics, all characteristics, are either inherited or caused by mutation: they are never acquired. It is still far from clear how a series of mutations, then, have caused trends, such as those morphological changes, whether the growth of the horse's hoof or the growth and development of man's brain. Nor is it clear whether speech, conceptual thinking, or abstract thinking, or human rationality, has evolved from some animal qualities, as Darwin insisted in his *The Descent of Man* — regardless of the means of descent. Of course, certain human developments, say the invention or rather the domestication of fire or of serial music, are not the result of genetic mutation, we presume.[61] Nevertheless, as long as we assume that an ape will not develop these, we thereby assume, as a condition for these, some genetic change. But the change may come at once or in a series. Assume rationality to be a function of the shape of the skull, or of the hand, or both, and the science of man falls into place within general biology, which describes the growth of the hand the way it describes the growth of the hoof.

We still do not have a neo-Mendelian explanation of trends, but at least we wish to see one trend, namely the growth of rationality, as rooted in a trend of morphology, or as rooted in a trend of behavior: perhaps the growth of man's mating calls and perhaps the growth of his skull makes him able to have descendants who invent fire and poetry; or perhaps the one growth interplayed with the other. In either case we can ask how does rationality, a novel characteristic, evolve out of old ones?[62]

What we want, generally, is to know whence the observed uniqueness of man? If it evolves from a unique characteristic, uniqueness as such is still unexplained; if it evolves from a general characteristic, why has it evolved only in man? Darwin himself must have struck upon this dilemma, since it made him consider the possibility that today some ape is evolving and his descendant in the not so distant future may become as rational as Neanderthal man was.

Such possibilities are not usually described in detail — nor did Darwin say more than a few words about such matters, and obviously because of his hostility to speculations, the hallmark of positivism. Yet in physical anthropology, where speculation is quite unavoidable, every time a skeleton is discovered and a speculation heralds another great-grandfather, there will be someone who will declare the alleged great-grandfather an imposter and a mere granduncle, a member of a line of descent which ended up in a blind alley.[63]

The disputes of this sort are quite metaphysical[64] and unresolvable: we have no criteria for humanity and no theory of its evolution mechanism. Moreover we cannot quite say how a mechanism which preceded humanity gave rise to it.

This difficulty is quite general and quite ancient. It was raised generally in antiquity by Parmenides who said that if in reality there is unity then where there is diversity in appearance, we find nothing but falsehood. And it follows that our theory of reality cannot explain appearances, since truth never entails falsehoods. There is one solution to the problem of how to explain diversity, and it belongs to Democritus who responded to Parmenides: assume the existence of a few elements whose diverse combinations may create a wide diversity. To take Aristotle's and Galileo's analogy, the few letters of the alphabet yield a rich variety of words. [65]

The problem may also be, how can we ever explain the ever-changing appearance of diversity? The answer of Democritus is, diversity and change may be explained as the outcome of (process of) combinations of various factors. In particular, to add a modern idea, when conflicting forces change, their balance may alter radically as the result of gradual change. Moreover, the gradual change may result from a process of two preexisting factors reinforcing each other. [66]

I put it all abstractly, because I think it is all too easy to apply this to myriads of cases. And it greatly puzzles and exasperates and amuses me to see how many writers discovered the special cases the hard way, when they could master the general abstract idea and then easily apply it anywhere. I do not wish to say this general idea is good enough – I have explained elsewhere why I think it is not. Rather, I wish to show here that its application to any concrete case will not do unless it be specific enough.

In particular, the application of the logical difficulty to evolution may be worth pointing out. It is said that man's hand and brain have helped each other to develop. This is very poor: apes have hands and brains and yet they did not partake in the process we underwent; why? Ancient horses lost their hands and developed their brains. Elephants and dolphins developed their brains too. Unless we have an initial position peculiar to man, we cannot explain why only man evolved on the path he did. The initial position may be less remote from other animals; the peculiarities may help each other evolve, but their initial combination must already be unique. If every element is not unique but their combination is, then the uniqueness of man is explicable.

To repeat, the peculiarity of man may be a great dose of a quality which grew over the ages. The quality itself, we assume, is a unique combination of factors which are not unique. The moment these factors have combined will be the moment of appearance of humanity. The earliest human may have looked more like an ape than like a man; but this is a matter of mere appearance.[67]

The theory of the missing link, then, is but a logical error.[68] The so-called missing link is an ape-looking human, namely a being satisfying certain criteria, but not obviously so. So, considering an ancient skeleton, the question is not so much, does it belong to a grandfather or to a granduncle; the question rather is, does it belong to a human or an ape? This question cannot even be attacked, let alone satisfactorily answered, prior to the presentation of the theory of the factors which made apes human and of the mechanisms which helped the factors reinforce each other into our own evolutionary path; indeed, until we have a better theory of evolutionary trends.[69]

We have an excellent example of a radical change of this kind in the current theory of the origins of life. According to this theory, the first living thing was a trigger which radically altered the atmosphere of the earth, thus enabling diverse life forms to evolve. Whatever the factors that entered in combination to make for the novelty − the living things − they were factors which, it is generally assumed, existed before life (amino acids, incidentally), which combined into such a living thing that could exist before as well as after the transition, and such that it much benefitted from the transition. The transition itself, it is assumed, was a moment when a spark − a bolt of lightning − hit an unusual combination of chemicals to make them combine into protein.[70] Let us consider the analog of this theory of the origin of life that should describe the origins of humanity. What animal factors put together created both language and conditions highly conducive for the evolution of language?

Let us take one other example, to illustrate these questions further. Consider Rudyard Kipling's *Just So* story about the origin of writing. Consider a member of an illiterate tribe in need to send a message and consider the presence of a mute or alien person as the only candidate for messenger; sender invents a pictogram which is delivered; recipients are worried about sender, read their worry into the pictogram, maltreat the poor benevolent messenger and send a contingent of warriors to help; discover misunderstanding, and rectify it; writing is here to stay.

Behind Kipling's charming story, built on this simple scheme, stands a problem not unlike that of the origins of life. There is a vicious circle which prevents the evolution of writing. Even if someone invents writing, there is the need for the convention of reading to make it work, but reading cannot precede all written messages. Kipling suggests, then, that under emergency, writing is invented without regard to the fact that the recipient will fail to read the message properly, that when the error was corrected the convention of reading was established to prevent the repetition of the error, and so reading and writing were established and incentive to develop them was created.

The theory, incidentally, could be reversed: a person could, under great stress, read a message where there was none, and his error was corrected. In either case the problem, how could two things be invented simultaneously, was solved by the assumption that a person assumed the invention of the complement to his invention and his mistake was corrected by the actual invention of the complement.

From all we know, Kipling's problem could be solved by a simpler theory. Writing was developed as an extention of systems of memorizing, such as the familiar knots and cuts, usually employed for the sake of keeping inventories. [71] That is to say, writing was initially less of a communication system and more of a diary system, used for inventory, for memorizing sacred texts, and for chiseling famous events on monuments, lest they be forgotten. (Up till today many simple folks can read only their familiar prayer books.) [72] The Kipling problem for speech seems harder, but it could be solved, again, when we search for a familiar context within which the novelty of speech could meaningfully emerge. The favored suggestion – due to Robertson Smith, I think – is that of magical ritual reenactments, in song and dance, of significant events, hunting, or funeral, or such, used as combined memory and preparation. [73] One has to add to this picture the known fact that expressive broadcasts of all sorts, from scaring competitors away to mourning to revelries, are extremely common in the animal world. And so, possibly, in the course of generations of reenactment of intense and precisely repetitious proceedings, the broadcasts have become signs for the situations which they normally accompany. [74]

The novelty of such solutions is in their evolutionism, yet this evolutionism is not in the least Darwinian. The logic of Kipling's story is confined to human understanding: we cannot apply it to blind evolution. We cannot say, that is, that though an animal could use only a couple of evolutionary traits together, e.g., a useful organ and a nerve to control it, a given animal did nonetheless evolve the one while thinking it had the other or while hoping it would soon have it. But, assuming that writing was, initially, an *aide-mémoire*, really means that an organ could evolve to facilitate an existing function and then find itself a new function or an extension of the old one. But Kipling's story could be true nonetheless and its logic is at times exhibited in

fact. Every time we show resourcefulness and invent a new idiom or
item of communication hoping that it would be caught on without
further ado, we see Kipling's logic in action. What, then, will Darwinism do about this logic?

Clearly, Darwinism will have to reduce every known case of a Kipling-type (evolutionary) logic to a more biological (evolutionary) logic.
Otherwise, Darwin's central idea, of making man an integrated part of
the animal world, will fail, just as much as the Darwinian idea of
eliminating purposes altogether (not by explaining them away but) by
explaining them causally. [75]

But then, the origins of the human species, just as the origins of any
other species within Darwinism, is a question of reproduction: the
new species evolves when its members are reproductively isolated. On
top of this, we can ask, when did we develop erect gait, round jaw, or
folk dancing — but *a priori*, these have nothing to do with reproductive isolation. If we want our theory to assert the existence of a link
between erect gait and reproduction, then we postulate such a link, as
a hypothesis or a speculation. We can also consider in this way the
emergence of a ritual, like reciting poetry to the bride-to-be, and make
the hypothesis that it became one day an essential precondition for
mating. Konrad Lorenz has shown us that such examples are far from
fantastic, but no one has advanced hypotheses of this sort as yet:
Darwin's hypothesis of sexual selection comes nearest, yet it is still
too sketchy.

When the view is put in its stark nakedness, it sounds incredible: are
we not more rational than apes? Can we not speak and read and write?
It took a long tradition to make such characteristics mere variants of
other behavioral characteristics: each animal species has its pecu-
liàrities. But is human intelligence just another characteristic? The
affirmative answer to this question is known as behaviorism.

Before discussing behaviorism I must say a word about Dr. John
Watson. The word "behaviorism" is his and his doctrine was for dec-
ades identified with behaviorism plain and simple. These days, however, even the most general and most fundamental assumptions of
Watson's theory are forgotten. But in another sense the label "behaviorism" gained wide popularity and the movement which has endorsed it is going strong. Nor was the movement started by Watson.
Even the methodological remarks made in the introduction to
Watson's *Behaviorism*, which are still the chief characterization of the
movement, even they are not new. A number of historians of philosophy repeatedly discover, and with a shock, the Spinozist character
of Watson's ideas. [76] Watson's methodology does not deny the exis-

tence of man's cognitive apparatus and his inner world, but it suggests that we can ignore these with no loss of either factual information or theoretical explanation of behavior.[77]

Here, then, Darwinism is pushed through all the way — human conduct is viewed strictly causally, and in a conspicuously animal fashion. Yet some of man's most significant traits are simply ignored. Here we have subtly crossed from man-as-animal to the animal-in-man. This is but a sleight of hand. Let me explain.

Notes to Section VII

35. The theory of the descent of man is part of the theory of speciation; this theory, however, is anything but complete and incontroversial. See, for example, Theodosius Dobzhansky, "Species of Drosophila", *Science*, Vol. 177, 25 August 1972, pp. 664–9 and bibliography there.

36. See Sir Francis Darwin, ed., *The Autobiography of Charles Darwin*, Chapter IV, Growth of the Origins of the Species, first entry, p. 120 of the edition of Henry Schuman, New York, 1950, reprinted in *Darwin on Man*, mentioned in note 15 to Section VI above, Notebook B 232, p. 47. See also B 231.

That evolutionism is older than Darwinism is common knowledge by now, perhaps due to the brilliant historical sketch in Shaw's preface to his *Back to Methuselah*. That the crux of Darwinism is just the idea of natural selection is a point made by Shaw there. The idea that the crux of Darwinian evolutionism concerns man's descent, is to be found in the final chapter, "Darwin and Adam", of John C. Greene's informative *The Death of Adam: Evolution and its Impact on Western Thought*, Iowa State University Press, Ames, 1959; Mentor, New York, 1961. See also Abraham Kardiner, *The Individual and His Society, the Psychodynamics of Primitive Social Organization, With a Foreword and Two Ethnological Reports* by Ralph Linton, Columbia University Press, New York, 1939, pp. 382ff. "Survey of Freud's Social Psychology", especially pp. 390, and 399–401.

37. The idea that Darwinism is true yet man is no mere animal is problematic from the viewpoint of traditional Catholicism, as explained best in James Blish's science fiction novel *A Case of Conscience*.

38. There is a science fiction novel by Fred Hoyle and Son suggesting that humans were hidden on this planet because their resemblance to apes may fool enemies to think they are natives. The novel springs, I suppose, from the difficulty to find the missing link. Yet it is, of course, quite out of the question. Even the non-Darwinian biologists today assume the animal ancestry of man. Evolutionism, then, but not Darwinism, is by now universally admitted.

39. See Bently Glass, "The Long Neglect of Scientific Discovery: Mendel's Law of Inheritance" in *Studies in Intellectual History*, Baltimore, 1953, pp. 148–60, quoted in Lewis Feuer, *Einstein and the Generation of Science*, Basic Books, New York, 1974, pp. 281; see also Elizabeth Gasking, "Why Was Mendel Ignored? " *J. Hist. Ideas*, Vol. 20, 1959, quoted in J. S. Wilkie, "Some Reasons for the Rediscovery and Appreciation of Mendel's Work in the First Years of the Present Century", *Brit. J. Hist. Sci.*, 1962–3, pp. 5–17 and by Lewis Feuer, *loc. cit.*

All these authors find the lack of relevance of Mendelism to classical Darwinism the cause of its neglect – and the discovery of the relevance to neo-Darwinism the cause of its appreciation. Needless to say, I think this is an error: a is not relevant to b if and only if there is neither deducibility nor contradiction between them; whereas Mendel's own view – Mendelism with no mutations – contradicts Darwinism. For the systematic confusion between the relations contradiction and irrelevance see section 14 of my *Towards an Historiography of Science*, mentioned in note 3 to the Introduction above.

The idea that the discovery of the DNA structure is the final location of the gene is questionable. Some writers prefer to do away with the gene altogether and label the fundamental unit of the genetic mechanism operon rather than gene in order to allot it different roles from those traditionally alloted to genes, especially roles of different kinds of interaction with the environment; others call some genes operons, others by other names.

40. The concept of mutation was first introduced in paleontology to designate phenomena seemingly, at least, inconsistent with Darwin's own continuism.

Paleontology and Darwinism is a broad topic. For a critical assessment, other than the run of the mill apologetics, one has to look a bit carefully, but it is not too difficult to find it. Marjorie Grene's *The Understanding of Nature: Essays in the Philosophy of Biology*, Synthese Library, Boston Studies in the Philosophy of Science, Vol. 23, Reidel, Dordrecht, 1974 should be mentioned as a philosophically, rather comprehensive work for a brief exposition for non-experts. For the latest see Martin J. S. Rudick, *The Meaning of Fossils, Episodes in the History of Paleontology*, Macdonald, London, 1972, Elsevier, New York, 1973. For later developments, with increased stress on modern ecology and on continental drift and such see the high-powered James W. Valentine, *Evolutionary Paleontology of the Marine Biosphere*, Prentice-Hall, Englewood Cliffs, 1973. I must confess much of all this is above my head and I cannot comment on it. See also Wilkie's intelligent and easy paper cited in the previous note.

41. In his *Autobiography* Darwin says he was unimpressed by Lamarck's, or by his grandfather's similar, views of evolution. "Nevertheless it is probable that hearing rather early in life such views maintained and praised may have forwarded my upholding them under a different form in my *Origins of Species* . . ." His objection, however, was not to the content, but to its paucity: The proportion of speculation" in his grandfather's book "being so large, the facts given." In his letter to J. D. Hooker of 11 January 1844 he says "Heaven forfend me from Lamarck nonsense . . . But the conclusions I am led to are not widely different from his . . ." For more about the Lamarckian aspect of Darwin see E. Mayr's

preface to the 1964 Harvard facsimile edition of Darwin's *Origins of the Species,*
and his "Lamarck Revisited", *J. Hist. Biol.,* Vol. 5, 1971, pp. 55–94, pp. 78 and
90.

See also the second quote in the next note, of a clearly Lamarckian passage in
Darwin. See also notes 56 and 60 below for the "official" recognition of this by
Sir Gavin de Beer.

42. See the following extracts from Charles Darwin, *The Descent of Man,* London, 1871:
"My object in this chapter [Chapter 2] is solely to show that there is no
fundamental difference between man and the higher mammals in their mental
faculties." (p. 35)
"The fewness and the comparative simplicity of the instincts of the higher
animals are remarkable in contrast with those of the lower animals. Cuvier
maintains that instinct and intelligence stand in inverse ratio to each other . . .
[But Darwin denies this; he does not deny, however] that instinctive actions
may lose their fixed and untaught character, and be replaced by others performed by the aid of free will. On the other hand some intelligent actions . . .
become converted into instincts and are inherited." (p. 37)
See also further quotes from the same work in note 46 below.
"Nothing exists in man, which has not previously existed in the amoeba." This
maxim, reminiscent of classical sensationalism, was ascribed to Darwin by Susan
K. Langer in her *Philosophy in a New Key; A Study in the Symbolism of Reason,
Rite, and Art,* Harvard University Press, Cambridge, Mass., 1951, pp. 28, 32. This
is an emergentist view, and it is strange to find it in Darwin. For its origins see note
57 below.

43. For Darwin on language see his Notebooks on Man etc., p. 18 but also his
endorsement of the onomatopoeic theory (for which see note 73 below) on pp.
20 and 31, yet p. 31 also has the theory of the origin of language in gesture, which
theory has only recently gained currency. See also his *Descent of Man.*

For Freud's view of the origins of language see his *Introductory Lectures on
Psychoanalysis,* 1916–17, Lecture 10, fifth paragraph from the end, *Standard
Edition,* Vol. XV, p. 167:
"A philologist, Hans Sperber of Uppsala, who works independently of Psychoanalysis, has put forward [1912] the argument that sexual needs have played
the biggest part in the origin and development of speech. According to him the
original sounds of speech served for communication, and summoned the
speaker's sexual partner; the further development of linguistic roots accompanied the working activities of primal man. These activities, he goes on, were
performed in common and were accompanied by rhythmically repeated ut-
terances. In this way sexual interest became attached to work. Primal man
made work acceptable, as it were, by treating it as an equivalent and substitute
for sexual activity. . . ."
and he goes on to explain why work and sex still share symbolism, especially in
dreams; thus, weapons stand for both work and sex-organs.

The interesting fact about the theory of the origins of language Freud offers is that it describes primeval man as already neurotic, as Freud himself hints a couple of paragraphs later, and in accord with his *Totem and Taboo* where humanity equals (primeval) guilt. See also Lecture 25, Anxiety (p. 406) where, describing infant phobias, he suggests that ontogeny recapitulates phylogeny. He also relates (p. 407) that children in the dark long to hear talk since their longing for company is transformed to fear of the dark.

The Darwin-Freud theory of language as evolving from music is defended ably by G. Révész in his *The Origins and Prehistory of Language*, 1956.

Révész says, p. 171, ". . . the call, appearing in the prelinguistic stage of human development as an especially important form of communication, became the common root and starting point for language and . . . music" "This conception", he continues in a note, "is in polar opposition to the theory, which has been repeatedly revived since ancient times, that the first language of mankind was song." He quotes Herder, and refers to Jespersen. He prefers Spencer's view which bases music on speech. Yet this idea is objectionable, too, since speech "does not use fixed intervals." By contrast, "music goes back to . . . the call, which, though it is not music, possesses its essential elements, the fixed intervals." This is a bit questionable in view of the existence of tonal languages, as well as of music with no fixed intervals, primitive as well as twentieth-century.

On the question, how much Freud was guided by neurophysiology and how much by autonomous psychology, the debate still rages. See, for example, J. O. Wisdom's highly favorable review of Harry Guntrip's *Personality Structure and Human Interaction: the Developing Synthesis of Psychoanalytic Theory* (London, 1961), in his "Mid-Century Developments within Psychoanalytic Theory", *Brit. J. Phil. Sci.*, Vol. 16, 53, May 1963, pp. 54–63, which he calls "unusual" and "of general interest" (p. 54, see also p. 63). His chief criticism "concerns the exegesis of Freud" which Guntrip offers (p. 58), from which "one gets the impression of Freud not as the outstanding psychologist who really did take mental disorder out of the realm of physiology and into the realm of pure psychology but as one who was still bogged down by physiological thinking." I do not comprehend the "but": Freud was both "bogged down by physiological thinking" and the one "who really did take mental disorder out of the realm of physiology into the realm of pure psychology" (nor is the word "pure" of much weight here). The difference between Guntrip and Wisdom is a matter of weight, of course, and Wisdom does say so. For my part, I think it is clear that Freud changed with age, never quite relinquishing his physiological reductionism, but allowing it to recede to the background. (For example, Wisdom refers to the Oedipus complex in this context, p. 60, quite overlooking that it came late in Freud's career.) Exegetes tend to ignore a man's change of opinion, much more so his change of (philosophy or) fundamental attitude.

See also notes 13 and 15 above.

44. Niko Tinbergen, "The Search for Animal Roots of Human Behavior", Chapter 16 of his *The Animal In Its World*, Vol. 2, Harvard University Press, 1972. He explains (p. 166) teachers' demand for respect by animals' preference to learn from superiors (on the pecking order). This is funny. Rather we should learn from this to tell our children to open up and learn from everyone! This is autonomy, a peculiar human trait! S. L. Washburn, speaks of the social life of primates in his "100 Years of Biological Anthropology", in J. O. Brew, ed., *One Hundred Years of Anthropology*, Harvard University Press, Cambridge, Mass., 1968, pp. 97–115, p. 109:

> "For example, monkeys normally learn to be social, and Harlow (1966) has described the stages of this learning and the devastating consequences of social isolation. Gibbons also learn to be social, but they learn a very different social system. It is useless to postulate a social instinct, but the relations of biology of a species, the situations, and the behaviors present a series of problems. Monkeys will learn to work for the sight of another monkey. They will make great efforts to stay with their troops. They make clearly observable efforts to sit near preferred individuals or to touch other individuals, and, in addition to mating behavior, many social behaviors appear to be highly rewarding. One aspect, or more correctly, a number of aspects, of the evolution of man's capacity for culture is the evolution of the biological bases for interpersonal relations. The diversity of cultures in no way alters the fact that in every pattern of culture it is biological organisms which learn human ways, are moved by human emotions, and adjust with human limitations."

45. The similarities between man — tribal — and apes is discussed by Leyhausen in Konrad Lorenz and Paul Leyhausen, *Motivation of Human and Animal Behavior, An Ethologic View,* translated from the German by B. A. Tonkin, Van Nostrand, Reinhold, New York, 1973, pp. 103ff., with a view to reducing man to animal, with a view to declare territorial rights natural, pp. 109ff., which nonsense the public should hopefully be soon tired of.

Adrian Kortlandt, "Chimpanzees in the Wild", *Scientific American*, May 1962, Vol. 206, pp. 128–140, reports such human traits in chimpanzees as deference to elders (p. 130), (who act as "security inspectors" (p. 137)), aesthetic appreciation (p. 131), and child rearing, as a major factor of social grouping (p. 132). "The main problem of primate research" he says (p. 133), "is to explain why the great apes did not become more nearly human than they are." And he refutes the "frequent answer" namely that chimpanzees "never came down out of the trees" (p. 133) or that they do not use weapons (pp. 134, 138).

For a review of the present stage of the animal sociology see Richard P. Michael and John H. Crook, eds., *Comparative Ecology and Behavior of Primates, Proceedings of a Conference, London, Nov. 1971*, Academic Press, New York, 1973, reviewed by Alson Jolly in *Science*, 12 April 1974, Vol. 184, pp. 149–50. See also Emil W. Menzel, *Science*, Vol. 184, 31 May 1974, p. 976:

> "Starting in the 1930's and up until the middle of the 1960's, the key themes were dominance, sex, and the attempt to be objective . . . The 1960's saw the rise of the Romantic Era, in which primate societies were gradually seen to be really held together by democratic and benign leaders, love of mother and kin, species-specific communication systems, play rather than fighting, grooming

rather than sex, and above all liking for each other . . . each species, if not each social group, had its own unique social culture. Authors became increasingly cautious about generalizing even to the same species of monkeys in a different forest — although this of course did not inhibit them from generalizing from squirrel monkeys or rhesus to man . . ."

46. See the following extracts from Darwin, *The Descent of Man,* London, 1871:
(p. 142) "But we know (and this is well worthy of reflection) that several kinds of apes are now actually in this intermediate condition . . ."
(p. 160) "Undoubtedly it would have been very interesting to have traced the development of each separate faculty from the state in which it exists in man; but neither my ability nor knowledge permit the attempt."
The speculation in the first passage, namely that apes are still evolving, conceals a problem. In one place, in his notebooks (B169), Darwin even adumbrates a hypothesis, evidently as a possible solution: "If all men were dead then monkeys make men. — Men make angels. —" That is, perhaps humans block simian evolution; but then what stops human evolution? See *Darwin on Man,* mentioned in note 15 to Section VI above, p. 446.
N. J. Berrill, "The Roots of Human Nature", *Atlantic Monthly*, June, 1966, pp. 92—6, reprinted in Hermann K. Bleitreu and James F. Downs, eds., *Human Variation: Readings in Physical Anthropology*, Glencoe Press, Beverly Hills, 1971, pp. 15—25, pp. 16—17:
"The more we see of the chimpanzee, the more we realize he is one of us . . . Other qualities in chimpanzees make certain human traits more acceptable and perhaps better understood. Not only chimpanzees but also monkeys will work for hours at solving simple puzzles with no reward other than the satisfaction gained. In fact, a chimpanzee if he likes a learning task will work at it incessantly unless he is hungry, paying no attention to offered food, just as a man engrossed will forgo a meal. This contraverts the tradition that there is an inborn aversion to work, whether mental or physical, and that some tangible reward is required in order to work to be done. What seems necessary is not extrinsic reward but intrinsic interest . . . monkeys and apes and humans enjoy the skill in using their distinctive combination of eye, hand, and brain for what it is worth. Winston Churchill was expressing this when he said, 'I like to learn, I don't like to be taught.' "
The fact that an infant of the most backward human society known to us will grow as a member of a civilized society if placed there, but an infant ape will not, is, in R. A. Wilson's view, a refutation of Darwin. "Darwin expresses surprise", he says, *The Miraculous Birth of Language,* New York, 1949, p. 181, "that some men should still think that there is any such barrier between the two." Nevertheless, he writes, "many authors have insisted that man is divided by an insuperable barrier from the lower animals in his mental faculties. Well, these authors, as a matter of demonstrable fact, are right and Darwin wrong." Yet what Darwin had in mind is that apes can evolve into humanity, though not in one generation; and he was wondering whether apes are now, in our own time, not evolving.

Here, then, is the limitation, the poverty if you like but not refutation, of Darwinism: it does not tell us the difference between an evolutionary plateau and an evolutionary trend. Look, says Schrödinger, at the bicycle: by comparison, at least, it has achieved a certain evolutionary stability "and has therefore pretty well ceased to undergo further changes". See his *Mind and Matter*, Cambridge University Press, 1958, p. 32.

Charles Hockett, "The Origins of Speech", *Scientific American*, September 1960, reprinted in *Human Variation and Origins, An Introduction to Human Biology and Evolution* (with introduction by W. S. Laughlin and R. H. Osbourne), Readings from Scientific American, San Francisco and London, 1965, pp. 183–190, offers (pp. 188–9) a more Darwinian view. By accident two natural messages, such as a food signal and a danger signal may be uttered simultaneously. Usually this will not be understood as a new signal but "once that did happen, the earlier closed system had become open and productive". Similarly, slight displacement may occur, such as delayed danger signals, etc. Such accidents, then, made us evolve, and the chimpanzees either did not experience them or could not use them. Why not?

Darwin could accept this theory on his assumptions that speech is prior to language, and that music is prior to speech. What Hockett seems to say, however, is perhaps that food and danger signals, even in the shape of specific sounds or calls, may be as primitive as mating calls and so not derivative of them, neither directly, much less via music. Révész might perhaps view these as musical, but then both music and language originate in calls and so this argument is of no avail.

See also G. McBride, "On the Evolution of Human Language", *Social Science Information*, 1968, Vol. 7, 5, pp. 81–5; also his "On the Evolution of Human Language: A Postscript", in J. Kristena, J. Rex-Debove, and J. Umiker, eds., *Essays in Semiotics* (T. A. Seboek, ed., *Approaches to Semiotics*, Vol. 4), The Hague, 1971. See also Charles R. Peters, "Evolution of the Capacity for Language: a New Start on an Old Problem", *Man,* 1972, Vol. 7, pp. 33–49.

47. Cf. Karl R. Popper, *Objective Knowledge, An Evolutionary Approach*, Oxford, 1972, pp. 269–70:
"The real difficulty of [neo-] Darwinism is the well-known problem of explaining the evolutions which are *apparently goal-directed* such as that of our eyes, by an incredibly large number of very small steps; for according to [neo-] Darwinism, each of these steps is the result of a purely accidental mutation. That all these independent accidental mutations should have had survival value is hard to explain. This is especially the case for the Lorenzian inherited behavior."
And on p. 271, note, Popper refers to the countless difficulties of Darwin's theory to which some neo-Darwinists seem to be almost blind.

M. Polanyi makes a similar remark in his *Knowing and Being*, Chicago, 1969, about the possibility to abuse one's function by ignoring just criticism. See notes 5 and 6 to the Introduction above.

The first to deny the Darwinian continuity theory seems to be one of the fathers of neo-Mendelism, Hugo de Vries, *Mutationstheorie,* Leipzig, 1901,

Species and Varieties. Chicago, 1905, and *Die Mutationen in der Erblichkeitslehre,* Berlin, 1912. See also J. S. Wilkie, "Some Reasons for the Rediscovery and Appreciation of Mendel's Work in the First Years of the Present Century", *Brit. J. Hist. Sci.,* Vol. 1, 1962–3, pp. 5–17, and G. Révész, *The Origins and Prehistory of Language,* translated from the German by J. Butler, Philosophical Library, New York, 1956, p. 175. See also Loren Eisley, *Darwin's Century, Evolution and the Men Who Discovered It,* New York, 1958, Chapter IX, Section 3; and my review of K. R. Popper, *Objective Knowledge,* note 58 to Section IV above.

48. Two issues are involved here, namely first the theory of the innate or inborn or native versus the acquired or the learned, and second the theory of racial memory. We may easily identify the two issues by identifying the innate with racial and contrast the two with the learned. The results of this are strange.

The *locus classicus* of the identification of the innate with the racial is Konrad Lorenz, "Kant's Doctrine of the A Priori in the Light of Contemporary Biology", originally published in *Blätter für Deutsche Philosophie,* 1941, Vol. 15, pp. 94–125, English translation in *General Systems,* Vol. 7, 1962 (Yearbook of the Society for General Systems Research, Mental Health Research Institute, University of Michigan, Ann Arbor, Michigan), pp. 23–35. The purpose of that paper seems to me to be the amalgamation of Uexküll and Groos, though, of course, this is a mere conjecture on my part. It is interesting that philosophically this is, clearly, Lorenz's best, and oddly of the same period as his very worst work, mentioned in note 30 above. Later on Lorenz changed his theory of animal learning under the pressure of valid criticism – see note 9 to Section I above – until it became increasingly clear that the dichotomy between the innate and the learned cannot be maintained. This dichotomy is the target of his attack to which he devotes his *Evolution and Modification of Behavior,* University of Chicago Press, University of Toronto, 1965. And, of course, without the dichotomy the identification of the innate and the a priori makes no sense. Yet this very identification is still held by Chomsky and his followers; and even when they deny it they still insist on the dichotomy. See previous note. Similarly the theory of the I.Q., invented at the end of the last century, of course accepted the dichotomy as a sacred tenet. All attempts to patch up this defeat are mere confusions. See my "The Twisting of the I.Q. Test", referred to in note 4 above.

Consider the innate and its equality with the racial. The innate was equated with racial memory with instinct by Darwin and by August Weismann. This is exactly what Freud considered the Id or the unconscious to be. It is important not to confuse the unconscious, which we may become conscious by reflection, but which remains unconscious and is not controllable, with the subconscious, which is the storehouse of all that we have acquired but wish to put aside, repress, suppress. The subconscious includes our moral sense, namely, our super-ego, since we repress it on account of its making us feel guilty.

Identifying the innate and the racial, then, will not permit us to consider the Oedipus complex, the root of our moral sense as well as sense of guilt, as racially transmitted, unless it is in our genes. Freud wanted at times to postulate racial memory of the Oedipus, but in the universal subconscious of Jung, not in our genes; that is to say he wanted to break this very identification of the racial and the genetically innate. Can this be done and, if so, how?

No doubt much of what Jung used as examples of the universal symbolism of the universal subconscious has turned out to be either some purely biological symbolisms of the sort that interest animal psychologists, or symbols which are very easily assimilated by members of diverse cultures even though they originate in given specific cultures, simply because they are quite primitive. Comics and such are good instances of these, and compare well with pictures drawn under Jung's inspiration and presented by him as good illustrations of his views.

The question, then, reappears, is it logically quite impossible to have racial memory not genetically transmitted? I think it is logically possible but not admissible given our general background knowledge. And so, identifying racial memory and inborn knowledge is not a revolutionary hypothesis. Its tenability or otherwise, however, depends on the tenability or otherwise of the dichotomy between the inborn or native and the acquired or learned. This is obviously false, and leads to fantastic results. See for example Gilbert Ryle's "Mowgli in Babel", *Philosophy*, Vol. 49, 187, 1974, pp. 5—11, which offers a terrific and most simple critique of Chomsky. "What seems to have gone wrong is this", he says (pp. 9ff.). "Chomsky . . . and many others, began by assuming that Pavlov, Skinner, etc., have worked out . . . the scientific and therefore mechanical theory of learning . . . Instead of sitting back to think ecologically . . . about learning . . . Chomsky . . . and Co. surrender the whole notion of learning to the mechanizers, and make do, as best they can, with the notion of evolutionary inheritance . . ." And, still further (p. 11), he adds, "Same input same output? Rubbish: But what of '[Tommy]cannot know at birth which language he is to learn, but he must know that its grammar must be of a predetermined form that excludes many imaginable languages. Having selected a permissible hypothesis, he [Tommy!] can use inductive evidence for corrective action, confirming or disconfirming his choice? ' etc., etc. (*Language and Mind*, p. 78). Here too – Rubbish! " and so both Skinner and Chomsky are declared "Rubbish! " and the field is wide open. The trouble, of course, is that there is a strong correlation, as yet unstudied, between the inborn and the ability to learn. See my "The Logic of Scientific Inquiry", *Synthese*, Vol. 26, 1974, pp. 498–514. See also next two notes.

49.   The view that a seeming continuity should be regarded as a discontinuity if in the process a radical change occurs in depth – a change of purpose, say – which takes time to manifest itself and which does so gradually: it has been expressed in G. Révész, *The Origin and Prehistory of Language*, translated from the German by J. Butler, Philosophical Library, New York, 1956, pp. 176–7. See also my "Continuity and Discontinuity in the History of Science", mentioned in note 8 to Section I above, where I claim that Hegel is right to claim that continuity and discontinuity intertwine and that obviously he is in serious error in feeling that somehow this conflicts with logic and/or mathematics, even though it is quite a general point that he makes here.

There is no doubt, the chief disagreement on the origin of language as well as on the nature of language concerns continuity: Darwin and Freud and Karl Buhler see antecedents of language in animal expression and communication, whereas Humboldt, Max Müller, and Révész and Chomsky too see here "an impassible chasm" (see note 75 below). For my part I cannot say I understand the disagreement to my satisfaction and think there is much to be gained by respectful attempts to sharpen it before discussing any further the arguments pro and con each side. See also notes 72–5 to Section VII below.

50. A very conspicuous example is Helmuth Plessner whose central idea is that we should replace Descartes' mind-body dualism with the dualism of the self that has a body with the self that is the body. This point about the duality of self comes from Freud's *The Id and the Ego* of 1923; it was taken up by his friend Paul Federn who explained schizophrenia as the loss of the sense of self in the second of the above two senses. Federn's *Ego Psychology and the Psychoses*, Image Publishing Company, London, 1953, started quite a trend in existential psychoanalysis which led to Laing's classic works discussed above, Chapter 1. See note 42 to Section III.

The prominence of this, then, both in circles of continental philosophical anthropologists and in psychoanalytic circles, makes this lack of recognition particularly puzzling. Indeed, the only person who shows awareness of all this is René Spitz, and he is, of course, steeped and well known in both traditions.

It may be curious to note that P. L. Berger and Th. Luckmann endorse Freud's theory in their famous *The Social Construct of Reality, A Treatise in the Sociology of Knowledge* (New York, 1966, 1967) but fail to ascribe it to him even where they praise him, i.e., in their notes 74 and 75 to Chapter II, though they manage to mention him while depriving him of his originality, i.e. in note 80 – all on page 202. The explanation may be found on p. 196 where Freud is (justly) dissented from on account of his psychologism (note 7). Even there (note 9) they declare their view of man's "sexual plasticity" not the same as Freud's view of "the original unformed character of the libido", but admit that the one view "has an affinity" to the other. Yet the very end of the volume, notes 46 and 48 of the last chapter, make ample amend for those who are in the know and may sense the injustice. Whom do they try to deceive?

There is an ambiguity which needs clarification here. It is possible that Freud thought all biological mechanisms specific and all diffusion psychological. Or, he may have thought simply that biology is not as diffuse as psychology. If he meant the first, then, clearly, Lorenz seems to have refuted him empirically – see notes 12 to Section VI and 44 to this Section – when he found biologically diffuse, i.e. ambiguous, mechanisms. It is also clear that holders of the postnatal fetalization theory should say, the more diffuse mechanisms are evolutionarily the higher. It is also clear that this is the central idea of learning by I.R.M. – see next note – namely that the inbuilt mechanisms have some ambiguities in them that "are meant to" be decided one way or the other in an empirical fashion depending on circumstances (= adaptability = ability to learn).

51. Konrad Lorenz developed a learning theory which combines Kantian nativism with traditional (inductivist) associationism. Consider the "educational" game (developed and popularized during Lorenz's childhood or thereabout) of fitting wooden blocks of diverse shapes into a board with holes of the same shapes. Consider the mind to be the board, and the qualities of the first block that go into a given hole to be associated with that shape. Thus, the first object that fits a given slate has qualities associated with the slate, so that by association, a square block is red and a round one green; or, rather, one person's mother is blonde, and another brunette. Also, the slate evolves, partly as the outcome of previous learning acts (blue-eyed blonde people are brave) and partly as the result of maturation (gentlemen prefer blondes). Also some slates appear only after some other slates get filled, and at times in ways which depend on past history (educated people can learn; rich people can invest).

Unlike (inductivist) associationism or (Kantian) Gestalt psychology, however, this theory does not clearly entail a view of scientific method.

An interesting fact can be viewed as an extension of Lorenz's moves. Often we teach our young some inexplicable or half-understandable items that they half memorize half have some vague intuition of — usually an incorrect one. Later on, when these are explained more fully, they fall into place. This experience has a positive side — one learns the experience of things falling into place — and a negative side: the things may, and are intended to, fall into place and stay put, partly as relegated to the unconscious framework, partly since sanctified by childhood memories. At times people who cherish the experience of a "click" can only alter their view when a bigger and better "click" occurs: they are dogmatists who merely alter a dogma. All this is simply creating new slates, new internal release mechanisms, which are later, indeed, released.

All this sounds sophisticated, yet it is the same as the traditional idea, shared by Jews and Chinese alike, that the values of the culture, and instances of them in narrative and in ritual, should be transmitted to the young well before the young can absorb them, and utterly regardless of the failure and frustrations that parents and teachers must suffer as a result. And the Sages even say that what they aim at are "clicks" to come later in the process of maturation.

For more detail on the problem of smooth intellectual development and the intentions that create these "clicks" see my "Sociologism in the Philosophy of Science", *Metaphilosophy,* Vol. 3, 1972, 62–73.

The conflict between Lorenz's theory of science or scientific learning or scientific method and his theory of animal learning by a mixture of imprinting and conditioning has been noted, for the first time, I am surprised to notice, in Karl Popper's "Autobiography", P. A. Schilpp, ed., *The Philosophy of Karl Popper*, La Salle, Ill., 1974, Vol. 1, pp. 160–161, note 44, and even Popper tries to minimize the place of inductivism in Lorenz's view of science in a manner which seems hilarious when that note is compared with Lorenz's somewhat infantile Nobel Lecture (*Science*, Vol. 185, 19 July 1974, pp. 229–234), e.g. (p. 230), "no such thing as a false analogy exists: An analogy can be more or less detailed and hence more or less informative . . ." and (p. 232) "Since we know that the behavior patterns of geese and men cannot possibly be homologous [i.e. of a common origin] . . . and since we know that the improbability of coincidental similarity can only be expressed in astronomical numbers, we know for certain that it was a more or less identical survival value which caused [e.g.] jealousy behavior to evolve in birds as well as in man." (Hence jealousy is "good"!)

Yet, why do birds learn by imprinting and conditioning but man by analogy and repetition?

The view which Lorenz offers in his Nobel Lecture is a variant of the Kalam theory that everything conceivable is realizable, and of Descartes' theory that all clear and distinct ideas are true. What all variants suffer from is a remarkable poverty of the imagination (as Maimonides has noted, and as Boyle and Bayle have).

52. Freud's theory of plasticity is the idea of diffuse psychological mechanisms based on fairly clear-cut biological functions or instincts; it accords with either Darwin's view that instincts may be replaced by capacities to learn or Lloyd Morgan's theory of instinct modification. Now, clearly, Sir Solly Zuckerman, *The Social Life of Monkeys and Apes*, London and New York, 1932, agrees about the possibility of diffusion but denies that the diffusion itself guarantees plasticity. As to the first point, he says (p. 312) that sex signifies less in monkeys than in humans because social sexual relations are "clearly demarcated . . . if . . . not naturally . . . at any rate enforced by the law . . . But in monkeys, sexual activities are primarily diffuse in character. Sexual responses develop early in life and then become expressed in an extravagantly varied manner within a social system based on dominance." Yet he also rejects the idea that diffusion guarantees plasticity quite offhand, noting (p. 31) that "plasticity in the individual and in the group is not determined by psychological factors alone. The mechanisms of reproduction may or may not be so fixed and sharply defined as to determine stereotyped forms of social response. Those of the monkey are less definite than those of the ground-squirrel, and this is directly correlated with its freer behavior." I do not think this was answered by the plasticity school, especially the Freudians among them. Róheim in particular, dismisses the point, saying (*Psychoanalysis and Anthropology*, p. 407) Zuckerman "is critical of many details but nevertheless assumes that [the foetalization] views in general are valid."

Zuckerman's claim that sex signifies more for humans than for simians because it is less specific in them opens the door to views opposed to all traditions, east and west, which recommend sex strictly for procreation. It really means that permissiveness is a stage in further diffusion which will make present-day sex obsession a mere cultural lag. "After all", says Dora Russell in her permissive and pro-sex *The Right to be Happy*, Harper, New York and London, 1927, p. 135, "there are other pleasures besides sex, though one might scarcely think so when one hears the Puritans and Freudians talking." Culturally, Freudianism is, here, an afterimage of Puritanism!

53. Sherwood L. Washburn, "Tools and Human Evolution", *Scientific American,*

September 1960, reprinted in *Human Variation and Origins, An Introduction to Human Biology and Evolution*, (with introductions by W. S. Laughlin and R. H. Osbourne), Readings from Scientific American, San Francisco and London, 1967, pp. 169—182, p. 180:

> "In man adaptation to bipedal locomotion decreased the size of the bony birth-canal at the same time that the exigencies of tools use selected for larger brains. This obstetrical dilemma was solved by delivery of the foetus at a much earlier stage of development. But this was possible only because the mother . . . could hold a helpless, immature . . . infant . . . the human type mother-child relation must have evolved by the time of the large-brained, fully bipedal humans of the Middle Pleistocene . . . The slow moving mother, carrying the baby, could not hunt, and the combination . . . imposed a fundamental pattern of the social organization of the human species."

For an overview of the development of the movement of present-day philosophical anthropology and for bibliography, see Géza Róheim, *Psychoanalysis and Anthropology, Culture, Personality and the Unconscious*, New York, 1950, 1968, Chapter 10, "The Unity of Mankind", also, Peter L. Berger and Thomas Luckmann, *The Social Construction of Reality, A Treatise in the Sociology of Knowledge*, Doubleday, New York, 1966, paper edition 1967, Chapter II, "Society and Objective Reality", and notes, especially note 1, pp. 195ff.; as well as Marjorie Grene, "Philosophical Anthropology", in Raymond Klibansky, ed., *Contemporary Philosophy, A Survey*, Florence, 1969, pp. 215—220 and bibliography there.

James Blish imagines, in his *A Case of Conscience*, a superhuman race whose total fetal development is outside the womb, with ontogeny recapitulating philogeny. Of course, the result is that fetalization in that case does away with the need for nursing. But if nursing is only a necessary condition for high plastic adaptability, we may well imagine a highly favorable environment, etc., where nursing is entirely dispensible with!

Shaw's *Back to Methuselah*, though, of course, anti-Darwinian, can be adapted, too. We may have a species with newborn better adapted than we are today yet in a sense quite fetal, i.e. in the sense of being still very highly adaptable.

The idea, then, is a bit confused: We see evolution as being both more mechanisms and each of them more open to further specifications. Here is the root of evolutionism's chief error. Evolution is not on a single scale — see note 4 above about scales.

The strongest argument against the theory of fetalization is the observation that sexual maturation arrives earlier in the young of the better-fed populations. See J. M. Tanner, "Earlier Maturation in Man", *Scientific American*, Vol. 218, pp. 21—7. Since the theory is vague it is hard to assess the strength of the criticism. Since, doubtlessly, if the process were the reverse authors like Róheim would claim great victory, the evidence should by the same token be deemed rather deadly. But I prefer to view zealous defenders of a theory more of a nuisance than of a meter of criticizability. Of course, one can doubt the evidence, but then the evidence for fetalization is more questionable than of early maturation allegedly due to better feeding. Incidentally, I suppose better feeding to be a meter for easier life all-round: general anti-fetalization arguments such as Shaw's *Back to Methuselah* is full of, would lead one to expect security to be as strong a factor for early maturation as food. Since early maturation is judged, empirically, by the first appearance of menstruation, it is relevant to mention that many women had their first menstruation in years on the week they left World War II concentration camps. See also Rose E. Frisch and Janet W. McArthur, "Menstrual Cycles: Fatness as a Determinant of Minimum Weight for Height Necessary for Their Maintenance or Onset", *Science,* Vol. 185, 13 September 1974, pp. 948–950, and references there. In that study only weight and fat content of women were considered, "other possible causes having been excluded".

It should be mentioned, likewise, that were the postnatal fetalization theory taken a bit more seriously opponents would ask, how come human beings are not marsupials? And, I am of the opinion, were humans marsupial, Róheim would see this as proof of the theory at hand. Are marsupials more plastic than their placental analogs? If not, why not? Joseph Campbell, "Bios and Mythos: Prolegomena to a Science of Mythology", in G. B. Wilber and W. Muensterberger, eds., *Psychoanalysis and Culture: Essays in Honor of Géza Róheim*, International University Press, New York, 1951, pp. 329–343, pp. 337–9 discusses this point most glibly.

54. Of course, what environmental factors contribute to the activity of the genetic mechanism and what not, is a general and difficult question. The autogenous regulation theory says that the products of the activity of the genetic mechanism are a major contributor: when the mechanism produces enough of a certain entity, for example, the presence of quantities of that entity impede production And so, whether the cytoplasm's contribution to the fetus' formation is strictly genetic or environmental I, for one, cannot say. Nor have I seen discussion of this anywhere. See also notes 39, 40, 61, 62, and 68 to this section.

55. The experiments in cloning have not been as successful as described here, but we may assume, with the whole literature on the topic, that this is a mere technicality, that soon cloning will become practicable even with large animals, perhaps even practiced in large breeding farms.

56. Sir Gavin R. de Beer, "Portrait in Science: Darwin's 'Origin' Today", in *Natural History,* Vol. 75, August 1966, pp. 62–64, reprinted in Hermann K. Bleitreu and James F. Downs, eds., *Human Variation: Readings in Physical Anthropology*, Glencoe Press, Beverly Hills, 1971, pp. 7–15, p. 9:
> "It remained for Ronald Fisher in 1930 to show the real importance of Mendel's discovery, which was that inheritance is particulate — which means that variance is preserved instead of being 'swamped', as has been assumed under the false notion of blending inheritance."

Yet, Sir Gavin recognizes in the next page, Fisher's work had to be supplemented by E. B. Ford's view of the transition of favored genes from recessive to dominant state. According to Richard Goldschmidt, who published in the early thirties and forties, even this did not suffice and the theory had to be supplemented by the hypothesis (which Sir Gavin rejects, *loc. cit.*) of some discontinuous or large-scale mutations.

To date the problem is still open. An excellent and brief report on the latest controversy between the natural selectionists and the neutralists can be found in Gina Bari Kolato, "Population Genetics: Reevaluation of Genetic Variation", in *Science*, Vol. 184, 26 April 1974, Research News, pp. 452—4 and references there.

The fact that Darwinism was in great difficulty is recognized by Darwinians like Sir Gavin only in claims that the difficulty has been solved (and even then not very frankly). See, for another example, *Human Variation and Origins, An Introduction to Human Biology and Evolution* (with introduction by W. S. Laughlin and R. H. Osborne), Readings from Scientific American, San Francisco and London, 1967, p. 52:

> "Darwin has presented the theory of natural selection in 1859, but it wasn't until the work of Bateson, Fisher and Wright that genetic explanations became possible. Similarly . . . population genetics did not develop as a biological subscience until Fisher's *The Genetic Theory of Natural Selection* was published in 1929, and Wright's paper, *Evolution in Mendelian Populations* appeared in 1931."

57. Leibniz is not usually associated with Darwin. Yet the Leibnizian character of Darwin's work, his bringing man into the fold of animal nature is discussed very sympathetically by an opponent, R. A. Wilson, in his *The Miraculous Birth of Language*, New York, 1948, pp. 100—2.

It is interesting to notice that it was this kind of unification that Kant sought in the *Critique of Judgement*, Part II, Appendix, §80, J. H. Bernard's translation, MacMillan, London, 1914, p. 337, in a passage on the analogy of forms of many animals, and on evolutionism proper (p. 338), quoted by Wilson, *op. cit.*, p. 71. Wilson offers the impression that the aspiration was very popular in the eighteenth and nineteenth centuries. See also A. O. Lovejoy's classic *The Great Chain of Being*, Harvard University Press, Cambridge, Mass., 1942. The same view is expressed in Loren Eiseley, *Darwin's Century, Evolution and the Men who Discovered It*, Doubleday, New York, 1958, Chapter X, Section II, p. 259.

Darwin had an early theory which he labeled monadism, which probably was the root of the continuity theory and the missing link theory he held throughout, and which may, in origin, be somewhat Leibnizian. But probably the Leibnizian remote connexion was lost on Darwin himself. See Howard E. Gruber, *Darwin on Man, A Psychological Study of Scientific Creativity, Together with Darwin's Early and Unpublished Notebooks*, transcribed and annotated by Paul H. Barrett, foreword by Jean Piaget, Dutton, New York, 1974, Chapter 7, pp. 139 and 146, and pp. 441 and 461. The origin of the new term, a passage from Sir Humphry Davy, is no doubt Leibnizian in part only.

58. The science fiction writer and philosopher Olaf Stapledon, in his *Star Maker*, gave stars and nebulae faint abilities to think and act, evidently *à la* Leibnizian

stones. Clearly, he thought with Copernicus, Kepler, and Galileo, that a star is more of a whole than a stone. Clearly, too, Leibniz ascribed a higher degree of rationality to a higher wholeness. In my own opinion wholeness is not one-dimensional and so cannot be properly ordered.

59. The human mutant, the superman, was conceived by Darwin already; see note 46 above. The mutant entered science fiction, and through it into public consciousness, via the works of H. G. Wells and G. B. Shaw.

For exosupermen, see the detailed history in "Extraterrestrial Intelligent Life", Lewis White Beck, Presidential Address, *Proceedings and Addresses of the American Philosophical Association,* Vol. 45, September 1972, APA, Clinton, New York, 1974, pp. 5–21. The references are very extensive and eminently clear. Beck quotes, p. 19, Wolfgang Philip, *Das Zeitalter der Aufklärung*, Bremen, 1963, p. xxvii, on Pascal's suffering from a "Brunonian shock"; he also quotes, p. 11, the "very sophisticated book", S. A. Kaplan, ed., *Extraterrestrial Civilizations*, Israel Program for Scientific Translations, Jerusalem, 1971, p. 257, on the Darwinian and Marxian encouragement to modern exobiology. Historians of science fiction now agree that the greatest impetus to this literature came from Erasmus and Charles Darwin.

60. Sir Gavin R. de Beer, "Portrait in Science: Darwin's 'Origin' Today", in *Natural History*, Vol. 75, August 1966, pp. 62–64, reprinted in Hermann K. Bleitreu and James F. Downs, eds., *Human Variation: Readings in Physical Anthropology*, Glencoe Press, Beverly Hills, 1971, pp. 7–15, p. 8, quotes Darwin's admission of the force of Fleeming Jenkins' criticism (the chance of one mutation occuring in two mates is infinitesimal), and adds,

". . . In the new (5th) edition of the *Origin* then in preparation, Darwin did the best he could, which was to lean more heavily on the position that variation was produced as the result — then supposedly inherited — of acquired characters, of the use and disuse of different portions of the anatomy, and of environmental action".

I think Sir Gavin is a bit vague here — since he is leading to the discussion of the problem in neo-Mendelian settings — quoted above, two notes earlier — whereas for Darwin the important factor was the creation of a cleavage between mutant and his parent group, so as to prevent a throwback. This is indeed the point made by Erwin Schröedinger in his *Mind and Matter*, Cambridge, 1958, pp. 26ff. on "feigned Lamarckism", where he says it is so important that a mutant go and make good use of his new mutation. For, here, indeed, a volition enters the picture and breaks away from strictly causal Darwinism (strictly causal, meaning not purposive, though not meaning non-statistical). See discussion of this passage in K. R. Popper, *Objective Knowledge*, Clarendon Press, Oxford, 1972, p. 268 and my criticism of it in my review of it mentioned in note 8 to Section I.

61. We reject, that is, the theory that all social life is genetically determined. Theodosius Dobzhansky, "Evolution — Organic and Superorganic", *Bull. Atomic*

Sci., 20 May 1964, pp. 4—8, reprinted in Hermann K. Bleitreu and James F. Downs, eds., *Human Variation: Readings in Physical Anthropology*, Glencoe Press, Beverly Hills, 1971, pp. 44—55, p. 47, says,

"One extreme is a thorough going genetic determinism . . . ' . . . the structure of society rests on the stuff in the chromosome and the change it undergoes.' This extreme is rather easily refuted; historical and social changes are sometimes far too rapid to be merely manifestations of genetic changes."

The refuted hypothesis is that of a "one-to-one correspondence between cultural forms and genetic traits" (*op. cit.,* p. 51); whereas the quoted theory is that the one is a function solely of the other (an ellipse, or a parabola, for example, is a function, but not a one-to-one correspondence). I am a bit embarrassed by this gross misrepresentation by a reputed author of a view which he himself quotes; I can only explain it thus: the author is convinced of the falsehood of the theory which he (positivistically) views as being easily refuted. In truth the theory in question is irrefutable, of course: we simply take it for granted that the theory in question is false.

62. The problem "why did man evolve?" is the same as "why did apes not evolve?". Clearly, Darwin felt it when he wondered whether apes are still evolving or not. For the history of the problem see Loren Eiseley, *Darwin's Century, Evolution and the Men who Discovered It,* Doubleday, 1958, Chapter XI, especially pp. 318ff. For Darwin on the possibility that apes are evolving, see note 46 above.

With what tools can such a question be tackled? Neo-Darwinism ascribes all mutations to accident, and so, by a rare accident some apes mutated, and by another rare accident some mutants survived, and by yet another, there was no throwback. How a mutant avoids falling back on the older pattern is a question which was raised in Darwin's time and caused him great troubles. See Loren Eiseley, *op. cit.,* pp. 210—13 (see index, art. Jenkins, Fleeming). See also notes 56 and 60 above.

63. For the fact that every ancient hominoid known is suspected to be a granduncle rather than a great-grandfather, see opening chapters and references of Sol Tax, Loren C. Eiseley, Irving Rouse, and Carl F. Voegelin, eds., *An Appraisal of Anthropology Today* The University of Chicago Press, Chicago, 1953, "Problems of Historical Approach: Results". David Plibean and Stephen Jay Gould, "Size and Scaling in Human Evolution", *Science*, Vol. 186, 6 December 1974, pp. 892—901, argue that "all australopithecines are versions of the 'same' animal" with the sameness left vague. See bibliography there.

64. *Human Variation and Origins, An Introduction to Human Biology and Evolution* (with introductions by W. S. Laughlin and R. H. Osborne), Readings from Scientific American, San Francisco and London, 1967, p. 5:

"Just as the concept of the "missing link" is meaningless without the larger parental concept of the Great Chain of Being, the names and sequences of the

Cenozoic epochs, the Eocene, Oligocene, Miocene, Pliocene, and Pleistocene, are irrelevant without the methodology of the intellectual framework that brought them into being. This framework has been authoritatively supplied by a major contribution to statistical analysis, Ronald Fisher (1953). Fisher suggested that statistical science was the peculiar aspect of human progress that gave the twentieth century its special character, and that the period of 'inconspicuous gestation' extended through most of the nineteenth century . . ."

This passage is very interesting. It is meant to say, original concepts such as those of epochs, are statistical, and were given meaning only in this century by Fisher's statistical theory. Does this also apply to "the missing link"? How? The Great Chain of Being, they say, has now become statistical; "The missing link", then, must be statistical too, or indeed, the whole concept of species. That the concept of species is statistical is, indeed, a fact, and without it one can hardly understand contemporary studies of statistical balance between interbreeding species, such as wild and domesticated plants or animals. But man cannot interbreed with other animals now; could he at certain stages?

(Some suggestions of possible frameworks are dealt with in the final chapter of John T. Robinson *Early Hominoid Posture and Locomotion*, Chicago University Press, Chicago and London, 1973.)

65. The solution offered by Democritus, and endorsed by Plato (who rejected the atoms but retained their forms), seems very congenial, as it enables us to see diversity — of appearances — within unity, or rather within reality, whether of atoms and the void, or forms and the void, or forms and primordial matter, or even more abstract entities, such as being and becoming or actual and potential. Yet the question remains just as Parmenides put it: if appearances are false and realities are true, how can the truth explain falsehoods? The question is utterly unanswerable as long as explanation is a sort of deductive relation since a falsehood can never be validly deduced from a truth. Aristotle's metaphor of the alphabet makes the solution plausible, except that the alphabet is a code and not an explanation. This is why all sorts of fictionalism repeatedly gain popularity: for fictionalists scientific theories are mere classifications, or codes — especially when they view theories as implicit definitions, of course.

The metaphor is to be found in Aristotle's *Metaphysics*, Book Alpha, and in Galileo's first dialogue, first day, last entry (by Sagredo) and second day, Sagredo's sixth entry — in a Platonist sentiment. Since I spoke in the text of the analogy to letters, let me say here that analogy is magical, indeed it is Frazer's chief characteristic of sympathetic magic, namely the law "that like produces like, or that effect resembles its cause", namely the law of similarity, or of homeopathic or imitative magic. The other law of magic mentioned by Frazer, magic by contact or contagion, is, indeed, imitative of the first (*Golden Bough*, Macmillan (abridged edition), 1922, pp. 12, 14). Plato's celebrated passage on the alphabet, *Phaedrus*, 274C–275B, relating the ancient Egyptian myth of the divine origin of writing, is magical no doubt, and relates it to the art of memory. It is quoted in Frances A. Yates, *The Art of Memory*, University of Chicago Press, Chicago and

London, 1966, p. 38. Yates traces some of its connections (I miss reference to Francis Bacon's *Abecedarium Naturae*, not to mention Thomas Harriot) with cabbalism and hermeticism through the ages, showing that the Platonism of cabbalism as opposed to the Aristotelianism of scholasticism is at least as traditional. The letters of the alphabet are both magical and scientific (even mathematical), both mnemonic devices and hints at the laws of nature, not to mention the *ars combinatoria*, exhibit confusion of magic and science which was so characteristic of the esoteric movement to which Copernicanism belonged until Galileo agreed – in the opening of his first dialogue – to do something about it. He did much, but science free of myth is impossible, see Section XIV below on the myth that science is utterly rational.

66. I cannot possibly do justice to the idea of conflicting forces and its history. The theory of the conflict originates in Kant, evolves into a system of philosophy of nature in Schelling and Hegel, who later develops it into Hegelian dialectic so popularized by both Marx and Engels, each in his own way. I have sketched some of the physics involved here in my *Faraday as a Natural Philosopher*; see also my "Continuity and Discontinuity in the History of Science"; both mentioned in note 8 to Section I above. See also note 10 to this chapter.

67. It is thus no surprise that the missing link can be better characterized by material culture than anatomically. See Emmanuel Anati, *Palestine Before the Hebrews*, Jonathan Cape, London, 1963, p. 77. See also there, pp. 50, 55, 57, and W. E. LeGross Clark, *The Fossil Evidence for Human Evolution*, University of Chicago Press, Chicago and London, 1955. Of course, the question, is a given skeletal remain that of a granduncle or grand-ancestor, is meant to signify, "is he an ape or a man?" Except that the two questions are not identical, since some humans are only granduncles and some simians are grand-ancestors. (We are speaking, of course, always statistically, see note 64 above, so that a skeleton is always a sample representative, we assume representative even in the statistical sense though at times only after some adjustments of presumed personal peculiarities, of a level of evolution which may be a link leading to us or not.) Indeed, calling a skeleton a granduncle enables us to leave open the question, was he an ape or a man. Yet this question presses no less than, is he our ancestor? Clearly, for that we need both more paleontological knowledge than we have and criteria for humanity – see note 63 above. These we do not have and it is a tradition in science – to be abolished – that unanswered questions are better not overmuch emphasized.

68. I would like to stress one point as much as possible, but I shall not explain it, since the explanation is highly technical and quite lengthy, yet bearing no relevance to materials handled here.

There are two theories about the meaning of a question. The one is Wittgensteinian, or a matter of the logical positivistic or the language analytic schools. I cannot fully articulate it, since I get quickly involved in obvious contradictions when I try. Roughly, everybody agrees that the meaning of a question is its range of possible answers. Now the positivists assume two further ideas about the meaning of a question. First, you cannot understand a question at all if you cannot conceive of any possible answer to it, or if you cannot imagine how to test empirically the truth or falsity of an answer which you can conceive of. Second, is such cases there is a grammatic error in the question (and the answer).

The other tradition is much younger, and is that of the formal logic of questions, or erotetic logic. It includes the idea of a pseudo-answer to a given question, which is not an indication as to which of the possible answers to it is true, but an indication that a presupposition behind it is false. For example, consider the question: that person over there, is he your older brother or your younger brother? The answer, oh, he is a friend of the family and is living here for a while, is a perfectly natural and reasonable reply to a visitor in one's home, observing the family friend, say, coming out of the shower. For a Wittgensteinian, then, the question is genuine. Yet, strictly speaking, the response is no answer at all but a pseudo-answer; and a pseudo-answer turns the question into a pseudo-question; and so it is not a genuine question.

It is only in the second sense, not the first, that I consider two or three classic questions in the present context to be pseudo-questions, particularly the classic mind-body problem and the missing link problem: in certain contexts they are quite legit, but in the context I am presenting here they are not. See my essays mentioned in note 68 to Section V above.

69. Human *Variation and Origins, An Introduction to Human Biology and Evolution* (with introductions by W. S. Laughlin and R. H. Osborne), Readings from Scientific American, San Francisco and London, 1967, introduction to Pt. III, p. 140:
"It is surprising, but unfortunately true, that even when accepting principles of Darwinian and genetic theory, social scientists tend to emphasize the word "natural" in natural selection, thereby thinking only of the physical environment and failing to recognize what an important selective force culture has exerted in the course of a large part of man's evolution. Many ethnologists consider culture to be above and completely separate from biological characteristics of the responsible [?] organism . . . .
The importance of . . . unique features of man's evolutionary history has been overlooked by some students in their eagerness to apply to humans the more simple ready-made formulations used for infra-human species, and there also has been a not uncommon misinterpretation of certain basic principles of population genetics."

70. A. I. Oparin, *The Origins of Life*, 4th edition, Oliver & Boyd, Edinburgh and London, 1957, and references there; Gosta Ehresvärd, *Life: Origin and Development*, University of Chicago Press, Chicago and London, 1962, and references in Chapter XIV there.

71. The problem of the origin of writing is rooted in the hidden assumption that writing is meant for communication, that the first written item was a message, if not a letter, then an open letter of sorts. Yet writing turns out to be a record, not a communication, or a letter to oneself, not to another, a piece of willful memory. Letters, then, are a later invention.

The same holds according to Robertson Smith (see note 74) for speech: the earliest speech, too, is a literary rather than a mating call. This may relate closely to the famous fact that children wish their fairy tales repeated *verbatim* — a fact all too often reported as typical infant conservatism, even though an anti-conservative child will exhibit this trait.

We have no record of the origins of writings other than Plato's narrative of the Egyptian myth, mentioned in note 65 above, and such records as preliterate people have, whether knots, cuts, or odd ideographs. Yet such signs, we know, overlap genuine writings, and the myth need not be rooted in the original event, but can rather be a later hypothesis. The records of the origins of speech must lie in the layers of language, and the dissection of language to chronological layers is barely begun, especially because the so-called Sapir-Whorf hypothesis is still too underdeveloped (see notes 11 to Section IX and 48 to Section XXIII below). See Owen Barfield, *Poetic Diction* (1927), third edition, Wesleyan University Press, 1973, Chapter 8, section 4, references to Max Müller and Anatole France, and to Rudolf Steiner on p. 207. His just critique should not be fused with his backward-looking views.

For the problem of the original contract see Section X and notes 72–75 to Section XV below.

72. The difference between mnemonic writing and communicational writing is very important and relates profoundly to the traditional difference between writing and speech. The major factor here is that of redundancy. Usually the mnemonic kind has less redundancy which is why at first one can read only familiar stuff. Indeed at times mnemonic writing has so little redundancy as to be useless (why did I make a knot in my handkerchief today?). Also the redundancy of mnemonic writing greatly differs from that of spoken sentences. The attempts to bring writing nearer to speech are in two very different directions, all too often confused by writers on style, namely the switch from a mnemonic type redundancy to communication type redundancy, and the attempt to make written words "sound" fresh and alive. Interestingly, the dialogue in foreign accent movies excludes certain kinds of native abbreviation but tends, in compensation, to produce certain spoken kinds of abbreviation and so it sounds more like the written word. See also note 55 to Section XXIII below.

73. Theories of the origins of language are the *bow-wow* theory (onomatopoeic theory); the *pooh-pooh* theory (emotive expressive); the *ding-dong* theory (innate or native meanings of certain sounds or sound-combination); the *yo-he-ho* theory (synchronizing work-effect by sounds); the *yam-yam* theory (remembering a good meal at times of hunger). The advantage of Robertson Smith's theory (see next note) is that the trill of the sound of the letter "l" as reflected in Hallelujah in the original speech conforms to all of them.

Criticizing all such theories as attempts to explain the beginning of language Otto Jespersen says, in *Language, Its Nature, Development and Origins*, George Allen and Unwin, London, 1922, 10th impression, 1954, p. 416:

> "It would seem to matter very little whether the first word heard by man was *bow-wow* or *pooh-pooh* . . . each . . . explains *parts of language,* but still only parts, and not even the most important parts . . . Again, with the exception of Noiré's theory [the *yo-he-ho*] , they are too individualistic and take too little account of language as a means of human intercourse. Moreover, they all tacitly assume that up to the creation of language man had remained mute or silent . . ."

The criticism is eminently valid if these theories come to explain the rise of language as such, but not if they come to solve Kipling's problem! What this criticism might indicate is that words conforming to any of these theories are more likely to be ancient than words not so explicable. This point is free of the criticism. (As to the criticism from silence, see next note.)

74. J. Robertson Smith, *Religion of the Semites*, end of the book. Smith found the prominence of the phoneme "l" in Hebrew calls like Hallelujah, as well as in Greek calls, very impressive as seemingly remnants of mere excited trills which became words. This may throw light on a totally different issue.

It was B. Malinowski who had the dilemma, what came first, word or sentence? See his review of M. M. Lewis's *Infant Speech: A Study in the Beginning of Language,* London, 1936, in *Nature,* Vol. 140, 1937, pp. 172–3, reprinted in Dell Hymes, ed., *Language in Culture and Society, A Reader in Linguistics and Anthropology,* Harper, New York, 1964, pp. 63–4. Both Wallace Chafe and A. S. Diamond assume the earliest speech constituted of imperatives, yet expressive short sentences are more like it. So, rather than the Hebrew Hallelujah, I suggest Alelai-li, which is expressive of a lament, in accord with Robertson Smith's idea but also with Max Müller, Karl Buhler, and others, of expressiveness as the lowest function of language.

It should be noted that the need to connect language to prelinguistic behavior is felt by both the Darwinians and the Humboldtians (see note 49 above and next note). Indeed, it was already noticed by Rousseau, no less: see note 46 to Section XIV. Of course this is but the problem akin to the one Kipling faced regarding writing.

That Freud, too, had his mind on the same question, may explain the passage, in his encyclopedia article on Psychoanalysis, 1923, *Standard Edition*, Vol. XVIII, pp. 235–254, p. 242:

> "Symbols, which raise the most interesting and hitherto unsolved problems, seem to be a fragment of extremely ancient inherited mental equipment. The use of common symbolism extends far beyond the use of a common language."

Of course, this is a cryptic passage, and were it not written by a highly influential thinker it would be better overlooked. As things are, it is interesting to ask how it relates to Robertson Smith's hypothesis, and to the current view of the primacy of the sentence (some symbolic expressions are, lo and behold, sentence-like, some alas! are not).

It should be noted that in all our discussions on memory and language the problem of truth, or even of propositions, hardly arises — as I think it should be since truth is a sophisticated idea, and comes to the fore only with the ability to show some critical acumen, namely, to go beyond the emotive and even descriptive level to that of criticism. (K. R. Popper, *Objective Knowledge*, Oxford, 1972, p. 120.)

75. The difficulty here outlined — of determining the origin or point of origin of mankind — is fully felt by a number of authors. I single out George Révèsz, *The Origins and Prehistory of Language*, translated from the German by J. Butler, Philosophical Library, New York, 1956. See, for example, p. 7 where language is declared a necessary condition for humanity and describes thought experiments to explain it: talking monkeys, non-talking humanoids, and the like. Révész discusses Humboldt's views of the origins of language (e.g. pp. 70, 76) in order to defend (p. 80) Humboldt's view "that language could not have been invented if something of its type had not previously been present in the human mind (*Über das Sprachstudium*, p. 247)"; and (p. 92) "in this sense W. von Humboldt is correct in believing that language arose 'at a single blow'. This idea was obviously not intended as a depiction of an historical fact, but simply as a way of representing the inseparability of the concepts of man and language." To stress this point Révész adds a note appealing to the fact that "one arrives at the same conception in principle on the basis of the theory of mutations."

The confusion still persists, and can be ascribed to empiricist prejudices. I say prejudices because associationism is meant to apply equally to man and beast and so it either explains language and is refuted by other animal's linguistic limitation or it does not explain language at all. See Ryle's critique of Chomsky quoted in note 48 above, and my review of the N. Chomsky/M. Black debate, "Listening in the Lull", *Phil. Soc. Sci.*, Vol. 2, 1972, pp. 317–322, p. 321.

On pp. 176–7 Révész explains how apparently continuous processes, such as the transition from high Renaissance to the Baroque are to be considered discontinuous if they are due to the appearance of new factors. This is, I think, the same view as advocated here.

76. See, for example, Stuart Hampshire's talk to the British Academy, "Spinoza and the Idea of Freedom", *Brit. Acad. London, Proceedings, 1960*.

77. An adequate description of the behaviorist's wish to ignore inner life can be found in Roger W. Sperry, "Mind, Brain, and Humanist Values", in John R. Platt, ed., *New Views of the Nature of Man, the Monday Lectures, 1965*, University of Chicago Press, Chicago and London, 1965, pp. 71–92, pp. 75f.

"The best way to deal with consciousness or introspective, subjective experience, they tell us, is to ignore it. Inner feelings and thoughts cannot be measured or weighed . . . or otherwise recorded or dealt with objectively by any scientific methodology . . .

. . . Consciousness, in the objective approach, is clearly made a second-rate citizen in the causal picture. It is relegated to the inferior status of (a) an inconsequential by-product, (b) an epiphenomenon (a sort of outsider on the inside), or most commonly, (c) just an inner aspect of the one material brain process . . .

Once we have materialism squared off against mentalism in this way, I think we must all agree that neither is going to win the match on the basis of direct, factual evidence."

Sperry's own view is emergentist and, in my opinion, unsatisfactory: yet his description of his opponents is a masterpiece of a fair yet damning report.

VIII   THE SUBTLETY OF BEHAVIORISM IS SHAM

Behaviorism is the best-known theory of man as animal.[78] Of course, it is most customary to view behaviorism as a branch of mechanism, and perhaps with justice. One of the most remarkable behaviorist scholars is, indeed, Grey Walter who has designed automata which can be taught by conditioning, and his famous mechanical tortoises are remarkably life-like in their attraction to light, in their ability to re-charge their electric batteries, in their ability to learn to circumvent obstacles, in their ability to surprise their makers.

Yet the leading behaviorist scholars, to wit, John Watson and B. F. Skinner, are staunch inductivists, and in their severe anti-speculative bent they refuse to pronounce their faith in mechanism, or even per-haps to commit themselves to such a faith even in the innermost of their minds.[79]

What both Watson and Skinner stress, and what the world unkindly and unjustly refuses to listen to, is a flat disclaimer.[80] They deny that they declare thoughts and emotions nonexistent; they deny that they find no room in the world for freedom and dignity.[81] Indeed, perhaps paradoxically, perhaps (as I think) illogically, Skinner's hope is to increase man's happiness, freedom, and dignity, by ignoring them, i.e., by doing his research while making no mention of them.[82] That is to say, he wishes to create more freedom by refusing to talk about free-dom, and likewise by preaching the faith in this refusal. This is a true advance over Christian Wolff who, we may remember, wanted to in-crease freedom and reduce suffering by the open denial of their very existence. I shall go further and say that there may, in principle, be some excellent sense in Skinner's idea, as the following discussion may illustrate.

That it is foolish to be a miser is a standard theme of all folk literature, historical or mythical, diversional or devotional — all to no avail. What is the moral which preachers draw from this failure? That the moral should be pushed ever harder, until it reaches its object. Yet why does the miser not listen? Because he thinks he can beat the system: other misers were unsuccessful, but he, being a better miser, will. And why does the preacher not take notice of the fact that the miser would not listen? Because he, too, thinks he can beat the system: other preachers were unsuccessful, but he, being the better preacher, will. The miser may also feel that unsuccessful as he is, he could be even worse off had he been too easy with his money. And, likewise, the preacher may feel that unsuccessful as his preaching is, it is better than no preaching. Neither will test his idea by desisting and looking at the facts to decide whether things deteriorate or not. Of course, they cannot: the experiment should be on a large scale, not regarding the vagaries of the fortunes of one man. And so the one person hoards and the other talks against hoarding; endlessly. Indeed, the one is part-and-parcel of the other's addiction.[83] (Generalizing this leads to anarchism: cops and robbers interact.)

Modern social science, more or less *en bloc*, declares its hostility to the preacher while having no love lost on the miser either. First came the Age of Reason and denied the existence in the last resort of all morality, all freedom and dignity, so as to get rid of the preacher once and for all. Then came those who felt it best not to preach, but without denying or affirming the existence of morality. Now they may be right. Perhaps we can see that by showing that the post-Wolffian stance of denying morality for morality's own sake is common to Marx, Freud, and Skinner. Perhaps, *à la* Marx, we should eliminate hoarding by eliminating insecurity, by instituting a socialist system; perhaps, *à la* Freud, we should psychoanalyze compulsive hoarding as rooted in anxiety; perhaps, *à la* Skinner, we can find the reinforcements which made a hoarder hoard and undo them by de-conditioning or by counterconditioning. Any act that will make an unhappy public menace into a happy and productive member of society surely beats preaching any day.

That perhaps there is no inconsistency here is very obvious: a thinker may speak on two different levels, and on the ordinary everyday level he may admit what on the more abstract and theoretical level he may deny. The moralist who denies morality is not necessarily different from the physicist who is willing to admit and deny, say, the smoothness of his desk or the existence of colors, almost in the same breath; meaning that we observe smoothness and colors yet in reality we only absorb electromagnetic energy deflected from arrays of atoms. Yet when it comes to behaviorism, things differ somewhat. Marx and Freud claim to be able to explain morality, good and bad —

the hoarder's and the preacher's, as well as their own. Not so Watson or Skinner.

It all began with Pavlov and his dogs.[84] What he illustrated is the thesis of associationism, and he did so by creating a new stimulus-response pattern by association, one which he viewed as a conditioned reflex, based on associations of unconditioned or natural reflexes. Briefly, the dogs heard a bell when food was offered and thus were led to salivate even when the bell rang with no food in sight. Moreover, Pavlov was thus able to convey the same message in different ways — sight, sound, smell — and so he could send some conflicting messages which drove his dogs crazy or neurotic as you wish.

The most surprising fact about this story is its utter insignificance.[85] One may well deny its insignificance offhand since it was hailed with great excitement and led to a series of waves of new psychological doctrines and sooner or later to a new psychotherapeutic method — Joseph Wolpe's — and is perhaps to date the most talked about psychological experiment. Yet what was new in it? After all, every mother knows that children salivate when they are told that food is coming just as much as dogs! We all associate faces with names, heat with fire — indeed associationists since John Locke and David Hume repeatedly claimed that the world was full of obvious instances of associations! If you do not like my examples because they are human and verbal, take cats and dogs in the literature of the Age of Reason and later. David Hume stresses that dogs associate fire with heat just as much as humans and just in the same associationist manner![86]

Perhaps one would object by saying that the pre-Pavlovian data are interpreted, and so less reliable than Pavlov's. One may say that here, in Pavlov's case, salivation was an unconditioned response to food which made by repetition a conditioned response to the bell. If so, this raises the question — it turns out to be central in post-Pavlovian psychology, especially that of Lorenz — what response of a dog, or a human, is unconditioned? The question sounds like, what response is inherited? But we know already that not every inborn response is inherited — indeed, we prefer not to talk of inborn response but of innate release mechanism: the very first operation of a mechanism already makes any later operation a response of one kind or another. And so we may never know what it is until we test it in all possible conditions that may release it! What response, then, is unconditioned? The peculiarity of Skinner is that he can overlook the question. He does not even have to know much about the existing responses of the subject, be the subject pigeon or child; as long as he knows some responses and can use them to create new ones, or to reinforce and weaken some old ones, he has work to do. And this keeps him busy. And this keeps him happy. (The work which, again, prevents thinking!)

One may also object that most associations we knew before Pavlov were cognitive, such as verbal responses. This will raise the question, was Pavlov's dogs' response to the bell cognitive or not? Did the dogs, in other words, think bells rang for food? The question is debated in the literature. What Skinner says to this is that he is not interested in the cognitive side of behavior, or the cognitive phenomena associated with behavioral ones: he plainly ignores them.

What Skinner learned from Pavlov, though, is the idea of positive and negative reinforcement. This, too, is not new. But simplified laboratory cases do begin with Pavlov.

Why is Skinner not interested in cognitive phenomena? He can do without them, he says; like Watson before him. This is plainly a mistaken view of his task: he is obliged to explain them, and he does not. He does not, because he deems it his job to construct theories on pure observations which are objective data. Are pure observations objective or subjective, though? Russell said that behaviorists are the most subjectivist since they only report their own subjective observations. On this he agreed with Kant.

Arthur Stanley Eddington spoke of his two desks in a classic passage: [87] there is my brown smooth wooden desk on which I rest my elbow, and there is the same desk, colorless, not smooth at all, consisting of myriads of nuclei and electrons in a vast vast vacuum. Which of the two shall it be? It can't be both! Eddington was no believer in induction. On the contrary, he believed that scientific theory is mere fiction. Man walks along the shore of the ocean of truth (Newton's metaphor) and sees mysterious footsteps in the sand (Robinson Crusoe's of course); following them he (Kant, of course) finds they are his own: scientific theories only reflect the mind of the scientist, not reality. The desk comprising protons and electrons is fiction, said Eddington, and the observed desk, the world of appearance, is the only one we know.

Eddington was in error. The desk which is a collection of electrons and protons does not explain away my observed desk. On the contrary, it is not any old collection of electrons and protons, it is that collection whose mass is so concentrated in a given space-time region, whose arrangement is so regular as to be, in the first approximation, a smooth surface, such a regular arrangement of atoms of such masses and distributions, that it is bound to reflect certain wavelengths of electromagnetic waves, thus appearing to be brown, etc.

Is vision objective or subjective? Does the world appear to the scientist without illusion? Is perception independent of who is the observer, or whether the observer is man or beast? Do we observe people and animals suffer? Behaviorism seems irrelevant to our attempt to explain the observed phenomena, such as those of suffering. Also it makes the scientist a special kind of being, who talks while he means what he says, yet who refuses to take notice of any meaning of any other behavior except the meanings of reports of other behaviorists. It is not surprising, then, that behaviorists reinforce each other positively even when they disagree (on secondary issues). Should a behaviorist succumb to negative reinforcement of anti-behaviorism? Not if his doctrine is true. But what is truth? Positive reinforcement? [88]

The behaviorist thinks he has a way out. He will appeal, again, to the two levels − of the everyday life where all speech has meaning, the speech of the behaviorist and of his subject alike; and of behaviorism, where meaning is totally ignored. But there is an error here. The two levels can both be employed either if one level explains the other − as an approximation, for sure, but not as a mere chimera − or if they are totally irrelevant to each other. Hence, the hypothesis the behaviorist employs is that meaning is irrelevant to speech. Indeed, how else can he claim to be able to study speech while ignoring meaning? Hence, whereas the behaviorist intends to suspend judgment about the unique in man, unintentionally he explains it away. Unintentionally he does what Koestler accuses him of doing, making man and pigeon inherently alike.

It was not my intention to demand that meaning should not be disregarded: for many studies it may well be ignored. Whereas when studying man as animal we cannot ignore his meanings, when studying the animal in man we often can − in studies related to his various mechanical, physiological, and neurological aspects. Of course, the effort is also extremely useful to push these studies as far as possible and see as much mechanics as possible even in what may have meaning. I mentioned already that this is what led Descartes to the marvelous (and true) conclusion that memory is mechanical; let me also mention the no less surprising result that epilepsy is neurophysiological and so can be induced in animals, that dreams occur in the animal world, that animal and man are excitable easily by certain very simple experiments. Indeed, these experiments may well exhibit what that incredible charlatan and mystic C. G. Jung called the universal unconscious symbolism. It is no accident that both artists and psychologists are looking for these and finding them, and showing that they relate to our good old internal release mechanisms (I.R.M.) which are themselves as devoid of mystery as any release mechanism made in the factory can be.

This raises a rather exciting problem. The mechanical aspect of us includes memory, and hence I can remember information I have never internalized, say if it belongs to a library accessible to me and if I know how to retrieve it from the library. This ability is in a sense privileged, as it is confined to the literate and even the trained in a fairly old-fashioned scholarly manner. In a sense, however, the ability is quite universal, as anyone can be trained to read and, at least, look up a dictionary or an encyclopedia, consult a trained librarian, etc. It is impossible here to draw a line between the universal, the I.R.M., and the specific — a specific language, training, literature available — since there is no innate literacy without a literature to be read and no literature to be read without some innate literacy. This seems to me a point of cardinal significance. Moreover, the I.R.M. is not fixed but given to development and deterioration, in the individual if not in the species. It looks Lamarckian to claim that acquired characteristics are inherited on occasion. As Schrödinger has argued,[89] that is not so: if the acquired characteristics of an animal make it alter its circumstances (say, by migration, or by rewarding literacy or physical prowess), the circumstances then may help alter criteria for him who is the fittest who, according to the rules of natural selection, shall survive. And indeed, we may well remember that the I.R.M. theory does come to replace a Lamarckian element in Darwin.

For a behaviorist who will only test memory performance, but refuse to discuss memory as such, the previous discussion makes no sense: yet, true or false, I would not like to disregard it; rather I would like to examine and explore it further.[90] To do so, all we have to see is how different a behavior pattern is when it involves meaning from when it does not. Let me try and show this.

Imagine that you are a migrant bird. One day you feel a strong urge to move. You cannot explain it, you do not know where you go. But you move, you keep moving, and each new position tells you with assuredness the direction that you should take, and not more than that. When you arrive at your destination the bond breaks and you know that you have arrived. But an accident happens to a friend of yours who has shared your experiences and he died on the way or, still worse, a broken wing forced him to settle in the wrong place which has the advantage of neither the old home nor the new.

Science fiction writers have often used this idea and embedded it in fine stories or dull ones, imbued it with the right atmosphere or the wrong one. Does this happen to mankind in reality, or is this a piece of pure fancy?

The answer seems to be dual: we do act like that, semiautomatically, both in adolescence and in obsession, both in cases where we act on racial memory of sorts (in the sense that migrant birds have it) and in cases of forcefully suppressed yet very active and serviceable memory.[91] And it is a very different kind of action from the one we still take as the paradigm under the classic rationalist influence, i.e., deliberate action. But what action is deliberate, what is compulsive or instinctive? Churchgoing of the most normal routine type is irrational to Søren Kierkegaard, instinctive to Konrad Lorenz, rational to Max Weber. Which is it? We simply do not know. Therefore, restriction on noticing deliberation and its significance is a great constraint on our attempts to comprehend ourselves.

All this may be fancy. Suppose you bare your teeth, I see this, and my adrenal gland starts secreting adrenalin into my blood in preparation for a possible clash with you. Lorenz will see this as an instinctive response. He defines instinct as reflex plus emotion; and, he would say, it is the reflex that matters. The behaviorist will say, when I see your teeth bared I need not think directly that it means you are hostile in order to release the adrenalin. Emotion is at most another side of secreting a hormone.[92]

This is why so much of the opposition to behaviorism is expressed in exciting experiments in perception. Contrary to the claims of the behaviorist, and in accord with much criminological data, especially courtroom evidence, I see you hostile, but I hardly see your teeth; we know of no correlation between a trigger and a response in humans as yet. Uexküll has argued that in some lower animals where a small number of responses is possible we can specify a one-to-one correlation between stimulus and response, and many examples have been adduced by him, by his disciple Lorenz, and by others. Suppose, as Lorenz does, that this is likewise true of man. Yet we do not know what stimulus relates in us to what response, and so we cannot avoid describing the stimulus, protem, as, it-looks-as-though-he-is-angry-with-me, or, she-really-appreciates-me.[93]

And this refutes Watson's celebrated claim that he can ignore with impunity all such expressions: when he ignores them he sinks into his own subjectivity.[94]

Notes to Section VIII

78. The behaviorist stress on the continuity of man in nature as expressed in the repeated analogy between human and animal languages has been noted in Chomsky's first Shearman Memorial Lecture in University College, London. See E. Gellner, "On Chomsky", reprinted in his *The Devil in Modern Philosophy*, Routledge, London and Boston, 1974, pp. 225–232, especially p. 231.

79. In a sense Freud and the behaviorists are worlds apart, the one ever so sensitive to innermost emotional states (as the movie *Freud* illustrates more vividly than any biography or pen-portrait except an occasional private letter by the master himself), the others vacillating between a cavalier dismissal of the inner world as irrelevant and an evangelistic dismissal of any claim for its existence as sheer humbug. Yet Freud, Pavlov, Watson, and Skinner, alike, saw man as a pleasure-seeking, pain-avoiding mechanism and preached enlightened self-interest. It is no accident that all of them denied the very existence of society in typical eighteenth-century mood. See also note 65 to Section XIX below.

The central behaviorist idea is the methodological view that introspection and such should be banished because they are not public data. It was repeatedly rejected by Bertrand Russell who said, in *Human Knowledge, Its Scope and Limits*, London and New York, 1948, Part One, Chapter V, The Science of Mind, p. 45, "This view", i.e. behavioristic methodology, "seems to me so absurd that if it were not widely held I should ignore it". Indeed, he thought it was solipsist.

80. I suppose it is Quixotic to hope that people will learn that behaviorism is not the denial of the existence of thought processes but the conduct of research while ignoring the question whether thought processes exist. See, for example Charles Taylor, "The Explanation of Purposive Behaviour", in R. Borger and F. Cioffi, eds., *Explanation in the Behavioral Sciences*, Cambridge University Press, 1970, pp. 49–79, p. 61 for the presentation of behaviorism as mechanism after it was correctly presented, p. 55, by the same author. Unfortunately, even behaviorists, such as Skinner, betray their mechanistic views at times – see note 77 to Section V above – and so make it hard for their readers to see the point of their subtlety. This is particularly so because the basis for behaviorism is inductivism; see R. A. Boakes and M. S. Halliday, "The Skinnerian Analysis of Behaviour", in Borger and Cioffi, *op. cit.*, pp. 345–374, pp. 346–7. Yet the very inductivism of these authors is presented in so lame a fashion that it is hard to complain about the public's inability to dissociate behaviorism from mechanism.

81. It is strange to note that Watson was particularly eager not to explain away language, or even thinking. "The behaviorist advances a natural science theory about thinking which makes it just as simple, and just as much a part of biological processes, as tennis playing" and "speaking overtly or to ourselves (thinking) is just as objective a type of behavior as baseball" pp. 238, and 6, 1930 edition of *Behaviorism*. Also quoted in R. A. Wilson, *The Miraculous Birth of Language*, New York, 1948, p. 90, note, where the author regretfully concludes that Watson nonetheless explains language away – as I conclude here, see below. Incidentally, tennis and baseball are not usually taken as paradigms of objectivity as they are by Watson — a remarkable Americanism, to be sure. Most social philosophers would take any specific game to be a local peculiarity and so not sufficiently objective. See Section XI below.

82. That Watson was preaching a specifically American version of the work ethic was noted by Bertrand Russell in "Behaviorism and Values", in *Skeptical Essays*, Allen and Unwin, London, 1928, 1934, pp. 89—98, especially pp. 93—4.

The moral attraction of Skinner, and its enhancement by a seemingly hard scientific stance has been observed by R. W. Friedrichs, "The Potential Impact of B. F. Skinner Upon American Sociology", *The American Sociologist*, Vol. 9, February 1974, pp. 3—8. See also Section IX below and notes.

83. The observation that preaching against addiction is an integral part of the addiction is in a sense ancient wisdom: "stolen water tastes sweet", says the temptress in *Proverbs* (9:17). Its full statement as an observation was made by W. Somerset Maugham, quite repeatedly, e.g. in his *The Razor's Edge* apropos of both drinking and hoarding and in his moving "Sanatorium" apropos of annoying a neighbor with a musical instrument. Yet the full statement I found only in Eric Berne, *Games People Play*, Grove Press, New York, 1964, pp. 75—8; I quote a brief passage from p. 76:

"There are a variety of organizations involved in "Alcoholic," some of them national or even international in scope, others local. Many of them publish rules for the game. Nearly all of them explain how to play the role of Alcoholic: take a drink before breakfast, spend money allotted for other purposes, etc. They also explain the function of the Rescuer. Alcoholics Anonymous, for example, continues playing the actual game but concentrates on inducing the Alcoholic to take the role of Rescuer. Former Alcoholics are preferred because they know how the game goes, and hence are better qualified to play the supporting role than people who have never played before. Cases have been reported of a chapter of A.A. running out of Alcoholics to work on; whereupon the members resumed drinking since there was no other way to continue the game in the absence of people to rescue."

This sounds very impressive, yet William Inge's 1950 play (1952 movie) *Come Back Little Sheba* should convince us that some throwbacks result from intense though perhaps unintended provocations and pressures. There is no doubt that obsession is extremely attractive to the obsessed, and that, following animal psychology's lead, we can take all obsessions as such to be throwbacks, regardless of whether and to what degree they are neurotic or psychotic. This is grudgingly admitted even by Eric Berne, who says (p. 78) "Nevertheless, A.A. is still for most people the best initiation into the therapy of over-indulgence."

Yet the real trouble is that most people were educated to be human robots, i.e. unable to decide, and this education survives all criticism of it. Indeed, a major means of perpetuating the existing educational method is to demand an unlimited number of further debates on the issue — see my "The Preaching of John Holt",

Interchange, Vol. 1, No. 4, 1970 — to demand that the reform should achieve more than is at all possible, and so on. All decidophobic techniques have been excellently exposed by Walter Kaufmann in his superb *Without Guilt and Justice: From Decidophobia to Autonomy*, Wyden, New York, 1973. But, of course, the decidophobe will first ignore this book and then subject it to endless disputes. The technique of endless disputes has been exposed in my "Was Wittgenstein Really Necessary?" unpublished because referees can open endless disputes. Our only hope, as Butler says and Russell agrees, is in the possible cumulative effect of the defects of the educational system: all autonomous rejects of the system, unite? Perhaps better not.

84. This is not to imply that Pavlov approved of his American followers. See the passage of his *Lectures on Conditioned Reflexes*, translated by W. Horsely Gantt, Martin Lawrence, International Publishers, London, New York, 1928, p. 329, quoted in Bertrand Russell, *The Scientific Outlook*, London and New York, 1931, 1962, Part 1, Chapter I, Section V, p. 52.

85. Bertrand Russell notes the utter banality of Pavlov's technique of driving his dogs into neurotic frenzy by the sad observation,
   "I am afraid a similar procedure is habitual in schools, and accounts for the apparent stupidity of many of the scholars."
   Bertrand Russell, *The Scientific Outlook*, London and New York, 1931, 1962, Part I, Chapter 1, Examples of Scientific Method, Section IV, Pavlov, p. 51.
   I wish I could consider the view quoted here as a joke, or at least as an exaggeration, yet I do think most professors surprisingly demanding and narrow-minded, pretentious and dogmatic, petty and moralistic, and opinionated even about the simplest questions concerning scholarship and its value or non-value.
   Pavlovian conditioning is extremely problematic even on the simplest laboratory level, and the story of dogs salivating at the sound of the breakfast gong is very misleading. For one thing, the example is question-begging in the sense that we do not know whether the conditioning is here of a reflex action, or not — see D. W. Hamlyn, "Conditioning and Behaviour", in Robert Borger and Frank Cioffi, eds., *Explanation in the Behavioral Sciences*, Cambridge, 1970, pp. 139—152. For another thing, we have not only stimulating but also inhibiting conditioning, and the two are intertwined — what looks as stimulating may well be deinhibiting, or even inhibiting! And from Pavlov to date the technicalities of inhibitions are unsurmountable. See S. Blough, review of R. A. Boakes and M. S. Halliday, *Inhibition and Learning, A Conference*, Essex, England, April 1971, New York, 1972, in *Science*, Vol. 178, 20 October 1972, pp. 295—6. (The way inhibiting may look like stimulating is the inhibition of a higher control that permits the release of a subdued lower and older one, as H. Jackson already noted.)
   R. B. MacLeod says, "to put it even more bluntly, the S—R models have seriously restricted the freedom of psychological inquiry", Joseph R. Royce, ed., *Toward Unification in Psychology, The First Banff Conference on Theoretical Psychology*, University of Toronto Press, 1970, p. 39.

86. David Hume, *A Treatise of Human Nature*, Section XVI, Of the reason of animals. "The resemblance between the actions of animals and those of men is so entire in this respect", he adds, "that any observation of any animal will do."

Sir Karl Popper quotes animal psychologists criticizing associationism in his *Conjectures and Refutations*, p. 44.

The interesting fact is that while Freud discovered neuroses Pavlov inflicted them on dogs, thus retaining the resemblance Hume was speaking of.

Not only in inductive knowledge, but also in non-inductive instinctive or *à priori* knowledge as it were, Hume compares men and animals,

". . . Though the instinct be different, yet still it is an instinct which teaches a man to avoid the fire: as much as that, which teaches a bird, with such exactness the whole economy and order of its nursery."

This passage is quoted by Noam Chomsky, *Problems of Knowledge and Freedom, The Russell Lectures*, Vintage Books, Random House, New York, 1971, 1972, p. 5, where Chomsky claims that twentieth-century empiricists still agree with Hume since his point is more or less part-and-parcel of empiricism (i.e. inductivism).

87. Eddington's classic double-faced — commonsense and scientific — desk occupies the Introduction to his *The Nature of the Physical World*, J. M. Deut & Sons, London, 1935. It came there, I suspect, from Berkeley's *Principles of Human Knowledge*, Section 3, perhaps via Russell's *Problems of Philosophy*, 1912, first chapter, fourth and second paragraphs from the end (the third paragraph in between appropriately enters the polarization between appearance and reality). What Eddington did was to replace appearance with common sense and reality with the scientific picture — of course in order to deny science of its traditional claim for realism. For more details see my "The Future of Berkeley's Instrumentalism", mentioned in note 54 to Section IV above.

88. Whether scientists are themselves conditioned is a real question. Russell quotes in the above-mentioned (note 85 above) *The Scientific Outlook*, p. 53, a very interesting passage from Pavlov's work, p. 41,

". . . At the beginning of our work and for a long time afterwards we felt the compulsion of habit in exploiting our subject by psychological interpretation . . . Gradually with the progress of our research these doubts appear more rarely, and now I am deeply and irrevocably convinced that along this path will be found the final triumph of the human mind over its innermost and supreme problem — the knowledge of the mechanism and laws of human nature."

And in his religious fervor Pavlov expresses his belief,

"Only science . . . will deliver man of his present gloom, and will purge him from his contemporary shame in the sphere of interhuman relations."

Pavlov's faith in science as the cure-all sounds fantastic to us, but it was prevalent both in the eighteenth century and, among those who were not swept by Romanticism, until World War II. Thus we see for example C. H. Waddington, *The Scientific Attitude*, Penguin, 1941, 1943, Chapter V, finds a severe defect in science that it has not solved all our problems, yet in Chapter X the same faith in science is reaffirmed.

Science fiction still keeps the faith alive. Thus, rather than solve educational problems, science fiction writers prefer to fill people's brains with libraries by sheer mechanical means. This accords with Descartes' theory and, at least, makes all science fiction writers know, what school teachers do not, that memory is not education. Back to Pavlov, and his teaching of dogs and his learning about them.

On the whole, it is amazing to me how insensitive thinkers are when discussing according to one set of rules the correctness of another set of rules. Hume, for example, in his *Treatise,* explicitly claims that his view that there is no confirmation, is confirmed. These inconsistencies can, of course, be resolved by the application of a different level's argument. But why do so? W. Kohler, for example, says, *The Mentality of the Apes,* translated by Ella Winter, 2nd revised edition, Routledge, London and Boston, 1973, pp. 3—4, 149, 228—9, 267, that perhaps apes' mentality differs from a human's (he believed in induction). Only Niko Tinbergen tried to apply his (Lorenzian) theory of animal learning to human learning — but not to his own development of his own theory of learning.

89. See note 48 to Section VII for the demarcation rejected here. For Schroedinger's argument see note 60 to Section VII above. See also my review of Popper's *Objective Knowledge,* cited in note 58 to Section IV above. In the same vein we may say, as more and more anthropologists do say, the interaction between hand and brain is via the invention and use of tools: the genetic advantage of a better brain is exhibited in its use, and the use is, in early stages, largely manual.

90. As to storage of remembered items proper, consider the following two ideas. J. Z. Young, *A Model of the Brain,* Oxford, 1964, p. 180, suggests that there is a genuine failure to store information in long-range memory banks; this, he says, explains why old people remember clearly old events but not equally well new ones. W. Fishbein has claimed that the act of such storage occurs in R.E.M. sleep (see W. Fishbein et al., "The Effects of R.E.M. Sleep Deprivation etc.", *Psychophysiology,* Vol. 7, 1971, p. 299; see also Z. Giora, "The Function of the Dream: A Reappraisal", *Amer. J. Psychiat.,* Vol. 128, 1972, p. 1067). If so, then we can test these two hypotheses by stimulating R.E.M. sleep in old people, etc.

91. The feeling of knowing every next step but not the whole way is commoner than expected. Mechanics and bank clerks concentrating on a job in the midst of distraction have it; so do trackers; so do scouts who walk on a barely familiar terrain; so do visitors of childhood scenes; so do beginning lovers. The sense of immense mystery is at times present, at times absent, but inessential. Such experiences, so common, defy our psychological knowledge as the greenness of grass defied physical knowledge but a century ago. (Freud discussed a pathology resembling cases of such memory — not believing that a true case exists. See note 31 to Section III above.)

A less obvious and more common behavior pattern of native knowledge than the move in a definite direction, as described above, is the inexplicable inability to concentrate on whatever one is doing, known as strange restlessness — which is explicable as a search for a definite yet unknown stimulus which starts a new chain of behavior. In the following Craig-Lorenz schema this restlessness plays similar roles. There are specific instances of a missing link in a complex, largely instinctive, chain of action; the links can be acquired only in the presence of a given specific stimulus. The animal will then become increasingly restless until the required stimulus accidentally occurs and enables it to proceed with its job to complete the schema and thus to be able to accomplish a complete meaningful task (such as building a nest).

What the Craig-Lorenz scheme clearly displays is the case where the act of learning and the act of keeping the business of living going — in the schema at hand the two coincide — may be met by no better means than sheer randomizing. This proves that randomizing is a form of learning and of improving and of performing a given task, yet that it is both a highly inefficient mode and a very rare one. Yet cyberneticists have no other way than programming or randomizing or partial programming and completing the task by randomizing. No doubt, there are other processes which are highly random and inefficient in the biological world; by and large, their conspicuousness is evidence of their rarity, and this *prima facie* leads us to question the truth of Darwinism. Darwinists, however, might take this in good grace as a set of challenges.

92. Konrad Lorenz, in his perhaps not very famous "Inductive and Teleological Psychology" of 1942, *Studies in Animal and Human Behavior*, Vol. 1, translated by Robert Martin, Harvard University Press, Cambridge, Mass., 1970, pp. 351—70, expresses hostility and contempt, unusual even by the standards accepted by Central European Professors, to anyone who dares deviate from humble induction and industrious and indefatigable search for causal explanation. (Self-righteous humility is, no doubt, the best cause for a chuckle.) The translator, Martin, says in his foreward (p. x), "Lorenz seems quite definitely to" — what a lovely expression of ambivalence in the form of a mixture of scientific caution and dogmatic fanaticism — " ... have ... remove(d) the last shrouds of mysticism surrounding the governing factors of behavior ...". In his foreword to Vol. II, 1971, Martin bitterly complains against those who view Lorenz as a reductionist, referring to Lorenz's own declaration that he is not. If the idea that all behavior can be causally explained is not reductionism, then there must be causal laws which are not a part of physics. I wonder if this is what Lorenz has in mind, but I suppose it is. It is a bit puzzling that Lorenz should seek causal mechanisms yet not be a reductionist; this, however, is indeed what he seems to assert. See final section of his "Establishment of the Instinct Concept", *ibid.*, Vol. 1, pp. 307—12. See, however, note 95 to Section IX below.

93. All this is similar to J. Fodor's critique of reductionism (*Psychological Explanation: An Introduction to the Philosophy of Psychology*, New York, 1968). Fodor says that defining an entity by its function allows us to construct it in very

diverse methods — as many as our imagination allows — and so even if it happens that a given function is performed by one given material thing they are not identical: suppose all air filters are today made of material x, it is still nonsense to say air filters are made of x instead of all air filters today happen to be made of x. Hence, says Fodor, even if each psychological state corresponds as it happens to some natural state, this does not ensure reductionism. The reductionist may retort that an argument good enough for filters is not good enough for gills, lungs, etc., since life is natural rather than artificial, and so not given to arbitrary variations. Yet the very same reductionist will be all too ready and willing to reduce ever so many seemingly functional moves to chance (see note 91 above). He will then have to explain why things are not chance-like whereas processes very much are. He may then take a different route and define air filter, artificial or natural, by describing all possible materials it can be made of, all structures it can have, itc. Yet the very reason for which he will lump them all together will still be the function of our air filter! I think this makes Fodor's argument unanswerable. The only ways open to a reductionist, then, are either to declare the lists — not yet available! — quite arbitrary, or else to omit all these lists and forget all about functions, here and now. Either move will impoverish his science beyond recognition.

Yet all this is hypothetical. For the time being we simply do not know what functions as what.

The claim that we know the stimuli which make us conclude statements of facts is a corollary of sensationalism, i.e. the doctrine of the primacy of sense data as sources of information. Indeed, sensationalism is a much more deeply seated prejudice than the claim that we know our primary sensa. For, when that claim was satisfactorily refuted, sensationalism was restored with the aid of an auxiliary (and quite *ad hoc*) hypothesis that we once knew them but now forget, just as it is conceivable that literacy may evolve to the point that readers may not notice the letters of the alphabet (indeed, beginners read letters and graduate to reading words). This *ad hoc* hypothesis is funny, because whereas we begin to read when we are conscious and aware enough about reading, we perceive before we have any degree of consciousness or awareness.

Gestalt psychology is largely a series of experiments in perception where subjects cannot discover the elements of perception that go into their perception as a whole, plus attempts at explaining these experiments. Now, the classical perception theory centers on physical objects and so, to a very large extent, do Gestalt experiments. Even so, Gestaltists have shown that a major component in my perception as a whole of a physical object is its meaning to me. But when the object is an animal, particularly a human being, then the meaning of his appearance to him, and my conjecture about it, become of a crucial significance for my perception of him.

This is where Jakob von Uexküll's conception of *Umwelt* becomes so crucial, not, as he thought, for the perception an animal has of its surrounding, but rather for the ethologist's perception of the animal. (Uexküll, to expand this point, was a Kantian who extended Kant's transcendentalism to animals, thereby hoping to "objectivize" Kantianism, though his followers took this to be a universalized subjectivism. See K. R. Popper, *Conjectures and Refutations*, London and New York, 1963, and later editions, Chapter 20, "Humanism and Reason", pp. 377–84. In truth, however, Uexküll was not Kantian enough.)

94. The critique of behaviorism presented here is composite and can be found in diverse works, from Russell's critique to Chomsky's. The odd thing about it is its obviousness: one should have expected a doctrine to be dead after such a flogging administered to it so many times. Yet, behaviorism is a strong myth, resting on the western intellectual tradition as a whole, on both inductivism and subtle moralizing, and on what Walter Kaufmann has labeled decidophobia.

The worst about behaviorism is that it has opened the door to vulgar behaviorism — a confusion some of its adherents are addicted to, between the habit that is the source of all learning according to Hume and all his modern followers, Skinner included, and the bad habit that is smoking, drinking, or lying to one's wife. I often wondered how a stern moralizing could also be a cheap means of condoning. That certain versions of Christianity share this quality only strengthens the puzzlement. Here we need both Freud's and Lévi-Strauss's theory of the reversal of symbolisms to their opposite (in the emotional and the cognitive senses, respectively), especially under stress (emotional and cognitive, again). It explains why people of poor emotional and intellectual makeups are given to such confusions, and to theories that seem — quite erroneously — to condone them. But vulgar behaviorism, like vulgar Marxism, is but an object of inquiry, not a target for any serious criticism.

IX BEHAVIORISM AS A STERN MORALIZING

Behaviorism is the most elusive doctrine in the field. Taken to mean Watson's theory, it is so obviously out of date. Lorenz said already in the thirties that it so obviously fails to apply even to bird behavior that he would not bother to refute it.[95] Even as taken to mean nothing but the doctrine of positive and negative reinforcement, it is out of date. In his *Beyond Freedom and Dignity*, B. F. Skinner quotes Koestler's characterization of this theory (behaviorism) in this way (positive and negative reinforcement) and says that in this formulation it is fifty years out of date (i.e. Pavlovian rather than Skinnerian; see above). But he does not add a correction, does not spot the error, does not compare it with a more modern alternative. This way Skinner can have the cake and eat it too (Skinnerism is really Pavlovian at heart; see above).[96]

There is an immense attraction to the theory that conduct is towards pleasure and away from pain, that conduct creates better conduct, i.e., learning is reinforcement, that knowledge is improved conduct.[97] Locke took it for granted, even Spinoza preached a moral variant of it (not regarding learning, though) as the doctrine of enlightened self-interest. Hume took it as both self-evident and commendable that passion is and should be the mistress of reason. Pavlov proved it empirically by contriving an exceptionally artificial experiment, whose very value as an experiment is highly questionable, yet the whole learned world applauded his effort as a real breakthrough.[98] Why this excitement?

The question was raised already by Nietzsche.[99] But he had no answer. He found the question, I suppose, when he read Heine's answer to it,[100] but he could not endorse that answer. Jeremy Bentham, said Heine,[101] really didn't believe in pain and pleasure, but in honest to goodness ethics; yet he found utility to be the best lever to lift John Bull.[102] The Englishman is most reluctant to appear upright but will gladly do the right thing when it looks useful. This idea has been endorsed recently by Karl Popper, Michael Polanyi, and Raymond Aron who see in Marxism such an attraction: Marxism demands self-sacrifice in the guise of self-interest.[103]

I think Heine's answer has more to it than meets the eye. The most terrible thing and the most hopeful thing about behaviorism is that it takes reward to be part and parcel of the process of learning, and learning of living. In a true Protestant manner it unfortunately takes reward not as something enjoyable in itself but as a stage pushing us towards still better things in life. Yet at least in that manner it fortunately does commend reward. Let me expand these two conflicting aspects.

Reward as a part of a development is very different from reward as a value in itself. Take Tolstoy's story of the two brothers. They were looking together for their places in the world and parted when they came to a crossroad, one leading to a warrior's life of fame and deeds, the other to a farmer's life of work and security. The warrior ended up as a refugee in the farmer's secure home. The farmer defended his choice as the better one since he had a humble fortune whereas his brother had nothing. The warrior protested with the story's punchline: but I have my memories. The story is disturbing, and it is not easy to find why. The reason why, I suggest, is that the pleasure of memories is not a part of any process, not a pleasure a Protestant may commend. The idea was enlarged in William Golding's *Free Fall*, where the hero cannot enjoy the fruit of his labor when the labor is over. The same idea is expressed more directly in Robert Louis Stevenson's *Apology for Idleness*, Jerome K. Jerome's *Idle Thoughts of an Idle Fellow* and Bertrand Russell's *In Praise of Idleness*, where Russell ruefully confesses an inability to enjoy pointless games and finds it to be a fault in his puritanical upbringing.

Nowhere is the difference between the pleasure as part of the process and the pleasurable end so poignant as in John Stuart Mill's *Autobiography* where he tells how he had a breakdown when he asked himself whether he would be happy had he achieved his end and answered his own question in the negative. Nor did Mill ever come as close to anti-puritanism as Russell; for, rather than praise pleasure as an end in itself and look for it, he gave it up as an end in itself and declared the smooth running of the machine to be just one of the many ends, rather than the one and only end towards which the machine operates!

And yet, even this is a concession, and so an improved version of puritanism. For, the initial moralistic work ethic prefers to see man work in the sweat of his brow and gnash his teeth yet go on working. The misanthropy of this idea was masked by the argument that pleasure makes man lazy, that if man learns to work under any condition then we need not fear the conditions that might relax his effort. This argument is so obviously false, that it only survives as a thin mask of misanthropy. As Freud has noticed, its application has ruined so many people and made them drop out of the labor force as criminals or as mental cripples.[104] And in his pitifully obsessive misanthropy the moralist always adds condemnation of the poor bastard who was too broken-up to work, even if what broke him up was the moralizing itself.

Bertrand Russell tells this in his *Autobiography*. Once, when his tutor left him to go home but was stopped at the door by Uncle Rollo for a brief conversation, young Bertie felt that they were talking about him and that they were pleased. He concluded that they were pleased with his studies and this was an enormous source of encouragement for him. It must have been an immense hunger for reward, for a positive reinforcement, that made the old Russell remember this incident of his youth and record it in the story of his life. He was not satisfied by the encouragement; he was suicidal as a youth, and hungered for positive reinforcement all his life. Of course, his being suicidal, etc., is only partly due to his upbringing — it is also partly due to his extreme sensitivity. Otherwise we would have many more attempted suicides on our hands than we do, since puritanism is still commoner among teachers than we would admit.[105]

The proof is in Skinner's teaching machines. Skinner has built them out of expediency, when he found that teachers behave so poorly even by comparison with the little that he expected from teachers. His machines fully comply with his expectations. The machines simply either tell the students that they have answered a given question correctly and deserve a compliment, or else they patiently repeat the question. Also, they correctly answer any well-formulated question put to them, without yelling at their students that they ought to know the answer by now.[106]

Considering teaching machines as teachers makes one shudder, yet comparing them with the average teacher of today one must admit they are far from being the worst. This gives us an insight into the tremendous power of goodness: how much schoolchildren depend on the occasional humane teacher they meet. It also gives us an insight into the power of the inertia in human nature: Skinner is but a disciple of the eighteenth-century school of psychology, yet the very mention of his machines suffices to throw many teachers into hysterical fits. It takes centuries to implement even marginally an idea that is so commonplace as that of humans as pleasure-seekers.[107]

But all hedonistic theories, old-fashioned or progressive, Hume's or Skinner's, have been amply refuted, not only in learned books of philosophers, psychologists, historians, and sociologists, not only in novels of highbrow quality, but even in detective novels.

I have in mind, most particularly, Raymond Chandler's last novel, *The Long Good-Bye*. Chandler's narrator himself refutes Hume's moral theory, in being a most unpleasant decent citizen. He plays the game by the rules as best he can, but his clients are crooks and he has to serve them and the law. He finds that he can play better and closer to the rules when he has a tough character, and he sees to it that no one else but he pays for the toughness of his character, though the price paid thus is very high, to wit, loneliness. In the novel at hand Chandler goes further and describes as the hero a Humean character, one who combines the useful with the agreeable, just as Hume prescribes, and who even plays by some sort of book of rules, yet who lacks moral fiber, or perhaps merely moral stamina, and whose friendship is finally rejected by the narrator.[108]

Skinner's *Beyond Freedom and Dignity* may be easily dismissed on the ground that its author thinks he explains freedom and dignity by explaining them away. Yet dismissing him we may overlook his all too just critique of what he calls the freedom literature. His strictures of the freedom literature are largely valid. It also tries to construct the essence of freedom (and of dignity) by what turns out to be a utopian dream, and rather a naïve one at that. Indeed, here he has a strong advantage, since his *Walden II* is not naïve at all, and quite realizable, heaven forbid. The conclusion to draw from this is that the freedom literature centers on wrong issues. Raymond Chandler knew this already, and Thomas Szasz has shown that real moral issues which teachers and school psychologists face are hardly different from Chandler's private eye's: when morality and the social order clash, what do you do then? It is silly to suggest that my duty to my aunt is the real moral issue; even if the sacrifice my aunt requires is much too high, the problem is hardly serious if convention sets a reasonable limit to it, usually in the form of a balance between the sacrifice I should make to my aunt and that to my wife and children; even to my own mental well-being, says Philip Roth.[109] But when a psychologist is forced by school to tell about a pupil who has confided in him, when a detective is forced by the police to tell about a client, what then? Ethics, then, is not the pursuit of an ideal, but the search for it through the struggle with the real.[110] Moralizing politics is not only politics, it is also ethics.[111]

Notes to Section IX

95. For Lorenz's contempt for behaviorism see end of his introduction to "The Establishment of the Instinct Concept" in Vol. 1 of his *Studies in Animal and Human Behavior*, translated by Robert Martin, Harvard University Press, Cambridge Mass., 1970, and *Instinct Behavior, The Development of a Modern Concept*, translated by Claire H. Schiller (introduction by Karl S. Lashley), International Universities Press, New York, 1957, where its label is more adequately translated, "The Conception of Instinctive Behavior". See aslo Lorenz's introduction to Vol. II of Martin's translation, 1971, pp. 15, 18, 23.

Whereas in his early works Lorenz identified the label "behaviorism" with Watson's theory and therefore refused to criticize it, in his *Evolution and Modification of Behavior* of 1965, beginning of Chapter 2, he defines the same term in the broad sense and devotes the whole volume to its criticism. Here even Lorenz, for whom criticism so often equals disrespect, shows that criticism is to be leveled only at respected opponents.

96. B. F. Skinner, *Beyond Freedom and Dignity,* Knopf, New York, 1971, pp. 165ff., paperback, Bantam, New York, 1972, pp. 157ff.

97. A discussion of the behavioristic temptation and the way to resist it by observing non-behavioristic facts is forcefully presented in Edgar Tranekjaer Rasmussen's beautiful "On the Concepts 'Being Conscious of Something' and 'That of Which One is Conscious' ", in Jaakko Jarvinen, ed., *Contemporary Research in Psychology of Perception, in Honorem Kai von Fieandt Sexagenari,* Porvoo, Werner, Söderstrom Osakeyhtiö, Finland, 1969.

98. For a history of detailed and quite devastating criticisms of Pavlov's experiment see Marjorie Grene, *Approaches to a Philosophical Biology*, Basic Books, New York and London, 1968. I am impressed with both the 1935 criticism of F. J. J. Buytendijk and Helmuth Plessner, as well as the 1934 criticism by Kurt Goldstein — Grene's pp. 128ff. and 243ff.

99. Friedrich Nietzsche, *Beyond Good and Evil, Prelude to a Philosophy of the Future*, 1886, translated with commentary by Walter Kaufmann, Vintage Books, New York, 1966, Part 8, pp. 252—3. Calling these ideas English, however, and the English the source of all European mediocrity, including the Enlightenment, is sheer rubbish, of course.

100. Friedrich Nietzsche, *Ecce Homo*, 1908, translated by Walter Kaufmann, Vintage Books, New York, 1967, Why I am so Clever, §4: "The highest concept of the lyrical poet was given to me by Heinrich Heine. . . . He possessed that divine malice without which I cannot imagine perfection . . ."

101. See Heinrich Heine, *Religion and Philosophy in Germany, A Fragment*, translated by John Snodgrass, Beacon Press, Boston, 1959, p. 65,
   "Materialism has fulfilled its mission in France. It is perhaps at the present moment busy accomplishing the same task in England; and it is on the system of Locke that the revolutionary sects in that country, especially the Benthamites, the apostles of utility, take their stand. These latters are men of powerful intellect; they have possessed themselves of the right lever with which John Bull may be set in motion. John Bull is a born materialist, and his Christian spiritualism is for the most part traditional hypocrisy . . ."
"To myself" says Sir Henry Sumner Maine in a similar vein (*Lectures on the Early History of Institutions*, Lecture XIII, 7th edition, Kennikat Press, Port Washington, N.Y., 1914, 1966, pp. 338—9), "the most interesting thing about the theory of utility is that it presupposes the theory of Equality . . ." And, on the last page, "Bentham was in truth neither a jurist nor a moralist in the proper sense of the word. His theories are not on law but on legislation . . ."

102. The utilitarian (or eudaimonic, perhaps) reduction of altruism to egoism must explain altruism as a brand of egoism. This leads many to think that there is no such thing as altruism, or even that every expression of altruism is a hypocrisy which is, of course, a special and intense and wicked version of egoism.
   The best refutation of this — sophomoric, need one say — view is the altruism exhibited in the relations between parent and offspring or between spouses, which are certainly both highly altruistic and highly egoistic.
   The classical eudaimonistic ethic, whether that of Socrates or of Spinoza, assumes the existence of altruism, right and wrong, egoism, right and wrong, and self-knowledge; it also takes it for granted that right altruism is both egoistic and rooted in self-knowledge.
   The problem of modern eudaimonism is, obviously, epistemological: what is self-knowledge and how is it attainable. But here I do not discuss epistemology

and take skepticism for granted; I discuss this in my "Unity and Diversity in Science" mentioned above, note 8 to Section I. A skeptical theory of knowledge — a theory of partial knowledge — is a matter for separate debate. See my "Imperfect Knowledge", in *Philosophy and Phenomenological Research*, Vol. 32, June 1972, pp. 465–477 (reprinted in my *Science in Flux*, Reidel, Dordrecht and Boston, 1975). I have discussed the reduction of altruism to egoism in my "On Pursuing the Unattainable", *Boston Studies in the Philosophy of Science*, Vol. 11, 1974, pp. 249–257.

103. The idea that Marxism is attractive because it is moralizing while denying that it moralizes, thus lending its preaching the authority of scientific fact is not new. It has been elaborated by K. R. Popper in Chapter 22 of his *The Open Society and Its Enemies*. It was repeated by M. Polanyi, e.g. in his *The Tacit Dimension*, Doubleday, 1966, Chapter 3, p. 59, and by Raymond Aron in his *Opium of the Intellectuals*, translated by Terence Kilmartin, Norton, New York, 1957, 1962, pp. 283–4; see also pp. 289 and 293 and comments below.

The view of H. B. Acton, *The Illusion of an Epoch*, London, 1954, p. 253 that Marx's theory of praxis "is a sort of idea in which ethics and science are mixed up together" is a better reading of both Marx and his ethos. As Acton notes (*loc. cit.*), a rudiment of this idea can be found in Bacon (*Novum Organum,* I, Aph. 129, *Valerius Terminus, Works*, eds. R. L. Ellis, J. Spedding, and Th. Heath, London, 1859, Vol. 3, p. 232).

It seems clear to me that the chief reason for the popularity of both eudai-monism and naturalism in the Age of Reason is, as Popper puts it, the view of the preacher as an evil hypocrite, so strongly expressed by Marx. It was Heinrich Heine who was first to ask, in his *Religion and Philosophy in Germany*, of every philosophy what is its moral import, and judge it on that ground. He thus discovered people's predilection for covert preaching, quoted in note 102 above. Yet his work was ignored, because it was deceptively easy. The same fate befell Russell's *Skeptical Essays*, which examines the ethical implications of Bentham's doctrine, "The Harm that Good Men Do", pp. 109–120, of behaviorism, see note 82 above, and of Marxism. He anticipated the discovery which Popper, Polanyi, and Aron make separately, and says, in Chapter XI, p. 136, "Although Marx professed to regard men as neither good nor bad, but merely embodiments of economic forces, he did in fact represent the bourgeois as wicked, and set to work to stimulate a fiery hatred of him in the wage-earner." See also note, p. 137, "The theoretical part of *Capital* . . . It's sole purpose is to make the reader feel . . . righteous indignation. . . ."

This comes close to George Orwell's analysis, in his diverse writings, see the Penguin edition of his *Collected Essays, etc.*, index, Art. Intelligentsia, that some intellectuals endorse left-wing political ideas and ideology, including Stalinism, out of sheer power worship. This view is in part endorsed by J. L. Talmon, *The Age of Violence*, and is opposed to the view of Popper, Polanyi, and Aron. Needless to say, Russell is cleverly situated in between allowing for diverse possibilities.

It is too early perhaps, to give an overall view of the history of the left wing in our own century, but I wish to draw attention to the fact that the personal testimonies, especially of Arthur Koestler and of Ignazio Silone, in R. H. Crossman, ed., *The God that Failed,* Harper, New York, 1949, 1963, are very convincing and indicative of as much sincerity and good will as can be expected of ordinary mortals; indeed, perhaps quite extraordinary. Also, both illustrate cases of individuals who had enough moral fiber to follow the dictate of their conscience when this was to join the Communist Party but not when this was to leave it. They explain it by reference to the confusion and corruption which the party manages to bestow on its members. This is somewhat different from Orwell's explanation by reference to left-wing intellectuals' power worship but agrees with his observation of the same facts. It is, I suppose, the fate of all fanatics that they are prone to bend morality for the good of the cause, and so to lie, and so to isolate themselves intellectually (lies and rational debate do not mix), and so to condemn themselves to intellectual stagnation and confusion.

The difference between nineteenth-century and twentieth century left-wing politics is obviously quite important. I do endorse Karl Popper's view of the older movement as a movement which often could and did show compassion to workers and their plight. Even Marx expressly advised his followers to join workers in their fight for any just cause, even though it be doomed to failure, as this will unite and educate them for the revolution. See his "Wage, Labor and Capital" and "Wages, Price and Profit". Likewise, Rosa Luxemburg saw the crux of the difference between orthodox Marxism and revisionism in their answer to the question, can trade unions succeed in their attempt to improve the workers' lot? See her *Selected Political Writings,* edited and introduced by Dick Howard, Monthly Review Press, New York and London, 1971, pp. 85ff.

Nowadays, however, Marxists oppose the democratization and the enhancement of the quality of working life. Having no compassion they are ready to sacrifice workers on the altar of the Revolution. See Judith Buber Agassi, "Morality in Industry: The Enhancement of the Quality of Working Life", first section, to be published in the proceedings of the Haifa International Symposium on Ethics in the Age of Pervasive Technology. See also her "The Israeli Experience in the Democratization of Work Life", *Sociology of Work and Occupations,* Vol. 1, No. 1, February 1974, pp. 52–81.

See also Raymond Aron, *Opium of the Intellectuals, op. cit.,* pp. 74ff. and 79ff. for the perverse attitude of left-wing intellectuals towards workers. I confess I find the book more of a plethora of very stimulating suggestions than a penetrating analysis. Especially as a portrait of the intelligentsia and as an answer to why are (some!) intellectuals fanatics, I find the analysis questionable. For example, it is quite conceivable that, as Russell has observed ("Faith and the Mountains"), fanaticism, or love of power, etc., are not more prevalent now than in earlier times, no more among intellectuals than in the population at large (though it may be more pernicious; which is the point of Julien Benda). The major thrust of Aron's *Opium,* and an excellent one at that, is against the view of Stalinism as a mere episode or aberration in the history of Communism (as noted too by Solzhenitsyn, *Gulag Archipelago,* I, Ch. 2). Yet the same ought to be said, *pace* Aron, about McCarthyism: the fact that the analyses of these two phenomena are so very different does not make either less indigenous to its own milieu: it is simply that the milieux are very different too; that, in particular, the disappearance of millions into concentration camps is inconceivable in the United States today, but at least possible if not actual in Russia today.

Since all this centers round the question, how much do intellectuals worship power, it may be relevant to mention an important view to the contrary, that of the opening paragraph of Preston King, *Fear of Power, An Analysis of Anti-Statism in Three French Writers,* Cass, London, 1967. He says that

"power is no more inherently evil than it is inherently good; that where social organization exists, political power exists too; that the power which such organization yields is not completely a matter of consent; and that neither force nor consent can serve as an exclusive criterion of just action in politics."

King's thesis is that some intellectuals hate power, preach keeping away from it, and thereby jettison social and political responsibility. (See also note 21 to Section XI below.)

I think it is true that both the love for power and the hatred of it are significant factors in individuals' — at times in the same individual's — political attitude. All this requires much further study, and seems to me to indicate that it matters less to which social class a person belongs than to which intellectual milieu he owes his prejudices. The philosophical, methodological, social, even artistic, parts of one's background tend to interact strongly even when — particularly when — producing sympathy with tyranny.

104. See George Santayana, *The German Mind: Philosophical Diagnosis*, Thos. Crowell Co., New York, 1968, p. 109:

"Both Christianity and romanticism had accustomed people to disregard the intrinsic value of things. Things ought to be useful for salvation, or symbols of other greater but unknown things: it is not to be expected that they should be simply good in themselves. This life was to be justified, if justified at all, only as servile work or tedious business may be justified . . . Unless some external and ulterior end could be achieved by living, it was thought that life would be vanity . . ."

There is a famous Talmudic saying that stopping one's study of the law to enjoy the beauty of a tree is already risking one's own soul (see also p. 178, "German religion and philosophy are drawn, by a curious irony, from Jewish sources . . .").

Freud noted with grim bitterness that stern moralistic education may push one into a life of crime, no less, and in a famous work of his — *The Id and the Ego.* Yet the social reformist in Freud still awaits discovery. Already Russell has complained that Freud's complaint about children's life of misery has been cruelly ignored. Indeed, I find that even George Orwell's moving autobiographical "Such Such Were the Joys", not to mention Butler's *The Way of All Flesh*, has done too little to alleviate the misery of excessive moralizing to children. I suppose unless the sensible attempt to democratize schools succeeds there will be little hope for radical change – not to mention the attempts to democratize both mental homes and jails, which are urgent in different ways, which proved possible and beneficial, (unless we are ready for the better reform of abolishing them) – but to no avail.

105. For Russell's lifelong strong need for expression of approval, see R. Crawshay-Williams Rupert, *Russell Remembered,* Oxford University Press, London, 1970: *The Autobiography of Bertrand Russell: 1872–1914*, Allen & Unwin, London, 1967, pp. 83–6, 93. These passages are discussed at length in B. Scharfstein's forthcoming *Philosophers As Human Beings.*

106. My account of Skinner's teaching machines is slightly oversimplified. I omit other commonsense factors. For example, Skinner says an obvious and old truth: "To acquire behavior a student must engage in behavior". See his "Why We Need Teaching Machines", *Harvard Educational Review,* Vol. 31, 1961, pp. 377–398, p. 389. Commonsense as this is, teachers are still not familiar with it. Speaking of elementary or common techniques, Max S. Marshall has, in *Two Sides to a Teacher's Desk*, New York, 1951, this to say about lecturing (p. 16),
> "Most lecturers use notes. Many have full notes from which they read ... Reading notes is like reading a textbook, except that the notes never got as much working over ..."
and were perhaps even rejected by some publisher. Adding jokes, says Marshall, does not alter the fact: the job of the notes is to prevent the speaker from seeing his audience. Marshall thinks most textbooks are horrid, but better than lecture notes.

Already in Locke's *Thoughts Concerning Education,* §94, we read that a teacher should only introduce a student to a subject and let the student take initiative to progress in it if he wishes, that he should rather develop a character, including the readiness to be disciplined and work hard. The same idea is endorsed by Kant in his *On Education.* But teachers in general refuse to accept reforms even three centuries old – or is it school programs designers, educational leaders, and such?

So much for praise of Skinner. This, however, does not mean that Skinner's behaviorism is not detrimental even to his own good works. Patrick Suppes, "Facts and Fantasies of Education", in M. C. Wittrock, ed., *Changing Education: Alternatives from Educational Research*, Prentice Hall, Englewood Cliffs, N.J., 1973, pp. 6–45, pp. 13–14, referring to Skinner's *The Technology of Teaching,* 1968, says sharply,
> "The crudeness of [Skinner's] talk about responses and shaping them without serious reference to how arithmetical concepts should be built up is typical of this strange and undocumented proposal of how arithmetic ought to be taught. ...
> No evicence is offered about the effectiveness of these ideas for the teaching of arithmetic. ...
> I challenge ... Skinnerians ... to produce genuine psychological theory of mathematical learning and thinking".

See also the comprehensive, but much too statistical paper by Dean Jamison,

Patrick Suppes, and Stuart Wells, "The Effectiveness of Alternative Instructional Media: A Survey", *Review of Educational Research*, Vol. 44, 1974, pp. 1–67, especially about the paucity of data. I do not doubt that once stupendous success will be consolidated, the demand for large-scale implementation will be overwhelming and schools on all levels will have to give in, teachers' union will have to offer courses for teachers, etc. And I propose careful experiments in free schools aimed more at avoiding pressure than at positive results will bring about stupendous results if only the experimental projects be flexible enough. See note 2 to Chapter One.

107. The standard accusation of standard educational techniques is that they force students into the rut and stifle originality. There are myriads of references to support this statement, but I trust the reader will not find any necessary.

My own complaint is that standard educational techniques force people, rather than that the place people are forced into is the rut; and that in addition to the evil of unnecessary forcing, this forcing stifles flexibility or adjustability. That creativity is normally stifled too, I am willing to concede; but I wish to qualify this by the willingness to admit, however reluctantly, that some of the vilest acts may lead to creativity and at times they have. Nevertheless, many responses to the standard educational techniques accord with the standard objection and have led to creative educational experiment.

In creative education the student is positively reinforced for some achievement or another. It turns out, that this amounts to the cruel starving of children for affection — which is withheld from them until they comply. Which is mentally most unhygienic. See text to note 105 above; see also note 106 above and note 83 to Section VIII and reference there and note 89 to Section XX.

Skinner's laudable assumption that knowledge is its own reward, which is built into the teaching machines bearing his name, may be true or false. If false, there may be no reward attached to the use of the teaching machines and so to play. If, however, parents and/or teachers conspire to put pressure on students to use the teaching machine and to use it well, then the old evils will reappear. The most important teaching machines experimenter in the U.S. today is Patrick Suppes and he is particularly concerned to create as many safeguards as possible to prevent such cases. Yet the fact remains: we can easily slip into using teaching machines to create a Skinnerian utopia. This is particularly dangerous if this is already a popular inclination among intellectuals anyhow. See Robert K. Lindsay's excellent review of William T. Powers, *Behavior*, Chicago, 1973, in *Science*, Vol. 184, 26 April 1974, pp. 455–7, penultimate paragraph:

"The trouble with Skinner's program, claims Powers, is not that the world will not accept his views, but that it already has accepted it, since there is no other means of control and control is what we demand. But constant diddling with control systems leads inevitably to conflict and ultimately to revolt. Salvation can be found only in stopping all attempts at control and influence."

Why, then, do teaching machines work? Powers, and with him Lindsay, stress that in truth stimulus-response systems crudely emulate feedback systems, and these explain the phenonema much better. This should permit us to improve greatly upon existing machines. And then there will be no fear of ill-effects of any misuse of the machines.

Prevention of coercion in experimental stages is much easier than when the system is universally implemented.

See Jamison, Suppes, and Wells, survey mentioned in previous note, p. 26, "student-to-teacher ratio has little influence on student learning". Yet the need for adult company is unquestionable, and all teaching machine programs combine human and machine instruction. The encouragement that is so essential, I propose, can come even in small doses. This is a very important fact and one which can be utilized similarly to programs of volunteers visiting hospitals and orphanages so as to provide children with adult contact. The science fiction *Mirror for Observers* by E. Pangborn says, one encouraging observer is better than many teachers.

108. What is so impressive about Chandler's description of the main character of *The Long Goodbye* is that he is a realist; he promotes the utility of everyone, but within reason, knowing that usually, but not always, honesty is the best policy. Hume himself notices, though only in the second half of the Conclusion of his *Principles of Morals*, that his utilitarian ethics covers most but not all cases of what we normally consider moral conduct: it excludes self-sacrifice. He then takes resort to the argument from peace of mind. This argument is not only problematic – see my "On Pursuing the Unattainable", referred to in note 102 to Section IX – but also question-begging, since peace of mind is attained by doing what is right and so cannot define it without circularity. Anyway, Chandler's main character is just the kind of man that emerges from Hume's *Principles*: he has no peace of mind and no special moral code, yet he is decent in his own way.

The amazing fact about the moral quality of the main character of Raymond Chandler's *The Long Goodbye* is that it is analyzed by the narrator, the detective, just in this manner. The detective has to analyze a case and, as a precondition, a character as well; and only in the very end he cracks both. Chandler thus makes a jigsaw puzzle both lowbrow and highbrow at one and the same time. The added peculiarity of *The Long Goodbye* is that its narrator, the detective, becomes the fall guy of the story, which is the greatest humiliation for a detective, simply because he refuses to be bribed. The bribe, to make the issue strictly moral from the start, is described as legitimate yet not quite moral; yet the narrator prefers to be the victim rather than compromise. In the end he understands the situation and knows the facts after refusing the bribe that was intended to keep him ignorant, and he realizes that he was the fall guy. But nothing happens: he simply severs his ties with an amoral man – and goes his own way.

Raymond Chandler's snoop is a secret utopian, as he admits in the end of his terrific *The Simple Art of Murder*. The snoop's nastiness is repeatedly and frankly used as a mask to enhance his ability to fight for his ideals, thus offering both artistic dynamics and a sharp insight that Popper, Polanyi, and Aron have observed. Raymond Chandler shares this characteristic with Dashiel Hammett, of course, just as much as the romanticism, which is at once enhanced and covered up by the stark realism of their description of poverty, misery, loneliness, and corruption that permeate the world. It is no accident that Chandler and Hammett were both Marxists; just as much as the fact that Durkheim, Malinowski, and Radcliffe-Brown were socialists but not Marxists. The moral motive is so strong and so obvious, yet cynicism all the more reigns supreme! This can only be explained by the polarization to nature and convention discussed in Chapter III.

109. Philip Roth, *Goodbye Columbus* and *Portnoy's Complaint.*

110. Thomas S. Szasz, "Mental Health Service in the School", *This Magazine is About Schools*, October 1967, pp. 114–34 reprinted in his *Ideology and Insanity*, Anchor Books, Doubleday, New York, pp. 140–166, Section III. That this sensational paper went unnoticed is one of the severest moral indictments of our present educational system.

111. See note 54 to Section XVIII below. It surprises me that such an important historical event as the search for a new morality, in the 19th century and, again, in the 20th, is hardly recorded except in novels, plays, and writings of odd, and often shallow, philosophers.

Friedrich Nietzsche thought he was proposing a moral revolution when he said (*Zarathustra*), let the dead bury their dead. Indeed, he had so much following precisely at the junction, when there was not enough affluence to raise the general level but enough to reward those who have talent and can accept the challenge. And Nietzsche told people to take the challenge, whereas Balzac in *Père Goriot*, for example, puts the challenge in the criminal's mouth and leaves the problem unsolved, and Victor Hugo solves the problem by calling the old to sacrifice themselves for the young, e.g. in *Les Misérables*.

It is clear, however, that what Nietzsche was fighting for was a moral cause, namely the right of the hopeful to survive the hopeless. He was not making a moral revolution but rescuing reasonable morality from the immoral demands tradition and elders made — and still make — on the able young ones.

X ANTI-INTELLECTUALISM EXPLAINED

When we envisage man as animal we may, for want of a better method, look at the animal in man, and try to explain as much of him in terms of animal nature as we can, thereby either explaining, say, language as animal or explaining every thing we can explain while disregarding language. Historically, the first option was closed and so the second option was avidly pursued. And it proved quite fruitful everywhere except where language is of a crucial importance. It is thus no surprise that much of the history of the social sciences looks distinctly anti-intellectual. This seeming anti-intellectualism is much due to the lack of clarity about the research program, the strategy of research, which was then employed. Alternative strategies surely were possible and employed in fields where language was of a supreme importance — e.g., the study of language and literature, of mythology and religion. An alternative strategy could be employed, for example, of taking language as given and treating sociology or politics pretty much as animal sociology or politics, with the added given language. Man to man is wolf, says the famous Latin proverb; a talking wolf, of course. And so, perhaps, Hobbes' *Leviathan* follows this alternative.[112] Assume men to be talking wolves, we may hear Hobbes say, and you will see that sooner or later they will talk peace. This is the doctrine of the original social contract. Hobbes assumed that the contract was between warrior wolves who convened and agreed on a strong monarchy; Rousseau thought it was between peace-loving apes who convened and agreed on a democracy strong enough to incarcerate the disturber of the peace, but not stronger. (There are two Rousseau's, of course, one who preferred the lawless state of nature and saw all society as decadent, and one who advocated democracy; I shall come to this later.)

Opponents to the original contract, in particular the two friends Adam Smith and David Hume, objected not so much to the claim that those who convened and signed the contract were wolves, or apes; not so much to the claim that the law specified in the contract was monarchy, or democracy. They felt that if society is mere convention it is no part of human nature, and so reductionism is blocked by contractualism — and they were reductionists.[113] Of course, if language is part of human nature and the contract an inevitable outcome of it, this objection might be answerable. But as to language, it encounters the difficulty of the vicious circle type which we already met in Kipling's story: language presupposes society and vice versa. Moreover, and independently, the naturalists felt, the conventionalists' taking society as derivative is false: it is of the essence — an immediate part of human nature, it is unexplainable but explains a lot.

And so, to Hume, to Smith, to Smith's most prominent disciple Jeremy Bentham, society is the product of man's social nature which is a primary animal drive.[114] For Bentham there is a universal law of gravitation, in the science of man just as in the science of astronomy: men naturally gravitate towards each other in search of companions. Hume already described company as useful and agreeable. Adam Smith spelled out the usefulness in a most sophisticated theory.[115] Productivity rises with specialization, specialization requires commerce — whether truck and barter or an elaborate market machinery.[116] Hence productivity increase is an incentive for sociability. What is common to these views — and many others — is that they rather sidestep language altogether: if sociability is taken to be more essential than language, then we can discuss its other consequences while making as little as possible of the fact that man is a talking animal.

There is a terrible optical illusion here. That all this is a terrible mistake may be more easily felt than expressly articulated. The unease about it fills volumes which fail to express it explicitly: is sociability or language or anything else a specifically human quality? If it is, why is it not manifest in other social animals?[117] If it is not, why is it part and parcel of the science of man rather than of all social animals? Strange as it may seem, in the whole relevant literature there is no discussion of this. Strange as it may sound, language was so successfully sidestepped that even a theory of learning was elaborated at the time, by Hume and many others, to wit associationism, in which language plays no role or a marginal one, and which thus applies to man and beast alike.

It is no accident that the contributor to the epoch-making French *Encyclopedia* article on nature had to explain that the return to nature is more than the mere return to the apes or the wolves, since man is rational by nature.[118] More revealing, still, is the fact that until fairly recently it was taken for granted that apes and wolves live in no organized society. It is revealing not merely in that a lacuna existed, filled by the new field of study — that of ethology or of the social order of animals. Considering that the classical sciences of man were oriented toward favoring the animal in man, and considering that the social aspects of the lives of certain animals are too conspicuous even to the casual observer, e.g., the division of labor among certain insects, in herd animals, or even in migratory flocks of birds, one may wonder how the misconception was maintained.

The truth of the matter seems to be very strange. It seems we were so drilled to think animals live in anarchy that the discovery of the pecking order, of the sociology of baboons' leadership and such, came to us as a shock. It seems that the desire to live with no political authority over us, the plain love of freedom, was projected by us into animals and only then "observed." Does a wolf at least earn his freedom in exchange for his living in a relentlessly hostile world? Does he have political freedom, that is? In a sense the question does not obtain, namely in the sense in which political life presupposes the existence of linguistic life, of verbal behavior. In a sense, though, we can insist on the question and define political life more primitively as the government (or its absence) of wolf by wolf. Is one wolf free of domination by another wolf? It is almost too much to believe, but it is

a historical fact easily ascertainable, that the pecking order was invented not by animal sociologists but by political philosophers, perhaps in
antiquity — Heraclitus — certainly in the Reaction to the Age of
Reason — Hegel — long before it was applied to animals: Hegel's
theory of domination and submission, or of the master-slave relation,
is a theory of a pecking order: every two individuals of the (human)
species establish as soon as they can who of the two is the superior
one in rank.[119]

Hegel argued that in human society this principle, the pecking
order, prevents the pack from being a mob and establishes order in it.
Of course, those who still loved freedom could not accept Hegel's idea
of order, and if at times they agreed with him on what order was, then
consequently they hankered all the more after disorder.[120]

The Age of Reason's idea of freedom as disorder and the Reaction's
idea that order is domination and submission, are, thus, the same
descriptive idea: the difference between the two is merely in matters
of preference. The critics of this idea are the seekers of orderly freedom or of a compromise between order and freedom. But compro-
mises are traditionally looked at with great suspicion, partly because
one cannot compromise a principle (or it ceases to be a principle),
partly because of a deep-seated principle of polarizing nature and
convention, of which I shall speak later at quite some length. Let me
conclude, however, with some remarks about the possibility of such a
compromise in the animal world.

Our image of animals as free, in the state of nature, may be bogged
down by a theory of instinct. How can an animal like an ant be free if
it is totally dominated by instinct and is highly predictable? Can the
conduct of a free agent be so very predictable?

On the more commonsense level we can say that worker-ants are
less free than queen ants or drones. Or, leaving the insects, we can
consider a stag or a cock who is inferior on the pecking order and so is
induced to live in a state of psychological castration, so-called, i.e., is
led to have no sexual desires whatsoever as long as he is in the same
social environment.[121] No one in his right mind will consider such a
society a good model for mankind to follow. On second thought —
but only on a second, not a first, thought — one will discover that
similar mechanisms, repressive ones, occur in human society, that
people can be made to resign to certain situations to the extent that
they will totally give up certain ends, no matter how desirable, and
will not pursue them even when they are easily attainable. Indeed,
when the temptation proves too much people are known to throw
hysteric fits rather than yield to the temptation. Some moralists, ad-

mittedly, will view this a virtue – but never gladly and always out of the (erroneous) recognition of necessity.

Of course, the moralist's attitude amounts to a compromise on the model of psychological castration we see in animals. Indeed, whether by a historical or a prehistorical development, we can say, Freudian repression is fairly common, at least in our own society, and amounts to something surprisingly similar to what was later discovered in animals. Admittedly, in animals we see cases where a mechanism operates in clear-cut ways. But Lorenz took pains to show that the clear-cut cases only stand out, that conflict abounds in animals, quite contrary to the claim of some physiologists (including Sherrington) and some psychoanalysts that it is obviously absent. Moreover, we do have clear-cut cases in humans too, such as slave mentality, total sexual impotence, total political indecision, etc.

That such mechanisms as Freudian repression mechanisms are fairly animal is indeed one of the triggers of the surge of studies of animal psychology and sociology. To be a bit more specific, it was the search of animal infant sexuality, Oedipal conflicts, and the like; yet clearly, by Freud's theory, these desires, and their more potent expression in adolescence, are the ones which cause repression and thereby also give rise to the very social order.

It is clear today that repression plays a great political role, in man and in other animals. (On this point muddled Freudo-Marxists are better off than orthodox Freudians: sex plays a great role in primitive politics!)[122] Whether in the other animals repressive mechanisms entirely suffice to explain at least animal sociology is an open question. Konrad Lorenz, for one, says not even that, since animals have evolved traditions. This is certainly true of humans, whose traditions, especially those linked with language, including cultural and religious ones, not to mention politics proper, far outweigh the merely innate psychologically given.

And so, to begin with, we must admit that the idea that we may imitate the freedom of animals is folly, that whether we are essentially animals or more than that is a question that can be postponed. I have no objection to the program of looking at man as animal, though I think it is less and less fruitful; but I think we should also have no objection to looking at man as a special kind of animal – a talking animal. If language is reducible to animal qualities, the reduction of language can be done later. If not, surely we cannot ignore it for that reason alone. Society is not a mob and language is what keeps it together more than any other single aspect of human life. And therefore we should not confine our study of man to the mere study of his

animal drives; even the admission of sociability as a major drive will
not do: it is not the drive for sociability but the facts of association
that we may wish to explain, and language enters almost every facet of
human society and association in a very significant way.[123]

In conclusion, let me recapitulate. The theory of man as mere
animal is the basis of a program to explain man, not an explanation
proper; and confusing the two may cause anxiety. We can explain the
novelty of specifically human traits, such as language, as caused by a
new combination of old animal traits, which combination makes the
traits reinforce each other. Hence the transition from ape to man must
be abrupt, and give rise to peculiarly human characteristics. Behaviorism is the pointless program to overlook rather than explain these
characteristics. Also, much of the program to explain man as animal
often rested on an unexamined assumption that animal society is
based on internal release mechanisms which preclude man's peculiar
characteristics, so that when social science takes animal sociology for
its model it is not allowed to make room for man's peculiarity. These
facts, I think, explain much that is puzzling in the irrationalism of past
and present researches into the nature of man.

Notes to Section X

112. J. W. N. Watkins, *Hobbes's System of Ideas, A Study in the Political Significance of Philosophical Theories*, Hutchinson University Library, London, 1965, p.
137, 1973, p. 98, presents man as an animal plus language. He adds that the distance is small — animals and men both associate experiences thus being able to use
signs; but men can also create artificial "signs" or "marks" or labels (p. 139, p. 100).

The question that springs to mind is, of course, does man's ability to use words
make him human, or does his contract? This is a particularly hard question, since
words require agreements to make their meanings interpersonal. See Michael
Oakeshott's "Moral Life in the Writings of Thomas Hobbes", in *Rationalism in
Politics and Other Essays*, Methuen, London, 1962, 1967, especially p. 256 and p.
257, note.

"In a word", says La Mettrie, *L'Homme Machine,* Open Court Classic, La Salle,
1961, p. 100. "would it be absolutely impossible to teach the ape a language? I do
not think so."

And attempts to teach apes to talk go on for nearly a century now.

It is amusing to observe that Freud makes man the result of a contract, not the
result of language proper; language, therefore, is one result of the contract (i.e. a
sense of guilt and a resultant taboo that makes all culture possible, language
included). One may see here in Freud's theory a solution to a Kipling-type problem: language and contract seem interdependent, but Freud says (rightly) pre-
verbal contract is possible.

113. This interpretation is most forcefully presented by Elie Halévy, *The Growth of Philosophic Radicalism,* translated by Mary Morris, Beacon, Boston, 1955, p. 433,

"The Philosophical Radicals wished to make social science a rational science; they held that all social phenomena are reducible to laws, and that all the laws of the social world are in their turn explicable by the 'laws of human nature'. But the laws of human nature are themselves of two kinds: physical . . . and psychological . . ."

114. For the naturalism of Hume, Smith, and Bentham, see notes 116 and 118 below.

115. Smith was not the first, of course, to argue that convention only hampers the economy. Already the physiocrats had this as their central idea. "Quensnay and his disciples", says Lord Robbins, in *The Theory of Economic Development in the History of Economic Thought,* MacMillan, London, 1968, p. 7, "saw the French economy burdened with a load of regulations which they regarded as inimical to productivity, and their analysis was directed to why this was so and how the removal of these regulations would lead to greater prosperity."

116. Of the naturalism of Smith's *Wealth of Nations,* see Elie Halévy, *The Growth of Philosophic Radicalism, op. cit.,* Chapter III, especially pp. 94, 97, 98, also pp. 100–101 for his (Smith's), at times, opposition to rent as unnatural, and p. 100 for his, at times, acceptance of it as natural.

Nevertheless, Smith's naturalism does not lead him to ignore given laws in their historical context, and even the laws governing his commonwealth are more organically grown than his French colleagues would allow. See Lord Robbins, *The Theory of Economic Development in the History of Economic Thought,* Macmillan, New York, 1968, section on Smith's system of natural liberty, pp. 99–102, especially p. 99, last sentence and p. 100, line 7, and contrast with Halévy, *op. cit.,* p. 487, last sentence. Yet, clearly neither Smith nor other and more advanced economists could incorporate a reasonable theory of money into their systems, since money is conventional. David Hume "proved" that this is no defect since, were the quantity of (liquid) money doubled, nothing will happen except that prices will double.

F. A. Hayek says, in *The Pure Theory of Capital,* Routledge, London, 1941, 1962, p. 31, quoted by B. A. Corry, *Money, Saving, and Investment in English Economies, 1800–1850,* London, 1962, p. 5, that it is "self-contradictory to discuss a process which admittedly could not take place without money, and at the same time to assume that money is absent or has no effect."

117. Darwin's wondering as to whether apes are today undergoing evolution similar to ours, and if not why not, has not in the least been allayed. On the contrary, the studies by S. L. Washburn and I. De Vore, by Adrian Kortlandt, and by Jane Goodall, have made us feel intuitively and emotionally much better disposed towards our simian "brethren in suffering", to use Darwin's early expression. See notes 45 and 46 to Section VII above.

The literature sometimes stresses continuity and similarity between man and animal, exhibiting, for example, bee language as akin to human language, and sometimes stresses the differences (such as E. Benveniste, "Animal Communication and Human Language", *Diogenes*, Vol. 1, 1952–3, pp. 1–7, on the absence of dialogue or even repetition by other speakers, in response to a bee's message). I think it is better to approach the question generally and make clear what we are after before looking for it.

Oddly, if the information is by smell it is a priori easier to transmit through intermediaries than if it is by gestures, yet intuitively we consider the latter more akin to human language. This despite the fact that already Dr. Johnson noted that sending a snuffbox for a refill makes the box a carrier of a fairly abstract message. This shows the force of the gesture theory of the origin of language, which theory is now enjoying a revival. For the debate on the question whether the bees' transmission of information is by dance or by smell or by other means, see *Science,* Vol. 185, No. 4154, September 1974, p. 814 and sets of references there. See also J. L. Gould "Honey Bee Recruitment: The Dance Language Controversy", *Science,* Vol. 189, No. 4204, 29 August 1975, pp. 685–693 and references there.

118. Naturalism is the doctrine defended by the *Encyclopedia* on "Natural Law" (by Diderot) and in the article on Law of Nature or Natural Law (by Boucher d'Argis, translated by Richard Popkin), which reads:

"In its broadest sense the term is taken to designate certain principles which nature alone inspires and which all animals as well as all men have in common. On this law are based the union of male and female, the begetting of children as well as their education, love of liberty, self-preservation, concern for self-defense.

It is improper to call the behavior of animals natural law, for, not being endowed with reason, they can know neither law nor justice.

More commonly we understand by natural law certain laws of justice and equity which only natural reason has established among men, or better, which God has engraved in our hearts.

The fundamental principles of law and all justice are: to live honestly, not to give offense to anyone, and to render unto each whatever is his. From these general principles derive a great many particular rules which nature alone, that is, reason and equity, suggest to mankind.

Since this natural law is based on such fundamental principles, it is perpetual and unchangeable: no agreement can debase it, no law can alter it or exempt anyone from the obligation it imposes. In this it differs from positive law, meaning those rules which only exist because they have been established by precise laws. This positive law is subject to change by right of the same authority that established it, and individuals can deviate from it if it is not too strict. Certain people improperly mistake natural law for the law of nations.

This latter also consists in part of rules which true reason has established among all men; but it also contains conventions established by men against the natural order, such as wars or servitude, whereas natural law admits only what conforms to true reason and equity.

The principles of natural law, therefore, form part of the law of nations, particularly the primitive law of nations ... From these general ideas on natural law it becomes clear that this law is nothing other than what the science of manners and customs calls morality.

This science of manners or of natural law was known only imperfectly to the ancients; their wise men and their philosophers have spoken of it most often in a very superficial way; they introduced into it errors and vices . . ."

119. Hegel's theory of domination and submission, his master-slave theory, or his theory of lord and serf, or his theory of the master-slave relation is expounded in his *Phenomenology of the Spirit*, B. Self-Consciousness, IV. The True Nature of Self-Certainty, A. Independence and Dependence: Lordship and Bondage; pp. 228–40 of the J. B. Baillie translation, Allan and Unwin, London, Humanities, New York. What the master has to do with his slave is very clearly stated at the very start of the chapter (p. 229): "It [the master] must cancel this [slave] its other [ego] . . . First, it must set itself to sublate the other independent being, in order thereby to become certain of itself as true being; secondly, it thereupon proceeds to sublate its own self, for this other [the slave] is itself." Hegel proceeds to describe self-hatred and self-destruction as a prime characteristic of this relation. No doubt the ugly movie "The Servant" of Harold Pinter and Joseph Lousey illustrates all this very well, with the subtle reversal from the accidental master-slave relation, to the true one, where the accidental master becomes the true slave and vice versa.

The Freudian element of Hegel's theory of master and slave has been noticed but hardly ever discussed. See, for example, John Plamenatz, *Man and Society*, Vol. II, Bentham Through Marx, McGraw-Hill, New York, 1963, p. 186, where Freud is declared to have viewed sublimation as rooted in man's need for recognition in Hegel's sense. This recognition, however, is Adlerian, not Freudian, though Hegel's passion and need for recognition is a compound of Freudian, Adlerian and other undifferentiated elements.

Perhaps the first to notice the Freudian element in Hegel is Robert Tucker; see note 61 to Section XIX below.

Hegel's theory of master-slave relation is as insightful as it is inhuman. He calls needs for things to consume desire (and this includes sexual desire). He notes that uncertainty regarding desires is vexing, and suggests that to create certainty we associate with other people. In other words, slavery is admittedly mutual destruction; yet it is preferred to freedom because there is certainty only in (destruction and) slavery. (There is, of course, the secondary question, who of the two partners should be the master, but this is emphatically a secondary question.) Hegel worked out the idea abstractly; its application to sexual partners is due to Sartre (*Being and Nothingness*).

Hegel and Sartre overlook some very important facts. It is admittedly the case that educators try to elicit certain obedience in their charges; that they try to achieve this by eliciting obedience as such. It is admittedly the case that ideologists often praise obedience as such, that even the theory that only he who can obey can command is very popular today as it ever was. It is also to be admitted that of those whom we fail to subdue, some become masters who assert themselves by treading on the heads of slaves. Nevertheless, there are people who are neither masters nor slaves, who do not feel the desire to assert themselves, much less so by imposing on others, much less on others who are willing to be imposed upon. I cannot see the attraction of the sado-masochism that fascinates Sartre so, and I find facile his claim that I only repress my fascination with it. He thus begs the equally facile claim that he is unfamiliar with the freedom from self-assertion. But I do not really think either facile claim is true.

The dichotomy between certainty and freedom is, of course, as ancient as it is obvious. See note 2 to Chapter III. It is expanded at some length in Popper's *Open Society*, where, rather than advocate freedom — which, presumably we all want, *ceteris paribus* — he advocates the relinquishing of the ideal standard of certainty so as to make freedom at all possible.

Hegel's view of the master as a slave to his passion is a romantic variant of the view that the master is as much a slave as the slave is. This latter is, of course, as old as the idea of Socrates that hurting others is self-damage. Yet how it was applied in antiquity to social reform is unclear. It is a central doctrine of Marx rejected by Vulgar Marxists in favor of a theory of a conspiracy by the masters (see K. R. Popper's *The Open Society* Vol. II, pp. 94, 101). Marx, of course, did not invent it: Rousseau states it in the very opening of his *On the Social Contract* and it is clearly enough present in Spinoza's *Tractatus* and adumbrated already in Hobbes's *Leviathan* (though Hobbes, of course, saw a high degree of submission to authority an unavoidable necessity, whereas Spinoza was a liberal).

In defence of the Vulgar Marxists I must say they were driven to it by the failure of Marxism. Even the Master himself, who explained the failure of the 1848—50 revolution as not radicalist enough, explained the failure of the Paris Commune by reference to a conspiracy for want of a better explanation. See Karl Marx, *On Revolution*, arranged, edited, and translated by Saul K. Padover, Karl Marx Library, Vol. I, McGraw-Hill, New York, 1971, pp. 159—164, 215, 224, for the former and compare with his praise of moderation of the Commune, pp. 357, 359, 367—8. Marx himself notices that conspiracy explanations do not quite make it. He also says, p. 357—8, "In every revolution there intrude" all sorts of people who do not belong there . . . "They are an unavoidable evil: with time they are shaken off; but time was not allowed to the Commune." And, surely, he would have said the same about opponents who hit below the belt. But the idea that history is not ready is only good for a limited period. Anyway, the remark makes it clear enough that here Marx allowed only a limited place for any explanation by the assumption of a conspiracy.

120. It is quite relevant in this context to mention Kropotkin's *Mutual Aid* and its stress on animal cooperation. See George Woodcock and Ivan Avakumović, *The*

Anarchist Prince, A Biographical Study of Peter Kropotkin, Schocken, New York (1950) 1971, Chapter VII, pp. 334ff. What impact Kropotkin had I cannot say, but see E. W. Wilson, *Sociobiology,* Harvard University Press, 1955.

Marx accepted Hegel's analysis of society in an interpretation of his own, but, of course, rejected the society so analyzed. This is the thesis of Robert Tucker in his *Philosophy and Myth in Karl Marx*, Cambridge University Press, 1961, 1972.

121. A. M. Guhl, "The Social Order of Chickens", *Scientific American*, Vol. 195, February 1956, pp. 43–6; C. Robert Watts and Allen W. Stokes, "The Social Order of Turkeys", *ibid.,* Vol. 224, June 1971, pp. 112–118.

For more complex patterns of sex, pecking order, and/or territoriality see the following works:

Fritz Walther, *Verhalten der Gazellen,* Zimsen Verlag, Wittenberg, 1968; David Mech, *The Wolf,* Natural History Press, Garden City, 1967; H. Klingel, "Social Organization and Reproduction in Equids", *Journal of Reproductive Fertility,* Suppl. 23, 1975, pp. 7–11.

There is also a forthcoming research of H. Mendelssohn on the African lizard.

122. I dare call the Freudian-Marxist school muddled because both Freud and Marx were monists, and combining their doctrines leads to a catastrophe. What the members of this school are right about is their acceptance of the so many observations that Marx or Freud has made in support of his thesis. It is much more common sense to accept the obvious part of each doctrine, but intellectually much better to ask which is better and perhaps reject both. The attempt to do so, to answer the Freudo-Marxist challenge is Géza Róheim, *The Origins and Function of Culture*, Nervous and Mental Disease Monographs, No. 69, New York, 1943. On p. 40 he notices that economic and psychological factors are interdependent. Yet he allows psychology to influence economics without further ado while insisting on a psychological explanation of the influence of economics on psychology. This is an apt description, I think, of the program which stems from psychologism. The only thing that is the matter with Róheim's argument is that, like most of his arguments, it is weak and displays no self-criticism.

123. The field of sociolinguistics is so explosive that even a brief survey of recent works is bound to get out of hand. See, for example, Allen D. Grimshaw, "On Language in Society", Survey Essay, *Contemporary Sociology*, Vol. 2, No. 6, 1973, pp. 575–85 and Vol. 3, No. 1, 1974, pp. 3–11, and references there.

Chapter Three

Man as Rational

In conformity with my anti-all-or-nothing-attitude I intend to reject in this chapter both the view that man is utterly rational and the view that he is utterly irrational.

Rationality has two or three meanings, which were historically closely linked, which recently went their separate ways, and which I think should come back together.[1] The central idea here is the idea of the rational man, as opposed to the irrational man, to wit the arbitrary man, to wit the capricious man, the unjust, insensible, wild man. There is the idea of rational belief or rational thinking, which I grudgingly must agree is the same idea, though rational thinking will do much better than belief, since, strictly speaking, it is difficult to speak of belief as rational or not. There is the idea of rational behavior, which is purposeful behavior. And it is not hard to see, at least not hard for the untutored to see, that one's rational behavior is linked both to one's purpose and to one's rational thoughts of one's situation and is opposed to one's capricious behavior, which is not linked to one's purpose or rational thoughts. There is, finally, the idea of the rational as the intelligible: the idea of what is given to rational explanation. Again, we can rationally explain a man's conduct by assuming his rational thoughts and rational conduct relative to his ends, and we find a capricious conduct quite inexplicable. All this is plain sailing, until we assume that the world, or Mother Nature, is not capricious, but orderly behaved, and is thus ruled by some law and order. Rational explanation — explaining the world as God's creation — becomes causal explanation, and total rationality becomes total causality. Namely, scientific determinism. And both belief and purpose then have to be explained away (Spinoza; Kant and Laplace; Darwin and Marx and Freud and Watson).

We see, then, a strange *volta face*. We have the intuitive idea that rational thought, action, and explanation, are all one. This leads to the opposite conclusion that really there are no rational thoughts and no rational actions, only rational explanations.[2]

The reason for this amazing *volta face* is the single added premise: there is nothing in the world except appearance and reality, there are two ways and only two ways of looking at any given thing in the world. Now, clearly, if one thing explains the other, then the one is more real than the other; and so it follows from the polarization of everything into appearance and reality that the explained, being the less real, has no reality at all, is merely an appearance.[3]

This is exactly why those who think they explain man as mere animal or mere machine thereby explain away man's distinct humanity, his dignity, language, rationality. This is an error, we saw, since chemistry is explained by physics but is not explained away. And the Greek polarization from which this error follows is also an error. And so, contrary to ancient Greek metaphysics and methodology, we have today a more moderate view, due to Faraday, Einstein, and Popper, a more gradualistic view, of approximation to the truth in stages. The most explicit expression of the moderate methodology of science was developed by Popper, in his theory of science as conjectures and refutations. This theory has no place for metaphysics except as an occasionally useful private heuristic device. This is where I start to deviate from Popper's view. For my part I see a place, both in principle and in history, a place for metaphysics more significant for science than Popper allows, yet more piecemeal, less comprehensive, than a grand scale metaphysics.[4] I wish to consider certain important doctrines metaphysical – in the (positivistic) sense that they are unscientific and in the (Aristotelian) sense that they offer first principles of physics; metaphysical also in the (Kantian) sense that they play a part as regulative principles for scientific research, not merely as heuristic devices. An example for meta-physics is Greek atomism; an example of philosophical anthropology, of meta-social-science, is the doctrine of original sin which is transformed into the so-called Protestant ethic or work ethic,[5] and accepted by positivists, who use it in their construction of their theories – both metaphysical and scientific.

What intrigues me in all this is the fact that the Greek polarization has led thinkers, both metaphysicians and positivists, to assume both that man is inherently rational and that he is inherently irrational.

For, in appearance, he is sometimes this sometimes that, and assuming that in reality he is this forces us to disregard as mere chimera the apparent fact that he is sometimes that. This explains, I think, the fact that what Claude Lévi-Strauss has characterized as mythical thinking goes on within the social sciences up till this very day.

Notes

1. For the views of rationality as both rational thought and rational action see references in note 70 to Section V above.

The idea that rationality is intelligibility is expressed in the first sentence of Kant's "Idea For A Universal History From A Cosmopolitan Point of View", in Lewis White Beck, ed., *Immanuel Kant on History*, translated by Lewis White Beck, Robert E. Anchor, and Emil L. Fackenheim, Bobbs-Merrill, Indianapolis and New York, 1963, p. 11: "Whatever concept one may hold, from a metaphysical point of view, concerning the freedom of the will, certainly its appearances, which are human actions, like every natural event are determined by natural law." (See J. B. Bury, *The Idea of Progress*, Chapter 15, first paragraph, quoted in J. Plamenatz, *Man and Society*, New York, 1963, Vol. 2, p. 417, about the historicist nature of this law.)

2. The reduction of freedom to necessity — whether that of a causal law or of a statistical one — is done in diverse ways. Either the reduction proves freedom to be a chimera, or it proves that freedom conforms to law. The second option means that a creature on a higher level of understanding may predict my free choice. This is considered by some as chimerical, since, they say, only unpredictability in principle is free. I reject this argument on the ground that we have case histories which we feel — perhaps erroneously — we could predict with little insight, yet whose participants felt very strongly about what they felt — perhaps erroneously — that they resolved by decisions. I think the existence of such cases is a) uncontestable and b) thought provoking.

For a very interesting argument against the reduction of freedom to necessity see Gellner's "Maxims" reprinted in his *The Devil In Modern Philosophy*, Routledge, London and Boston, 1974, pp. 67–77, where the role ideas play within causal chains is analyzed. This is question begging for the reductionist, of course, but that is another matter, as even reductionists must speak of ideas they cannot reduce as yet.

Popper has offered a by now celebrated argument about the impossibility of self-prediction, published in his "Indeterminism in Classical Physics and in Quantum Physics", *Brit. J. Phil. Sci.*, Vol. 1, 1950, pp. 117–133 and 173–195, reported in the Preface to his *Poverty of Historicism*, Routledge, London, 1957, where he says he is "no longer satisfied" with it and promising "a more satisfactory treatment" in his still unpublished *Postscript: After Twenty Years*. Popper intended to criticize Bohr's claim that classical physics but not quantum physics is deterministic, and defeat historicism, the doctrine of scientific inevitability; and also to throw light on the mind-body problem. Popper thinks that freedom is incompatible with determinism and that the purpose of mentalism is to establish freedom. He is aware of the fact that determinism is irrefutable but claims to have refuted scientific determinism.

I cannot go here into the detailed discussion of Popper's views on the matter. Let me report that they have gained great popularity. For my criticism of his views see my forthcoming "Determinism: Metaphysical and Scientific", in the forthcoming *Proceedings of the 1975 London Ontario International Congress of Logic Methodology and Philosophy of Science.*

3. The Greek thinkers themselves had great difficulties due to the polarization, and from the very start. See Daniel Gershenson and Daniel Greenberg, "The 'Physics' of Eleatic School: A Re-evaluation", *The Natural Philosopher*, Vol. 3, Blaisdell, New York, Toronto, London, 1964, pp. 95–111. This paper is perhaps the best on the topic at hand and I am happy to acknowledge my profound indebtedness to it.

The most important attempt to escape the dichotomy was the attempt to save the phenomena not by a real explanation but by mere fiction – fictionalism or instrumentalism so-called. See my *Faraday as a Natural Philosopher,* University of Chicago Press, Chicago and London, 1971, my "On Explaining the Trial of Galileo", *Organon*, Vol. 8, 1971, pp. 138–166, and my "The Future of Berkeley's Instrumentalism", *Studi. Intl. Filos.*, 1976, pp. 166–177.

4. See references in previous note. See also my "The Nature of Scientific Problems and Their Roots in Metaphysics", in Mario Bunge, ed., *The Critical Approach, Essays in Honor of Karl Popper*, Free Press and McMillan, New York and London, 1964, pp. 189–211; "The Confusion Between Physics and Metaphysics in Standard Histories of Science", in H. Guerlac, *Proceedings of the Xth International Congress in the History of Science*, Ithaca, 1962, Paris, 1964, pp. 231–250; "Science in Flux: Footnotes to Popper," in R. S. Cohen and M. W. Wartofsky, *Boston Studies in the Philosophy of Science*, Vol. 3, Reidel and Humanities, Dordrecht and New York, 1965, pp. 293–323; "What is a Natural Law?" *Studium Generale*, Vol. 24, 1971, pp. 1051–1056. The papers mentioned in this note are reprinted in my *Science in Flux, Boston Studies in the Philosophy of Science*, Vol. 28, Reidel, Dordrecht and Boston, 1975.

5. As noted in note 16 to the Introduction above, it is simplicist to speak of the work ethic as one, since it has historical branches of great variety. Also, it is, of course, always possible to find many variations even within a very narrow compass. Kinsey's passion for work and for science in the most old-fashioned manner did not prevent him from being a pioneer. In spite of his many old-fashioned traits he found a new field of study, and one where his very conservatism was put to excellent use for an advanced, even revolutionary, cause: frankness about sex. See Frank A. Beach's excellent review of Wardell B. Pomeroy's *Dr. Kinsey and the Institute for Sex Research*, in *Science*, Vol. 177, 4 August 1972, pp. 416–8.

XI   GREEK METAPHYSICS TODAY

So much for the summary, which, I see now, is involved in a serious difficulty. It is a difficulty that I do not see how I can avoid, and it is going to get worse in this chapter. The difficulty, in brief, is this. I shall soon contend that historically people held a view about rationality which they did not always strictly conform to; that, to make things worse, they did not always strictly conform to it even in their deliberations – which is to say that I ascribe to them a view which they themselves at times contradicted; to make things still more impossible, they sometimes failed to articulate this view to the full – and yet I ascribe this view to them all the same. Is this not too arbitrary? Should I not say that their not conforming to the view is the evidence that they never held it? At least that they never held it seriously? Some quotations may prove that some people held given views; but these quotations will not help: I cannot quote everybody and I cannot even claim, let alone show, that those I have quoted believed in what they said in the sense that they never retracted and always attempted to practice it. Whether I discuss certain views of certain writers on Greek metaphysics, or any other views of any individuals or groups, the same questions inhibit the discussion quite *a priori:* Do people say what they believe in, and so they act on it? Are they consistent, honest, and at all able to act on their views? How is rationality expressed, then? Are people at all rational?[6]

This is the question of this chapter. My thesis is not that people are rational and also it is not that they are not. My thesis is more preliminary than that: all too often when asking this question philosophers slide from one question to another question: from, "Are people rational? ". to, "Are people really rational? ". Now, "Are people rational?" and, "Are people really rational?" are two quite different questions – as everybody knows. 'Really' refers to reality as above, to the ultimate level of reality, to the hard core, whereas without 'really' the question refers to mere appearances, or to some level of reality between reality and appearances, not at all to final reality. It is a fact, not always noticed, that about appearances and about intermediary levels, we all agree well enough: seemingly, at least, men are irrational, erring, evil, etc., and the apparent shortcoming of men is, unquestionably, often enough exposed for all to see. The optimists are not blind to the sad facts just mentioned, nor to their relatively deep roots in reality. What the optimists deny is that any man be *really* irrational, erring, evil, etc., that he is so in the very last resort. Now, very often the attempt to go to reality led people to explain away instead of to explain satisfactorily, the observable and oft disappointing, normal ways of normal men. I shall soon come to this. Meanwhile, let me come closer to the heart of the present chapter. Often philosophers made two moves: while moving away from the question, are people rational? to, are people really rational? , philosophers also confused it with the question, is man by nature rational? Here an entirely new moment enters, a hidden or not-so-hidden assumption that the nature of things, their very essence or substance, differs from the appearance of things. We also here contrast nature with mere convention[7] and this makes us tend to equate convention with appearance.[8] But we should not rush to assert this equation. For, we have here a triad, in the terminology of Lévi-Strauss:

truth : falsehood :: reality: appearance :: nature : convention

and

truth > falsehood.

Let me explain. Truth is the same as reality, the same as nature; while falsity and appearance and convention, again, go together. And truth is good, falsehood bad. Hence, for example, natural conduct is good, conventional conduct is hypocrisy and thus bad. To be more cautious, truth is to falsehood as reality is to appearance. Moreover, even this is not the full picture. Things are not so simple: table manners are conventional and good, and ones without them are not natural (= good) but wild (= bad). But spontaneous emotion is wild (= natural = good) and inhibition is control (= convention = bad).

Now I am in such a great difficulty, I do not know where to move. To begin with, I have to explain a point or two of Lévi-Strauss's theory of mythology. And I think any proper exposition of this theory makes one dizzy.[9] Roughly, according to him, myths are expressions of polarities which create tensions[10] (both intellectual and emotional, of course). Polarities can associate with, or slide into, or receive symbolic expressions from, other polarities; they do so often in Freudian ways, sometimes even switching roles.[11] Also the tensions can be resolved by what Lévi-Strauss calls mediation. A mediation is a compromise third pole or a sort of compromise polarity — the third element is sometimes a pole into itself, sometimes a compromise between two poles, artificially created to this effect.[12] And, to add the proper Marxian component to Lévi-Strauss's doctrine,[13] there is a parallel in reality, he says, in daily life, to each polarity as well as to the mediate case. In the case of nature-culture polarity, symbolized by the raw-cooked (culture) and fresh-putrid (nature) as well as by (a conflict of) burned-cooked. And roasting seems to mediate, i.e., to be a compromise between, burned and cooked. As Edmund Leach notes in his comments on all this, roasted food is aristocratic and cooked food is plebeian. But let us return to our own example. Let us look at convention as a compromise: again and again the social scientist discovers that though convention falls far short of nature and so of truth, it may well be better to record and observe it than any other arbitrariness. And so, shamefacedly at first, perhaps, I may record diverse conventions or customs, first as an amateur ethnographer or folklorist, and later as a social anthropologist or sociologist. This ploy is already ancient too: in Plato's *Protagoras* the conflict between nature and convention is mediated by the arts, represented by Prometheus — in a manner echoing passages from the ancient epic of Gilgamesh, no less.

This has deep roots in modern thought. When Descartes goes on his grand search for Truth by first rejecting all he learned, he asks what shall I do by way of everyday life until I find the truth? And he answers, hold on to convention. Truth is, nevertheless, the opposite of conventional thought: whatever I think because I am a Frenchman rather than a Chinaman, he said, I wish to give up.[14] He wanted nothing short of the nature of human thought, the real humanity which is thus essential to any man and thus universal. And yet, short of it, he fell back not on the arbitrary but on the merely conventional. The same holds for Descartes' successors. We find that all 18th-century thinkers opt for nature, for man's deepest drives, rationality, etc. Even skeptics like Hume held an *a priori* theory of human nature considered as a system powered by inborn drives and which uses reason to study and manipulate the environment. Yet at the very same time, the process of recording ethnological information about strange conventions of strange people started — as scientific data. A little later European folklore, equally strange, was discovered too. The good image of the noble savage, from the start, conflicted with the image of the primitive savage, which image is sometimes good and sometimes bad.

But, to come to my problem. We are torn even today. Lévi-Strauss, whose theory of myth I have just applied to the tradition of Western science, is himself a Western scientist. He tries to explore *not* the particular myths of particular tribes, but that which is universal to all myth — to the savage mind if not to the human mind in general (he is uncommitted on this point).[15] He tries to find the universal by a special technique of superimposing diverse myths on the same topic; employing ideas from information theory, he considers diverse myths as distortions of a primeval myth and he superimposes variants of the same message to get rid of the noise.[16] This is, I think, a vestige of Greek science which he need not insist on — he explains satisfactorily at best the main myth, not the noise which is thereby merely eliminated.[17] This makes his work obscure and pseudo-scientific even according to the ideas of Edmund Leach, his main admirer and expounder in England.[18]

Now, my difficulty is clearly very embarrassing. Is my technique also not too arbitrary? I first declare that convention is seen as falsehood and thus rather explained away than treated scientifically; and then, I see it as scientifically investigated. I see its study, in part, as a compromise between explaining satisfactorily and explaining away; and, in part, in the work of the historical school proper, as an irrationalistic activity, as going to the folklore to imbibe folk-wisdom.[19] I do go with Leo Strauss in admitting that the historical school had a positivistic — hyperscientific, that is — aspect to it, expressed in the slogan, 'history as she really was'; a-moral and so relativistic, a-rational and so relativistic, ending up, perhaps, as nihilistic.[20] Of course, finding a measure of rationality in the ir-rationalists and vice versa is a standard mythological ploy. Indeed, already Edmund Leach has claimed that there is a surprising similarity between Lévi-Strauss and Leo Strauss. But to return to my question, where am I to end up? Is my story not thereby proven totally arbitrary?

Perhaps it is. But then we encounter the difficulty not only in philosophy but also in daily life, perhaps more clearly when under stress (in accordance with the claim of Lévi-Strauss that high tension is conducive to mythology). Take the classic case of a soldier under the first test of fire, discovering with a shock, all of a sudden, what was at the back of his mind all the time, namely, that 'the brave' is not the same as 'the decorated for courage', that the natural or real or the true leader is not the one who is acknowledged by his military rank to be the leader. This is one part of the polarity. Stressing it forces also stressing the other: back in the barracks, not acknowledging the conventional leadership,[21] i.e. rank, soon lands our brave novice into a military jail which is not less real than the battlefield, and whose reality lends bitter reality to the very conventions which the battle-field has so sordidly mocked at. The literature about life in the army, whether regular army or not, is full of stories which are variants of this schema, which air the sense of bewilderment of a young person under trying conditions trying desperately to differentiate the real from all else and thus only making his own life more of a nightmare. If such stories have a happy ending, the ending is outside the schema: the novelist has no solution to the problem giving the schema its artistic dynamics.

The dynamics belongs to real life, I say, and so does the solution if and when it takes place. Not only individually, but, even as a culture, we all see a pendulum-like movement between the poles of nature and convention.[22] Since World War II alone we have had the beatnik movement (nature); the conventionalism of McCarthy era: the hippie fads and the new left (nature); the mid-American and the silent majority (convention), and back. Those of us who have relieved themselves of the tension have either left the problem alone, or gone to the Ivory Tower to contemplate it quietly. Is leadership a mere convention, stupid and full of arbitrariness, or is it a natural and true quality? We still do not know, and the very polarization in terms of which we pose the question makes it not open to satisfactory answers. Yet the question is lived, and so are its known unsatisfactory answers. This makes life so very wasteful.

Notes to Section XI

6. In particular, writers usually took it for granted that the Greeks, at least the Athenians, were perfectly rational. See Martin P. Nilsson, *Greek Folk Religion*, 1940, Harper Torchbook, New York, 1961, p. 111:

"The general opinion is that the Greeks of the classical age were happily free from superstition. I am so sorry that I am obliged to refute this opinion. There was a great deal of superstition in Greece, even when Greek culture was at its height and even in the center of that culture, Athens."

Nilsson rejects this view, of course, on general grounds. On p. 120, he says,

". . . Man needs some kind of religion. If his old faith is destroyed, he turns to superstition and magic and to new gods who are imported from foreign countries or who rise from the dark depths of the human mind. There were such depths in the Greek mind also. That mind was not so exclusively bright as is sometimes said."

See also note 71 to Section XV below on the disastrous results of attempts to implement the view of man's perfect rationality.

The claim that classical — Greek or 18th-century — rationalism is false in that it makes man utterly rational has been stressed in many writings of Russell, Hayek, Polanyi, and Popper. Of these, Russell and Popper still call themselves rationalists, though in a new and qualified sense. Hayek denies that he is a rationalist though his views are very close to those of Popper's except that he is less willing to see state intervention than Popper (Popper sees it a necessary evil, but unavoidable all the same, whereas Hayek believes it better not to have any state intervention except by legislations that may alter, say, property rights and duties), and Polanyi has come down on the side of irrationalism. But later on Hayek endorsed Popper's label of "Critical Rationalism" ("Kinds of Rationalism," *Studies in Philosophy, Politics and Economics*, Chicago University Press, Routledge, Chicago and London, 1967, p. 94).

7. Rational thought is contrasted with
    pre-rational thought
    arbitrariness, caprice, and thoughtlessness
    dogmatism, closed mindedness, blind authoritarianism
    myth, legend, blind traditionalism
    irrationalism or anti-rationalism or unreasonableness
    post-rationalism or trans-rationalism.

Assuming the rational to be critical — among other things — we may then make the following psychological observation.

The pre-rational is the pre-critical, as we are familiar with in ourselves when we catch ourselves having taken for granted a thought which does not stand in our critical scrutiny. The arbitrary or the capricious is also familiar to us as a voluntary pre-critical, as what we know we may scrutinize and prefer not to. Both these categories are quite within common experience. The dogmatic is the attitude towards a view which has passed critical scrutiny with flying colors and is thus (allegedly) in no need ever for further scrutiny. This is the use of the words "dogma," "dogmatist", etc. in Sextus Empiricus. In this sense most philosophers since Bacon were dogmatists. The Catholic Church added to dogmatism the attitude of resisting further scrutiny in spite of carping doubts and regardless of sufferings and mental anguish. This makes Catholic dogmatism in part but only in part irrationalist, i.e. anti-rational. The idea of a post-critical philosophy is largely Michael Polanyi's, and is a synthesis between Catholicism and criticism. As to myth, I think it is hardest to describe and is psychologically similar to quite a few mental aberrations though it is anything but aberrant: a myth is what we half-understand and/or half-believe. The psychological difficulty of describing the mental state of holding a myth is a very curious phenomenon, which will be discussed at length below. For further details see my forthcoming "Was Wittgenstein Really Necessary? "

The idea that polarizations are ever into good and bad, rational and irrational, etc., must be — and is — modified to accomodate ambiguity and ambivalence. Indeed, myth is always ambiguous as compared with the moral from it, and many jokes are of the type: the moral from this myth is the opposite of what it seems. When the nine enchanted stags of the Hungarian folk-tale, for example, refuse their father's plea to return to humanity, it is perhaps because their taste of freedom in nature made them unable to return to the age of culture; perhaps, however, it is simply to say that the father's inadequate treatment is the initial cause of the fall of his sons to the state of wild beasts. Culture is, thus, uncomfortable but hopefully redeemable.

For my part I feel that on the topic of ambivalence Freud gave us his most useful insight into primitive culture, regardless of the fact that he does not speak of it in his *Totem and Taboo*.

8. The reader may be reminded that the Greek word "nōmōs" is used even more than the English word "convention" as a technical term, often signifying just non-nature, or non-truth, but conveying much force because of the idea that truth = nature = logos as opposed to falsehood = convention = mythos. For a striking example note that Democritus declares (Fragments 9 and 125) that secondary sensations, such as colors, are "conventions"! All in all, the use of the words as used in the above equations, plus the synonyms for nature such as substance, essence, and even character, are used at times more vigorously and at times more loosly; that is, at times their use fully reflects the two equations and the contrasts; at times, not fully, or even not very much.

9. Lévi-Strauss says in his *Mythologique,* I, *Le Cru et le Cuit*, Plon, Paris, 1964, p. 14, "Ainsi ce livre sur les mythes est-il, à sa façon, un mythe," and on p. 20 he presents his own book as "le mythe de la mythologie." See also notes 10, 15 and 18 below.

Percy Cohen, in his review of *The Anthropologist as a Hero*, in *Brit. J. Soc.,* Vol. 22, September 1971, p. 331, judges Lévi-Strauss as both a pseudo-scientist and great. Likewise, *The Savage Mind* was called a great book and a very bad book, John Greenway, *Book Week*, Vol. 4 (18), 1967, p. 1.

H. Stuart Hughes, in his review of *The Savage Mind*, in *The American Scholar,* Vol. 36, 1967; *Psychiatry and Social Science Review,* September 1967; as well as in *Claude Lévi-Strauss: The Anthropoligist as a Hero*, ed. E. Nelson Hayes and Tanya Hayes, MIT Press, Cambridge, Mass., and London, has voiced the same criticism, I think.

"The trouble with this method . . . is that in the end all relationships turn out to be equally meaningful or perhaps equally lacking in significance, content matters not at all — only the way the different elements are combined. And even these elements, as in the performance of a computer, are limited to the small number that are capable of unambiguous manipulation. The result, as the philosopher Paul Ricoeur has complained, is a discourse that is at once fascinating and disquieting — an 'admirable syntactic arrangement . . . that says nothing'."

In "A Conversation with Claude Lévi-Strauss" by George Steiner, *Encounter*, Vol. 26 (4), April 1966, p. 34, Lévi-Strauss contrasts his view with Marx's.

"My outlook . . . is devoid of any kind of mysticism" he says. "History has a meaning and should have . . . [yet] I can perfectly well claim at the same time that while this is true inside the society of the observer it ceases to be true when we try to reflect a broader point of view and look at it from the outside. It is exactly [*sic*] like Euclidean geometry which is absolutely [*sic*] true within certain limits at a certain scale, but which cannot be used when we are trying to widen our experience to make it include greater dimensions."

For the sophisticated, it is very easy to dismiss Lévi-Strauss as a charlatan, by drawing attention to the many confusions in passages the like of the above one (which is rather characteristic I am afraid). I am not so cavalier as to consider the damage caused by such talk negligible, but I am not such a militant rationalist on a white charger as to mind. I think, and this I consider my deepest disagreement with Popper, that damaging as all this may be *prima facie* it should be overlooked everywhere except where training is concerned. Moreover, there is an important point here about seeing a custom from the inside and the outside: it is not true and false, but natural and unnatural, respectively. See Section XX below.

10. The main defect of the dichotomy between nature and convention lies in the fact that as nature is unknown, convention is a substitute for nature, not an alternative to it. And so convention is often in need of modification in the light of progress in our views of nature. Thus, marital and sexual conventions may be based on false views of the nature of reproduction (e.g. that conception is due to spirits and males only facilitate the process) as well as of the nature of ties between parent and offspring. What happens when nature clashes with convention? As a result of such a clash one may win or lose by the books, knowing well enough that one's ill-luck or good luck is based on an institutionalized error. One may even rush to court before the law is reformed. In primitive societies, as E. E. Evans-Pritchard tells us, this is impossible. In modern societies, however, there is an increasing tendency to notice this element of nature in convention (convention as substitute nature) and the element of choice involved. The extent of each element is not easy to assess, of course; but it is worth inquiring into. In particular, there is no reason to be cynical about the frankly arbitrary element in our convention. There is a natural aspect and a choice aspect to, say leash laws, and as long as one can choose, with not much penalty, between a community with a leash law and without, I should find this most commendable.

Perhaps, indeed, it is in our experimentalist nature to adopt diverse conventions. Hence, the Greek dichotomy, as well as the cynicism towards convention plus reverence to nature, eminently reasonable and liberal as it once was, is no longer so.

For all this and the source of the reformist breakaway from the nature-convention dichotomy, see my "Conventions of Knowledge in Talmudic Law," *J. Jewish Studies,* Vol. 25, February 1974, pp. 16–34.

11. Lévi-Strauss's polarities, I think, have an ancestry in paleolinguistics where it was noticed that antonyms are often identical words: a clear example is the word which denotes the holy and also denotes the untouchable, unclean, unholy: taboo. Intellectually, no doubt, what polar concepts one has when one approaches reality much influence what one sees. That one is biased in favor of one pole rather than another is often stressed more, and may in everyday experience count more (since the comceptual scheme is there given), but in intellectual matters it is the polarities themselves, not one's bias in one direction, that cannot but obscure the facts that do not fit the set of polarities as a whole.

Strangely, Sir Francis Bacon was aware of both kinds of bias and so demanded the removal of all abstract terminology prior to empirical research so as to prevent all bias. See his *Novum Organum,* Book I, Aphorisms 15–17, 25, 43, and especially 59; also 60, 90, 97. Of course, his prescription cannot be accepted, for logical reasons, for empirical reasons, for practical reasons. It is the most popular one among natural and social scientists nonetheless.

A promising start in the effort to develop a prehistory of ideas seems to me to be this. Suppose we could divide language into layers; suppose we could then cluster words in a given layer into natural kinds; we could then develop a plausible world view with the given natural kinds and make the hypothesis that it was, indeed, the established view of native speakers. Of course, we have too much leeway here, as we cannot divide language into layers without error, and as there is a jump from natural kinds to a world view. Yet we have some external constraints in the form of archeology, of social anthropology, and ethology, and in the form of a theory of myth, of the origins of language, of theories, of concepts, of preliterate poetry, and so on.

It should be noted that such a dynamic approach has not been tried yet. The nearest to it is Chomsky's excellent critique of Whorf in his Introduction to Adam Schaff, *Language and Cognition*, edited by Robert S. Cohen, based on a translation by Olgierd Wojtasiewicz, McGraw-Hill, New York, 1973, where Chomsky finds in English an old layer exhibiting the same view of time as that which Whorf found in Hopi Indian. See also reference in note 71 to Section VII above.

12.   Let me notice here Lévi-Strauss's Freudian trait. But first a clarification may be called for.

The word "symbol" has different meanings in semantics and in psychology. In both cases a symbol is an entity with meaning, and the word "meaning" again has different meanings in semantics and in psychology. The object which has meaning is, usually, in semantics a signal and in psychology an object. But this is not intrinsic and is so for technical reasons only. In semantics an object can be given the meaning of a message, as already Dr. Johnson noted and as is obvious enough for the advertizer to use in his slogan "say it with flowers". In psychology, all too often the symbol is not a thing, but its name, as, for example, when we use a floral metaphor. The technical reason for the fact that in language we use signals rather than things is obvious: it facilitates speech. For the very same reason we replace in psychology the thing (the fetish, for example) with the metaphor; with the signal which is used for its name. We can speak, then, of the emotional content and of the informative content of a symbol, or, of its meaning.

Freud spoke of the emotional content accompanying the informative content of an imagery which is the original meaning of a word used in a borrowed meaning — which we usually call a metaphor. Lévi-Strauss spoke of the informative content of an emotionally charged imagery very closely linked with what we usually call a myth. Freud spoke here of emotional function, Lévi-Strauss of intellectual functions; Freud thus brought the abnormal to the normal, Lévi-Strauss the savage to the civilized. Both, however, put some constraints on the objects of their study. Thus, Freud had to ignore the artistic value of metaphor and altogether the artistic use of sex and of dreams and of the aberrant; Lévi-Strauss had to ignore the narrative (as opposed to pictorial) aspect of myth. Thus, Freud failed to discuss the psychology of art (as sublimation or therapy) and Lévi-Strauss failed to discuss the intellectual value of mythical thinking for a civilized man (e.g. as in Plato). Both forget the difference between myth and metaphor and the metaphorizing of a myth usually called demythologization (not in Boultmann's original − mythopoietic − sense). Both forget the question, "When do we think better while enhancing emotional overtones, when not?" Evidently, all these put a wedge between the normal and the abnormal, the civilized and the savage, whereas these two thinkers were motivated by the desire to enhance the unity of mankind.

The question Lévi-Strauss shuns and evades most is, "Are we all savage in our thought?" He shows that at times we are, that even the French Revolution has a mythical value for us. Yet, he is too cagy to express a clear opinion. Clearly, there is a catch here. For Lévi-Strauss a mythical mode of thinking consists of two different aspects. One, an axis of two extremes, each false, which we use in different proportions so as to describe reality. Second, we have a symbolic semi-conscious representation of all that. The second aspect is characteristic more of preliterates and aberrant literates (aberrant both as, say, poets, and as, say, hysterics). Lévi-Strauss views the second as less significant than the first, so as to minimize the difference between literates and illiterates. This is apologetic, but permissible. As to the first aspect, the axis of two extreme polarities, he is not sufficiently articulate about it, so let me say something on it.

The more sophisticated we become, the more dualities we can develop, and we learn to connect them not merely associatively, but abstractly, along certain principles. Here Lévi-Strauss does see a fundamental difference between the savage and the sophisticated, though he mystifies it. See the last paragraph of his *Savage Mind*, Chicago University Press, Chicago and London, 1966.

The difference lies in two aspects. First, a scientist does not simply blend opposites intuitively but measures the blend and subjects it to precise and refutable hypothesis. Second, when developing a new abstraction certain opposites (such as Aristotle's of gravity and levity) have to go and new ones replace them (such as Newton's attractions and repulsions), until the new abstraction itself is replaced − perhaps due to refutation or some other criticism. Also, we must admit, new oppositions are added like Jung's contrast between introvert and extrovert people, or Marshall MacLuhan's hot and cold media, or Lévi-Strauss's hot and cold societies, which are doubtlessly exciting as myth-like and so, also, arousing much (silly) hostility.

Of course, modern myths lead to hostility because of the flow of irrationality and the frustation of attempts to refute them (since they are irrefutable). But hostility is not an intelligent response nonetheless.

13. For the alleged influence of Marx on Lévi-Strauss and its actual paucity, see Octavio Paz, *Claude Lévi-Strauss: An Introduction*, Cornell University Press, Ithaca. N.Y., and Cape, London, 1970, 1971, fifth and final chapter. Marx's theory, says Strauss, applies to historical, i.e. literate, societies but not to ahistorical, i.e. preliterate ones. Here, clearly, Lévi-Strauss is not troubled with the question of the unity of mankind and untroubled he divides men into historical and ahistorical. Yet the question is, does Lévi-Strauss at all admit the difference between the historical and the ahistorical, or does he only use it in order to shun Marx and then forget it? In his *Structural Anthropology*, translated by Claire Jacobson and Brooke G. Schoepf, New York, 1963, London, 1968, p. 17, Lévi-Strauss says, "the methodological parallels which are sought between ethnography and history, in order to contrast them, are deceptive." The difference, he adds on p. 18, is, "principally, in their choice of complementary perspectives. History organizes its dates in relation to conscious expressions of conscious life, while anthropology proceeds by examining its unconscious foundations." This is quite Freudian, but hardly Marxist. Lévi-Strauss adds, unabashed (p. 23), "In this sense, the famous statement by Marx, 'Men make their own history, but they do not know that they are making it,' justifies, first, history and, second, anthropology. At the same time it shows that the two approaches are inseparable." Yet here he ignores Marx's claim that the anthropology of history is economic, not semiotic. Later on (pp. 297–8) he is thrilled by the economic aspect of games theory in which he sees "certain aspects of Marxian thought." This is quite a disappointment.

The dichotomy natural-artificial is attacked by Thomas S. Szasz in his brief and very scholarly "Men and Machines", *Brit. J. Phil. Sci.*, Vol. 8 (32), February 1958, pp. 310–317, where a large list of relevant material is discussed, and where the relevance of the dichotomy to mechanism is used to express an anti-mechanistic view based on the requirement for responsibility and relating to the problem of identity: men but not machines have ego crises, suffer from anomie, etc.

Szasz's major point — that mechanism fails even to explain the fact that machines are functional (a piece of wood becomes a machine when used as a lever) was taken up by Michael Polanyi later on, on his *The Study of Man*, The University of Chicago Press, Chicago and London, 1958, pp. 47ff.

Leach was puzzled about this. See his *Lévi-Strauss*, Fontana/Collier, London, 1970, p. 113:

" 'What is *universally* true must be *natural*' he says, with his own emphasis, but this is paradoxical because he starts out with the assumption that what distinguishes the human being from the man-animal is the distinction between Culture and Nature, i.e. that the humanity of man is that which is *non-natural.*"

The paradox is easily resolvable: the dichotomy nature-convention, being the same as truth-error, is greatly different from the dichotomy natural-artifact. When Protagoras says the fire burns the same everywhere but custom varies he refers to two kinds of laws, and the dichotomy natural-artificial refers to two kinds of origins of things. Yet, of course, the law of the land is false in its misleading claim for universality, and so is the artifact as opposed to the natural. Also, of course, following the law of the land we create artifacts whereas following the law of nature alone we do not. Here is the great origin of that idiotic aesthetic theory which says that all folk-arts are the same, that all great artists have universal appeal (and so Tolstoy was a folk-artist; well at least he aspired to be). See Ian C. Jarvie, "Is Technology Unnatural?" *The Listener*, Vol. 77, March 9, 1967.

The polarization natural-artificial is attacked head on by Helmuth Plessner in his discussion of the fundamental laws of philosophical anthropology, as he calls them, the first of which, he says, is that of natural artificiality: it is in man's nature to seek and create his equilibrium by making artifacts. See Marjorie Grene, *Approaches to a Philosophical Biology,* Basic Books, New York, London, 1968, p. 109 and Helmuth Plessner, *Die Stufen des Organischen und der Mensch,* Berlin, 1928, 1965, pp. 309ff.

14. René Descartes, *Discourse on Method*, the second part, 5th paragraph (Paul J. Olscamp's translation):

"But I had learned, ever since College, that we can imagine nothing so strange and unbelievable that it has not been said by some philosopher; and I had recognized in my travels that those who have feelings very contrary to ours are not, for that alone, either barbarians or savages, but that many of them use reason as much or more than we do; and I had considered how the same man, with the same mind, being raised from childhood among the French or Germans, becomes different from what he would be if he had always lived among the Chinese or cannibals . . . therefore I was unable to choose anyone whose opinions were preferable to those of others, and I found myself forced to undertake to guide myself."

15. Lévi-Strauss himself will not be offended if we call him a myth-maker ". . . it would not be erroneous to regard this book" i.e. his *The Raw and the Cooked,* "itself as a myth: in some manner, the myth of mythology." As usual with Lévi-Strauss, this is both an attempt to stress that no science is free of myth and an attempt to get away with anything that pleases him. Science is doubtlessly myth-ridden, but it needs no extra helping of myths. Perhaps Lévi-Strauss himself feels that this is not enough, since in his *Savage Mind* he claims more for himself: he contributes, he says, to "the mythology of our time" — meaning, I suppose, a positive contribution. Hence, he is willing to abide by some criterion of progress — he does not stop at "the mythology of our time" but wishes to advance it.

Lévi-Strauss's distinction between science as a world view and myth as a world view centers on one point: science is explanatory and myth is associational-classificatory. This, I think, is true. There is always Aristotelian classificationism which falls between stools, since it does allude to an explanation of sorts which lurks behind it, and its claim for certain systematic unity is more than mere arbitrary association.

The arbitrary element in mythology is extremely important as arbitrary. Prohibitions and ordeals of momentous significance are presented as mysterious, inexplicable, and yet pregnant with meaning. In a way this truthfully reflects the child's experience of some crucial moment in life. Indeed, scientists too, when deeply puzzled about a strange phenomenon, may encounter the same feeling, yet with the intent to break the spell. It is not surprising, then, that the scientific tradition was averse to arbitrariness — with a hostility betraying fascination — and strongly inclined to determinism. Indeed, even science's hostility to history — until the advent of scientific history — is of this brand. Here Lévi-Strauss is in error: myth is both the arbitrary-historical and meaningful-timeless, whereas science is only the latter, though with Lévi-Strauss in the scientific tradition, quite contrary to his own protestation and intention to be a bridge.

For the importance of the inexplicable as inexplicable see E. Gellner, *The Devil in Modern Philosophy*, Routledge, London and Boston, 1974, Chapter 5, "Is Belief Really Necessary?" and Chapter 9, "Morality and 'je ne sais quoi' Concepts."

16. This idea from information theory is used to present Lévi-Strauss's idea that the superposition of various versions of a myth seems to Edmund Leach to be the true core of his ideas. See his *Lévi-Strauss*, p. 59. Lévi-Strauss himself uses a slightly different metaphor, and stresses the information theoretical aspect a little less. He says in his "The Structural Study of Myth," *J. Am. Folklore*, Vol. 67, 1955, pp. 428–444, reprinted in Lessor and Vogt Reader in *Comparative Religion, An Anthropological Approach*, 2nd ed., Harpers, New York, 1965.

"4.4 The myth will be treated as would be an orchestral score perversely presented as a unilineal series and where our task is to reestablish . . .
2.1. . . Ancient philosophers were reasoning about language the way we are about mythology . . . it is the combination of sounds, not the sounds themselves, which provide the sufficient data.
2.3. . . This is precisely what is expressed in Saussure's distinction between *langue* and *parole*...
2.4. . . the French revolution is both a sequence belonging to the past . . . and an everlasting pattern which can be detected in the present French social structure . . . See for instance, Michelet . . . He describes the French Revolution thus: "This day . . . everything was possible . . . Future became present . . . that is, no more time, a glimpse of eternity."

17. ". . . superstructures are *faulty acts* which have 'made it' socially. Hence it is vain to go to historical consciouness for the truest meaning", says Claude Lévi-Strauss (*The Savage Mind*, University of Chicago Press, 1966, p. 254), thus eliminating the specific from his explanatory scheme.

The idea was anticipated by F. A. Hayek, who considers society as an unintended consequence of individuals' actions, Incidentally, he views this fact a sufficient refutation of the dichotomy between nature and convention, and the chief reason for people's reluctance to admit it. See his "Kinds of Order in Society," in *The New Individualist*, Vol. 3, No. 2, 1963, pp. 3–12, especially pp. 5–6. Yet, of course, Hayek's conclusion from this is diametrically opposed to that of Lévi-Strauss, and he finds history very relevant and historical explanation very much in place.

18. Edmund Leach, *Lévi-Strauss*, Fontana/Collier, London, 1970, p. 50, mentions two major difficulties. One concerns the ease with which one can fit together theory and facts. "Logical Positivists can therefore argue that Lévi-Strauss' theories are more or less meaningless because, in the last analysis, they cannot be

rigourously tested." The second concerns the collectivist aspect of Lévi-Strauss's theories, the abstractness and metaphysical character of his chief idea etc. It is entirely unclear how much Leach endorses Lévi-Strauss's ideas in spite of these two objections, how much he clings to the objections, and what he does about the conflict if he is in a conflict here. The very fact that he puts two positivistic objections separately, because only the first is modern and the second both modern and classical, without explaining what he does, is endearing. For his rejection of Lévi-Strauss's Durkheimian collectivist view see the opening of his "The Legitimation of King Solomon." As for the other objection, the modern one, it seems clear that he is ambiguous about it, and confused too — since he by implication views Popper (whom he does not mention) as a member of the Logical Posivist school. First, on p. 54 of his *Lévi-Strauss*, he uses Popper's view and compares Lévi- Strauss with Freud: "The same fascination . . . and the same kind of weakness too." Namely, both are unfalsifiable. On p. 82, however, he condemns the "reckless sweep with which himself is prepared to apply his generalizations" as "a kind of verbal juggling . . . quite typical of Lévi-Strauss' . . . procedure [which] cannot show us the truth." Here, clearly not falsifiability, but verifiability is what Leach is after, as the end of the quote betrays: "they only lead into a world where all things are possible and nothing sure."

19. Unlike the Renaissance, the Age of Reason viewed science as descriptive and art as affective or expressive. What the Romantics claimed was that art and religion are descriptive of man's inner world and are thus, even as descriptive, superior to natural science. This led to a great confusion about the words "science" and "natural science", which are used at times as synonyms and at times not: thus positivistic empirical psychologists wish at times that their science be considered natural, at times they declare it social and so in a sense not "natural"; the Romantics declare history a science, and even "dogmatic science" is not an unknown expression on the Continent. Romantics love to protest against the English use of "science" as synonymous with "natural science", as a veiled plea to admit the history of culture and art as scientific, not to mention theology.

20. See Leo Strauss, *Natural Rights and History*, University of Chicago Press, Chicago and London, 1953. Leo Strauss's observation that Romanticism had a positivistic and scientific-empirical pretension seems to me to be astute and very useful. Consider, for example, Jacob Grimm's revised preface to second edition of his *Grammar*, quoted in John T. Weterman, *Perspectives in Linguistics*, University of Chicago Press, Chicago, 1963, p. 20, "I am hostile to notions of universal logic in grammar. They apparently lend themselves to exactness and solidarity of [a priori] definition, but impede [empirical] observation, which to me is the soul of linguistic science". See also note 34 to Section XII below.

21. The discussion of nature versus convention relates to both the law of the land and to the legitmacy of the government. The two look the same, but are not.

The political import of the polarization of all societies into nature and convention, unlike the earlier polarization into nature and culture was, first and
foremost, to question the sovereign rights of government, and to declare only
nature to be the legitimizer of sovereignty. Rule by convention was arbitrary and so
no better than highway robbery, to which one submits, if at all, only under the threat
of the use of brute — i.e. illegitimate — force. See also note 103 to Section IX above.

(Sir Karl Popper sees contractualism as a version of conventionalism and so
present in some ancient Greek texts. I think here is the most serious flaw in his
Open Society, both historically and philosophically. I have aired my philosophical
misgivings in my "Modified Conventionalism is More Comprehensive Than Modified Essentialism" in P. A. Schilpp, ed., *The Philosophy of Karl Popper,* 1974, and
in my "Modified Conventionalism", *Science in Flux,* Reidel, Dordrecht and
Boston, 1975. I shall not discuss Greek history for want of scholarship.)

The root of contractualism came in a roundabout way in Machiavelli's *Prince.*
Already Lucretius, *The Nature of Things,* Bk V, lines 1137–1158, likewise
Machiavelli pursues the idea of the arbitrariness of brute force with cruel logic and
brings hope out of the very depth of despair: the prince who may do all to achieve
power may also desire to be loved since government by love is more stable than by
fear and he may want peace since in peace he may strengthen his control even
further. Hobbes turned this around: the population submits to the sovereign king
because he promises peace, and indeed the legitimacy of his rule is in his control
and prevention of internal wars. If so, said Locke, we should make it always
possible to dismiss an undesirable government, i.e. one which does not keep its
obligations; this is his checks and balances theory. The principle of all this is
Rousseau's: We willingly give up a part of our freedom, he said, but as little of it
as necessary for the maintenance of the peace.

The contractualist idea became, then, the view that the government obtains its
mandate from the people or else it is a gang of highway robbers. That means that
by nature the mandate is in the hands of the people, and the people is sometimes
every individual, sometimes "the general will" or the group as a whole.

Even the individualistic view enables us to ask, but is the law of the land
convention? And democrats like Kelsen and Delvin say, yes, the people's whim
binds: they are still conventionalist regarding law even though naturalists regarding sovereignty or the rights to govern.

The most important corollary to Lord Devlin's view is that a change in public
morality due to rational debate is as good as change due to any other cause. Yet,
he would argue rationally that sovereignty naturally rests in the people but their
wishes in matters legislative are arbitrary. It was the rational debate on this point
of his that helped bring about significant legal reform, the abolition of sexual
victimless crimes so-called. Now the abolition of the prohibition against alcohol
was effected after much damage was caused to American society, and many
people feel that unless the prohibition against canabis — or any other drug —
becomes equally harmful, it should stay in the books. Others argue that this evil
should be anticipated and prevented. See, e.g., Norman E. Zinberg and John A.
Robertson, *Drugs and the Public,* Simon and Schuster, New York, 1972. Now Devlin

must admit that a rational debate on the good or evil that victimless crime laws – in matters of sex, gambling, and drugs – bring about changes in the law, at least on the view that people's tastes suffice to decide criteria of good and evil. Yet Devlin insists that it is popular revulsion against victimless crimes that suffices to make them crimes. On this he is plainly in error: a rational man can weigh the cost of prohibiting whatever is objectionable, and at times find it even more objectionable. See H. L. A. Hart, *Punishment and Responsibility*, Oxford University Press, New York and Oxford, 1968, Postscript, and references on p. 267; see also H. L. A. Hart, *Law, Liberty and Morality*, A Vintage Book, Random House, 1963, the first and only text to break away from the nature-convention dichotomy in legal philosophy, and while discussing and criticizing Devlin's views; see also references there. As Hart notices, the recommendations of the Wolfenden committee to abolish victimless crimes is based on liberalism proper, not on legal principles that go back to nature or to convention. This raises an interesting contrast between Greek and modern democracies. The standard view of Greek democracy as direct, unlike modern representative democracy, is true but not deep as it overlooks the fact that representative government is very widespread all over the earth, in primitive and not so primitive societies. But the Greeks were tolerant either with no ideological basis for their toleration or with naturalism, the brotherhood of men, as its base. Liberalism is a modern creation, rooted in reformist parliamentary practices and the checks and balances system. The checks and balances are Locke's. The reformism comes from ancient Roman and Talmudic practices. See my "Conventions of Knowledge in Talmudic Law", in Bernard S. Jackson, ed., *Studies in Jewish Legal History: In Honour of David Daube*, Jewish Chronicle Publications, London, 1974, pp. 16–34.

The major practical difference between the Greek and the modern radicals is, indeed, in the modern parliamentary practices. The very ancient Greek discovery that law is mere convention led to instability because individuals found themselves not bound by laws that are mere conventions and errors. The public debates, say, on Devlin's and Wolfenden's views were conducted in a totally different spirit, of the democratic view that we abide by laws even while combating them by rational means. In many ways the modern world has gone far beyond the Greek ideas on which it bases its theory and practice. Yet inductivist philosophy of science in the twentieth century is still ancient Greek: it assumes that one acts on one's beliefs. It was, thus, Russell's inductivism that repeatedly pulled him back to radicalism.

This, to conclude the discussion, may raise the question again: who is the sovereign? Where does sovereignty lie? What is the proper exercise of sovereignty? It seems that the more decentralized and democratic government is and the more active citizens are in participation in the process of government, the less important the question becomes, and the more one tends to say, intuitively but not very clearly, that sovereign power lies in the people when they exercise it well. This is, I think, much in the spirit of Popper's *Open Society*, though somehow the aspect of participation is hardly mentioned there. For, he says, the question is not who should rule? but how should the abuse of government be curbed?

22. The example of the post–World War II pendulum swing of public opinion from one extreme to the other is not the only one. The first modern instance is the Puritan Revolution in England, as discussed in J. W. N. Watkins, "Revolutionaries and their Principles, Milton's Vision of a Reformed England", *The Listener,* January 22, 1959, pp. 168–9, and 172, which I consider classic. Other instances are, of course, the French Revolution, the Russian revolution, etc. Also, as Watkins notes, the failure of a revolution may swing the pendulum either to the right or further to the left. Hence, for example, anarchism and syndicalism, or Luxemburgism and Trotskyism.

The most important and powerful and conspicuous vacillation is in attitudes towards family ties which Plato denounced and Aristotle extolled – both in the name of Nature. The pendulum keeps swinging. Thus we read in a recent publication, Robert Nisbet, *The Social Philosophers, Community and Conflict in Western Thought*, Thos. Crowell Co., New York, 1973, p. 447:

"...kinship ... is enjoying one of its periodic recrudescences... Only a generation or two ago, imposing voices were declaring the bankrupcy of the family and its replacement by other, more individualistic transitory ties. Events have proven these voices mistaken ..."

Needless to say this is not the last word, and the literature on group marriage and other experiments based on dissatisfaction with traditional forms of kinship is swelling. See Gordon F. Streib, ed., *The Changing Family: Adaptation and Diversity*, Addison-Wesley, Reading, Mass., and London, 1973. See also notes 51 and 52 to Section XIV and note 65 to Section XV below.

XII SCIENCE AND PSEUDO-SCIENCE ARE ENTANGLED

The Ivory Tower has libraries full of debates on the questions just posed. The major disagreement on it is between rationalists, the children of the Enlightenment, and the irrationalists, the romantics. In more recent times, authors either still belong to one of these two schools, or they concoct mixtures of ideas borrowed from both, or they are forging a new and alternative philosophy. The chief point of departure for the romantic school from that of the Enlightenment was a new attitude to history. Indeed, this is why the romantic school is often called the Historical school. But let me approach matters slowly, beginning with the Enlightenment's hostility to history and its roots in the Enlightenment's extremist theory of rationality.

Much has been written about the hostility which men of the Enlightenment showed towards history – human history, they said, is a record of sad accidents and of meaningless events:[23] folly, ignorance, superstition, war, pestilence; soon, however, the millenium will come: enlightenment and universality, science and technology, universal understanding, and good will. Why should we delve into the

past? — Yet, we have records that show clearly that the past positively
haunted the men of the Enlightenment. Did they wish to forget
history, convention, the valley of the shadow of death, and totally
immerse themselves in their search for the Enlightened millenium; or
did they wish to remember and maybe even preserve a little? Perhaps
the strongest image of Jewish Enlightenment is of the Jew who broke
the taboos but studied the Talmud devoutly. History is less easily
forgotten than was assumed; people discover in themselves a passion
for history. Is this passion rational? The problem is standard, and
there is much arbitrariness possible in any answer to it. We have thus
replaced the question, is man in fact rational? with the question, is
the social scientist in fact rational? Or, is he, perhaps, only partly
rational?

The very polarization

truth : falsity :: nature : convention :: reality : appearance

makes it impossible to talk of degrees of rationality; we must therefore observe in the traditional mode also the polarization

truth : falsity :: rationality : irrationality.

Now this last duo is much more common than the duo,

reality : appearance :: nature : convention.

Indeed, the parallel between the true and the rational is pre-
scientific, whereas the parallel between convention and falsehood goes
back only to Greek science. We can find the first parallel in primitive
cultures and in non-Greek civilizations, and we can find it even in the
most extreme cases around.[24] One extreme is the theory of original
sin encountered already, though in its medieval garb: while it is most
rational for man not to sin and most irrational for him to sin, because
the fun of sin is at best momentary and the damage it causes is
everlasting, nevertheless, sin he will.[25] The other extreme is the per-
version of the positivistic version of the classic eighteenth-century
doctrine of enlightened self-interest, known as De Finetti's doctrine of
revealed preferences.[26] It consists of the elimination of belief and
elimination of the profession of any belief and substituting the
practical articulation of it; action speaking ever so much louder than
words, and, action always betrays belief. If, in particular, a man bets
in favor of a prediction, he thereby expresses the degree of his belief
in its happening — which belief is *eo ipso* rational. Rationality, however, here totally lost its universality: each man has his own scale of
probability. Since, in fact, people's probabilities are inconsistent (e.g.

they erratically bet on horses with no idea about odds or about the facts of the matter), De Finetti would have to hide behind some excuse, e.g. that people change their subjective scales of probability, etc. But rational they are, he insists.

What is common to both extremes, to the ultra-modern and to the medieval, to the one which condemns man to utter rationality and to the one which sees him as hopelessly irrational, is the correlation

truth : falsity :: rationality : irrationality.

No doubt, the medieval thinker, but not the holder of the theory of subjective probability, believes in the existence of heaven and hell. This is immaterial. The medieval thinker ascribes this belief to his fellow men and concludes that they are irrational; the modern one assumes that they are rational and concludes that they reject this belief, all lip-service to it not withstanding. Both agree that rationality links belief to action. De Finetti, it is true, speaks not of a belief but of a subjective probability — yet, the object of the subjective probability is still the truth or falsity of a prediction, and the probability is a refined measure of the degree of a belief. De Finetti has not yet heard of self-deception, not even of the one practiced by all obsessive gamblers. Or rather, he has not yet taken account of it, but hopes he will — he deceives himself that his work is scientific etc. Or perhaps he simply explains 'self-deception' away.

Is at least science, if not all of human activity, not rational? Can we not delineate science from pseudo-science as to retain at least the rationality of science? I think the last shot in this direction, and a most exciting one, was that of Sir Karl Popper. I would compare his failure to Maxwell's failure to construct a model of the aether: it is a failure that may be viewed as terminal. Popper's delineation is valid and important, but it fails to purify science from all pseudo-science. His very examples of pseudo-science, namely Marx's theory of society and the economy, as well as Freud's or Adler's psychoanalytic theories, turned out to be, by his own very criterion (of empirical refutability), in part scientific and in part not, and in quite un-expected ways. And so I think the game is up. Popper expresses too much wishful thinking, and what he wishes — a clear demarcation — is anyway not too desirable. His erstwhile disciple, Imre Lakatos, has expressed the hope, as well as the difficulties, in attempting a proper demarcation. His expression of the tension of the theory of rationality, to use Lévi-Strauss's mode of speaking again, came as a wonderful quip, which had by now become internationally famous.[27] The history of ideas, he said, is a caricature of its own rational reconstruction. The rational reconstruction of the history of ideas, that is, signifies more than the real history, since it is, so-to-speak, the essence of the history of ideas. I like this bold idea, since it at one go notices that inevitably rational reconstruction is so very different from reality, so much of a distortion, and yet it condones that distortion. In this manner, there is both recognition of the fact that rationality is only partial, and indulgence towards the exaggerated rationality of the reconstruction — for the exaggeration is still defective even if reality is but a caricature of it. No doubt, historians of ideas who ignore blind alleys, and pass quickly over dull periods and center on exciting ones, get what Lakatos has labeled "instant rationality", and which is quite misleading.[28] Yet, Lakatos is right; this misleading image is justified, since thinkers work hard in order to achieve, at least in retrospect and through some modification, just the very rational story that the one who reconstructs it is after. It is a fact that intellectual autobiographies are usually more reconstructed than intellectual biographies; and one can hardly call this lies.

Yet, in spite of my sympathy for Lakatos' views, I have one grave misgiving: rational reconstructions themselves may have to be rejected. I do not mean streamlined, I do not mean improved by some internal criterion of improvement or other. I mean we may have to send a rational reconstruction back to the drawing board. We may even have to revolutionize our view of the very rationality of the reconstruction, not merely the reconstruction itself. In particular, I contend, the very system of social thinking within which we reconstruct its history, has been superseded. The very polarization between rationality and irrationality, the very claim that the one is to the other as truth is to falsehood, has to be given up and, consequently, all rational reconstructions of social ideas have to be redone.

It is a historical fact, I contend, that the irrationalist historical schools of the 19th century led up to Marxism[29] and to functionalism, as well as to social Darwinism and to phony animal psychology, and to other irrational activities (including nationalistic politics and myth-making). All these concoctions made the study of existing conventions so much an integral part of our rational heritage, that I start to wonder whether we are not drastically unfair in viewing the nineteenth-century historical school as no more than irrationalistic. It is all too well-known that both the classical positivists and also those of our century suffered from a lack of historical perspective. Indeed, Otto Neurath, the leader of the Vienna Circle, frankly and repeatedly lamented the lack of it amongst his colleagues.[30] And if rational scientific attitudes do not go well with the historical approach, I do not know which of the two should take the blame; or why.

There may, then, very well be a grave injustice towards the historical school in the very fact that their doctrines were not rationally reconstructed (regardless of their own irrationalism, of course).

The historical school, beginning with Edmund Burke,[31] found it most important not just to denounce the universal in man, but to do so in a positivistic (antiessentialistic) mood, and also to replace the universal view with an alternative. In a positivistic mood, the historical school could, and did, reject the universal, the true ultimate reality, the substance; and as metaphysical, no less. And on top of this insult, in the crazy inconsistency shared by all good positivists, they developed a new metaphysics − that of the inequality of men. This metaphysics started in Burke with cultural inequality; this was followed up by his German disciples with national inequality, and it all ended with racial inequality and the greatest disaster in the whole history of mankind. How much we can blame the tradition of such wild theorizing for the brutalities which followed I cannot say. Yet, it turns out, at least according to some historians, including Shmuel Ettinger, that even in the irrational mode of thinking the nineteenth-century romantics found trailblazers among their Enlightened predecessors. Not only so much of the obscure in Hegel had allusions to the little which is obscure in Kant; not only, as both Hayek and Leo Strauss have noticed, has the historical school made positivistic claims just like those of their Enlightened predecessors; not only did all positivists − of the 18th and the 19th centuries − combat metaphysics in general while defending their own metaphysical doctrines with equal zeal. Even in the deployment of cheap propaganda, such as cheap anti-Jewish arguments, the Enlightenment only fell short of romanticism, but was itself not idle. The Enlightenment, as I said, was millenarian, and its adherents found it easy to gloss over a detail here, to indulge a point there, only *pro tem*, of course, until salvation come.[32]

If so, there is a difference between the romantics and the Enlightened, but merely one of degree. And in degrees not of inhumanity, insensitivity, or sheer indulgence in propaganda − but in degrees of rationality. This is so very significant because if you take away from the Enlightenment its right to claim perfect rationality nothing remains of it *by its own light*. So back to the drawing board, and let us reconstruct both movements, the Enlightenment and romanticism. Moreover, the pessimism of the romantics, explicable as an outcome of their own irrationalism, may alternatively have been caused by the recognition that the millenium is not so near. Perhaps, as I once thought, the failure of the millenium, i.e. the failure of the French Revolution, caused first irrationalism and then the pessimism of the same first irrationalist. Perhaps. Reading Leo Strauss I am willing to reconsider and posit this view: the failure of the French Revolution was rationally interpreted as the failure of the expected millenium; as the refutation of both the expectation and the theory of the Enlightenment which gave rise to it. The failure thus led to a revision in expectation, to more caution in expectation. Hence, rational revision led to both pessimism and an increased attention to history — as to the history of human folly which is more than a passing accident.[33] The history of human folly was now considered the natural history of man, the stock of facts upon which to erect a more solid system of human science. This view of history as human science par excellence was backed by relativism which, says Leo Strauss, led to nihilism.

It was my initial intention to say nothing about relativism and nihilism. Indeed, I wanted to use nihilism as nothing but the absurd to which both conventionalism and relativism take us with a logic of their own. And, relativism regarding the truth is a super-sophisticated view which rests on intellectual rubbish (the phrase is Russell's). We can, of course, define degrees of truth. We can easily speak of truth within a given system and make the different systems incomparable. We can also define the absolute truth and correlate the relative and the absolute. Those who make truth relative, then, accomplish nothing unless they declare the absolute truth meaningless; and when they do so they simply commit an error.

The positivists would shun the absolute truth unless it were attainable. The romantics would endorse this — hence the importance of Leo Strauss's view of romanticism as perverted positivism[34] — and they add the following dilemma. If the absolute truth is attainable and attained then it makes one culture, the one which has attained it, privileged; and all other cultures, and all history, become then utterly irrelevant. If absolute truth is unattainable, or attainable but not attained, or even merely possibly not attained, then the skeptic wins and we have no knowledge at all. Thus the misguided fear of nihilism which might creep through skepticism is the possible cause of the nihilism which creeps through relativism. This, however, is a rational reconstruction of romanticism as an attempt at rescuing its rationality.

Indeed, according to this reconstruction, the romantics shared with the Enlightenment the polarization of truth and error, nature and convention, the rational and the arbitrary. It is only with a new theory which rejects the polarization that we may try a new way to ratio-nality. We may recognize, even with ease, that rationality is not utterly binding; that not all irrationality is caprice; that some error is reasonable some not; that some error is nearer to the truth than other; that not all convention is equally irrational, arbitrary, erroneous.

Yet there is much opposition to all this. Even Leo Strauss, who is willing to see romanticism as in a sense not so much arbitrary as overrationalistic (positivistic, scientistic), even he polarizes nature and convention; and easily concludes from the failure of the Romantic school's conventionalism that naturalism is true, that we must return to naturalism, though naturalism has now failed too. So, he wants naturalism to function as a mere regulative idea, as an ideal. Of course, he arrives there by equating the absolute truth with nature. I too want the absolute truth as an ideal, but I refuse to equate it with nature. I prefer another way. Let me describe in brief the polarization between nature and convention and how Lévi-Strauss may help us overcome it as sheer mythology — the naturalism of Lévi-Strauss himself notwith-standing.

Notes to Section XII

23. One of the major traditional contrasts between myth and science is the claim that myth is an inadequate explanation because it is a historical explanation. This theory is a stumbling block which is hard to get rid of (see Jarvie and Agassi, "The Rationality of Magic", mentioned in note 70 to Section V above). Lévi-Strauss quite completely overlooks this, though he does opt for universalism and he does claim that myth is universal, the science of the concrete. So to speak, it comes as a story because as a story it is more tangible. This, of course, is a more sophisticated version of F. M. Cornford's earlier views (see references 56 to Section XIV and 58 to Section XV below); yet it is still positivistic.

It seems to me that the polarization universal-historical does not hold for myth. A specific quality of all myth, I suggest, is that it fuses the universal with the historical, thereby intimating the myth of the eternal return. That eternal return is a central theme of ancient mythology was noted by Cornford (see the end of his "The Unwritten Philosophy"). It is repeatedly used as a standard ploy in science fiction. The myth of eternal return is very rich in promising safety and tragedy at one go, enormous peace of mind and a touch of hysteria. But this is not to say that the myth of eternal return was gone when the idea of progress took over. In a passage very anticipatory of Lévi-Strauss's theory of myth as a language, R. G. Collingwood concludes his essay on Oswald Speng-ler's cyclic myth (*Essays in the Philosophy of History*, University of Texas, 1965, paperback, McGraw-Hill, 1966, p. 75):

"Thus the historical cycle is a permanent feature of all historical thought; but

whether it occurs, it is incidental to a point of view. The cycle is the historians
field of vision at a given moment . . ."
Without making it equally clear, however, Collingwood contrasts the cyclic view
with that of progress. He explicitly contrasts the two views in his essay on Croce's
philosophy of history (p. 16) and more openly in his essay on a philosophy of
progress (p. 105). Lévi-Strauss enables us to paraphrase, cyclicity and progress are
the two poles of the historian's myth, the contrast which, perhaps, may be mediated by "the meaning of history" (p. 112). For more on the meaning of history
without the myth of progress see Popper's *Open Society*, final chapter.

24. The fact that the Greek philosophical dichotomy nature-convention has its
parallel in the primitive nature-culture, as Lévi-Strauss says, does not make the
primitive dichotomy a precursor to the Greek philosophical one. For, whereas the
Greeks equated nature to truth and reality and convention to falsehood and
appearances, primitives live in their culture as the very bosom of the real. See
Mircea Eliade, *Cosmos and History,* translated by W. R. Trask, Harper Torch,
1959, p. 95:
     ". . . Archaic man . . . living at the heart of the *real* . . . amounts to respecting
     the "law". . . he nonetheless lived in harmony with the cosmic rhythms . . ."
This may mean that Eliade ascribes to archaic man natural monism, or that he
ascribes to him the will to dominate nature by magic rites. His presentation of the
law, pp. 31–3, is systematically vague, and his discussion of "Map philosophical
myths and the more or less scientific cosmologies . . . which begins with the pre-So-
cratics" (p. 118–20) avoids the issue of myth versus science or the nature-convention dichotomy altogether. Yet in his *Myth and Reality*, Harper and Row, New
York, 1963, p. 112, he says, "with 'demythicization' . . . did we finally do away
with mythical thought."

25. Two delightful descriptions of medievalism I would like to recommend,
perhaps as not very scholarly, but as profound and insightful in all their deceptive
simplicity: H. Heine, *Religion and Philosophy in Germany*, and B. Russell, *Marriage and Morals*, London, 1929. Even Friedrich Heer, *The Mediaeval World,
Europe 1100–1350,* translated by Janet Sondheimer, Weidenfeld and Nicolson,
London, 1962, World Pbl. Co., Mentor, New York, 1963, the latest praise of the
Middle Ages, is harsh in Chapter 13 on Jews and women (!).

26. The literature on De Finetti's theory is so vast that even bibliographies on it
are bulky. For my part I recommend D. Gillies' review of De Finetti's *Teoria della
Probablitià*, called "The Subjective Theory of Probability", in the *British Journal
for the Philosophy of Science*, Vol. 23 (2), May 1972, pp. 138–157. See also my
"Subjectivism: From Infant Disease to Chronic Illness", in *Synthèse*, Vol. 30,
1975, pp. 3–14; see also there, pp. 33–8.

27. Lakatos' quip is quoted in I. C. Jarvie, *Concepts and Society,* Routledge,
London and Boston, 1972, p. 181, note 15. No doubt it appeared elsewhere as
well; it is however, more a matter of oral tradition than of publication.

It is interesting to compare Lakatos' quip with the remark he published ("Proofs and Refutations", IV *Brit. J. Phil. Sci.,* Vol. 15, 1964, p. 315), which is much more guarded and so not at all as striking as the one attributed to him by oral tradition: "actual history is frequently a caricature of its rational reconstruction." The word "frequently" makes the printed version perceptive; its omission makes the oral version Hegelian or quasi-Hegelian. Also, I. Lakatos "Methodology of Scientific Research Programs", in *Criticism and the Growth of Knowledge,* eds. I. Lakatos and A. Musgrave, Cambridge University Press, 1970, pp. 91–196, p. 138, says that one has to check both one's rational reconstruction for its lack of historicity and history for its lack of rationality. Also, Lakatos said in a seminar discussion following a paper I read in his seminar in June 1973, in response to my rejection of his view as too Hegelian, that one must endorse Hegel's doctrine of the cunning of history since all it means is that we are allowed to ascribe to historical figures the rational yet unintended adherence to what we today consider to be the proper rules of conduct. For my own objection to this very claim and to the Hegel-Ryle-Polanyi-Lakatos view, see my "The Logic of Scientific Inquiry", *Synthèse,* Vol. 26, 1974, pp. 498–514.

28. Lakatos' discussion of instant rationality can be found in his "Methodology of Scientific Research Programs" cited in the previous note, Section (d), "A New Look at Crucial Experiment: The End of Instant Rationality", pp. 154ff., and in later publications of his. As for my view of instant rationality see my *Towards an Historiography of Science,* cited in note 3 to the Introduction, above, Section 13, "The Advantage of Avoiding Being Wise After the Event."

29. Arnold Hauser, *Mannerism, The Crisis of the Renaissance and the Origins of Modern Art,* Routledge, London, 1965, p. 100:
> "Marx was also guilty of romanticizing the past in his assumption that mechanization and mere machine-winding led and were bound to lead to the worker's intellectual frustration. In reality, however, work on a machine was mentally more demanding than ploughing a field, and called for more intelligence than handling a hoe or shovel, or doing the work of many artisans on feudal estates or in small village communities."

The view that science is descriptive and not expressive is common since the Age of Reason. Feuerbach conceded to the romantic idealists that even science has an expressive component and Marx, following Feuerbach, added that even art, especially narrative fiction, has a descriptive component even when attempting to be as nondescriptive as possible. Both have viewed religion as expressive — simply because they were atheists: Fichte who was an idealist viewed even science as merely expressive.

R. G. Collingwood, in his monumental *Speculum Mentis,* Oxford, 1924, presents religion, art, and science as man's efforts to comprehend the universal and the particular — and he concludes that art has been thus for the least unsuccessful for some very general reasons. See my "Unity and Diversity in Science" referred to in note 9 to Section I above, end of Section V there.

30. See Barrington Moore, Jr., *Political Power and Social Theory*, Cambridge,
Mass., 1958, p. 123.

"When we set the dominant body of current thinking against important figures
of the nineteenth century, the following differences emerge. First of all, the
critical spirit has all but disappeared. Second, modern sociology, and perhaps
to a lesser extent also modern political science, economics, and psychology, are
ahistorical. Third, modern social science tends to be abstract and formal. In
research, social science today displays considerable technical virtuosity. But
this virtuosity has been gained at the expense of content. Modern sociology has
less to say about society than it did fifty years ago".

Neurath's lament cited in the text belongs to oral tradition.

Radicalism and its cognate positivism were ahistorical from the start, but
became historical in the nineteenth century due to the intrusion of historicism.
See note 2 to this chapter. The modern rejection of historicism naturally led to
the return to the neglect, noted by Barrington Moore and others. What is remarkable, then, was not the Vienna Circle's neglect but Neurath's interest in history.
See Robert S. Cohen's sympathetic essay on him in Paul Edward's encyclopedia of
philosophy. Yet, both Neurath and Edgar Zilsel showed interest in both the
history of science and Marxism: their interest was a survival, to use the anthropological term.

Can there be an interest in history not rooted in conservatism and not historicist? (This apart from the fact that historicism is willy-nilly conservative, as
Popper, Robert Tucker, and others have noticed.) I think it is clear that the
answer is affirmative. But how exactly? On what ideological foundations?

I think the reason J. H. Plumb, *The Death of the Past*, Boston, 1970, is so
famous because it purports, however indirectly, to answer this question. On page
60 Plumb declares the interest in history to be – *prima facie*, I presume –
conservative: on page 65, in a note (!), he declares scientific history to be of a
different ilk. What he thinks is scientific, however, is revealed on p. 106, where he
offers a naive inductivist view of science, on pp. 133 and 135, where he expresses
crypto-neo-Marxist views, and on p. 134, note (!) where he regresses, against his
intention, to old-fashioned historicism.

31. Burke is the author, in his *Reflections on the French Revolution*, of the myth
that the French are apriorists or speculative thinkers and the British are true
empiricists, whereas in truth radicalism had been shared till then by both empiricists and intellectualists. (Admittedly, his chief opponent, Dr. Richard Price,
was an Englishman and "a non-conformist minister of eminence"; and he branded
him "a dogmatist", "who seems to have speculated himself into no small degree of
fervor upon this subject" – pp. 27 and 66 of the Doubleday Dolphin edition, New
York, 1961. But he dismisses him as one of "this society of the Old Jewry and the
London Tavern", p. 98.) In criticizing the French he says (p. 73) "The science of
constructing a commonwealth, or renovating it, or reforming it, like every other
experimental science, not to be taught *a priori*". He requires cumulative data,
adding (p. 74), "The nature of man is intricate . . . The simple governments are

fundamentally defective . . ." He adds irrational arguments (p. 75): "The rights of man are . . . incapable of definition" but concludes "Men have no rights to what is not reasonable" and "these theorists" who justify the Revolution demand rationality, which is unreasonable. Empiricism becomes in Burke's hand not a matter of inductive evidence but of that trial and error which George Bernard Shaw praised (*The Devil's Disciple*, preface) as "muddling through" (and as typically English). He continues with declaring (p. 90) the idea that "a king is but a man" a "barbarous philosophy". In his view the Enlightenment is unenlightened because it ignores "the wisdom of others" (p. 101) and the fact that "man is by his constitution a religious animal" (p. 104), whereas the rights of man are but a speculative idea (p. 44):

> "for reasons worthy of that practical wisdom which superseded their theoretical science, they [Parliament in the days of Charles the First!] preferred this positive [*sic*], recorded, *hereditary* title to [freedom] . . . to that vague, speculative [*sic!*] right which espoused their sure inheritance to be . . . torn to pieces . . ."

He calls "this policy" (p. 45) "the happy effect of following nature, which is wisdom without reflection, and above it". But in addition to hostile irrationalism allegedly justified by rational skepticism, he also offers a favorable attitude (p. 71):

> "Far am I from denying ["the rights of men"] in theory; full as far is my heart from withholding in practice (if I were of power to give or to withhold) the *real* rights of men. In denying their false claims of right, I do not mean to injure those which are real . . . "

He admits the right to abide by the law, to have justice administered, etc. But not the right to equality. One's share in a venture, he concludes the paragraph "is a thing to be settled by convention".

This raises the question, does Burke believe in nature or in convention? The answer is, in both. I quote a passage which I think is very clear, and one which uses, as the one above (p. 44), the word "positive" which I think Burke gave currency to.

> "The rights of *men* — that is to say the natural rights of mankind — are indeed sacred things; and if any public measure is proven mischievously to affect them, the objection ought to be fatal to that measure, even if no charter at all could be set up against it. If the natural rights are further affirmed and declared by express covenants . . . by written instruments and positive [*sic*] engagements, they are in still better condition . . . Indeed, . . . formal recognition . . . can never be subverted . . . "

(Speech on Mr. Fox's East India Bill; reprinted in *The Philosophy of Edmund Burke*, A Selection from His Speeches and Writings, edited, with Introduction, by L. I. Bredvold and R. G. Ross, The University of Michigan Press, Ann Arbor, 1960, p. 68.) I do not quite understand Burke's term "positive"; in his expression (p. 73), for example, "suffer any artificial positive limitation upon those rights", the word "positive" seems to me quite redundant; the dictionary suggests "positive" is the same as "factual" when opposed to "speculative" (as in "positivism", though much older). Not much later Saint-Simon introduced the word "positive" to mean fully demonstrated. See Emile Durkheim, *Socialism*, edited with an introduction by Alvin W. Gouldner, from the edition originally edited with a preface by Marcel Mauss, Collier Books, New York, 1962, p. 134. See the concise and clear book by Frank O'Gorman, *Edmund Burke: His Political Philosophy*, George Allen and Unwin, London, 1973, and Indiana University Press, Bloomington, 1974, especially about the development of his reactionism and empiricist methodology so-called, before the French Revolution. See Index Art. political philosophy, method; and radicals.

32. See S. Ettinger, "Jews and Judaism as Seen by the English Deists of the 18th Century", in Hebrew, *Zion*, Vol. 29, 1964, pp. 102–207 (with English summary). See also his "The Origins of Modern Anti-Semitism," in *Dispersion and Unity*, No. 9, pp. 17–37.

See also Nathan Rotenstreich, *The Recurring Pattern: Studies in Anti-Judaism in Modern Thought*, Weidenfeld and Nicolson, London, 1963.

It is a fascinating fact that Feuerbach's final verdict — Christianity is the best established religion yet is still too sectarian and so not good enough — is used by a few front-rank science fiction writers to resolve their ambivalence. It allows them to endorse both the universalism of science and a bias in favor of Christianity, especially as compared with Judaism, i.e. it enables them to condone their own hostility to Judaism as being — no doubt — of the rather mild variety. It is mild hostility, incidentally, which is a significant positive contributor to the eruption of violent and brutal genocide. This is Ettinger's thesis which I have been presenting in the text. It is amusing, then, that Feuerbach's final achievement is both the articulation of the mild hostility of his Enlightened predecessors (including Voltaire and Kant) and the spearhead of modern social anthropology, beginning with Taylor and Frazer. For the religious bias of these see E. E. Evans-Pritchard, *Theories of Primitive Religion*, Clarendon Press, Oxford, 1965. See also his remarkable "Religion and the Anthropologist," *Social Anthropology and Other Essays*, Free Press of Glencoe, 1962, pp. 155–171.

33. Collin Wilson's science fiction story *The Mind Parasites,* though rather disappointing as a whole, and though it rather irrelevantly drags in phenomenology, Husserl and all that, though he refers to Jung (of whom see more in note 48 to Section VII above) and ignores Freud, is all the same a remarkable book both in its theory of romanticism and in its successful integration — in the first half or so — of abstract theoretical deliberations into the mood, texture, and even narrative, of the tale. The novel gets out of wind when romanticism is done away with. As a disquisition on romanticism it surpasses not only Wilson's other works, non-fiction and fiction alike, but even serious studies of the topic. It is nothing as systematic as the study of George Herbert Mead, nor as penetrating as the studies of Heinrich Heine and Friedrich Nietzsche; but, strange as it sounds, it is one of the first post-Freudian studies: all Freudians were busy in proving the universality of Freud's vision or in applying it to the twentieth-century cultural and political science. And even Wilson himself fails to mention Freud or to do him much justice. Yet the fact that romanticism is an expression of an anti-positivistic ambivalence of a peculiar nature is brought about by Wilson who speaks of a vision of man as a god and the resultant revulsion against the humdrum of the everyday — the love of the gulf between the desert which is magnificent to the eye and the desert that kills one's feet.

The romantic syndrome has two different and closely linked aspects. One is the preference for ambivalence. The other is the return to the myth-world. Now the conscious aspect of living in a myth-world is already the destroyer of the myth-world as it was once felt — naively. Yet it can be revived in the arts. For, the feel of the myth-world is the feel of the world polarized, is expressed strongly in special brightened moments, in sessions of recital of myths or of poetry of certain sorts, and in magic sessions, seances, etc. The subject then intentionally and intensely concentrates on the two pure extreme states of mind. The reader can easily experience this for himself by contemplating together any two polarly opposed situations; for example, the security and comfort and relaxation of one situation and the horror of an opposite situation; mothers in whose laps one rests one's weary head turning into rotting corpses or black widows or any other revolting and tensing entities and back; tender and alluring women turning into vampires and back; robots becoming demons, etc. The experiment has to take some time, time needed to heighten either sense by itself — that of security and that of anxiety — and then both together.

Notice that both some of the world's greatest works of art and some of its worst works of art are so built. Homer's story of the sirens; "the Lord is my shepherd . . . on restful water He will guide me . . . the valley of shadow of death . . ."; Frankenstein; the dangling corpse of a mutilated beauty queen in ever so many detective novels good and poor. Of course, this is not to say that the function of myth and magic is poetic, merely to use the atmosphere of poetry known to the modern reader so as to conjure the atmosphere of myth and magic. Nor is it to say that this atmosphere is what makes for good art, as R. G. Collingwood well explains in his *Principles of Art*. Yet when he said that magic is rather art than science he was in error. See I. C. Jarvie and J. Agassi "On the Rationality of Magic," mentioned in note 70 to Section V above. Nor is all art magical, nor all magical art particularly good or particularly bad; nor are all contrasts magical, poetic, or anything else. All one can say here, I think, is that strong contrasts are strong stuff to be handled carefully.

Inasmuch as neurosis and magic share the mixture of comfort and anxiety, Freud's ability to psychoanalyze ancient myths and neurosis etc. in savage people is amply explained.

The enormous attraction scholars feel towards totemism has already been noticed by Claude Lévi-Strauss in the very opening of his *Totemism* (translated by R. Needham, Beacon Press, Boston, 1962). There he says that the students of either hysteria or totemism tried to make them "more *different* than they really are"; that like hysteria, totemism was isolated in the late 19th century" — as though it constituted a natural entity — which scholars preferred to regard as alien to their own moral universe, thus protecting (themselves against acting on) the attachment which they felt toward it."

34. For more details see my "On Pursuing the Unattainable", referred to in note 102 to Section IX above.

An example of Hegel's positivism is his treatment of physiognomy *(The Phenomenology of the Mind, V A 3 C)* as a pseudo-science and hence as metaphysical. He quotes Lichtenberg, who lumps superstition, pseudo-science and metaphysics together, using as an example the case where a man who behaves well is declared nonetheless a rogue at heart. Endorsing Lichtenberg's view, Hegel adds (the J. B. Baillie translation, Allen and Unwin, London, Humanities, New York, revised edition, 1931, 1966, p. 349), "The true being of a man is, on the contrary, his act, individuality is real in the deed, and a deed it is which cancels both aspects of what is 'meant' or 'presumed' to be." Interestingly, it was Bertrand Russell who viewed this activism as the most prominent aspect of modern irrationalism, including that of Bergson and William James. See his "The Philosophy of Bergson", *Monist*, Vol. 22, July 1912, pp. 321–347, reprinted in his *The Philosophy of Bergson*, MacMillan, London, 1914. See also the end of his chapter on Bergson in his *A History of Western Philosophy*, and the end of the chapter on William James there. In his chapter on Marx he says, "so far as I know, Marx was the first philosopher to criticize the notion of 'truth' from the activist point of view" (p. 784); yet the first was Hegel. That Bergson's activism is Hegelian was already noticed by Popper, *Open Society*, Chapter 12, note 25, Vol. II, p. 307, where he quotes from Hegel "The very essence of Spirit is activity".

George Lichtheim points out in his *From Marx to Hegel*, New York, 1971, pp. 202–4, that positivism and Hegelianism – including the Frankfurt Marxist school, especially its leader Theodor Adorno – share the identification of rationalism with the appearance-reality polarization as well as the instrumentalist philosophy of science which confines science strictly to the world of appearances, leaving reality to metaphysics (regardless of positive or negative attitudes towards metaphysics). He then adds (p. 205) that this idea is not new.

But perhaps I flatter Lichtheim too much; as he is aware (p. 201), the Frankfurt school's "Hegelian logic . . . is enough to make any decent empiricist despair; and . . . despair is indeed the uppermost among the sentiments with which the disciples of Karl Popper have greeted the new phenomenon" of the "new" Hegelian "logic". Were Lichtheim as clear elsewhere as in this passage, we would not despair so easily. Meanwhile, I am not able to examine the correctness of the previous paragraph, and can only hope it is not too distorting.

The idea that act, not thought, matters, is arch-positivist and arch-functionalist; see note 56 to Section XIV below.

XIII SCIENCE IS TRADITIONALLY BASED ON A MYTH

The story as told by a few modern philosophers, beginning with Burnet and Field, I suppose, and including both Popper and Leo

Strauss, is this.[35] Philosophy introduced the dualism of nature and conventions, of facts and mores. Before Philosophy we had natural monism, not nature versus convention. The word "Law" (or, say, its Greek or its Hebrew cognate) denoted both natural law and social law, and this indicates their common origin, natural monism.[36] According to monism there is no law which is breakable, and so there is no law which says, thou shalt not sin; as sin was often committed. Rather, the law said, sin entails punishment. Taboo was generally supposed to be just that: a primitive concept of prohibition, an idea of prohibition which, when broken, inevitably leads to calamity.[37] If God himself wants to avert the calamity, some have observed, He cannot break or abolish the taboo but He can, and did, take the calamity on Himself. Whatever sophisticated Christians think, I have heard quite a few Christian missionaries of diverse denominations explain the crucifixion this way. And this is, exactly, the classical anthropological interest in tabooism as an expression of natural monism — this was shown, *inter alia*, by Malinowski and by Freud. It is well-known that Freud was attracted most to what he attacked most powerfully: Christianity.[38] And likewise Malinkowski, though with him it was not Christianity but sex.[39] Which brings us back to Lévi-Strauss. Lévi-Strauss's lack of interest in the penal or restrictive character of taboo even when studying the meaning of taboos, such as those relating to incest, is by contrast to Freud and to Malinowski quite remarkable.[40] It indicates, I suppose, that taboo is not the one pole which interested Malinowski and Freud, but that it is spread on two or more poles. On the pole which interested Malinowski or Freud Lévi-Strauss had nothing to say.

The most famous statement in response to natural monism is that of Protagoras: the fire burns the same everywhere, but convention varies from place to place. This is not the discovery of diversity but the resultant contempt for it, a contempt still expressed by Russell who, in his *Skeptical Essays* for example, illustrates the futility of convention: Mohammedans are polygamous, Tibetans are polyandrous; a little knowledge of the diversity of customs, he says, "must soon reduce any candid person to complete skepticism, since there seem to be no data enabling us to say that one marriage custom is better or worse than another". In Russell's science fiction "Zahatopolk", the young Incas of the distant future are shown foreigners who eat peas — which they are told are disgusting — in order that they should feel the great superiority of Incas who, of course, abstain from peas. Here we see a few factors persist, from antiquity to date: contempt for plurality because it is a plurality; natural monism sustains my culture as the natural one, and denounces yours as corrupt; even my tolerance to-wards you may still be condescending; the shock of discovering the dualism of nature and convention, namely the shock of discovering the falsity of my own culture and my resultant ability to denounce it. We cannot acquire open-mindedness with ease, says the philosopher, we must first be able to tear ourselves from the preconditioning of our own culture. Hard as this is, it is worth it; it opens the possibility of finding truth, of meeting our real nature, etc. The ancient myth, then, best expressed by Plato, can be put in modern words thus: natural-ism must first be denounced in order to be regained; it is of little doubt that modern radicalism is rooted in this very ancient myth.[41]

In his essay on John Stuart Mill,[42] Sir Isaiah Berlin illustrates the conflict that radicalism creates in the minds of liberals. "Toleration, Professor Butterfield has told us . . ., implies certain disrespect . . . Mill would, I think, have agreed . . ." Berlin argues that Mill succeeded, by and large, in squaring his radicalism with his tolerance. More inter-esting, he sees in Mill a more difficult, and less successful, attempt to square radicalism (or rationalism, as he calls it) with romanticism. And he views Mill's sudden praise of the pluralism of the Middle Ages as "anti-egalitarian". This is quite a confusion, especially since Berlin compares Mill here to Burke rather than to egalitarians renown for pluralism, such as Max Stirner.[43] It is quite obvious that pluralism was always opposed to classical radicalist rationalism and dependent on toleration. We do not need romanticism to support this conflict; the conflict is rooted in the radicalist rationalist support of nature as against mere convention. If anything, romanticism exploited the con-flict and attempted to resolve it by the presentation of a new theory of rationality — a new relativism of truth, of nature, of anything.

I will go further. Bertrand Russell, Karl Popper, and Leo Strauss were of the most bitter recent opponents of Romanticism: its new doctrine of rationality leads to cynicism. Russell was a radicalist rationalist who could not offer better reasons for the toleration of foolish ideas than Mill, and who only advocated active pluralism on matters on which science was not determined, and he definitely recommended that we should decondition ourselves and get rid of our speculations and customs and such. Even the pluralism permitted by science is a rather shaky matter according to Russell. As to Popper and Strauss, both of these thinkers openly oppose radicalist or traditional rationalism, and are even more in favor of toleration and pluralism than their predecessors. Yet, regardless of their opposition to radi-calism, they repeatedly open the way to it by their very acceptance of the dichotomy between nature and convention. Admittedly, Strauss recommends return to a modified naturalism, and Popper to a modified conventionalism. (They are more or less the same.)[44] And I have tried to make as much use of their ideas in order to combat the dichotomy between nature and convention. Yet, I cannot deny the fact, that both Strauss and Popper still partly endorse the Greek myth of polarity − namely, when narrating the myth about the history of the idea of nature versus convention.

Again, I feel uneasy and with the same difficulty as before. I just said that the ancients and the thinkers of the Enlightenment explained away all convention. Yet there were studies of conventions already in antiquity, such as Aristotle's studies of constitutions (which were lost, though found in part, in the last century). Even attitudes to conventions, as Strauss and Popper note, vary widely. Some are nihilistic or cynical about all convention, others find in certain conventions something not wholly arbitrary, namely, something rooted in human nature, and thus something ameliorating. Now, obviously, the rooting of the good convention in human nature is the myth of the original contract − a myth which was attacked by naturalists such as Hume and defended by Rousseau who was a naturalist turned conventionalist and thus, according to Leo Strauss, both the peak of the Enlightenment and the beginning of the romantic school.[45] Popper offers his contractualism with no original contract.

But I wish to stress my unease. According to Leo Strauss, according to most historians of ideas, Rousseau is not in between the two poles of nature and convention: he is inconsistent in being torn between the two; he does not find a place between the two poles but tries to inhabit both, which is illogical. And all this maneuver because, we say, he accepted both naturalism and the dualism of nature and convention; and then tried to get out of the difficulties that he thus landed into. But perhaps the fault is ours, and he *is* in the middle. Perhaps at least Strauss and Popper should be. Are they?

Notes to Section XIII

35. See G. C. Field, *Plato and His Contemporaries, A Study in Fourth-Century Life and Thought*, London, 1930, 1967, end of Chapter 6, pp. 97−8:

   "... The notion that the laws of the city contained all that was necessary for the right conduct began to be questioned ... Sophocles revealed in *Antigone* a vivid appreciation of the possibility of conflict between ... laws ... and ... moral law. From another direction, also, doubts began to be raised about the supreme claims of the law and custom of any particular city ... There is a familiar story in Herodotus of the horror which a group of Greeks ... while a group of Indians . . . different people may observe and respect entirely opposite rules of conduct . . .

All this does not yet amount to a philosophical view. We get to this by the elaboration of a distinction . . . between Nature (physis) and Law or Convention (nōmōs). The origin of the ideas which based themselves on this distinction is extremely obscure . . . "

The development of the ideas based on the philosophic distinction between Nature and Convention, says Field, led to political demoralization. He says (*ibid.* p. 89) of the line of thought developed from the distinction:

"without putting anything positive in its place [the. place of the law of the city-state] it [the line of thought based on the distinction] seems to have exercised a dissolvent effect on the moral outlook that already existed. We, in modern times, are so accustomed to make a sharp distinction between the moral law and the laws of the State that if our faith in the one was weakened it would not necessarily affect in any way our belief in the other. But with the Greeks, as we have seen, it was not so . . . It is very instructive to read the remarks of Thrasymachus in the *Republic,* or, still more perhaps, Calicles in the *Gorgias,* who represent this kind of immoralism. They draw the distinction between natural and conventional morality and identify the natural morality with immorality [which today we call cynicism]."

And again, speaking of the beginnings of the first buds of collectivism in fourth century Greece, Field says (p. 116),

". . . the mention of it may help to remind us that the century which saw such widespread moral decline also saw a widespread interest in moral problems and some of the most serious and interesting moral contributions to their solution which have ever been made . . .

What is of particular interest to trace is the development of that line of thought which expressed itself in terms of the distinction between Nature and Convention. . .

On the negative side we find criticisms of institutions and ideas which had hitherto been taken for granted. Thus there are traces of attempts to limit the functions and powers of the State . . . Lycophron . . . regarded the whole function . . . as consisting in protection of the citizens from violence and wrongdoing . . . There are signs also of protest against the ideals of patriotism . . . The distinction . . . between Greek and Barbarian was attacked as purely conventional and as having no basis in the nature of things. Other distinctions also . . . equally profound to the ordinary Greek . . . between well-born and lowly as having no real ground in nature . . . the universal institution of slavery . . .Nature has made no man a slave . . ."

Field goes on to speak (p. 119) of a "positive side", the search for a higher end for man, whether political salvation (Plato) or salvation of the individual "in the life of contemplation" (Aristotle). "But the typical expression of this point of view", continues Field, "is to be looked for in the Cynic movement." The reason that the name of the movement was so twisted is (see on this p. 120 note) that whereas their preaching of poverty so resembled that of Christianity they preached an attitude towards sex as similar to that towards food as possible.

I much recommend Sir Ernest Barker's *Greek Political Theory, Plato and His Predecessors*, University Paperbacks, Methuen, London, 1918 etc., 1960 etc. See index, Art. Nature; see especially Chapter IV, the section on the antithesis of physis and nōmōs, pp. 74ff.

Barker refers to Burnet (*Int. J. Ethics*, Vol. 8, p. 328) as the source of the current view of the importance of this distinction. Popper, in his *Open Society*, refers to Burnet's *Greek Philosophy*. Yet neither Barker nor Burnet stresses that the view of the contrast nature-convention as central to Greek philosophy is quite modern. Indeed, as is often the case, the emphasis on the claim of novelty for the distinction bespeaks the beginning of the modern deviation from this claim.

See John Burnet's remarkable "Law and Nature in Greek Ethics", *International Journal of Ethics*, Vol. 8, 1896–7, pp. 328–333. Burnet refers there a few times to his classic *Early Greek Philosophy*, 1892, 4th ed., 1930 (which Guthrie and others consider "*the* standard work"). Yet the thesis is not clear enough in that book, especially in view of Burnet's inability to apply his own thesis clearly enough to Parmenides and Heraclitus – no less! – because he tried to beautify them, I imagine. See K. R. Popper, *The Open Society*, Vol. 1, Chapter 2, note 2 and Chapter 3, note 22. Indeed Burnet himself opens by saying he wanted "to throw a little fresh light upon" the famous nature-convention distinction. Noticeably, his reading of pre-Socratic physics, including Parmenides, is better (and nearer to Popper's taste). He also argues that it is the very nature of the nature-convention distinction that makes Greek ethics the search for natural law, and also links science and ethics, via the theory – which Popper has labeled "the pedigree theory of knowledge" (*Conjectures and Refutations*, Chapter 1, Section XV) (which Burnet ascribes to Natorp) – that the natural scientific theory is true-born, not bastard. This theory is ascribed to Democritus who said, by convention the sweet is sweet etc., but in truth there are atoms and the Void. The passage in Burnet is not clear to me, and his rendering of nōmōs here as use rather than as convention is highly questionable. Still, he insists that the nature-convention distinction should make sense of this passage, and he is right; but he requires too much. (See note 8 to Section XI above.)

The clearest expression of natural monism occurs in the very work that is intended to be the means of its rejection, to wit, Aeschylus' *Eumenides*. In it the *Erinyes*, the furies, demand revenge regardless of all mitigating circumstances, perhaps even punishment for one for whom by sheer bad luck there is no proper option! And they quarrel with the Olympian deities who are less harsh than they. Yet from the start the dramatist mocks at them, showing them like dogs who will not let the prey go, who whine and whimper, etc. Finally Pallas Athena strikes a compromise and the *Erinyes* become the *Eumenides* of the play's title, kind ones, even though they still take revenge.

It is curious that discussions of natural monism shun Aeschylus entirely, even though philosophers and historians of thought are not always so blasé. The reason for this may be found in the view of Aeschilus as a mythmaker whose myths are not all consistent with each other, as expressed in Chapter IV of H. D. F. Kitto, *Greek Tragedy, A Literary Study*, Methuen, London 1939, 1950, 1961 and many reprints (compare Chapter IV in 1st and 3rd editions in this respect). Now thanks to Lévi-Strauss we have come to expect myth systems to include conflicting myths, and thanks to the erosion of the nature-convention dichotomy it is possible to suggest, as I do, that it was a myth, and the myth to end all myths. Hence, its mythic origin is now no longer inconceivable. Surprisingly, Gilbert Murray already knew this, yet disappointingly he did not use it to connect the *Eumenides* with the nature-convention polarization. See his *Aeschylus, The Creator of Tragedy*, Clarendon Press, Oxford, Oxford University Press, New York, 1940, 1962, pp. 201–4. See also note 51 to Section XIV below.

First to deviate strongly from the nature-convention dichotomy seems to me, however, to be Popper. Yet, I find his break from the Greeks not clear enough. In particular he does not relate his breakaway from the reality-appearance dichotomy to his breakaway from the nature-convention dichotomy. These two have also to relate to his break from the (justificationist) identification of truth with rationality.

36. On natural monism see K. R. Popper, *The Open Society and Its Enemies*, index, Art. Monism. See also next note.

37. A. A. Radcliffe-Brown, *Taboo*, The Frazer Lecture, 1939, Cambridge, 1939, defines taboo, or, a ritual prohibition, to use a term he prefers, as:
> "a rule of behaviour which is associated with a belief that an infraction will result in an undesirable change in the ritual status of the person who fails to keep to the rule. This change of ritual status is conceived in many different ways in different societies, but everywhere there is the idea that it involves the likelihood of some minor or major misfortune which will befall the person concerned."

(Also reprinted in William A. Lessa and Evon Z. Vogt, eds., *Reader in Comparative Religion, an Anthropological Approach*, Harper and Row, 1959 and 1965.)

The background to this theory is deeply rooted in the classical view of magic as pseudo-science. G. J. Frazer says (*The Golden Bough, A Study in Magic and Religion*, Vol. 1, abridged ed., MacMillan Paperback, New York, 1960, p. 22),
> ". . . taboo is so far a negative application of practical magic . . . taboo says 'Do not do this, lest so and so should happen'. The end of positive magic or sorcery is to produce the desired event; the aim of negative magic or taboo is to avoid an undesirable one. But both consequences, the desirable and the undesirable, are supposed to be brought about in accordance with the laws of similarity and contact".

Yet at once Frazer is at pain to explain that the evil of a taboo must be imaginary, or else breaking a taboo will be exactly as punishable as putting one's hand in the fire: taboo is a fallacy, as all magic is — according to Frazer, that is (p. 23). It is interesting that hence, even though Frazer glosses over it, magical beliefs are to him myth-like, only half-believed by their believers. This was made more explicit by Malinowski, who took pain to modify the tabooist theory of natural monism – all crime must be punished – in a very reasonable way in one of his most reasonable and moderate studies, *Crime and Custom in Savage Society*, Routledge, London, 1926, see index, Article "Taboo," especially Part II, Chapter II, penultimate paragraph, "We have found that the principles according to which crime is punished are very vague ... Crime ... can be but vaguely defined ... the most definite prohibitions are elastic, since there exist methodical systems of evasion."

This is a curious affair. I cannot go into the history of the rise of the idea of taboo in social anthropology; I think the above quotations indicate, however, that the view of primitives as natural monists was on its way out in anthropology while it was picked up by historians of Greek philosophy. (Now, with the rejection of this view on the strength of Lévi-Strauss's theories, things are not very clear but at least they are fluid again.)

The idea that moral conventionalism transcends moral naturalism, which in turn equals tabooism, is perhaps due to L. T. Hobhouse. See his *Morals in Evolution*, London, 1906. The same idea is endorsed in Westermark's *Ethical Relativity*, 1932, and in Popper's *The Open Society and Its Enemies*, London, 1945, which, in addition, includes the view of the rise of Greek philosophy from naturalism to dualism.

Lawrence Kohlberg observes empirically a scale passing, both onto-genetically and phylogenetically, from naive naturalism which is more pragmatic than tabooistic, to the uncritical acceptance of one's environment's norm, to contractualism, to Universalism (justice, equality, dignity). I think he has not yet offered a schema good enough to test empirically, and not a clear hypothesis behind the schema. See Theodore Mischel, ed., *Cognitive Development and Epistemology*, New York, 1971, Kohlberg's "From Is to Ought" (pp. 151–235) and comments by R. S. Peters there (pp. 237–267). Yet, no doubt, his work is of great importance as a serious empirical comparative study of morals.

38. David Bakan, *Sigmund Freud and the Jewish Mystical Tradition*, Van Nostrand, Princeton, Toronto, London, 1952, Chapters 21 and 22. See also Sigmund Freud, *Moses and Monotheism*, trans. Katherine Jones, Vintage ed., New York, 1955, pp. 114–15, "... The poor Jewish people ... Over and over again they heard the reproach. 'You killed our God'. And this reproach is true, if rightly interpreted ..." Quoted in H. Stuart Hughes, *Consciousness and Society, The Reorientation of European Schools of Thought*, Vintage ed., New York, 1958, p. 147.

39. Commenting on the immense contrast between Malinowski's *A Diary in the Strict Sense of the Term* with its hostility to the natives and Malinowski's monumental studies with their strong and persistent egalitarian bias, Clifford Geertz, himself a well-known anthropologist says (*New York Review*, and *Psychiatry and Social Science Review*, Vol. 2 (61), 1968, pp. 7–11), that "the insight into Trobriand life Malinowski apparently was unable to gain by human contact he gained by industry" thus endorsing both Malinowski's Calvinism and his egali-

tarian theory of field work. What seems to me quite obvious is that both Malinowski's academic works and his diary abound with instances of human contact
plus insight. But, Malinowski separated the good vibes from the bad vibes and
stuck to his theory that field work must be rapport which in turn must be all
good vibes. And thus the diary poses a problem which Geertz notices. Though
Geertz seems to be critical of Malinowski, he struggles with the refuting fact that
Malinowski was no angel and ends up by disposing of it the same way Malinowski
did: hard work restores good vibes and the bad ones should be kept private and
lead to self-exhortation.

40. Claude Lévi-Strauss accuses Malinowski in his *Totemism* (Boston, 1962) of
"hasty generalizations" and of "naturalism". If totemism is natural, the question
arises, "why it does not exist everywhere . . ." (pp. 56, 58). Early Radcliffe-Brown
suffers from similar naturalistic tendencies (pp. 61–2). A little later (p. 82) he
says Evans-Pritchard's "fertile views . . . are . . . subject to reserve in two respects."
One was that he restricts his theory to the theologically minded tribe he was
studying, assuming that theology was not insignificantly a factor in history: "he
presents a general interpretation in the language of a particular society, thus
limiting its scope". Later Radcliffe-Brown introduces the comparative method in
order to attain "general propositions" (p. 83) which is what Lévi-Strauss himself is
after. The theory, partly Radcliffe-Brown's, extended by Lévi-Strauss, is that
totemism is "a principle consisting of the union of opposites" (p. 88). There is no
totemism, really, but:
> "the alleged totemism is no more than a particular expression, by means of a
> special nomenclature formed of animal and plant names [in a certain
> code . . .] . . . of correlations and oppositions . . . sky/earth, war/peace . . . The
> most general model . . . is . . . in China . . . Yang and Yin . . . Totemism is thus
> reduced to a particular fashion of formulation of a general problem, viz., how to
> make opposition . . . "

Now the problem is general; but the totemic expression of it is particular and
so the question Lévi-Strauss throws at Malinowski can be raised for his view: the
totemic expression of the universal problem "why it does not exist everywhere".

41. The distance between all men as brothers and having no brothers is really
very small. Thus, when Plato makes (*Prot.*, 337c) a cosmopolitain say "I consider
you all kinsmen and friends and fellow countrymen, not of course by law but by
nature," it sounds heart-warming; and when Stalin calls the Russian Jews rootless
cosmopolitans without a homeland its cruelty is manifest in the fact that he was
poking fun at their misery. Yet it is an old truth that having no home and having
the whole world for a home is the same thing: except that the feeling of being at
home in the world or the absence of that feeling are two very different feelings
indeed. And there are people at home nowhere, somewhere, or everywhere, and
these are cosmopolitans or not – each of these six possibilities is realized. Yet
clearly the early cosmopolitans assumed that the true cosmopolitan is at home
everywhere in his feelings too, thus anticipating Socratic (and Spinozist)

eudaimony. The passage from Plato's *Protagoras* is so impressive because it expresses the boundless optimism and good will of the early radicalists. That this quality is quite generally characteristic of radicalism has been stated by J. W. N. Watkins' moving "Milton's Vision of a Reformed England," *The Listener*, January 22, 1959, pp. 168—169 and 172.

Bertrand Russell, especially in his *Skeptical Essays* (the passage quoted in the text above is from the Introduction, p. 15 of the 1934 Allen and Unwin, London, edition), as well as his *Unpopular Essays*, has a very peculiar quality when expounding his radicalist philosophy. To the last he felt that the radicalist utopia is ever more realizable from the technical point of view yet ever more remote all the same because of human folly. At times he writes as an observer belonging to an altogether different species yet at times the pain of his alienation from the common man is too obvious to conceal. See my "The Last Refuge of the Scoundrel," *Philosophia*, Vol. 4, 1974, pp. 315—17.

The attempt to retain radicalism while denying that radical changes are at all possible, for instance in the philosophy of Herbert Marcuse, is quite different from Russell's view: whereas Russell still pleads for rationalism, and still thinks that rationalism makes a radical change possible, Marcuse thinks that one should settle down in one's radicalist convictions even after disillusionment, simply as a weakness, an inability to jettison one's view and search for a radically new one, an inability justifiable by the Hegelian adoption of contradictions. I do not, of course, expect his followers to declare the previous sentence fair, even though he will bravely view it both fair and unfair at one and the same time.

42. Sir Isiah Berlin, *Four Essays on Liberty*, Oxford University Press, London and New York, 1970, p. 184.

Regarding democracy and disagreement, see the significant paper by J. W. N. Watkins, "Epistemology and Politics," *Meetings of the Aristotelian Society*, 1957, Suppl. Vol. No. 1, pp. 81—102, pp. 83—88, where disagreement without distrust and without bickering is taken as the foundation of democracy. He links this with fallibilism since any epistemology whatsoever leads to the view that those who differ from orthodoxy are plain deviants (p. 89). Here, then, Watkins bluntly clashes with Mill, Butterfield, and Berlin, and of course he is so very commonsense that one has to explain the fact that they did not hold the same view. And the explanation is, indeed, not far to seek and is rooted, as Watkins argues, in an epistemology which precludes all serious prolonged disagreement. It is no surprise that Watkins was so well anticipated by that arch-skeptic, Voltaire; see his *Notebooks*, ed. Th. Besterman, Tome I, Voltaire Institute, Geneva, and Toronto University Press, Toronto, 1952, p. 43, 2nd ed., 1968, p. 65.

"... write strenuously one against another, but deal together freely and with trust and peace; like good players who after having humour'd their parts and fought one against another upon the stage, spend the rest of their time drinking together".

43. For Max Stirner's favoring of medieval pluralism see, for example, Eugène

Fleischmann, "The Role of the Individual in Pre-Revolutionary Society: Stirner, Marx, and Hegel", in L. A. Pelczinsky, ed. *Hegel's Political Philosophy,* Cambridge University Press, 1971, pp. 220–229, especially pp. 221ff.:

> "True, he says, the feudal political system was far from being an ideal set-up, but at least it carried with it the advantage of being a pluralist one: when a man was not happy with a prince, he could always turn to the bishop; when the bishop proved too exacting, he could solicit the protection of the city; and against the city he could request the aid of the corporations; and so on. But what is a man to do in a state which is based on a single principle, on an idea (as, for example, with Hegel, whose state is the active reality *(Wirklichkeit)* of the moral idea)?"

44. See my "Modified Conventionalism", referred to in note 21 to Section XI above. Notice that holding a modified view is a deviation from the dichotomy; yet, I think, this is not enough: one has to cotton it.

45. That Rousseau is in part a radicalist in part a romantic is, I suppose, agreed upon by all historians and commentators. Yet this hardly makes them put him in the middle. The first somewhat non-polarized social theory was, nevertheless, romanticism, which, traditionalist as it was, being a reaction to radicalism, recognized the existence of changes, often created by heroes, who are the equivalent within romanticism to the radicalists' rational men. Hegel and Marx saw history as the succession of traditions and so a new component was introduced which is neither nature nor convention but a matter of degree. This, in the hand of Marx's successors, developed into political gradualism much akin to that advocated by Popper in his *Open Society* and close to his methodology which denounces the division of theories to (verified) truths and (objectionable) errors.

See Peter Gay, "The Inevitability of Gradualism", in his *The Dilemna of Democratic Socialism: Edward Bernstein's Challenge to Marx,* Columbia University Press, New York 1952, pp. 220–252, reprinted in J. V. Downton Jr. and David K. Hart, eds. *Perspectives in Political Philosophy*, Vol. III, Hindside, Ill., 1973. See also my "Genius in Science", *Phil. Soc. Sci.,* Vol. 5, 1975, pp. 145–161, for the romantic theory of the hero, especially pp. 149–152. See Walter Kaufmann, *Without Guilt and Justice*, Wyden, New York, 1973, for the contribution of this theory to the modern autonomism.

XIV THE MYTH THAT SCIENCE IS UTTERLY RATIONAL

If Rousseau *is* in the middle, then he was sadly misunderstood by all his readers, of his days and of later generations. Perhaps he is in the middle and we all fail to read him properly because we are not in the middle, because we do not even know how things look from the middle (often a thinker is misunderstood by those who can't share his vantage position). It is of a great importance that we do develop our middle position — not so much in order to have, perhaps, a better understanding of Rousseau, as to come nearer to the truth in many other respects. It is a fact that the polarization is still very popular, that is, the view that there are two and only two views of nature and convention, the one being the primitive man's natural monism and the other being the philosopher's dualism of nature and convention. It will be very helpful to overthrow this view.

There is ample evidence that dualism existed amongst the myth-minded predecessors to the Greek inventors of philosophy and, thus, of the nature versus convention polarity. We need not go to the American Indians studied by Lévi-Strauss.[46] G. S. Kirk is quite right in showing that the epic of Gilgamesh is full of it, with Enkidu representing raw nature turning cultural or civilized and Gilgamesh as cultured, though on occasion returning to the wild for a while.[47] No doubt, there is nowhere in the Gilgamesh epic a contrast between customs of different people. Nevertheless, I say, the epic of Gilgamesh does disprove the dualistic myth that the predecessors of dualism were monists plain and simple.

I do not deny that the beginning of philosophy is identical with the philosophical nature-convention distinction, even though Kirk is right when saying, in the wake of Lévi-Strauss, that some nature-culture distinction is older than previously suspected, and is much older than philosophy, since it permeates mythical thought of all kinds. I reconcile this apparent contradiction by the claim that the distinction in question is manifest in two utterly different myth systems, the mythical and the philosophical. I suggest we have to view it, then, as two different claims, and perhaps translate both of them, modified or not, into a third and a hopefully better system.

That the philosophical myth is as old as philosophy is corroborated by Field[48] and by Leo Strauss[49] in the way they read Herodotus. Herodotus tells a myth, according to which the Persians became philosophical only after they expelled the Magi from their midst. I remember, incidentally, in my childhood, hearing or reading an echo of the classical rationalistic debate about Herodotus' method. Was he a liar? Or was he a credulous reporter? Perhaps he was such a sophisticated recorder of fact, so disinterested and comprehensive a recorder, that he deliberately ignored the question of the truth of what he had heard? Clearly Herodotus was a myth recorder-maker in the style of his day, and clearly the polarization of all historians to recorders and myth makers leaves him out as a man of a period of transition;[50] perhaps it even leaves most historians out. Now the polarization itself has its early clues in Herodotus himself. He tells the story about how a king proved the nature-convention distinction – in myths it is always a wise king who proves, of course – by confronting members of different traditions on the customs of burial of their dead. I once thought that this specific example was chosen by Herodotus because emotions went deep and so obscured the fact that burial customs were mere conventions – so that illustrating the thesis by reference to such a case makes sure that the lesson will be driven home. But why was the matter of burial so emotionally laden? Oh, well, as Herodotus hints, we all feel terrible when our loved ones die and so we wish to treat their remains as respectfully as possible. But this does not in the least explain why respect cannot be expressed by purely conventional means. This is not to contest the fact, of course, but to wonder about it. Anyone familiar with Evelyn Waugh's *The Loved One* knows how easily he expresses contempt for the American way of paying last respects by portraying it not so much as distasteful but as a vulgar convention. Why is conventional respect not sincere? The answer is, obviously, because sincerity comes from nature if it is to be true; otherwise it is hypocritical.

Now we all know, yet in this context forget, that, in truth, matters of burial are matters of taboo and mythology, today and more so in antiquity. And this is exactly the target of the nature-convention dichotomy; this is exactly what was exploded by the nature-convention distinction as meaningless: the dichotomy is positivistic as well as radicalist: when the philosophic nature-convention distinction is applied to the old ways wholesale, much has to be reoriented, and taboos become mere silly customs and myth becomes mere fable. On one thing we all agree: if taboo and myth exist, they exist between nature and convention.

This, let me stress, is what is wrong in contemporary studies of myth and taboo. It is positivistic, and is thus a denial of the existence of the very objects to which it directs our attention. In their attempting to explain myth and taboo, positivists repeatedly explain them away.

It is a strange fact regarding students of myth that they are so absorbed in their observations of myths that they hardly observe their colleagues – except to criticize them. Again and again one student of myths attacks the narrowmindedness of a colleague who cannot stomach one myth or another; and yet they do not generalize this. Everybody knows that the myth-world – myth associated with taboo and ritual – hardly makes sense to the traditional philosophically minded man. This is most conspicuous in all religious studies in elementary and middle schools, religious or not. In places of higher learning it gets wrapped in sophistication. Sir Henry Maine,[51] whose studies are of such importance, declared in the mid-nineteenth century that ancient man had no law at all, hardly even custom — merely habits. And Maine saw in the family, historically, nothing but the brute expression of lawless authority, the authority of the father, and thus the opposite of the individualism which he so cherished and which he equated with civilization *tout court.* But why do individualists have families? Ah, well! They have a different type of family — of course.[52] Those who could not take such a mediating compromise suffered terribly. Just think of Franz Kafka dismissing all kinship, including fraternal warmth, as mere convention! Once a myth is criticized, it seems, it at once vanishes as mere convention! There is no doubt that at the same period, when Romantic irrationalism developed and myth-mongering became quite a philosopher's profession, rationally minded people were almost constitutionally unable to take the myth world seriously; and even Sir James Frazer, a nineteenth-century man, though he died near the middle of the twentieth century, who showed great distinction in his effort to make some limited sense of some myth and ritual — even he (so say his disciples) did not try overmuch.[53] It is no accident that rationalists, especially late Victorians, stuck to their own customs so desperately; the very thought that these may perhaps be overthrown amounted to their overthrow *de facto:* so strong was their own faith in the polarization between unalterable nature (good) and mere convention (bad).

Today, perhaps because of Freud and Malinowski, or perhaps because of Lévi-Strauss, I think the tide had gone the other way. There is little doubt in my mind that the intense and deeply sad concentration on myths where animals look human and on totemism and all that is at times a vain effort to remember how we — I mean the researcher himself — used to talk to a cat with all seriousness and absolutely unaware of the cat's inability to comprehend. And, I suppose, the persistence of Taylor's myth about myths as childlike mixtures of facts and fiction, though criticized early in the day, is largely due to the wish of the student of myth to return to his childhood.[54] This is clearly indicated by recent writers who recapitulate Taylor's myth, including Martin Buber in His "Problem of Man" of the 40's and Géza Róheim in his *Gates of Dream* of 1952.[55] The connection of some myth with rituals is so reminiscent of psychodrama that the insistence of so many anthropologists and historians on Malinowski's and Cornford's myth of the identity[56] of myth and ritual, all evidence and arguments to the contrary notwithstanding, can likewise be viewed as a very strong emotional attachment to, as no less than an expression of, a purely positivist ethos. (The positivism of this is clear: belief, especially mythical, is elusive; and only ritual is tangible.) I do not mean to offer here a quasi-Freudian analysis of the students of myth. I only observe that their own method of analysis of myths applies with greater ease to itself than to the myths it allegedly analyzes. In brief, I think it is clear that mythical quality is a matter of degree, that we cannot completely avoid it, and that any attempt to see in this fact license to make myths is foolish: we make enough myths without really trying.[57]

Notes to Section XIV

46. It is quite obvious, I think, that most of Lévi-Strauss's theoretical ideas are hardly more than rejections of old and established ideas. At times it is not clear how − or even whether − he does so; at times he is quite successful. At times he does not even attempt to do so even when his approach necessitates it. One of his clearest expressions, his *Totemism* (Boston, 1962), culminates with the rejection of the nature-convention dichotomy by rejecting the myth of the origins of society while yet rejecting psychologism in favor of sociologism rather than to-gether with it. He says, p. 70:

> "We do not know, and never shall know, anything about the original beliefs and customs . . . but as far as the present is concerned, it is certain that social behavior is not produced spontaneously by each individual, under the influence of emotions of the moment. Men do not act, as members of a group, in accordance with what each feels as an individual; each man feels as a function of the way in which he is permitted or obliged to act. Customs are given as external norms before giving rise to internal sentiments, and these non-senti-ment norms determine the sentiments of individuals as well as the circum-stances in which they may, or must, be displayed."

Clearly, though it is true that a society's customs are indeed internalized by its young members, it is false to say, as Lévi-Strauss says here, that in a ritual the individual acts in accord with custom, not impulse; on the contrary, the ideal of the society, which is at times realized, especially by individuals who are priests and other model members of society, and especially in primitive and collective societies, is that the individual acts completely impulsively, utterly unguided by any thought or circumstance, yet performs the ritual or otherwise acts in perfect accord with his social norms, his tradition, etc. (We see this among leading mem-bers of the youth culture, the kibbutz, etc.) In Freudian terms, the ideal is to act not on the norms but on their internalized counterparts which should be their faithful copies. Only when internalization is unsatisfactory is the second best requirement the one described by Lévi-Strauss; acts in accord with accepted norms. Yet the reformer exists, even in primitive society, whose feelings, thoughts, impulses, etc., run contrary to custom and who recommends its breach or alteration.

Lévi-Strauss continues the passages quoted above thus:

"Moreover, if institutions and customs drew their vitality from being continually refreshed and invigorated by individual sentiments, like those in which
they originated, they ought to conceal an effective richness, continually replen-
ished, which would be their positive content. We know that this is not the case,
and that the constancy which they exhibit usually results from a conventional
attitude."

Here, clearly, Lévi-Strauss uncharacteristically endorses a false dichotomy
rooted in ancient philosophy. Clearly custom is sustained by both emotional
content and convention. Indeed, we can see that convention is invoked when
emotion runs low, as an empirical fact. But to continue the quote from Lévi-
Strauss, which is so interesting because he is usually considered an arch-naturalist,
yet here he is a conventionalist.

"To whatever society he belongs, the individual is rarely capable of assigning a
course to his conformity: all he can say is that things have always been like
this, and he does what people before him did."

This, again, is an error: a man speaks of his conduct usually as of one which
suits him, or as one which he adopts because conformity suits him — and in both
cases he says that things have always been like that. This is true of primitive and
not so primitive people alike; with the exception of innovators — again, primitive
or not.

To return to Lévi-Strauss, he ends by again pooh-poohing the psychological
side of things, saying the false statement:

"Emotion is indeed aroused, but when the custom, in itself indifferent, is
violated . . .

Actually, impulses and emotions explain nothing; they are always *results* . . ."

For my part, clearly, in explanations, all to often we use *both* custom and
emotions; as to which comes first, it is the hen and the egg.

Inasmuch as Lévi-Strauss notices and answers this question, he does so in his
final three pages. He quotes (p. 102) a remarkable passage from J. J. Rousseau to
say that man's earliest speech had more motive than reason and so was more
poetry than prose, metaphoric rather than descriptive. Totemism minus "the
illusion of totemism", namely, the mere fact that totemism is a peculiar expression of a general situation, is thus merely a relic of the past, a genuinely primitive
or primeval phenomenon, an expression of childhood — of mankind and of every
one of us.

Lévi-Strauss ends his book with the accent on the unity of mankind. Rousseau
could imagine totemic phenomena, however remote he was from them, because all
human minds are similar (p. 103). This, clearly, is a lame admission of the fact
that there are also enormous differences. I do not like it at all that the admission
of the difference is only made, tacitly, when stressing the similarity.

Yet the similarity does exist, and whatever the origin of society may be, we
may perhaps say this of the origin of a convention in primitive society as well as in
some fairly modern and sophisticated ones, including even the society of scientists

(to the extent that Polanyi's theory of science as tacit knowledge can be illustrated, that is). For, I find in the literature an important anthropological hypothesis that guides much ethological work, yet which is only implicit, and which I wish to state explicitly. It is the one or two following ideas. 1. When primitive leaders declare some new or old customs incomprehensible yet and they impose it by authority, they are right: the tribes which have no customs of that sort get eliminated *à la* Darwin and Spencer and Malinowski, yet there is only brute authority, no reason, to impose them. The reasons were (will be) only recently (soon) discovered by ethologists. 2. Of course, we should add, not knowing the true rationale of a custom, elders have imposed it with all the accretions that it came with at the time. This is how comparative anthropology discovers the universal (animal) core and peels off its accretions which are mere noise (Lévi-Strauss). The same may perhaps be done with the noise of the history of science (Lakatos; see note 28 to Section XII above).

I have tried to present in the previous paragraph a view which stresses as much as possible the reactionary variant of the originally radicalist view of the unity of mankind granting it as much plausibility as possible. But I found it extremely difficult to extract from it what seems to me to be reasonable. I found the formula which does more — which justifies up to a point both traditionalism and radicalism as against skepticism — in the succinct wording of the arch-skeptic Arne Naess, *The Pluralist and Possibilist Aspects of the Scientific Enterprise*, Universitetsforlaget, Oslo, Allen and Unwin, London, 1972, p. 109, note 7:

> "From a biological and ecological point of view humans have a built-in need to combat uncertainties that have daily threatened their lives in an inimical Pleistocene environment. The frantic effort to increase levels of certainty is no longer functional, but is sustained by instinctual mechanisms."

I confess I find such stuff heady, and wonder whether it is not too advanced for our age.

47. G. S. Kirk, *Myth, Its Meaning and Function in Ancient and Other Cultures*, Cambridge University Press, Cambridge and University of California Press, Berkeley and Los Angeles, 1970. In the preface he says that some "will find it less easy . . . to accept the relevance of Lévi-Strauss to some of these matters; but his theory contains the one important new idea since Freud . . ." On p. 7 he rejects Lévi-Strauss's idea of mediation. The new idea, on p. 43, is declared to be "that myth is one mode of human communication — economic exchange and kinship exchanges by means of women, being others".

48. For G. C. Field, see note 35 to Section XIII.

How much the distinction between physis and nōmōs is universally Greek is asked in Joseph Needham's "Human Law and the Laws of Nature", *J. Hist. Ideas*, Vol. 12, 1951, reissued in his *The Grand Titration, Science and Society, East And West*, Toronto, 1969.

49. Leo Strauss, *Natural Right and History*, University of Chicago Press, Chicago and London, 1953, p. 85:

"Before the advent of philosophy, natural rights were deemed divine; and . . . in a community governed by divine laws, it is strictly forbidden to subject these laws to genuine discussion, i.e. to critical examination, in the presence of young men. Socrates, however, permits himself to do so, as he comes after the advent of philosophy. Herodotus . . . indicated this state of things by the place of the only debate which he recorded concerning the principles of politics: he tells us that the free discussion took place in [mythical!] truth-loving Persia after the [mythical!] slaughter of the Magi. Herodotus, iii 76 (cf. i, 132)."

50. Since the polarization of mythos and logos is radicalist, it allows for no period of transition, in principle, though a reasonable period of rapid change is always allowed. This idea is retained even by some who wish to retain the value of some myth and not write it all off. Let me mention one example.

Pierre Smith, "The Nature of Myth", *Diogenes*, No. 82, Summer 1973, pp. 70–87, Section VI, 'The Myth as Belief', p. 84, says that anthropologists distinguish myth from story in that it is believed in and from history in that it is false, indeed simply incredible: "in our tongues the word *myth* has become synonymous with error, while wherever it is operative a myth is considered the very vessel of truth." Smith goes on to provide an explanation *à la* E. E. Evans-Pritchard: myth is a language; we cannot question it while using it.

The obvious question is, can we use different languages and compare them? If so do we believe in them? Can I be described as a believer in Marxist mythology while talking with a Marxist in his own "language" and in Jewish mythology while talking with Jews? I was once a true believer in this system, once in that, and I do, as a matter of empirical fact, retain the ability to talk the language, i.e. to talk on the presuppositions characteristic to Jews or to Marxists; yet I do not think while exercizing this ability I am a believer. Whatever there was when I was a true believer is gone forever.

Yet, for Smith, two languages divorced from each other allow only conversion from one to the other and the loss of the use of the older one.

Paul Friedlander, *Plato, an Introduction,* Harper Torch paperback, New York, 1958, Chapter 9, on myths, declares that it was during the period of the sophists that Greek thought was liberated from mythical thinking. It is not clear to me, however, whether Friedlander opposes mythical thinking or not. For, obviously, Plato narrated and even invented myths yet he was well aware of any achievement of the sophists. Socrates, he says (p. 172), does not "dissolve" or "destroy" myths as the sophists do, but rather uses them "in the service of his single goal — self-knowledge." I do not understand whether this makes him oppose all "mythologists" or not, and think Friedlander is dodging the issue here.

"When Plato accepted Socrates' quest as his own, he burned his [mythological] tragedies", continues Friedlander, now seemingly suggesting that Plato understood Socrates to disapprove of myth-making (even though he would not spend his time in combating it). But he was unsuccessful, adds Friedlander, both because he was a poet and because he needed poetic intuition in order to philosophize. Here, I am afraid, Friedlander is too confused, and, influenced by inductivism, declares all free intuition as myth-making. And so he concludes that Plato "created the myth of Socrates". Here, then, the reading becomes clear: Plato burned his tragedies as he misread Socrates to oppose all myths (which Friedlander confuses with free intuitions). Friedlander, then, opposes the contrast mythos-logos with the idea that even logos needs intuition. This is a poor (inductivist) way of opposing this contrast.

Popper contrasts mythos with logos as the uncritical and the critical. In his system, the opposition of the contrast, then, equals the destruction of all criteria for demarcation of the critical. This can be done and was even done by Friedlander himself on the following page (p. 173) though not at all clearly (whether by inductive standards or critical ones). For, he mentions as arguments against the contrast, both the fact that there were many myths to choose from, and the best ones were chosen as explanations, and the fact that poetry too meets with criticism and competition. (But, of course, he does not mention Popper.)

One page further (p. 174), Friedlander implictly endorses the usual view of myth as not only intuitive and/or uncritical but as somewhat supernatural or "of transcendent world", which is (p. 175) "the world below", "of the judgment of the dead". (The concepts of the trans-rational or trans-critical are common in the diverse existentialist works, philosophical, methodological, even psychological.)

51. Gilbert Murray, *Four Stages of Greek Religion*, Columbia University Press, New York, 1912, Chapter II, "The Olympian Conquest", Section II, "The Religious Value of the Olympian", especially pp. 80, 95, presents Homeric religion as a religious reformation intended to celebrate the victory of culture over brute nature. This is, of course, in no conflict with the claim that the more ancient, Pelasgian religion itself included the contrast between nature and culture, as Lévi-Strauss has led Kirk to assert. It is interesting that so much of Lévi-Strauss is implicit in Gilbert Murray, yet he never came to question the view of philosophy as the contrast between nature and convention.

Sir Henry Sumner Maine, *Ancient Law, Its Connection with the Early History of Society, and Its Relation to Modern Ideas*, 1861, third American edition, from the fifth London edition of 1873. His views of ancient law as customs are in sharp contrast to the above quoted modern views of ancient law as divine. They appear in Chapter 1, pp. 5–19. His view of family ties comes in Chapter 5, on aguation and cognation, where (p. 143) due to adoption or aguation of relatives from the female side, the family becomes not quite a natural thing and so a mere artifact – "arbitrary", "so elastic as to include strangers" – a design to impose (p. 144) the authority of fathers, while (p. 149) a woman is strictly subordinate, and legally becomes her husband's daughter after marriage.

52. Sir Henry Maine, *op. cit,* p. 162, speaks of "the gradual dissolution of family dependence and the growth of individual obligation in its place". "Nor is it difficult to see" he adds, "what replaces family ties: it is Contract."

The problem, why are family bonds so very strong, is generally aired in the literature, yet is seldom forcefully stated. It is forcefully stated in I. C. Jarvie's

The Story of Anthropology, McGraw-Hill, N.Y. 1972, Chapter 2, "Family and Kinship", pp. 43—4. He answers it differently for primitive and modern societies. For primitive societies, he says, articulating a classical hypothesis, the kinship system sustains all other social sub-systems. For modern societies this does not hold, as seen by the weakening and dissolution of family bonds in modernizing societies (p. 71). Yet even in modern society the institution of kinship survives — as all institutions tend to do — as long as they serve some function and until "someone comes up with a better idea" of how to fulfill this function (pp. 70—71).

This explains, I suppose, the survival of the family in modern society, but not its very strong bonds. Nor does it explain why in some parts of modern society bonds to a wider family are stronger than in others. The first point was, perhaps, taken up by Freud and his followers, especially Melanie Klein and Konrad Lorenz. The second point is still very unstudied; even the bare facts are only slightly noted, though to a sufficient extent to raise the problem.

Broadly, let me conjecture so as to fill the gap in Jarvie's theory, there is a function to irrevocable pseudo-natural institutional roles. This function is filled in some societies by kingship and priesthood which are irrevocable; and it may be only semi-hereditary, see E. Gellner, *Saints of the Atlas,* Chicago University Press, Chicago, 1969, pp. 74ff. and pp. 261ff. Kinship, in the sense of the extended family is also partly alterable, as noted by Sir Henry Maine, see quotation in note 51 above; see also E. E. Evans-Pritchard, *Social Anthropology and Other Essays*, Free Press, Glencoe, 1962, for example, "Zande Blood-Brotherhood", pp. 257—287, especially the two or three final paragraphs: blood-brotherhood is manufactured kinship, magically enacted.

53. See I. C. Jarvie, "Academic Fashions and Grandfather Killing", *Encounter*, 26 April, 1966, pp. 53—55, for the claim that social anthropologists are given to the ritual of killing Frazer repeatedly. See also J. Agassi and I. C. Jarvie", "Magic and Rationality Again", mentioned in note 70 to Section V.

54. For Taylor's theory and its background see E. E. Evans-Pritchard's delightful *Theories of Primitive Religion,* Clarendon Press, Oxford, 1965, Chapter 2, "Psychological Theories", especially pp. 20—25. See also note 56 below.

55. Martin Buber, "Ba'ayat Ha'adam", *Ma'arachot Lesifrut*, Tel Aviv, 1943, English translation, "The Problem of Man", in *Between Man and Man*, translated by R. G. Smith, Routledge, London, 1947, § 10, p. 143.

Buber is one of the few writers who not only studies myth, but also finds such study essential for philosophical anthropology. A reason for this is offered by Philip Wheelwright, "Buber's Philosophical Anthropology", in P. A. Schilpp and M. Friedman, eds., *The Philosophy of Martin Buber*, Open Court, La Salle, Ill., and Cambridge University Press, London, 1967, pp. 69—95, p. 71: ". . . Now while Buber does not even disparage man's rational faculty, and indeed there is plenty of evidence that he prizes it highly, he is unwilling to accept it as the determinative factor in establishing what man essentially is. For, he holds, it is not by his reasoning alone that man differs from his animal cousins . . ."

Géza Róheim, *Gates of Dreams*, International University Press, New York, 1952, p. 401.

The theory is already stated by Róheim in his *Origins and Function of Culture*, New York, 1943, p. 93, and quoted approvingly by Joseph Campbell in his "Bios and Mythos: Prolegomena to a Scientific Mythology", in G. B. Wilbur and W. Muensterberger, eds., *Psychoanalysis and Culture, Essays in Honor of Géza Róheim*, Humanities Press, New York, 1951, pp. 329–343, p. 343.

See Owen Barfield's work mentioned in note 71 to Section VII.

56. For a detailed criticism of the doctrine that myth is not to be taken literally see Ernest Gellner, *Cause and Meaning in the Social Sciences*, Routledge, London and Boston, 1973, especially pp. 37ff. and 168ff. F. M. Cornford, *The Unwritten Philosophy and Other Essays*, Cambridge University Press, 1950, paperback, 1967, the very end of the essay "A Ritual Basis for Hesiod's *Theogony*":

"What excites me was the idea (which I got from Hooke's books) that early philosophic cosmogony is not only a transcription of mythical cosmogony, but finally [i.e. at long last we have vindicated the old thinkers and our own selves!] it has its roots in *ritual*, something tangibly existing, not baseless 'fancies' and speculation."

It has to be stressed that whereas positivism usually tends to dismiss causal nexus and ontological identifications as mere functional correlations, at significant junctions positivism insists on identity – whether of all mental with some physiological processes or of all beliefs with some rituals. This makes positivism wishful thinking rather than a doctrine proper.

Also, when positivism becomes less fashionable, there is a tendency to keep some of its tenets alive as metaphysical. And metaphysical they certainly are, yet they are of no interest to anyone except to positivists and their critics, not to metaphysicians.

See, for example, S. Morgenbesser, P. Suppes, and M. White, eds., *Philosophy, Science, and Method: Essays in Honor of Ernest Nagel*, St. Martin's Press, New York, 1969, or a comprehensive review of it, e.g. by Marshall Spector in *Metaphilosophy*, Vol. 2 (3), July 1971, pp. 251–267, especially of Hempel's contribution, "Reduction: Ontological and Linguistic Facets" (p. 179 of the volume, or 254 of the review).

It is customary to dismiss the critique of reductionism by the Duhem-Popper argument that the explanation modifies the explained statement and so, strictly speaking, does not explain it at all. The dismissal is by the claim that the modification of the explained statements, and thus of the explanation schema, is small (see p. 257 of review). This seems to me a silly inconsistency: the modification is small when measurement is concerned but unmeasurable when ontology is concerned: identity is not a matter of degree.

The identity of beliefs and rituals as a link between positivism, relativism, and pragmatism has been discussed at length by diverse writers, I. C. Jarvie's *The Revolution in Anthropology* (London, 1963) being the most elaborate and easily accessible.

57. The fact that the philosophy (and history) of science is the body of myth or religion of men of science can be presented both diachronically and synchronically. The history of the organization of the commonwealth of learning is shrouded in developments of myth and taboo, partly necessitated by a hostile bigoted environment, partly required by participants, partly caused by most unwise great men of science such as Newton and Laplace, partly by mere historical accident. (That the views, metaphysics, quirks and mannerisms of geniuses become sacred is a general fact.) The fact that today the philosophy of science is still the living myth of men and science can be presented by statistical surveys — these have started being performed now, but the questionnaires I have seen are rather poor and the sampling methods no better. My own evidence is very simple and obvious: men of science whom I meet for the first time often have a strong urge to give me lectures in the philosophy of science for the sole reason that they hear that I am a philosopher of science. Poor scientists, good scientists, at times even first-rate ones, have delivered to me lectures of the intellectual level of a mediocre if somewhat spirited sixth grader at best. Perhaps the word lecture is a euphemism — homily may be more like it. Yet some very prominent lectures of very prominent men of science get published and they are of genuinely poor quality.

See my "The Origins of the Royal Society", *Organon*, Vol. 7, 1970, pp. 117–135. See also my *Towards an Historiography of Science*, mentioned in note 3 to the Introduction above, Section 2, The Function of Inductive Histories of Science.

XV SOCIAL SCIENCE WITHOUT THE MYTH OF SCIENCE

The distinction between nature and convention is thus the same as the distinction between logos and mythos. Myth is thus convention and thus a chimera. It is not explained but explained away.[58] Appearance, then, is not to be explained at all! It is hardly possible to ascribe this to Greek philosophy, with its enormous concern for explanation. But I cannot escape this conclusion.

Be this conclusion valid or not, and the temptation is to declare it invalid because of the Greek concern with explanation, the fact remains that the Greeks never attempted to explain myths, let alone explore them,[59] and that their heirs in the Age of Reason even denied the existence of the myth world amongst primitives, that these heirs noticed myths and such only on occasion and only so as to feel revolted by them and dismiss them as prejudices and superstitions worse than ours.[60]

Today we are not as free of all this as we would wish to congratulate ourselves that we are.[61] But we have enough distance from the myth world to want to find explanations of it rather than explain it away. But we are frustrated. We want to eliminate the irrational, at least from our conduct, and we thus accept unwittingly the polarization between the rational and the irrational, the natural and the conventional; and we then cannot help but view the myth world as somewhat natural, as rational no less than our world, and we thus let in relativism, subjectivism, cynicism, etc. And these are reinforced by positivism, which is the vacillation between them and their extreme opposites. And this is the story of a vast portion of our present-day intellectual and cultural heritage.[62]

It seems to me fairly obvious, then, that the ancient polarizations are still alive and kicking; that we do not have to be much on the outlook to meet the ancient polarization,

falsehood:truth::mythos:logos::appearance:reality::convention:nature.

Yet in order to avoid it, all we need remember is that explanation moves towards reality and away from appearance, but still it occupies the middle ground. The middle ground is between appearance and reality, yet it alters appearance; it is likewise between mythos and logos, yet it engenders new mythology; it is likewise between convention and nature, and may help us improve convention — on which more in the next chapter. It is, finally, not the whole truth and nothing but; and so it is false, although, we hope, to decreasing degrees of falsehood (Einstein, Popper).[63]

Yet, I confess, easy as it is to remain in the middle ground, I should not overlook the tremendous attraction of the extremes, and of the practice, the great discovery of which belongs to Lévi-Strauss, of covering the middle ground by mixing the extremes in proper proportions and unnoticingly.[64] Here, then, we see exemplified in our own ethos Lévi-Strauss's thesis that polarizations have a logic of their own, that mythology thinks for us all by itself. (Except that the logic of myth is less prevalent in the West, at least in the natural sciences.) It is no accident that even Franz Kafka, not quite a philosopher, yet a person who was extremist in his bold polarization, lost all sense of the significance of the family once he looked at it as at a mere convention; yet, he was trapped in it all the more. We know and he knew that he could never rid himself of the ghost of his domineering father, and his declaring it as meaningless only made it harder for him to see what was the matter.[65] We see that from his short story "The Judgement" on a father's verdict, and we see it from his self-torturing *Letter To My Father*.[66] The same holds for another person, a positivist who terrified his followers in his demand to see only the tangible and no chimeras, namely Ludwig Wittgenstein. Wittgenstein, the father figure of English philosophy for a whole generation, said both of the two opposite polar things as regards his relations to his followers. On one pole he said, there is no such thing as philosophic ancestry; and he complained bitterly about his disciples, saying that had they comprehended him they would have deserted him and philosophy in order to go and do other things. On the other pole he was a most demanding father who never tired of making it clear that they never sufficiently aknowledged their debt to him, that he was all and they nothing: just as described by Kafka in his *Letter To My Father.*

It is not true that family relations and schoolmates are nothing to us.[67] Customs may change randomly from place to place, yet local customs are not at all random to the inhabitants of a locality: they are childhood memories, no less.[68] This, strangely, is quite a universal truth, from which the radicalist giants of the Age of Reason failed to break away. They tried. They were profoundly convinced that scales can come off people's eyes by the mere acceptance of reason, and thereby childhood memories can be relegated without any further effort to the realm of poetry and folklore devoid of rational force. They failed. Diverse thinkers then tried the idea of custom as a second nature.[69] But second nature is just a name for an attachment and dependence. As long as one hopes that this attachment will vanish in one generation — the desert generation, so-called — the problem is not pressing. But the attachment is transmitted from one generation to the next. For, to express and rationalize the emotional attachment to, and dependency on, local custom, is to make a myth; and myth, as expression and as part of local custom, is not something which vanishes like a ghost does when we bring a candle to the dark room; it does not vanish after a generation; it does not vanish by radicalizing education.[70] Moreover, the very claim of the Enlightenment that convention is sheer chimera which vanishes when the fact that it is chimera is understood, plus the feeling that one given convention — mine — is deeply rooted, may invite the myth that this very convention is something extra special.[71] We never know what is rational and what is a rationalization, and excessive rationality simply imposes rationalization. The excesses of the Enlightenment thus became pillars of romanticism with but the slightest and most welcome modifications.

All this is simply to update the best criticism of conventionalism to our own day. David Hume and Adam Smith, the naturalists, said in their respective books of essays,[72] that the sole argument of the conventionalist is the claim that a member of society is in principle at liberty to leave it and so, as long as he stays, he stays by agreement. This claim, say Hume and Smith, is as true as the claim that a passenger in a ship can jump overboard.[73] I often wondered how a man like Smith, who stressed that since every transaction is voluntary there is an expected gain on both sides, how he did not apply the same to society at large. But I was in error. His economic model was not descriptive but prescriptive — millenarian, even — and he dismissed all existing models, even if true, as irrational and superstitious. Yet naturalism need not blind us to the validity of the critique of conventionalism: on the one hand, it is not enough that in principle a convention can be willed; yet on the other hand, if, in fact, it is hard to break a convention, then it no longer rests on mere arbitrary agreement.[74] *At least the very difficulty of nullifying a convention is real, and so, to some degree, is the convention itself; hence equating convention with arbitrariness is an error.*

Hume and Smith rejected conventionalism, however, not the equation of convention with total arbitrariness. And so, they accepted society as natural — ignoring the myriads of arbitrary or semi-arbitrary conventions which keep society together. No, naturalism is equally false, since the passenger can, indeed, jump ship if another ship happens to pass by.[75] What remains, then, is simply non-arbitrary convention.[76]

And so, convention does not by its opposition to nature become falsehood, much less a chimera. We can study it and try to explain it rather than pooh-pooh it and hope it goes away. We can even try to explore the question, at what expense can we replace one custom or parcel of customs by another, and with what expected gain? This, I suggest, is much more rational. Moreover, it enables us to hope that we can simplify and universalize much that has thus far been tried only on limited scales in limited areas. It is hard to decide whether this makes us more natural and less conventional by simplification. Perhaps what is natural is savage society with its highly complex vastly associationistic mythical mode of thinking. We have, either way, gone far away from Herodotus' myth about philosophy as the rejection of myth as mere convention, and so, it is time we stop teaching it as if it were true.

The question may now rise again: are people rational? The question may be answered with the word "rational" having its strong ancient radicalist sense: if the rational is the real is the true is the natural, then, by God, no: we are not rational even if we know what it means. But men are rational in varying degrees depending on a more common sense of the word, and degrees of rationality is what I am after as a part of the new philosophy of man. And, again, are conventions utterly rational? Never. Are we free of convention? Never.

Does that preclude utter rationality? Yes. Does this make us all irrational? No. Why are we tempted to answer the last question differently? Because of the stronghold that the polarization of men to
rational and irrational has on us. We can break the spell of polarizations,
however. It will open to us, I think, new vistas and new avenues for research; not to mention some that have already been undertaken along these avenues, which may be greatly enhanced and encouraged.[76]

Here are good questions which cannot be grounded in either naturalism or conventionalism. How can we increase our rationality? When is it
more rational to change from one convention to another? If we refuse to
endorse our conventions as ideal or reject them as chimera,
how else should we relate to them in an effort to make both ourselves
and them more rational? These are the questions I shall take up in the
next chapter.

Notes to Section XV

58. F. M. Cornford, *Before and After Socrates,* Cambridge University Press, 1932
and many reprints, contrasts rational and mythical thinking dividing between
them with the act of "detachment of self from object". That is to say Cornford
considered contact with the outside world the prime error of all mythical thinking. In Freudianism this, naturally, has an easy connection with projections of
hopes and fears and good and bad intentions. Hence magic and hence mental
illness. Frazer identifies all magic with pseudo-science, namely with theories only
half-believed (since they are so easily refutable). See note 37 to Section XIII
above. Federn identified schizophrenia with the loss of sense of the body's
boundary. See note 42 to Section III above.

No doubt all this reflects more on the modern Western man and his need to
have his ego walled like a city by his skin than on the world of myth, magic, or
madness.

Nevertheless, it is to be admitted that a modern sophisticated man can be truly
attracted to magic and myth only when he disintegrates, whether as a society or as
a disintegrating individual. See Y. Fried and J. Agassi, *Paranoia, Boston Studies,*
1976. And so, admittedly, to us — but not to myth believers — myth is a chimera,
an appearance and less than an appearance since we have to make an effort to
visualize a myth.

The first essay of Henri Frankfort and others, *Before Philosophy*, Pelican,
1946, 1949 and many reprints, gives an admirable characterization of myth as
preceding the distinction between nature and convention. I think it is a very
important task to square Lévi-Strauss's denial of this claim with the rest of that
characterization. Of course, the key is that myths are held true when well applicable but allegorical when severely questioned, and back again — a fact crucial
for Frazer, also exploited, but never mentioned, by Lévi-Strauss.

59. See paper by D. Gershenson and D. Greenberg, mentioned in note 3 to this chapter.

60. The American literature on the American Indians is traditionally torn between viewing them as noble savages and as primitive savages. The culmination of this is in Fenimore Cooper's works which make some tribes this, some that. Mark Twain knows this, yet he does not note this in his celebrated list of Fenimore Cooper's "Literary Offenses". He prefers, rather, to contrast Cooper's claim for their cleverness with his own display of their stupidity. Perhaps this is so merely because he analyzes a couple of scenes from Cooper rather than Cooper as a whole. But I think it is because Mark Twain had his own problems with the Indians. See Louis J. Budd, *Mark Twain: Social Philosopher*, Indiana University Press, Bloomington, 1962, p. 45:

> *"Roughing It* (1872) also gave darker signs of misdirected bias from Twain's western years, especially when Indians slouched across its pages. From time to time he crossed the plain and felt only contempt for the redmen, and loudly and so often said so . . . In the *Galaxy* he derided the Indians with a white settler's passion as a "filthy, naked scurvy vagabond" whose extinction by the army should continue in spite of the "wail of humanitarian sympathy" from the older section of the country. There is no good reason why he reacted so violently."

On p. 67, and five years later, the author speaks of

> ". . . a sign that his glacial contempt for the Indian was thawing around the edges under pressure from neighbors, who were ahead of the national opinion . . ."

On p. 107, in 1887, Twain is "trying to see their [the Indians'] point of view" and on p. 189, in his posthumous notes we see him as an advocate of an unqualified brotherhood of men.

61. See Judith Buber Agassi, "Comments on Theory and Practice of Participant Observation," in R. S. Cohen and M. W. Wartofsky, *Boston Studies in the Philosophy of Sciences*, Reidel, Dordrecht, and Humanities, New York, Vol. 4, 1969, pp. 331–340, and "Objectivity in the Social Sciences", *ibid.* Vol. 11, 1973, pp. 85–96. See also her "Objectivity and Participant Observation", *op. cit.*, pp. 305–316. See also I. C. Jarvie, "The Problem of Ethical Integrity in Participant Observation", *Current Anthropology*, Vol. 10(5), December 1969, pp. 505–523.

62. Pierre Smith, "The Nature of Myths", *Diogenes,* No. 82, Summer 1973, pp. 70–87, p. 77, puts Lévi-Strauss's theory succinctly:

> "In short, there is no key to myths. These, taken as whole, aim not so much to depict the real as to speculate upon its latent potentialities; not so much to think something through as to walk the boundaries of the thinkable."

This is powerful stuff. The next stage is to think the real, and usually to deny potentiality: "what is is" says the mystic formula east and west. But Greek philosophy broke through with the doctrine of reality and appearance which reduces the potential to the real. This was noticed by Aristotle whose meta-physics, in one version is, actual : potential :: reality : appearance.

And so, even the Greek mystics, the Eleatics, had to explain but failed; see the Gershenson and Greenberg reference in note 3 to this chapter.

All this explains the great tenacity of the reality-appearance dichotomy: it is two steps ahead of everybody else.

63. See my "The Novelty of Popper's Philosophy of Science", mentioned in note 58 to Section IV above.

64. What Lévi-Strauss describes as mythical thinking, i.e. using opposite poles and at time mediators, is common in modern society too – as has amply been observed. Pairs of conflicting myths, fables, and proverbs have been noted. The question is regularly posed, however, are scientists mere myth-makers, are scientific theories myths? The answer is, definitely no; but this does not end matters, contrary to the most popular views on the matter. For, scientists hold myths just in the Lévi-Straussian sense: they vacillate between inductivism and instrument-alism (see my: *Towards an Historiography of Science*, mentioned in note 3 to the Introduction above, Section 14), between reductionism and anti-reductionism, etc., etc. Engineers vacillate between the view that every experimental set-up is repeatable to any desired degree of accuracy (when successful) or never quite repeatable (when faced with a failure). Until I read Lévi-Strauss I found such inconsistencies very disturbing – more so than even the tribalism of certain groups of scientists, engineers, and philosophers. Now I see the two – inconsistency and tribalism – as one: Gellner has shown that loyalty is best shown by endorsing inconsistencies. See note 15 to Section XI above for reference.

In science-oriented societies myths are often couched in tautologies. For example: 'you get what you pay for' means the price is right; and 'business is business' means you must accept being gypped without complaint. Also, it takes little effort to reconcile the contradiction between any two myths – which is done by explaining away one pole; whether the gypping or business ethics, it matters little which. The most awful and contemptible myth put as a tautology is, 'the end justifies the means'. Its opposite, incidentally, is, 'you can only do your best, and if what you do is right then certainly it's ok'.

It is therefore hard for me to understand how Kirk can accept Lévi-Strauss's theory *sans* mediation, as he does (see note 47 to Section XIV above).

65. Franz Kafka, *Letter to His Father*, Schocken, New York, 1953, 1966, p. 71:
"Not only did I lose my family feeling, as you say; on the contrary, I did indeed have a feeling about the family, mostly in a negative sense, concerned with the breaking away from you (which, of course, could never be done completely)."
A different sentiment is expressed, for example in *Letters to Felice*, ed. Erich Heller and Jürgen Born, trans. James Stern and Elisabeth Duckworth, Schocken, New York, 1973, November 11, 1912, pp. 35–6, where he describes his relations with his mother, where he says his relations with his sisters are good or friendly,

and professes mutual hatred with his father. But, quite possibly, it was when he tried to control his hatred that he found nothing but estrangement.

All this is still unsatisfactory. It is odd that he lost all family feelings, as he says repeatedly, when speaking of his own family, even though he could easily partake in others'; see *op. cit.*, March 16, 1913, p. 223, ". . . even if . . . I knew only that she was your sister, I should have to love her . . ."

66. As to the autobiographic character of "The Judgment", if evidence for it be needed, Kafka's *Letters to Felice*, cited in the previous note, December 4–5, 1912, p. 87, where the status of "some inner truth" is claimed for that story. See also the detailed analysis in Martin Greenberg, *The Terror of Art, Kafka and Modern Literature*, Deutsch, London, 1965, 1968, Chapter 3, especially p. 52.

See also Fredrick J. Hoffman, "Escape from Father", in Engel Flores, ed., *The Kafka Problem,* New Directions, New York, 1946, pp. 214–246.

Even a cursory bibliography on Kafka's relation to his father is too large a bibliographic work to attempt here. Let me, then, merely mention a caution which has been made by Charles Neider in his *The Frozen Sea, a Study of Franz Kafka,* Oxford University Press, London and New York, 1948. I mention Neider's book not because of its psychoanalytic interpretation and his view of Kafka's relations with his father as a predominant theme and as an inherently conflict situation. Rather, I mention Neider because of his more critical attitude. "In a curious sense," he says (p. 10), "Kafka is Max Brod's creation." (This was later corroborated by Brod's suppression of Kafka's relations with Milena.) "Brod is largely if not altogether responsible for the theological interpretation" of Kafka. "Brod introduces extensive excerpts from Kafka's *Letter to My Father* . . . He values the *Letter* highly, yet accepts only . . . portions . . . He is biased not only against psychoanalysis but against scientific method as a whole . . . The fact is that Kafka was secretive. One wonders whether Brod possesses sufficient information regarding Kafka's personal life . . . to warrant making judgments contrary to Kafka's own . . ."
See also pp. 31ff. For my part I do not see why we have to assume that either the cabalistic or the psychological interpretation must prevail or even dominate. Especially in the light of the good traditional psychoanalytic view that neurotics seek symbolisms we may weld the two readings of Kafka.

67. The inability of individuals to break loose so completely from established institutions as to ignore family relations (spouses, parent-child, siblings) is discussed at some length in Hegel's *Phenomenology*, VI, A a, "The Ethical World: Law Divine and Human: Man and Woman." It is an incredibly incomprehensible chapter, yet highly suggestive. One can read there, if one wishes, even the view that ancestor worship is universal and necessary and divine. The chapter, on the whole, reads as favorable to both women and sex, although it views as best sex, that latent sex which has no chance of becoming actual — a sister's love to her brother. The diatribe against women comes in the next chapter on guilt and destiny: women, says Hegel (p. 497 of the J. B. Baillie translation, Allan and

Unwin, London, Humanities, New York, revised second edition, 1949, 1966), extol their sons and young husbands; it seems that Lysistrata is in his mind though he does not hint (he does allude to Greek dramas in adjacent passages). He says, "The community, however, can preserve itself only by suppressing the spirit of individualism," the community needs it but also seeks to "suppress it as a hostile principle." Quite remarkable for a pre-Freudian! See also note 119 to Section X above.

68. Géza Róheim, in his *The Origin and Function of Culture,* Nervous and Mental Disease Monographs, No. 69, New York, 1943, Johnson Reprint, New York, 1968, though his thesis is extremely rationalistic ("in 1912 Freud ... *Totem and Taboo,*. . . showed that savages in certain cases act and think like neurotics ... the analogy lies between savage *cultures* and the neurotic ...", opening paragraph), sees the shortcoming of the rationalistic view and even suggests the crucial difference between inside and outside views (p. 9, italics mine):

"It is true, of course, that civilization is a mode of group living (Margaret Mead) but we must add to this definition that *when viewed from the outside,* it is always a peculiar mode. A rationalist might imagine that human beings living in a group, find a way to combine their energies in the struggle with the environment and that the most effective means are finally employed in this struggle. Variations of culture would in this case arise as variations in those means conditioned by a varying environment. But this is far from being true. What we really find is that human groups are actuated by diverse group ideals, led on by dominant ideas, which may be *supremely important for them but incomprehensible or devoid of value for their neighbors.* Ruth Benedict . . . I tried to go beyond this and to show that these collective psychical system formations were . . . defense mechanisms . . ."

And Róheim does not see that he only deviates from the exceedingly rational view of society to the extent that he denies that *from the outside* a society seems rational; but he concludes that society is therefore neurotic and irrational. Bacon identified irrationality with preconceived notions or prejudices and explained their persistence by the fact that facts can always be twisted to fit a theory and nobody wants to admit a mistake and take the ensuing humiliation. Marx modified this by equating prejudice with class-prejudice and declared economic interest to act as blinkers; Freud described neuroses the same way Bacon described prejudices, only with the censor being not one's peer group but internalized; Róheim describes primitive culture − any culture (p. 25), in fact − as infested with irrationality and as a neurosis.

69. A note regarding custom as second nature may be in order here, as customs matter in many fields, including ethnography and the law.

As phenomena, convention and custom are different in a clear manner: whereas a convention binds only the parties which draw it, customs pass from generation to generation. When a conventionalist philosopher says, customs are really only conventions, he means, the individual member of a society undertakes to observe its custom, or else, if enough people do not, the custom dies. Hence, he concludes, in reality, custom is convention. The conventionalist view of custom as convention widely differs from the naturalistic view of custom as habit, where habit is second nature, since habit unlike undertaking, has no component of obligation; its necessity is natural and so needs no reinforcement (in adults!). This is why lawyers and legalists are rather conventionalists than habitualists. Hence the Talmudic Myth of the Presence — all souls of the Children of Israel of all generations were present at the original Covenant at Mount Sinai — which comes to stress the obligational aspect of the Law. Habitualists, incidentally, may enter the obligatory component by an appeal to the fact that the individual has to observe or even endorse habits of his society which, being widespread enough are implicitly taken for granted in every venture unless explicitly excluded. Hence the Talmudic Myth of Compulsion — at Mount Sinai the Children of Israel were offered the choice between the Covenant and extinction.

What is common to the conventionalist and habitualist is, of course, the polarization of nature and convention, where habit is a mixture of nature — a disposition to develop patterns of conduct — and accident or convention — of choice of a particular pattern. Now in truth custom is not a convention, since it evolves before the age of consent, and not naturally compelling as we can break a habit. But the degree to which I view a habit as a second nature is the cost of breaking it. I have thus endorsed a gradual view instead of the polarized, all-or-nothing, Greek view.

The ethnographic corollary relates to the observation of change: how deeply rooted a custom is and at what cost it is alterable is a matter that contemporary anthropologists (e.g. Raymond Firth, Margaret Mead) observe and report in the literature.

The legal corollary, again, may relate the obligation to observe the custom with society's readiness to consider the possibility of altering it. Examples abound.

The legal problem however, is not thereby solved. Custom, to the legalist, is an unwritten law. But there is no law without sanction. Who, then, sanctions custom breakers? All 19th-century female novelists, English and French, provided the solution: the policeman who imposes sanctions on custom breakers is the parish-pump. Now all custom breakers know this theory and its refutation: they simply get on the better side of the parish-pump and get a favorable treatment which no police or court can offer without thereby becoming corrupt, yet this does not corrupt the parish-pump (who is too corrupt and stupid to begin with).

70. John Locke, *Some Thoughts Concerning Education,* 1693, p. 138 (Peter Gay edition, Classics in Education, No. 20, Teachers College, Columbia University, New York, 1964, p. 100)

"... always whilst he is young, be sure to preserve his tender mind from all impressions and notions of spirits and goblins, or any fearful apprehensions in the dark. This he will be in danger of from the indiscretion of servants, whose usual method is to have children, and keep them in subjection, by telling them of raw-heads and bloody-bones, and such other names, as carry with them the idea of something terrible."

The optimism of this view is very obvious. It begins with Bacon's claim that once people realize how much promise they miss because of prejudice they will be only too glad to start afresh. It ends, as Anna Freud notices in her 1954 Anniversary Lecture, with the optimism of early Transitionism when it was assumed that parents can learn to avoid inflicting neuroses on their children so that the next generation would be healthy post-Freudian. Radicalism, we remember (see note 50 to Section XIV above) believes in no need for a transition period.

Bertrand Russell notices in the beginning of *On Education* that ideal education is impossible without ideal society and vice versa. This has led him away from radicalism. Thus, he says (*Portraits From Memory*, "Reflections on My Eightieth Birthday"), "institutions mould character and character transforms institutions. Reform in both must march hand in hand". Nevertheless, he was repeatedly driven back to radicalism by his inductivist epistemology. His acceptance of the dichotomy was his greatest obstacle. He refused to see in ethics mere arbitrary convention and he refused to declare his ethical system the only true and natural one; he confessed he saw no way out of the dilemma.

71. At times, one's defense of one's prejudices as universally valid may mean no less than that those whom one discriminates against are not really human. This is, for example, the conclusion of George M. Fredrickson's review of Winthrop Jordan's *The White Man's Burden: Historical Origins of Racism in the United States* (O.U.P., 1973) in the *New York Review of Books*, Vol. 21 (1), Feb. 7, 1974, pp. 23–4: the very Declaration of Independence, he says, forced people in the name of consistency either to destroy all race prejudice in America or declare the victims of prejudice sub-human; and as long as the first option was too hard to be practicable, the Declaration helped people favor the second option. The same logic forces Chinese educated people to conclude that coolies have no "face." See Agassi and Jarvie, "A Study in Westernization", in I. C. Jarvie, ed., *Hong Kong, A Society in Transition*, Routledge, Praeger, London, New York, 1969, pp. 129–163, p. 146.

72. D. Hume, *Essays*, "Of the Original Contract", A. Smith *Lectures*, pp. 11–13; Wm. Paley, *Moral and Political Philosophy*, Book 3, Chapter III; J. Bentham, *Fragment on Government*, all quoted by E. Halévy, *The Growth of Philosophic Radicalism*, translated by M. Morris, Beacon, paperback, Boston, 1966, p. 133.

73. Hume's opposition to conventionalism in his famous essay "Of the Original Contract" includes diverse arguments, philosophical, commonsense, and historical. Let me quote this one only:

"Can we seriously say that a poor peasant or artisan has a free choice to leave his country when he knows no foreign language or manners and lives from day to day by the small wages which he acquires? We may as well assert that a man, by remaining in a vessel, freely consents to the dominion of the master, though he was carried on board while asleep and must leap into the ocean and perish the moment he leaves her."

Hume's essay is brilliantly summed up by Halévy, *op. cit.* (previous note), pp. 131–3. There are two arguments here, one against the original contract expressly not opposed to contractualism ("Two men, who pull the oars of a boat, do it by agreement or convention, though they have never given promises to each other") and one opposed to contractualism, quoted above.

See also Halévy, p. 133:

"Adam Smith and Paley adopted Hume's formula, almost textually, by criticizing the idea of the original contract. The same is true of Bentham . . . "

Hume's criticism from the limitations of simple folks is valid and moving. It is strengthened by educators' persistent effort to make their charges dependent, by the nationalistic discouragement of the study of foreign languages, etc. Yet, every time educators fail some individuals become able to leave and so their stay is voluntary.

Ernest Gellner has a communication-theoretic view of nationalism as generalized irridentism, of the emergence of a coherent communication system based on standardized education; see his *Contemporary Thought and Politics*, Routledge, London and Boston, 1974, Chapter 11, especially pp. 142, 153. This makes nationalism partly liberating, in that it enables one to move freely within one's country, and partly constraining. It raises the painful question, do all nations have to go through all stages of nationalism? This is a question with a historicist flavor, yet it makes ample sense, and, I have tried to show, can be asked without historicism and perhaps even be given better answers in the not so distant future.

It is too much to hope for an answer right now, but, clearly, one obstacle on the way to it is perfectionism which, in the present context demands that each stage should be passed through with all due care, that everyone devote oneself exclusively to the culture given to one, since one will never be able to master well any other culture.

This erroneous view is forcefully advocated by Michael Oakeshott, *Rationalism in Politics and Other Essays*, Basic Books, New York, 1962. He argues that the greatest error of radicalism – he calls it rationalism – is the view that one can rationally acquire with ease what in fact only proper upbringing and care can achieve. The example for such rationalism is Shaw's *Pygmalion* which is, doubtless, sheer fantasy. It is strange that Popper's follower and colleague, E. H. Gombrich, endorses Oakeshott's view. See his "The Tradition of General Knowledge", in Mario Bunge, *The Critical Approach: Essays in Honor of Karl Popper*, Free Press, MacMillan, London and New York, 1964, pp. 431–444, p. 434.

Of course it is all a matter of degree, and much depends on how much one aims to achieve: contrary to almost all of our barbaric educational methods, we should teach one to play the piano or read a mathematical text quite differently if he aims at modest success than if he means to excel in it. And, it is a fact, with little common sense one's achievement in a little time can be remarkably high, even though diminishing returns do set in fast. Those who know this fact have hobbies and amateur interests galore, whereas pedants can hardly have any. And pedantry is the offspring of the misanthropic work ethic.

74. Hume's strongest attack on contractualism seems to be his claim that keeping a promise is a convention on which the contract rests.

The new Misessian *laissez-faire* school of economics (the Chicago school) allows for all producers' violations of ethics, including mislabeling of products, to be penalized by consumers' abstention. They insist, however, that contracts honoring should be enforced by the law, rather than that the market eject the dishonest enterpreneur. They are inconsistent exactly where Hume saw the weak point of contractualism, yet they are, of course, naturalists. The new libertarians in the US are now willing to go even further and allow for private armies as the best means of enforcing contracts; this overlooks the possibility that the strongest will not be bullied to keep his word. This is a far cry from the doctrine of the natural goodness of man from which their doctrine has sprung.

Sir Karl Popper has explicitly dealt with Hume's objection, and offered a solution to it which he ascribes to Lycophron (*Open Society*, Chapter 6, Section VII), and labels "Lycophron's protectionism". He says, there is no reason why citizens should not will to be decent. I find this answer besides the point: if people willed to be decent and so kept the convention, then convention is based on moral rules. Are these arbitrary or natural?

Of course, the crux of the matter is that both naturalism and conventionalism are justificationist, and Popper is not. (As to Lycophron, I cannot say.) Hence, Popper is not a conventionalist proper, but, I propose, a modified conventionalist.

75. Hume's and Smith's argument against contractualism is that we cannot really leave a ship and so we are forced to stay. The answer is that if we can leave one ship and transfer to another then we have some relative freedom. This answer can be translated, like the original metaphor, back to social discourse. "That the ancient Athenians", says Mordechai Roshwald, (in "The Idea of the Promised Land", *Diogenes*, No. 82, Summer 1973, pp. 45–69, p. 49),

"... and the modern Anglo-Saxons retained their rather detached attitude to the fatherland is probably due to the fact that, in both cases, we have to do with maritime nations ... used to the idea of movement ... The experience of contact with distant places, the inevitable comparison ... create a frame of mind which is more objective and less loco-centric."

76. The content of this paragraph is an exposition of ideas I have received from Karl Popper, yet for me that paragraph leads to the next one which, I think, conflicts with Popper's theory of rationality. See my "Criteria for Plausible Argument", *Mind*, Vol. 83, 1974, pp. 406–16, reprinted in my *Science in Flux*, Reidel, Dordrecht and Boston, 1975, and "The Logic of Scientific Inquiry", *Synthèse*, Vol. 26, 1974, pp. 498–514. See also J. W. N. Watkins, "Imperfect Rationality," in R. Borger and F. Cioffi, eds., *Explanation in the Behavioral Sciences*, Cambridge University Press, 1970, pp. 167–216, and my review of it, "Listening in the Lull", *Phil. Soc. Sci.*, Vol. 2, 1972, pp. 319–332.

Chapter Four

Man as Social

In conformity with my anti-all-or-nothing-attitude, I intend to reject in this chapter both the reduction of sociology to psychology and the reduction of psychology to sociology. Man is indeed a social animal, but not only that.

Man was defined by Aristotle once as a rational animal, once as a social animal. What is common to both is that both were declared illusory by those who claimed that they are explicable. In particular, both the Enlightenment movement and the Marxist movement declared the state as non-existent because it is explicable — whether as the sum-total of individual interactions or as a means of class-oppression.[1] I shall not bother to refute again this identification of explaining with explaining away.

Now, is man's social nature the same as his rational nature? In tune with the theory of Lévi-Strauss we have both answers operating in our society, the affirmative as well as the negative. The affirmative answer sees in politics the art of planning a political and social utopia,[2] the negative one the art of adjusting, of swaying with the winds of change, of drifting on the waves of history.

But, as usual, rather than endorsing uncritically the two extremes, we can strike a middle-ground proper.[3] For my part, I wish to make it clear that, in my opinion, politics is only that part of political phenomena that can be properly classed as political behavior, which is open to choice, i.e. to rational action. And I wish to add that even this slim part of the political arena, namely political action, can never be wholly rational. That, likewise, the rationality of individuals can never be divorced from the social setting, and that even within the constraint of the social setting rationality is never complete. Yet it is the very interaction of individual action and the social setting that is the hallmark of the new philosophical anthropology.[4]

To return to our very starting point, Man is both a rational and a social (or political) animal. The question immediately arises: Are Man's social qualities animal rather than rational or the other way round?

It is strange that, though the definitions of Man both as a rational animal and as a social animal are at least as old as Aristotle, the further question,[5] is rationality social, was neither asked nor answered. On the contrary, it was taken for granted, we remember, that man's social nature is animal,[6] and that hence thinking is strictly individual. Indeed, the point most fully shared by both classical rationalists and their romantic heirs was just this. The rationality of society as a whole, namely the wisdom of the ages, was indeed postulated, but it was never ascribed to society, since society was never presented as a rational thinking super-individual, even by those who did view society as a super-individual. Rather, the rationality of society was variedly ascribed to blind Fate, to God, to the Cunning of History, or to some individuals, known as the Great Leaders; and finally, after Darwin gained popularity, to the forces of natural selection. Somehow even the romantics refused to give the group-mind the ability to generate rational thoughts like an individual.[7]

Perhaps the most significant point made by modern methodology is, paradoxically, that thinking is social, not individual.[8] This seems to put chains on the individual more than even the most reactionary romantic thinkers ever dared suggest. What I shall try to show here is that in this startling fact lies the liberty of the individual and the hope of resolving the ancient conflict between individualism and collectivism on more rational lines than either of these two extreme schools have hitherto suggested.

Notes.

1. Even if an institution were "nothing but" a label facilitating one's interaction with one's complex neighborhood, or facilitating class oppression, or anything else, even then, they cannot be explained away without loss. For, even labels are functional. Thus, the very fact that a label such as the name of a neighborhood in a city interacts with decision-making processes, particularly because a name becomes an instituted entity influencing the choice of boundaries to neighborhood in a uniform way, etc. Similarly, the fact that the unit of weight is grain in one country and milligram in another is a factor determining to some extent the size of pills, such as aspirin. Of course, such determinations may be marginal in

the sense that when it matters we may disregard names of neighborhoods or redefine them, etc. Yet the unintended consequences of one's decisions which are of marginal import to one may be of crucial import to another.

See Gerald D. Suttle, *The Social Construction of Communities,* University of Chicago Press, Chicago, 1972.

2. Tom Paine, for example, defends naturalism by the natural need of men to gravitate towards others. *The Rights of Man,* Part II, Chapter 1, p. 17, as quoted in Elie Halévy, *The Growth of Philosophic Radicalism,* translated by Mary Morris, Beacon Press, Boston, 1955, p. 189. Of course, Paine's naturalism was utopian (see Halévy, *ibid.,* pp. 191–2) in that he saw the ideal society in that which but comes to satisfy man's social needs in a free association. He thus explained away all existing society, as was common in his day, and also wished away all existing organized society on the ground that all organized society prevents utopia.

It is in this sense that the Enlightenment was not at all Spinozist. See B. Spinoza, *A Political Treatise,* R. H. M. Elwes' translation, Chapter 1, Introduction,
"Philosophers conceive of the passions which harrass us as vices . . . And so they think they are doing something wonderful . . . when they . . . praise such human nature as is nowhere to be found, and to make verbal attacks on that which, in fact, exists . . . instead of ethics, they have generally written satire, and they have never conceived a theory of politics, which could be turned to use, but . . . Utopia, or . . . golden age . . .
But statesmen, on the other hand, are suspected of plotting against mankind, rather than consulting their interests, and are esteemed more crafty than learned."
The claim that the image of man endorsed by the Enlightment is utopian is quite common a twentieth-century reading. See the works of Cassirer, e.g. *Rousseau-Kant-Goethe,* translated by J. Guttman, P. O. Kristeller, and J. H. Randall, Jr., Princeton University Press, 1945, especially pp. 10, 20, 22; *The Philosophy of the Enlightenment,* translated by F. C. A. Koelln and J. P. Pettegrove, Beacon Press, Boston, 1955; or Carl L. Becker, *The Heavenly City of the 18th Century Philosophers,* Yale University Press, New Haven and London, 1932, 35 printings to date. See also Frank E. Manuel, *The Age of Reason,* Cornell University Press, Ithaca, 1951.

So much for the eighteenth-century individualists. That the nineteenth-century collectivists were so often utopians has become commonplace due to Marx and Engels. The opponents of utopianism were mostly the negativists, the reactionary defendants of the *status quo.* What remains are the nineteenth-century individualists who, like John Stuart Mill and de Tocqueville, held the fort and kept liberalism alive. Yet they were historicists in the tradition of Saint Simon and Comte. See note 2 to Chapter Two, and note 2 to Chapter Three.

Yonina Talmon, "Pursuit of the Millenium: the Relation Between Religious and Social Change," *Archives Européennes de Sociologie,* Vol. 3, 1962, pp. 125–148, Section 3, "On the whole, millenarism appeared mainly in countries which had direct or indirect contact with the Judeo-Christian Messianic

traditions." Talmon was a functionalist who found millenarism a religious phenomenon with a social function. She says, section 4, "The revolutionary nature of
millenarism makes it a very potent agent of change." This is functionalist in a
most pickwickian sense of the word. For my part, I see millenarism as a degenerate version of radicalism, and so Greek, not Judeo- and not Christian. True,
everybody quotes Isaiah's millenarism. But if Isaiah is a millenarist, then so are
Confucius, Lao-Tze, and Chuang-Tze. Indeed, Confucius is more millenarist than
Isaiah in that he says, virtue brings heaven on earth.

3.   It is far from clear what the middle ground in politics should look like. When
tradition and reason clash, the radicalist chooses the one and the conservative the
other. (The reactionary, particularly the Hegelian, denies that there is a real clash,
presenting the seeming clash as a give and take.) Now Popper presents a theory of
a compromise: do not abolish tradition, but cautiously modify, piecemeal, in the
light of reason. More and more young Popperians find this solution conservative.
Their view is still in the making. I. C. Jarvie has already offered
a germ of it in his view that we can conceive or plan a society on a blueprint and
try to implement it, as a whole, not by cleaning the slate first (as radicalists would
have it) but by well-designed step-by-step transitions. This, needless to say, is a
constraint on the blueprint. See Jarvie's "Utopian Thinking and the Architect", in
Stanford Anderson, ed., *Planning for Diversity and Possible Futures and their
Relations to the Man-Controlled Environment,* MIT Press, Cambridge, Mass.,
1968, pp. 8–31. See a similar remark by Daniel Bell quoted below, note 66 to
Section XXIV and next note.

4.   Attitudes towards tradition are obscured by the fact that they are summed up
in a slogan – three attitudes, and one slogan! The traditionalist T. S. Eliot (*Points
of View,* Faber and Faber, 1941, p. 22), the liberal Sir Karl Popper ("Towards a
Rational Theory of Tradition", in *Conjectures and Refutations,* 1963), and all
radicalists (see quote from Descartes, note 14 to Section XI above and Locke,
Conduct of the Understanding, Section XXIV), all say, take from tradition what is
good and reject what does not stand up to rational examination! Yet they disagree as to what stands up to examination not only in detail but also systematically. Radicalists not only view the rejection of what is wrong in tradition
imperative and urgent, they view most of tradition as erroneous, since baseless.
Traditionalists believe that most things in tradition are founded and so, even if not
perfect, the best we have; and, do not throw away the old dirty water before you
have new clean water. The liberals are of diverse temperaments from radicalist to
traditionalist, but deny both views – you cannot reject all old errors at one
sweep, but what you can reject maybe you should, maybe even prior to having an
alternative, maybe not. Also, liberals defer to public sentiment in preference to
their own, even while trying to sway public feelings. At least this is how I feel, and
my temper is as radical as can be while remaining consistent with liberalism, and
errs a bit on the radical side – except that I am a passionate student of traditions
and histories. I never could understand why lovers of the study of traditions are so

often traditionalists. See note 30 to Section XII above. I should also mention the fact that some traditionalists, e.g. Burke, are reactionary and irrationalistic enough to allow tradition to overrule reason. See note 31 to Section XII above. But then some radicalists, e.g. Sorel, are likewise irrationalists. See note 36 to Section XXII below. Irrationalism, anyway, cannot be taken seriously; see my "Scientists as Sleepwalkers", in Y. Elkana, ed., *The Interaction Between Science and Philosophy*, Humanities Press, 1974, pp. 391–405, and "Rationality and the *Tu Quoque* Argument", *Inquiry*, Vol. 16, 1973, pp. 395–400.

5. It is quite possible that Aristotle already asked the question, if man is by nature a rational animal and a political animal, does his political essence reside in his rational or in his animal essence? For, Aristotle clearly tried to block an answer in his saying that man is by nature political since otherwise he is either inferior or divine (*Pol.* 1253a2); either an ass or an angel, that is, so that politics is not in rationality or in animality but in their very juxtaposition. What kind of essence can be the outcome of a juxtaposition, I cannot say, except that Aristotle's theory of genus and differentiae does not seem to allow for it.

6. One of the few places where unease is expressed at man as social animal and man as rational animal is in Philip Wheelwright, "Buber's Philosophical Anthropology", in P. A. Schilpp and M. Friedman, eds., *The Philosophy of Martin Buber*, Open Court, La Salle, Ill., and Cambridge University Press, London, 1967, pp. 69–75, pp. 70ff. First, "Aristotle's double characterization of man . . . seems to stand pretty much as a basis of all the serious views that he puts forward." Buber, he adds, claims that "only in our time has the anthropological problem reached maturity, that is, come to be recognized and treated as an independent philosophical problem" (*Between Man and Man*, London, 1947, p. 157), both because society became too big to be a real community and so broke down, and because man has lost control over his own creation, i.e. science. Yet, adds Wheelwright, the main asset of modern anthropology is its search for a unified view of man, not a dual definition like Aristotle's.

7. A concrete example is an analysis of the psychology of knowledge and its reduction to sociology *tout court* by Emile Durkheim and Marcel Mauss, in their *Primitive Classification* (originally published in 1903), translation and introduction by Rodney Needham, University of Chicago Press, Routledge and Kegan Paul, Chicago and London, 1963, opening paragraphs. See also their conclusion, pp. 86–7 where they assert the following views.

It has quite often been said that man began to conceive things by relating them to himself. The above allows us to see more precisely what this anthropocentrism, which might better be called *sociocentrism*, consists of. The center of the first schemes of nature is not the individual; it is society. It is this that is objected, not man. At the end of their study, however, they open the door to totally new ideas. First, they seem to say, classification is partly conceptual, partly emotional. Then, they add this:

"... Now emotion is naturally refractory to analysis, or at least lends itself uneasily to it, because it is too complex. Above all, when it has a collective origin, it defies critical and rational examination. The pressure exerted by the group ... does not permit individuals to judge freely. ... Thus the history of scientific classification is, in the last analysis, the history of the stages by which ... social affectivity has progressively weakened, leaving more and more room for the reflective thought of individuals. But it is not the case that these remote influences ... have [altogether] ceased to be felt today. ..."

What worries the authors here seems clear: if thinking reflects society, is there objectivity in science? They say, first, objectivity is a matter of degree; and this is quite revolutionary. Second, they say, the degrees of objectivity reflects degrees of individual freedom, another social element. But then, as long as individual freedom is allowed, total reduction fails. Nevertheless, the concluding paragraph reaffirms the program of explaining all thinking sociologically, thus defeating both currently contending parties, "the metaphysicians and [the] psychologists". And so a new idea is lost in the mist.

8. Colin Cherry, *World Communication: Threat or Promise?*, Wiley Interscience, London, New York, Sydney, Toronto, 1971, p. 3, says:

"... As Charles Peirce pointed out, talking with oneself is also a social process, a form of conversation. Thinking, that is to say, is also a social activity ..."

thus making the present view a kind of commonplace. I hope he is right.

XVI THE RATIONALITY OF SCIENCE IS PARTIAL

I have spoken critically of the accepted framework of the social sciences. Accepted, that is, in general outline, from Antiquity to date, though with sufficiently many deviations to somewhat obscure the general outline. Indeed, the aim of the present study is to attempt to find a new framework within which to fit these deviations; or which is hinted at by these deviations; or which "emerges inductively," so-to-speak, out of them. This, I suppose, is the salient point of the present exercise. When an alternative framework is presented, it may, of course, be a revolutionary one, aimed for future science and having no example to illustrate it; or it may claim a more realistic standing; it may claim to fit existing scientific activity better than the old established framework which it comes to replace. The present case, I suggest, is somewhere in between. I suggest that the better and more interesting scientific social studies fit the old framework less and less, and I hope that they naturally fit the framework I wish to see develop, so that the new framework will stimulate newer and better research projects, especially in diverse fields of education, before it is superseded.

Causal explanation, in the social sciences or otherwise, it is well known, places some simple restrictions on our assumptions. We cannot explain the less universal by the more universal alone; and we cannot explain anything satisfactorily except by an assumption more universal than that which we wish to explain. Hence, a satisfactory explanation is one which employs different levels of universality: the level of that which we wish to explain, and the higher level of that which explains (not necessarily the next one up, whatever this may be). Though this is well known and quite generally accepted, it is constantly violated — for various reasons. One reason, and it is the one I shall explore, is the view that a causal explanation should not be in the least arbitrary and to that end it should contain no assumptions except the most universal ones. The most universal is identified with metaphysics. Here is a conflict whose source is found in Antiquity, when it was postulated both that explanation is desirable and that assumptions should be the most universal and hence the least arbitrary.[9] According the Gershenson and Greenberg this conflict is expressed in the debate between the Eleatic-Parmenidean school and the Platonic one: if we assume only the most universal we cannot explain and vice versa. This same conflict led Noam Chomsky as recently as in 1965 to give up the demand for explanation.[10]

I sympathize with Chomsky's position, both on philosophic grounds — I do not approve of rejecting an idea out of hand just because it is not explanatory — and on the basis of common sense — as he is less pretentious when he says he does not explain much than when he says he does. But little virtue accrues to a confession of inability when the inability is declared universal. The reason Chomsky offers for the inability to explain is a philosophic error — he wants to concentrate so much on the universal elements in language that he ends up leaving almost all that is specific to a language hopelessly unexplainable.

The error Chomsky commits is not only a matter of philosophy, nor is it an error which affects merely his own research. This would only be the case if the fruits of his and his collaborators' labor were nothing but universal theory on the one side, coarse empirical facts on the other, with nothing in between. As a matter of fact, it is well known about Chomsky's own department at M.I.T. that it is seldom, if ever, that two of his followers analyze the structure of the same sentence in the same manner. The facts are presented, then, under interpretations; the interpretations are, then, explanations of the coarse facts, and may be or may not be rendered testable.[11] These explanatory interpretations are neither at the level of the most universal nor are they mere low-level generalizations; rather, they are exactly the kind of *axiomata media* which Bacon once complained were missing in the natural sciences. Ironically, four centuries later, diverse writers have complained they were missing in the social sciences. But whereas these diverse thinkers agreed that high-level universal (metaphysical) doctrines should not be proposed before the *axiomata media,* Chomsky takes the opposite stand and starts with his high-level universal doctrines. And thus far I am in agreement with him. Further, mere restatement of facts in the light of given metaphysical doctrines, particularly facts which (rightly or wrongly) seem anomalous, creates opportunities for the development of various *axiomata media,* explanations between the most specific and the most general. [12]

All this, I think is true of all science. It is especially significant in the social sciences, where specific models are needed to cope with the diversity of societies while not allowing the diversity to create too much arbitrariness. Attempts are sometimes made to exclude arbitrariness by so-called comparative studies. These use geographical area, language group, culture area, etc., as bases, hoping to be free of (metaphysical) guiding principles. [13] It obviously does not work and the comparative study all too easily degenerates into catalogues based on arbitrary classifications. It is a different matter if they are undertaken from the point of view of a general principle, a definite philosophical anthropology. This is especially so, to repeat, if a specific model seems to clash with the general principle and the seeming clash calls for either a modification of principle or a reinterpretation of a model by what soon may become a competing model subject to a crucial experiment between it and its predecessor. [14]

This use of specific models and general principles, then, may break the traditional polarization between the utterly universal and the uttely particular, and offer a middle ground — a genuine and in part testable comparative social science. Inasmuch as we manage to break the polarization between the utterly universal and the utterly particular, I contend, we also thereby manage to break the polarization between nature and convention, where nature is the utterly universal and convention the utterly arbitrary or capricious. For, the arbitrary and particular is contrasted with the rational (or social) and the rational with the universal or necessary. Hence rationality (or society) mediates between the particular and the universal.

As far as I can see, to view a specific society as merely arbitrary is an error because although from the outside a custom in a given society may look quite arbitrary, from within it may look quite rational, quite given for good reasons. We often ridicule ethnocentricity — that

naïveté, which takes its own social circumstances to be God-given —
and admittedly with some justice. But then we explain that away
instead of taking it seriously, and we thereby take our own canons of
social thinking as God-given. The prevalence of ethnocentricity was
dismissed by Herodotus and by Malinowski alike; it is time to explain
this prevalence, or at least take it seriously. [15]

Notes to Section XVI

9. See Gershenson and Greenberg, paper mentioned in note 3 to Chapter Three
above. See also final section of my *Towards an Historiography of Science* mentioned in note 3 to the Introduction above; also my "Logic of Questions and
Metaphysics" mentioned in note 68 to Section V above.

10. Popper claims that explanation increases with refutability. I doubt that this
is always so, but by and large I agree. And so, we should expect Chomsky's views
to be irrefutable. The irrefutability of Chomskian, old or neo, linguistics has been
forcefully presented by John King-Farlow, "Pronouns, Primacy and Falsification
in Linguistics", *Philos. Soc. Sci.,* Vol. 3, 1973, pp. 41–61.

   For the specific character of Chomsky's *Aspects of the Theory of Syntax,* MIT
Press and Mouton, Cambridge, Mass., and The Hague, 1965, see Judith Greene,
Psycholinguistics, Chomsky and Psychology, Penguin, 1972, Chapter 3,
Chomsky's Theory: 1965 Version, pp. 51–89, especially p. 55; see also pp. 177,
180, 190, 192ff.

   Note 24 of Chomsky's *Aspects* says it is hard to justify any hypothesis, including linguistics.

   In Chapter 1, §6, pp. 34–6 Chomsky disclaims ability to explain, and on the
ground that he overlooks the specific and centers on the universal. I think this is
fair enough.

11. All this is discussed in detail in my "The Nature of Scientific Problems and
Their Roots in Metaphysics", mentioned in note 8 to Section I above.

12. "For some time now it has been quite popular in our profession", says the
sociologist Ralf Dahrendorf, *Essays in the Theory of Society,* Stanford University
Press, 1968, p. 120, "to support T. H. Marshall's demand for 'sociological
stepping-stones in the middle distance' or Robert K. Merton's plea for 'theories of
the middle range.' I cannot say that I am very happy with these formulations."
And, adding some pacifying and explanatory remarks, Dahrendorf adds in a note,
"My objection to their formulation is therefore directed . . . against their explicit
assumption that nothing is wrong in recent theory but its generality, and that
simply by reducing the level of generality we can solve all problems."

13. For the defects of unguided comparative sociology see I. C. Jarvie, *The*

Revolution in Anthropology, Routledge and Präger, London and New York, 1964, pp. 20ff.

14. For the fruitfulness of cases of clashes between science and metaphysics see my works cited in note 4 to Chapter Three.

15. I wish to consider seriously both ethnocentric feelings and anti-ethnocentric feelings. For sophisticated intellectuals anti-ethnocentrism can come as naturally as others' ethnocentrism. As Gellner and Jarvie would put it — and they did put it so, though not exactly in these words — anti-ethnocentrism is the very ethnocentric bias of today's social anthropologists. We can see it thus. The ethnocentric may be surprised to learn how different foreign languages are and even that a foreign language is someone's mother tongue. (As Gogol puts it, in France even peasants speak French.) The anti-ethnocentric may be surprised to learn how ethnocentric the ethnocentric is — so much so that he may think his own mother tongue's grammar to be universal.

In brief, anti-ethnocentrism comes as intuitively to some as ethnoncentrism to others. And, in my opinion, the one is an inversion of the other and is equally erroneous, as Gellner and Jarvie have amply argued. For Gellner, see his *Cause and Meaning In The Social Sciences*, Routledge, London and Boston, 1973, pp. 198—202. For Jarvie, see his "Understanding and Explanation is Sociology and Social Anthropology" and "Reply" in R. Borger and F. Cioffi, *Explanation in the Behavioral Sciences*, Cambridge University Press, 1970, pp. 231—248, and 260—270.

The situation becomes obvious when a person is both the anthropologist and the informant. One reason for imposing fieldwork on anthropologists is to force them to shed their ethnic background, and with it, their ethnocentrism (see reference in note 61 to Section XV above); this reason obviously disqualifies an anthropologist from being his own informant. Yet, as Jarvie observes, some anthropologists do not need anti-ethnocentric training, and then being one's own informant is an asset. See Fred Eggan's Foreword to Alfonso Ortiz, *The Tewa World, Space, Time, Being and Becoming in a Pueblo Society*, The University of Chicago Press, Chicago and London, 1969, 1971:

"The author . . . is a relatively new type of social anthropologist . . . Such studies are particularly difficult for most of us since they normally require a certain degree of detachment, but under favorable circumstances . . . more than compensate . . ."

Regrettably, Alfonso Ortiz, the author, is more uncritical towards Claude Lévi-Strauss than towards his native Pueblo Indian system which he describes so ably.

XVII ASSUMING TOO MUCH RATIONALITY IS SILLY

There is an important fact, I contend, which we cannot easily alter, and which we even entrench by ignoring it: however arbitrary a custom looks from the outside, from the inside it looks very natural, pleasant, self-understood, reassuring. Knowing that other societies are different does not necessarily make one feel different about one's own society (unless one is alienated anyway); one does not feel unhappy about a custom simply because it is not universal (no custom is). At times this is so out of sheer *naïveté,* or out of ignorance and narrow-mindedness, and bigotry, and local mythology. But it is also the fate of enlightened people.

An enlightened person may become embarrassed by his preference for his own custom and be induced to rationalize it as the best for all societies, thus becoming a superbigot.[16] I wish I could present this case as purely hypothetical. It is, alas! quite common. I mention only one case. Dr. Isaac Watts said it was a shame that so many of his contemporaries were Christian for no better reason than mere accident of birth. It is charming to see such a broad-minded attitude, yet one shudders at the implication that Christianity should be endorsed by all as the edict of reason. And, one wonders, did Watts hold any Christian sect most rational, or his own? In the next generation, Dr. Joseph Priestley invited the Jews to debate religion amicably, and himself defended unitarianism which many viewed as not Christian at all — yet he implied that the Jews were irrational. Not much later Ludwig Feuerbach gave up religion, saying that Christianity was the most rational religion, but that it was not rational enough.[17]

I have taken attitudes to religion as an example of attitudes to institutions which are neither universalist nor blatantly irrational;[18] attitudes, in addition, which are neither free of bias nor necessarily bigotic, indeed at times hypersophisticated. No doubt, even some thinkers hostile to religion (say Marx) were not ready to condemn all religions on equal terms, and most of them were not equally hostile to all religions.

The resolution of the dilemma — the preference both for universalism and for one's own society — was relativism: each to his own faith.[19] As I said in earlier chapters, I shall not discuss relativism extensively. I should however, mention the fact that relativism gave birth to functionalism, which is a sociological-anthropological version of relativism. Not each to his own faith, but each to his own customs. Each custom, functionalism says, should be viewed from within, and indeed seen as natural. Social anthropologists of the functionalist persuasion attempt to explain inheritance laws as related to incest laws, for example: the two go together, and so, though each is inexplicable, both, and many others, which form a coherent whole, a comfortable habitat, are explained as natural — though only from within.[20]

It looks as if functionalism succeeds in its attempt to avoid the polarization between nature and convention. But, alas! , even at the cost of relativism, functionalism has not managed to avoid polarization. The polarization it postulates is between the functional and the nonfunctional. Every custom, every institution, functionalism claims, is one hundred percent functional.[21]

It seems clear that there are levels of functionality. Thus, in any modern monarchy monogamy seems to me to be much more functional than the monarchy itself. And the two can and occasionally do clash. More generally, we may consider the possibility of transporting a custom or an institution from one society to another and assess its functionality and coherence with the new habitat, as the feasibility of the transfer taking place without too many consequent changes. It is a fact that transfers do take place. The functionalist theory is that the transfer of one item changes the whole society; indeed, this is just a reformulation of functionalism. An example is held up to illustrate functionalism as just formulated: a metal axe was introduced into a primitive society, one measely metal axe, and it transformed the whole society.[22]

To prevent misunderstanding, let me say expressly, I think the axe story is true, yet a myth, a story elevated to the rank of a myth and so one whose historical truth matters little.[23] For the classical rationalist a true myth is almost a contradiction in terms, since they usually accused priests for having fabricated myths (and possibly but most unlikely a myth may turn to be true by sheer accident, for example the myth of the flood). Today we can say that science is ridden with myths. George Bernard Shaw already noticed this fact, but he considered it innocuous. His example was Newton's apple. Now, innocuous or not, myths of science are usually true. Newton did show people the very apple tree which dropped its mythical apple while he sat under it.[24]

The story is repeatedly told about an enthusiast beginner Freudian who cured a paralytic hysteric by the use of a ready-made analysis in one day — only to bring him to suicide at nightfall. This story is very similar to that of a man trying to help aborigines by letting them have some steel axes but destroying their society. In other cases of Stone Age tribes, incidentally, there are records of mistrust and taboo and other kinds of refusal to take a steel axe. All these stories are true, I suppose, or may very well be true, I am sure; yet they signify only for their moral — for their having been elevated to the rank of myths.[25]

The way to counter functionalism, to follow Lévi-Strauss, is to offer a different pole.[26] We may look for a case where a custom was introduced, absorbed, and led to no consequent change whatsoever.

Needless to say, we have such cases ready-made for us. But let us take cases of change. Perhaps the most conspicuous is the introduction of Christianity and Islam into diverse pagan countries, grafting them on to paganism, thus changing both the society and the religions. Similarly we have the myth — again, largely true — of the vast changes that the introduction of gunpowder to Europe caused in European social structure. The myth began already with Hegel.[27] Now, how much social change should gunpowder bring in its wake in order to comply with functionalism? Functionalists do not even know how to begin answering this question. It simply suited Hegel to say that gunpowder caused a lot of change — more or less single handed (here the mythical element is strong). It suited the Hegelian Sun Yatsen to believe that China could remain traditional even after adopting modern western (war) technology, and so he adopted that belief.[28]

What went wrong with functionalism? What made it adopt Hegel's idea that gunpowder alone must change the whole society to which it is introduced, is that functionalists still maintained the polarity of nature and convention and declared all properly functioning societies to be natural — only in a relativized sense.[29] For my part, I would rather keep the poles nature and convention, and try to locate all we have somewhere on a spectrum between the two poles. In particular, rather than defend each society on its own terms, as the functionalists do, I much prefer the classical Enlightenment aspiration towards the universal.

We see again that the classical or traditional approach has two components, moral and theoretical, and that the Enlightenment, like ancient Greece,[30] was radicalist in both. And the functionalists (like their romantic predecessors) move from radicalism to extreme conservatism.[31] Is it not easier to take a position in between? The answer is, no. All our intellectual tools were forged for different ends.[32]

Notes to Section XVII

16. The ethnocentrism of the Enlightenment was discussed to some extent and with deep sympathy, and critically by Sir Leslie Stephen, *History of English Thought in the Eighteenth Century*, 3rd edition, New York, 1902, 1927, Vol. 1, pp. 19ff. See also Basil Willey, *The Eighteenth Century Background: Studies on the Idea of Nature in the Thought of the Period*, London, 1940 and Paul Hazard, *European Thought in the Eighteenth Century, From Montesquieu to Lessing*, translated by Lewis May, Yale University Press, New Haven, 1954, World Publishing Co., Meridian Books, Cleveland, 1963. See also the next two notes.

17. Isaac Watts, *Logic or the Right Use of Reason in the Inquiry After Truth,*

London, 1724, Part II, Chapter III, Section IV. Joseph Priestley, *Letters to the Jews, Inviting Them to an Amicable Discussion of the Evidence of Christianity*, Birmingham, 1786. Ludwig Feuerbach, *The Essence of Christianity*, translated by George Eliot, Harper, New York, 1957.

Notice that whereas John Locke, with all his doctrine of toleration and its serving as a basis for his ethical and political doctrines, could not tolerate non-Christians, whereas Watts was blamed, even as late as by his biographer in the *Dictionary of National Biography*, for his weakness for nonconformists of all sorts. Hume observes in his *Dialogues Concerning Natural Religion*, "Locke seems to have been the first Christian, who ventured openly to assert, that faith is nothing but a species of reason, that religion is only a part of philosophy". But, of course, the modern rationalist defense of Christianity began with modern rationalism. See, for example, Robert Boyle, *The Excellency Theology, Compared with Natural Philosophy (As Both Are Objects of Men's Study)*, 1674, as well as his other theological works.

18. What shall we contrast with the rational? The pre-rational primitive, the non-rational believer, or the post-rational irrationalist? In truth this question does not make any more sense than any other question of contrast which is raised not relative to an ordered set of possibilities. Indeed the question can only mean, which set of possibilities are we to operate with, since whatever the set is, we have already made up our minds to put rationality on top as first priority.

Yet the choice of set is very relevant as a reflection of the alternatives we consider serious contenders. For me, therefore, the problem simply does not arise since I do not think there are any contenders. See references at the end of note 4 to this chapter.

Nevertheless, I should add, in the past, the image we had of the contender always was the reverse — or complement, or converse, or obverse (all these terms are precise but used here loosely and even metaphorically) — of our image of ourselves. And it starts with us as Christians and them as pagans. When in 1956 President Eisenhower was attacked for his criticism of the Israelis who were invading the Sinai desert and not the Russians who were invading Hungary he answered in an hour's speech televized on all networks from coast to coast, saying, you can criticize the Israelis who are Christians, but not the Russians who are pagans. Oh, he did not use the terms, and this is why his speech was so unnecessarily long; it is always shorter to call a spade a spade. Now for those who view President Eisenhower as too naive there is T. S. Eliot and his *The Idea of a Christian Society*, 1939, arguing for the same view, only while conceding that us are not as free of paganism as behooves us.

Both these eminent people are a few centuries out of fashion. For, the influence of Francis Bacon, who branded western science as a bunch of superstitions, led to the eighteenth-century view of our society as corrupt. Savages were then viable and free. China, then, was savage; Jews and Moslems did not exist. When the savage became a mere primitive and tradition was reinstated and ennobled, the local superstitions of the local European simple folks were discovered and honored. The superstitions, observes Shmuel Ettinger, merely reinforced popular anti-Jewish sentiments. But at least China came out all right. China ceased to be a country of noble savages and even the Moslems came to exist. The culmination of the Hegelian Feuerbachian refined anti-Judaism seems to be in A. J. Toynbee's views of the Jews as a fossil, a survival. The anthropologists, who have meanwhile banished survivals as a category (the refuge of the ignorant, or the apologist), have soon moved on, first to relativism which puts all cultures on a par, and second to the Lévi-Straussian dichotomy between myth and science. To be more precise, Lévi-Strauss has the division between science and myth as one pole, as another pole their identification, and as a mediation some gradation. For, us are scientists mingled with simple folks! As José Ortega y Gasset says in his "Notes on Thinking", *Concord and Liberty,* translated by Helene Weyl, W. W. Norton, New York, 1946, 1963, pp. 49–82, p. 63,

> "The discovery that our thinking is much less logical than we supposed has opened our eyes to the fact that primitive thinking is much more logical than we supposed."

Readers of science fiction literature may be surprised. The gradation view, the idea that even savages are rational though in a rather limited way, the idea that Christianity is a clever little piece of primitive philosophy (much superior to Judaism, some say) — all this is commonplace in science fiction yet it is only gradually entering the conscience of all sorts of social scientists, and of the authority of big guns like Lévi-Strauss who himself rests on the authority of cybernetics, linguistics, etc. (see his "Language and the Analysis of Social Law", *American Anthropologists,* Vol. 53, 1951, pp. 155–163, p. 155).

19. The modern employment of reason to buttress any faith seems to me rather crude. I have discussed the matter at great length and patience in my "Can Religion Go beyond Reason?" *Zygon,* Vol. 4, 1969, pp. 128–168, reprinted in my *Science in Flux,* Reidel, Dordrecht and Boston, 1975, but frankly I find all this rather tedious since the arguments I discuss there seem to me blatantly disingenuous. I find the cleverest writers demean themselves when they defend the defense of faith by reason. Let me offer one example. "To the unbeliever, this method seems disingenuous and perverse", observes T. S. Elliot ("Pascal's *Pensées*", in *Points of View,* Faber and Faber, London, 1941, p. 104) and explains: "for the unbeliever is, as a rule, not so greatly troubled to explain the world to himself, nor so greatly distressed by disorder, nor is he generally concerned (in modern times) to 'preserve values'." The explanation is terribly clever, and even quite true: most people, believers or not, do not care for explanation and the preservation of values. Hence, the facts referred to are irrelevant. Eliot continues with more relevant facts, as if they were elaborations: the unbeliever does not conclude from the goodness of saintliness (as if he accepts it!) that it is "real" and explanatory. He further speaks of the unbeliever's disbelief in miracles, though all sophisticated unbelievers declare them as irrelevant as sophisticated believers do. (See, for example, Shaw's preface to his *Androcles.*) Eliot ends the passage by simply misrepresenting Voltaire's skepticism as a mild version of liberalism: "in the end we must all choose for ourselves" — true and universally agreed upon, and so highly misleading. I think it will take a long study to expose one page of Eliot for the deception that it is; and if this be sophistication I'd rather go without it.

20. The view of a society as a whole was never achieved. And so even function-alists could feel the fragmentary nature of their functionalism. They did try to offer more general theories of aspects of primitive life, from magic to economics. This, however, is quite problematic. It would be too good if each item, say a spell, should conform both to a general theory of magic and to a functional pattern of the society in which it occurs, since this is overdetermination. Consider, for example, Radcliffe-Brown's view that each kinship term represents a specific category of kinship relations which is defined functionally. (Here the function is not immediately social, by the way, but immediately meaningful to the individual user of the term.) This is a testable and refuted theory, as Percy Cohen notes, which is still very important and may be qualified and rescued, say by allowing the view of the refutations as survivals (e.g. the Arabic distinct names for maternal uncle and paternal uncle show that once these two roles were different), coupled with a theory of what terms survive after their use is gone and what terms drop out of language. This, however, will introduce a linguistic theory that limits functionalism. Radcliffe-Brown himself had no theory of language in general, only of kinship terms. Had there been an absolutely functionalist theory of language, of magic, etc., we would barely escape overdetermination and so the conclusion that there can be at most one society. Since functionalism presents societies as perfect, anyway, this should not be too surprising.

21. The most incredible thing about the classic functionalist's views of conflict, especially Durkheim and Evans-Pritchard, is the absence of any discussion on or even explanation of the point at hand. Their most blatant remarks about crime being functional are even unexplained. Even Georg Simmel, whose view on the matter is moderately functionalist for no good reason, says more. See his *Conflict and the Web of Group-Affiliations,* 1908, translated by Kurt H. Wolff, Free Press, Glencoe, Ill., 1956, pp. 13ff., reprinted in his *On Individuality and Social Forces,* ed. Donald N. Levine, University of Chicago Press, Chicago and London, 1971, pp. 70–95, p. 71,

> "Conflict itself resolves tension between contrasts. The fact that it aims at peace [!] is only one, an especially obvious, expression of its nature: the synthesis . . . conflict contains something positive. Its positive and negative aspects, however, are integrated; they can be separated conceptually, but not empirically . . . social phenomena appear in a new light when seen from the angle of the sociologically positive character of conflict . . ."

In what goes on, however, quoted in note 79 to Section XX below, he rejects functionalism on the ground that, like psychologism, it postulates a harmony, which is "not only empirically unreal, it could show no real life process". He elaborates, in his section on "Conflicts as an Integrative Force in the Group" where he shows that letting steam off is important.

22. Lawriston Sharp, "Steel Axes for Stone-Age Australians", *Human Organization*, Vol. 11, 1952, pp. 17–22. (Notice that I am reporting the story in an exaggerated version, as if only one steel axe was involved.)

For a study of the place of this story in the functionalist lore and for a critique of that lore see I. C. Jarvie, *The Story of Social Anthropology, The Quest to Understand Human Society*, McGraw-Hill, New York, 1972, Chapter 4, especially pp. 106, 108. Michael Banton, *Roles, An Introduction to the Study of Social Relations*, Basic Books, New York, 1965, pp. 45–50, uses the same story to show that a society more in accord with the functionalist anthropologist's view is "fragile". I suppose fragile and overdetermined (see note 20 above) are intuitively fairly interchangeable here.

As far as Sharp himself is concerned, I suppose his chief concern was practical, even though he uses, of course, a functionalist system within which to couch his data. Not only is *Human Organization* published by the Society for Applied Anthropology. The thrust of his brief paper is, I think, in his conclusion (p. 22):

"For the Yir Yorout still in the bush, a time could be predicted when personal depravation and frustration in a confused culture would produce an overload of anxiety. . . . Without the past the present would be meaningless and the future unstructured and uncertain . . . the missionary with understanding . . . would . . . introduce his forms of religion and help create a new cultural universe."

No doubt, Sharp's concern is moving, and the paper is very thought-provoking — I cannot possibly go into all the important issues it raises, theoretical and practical.

Yet, as a confirmation of a myth this is too little to go by. It puzzles me that the tragic story of the axe (and of the quick cure of paralysis) strikes one as anthropological (or psychological) and scientific, whereas it belongs to wisdom literature and common sense. King Midas; Hans Christian Andersen's man with the glasses with which he can read thoughts; R. L. Stevenson's man who was God; Maugham's Catalina; The Man in the White Suit; a couple of stories by Theodore Herzl, and many more examples illustrate the same moral which either presents the fact that all progress is problematic or, more often, tells us the moral that progress, or at least too much of it, is harmful and therefore preaches a Luddite conservative outlook. Indeed, all retelling of the Golden Age stories in modern times must be counted as reactionary, a point noticed as early in the modern age as possible, e.g. by Shakespeare and by Cervantes who were each critical of it in his own way.

23. A true myth, invented by Popper, is that of the unique invention of the method of rational discussion by Thales, allegedly by his encouraging dissent in his own school. See his classic "Back to the Presocratics", in his *Conjectures and Refutations*, London and New York, 1963.

It is quite obvious that the story of the event cannot explain a tradition, except as explanation by origin.

The invention had to take root. How did it? Is taking root necessary? No; we have cases where the invention was imported and did not take root. Hence the story does not explain why, in Greece, it did take root. Once we can explain this, we need not assume unique invention, only unique conjunction of invention and the Hellenic conditions, whatever these were.

It seems to me more testable to contend that the Hellenic conditions – once they are specified in universal terms, of course – are rare enough then to say that the invention of rationality is rare enough; and either will do for the explanation of the uniqueness of the tradition of rational debate.

As to the specification of the Hellenic conditions, let us consider the hypothesis that they are conditions of a pre-democratic society with no rational tradition, yet with a politically powerful public opinion; and also, a fairly liberal and stable society where the tradition can take root. This is, I think, a fairly acceptable view of pre-democratic Greece, and if it is unique, then if many serve as the desired explanation.

"The significant fact" about morals and values in Homer, says M. I. Finley in his *The World of Odysseus*, 1954, Pelican, 1956, pp. 132f.,

"is that never in either the *Illiad* or the *Odyssey* is there a rational discussion, a sustained, disciplined consideration of circumstances and their implications, of possible courses of action, their advantages and disadvantages. There are . . . quarrels, not discussions . . . threats . . . emotional appeal, . . . harangue, and . . . warning. Skill with words had its uses . . . in the struggles for public opinion. Never, however, was a dispute resolved by talk, but always by decisions of the gods carried out through the prowess of the heroes."

This observation explains why Socrates bragged that when he served as a chairman of the Assembly, he sabotaged an unjust act of violence even though the majority was for it.

Democracy was not public opinion – this is pre-democratic and Homeric – but the settlement of disputes by rational means instead of violence. This, however, is shortcircuited when the difference between democracy and the (violent) pre-democrats has to be settled by violence. Greek democracy inherently could not withstand the pressures of opposition and so vanished even though militarily it was at times the stronger of the two.

See also note 19 to Section XXI below on the exceptional insignificance of religion in Greek tradition.

24. G. B. Shaw, Preface to *St. Joan*, "Lesson to the Church from Science".

25. In the modern use of the word "myth" as applied to modern writers by rationalist writers, certainly its main connotation still is that of an obvious falsehood which some dogmatic blockheads will not give up. See notes 50 to Section XIV above and 47 to Section XVIII below, and compare with Ben Halpern, "Myth and Ideology in Modern Usage", *History and Theory*, Vol. 1, No. 2, 1961, pp. 129–149, e.g. p. 143:

	Sorel's usage	*Mannheim's usage*
Myth	revolutionary	reactionary
Utopia	reactionary	revolutionary
Ideology	revolutionary-reactionary	reactionary

Of course, when Claude Lévi-Strauss ascribes myths to modern writers, he means nothing of the sort; thus, when he sees the French Revolution as a timeless quality in some radical writings, he does not wish to speak for or against it but to observe the function of the revolution as a symbol.

26. Functionalism moves towards structuralist functionalism with a simple inner logic. This was noticed long before Lévi-Strauss by Ernst Cassirer. See, e.g. his *The Logic of the Humanities,* translated by C. S. Howe, Yale University Press, New Haven, Conn., 1961, p. 174,

> ". . . the "nature" of language, religion, and art. First, what "is" and what is the meaning of each of them? And what function do they fulfill? Second, how are language, myth, art, and religion related to each other? Here we arrive at a "theology" of culture which, in the end, must seek its realization in a philosophy of Symbolic Form."

Since Cassirer himself provided such a "theory" and his volumes of *Philosophy of Symbolic Form* are not so unknown, one may well wonder, what has become of them. Nothing, in my opinion. Cassirer's view is worthless as too obviously inconsistent. On the one hand, his view of the nature of culture and civilization is dynamic in a Hegelian sense, as he explains in the concluding chapter of his *Logic of Humanities.* On the other hand, his view is as static as all functionalism of his day. See John Herman Randall's review essay of *Logic of Humanities,* in *History and Theory,* Vol. 2, 1, pp. 66–74. Hegelianism sees perfection in each stage of history, and progress in stages towards perfection; the former is relative and the latter is absolute, of course. Relativism is thus the legitimization of inconsistency.

27. For Hegel on gunpowder, see his *Philosophy of History,* Part 4, Chapter 3. One cannot gain the full impact of the book unless one notices that it is divided into four parts – the Oriental, Greek, Roman, and German Worlds, and that the German World comes into being out of the dark night of the Middle Ages by becoming a monarchy. See note 61 to Section XIX. See also Popper's *Open Society,* Chapter 12, Hegel, especially pp. 29ff.

28. For Sun Yatsen see Agassi and Jarvie, "A Study in Westernization", in I.C. Jarvie and J. Agassi, eds., *Hong Kong, A Society in Transition,* Routledge and Präger, London and New York, 1969, pp. 129–163, pp. 156–9 and references there.

29. Ernest Gellner has observed in his "The Danger of Tolerance," Chapter 13 of his *Contemporary Thought and Politics,* Routledge, London and Boston, 1974, pp. 175–181, that it is too facile to defend each system from within while being able to look at it from without: it amounts to admitting that a system is criticizable yet refusing to see it criticized. Gellner quite rightly says that a number of contemporary schools in sociology and in anthropology, as well as in general philosophy, hold this view, as well as some philosophers of science. He adds that this kind of approach leads thinkers to explain away a lot — whatever a system is observed to be unable to digest, indeed. And, he says, there is a sleight of hand here: when one explains things away one wants one's audience to pay attention to what is going on here, whereas the important question is where do things explained away finally go and whatever happens to them after they are sent away.

It is interesting to observe not only the penetration and practicality of Gellner's observation but also the reason for the mistake he points out: one can see a system from without only by transcending it, by refuting its claim for universality.

This is why, though I object systematically to the all-or-nothing-attitude, I do think it always useful to keep in mind both the all-attitude and the nothing-attitude as limiting cases. It is no accident that many systems, including Einstein's and Keynes', began by taking older views as limiting cases.

30. Pierre Levegne, *The Greek Adventure,* 1964, translated by Miriam Kochan, Weidenfeld & Nicholson, London, 1968, p. 299:
"It is difficult to form a balanced judgment on a movement such as this [i.e. sophism] . . . Born of doubts which preceded it, the movement consolidated them and drew from them their ultimate consequences . . . Basically, this was the triumph for the individual, of man armed only with reason, over the imperatives of the state and tradition . . . This was already the Aufklärung, with its destructive power and undeniable greatness."

31. See Steven Lukes, *Emile Durkheim, His Life and Works, A Historical and Critical Study,* Allen Lane Penguin Press, 1973, p. 338, note. Lukes refers to a remarkable paper by S. Ranulf, "Scholarly Forerunners of Fascism", *Ethics,* Vol. 50, 1939, pp. 16–34, where the author argues that not only Toennies and Durkheim, but even Comte, can be viewed as forerunners of Fascism. He quotes Marcel Mauss, Durkheim's collaborator, to say "I believe that all this is a real tragedy for us, too powerful a verification of things that we had indicated and the proof that we should have expected this verification through evil rather than a verification through goodness." Lukes also quotes Raymond Aron quoting to him a private remark by Léon Brunschvicg. "Nuremberg is religion according to Durkheim, society adoring itself" (*op. cit.,* p. 33, note).

32. For extended discussions of this thesis see my "Modified Conventionalism", mentioned in note 62 to Section IV above, and my "Conventions of Knowledge in Talmudic Law" mentioned in note 6 to Chapter Two above.

XVIII EQUALITY IS HARD TO DEFINE

How, for example, should we view equality?[33] Radicalists saw all men as naturally equal,[34] and traditionalist rejected this view.[35] Should we, like Orwell's *Animal Farm,* compromise and grade equality itself?

There is promise in the new liberal suggestion of legalistic egalitarianism, namely the suggestion that we take egalitarianism to mean nothing but the legal requirement to abolish privileges, especially aristocratic ones. This is not naturalism, as it does not assume the existence of equality, and not conventionalism, since it is rather a proposed constraint on conventions than the view of them as utterly arbitrary. Unfortunately, however, this proposal is not just. There is no doubt that the law discriminates between the rich and the poor. [36] Or, as Anatole France said (*Crainquebille*), the law, in its majestic equality, forbids both the rich and the poor to sleep under the bridge. What he meant, of course, is that the luxury of a hotel room is available to the rich only. This is true, no doubt. But is this discrimination? [37] The law, it is repeatedly said, does not discriminate in favor of the rich but in favor of their money: who holds the money and how he came to hold it is not recognized by the law (whereas it is different with titles of nobility). This, I think, amounts to no less than the ancient maxim, money does not stink. [38] It is easy to see that this will not do. We all see compulsory education as part of our egalitarian system. [39] And compulsory education is meant for the poor, of course, not for the rich. [40] And if discrimination in favor of wealth is not anti-egalitarian, then there is no need to secure education for the poor. [41]

It follows, then, that there is a socialistic element in egalitarianism as egalitarianism. [42] Indeed, this can be seen expressed even in the egalitarianism, even small measures of egalitarianism, of countries avowedly hostile to socialism, which oppose socialism in all its manifestations systematically and aggressively. I have in mind the Soviet Union and the United States of America, of course. [43]

I do not mean to endorse, in this observation, the classical communistic formula of socialism, shared by Plato and the early Christians, [44] by the Marxists [45] and the kibbutz movement. [46] For, I consider the idea that equality is secure only by the abolition of private property to be sheer myth. [47] It comes, incidentally, from a schizophrenic view of economics — the combination of a naturalistic view of property and a conventionalistic view of accumulated wealth. The inconsistency is explained away by viewing natural property — my own body, my food on my table, my food in the field I till — as just; but the accumulated property — the wealth of the miser which is economically idle while people are hungry — as arbitrary and thus wicked. [48] Even Adam Smith justifies the entrepreneur's wealth as risk-taking active participation in the economy, but condemns the wealth of a landowner who lives on rent. This combination of naturalism and conventionalism in economics is expressed in many myths, including folk-tales and parables (including Tolstoy's), political doctrines and ideologies, religious and metaphysical systems. What Marx understood by property was not the complex bundle of rights and duties that it is but control akin to a person's control over his body. Throughout classical economics, property was seen, indeed, as an extension of a person's control over his body. This is why Marx's materialism expressed itself as econ-omism: the natural tie between man and machine (capital) could be either property (capital) or production (labor); and preferably both, said Marx.[49]

The most common new form of egalitarianism demands equality of opportunity.[50] It is difficult to discuss this theory except when the range of opportunities is specified. For, when all opportunities are declared equal, the thesis of equality of opportunities becomes the same as the naturalistic thesis of the Enlightenment. Yet the range is usually left unspecified. It is not difficult to see that people may indeed prefer to leave it this way, as it leaves ambiguous the crux of the matter, the question whether the equality is of nature or convention, whether it is a universal matter, or pertaining to opportunities specific to a specific society. In particular, the most vexing problem pertains to the opportunity to purchase new opportunities, which is often the main point of the opportunity for education.[51]

This point, that we purchase opportunities, pertains to modern economics, to modern linguistics, and to the classical dispute about nature and conventions. It was David Hume and Adam Smith who repudiated conventionalism by saying that a member of a given society is no more free to leave than a passenger in a boat in the middle of the sea. And they used this argument to support natural-ism.[52] Of course, only under polarization does a critique of con-ventionalism support naturalism. And so, under the polarization, a major idea was lost.

It is, indeed, no more than a small advantage for an individual to have the opportunity to leave his own society, but the advantage of that opportunity may be enlarged by enlarging that opportunity, namely, by the development of techniques of acquiring foreign languages, by having neighbors who welcome immigrants, etc. And, need one say, with the facts of increased opportunities for migration – however marginal migration still is in many countries – there may come a change in the state of the individual in his society even if he does not migrate; this is well in accord with modern economic theory. We have seen this clearly in Great Britain, in the famous brain-drain case, where the government had to improve the conditions of scientists in Britain so as to reduce their rate of migration to the

United States, yet this could not be done without far-reaching socio-economic changes. What mobility of the individual gives, incidentally, is both higher flexibility of the individual — which opens to him more social options — and higher flexibility of the society, which may but need not lose him. This is exactly why Russia restricts emigration: it does not possess the flexibility that the freedom of movement requires.

The flexibility of society seems to me to be of high moral value, especially since it enables us to alleviate the suffering of the marginal individual.[53] Here again we have arrived at a doctrine — this time a moral doctrine[54] — which is neither strictly confined to a given social code as in the conservative approach, nor declared utterly universal and applicable to all men as such — for it pertains to given societies and their given degrees of adjustability to certain individual wants.[55]

I think I have illustrated thus far how the hardy[56] old demand for equality is linked with the ancient polarizations and how the new idea of equality of opportunity either collapses to older ideas or is unfolded — in a new nonpolarized philosophical anthropology — in quite a new manner. The development will bring about some problematic ideas which will have to be worked out in much detail before we have even a reasonable feel for what it is that we are requiring, not to mention explicit criteria for equality.

But equality was here but one example of a broader issue.[57] I am more anxious to speak of the adjustibility of the individual and the society as the means by which we evolve a philosophy significantly between the poles of naturalism and conventionalism. It will, of course, have to be politically neither radicalist (naturalist) nor conservative (conventionalist or naturalist); though, without being radicalist it should enable us to effect radical changes the like of which have never seriously been planned as yet.

Notes to Section XVIII

33. The idea that the perceived intellectual inequality in men is but the outcome of the inequality of opportunities is ancient (see Plato's *Meno*) and modern (see Locke, e.g. his *Conduct of the Understanding*, Section VIII). The debate over the Jensen report shows that the issue is still alive (see on this issue my "The Twisting of the I.Q. Test", *Philosophical Forum*, Vol. 3, 1972, pp. 60–72).

Popper's theory of learning as conjectures and refutations puts the whole issue into a new position: is everyone an equally good potential critic? Popper says, yes. In this Popper endorses essential equality, no matter on what ground, well within the tradition. This raises traditional problems — see next note.

34. Equality, or natural equality in "all men are equal" is essential, or potential, not apparent or actual, of course.

The Socratic doctrine of knowledge as inborn and of morality as knowledge makes men equal, but only in essence, i.e. knowledge. The reason that equality is not always apparent is confusion and can be lifted. Hence Socrates could not teach; he could not even lift the veil but only help lift it.

This doctrine is still very powerful in each of its departments – knowledge, ethics, teaching, healing, clarifying.

All knowledge, said Bacon and Descartes, is entirely up to the individual. Even the role of a midwife they found unnecessary. The strongest criticism, then, of all classical theories of knowledge is that of Michael Polanyi: those who want to know go to schools and universities. See my "Sociologism in the Philosophy of Science", *Metaphilosophy*, Vol. 3, 1972, pp. 103–122.

The theory of morality as knowledge is best embodied in Kantian ethics which is made to apply to all rational beings as such, even Martians (which is not consistent with his anthropocentrism). It is the doctrine of moral and intellectual autonomy and it is no accident that it is now applied to cases of claims of exemption by the force of superior command. Indeed Nuremberg and Jean-Paul Sartre and the Algerian struggle and May Lai have made Kant the leading moral-ist.

The attempt to lift the veil of confusion and have clarity triumph is, of course, the hallmark of the Wittgensteinianism militant. I shall let it ride.

The modern psychiatrists or psychotherapists have all accepted the Freudian idea of their task as that of the one who helps unveil – who is a midwife. Here there is a slight concession to the inequality of the patient. This has been violently attacked – quite correctly, I think – by Thomas S. Szasz in his numerous works as the unequalitarian, illiberal, often illegal paternalism of the psychiatrist. It is very interesting to notice what part of this illiberalism comes from pre-Enlightenment paternalism, what was condoned by Freudian midwifery. Szasz also argues that Freud himself had paternalist elements in him; but this is another matter, of one not living up to his too high standards. See his *Myth of Mental Illness* and other writings.

The excess of standards becomes a disaster in education. The Enlightenment idea of an Emile learning only from Nature herself is too naive to practice. Even Emile himself had a mentor. And so schools simply remained, to date, in paternalistic hands. Kant himself, his great admiration for Rousseau notwith-standing, supported this. He said, either children are not human or teaching them is immoral, which is correct, and concluded that they are not human – incorrect, of course – because they have no self-discipline and so cannot act morally. (This is a Prussian view of manliness.) It is a sad reflection on our culture that until recently the liberal schools were almost all reform schools or orphanages – Homer Lane, Mgr. E. J. Flanagan, Janusz Korczak, Anton Makarenko – or else schools for difficult children – A. S. Neill and even Bertrand Russell.

35. Not only traditionalists reject equality. The American Constitution is called

Utopian by Sir Henry Maine, *Ancient Law,* quoted above, because it assumed the natural equality of all men. And Maine was a staunch individualist.

The same holds for F. A. Hayek, who in his *Individualism and Economic Order*, University of Chicago Press, Chicago, and Routledge, London, 1948, p. 15, says, "Only because men are in fact unequal can we treat them equally. If men were completely equal in their gifts and inclinations, we should have to treat them differently in order to achieve any sort of social organization." I am afraid this is Plato's claim that justice is served when the shoemaker makes shoes and the philosopher rules. Of course, Hayek is no Platonist; he simply fails to handle the difficult problem of equality; Plato, on the other hand, is not an egalitarian to begin with. And so, on p. 30, Hayek says he is not "egalitarian in the modern sense of the word." He could "see no reason for trying to make people equal as distinct from treating them equally." No doubt, the fear of levelling is genuine, see next note, but Hayek even rejects, p. 31, equality of opportunity. Even equality before the law is "difficult to define", says Hayek, *The Constitutional Liberty*, University of Chicago Press, Chicago, and Routledge, London, 1960, p. 209. An exciting though biased review of the literature on equality is contained in Chapter Six and notes there.

36. It sounds trivial enough to say that equality is not *Gleichschaltung*, not the levelling of talents to the average. This, indeed, is the way K. R. Popper presents it in his *Open Society.* Yet, not only did de Tocqueville warn against this reading. When Salvador de Madriaga in his declaration in *New Frontiers of Knowledge, A Symposium of Distinguished Writers, Notable Scholars and Public Figures,* Public Affairs Press, Washington, D.C., 1957, p. 49, speaks against "deadly equality and the nightmare of murderous nationalism" as the two current extremes, and when Brian Aldiss, a doyen of science fiction writers, says the same thing about equality in *The Year's Best Science Fiction No. 4,* eds. Harry Harrison and Brian Aldiss, pp. 217–18, "This sort of equality is bad for all", one wonders whether it really is so trivial after all.

The attack on equality is, more philosophically, the attack on universalizability. E. Gellner is loath to join it, as it opens the floodgate to arbitrariness, irrationalism, fascism. But he is equally loath to deny the strength of the criticism of universalizability. See E. Gellner, *The Devil and Modern Philosophy,* Routledge, London and Boston, 1974, p. 109, Chapter 7–9, especially end of Chapter 9, "Morality and *'je ne sais quoi'* concepts".

37. In assuming the desirability of equality and discussing the difficulties of pursuing it, I take a route quite similar to that of T. B. Bottomore. "It is not my purpose here", he says in the concluding chapter of his *Elites and Society,* C. A. Watts, London, 1964, Penguin, 1966, 1967, p. 131, "to set out the moral case for equality, but rather to consider the social and political problems which beset the pursuit of equality, and the criticism, other than moral objections, which the elite theories bring against it." In a note, on p. 149, he adds, the moral case for equality "is admirably expounded in R. H. Tawney's *Equality*," Allen and Unwin, London, 4th ed.,

1952. For my part, I would rather refer to Popper's *Open Society* as the modern egalitarian manifesto; this, however, does not mean that I endorse either writer's ethics, and certainly politically I am in between the two. And, of course, I here explain my dissent from Popper's legalistic reading of egalitarianism. His view that we are all ignorant and anyone may come up, perhaps, with a good criticism or a good alternative idea is, to me, the only foundation of equality. See also note 40 below.

38. The view that the modern world was egalitarian in its abolition of the privilege system but not egalitarian enough to abolish poverty and richness is, of course, as old as the abolition of the privileges. Yet it comes as a revelation to diverse writers. Marx devoted a study to it, his pamphlet on the Jewish question, where the Jews are given the dubious compliment of being just as bad as the Christians, and the ones who worship gold and thus the source of capitalism. Marx's utopia is where there is no money, and no division of labor, and no social structure. Needless to say, the official Communist view was — perhaps still is — that since the Marxian utopia has no blueprint, Marxism has no blueprint for utopia; and hence is not utopian; and hence is scientific. Needless to say today one hardly needs notice that each of these deductions is fallacious.

39. See C. Jencks et al., *Inequality*, Basic Books, New York, 1972, for the inter-connectedness of education and inequality. The accent there, however, is on education as means — adequate or not — for equalization. Also, the authors are socialists; this, however, is not surprising, as I explain in the text.

40. The claim that "private property" may mean different things and we may make it mean what we think is proper, is advocated forcefully by F. A. Hayek, e.g. in his *Individualism and the Economic Order*, University of Chicago Press and Routledge, Chicago and London, 1948, p. 20. He thinks the only way for governments to properly interact with systems is via legislation, and legislation merely alters "private property" rights and duties, but this is legal egalitarianism all the same. Now, doubtless, this is unsatisfactory, not only because laws can be made to assign privileges, but also because the old Whig philosophy that Hayek professes rested on the hope that making minimum laws and only protective ones will soon let men's natural equality come to fore.

41. See John E. Coons, William H. Clune, and Stephan C. Sugarman, *Private Wealth and Public Education*, Harvard University Press, Cambridge, Mass., 1970. In his review of this volume in *Am. Pol. Sci. Rev.,* Vol. 65 (3), 1971, p. 798, Earl F. Cheit says,
> "In the United States ... the conflict between [the desire for equal op-portunities in education and the desire to offer one's best for one's dependents] ... is reflected in the methods in which public schools are financed. School finance is primarily a local matter. ... To offset some of the gross inequities between rich and poor local districts, most states have

developed financial aid programs . . . Until very few years ago, it seems that most citizens assumed that these programs more or less managed to equalize school resources. . . .

Briefly what the authors recommend is that the states . . . use the wealth of the whole state as a base. Why the state and not the Federal government? Because the constitutional responsibility is more easily fastened on the state. . . .

The authors . . . put their hopes in the courts. In their view, the best hope for their program is that the Supreme Court will support it on equal protection grounds."

For the court decision, and its immediate impact, see note 43 below.

42. The admission of the prevalence of a socialist impetus seems to me so obvious yet for so many authors it seems so hard. See, for example, Popper's admission of his youthful socialist tendencies which he contrasts with his mature liberalism, and legalistic egalitarianism, though at least in one place, *Open Society*, Chapter 18, especially p. 139, he fully stresses that were nineteenth-century socialist movements more liberal we could be living today in a much better and socialist world. See his "Autobiography", in P. A. Schilpp, ed., *The Philosophy of Karl Popper*, Open Court, La Salle, 1974.

Russell, I think, got the picture quite right when he equates (in diverse works) the march towards socialism with industrial democracy. The point was fully noted and even endorsed, I suppose, in Noam Chomsky, *Problems of Knowledge and Freedom*, The Russell Lectures, Vintage Books, New York, 1972, pp. 58–61, even though Chomsky seems to me to be more of an anarchist than Russell ever was, and hardly a liberal in the sense that Russell was, not to mention his clandestine Maoism (see, e.g. *op. cit.*, p. 65).

Still, even Russell's ideas of industrial democracy were too naive and not worked out at all. But this is hardly a critique.

43. Socialism as practiced today offers examples of regimes either with no egalitarianism or with uniformism – both, of course, quite unacceptable to any individualist.

The idea of equality is, of course, at the basis of socialism – not vice versa. That is to say, all socialists frown at the idea of socialism without equality or even declare it fake-socialism; whereas any socialist who is open-minded will concede with ease and quite *a priori* that if one could design equality without socialism then socialism would be redundant. That is to say, first and foremost, they wish to institute socialism in order to institute equality. Hence, other considerations (such as those pertaining to modernization and/or high productivity) are secondary. Second, if socialism is a necessary condition for equality and equality is a necessary condition for true socialism then (given universal conditions of some sort) egalitarianism entails socialism and is logically equivalent to true socialism. Someone ought to check the logic of all this.

Even equality of opportunities seems to be both dangerously problematic and quite socialistic — especially with regard to education. I contend that this point is quite obvious. My evidence is from *Newsweek*, not prone to philosophical subtleties, of September 13, 1971, p. 61, comments of the California Supreme Court ruling against local property tax as the means of financing public education: "dependence on local property taxes . . . discriminates against the poor" ruled the court, and "makes the quality of a child's education a function of the wealth of his parents and neighbors". Of the three or four commentaries *Newsweek* reports all concern the question what degree of equality is required and whether this will not impose uniformity. Is equality without uniformity possible? This is the classical question that is now comprehended by all. See also James W. Guthrie et al., *Schools and Inequality*, M.I.T. Press, Cambridge, Mass., 1971.

See also note 50 below.

44. Why did Christian Communism fail? Karl Kautsky gives a Marxist explanation in his *Foundations of Christianity* (translated by Henry F. Mins, New York, 1953). Christian Communism was of consumers, not producers (p. 292). Productive Communism, he says, could (and did) develop in agriculture, not in towns where work was dispersed. This is obviously deficient, as it is clear that when the Christian communities grew they had the choice between urban Communism of production and private property. This, I suppose, is why Kautsky takes recourse to explaining the absence of productive Communism by reference (p. 293) to Jesus' contempt for work (behold the lilies in the fields . . .). But contempt for work itself needs a materialistic explanation. Indeed, Kautsky stresses that both the free Roman poletariat, p. 122, and the early Christians, pp. 292, 293, were parasites who hated work and milked the rich. His explanation is that workers in antiquity were very poorly educated (p. 166). So were Marx's workers, of course, yet ancient workers could be content with their small lot (p. 167); quite unlike Marx's industrial workers whose poverty and work in large plants led them to revolt. That is to say, the iron ceiling of workers' income under capitalism forces them to be progressive; the law of increased misery under capitalism is thus central to the difference between Christian and Marxian Communism, and explains the failure of the former without depriving the latter of its chances. This is why the success of unionism in capitalist countries is such a severe blow to Marxism, and this is why the law of increased misery had to be rescued by the *ad hoc* hypothesis about imperialism.

(Whereas in Marx the law of increased misery is secured by competition, in Lenin's capitalism, where the system is run by monopolies and finance capitalists, there is no such safeguard. But the idea was taken on faith that only the metropolitan workers get better off, not all workers. This latter idea was conceded by Marcuse in his *One-Dimensional Man,* where he dismisses the working class as a whole and pins the hopes of the revolution on minorities, intellectuals, and youths.)

Why did Essene Communism fail? Unlike urban Christian Communism, admits Kautsky (pp. 292, 352), agricultural Communism could be, and, with the Essenes, was, both of production and of consumption. Yet, it could not persist without urban Communism. It is regrettable that he does not explain why. Why does a movement that can last a few generations not persist for more generations? The more one tries to apply Marxism to historical details the more baffling it becomes: it is better to stick to vague generalities.

45. The thesis that socialism, especially Marxism, is rooted in the egalitarian thesis of the unity of mankind is drummed in with a sledgehammer in Erich Fromm's introduction to his collection *Socialist Humanism, An International Symposium*, Doubleday, New York, 1965, Anchor, Graden City, N.Y., 1966, as well as in most of the diverse contributions to that volume. In spite of all the atrocities that ensued the diverse attempts to implement ideas of Marx and his followers, it still is, I believe, an uncontested thesis which that volume is defending: in its intention, western Marxism and western socialism (not that of Chairman Mao) is in its intent both individualistic and humanistic. See for example, p. 54, where President Léopold Senghor quotes, in the introductory remarks of his remarkable paper ("Socialism is a Humanism", pp. 53—67), both Lefebvre and Lucien Goldman, both leading Marxist scholars, to say, that Jesuit studies of Marxism are most prominent in this kind of literature. He further (p. 65) exposes the absence of Marxian historical attitude to Marx; he sees more of it in the Jesuit works. Senghor's own thesis is that Marx's central thesis is the anthropological view of man as a producer, a creator (p. 57).

It is nowadays quite common to follow Lukács and Marcuse: disregard history, tone down (Marx's) economism and (Engels') materialism, and overstress the Hegelian side of Marx, especially his sociology *sans* economics and even *sans* politics — particularly his theory of alienation. It goes so far as to declare *Das Kapital* incomprehensible without the early manuscripts. And, disappointingly, even Senghor endorses this view (p. 56). Needless to say, this is quite an exaggeration: after all, the fact is that Marx published his *Kapital,* not these manuscripts, and the fact is that the new interpretation of Marx as a Hegelian precedes the "rediscovery" of these manuscripts: so, then, he could not be so misunderstood.

Of all contributors to this volume, only Eugene Kamenka claims (p. 119) — erroneously, I think — relying on Marx's *Critique of the Gotha Programme,* that Marx contrasted freedom with distributive justice. Now there is no doubt that Marx's image of the free member of the classless society makes no room for injustice. Hence, the question is not what was Marx for, but what was he more avidly against: slavery or injustice. It seems to me, contrary to Kamenka, that whereas Marx saw freedom going hand-in-hand with justice, he felt that the struggle should be for freedom, not for equity: this is Marx's uncompromising revolutionism. Even joining the struggle for wage improvement he found permissible only because he thought it is doomed to failure and because he hoped that those engaged in the doomed struggle for redistribution will learn from the failure that they should fight for freedom and thus become revolutionaries. This, incidentally, is Marx's theory of education, also strongly reflected in the same *Critique of the Gotha Programme.* If there is one theory of Marx I endorse it is his theory of education as self-education through trial and error and as a social rather than a private phenomenon.

46. For the egalitarianism of the kibbutz movement and its utopianism see M. Buber, *Paths in Utopia,* translated by R. F. C. Hull, Routledge, London, 1949, Beacon Press, Boston, 1958, Epilogue: An Experiment That Did Not Fail. Cf. Judith Buber Agassi, "The Israeli Experience in the Democratization of Work Life", *Sociology of Work and Occupations*, Vol. 1, 1974, pp. 52–81, pp. 63–72 on the kibbutz.

47. The use of the word "myth" is, of course, problematic. I do not mean that the idea is merely an error, or even an obvious error. Rather, that it is a symbolic narrative of imagined future events that "thinks for us", and rather naive and poor thoughts, at that. For one thing, private property is a different thing today from what it was in the last century, and even then Marx and others misunderstood it: indeed, the abolition of it means different things to a kibbutz member (where the kibbutz itself is quite a sizeable property belonging to its members) and to a communist in Russia or, again, in America. Indeed, for many it symbolizes the freedom to pick any flower without someone calling the police on the ground that the flower grew in a garden that was his private property. And the feel of this freedom, rather than its social analysis, has the quality of a myth as the reader may see for himself by the mere concentration on this feeling for a while.

48. Marx's view of greed as the chief vice of man (and as Jewish) is very central to his doctrine as Robert C. Tucker argues in his *Philosophy and Myth in Karl Marx,* Cambridge University Press, Cambridge, 1961, 1972. He saw greed as very important since the profit motive is what keeps capitalists going; but as dominated by social forces and so as not of the essence. I think Tucker could have worked this point better had he stressed Marx's sociologism, or anti-psychologism.

49. For Marx's economism see, for example, Popper's *Open Society.* It is doubtless a fact that for Marx materialism was an extremely important matter, and he felt the best expression of it is in economism, which thus very strongly binds together metaphysics and social science. It is distressing that this obvious and important fact is nowadays overlooked since most Marx scholars are apologists who wish to ignore his defunct economics and economism. This makes Marx scholarship ahistorical, as Senghor says (see note 45 above) – or mythical, to use Lévi-Strauss' category.

For all this see E. Gellner, review of R. E. Money-Kyrle, *Man's Picture of his World, Inquiry,* Vol. 4, 1961, pp. 209–214, p. 213:

"The East prefers its Freud young and Marx old, unlike our own metaphysical leftists (Marcuse et al.), who like their Freud old and Marx young."

50. An enlightening discussion of the doctrine of equality, including equality of opportunity, can be found in Yves R. Simon, *Philosophy of Democratic Government*, University of Chicago Press, Chicago, Cambridge University Press, London, 1951. Simon discusses on pp. 222ff. equality of opportunity and its far-reaching, even absurd, implication for the education of the young: "The whole of his upbringing must be taken over by society" (p. 225). And so "We may have many reasons to be grateful to the Saint-Simonists. These antidemocrats, by the fact that they adhere so thoroughly to the theory of equal opportunity, reveal that this theory . . . does not proceed from democratic principles. It is not so much a democratic theory as a rationalistic theory" (p. 226). The collection of papers *Language and Poverty: Perspectives on a Theme*, ed. Frederick Williams, Chicago, 1970, illustrates how subtle is the disadvantage which poverty at home causes a pupil in school. I suppose Shaw's *Pygmalion* already showed the way to such researches. Anyway, it shows how right Simon is about the Saint-Simonists.

But, of course, the *locus classicus* for all such discussion must now be Walter Kaufmann's *Beyond Guilt and Justice*, Wyden, New York, 1973. Kaufmann rightly considers equality a version or a case of distributive justice and that a version or a case of justice. And, he argues, justice can never be satisfactorily administered. Yet, I must confess I am not convinced by his arguments. Briefly, I think, this is how things stand. Kaufmann argues (pp. 70–71), thus: we can easily arrive at an unjust decision by unfair means; we may also arrive by fair means at diverse adequate decisions; and so we can call none of them just (in the distributive or in the retributive senses). Hence, he says, the disturbance that diversity causes is that of decidophobia. Hence justice is redundant and is supported by the decidophobe.

One may argue against this, that if we have diverse adequate solutions we may consider our criteria not tight enough and so not good enough and so wish to replace them. Surely the readiness to try new criteria is nothing decidophobic!

To this Kaufmann should retort, why should our criteria be so tight as to offer unique solutions? Is it not enough that they exclude solutions that are undesired and offer diverse solutions?

To this one might retort, and should the choice between them be made arbitrary or might we not seek a new way of improving the choice by trying out more criteria?

See also note 43 above.

51. I suppose this is what is meant in the following, rather obscure, passage by Raymond Polin, "The Sense of Human", in Paul Kurtz, ed., *Language and Human Nature, A French-American Philosophers' Dialogue*, St. Louis, 1971, pp. 87–112, pp. 110–111:

> "But with the potential equality among men correspond, according to the hazards of aptitudes, the successes of educational formation and the chance of events, profound and real inequalities among them. The equality of men among themselves has become a common bond and we have made of egalitarian ideas the mark of our time. Egalitarian ideology, which sometimes takes on the form of a myth, masks the abstract quality of all equality among men . . . philosophers, like Hobbes or Rousseau, have sought out very subtle means of determining the equality which they consider necessary to the realization of a social contract. And, within the framework of equality of civil and political rights, we witness around us, in numerous modern regimes . . . an equality . . . which

applies the law to the actual inequality of powers, merits, accomplishments and situations."

52. The theory that what is natural is right is traditionally based on the theory of the brotherhood of men. See, for example, K. R. Popper, *The Open Society and Its Enemies*, Index, Arts. Nature and Brotherhood of men. In modern times, Darwinians from Herbert Spencer to Konrad Lorenz took nature to be, on the whole, good since on the whole conducive to survival. But, on the whole is not good enough, and we can be naturalists on the whole and condemn a specific natural instinct. We can even use a Darwinian argument to say that jealousy and the herd instinct were conducive to survival, say in a society where the law is a law of feud and revenge, but on the contrary, an impediment in civil society.

Is the brotherhood of men natural? It does have a natural component, see quotations in notes 41 and 42 to Section XIII above. And are xenophobia, suspicion, hatred, jealousy, etc., natural? Conducive to survival? Are love and trust and kindness and generosity, etc.?

Nobody knows, and so the literature on naturalism, ancient, modern, and contemporary, is usually just too pretentious to cut much ice. Since we all agree today that the truth is expressed in Bertrand Russell's *Education and the Good Life*, Boni and Liveright, New York, 1926, p. 136, "Neither the old belief in original sin, nor Rousseau's belief in natural virtue, is in accordance with the facts", it is difficult to see what force naturalism can have. See also J. W. N. Watkins' most remarkable "The Strange Face of Evil", *The Listener*, Vol. 52, September 30, 1954, pp. 522–3, where Watkins concludes that human nature is morally indifferent and therefore irrelevant to ethical considerations.

Since we view nature not as pure instinct but a complex I.R.M. system, the question, really, has lost its meaning: we know for sure enough that we can create different quasi-instinctive responses as we think fit; we can also break them as we see fit, though at certain cost.

53. This is what seems to me, for better or worse, but in retrospect and with some measure of surprise, the core of my philosophical work and interest. I think I am concerned with the penalties of being an outsider (suffering from anomie, or from alienation), which is a hackneyed theme, no doubt. I am likewise concerned with the facts that one may be an outsider through choice or through no choice of one's own, or through making a virtue of necessity – again, quite hackneyed material. Further, the choice which makes one an outsider is often what one is, socially, and psychologically, and is to a large extent one's work and one's attitude towards it. And so one's alienation may be the inability to have a task, or a peculiar task, or one's own work – be it religious, artistic, scientific, techno-logical, or social – again, a fairly well-known fact. Now, for my part, it seems to me quite clear that the differences between these diverse sorts of estrangement or alienation are merely accidental. Moreover it seems clear to me that some out-siders, indeed most scientists of note, win much acclaim, deservedly or not, and that these are also accidental. I wish to dissociate myself from the doctrine that alienation is essential to creativity, that these two — or either of them — and suffering — are related in any inherent way. Likewise I think we should neither reward nor punish people for their estrangement and/or creation, good or bad as we may deem it: rather we should use more common sense in such matters, and much more toleration. See for more detail my "Functions of Intellectual Rubbish", forthcoming.

54. Philosophers from Schopenhauer and Nietzsche to Maurice Ginsberg and Sir Karl Popper agree that ethics is trivial, that it consits in nothing but the golden rule: harm no man and help all men as you can. I find this idea tolerable in the eighteenth century for thinkers who believed one can build a social philosophy on psychology plus enlightened self-interest. I find it a bit amazing to meet people who still believe in it. It seems to me clear that we are morally obliged not only to avoid harm and help but also to fight injustice and administer justice. Of course, Popper will say this is political philosophy, not moral philosophy. And, he adds, we should moralize politics. And so Popper implies that the realm of ethical injunctions cannot remain confined to interpersonal adjustments; the realm of the ethical has to include all injunctions regarding the individual's sense of duty (as opposed to the injunctions the individual takes as a part of his contractual undertaking — with the state or with his fellow-men). I think it is obvious that the problems posed by equality are partly political, partly moral: not, as Popper would have it, all political. In brief, though Popper's claim, that we ought to moralize politics, not politicize morality, is correct in its collectivist sense of "politicize", it is nonetheless misleading: we must politicize ethics.

Notice, that, though Nietzsche disapproves of all morality, he views morality (*Beyond Good and Evil*, § 186) just like Schopenhauer, who approves of it. And how can two serious writers disagree on an issue and yet call it trivial? Nietzsche himself sees his own amoral man as a mutant; a "tropical monster" he calls him (*op. cit.,* § 197). But at least the superficiality of his view of morality is justified by his lack of interest in morality — a lack of interest rooted in rejection. Yet things get complicated on every turn: even Nietzsche's very rejection of morality, his very declaring of Socrates to be "that famous old serpent", has in it a noble aspect. For, Nietzsche sees in the very triviality of morality, in its very widespread acceptance (albeit merely hypocritical), nothing short of "the instinct of the human herd-animal": "Morality in Europe today is herd-animal morality . . . *one type* . . ." (*op. cit.,* § 202; italics in the original). See also his § 250: "What does Europe owe the Jews? . . . the high style of morality . . . infinite interpretation . . . moral problematics . . . We . . . are grateful for this to the Jews." And so, in an aside, he capitulates. (No doubt here, as in may places, Nietzsche indirectly acknowledges the influence Heine had on him, an influence which has hardly been noticed: Heine's idea of the death of God, *Religion and Philosophy in Germany,* end of Part II, for example, is widely acknowledged to Nietzsche; his idea of religion as opium for the masses, essay on Ludwig Börne, to Marx, etc.) But, with all this influence Heine had on Nietzsche, and regardless of Nietzsche's own many brilliant and adroit observations, I confess I find him, in the last resort, simply sick. I do not mean his obviously poisonous racism and antifeminism and authoritarianism alone; I mean more particularly his deep contempt for Socrates, Rousseau, Mozart, Heine; in short, for the very same things which he also had a deep appreciation for (consigned in his writings to a mythical country called "the South"). And, I suppose, he even knew he was sick, for he longed for "Man's Maturity: to have regained the seriousness that he had as a child at play" (*op. cit.*, § 94).

I have often wished to quote Nietzsche as one of the forefathers of what I here call — see Section XXIV below — the new image of the democratic man. But the more free, insightful, and imaginative his philosophy is, the more infuriating and stupid is the anti-egalitarian, racist, antifeminist constraint he puts on it; the more logically far-reaching and anti-academic his arguments become, the more they are vitiated by his own illogicalities and absurdities. One day we will have to take stock of Nietzsche's contributions to both liberty and brutality. The time has come to take interest in such stock-taking but the opportunity for it is not yet here. In particular, I find it fortunate that W. Kaufmann has kept the problem alive, but cannot consider his partisan attitude much of a contribution to a solution.

Russell held a straightforward political view of morality. In his *The Scientific Outlook*, 1931, Norton Library, 1959, Chapter 13, p. 216, he says,

"Traditional morality gives very little help in the modern world. A rich man may plunge millions into destitution by some act which not even the severest Catholic confessor would consider sinful, while he will need absolution for a trivial sexual aberration . . . There is a need for a new doctrine on the subject of my duty to my neighbor. . . ."

Walter Kaufmann broke new grounds in moral philosophy. His *Without Guilt and Justice* is an application of non-justificationism to old problems in a delightful manner. See also note 50 above. Here, I think lies the future of moral philosophy.

55. However small is the portion of the population who are institutionally in a position of disadvantage (the poor, the low caste, etc.), their attitude to their own society is the main factor in the stability or instability of their society. See S.M. Lipset, *The First New Nation,* Anchor, New York, 1967, pp. 310ff. Lipset sees religion, mobility, and participation as the major contributors to stability, noting, of course, the political aspect of religion. Now in a highly mobile society, where mobility is both vertical and horizontal, surely toleration towards others' beliefs is a more important stabilizing factor than one's own beliefs. In some authors' writings, especially Huntington's, belief in stability leads to relativism; in fact toleration both goes deeper than belief in stability, and avoids relativism on its toleration of tyranny — not to mention the fact that many revolutions of the worst kind were executed in the name of stability. See Samuel P. Huntington, *Political Order in Changing Societies*, Yale University Press, 1968, where all ideas are viewed only as means of stability and so good or else bad. Yet this very idea is quite conducive to instability and so bad by its own lights.

In line with the general idea that ethics gets politicized, let me observe that these days concern for equality among men is replaced by concern for equality among nations. This is so partly because the dominant members of backward nations can and wish to divert attention from home to foreign politics. It is possible, then, for backward nations to act in all sorts of ways, from trying to improve to pestering and even terrorizing advanced nations in attempts to force them to do the job of improving the backward nations. This prompts reactionaries in advanced nations to preach isolationism, at times on the valid and strong argument that lowering the economic, moral, etc., level of the advanced nations helps no one. They conclude by seeing advanced nations as islands of civilization to be defended at all cost. But this very conclusion, if enacted, will make the advanced nations uncivilized as it runs contrary to the thesis of the brotherhood of men.

56. Here, again, Kant has the last word, when he calls "inequality among men" a "rich source of much that is evil, but also of everything that is good" (*Populare Schriften,* ed. P. Menzer, Reimer, Berlin, 1911, p. 325, as translated by Ralf Dahrendorf in his "The Origin of Inequality", *Essays in the Theory of Society,* Stanford University Press, 1968, pp. 151–178, p. 152).

57. "The problem of [choice between] individualism and collectivism is closely related to that of [choice between] equality and inequality" says Sir Karl Popper, *The Open Society and Its Enemies,* Routledge and Kegan Paul, London, 1945 and many later editions, Vol. I, Chapter 6, Section V, opening sentence (p. 99).

XIX PSYCHOLOGISM AND COLLECTIVISM EXPLAIN AWAY EACH OTHER

To begin with, we have to observe that some conventions are more easily alterable than others. We call the easily alterable ones "fashions". Even to change the law about which side of the road cars are driven is not too difficult yet requires much forethought — as the recent Swedish change from left to right illustrates. Other changes are harder to effect, such as the one from bargaining in the marketplace to fixed price tags. Examples of still deeper changes may be the disappearance of fashions which express very strong passions, such as that of chivalric dueling so-called — for the sake of a woman, or as a response to an insult. Perhaps also idolatry and even churchgoing.[58]

The change which included the decline of the practice of idolatry surely connects with the transition from mythical thinking; the transition was, at least in part, into that philosophical thinking which polarizes sharply nature and convention. Whether the one mode of thinking — mythical — is more natural than the other — polarized — I would not know; I would not know even how to approach such a question. Of course, naturalism will force us to denounce myth as unnatural except when it happens to be true. This idea, to continue on the line pursued in previous chapters, led those philosophers who favored primitive man or his mythology to declare myth to be natural and hence true. And so the defenders of myths turned out to be philosophical relativists.

Some functionalist philosophers, incidentally, tried to categorize myth as neither true nor false — in a vain effort to defend myth without falling into relativism. But this won't do. For some people are myth makers, some are not. These functionalists especially have to view themselves as free of all mythology, since they polarize science and myth by taking science to be true and myth, though not false, devoid of truth.[59]

The rationalism of classical philosophy which identifies truth with nature, and falsehood with convention, persisted in polarizing even the unpolarizable. If it is not natural to drive one's car on the right rather than on the left, then at the very least it is natural to prefer uniformity in matters of driving. It must be natural or not natural to abide by the law, whether the law is natural or not, as the case may be. It doesn't matter whether it is deemed natural or whether it is deemed unnatural: what matters a lot is the demand that it has to be deemed one way or another — or else the traditional polarization is exploded.

And so the decision about the question, is it natural for man to obey the law, was polarized into two traditional schools, psychologism and collectivism.[60] Psychologism views the individual and only the individual as the natural entity and so man is substance and true. Society, then, is mere phenomenon, mere appearance. It may be untrue or it may be merely the outcome of the superficial manifestation of the truth, as something which may be explained by, and so explained away by, or reduced to, the individual. Society, according to psychologism, is no more real than lines in a *pointillist* picture. The lines in such a picture may be compared to society and the specks to individuals. We only have to assume the specks unalterable but mobile and so the picture alterable by the motion of specks and so quite accidental and even ephemeral. Each speck in a *pointillist* picture is, we may note, made of one color and this represents its true defining nature and its unalterability.

Order is a relation — whether between points or between people. Classical psychologism sees the social order as the outcome of individual people's rational action. People move about and wish to avoid accidental bumping into each other. And so they travel on the right-hand side of the road, talk to each other politely, make friends.

Now, the most obvious and best-known criticism of psychologism is the observation that an individual interacts not only with other individuals but also with social institutions, that when an individual acts rationally often enough his major considerations are not other individuals but certain social institutions, customs, laws, or whatever. Now a follower of psychologism may, like Adam Smith, declare existing institutions mere conventions and so not true or rational, and so not given to rational considerations. [61] Or a follower of psychologism like John Stuart Mill may explain the fact technically: it is hard to take into account ever so many individuals with whom one interacts and for the sake of simplification of one's calculation one may look at them *as if* they constitute an institution. For institutions are there allright, but as mere phenomena, as poor reflections of the real world populated by real individuals.

The same idea[62] is expressed more crisply in the writings of F. A. von Hayek. Of course our explanations include statements about institutions. But, he suggests, we shall not deem these explanations as final. Meanwhile, truth to tell, Hayek has given up finality as a viable option and, following Popper, he sees it as a mere ideal. [63] And so the edge of his psychologism is gone; indeed, if we follow Popper we have to admit that the edge of all reductionism is gone. And so, again, we see how nature, truth, explanation, reduction, all tie in well within the traditional mode. In the traditional mode, then, it may be claimed that society can be explained and so explained away or reduced – to the individual, of course. This, then, is traditional psychologism.

The critique of psychologism which seems to me weightier than the observation that man interacts with society is based on the observation that people reform society. This may be answered too: reformers are concerned with the reform of man, not of society; the reform of society is but a means for the reform of man, not an end itself. [64] Therefore, we may eliminate society even while explaining cases of social criticism. Now, this is only one case; quite another is that of one who insists, with all the collectivists from Plato to the last member of the kibbutz movement, that he wishes to reform society first, that he wants justice – which means a just society. Well, we may call the person of the second case irrationalist – and so ignore him. In the first case we explained away the society which people wish to reform; in the second case we explained away the people who have the wish.

I hope I have here illustrated the mode of thought of psychologism and shown how easy it is to answer all criticism of psychologism by explaining away anything which does not tally with it; anything social, that is.

Psychologism, able to explain away everything,[65] is thus irrefutable; but as explaining away is not explaining, psychologism must, by the same token, remain highly unsatisfactory. Why is there anything like a society anyway? Why is society there, even as a mere phenomenon, a mere apparition? Yes, the adherent to psychologism must repeat: the appearance of society is due to the existence of a multitude of people. Ah! But why at all do we have a multitude?

This powerful criticism is not mine, though I have presented it as a case of unsatisfactoriness rather than refutation. It is due to the great skeptic philosopher of the late seventeenth century, Pierre Bayle. [66] According to Bayle the question, why is there more than one mind in the universe? is the hardest question one can demand of Cartesian philosophy to answer. If the mind is one essence, it can be realized by one man alone, just as the essence of matter, extension or spatiality, is satisfied by the existence of one space only. The difficulty is much wider, we have seen. If there is one essence, all men are equal and even identical. If more, then, how can people interact? [67] Once we realize that different pieces of matter need one space as a stage of interaction, we may quickly conclude that minds need one mental space as a stage of interaction. This mental space, or its sub-spaces, are social entities, social wholes, group-minds, collectives.

It is a tribute to psychologism that so many of us feel mystified by collectivism.[68] Where, we ask, is the group-mind? What is it made of? How does it affect me or you? These questions are unfair. Where does the individual mind reside? What is it made of? How does it affect the body? These are equivalent questions, for which we also have no answers. Yet we all admit that individual minds are intuitively acceptable — whether we think we ought to explain minds away or not, whether we think man is or is not a machine, whether we think man has or has not got a mind, we agree that individual minds are intuitively acceptable. Let me observe the hard and fast fact (commonsensically speaking) that the group-mind is no worse off, as far as intuition is concerned, than the individual mind. It comes in diverse forms, whether as the *esprit de corps,* the national character, or the national interest. We all speak quite unselfconsciously about healthy and sick societies[69] — even healthy or sick economies; and health, of course, is but one more guise of nature. We have, as in Rousseau, healthy society and decadent society, nature and convention. There is no mystery about it, regardless of whether or not we postulate its existence as a reality.

The philosophically minded adherent of psychologism will have a simple answer: in everyday language, he will say, we shall observe a sick society and blame the devil for it; but philosophically we shall deny that either really exists, and as a matter of course. For my part, I say, it is quite allright for the adherent of psychologism to deny existence to societies or to spaces or to anything else. Yet as long as he admits that whether physical space exists or not is a serious legitimate question, he must admit the same about societies though he need not admit the same about the devil. Hence he is in error when coupling society, a priori, with the devil rather than with physical space. And so, the question, does society really exist, is as good as any, regardless of whether one answers it in the affirmative or in the negative.

This is not to deny that in the West collectivists were traditionally a reactionary lot who preached paternalism and deprived the individual of his sense of responsibility[70] unless he aspired to a position of leadership. Nor is it to deny that collectivists could not explain the interaction of the individual and his collective except when the individual acted in a strongly tribalist fashion.[71] The whole theory of alienation, incidentally, came to explain all other modes as deviations from tribalism and thus as anomalies to be explained away as unnatural and sick.[72] Of course, the fascination of the doctrine of alienation is that it justifies the indulgence of the alienated – i.e. the detribalized intellectual's self-pity. But that is by the way. What is more to the point is that, of course, it was our intellectual tradition which told us to be cosmopolitans, and so we yearn back to the tribe and secretly wish to relinquish our cosmopolitanism and our intellect for the sake of parochialism.[73] The pitifulness of it all led some to the brillant idea that now the whole world is one village, a global village so-called, so that we can have our cake and eat it too, we can be both tribalists and cosmopolitans! Hurray![74]

The obvious weakness of collectivism is its helplessness, its impotence, its historicism (doctrine of historical inevitability). Psychologism has two versions, one which looks to an ideal society with no constraint; one which accepts existing society as it is and merely reduces it to individuals. Collectivism in all its versions merely justifies whatever there is[75] and only allows us to pity those of us who are left out, especially the intellectuals. Psychologism either accepts society and so does the same, or ignores society and so can do nothing. Both traditions ignore the fact that some social change is easy to implement, some not so easy to implement.[76]

Notes to Section XIX

58. N. Ahlgren, "Lessons to Be Drawn from the Change of the Rule of the Road in Sweden", The World Touring and Automobile Organization, *Ninth International Study Week in Safety and Traffic Engineering, Proceedings of a Conference*, O.T.A., London, 1969, pp. 15–22, p. 15, narrates the history of the change: it was discussed since 1922, was the subject of a referendum in 1955 and made law in 1963; it came into effect in 1967. See also Krister Spolander, *One Year with Right Hand Traffic*, National Road Safety Board, Stockholm, September 1968; Swedish Safety Council, *Right Hand Traffic in Sweden*, Stockholm, 1968; National Road Safety Board, *A Brief Review of Investigatory Work Carried Out in Connection with Road Safety Campaigns Before, During, and After the Change to Right Hand Traffic in Sweden*, Stockholm, 1970.

For department stores retail price fixing see, e.g. *Encyclopedia Britannica*, 1966, Article "Retailing", p. 237, Department Store, and references there.

For chivalric dueling see Robert Baldick, *The Duel*, or his Article "Duel" in *Encyclopedia Americana*, International Edition, American Corporation, New York, 1972 ed.

There is a much cited paper – I have found many references to it – by H. Richardson and A. L. Kroeber, "Three Centuries of Women's Dress Fashions; A Quantitative Analysis", *Anthropological Records*, Vol. 5, 1940, pp. 111–153. I have seen no follow-up and no reference to a follow-up to this paper which thus seems to have the quality of a myth within science.

The importance of the paper – true or alleged – is that it puts even such frivolous things as fashions into a solid framework.

We see here again the tension of the polarization: if rationality means universality, then history is meaningless and can be safely ignored. Or else, history can be studied as series of random events. Historicism seems to offer a way out by offering a theory of historical sequences that make sense as sequences. But by now this theory is given up by almost everyone, yet Kroeber, one of the sturdiest historicists, still has his influence: fashions may be sequences or cycles and cycles may follow universal laws. (The mythical polarity between sequences and cycles has been noted by R. G. Collingwood; see note 23 to Chapter XII above.) Of course, once we allow for partial, and even for improved, rationality, we can have histories, especially intellectual history; and if fashions either rationalize – especially food fashions under the development of theories of nutrition and of hygiene – or result from rationalization of other matters – especially attitudes to sex – and so can have their place in history proper. History proper, then, is a story of progress (or its absence), in the sense that is not rational and not devoid of rationality but of movement towards (or away from) rationality as we think it happens to have taken place. For this idea of history see K. R. Popper, "Back to the Presocratics", in his *Conjectures and Refutations*, Routledge and Basic Books, London and New York, 1963.

59. This was stated forcefully by E. Gellner and I. C. Jarvie; see reference in note 15 to Section XVI.

60. For more detail see my "Methodological Individualism" mentioned in note 8 to the Introduction above.

There are very few analyses that are individualist or collectivist all the way: sooner or later a student of a concrete problem has to borrow from the paraphernalia of the opposite camp. And, of course, what he borrows is often perfectly legitimate on its own ground; the question is, can it be legitimized within the philosophy the student has chosen to work with? This question he leaves unanswered.

A glaring example is the Marxist collectivist conception of a class. Much was said about the fact that the two definitions of class — in relations to means of production (work) and in relation of ownership (exploitation) — are not always coextensive; that other social entities, like the state, are not reducible to classes. Yet the *Communist Manifesto*, Part I, 14th paragraph from the end, uses another, non-collectivist and much better, sense of class, when it speaks of the "organization of the proletarians into a class": a class, here, is an active political interest group, perhaps a political party.

Of course, one can speak of classes in two senses, "objective" and "subjective" Rosa Luxemburg called them, and to say, the objective class is there, organized or not, and the subjective class organizes into existence with class consciousness. No doubt. Yet to the extent that the objective class can act only when the subjective class is evolved is the contribution of the individual, not of the collective. And so, in a sense, in Marx's philosophy collectivism and individualism are both used. This is the point made in G. Plekhanov's classic *The Role of the Individual in History*. The question is, if this is the case, can individual action be reduced to that of the collective? Is Marx's reductionism really all the way? I think the answer is obvious: his logic is very weak. Bertrand Russell ("Why I Am Not a Communist") called Marx a muddled thinker.

The dynamic concept of class in Marx is discussed at length in Reinhard Bendix and Seymour Martin Lipset, "Karl Marx's Theory of Social Class," in their *Class, Status, and Power*, The Free Press, New York, 1953, 1966, where they quote from other early works of Marx. They conclude,

"It is apparent that Marx's theory of social class, along with other parts of his doctrine, involved a basic ambiguity which has bedevilled his interpreters ever since."

The ambiguity they notice is the conflict between historicism, or the doctrine of historical inevitability, and that of the need for class consciousness. But this can be settled by declaring the growth of class consciousness an inevitable process. The inevitability was seen by Marx as the necessity of man's acting in accord with his interest as he sees it. Rational action, thus, is voluntary as well as predictable; hence free as well as predetermined. This is the Spinozist element in Marx.

61. The view that the Enlightenment attacked all priesthood as superstitious in the name of universalism, as well as that it attacked error as particular and so superstitious, is clearly stated in Hegel's *Phenomenology of the Mind,* part on Spirit, B, II b, The truth of enlightenment, in the J. B. Baille, Allan and Unwin, London, 1931, Humanities Press, New York, revised ed., 1966, pp. 561ff.

What Hegel himself thinks of complete universality is very funny (The ethical world: Law human and divine: man and woman, p. 470 of above named edition): "The condition of universality, which the individual as such reaches, is mere being, death." Now, of course, death is mere nothingness. But for Hegel, from his *Phenomenology* on, although expressed strongly only in *Logic*, mere being = mere nothingness. Anyway, the sentence equates, rightly, individualism and universalism, and sees the desire of the individual to assert himself with no constraint at all as rooted in the death wish. The echoes of Freud in the young Hegelians, noted by diverse historians and biographers, is rooted, I think, in Hegel.

The fact that Hegel's works provided the young Hegelians with a rich mine of psychological insights reminiscent of modern psychology — Freud's, Adler's, and others' — is described in Robert C. Tucker, *Philosophy and Myth in Karl Marx*, Cambridge University Press, 1961, 1972, especially Chapter 5, but also in many other passages.

But, of course, for Hegel all discourses had to have political implications — which I like — and authoritarian ones — which I don't. And I wish to quote from Hegel a powerful argument in defense of authoritarianism, rooted in his poor view of the individual specimens of mankind. I wish to quote from his *The Philosophy of History*, Part IV, Chapter 3 (p. 399 of the Dover ed.) translated by C. J. Friedrich:

"Resistance to kingly authority is entitled liberty, and is lauded as legitimate and noble when the idea of arbitrary will is associated with that authority. But by the arbitrary will of an individual exerting itself so as to subjugate a whole body of men, a community is formed; and comparing this state of things with that in which every point is a centre of capricious violence, we find much smaller number of points exposed to such violence."

This thesis of Hegel, that modern central authority must be less violent than that which a decentralized society experiences, was criticized by Max Stirner, see note 43 to Section XIII, and is best refuted by twentieth-century experiences. I have no wish to exonerate followers of Hegel who helped the rise of Germany to the state of centralized monarchy and of more centralized tyranny, nor do I wish to exonerate the anti-Stalinist Russian Communists who found themselves defending Stalin while he got them liquidated. Yet, I feel that fairness demands the notice of a mitigating circumstance: the polarization of political philosophy to nature and convention, and/or to force and consent, gave plausibility to Hegel's inhuman argument when he showed that neither nature nor consent will do as a foundation of political philosophy — a point easy to make after the failure of the noble French Revolution.

No doubt Edmund Burke already criticized the Enlightenment in a manner similar to Hegel's — see note 31 to Section XIII above — and espoused a similar traditionalism and authoritarianism. No doubt, also, Burke had a different kind of audience and of influence from Hegel. Also, his *Reflections* were fresh after the Revolution, whereas Hegel could look at it through a perspective. What is astonishing about Burke, incidentally, is that his views were largely expressed prior to the Revolution, which only confirmed his fears.

62. See I. C. Jarvie, *Concepts and Society*, Routledge, London and Boston, 1972, for the clearest statement of the diverse contemporary views regarding individualism.

63. I cannot here do justice to my indebtedness to Popper's theory of science, regardless of the fact that I view myself as one of its severest critics. Let me merely say that he is the first to view scientific views seriously as putative truths which, however, are not likely to be true. This is a far-reaching idea, and I feel that even Popper himself fails to cotton it.

Popper's latest on reductionism can be found in his "A Realist View of Logic, Physics, and History", in Wolfgang Yourgrau and Allen D. Breck, *Physics, Logic, and History, Based on the First International Colloquium Held at the University of Denver, May 16–20, 1966*, Plenum Press, New York and London, 1970, pp. 1–38 (reprinted in his *Objective Knowledge*, Clarendon Press, Oxford, 1972). On p. 6, Popper takes the reduction of chemistry to physics as a paradigm: "by a reduction I mean, of course, that all the findings of chemistry can be fully explained by (that is to say, deduced from) the principles of physics." His thesis comes on page 7:

> "Now I want to make it quite clear that as a rationalist I wish and hope for a reduction. At the same time, I think it quite likely that there may be no reduction possible; it is conceivable that life is an *emergent* property of physical bodies [i.e., as Popper defines it, with a 'complete theoretical understanding in physical terms'] ".

This amounts to the view that an explanation must be true, or an understanding, or premises from which to deduce our knowledge, must be true. It is a terrible confusion, and it is distressing to see that Popper here fails to apply his ideas consistently. If we read this in a more Popperian way, we can say, since explanations have to be refutable, it does not matter whether or not an explanation is reductionist as long as it is refutable. Here I argue that refutability is not enough, that we may wish an explanation to conform to a given metaphysics, reductionist or not as the case may be.

64. The argument, that whereas men are ends in themselves, societies are mere means to ends, is forceful and obvious. Yet we do sacrifice men so as to save societies, even social orders, or freedom in a given society. Of course, there is the retort that in a war we sacrifice a few so as to save many. But the few are here concrete and the many are not. Moreover, we do all feel that the new imperative is valid to keep the species from destruction. And you can destroy the species without destroying any individual, say by total abstinence, so that not only individuals are ends in themselves but possible ones too. It is clear that society represents them better than any concrete individual. And so, it is not true, or rather it is too unclear, that only individuals are ends.

The argument that as society without individuals is impossible individuals are primary is very poor: the converse holds equally well.

The argument that since only men should be reformed since only men are primary or ends in themselves, but not societies, is thus invalidated by the previous two paragraphs. Nevertheless, this very argument has an interesting and important history, beginning in the individualist camp and then, in reverse, in the opposite camp. It led many individualists to declare that people who reform institutions with too much single-mindedness are suspect of being inhuman, obsessive, or collectivists. Though they often are, to conclude that they always are is a bit unfair. The moral problem a person faces who must choose between helping an individual and working for a worthy cause is truly tragic, and the tendency — I should say, natural tendency in the full ordinary sense of the word — is to attend the concrete individual in preference to abstract cause, even if, quite probably, many distant individuals who will only be born after one dies will suffer as a consequence. (*Isaiah*, 39:8.) Oh, it is easy to say, who knows what is probable. And it is easy to go mad and trust ones' intentions too. But I feel that some sympathy for victims of such problems is quite in place.

This, however, is not to say that the criticism is not valid. Some people are just fanatics who suppress even strong personal feelings. "Viewed in historical perspective, the figure of Rosa Luxemburg has become more and more appealing", tells us Ossip K. Flechtheim (in his "The Role of the Communist Party", in *The Path to Dictatorship, 1918–1933, Ten Essays* by Theodor Eschenburg et al., Anchor, Garden City, N.Y., 1966). "The 'Bloody Rosa' who was once the terror of the bourgeois and the compromisers has almost completely faded from memory. Today, the author of *Letters from Prison* and *Letters to a Friend* appears as an exceptionally kind and gentle woman." And the passage continues with a panegyric to Rosa unclouded by anything even slightly offensive. For my part, I think the polarization in Rosa — of the powerful cold political organizer and the sentimental moral private citizen — is a dangerous polarization and a horrifying mixture of rationalistic theory of the willpower with romantic sentimentalist theory of civil morality. This concoction is characteristic of the Communist novels of André Malraux which are at once powerful and moving propaganda, as well as poor literature. Consider the ethic of Malraux's ideal of a strong realistic politician who is self-denying in his politics yet in a rare private moment so kind and understanding. He is, indeed, so similar to the proverbial SS officer who kindly strokes his cat or his offspring in so many anti-Nazi movies. The only possible justification for Rosa or for Malraux's heroes is that the polarization was objectively created, that times were of crisis, of a total war. Perhaps. I cannot judge. Anyway, the ingredients of fanaticism and sentimentalism are in both, yet the fanaticism of the best Communists came from a sense of justice and compassion, the like of which were absent in other contemporary fanatic movements. See also note 103 to Section IX above.

65. It is delightful to quote an unbelievably naive passage from William McDougall, *An Introduction to Social Psychology* (University Paperbacks, Methuen, Barnes & Noble, New York, 1908 to 1960 onward), Table of Contents, "Chapter 1, Introduction, The position of psychology at the basis of all the social sciences now theoretically recognized but practically ignored. . ." and the preface to the 23rd edition:

"The Psychoanalysts, the Gestaltists, the Behaviorists, the Connectionists, the Characterologists, the Social Psychologists of America, the cautious middle-of-the-road men, all these have moved further towards the principles first clearly propounded in the first edition of this book. But, we are still very far from a general agreement."

McDougall is right though, in claiming that social psychology began as attempts to reduce sociology to psychology. Yet already in the thirties it developed to include studies in socialization, still from an individualistic viewpoint, but soon, when it got going, it was also adapted to the collectivist viewpoint. This is very conspicuous, as the following may illustrate. G. Duncan Mitchell, *A Hundred Years of Sociology*, opens his chapter (Chapter 13) on "The Origins of Social Psychology" with a paragraph which shows ignorance of this trend; yet the details of that chapter and the following amply illustrate this development. See there pp. 177, 195 and 228 for psychologism, the new trend, and collectivism, respectively.

On this matter, of course, Freud was in full agreement with McDougall. He expressed a very similar and similarly naive sentiment in his "Group Psychology and the Analysis of the Ego" of 1921. Yet, his very view of socialization as oppressive is more in line with eighteenth-century radicalism. It is no surprise to me that the critic of over-socialization, Dennis Wrong, is a Freudian of sorts. See "Group Psychology etc.", III, Standard Edition, Vol. XVIII, pp. 83–7, for a favorable discussion of McDougall's *The Group Mind* of 1920.

66. Spinoza argued the parallel between mind and matter thus: the substance of any material object is space, and space is a necessary being; but the essence of that same material object must be different, because that thing need not exist. And so, whereas to say of a thing that it is a substance entails that it exists, to say that it is an essence does not. Now the existence of a definite human being is not necessary, and so we have to define any definite human being by his essence, not by his substance. The substance of humanity, which is necessary, therefore, is as different from one man as space is different from any material object. See *Ethics*, Part II, Axiom I, and Props. VIII to X and his *Book of God*, God and Man.

Pierre Bayle viewed Spinoza as a mere simplifier and improver on Descartes – see his *Critical Dictionary*, Art. Spinoza – as more Cartesian than Descartes. (This gave license to the many Spinozists to call themselves Cartesians.) Bayle also notices that Spinoza moved Cartesianism towards Averoes' monopsychism – we all share one mind – and that the move must go all the way. He criticized Spinoza's parallelism by saying that parallelism allows for my soul to run in parallel to your body and vice versa. (This criticism was repeated by Euler against Leibniz and moved Kant towards a more critical view of things.)

In brief, Bayle notices the force of Spinoza's critique of Descartes and he acknowledges the similarity of the resultant view with that of Averoes, namely monopsychism – we all share one and only one mind – which was popular for many generations in spite of its being a heresy. Today it is still a heresy, though against science rather than established religion. Yet, it grips many audiences and is known in its Jungian variant of the collective unconscious. Any reader familiar with science fiction knows how popular Jung is.

For the popularity of monopsychism in the Middle Ages, see *Philosophical Forum*, Vol. 4 (1), Fall, 1972, especially Alfred L. Ivry, "Towards a Unified View of Averoes' Philosophy," pp. 87—113.

Reading this interesting issue is a pleasure, since each contributor is deeply aware of the Greek polarizations and their great impact on all of our thinking; it is also sad since the authors also take these polarizations to be true, and as a matter of course. They gently insinuate that dissent here is sheer ignorance and/or superficiality.

67. I take here substance to be the same as essence. I must admit I am not clear how Aristotle related substance, essence, and cause. See my *The Continuing Revolution, A History of Physics From the Greeks to Einstein*, McGraw-Hill, New York, 1968, chapter on Aristotle, and my "Who Needs Aristotle? ", in R. S. Cohen and Marx Wartofsky, *Boston Studies In the Philosophy of Science*, forthcoming. If substance is the same as essence, then just as matter and mind cannot possibly interact, so is it with mind and mind. The monad, concluded Leibniz, has no windows.

68. For a complaint about the fact that for so many scholars in the English-speaking tradition the existence of collectives is a priori incomprehensible — existence, perhaps in an intuitive sense, perhaps in the sense of irreducibility — see, for example, Gregory Baum, "Science and Commitment: Historical Truth According to Ernst Troeltsch", *Phil. Soc. Sci.* Vol. 1, 1971, pp. 259—277, esp. pp. 263—4 and 276.

69. J. O. Wisdom pushed the analogy between individuals and groups farthest than anyone else by applying the tools of psychoanalytic diagnosis to Britain. See, e.g., his "Situational Individualism and the Emergent Group Properties", in Robert Borger and Frank Cioffi, *Explanation in the Social Sciences*, Cambridge University Press, 1970, pp. 271—296, and my review of it, "Listening in the Lull", *Phil. Soc. Sci*, Vol. 2, 1972, pp. 317—332.

70. The view that the sociology of the nineteenth century tended to be collectivist and as collectivist it was an attempt to reduce the individual to society, is made in Albert Solomon, *The Tyranny of Progress*, The Noonday Press, 1955, Chapter Six. On p. 100, in particular, Solomon quotes Maine de Biran, *Oeuvres Inédites*, 1859, Vol. 3, pp. 207—209, to say,

"Not the human mind, not the individual understanding are the true subjects of the notions and verities of human existence. Society, however, gifted with a kind of collective mind, different from the individual's, is imbued with such knowledge. The individual, the human being is nothing; society alone exists. It is the soul of the moral world. It alone has reality, while individuals are only phenomena . . . If this is true, all philosophy of the past was wrong. One must recognize the failure of the science of the intellectual and moral man, one must admit the failure of psychology which has its basis in the primitive fact of conscience."

The passage is also partly quoted in Thomas S. Szasz, *The Manufacture of Madness,* Dell, 1970, Delta, 1971, p. 222. It was Count Gobineau, I understand, who already drew the conclusion from the reduction of the individual to society and from reductionism as a sort of explaining away; for he spoke of a future with "no nations anymore, but human droves." But as I do not have any knowledge of this writer I hesitate to ascribe to him this as a conclusion rather than as merely an evil vision.

71. An example of a statement that collectivism reduces the individual to society is in Clifford Geertz, "The Impact of the Concept of Culture on the Concept of Man," in John R. Platt, *New Views of the Nature of Man, The Monday Lectures,* 1965, Chicago University Press, Chicago and London, 1965, pp. 93–118, 115–6:

> "It is here, to come round finally to my title, that the concept of culture has its impact on the concept of man. When seen as a set of symbolic devices for controlling behavior, . . . culture provides the link between what men are intrinsically capable of becoming and what they actually, one by one, in fact become. Becoming human is becoming individual, and we become individual under the guidance of cultural patterns, historically created systems of meaning in terms of which we give form, order, point, and direction to our lives. . . . As culture shapes us as a single species . . . so too it shapes us a separate individuals."

The heavy technical language of the passage hardly conceals the strong totalitarian character of the view it expresses.

72. Durkheim's alleged explanation of suicide, for example, is a pseudo-scientific panegyric to collectivism. He "explains" suicide as either excessive egoism or excessive altruism or as anomie. This is puzzling, from the start. At first one might look for the analogy to the contrast between excessive-egoism and ex-cessive-altruism and hope to find its parallel between no-integration (i.e. anomie) and too-much-integration. On a second look, clearly for Durkheim excessive-egoism = no-integration and excessive-altruism = too-much-integration. It seems to me that the main point of Durkheim's *Le Suicide* is just the implicit thesis egoism = anomie, i.e., classical rationalism is sick; a Hegelian thesis (see note 61 above) displayed in a clumsy classification! Moreover, it is difficult to find him condemn too-much-altrusim or praise egoism, though he equates egoism with moral autonomy (since he equates nōmōs with the social entity, he equates auton-omy with anomie as a mere corollary). And only for the pendant did Durkheim distinguish, in nuance, between egoism and anomie. For Durkheim, egoism is rather self-conscious, rather accompanied by self-awareness (i.e. it is rather autonomous or enlightened). By contrast, anomie, is for him, drifting — akin to the alienation which Hegel and the young Marx saw in a peasant who somehow has strayed into town, or akin to the expression of the emptiness of the pursuer of the pleasures of the flesh in the older (and the newest) wisdom literature.

R. K. Merton's definition of anomie is more social than individual: not an individual free of legal bonds and so lost, but a society which has lost its legal bonds and so itself. See Raymond Aron, *Progress and Disillusion, A Dialectics of Modern Society,* Mentor Books, New York, 1968, 1969, pp. 155–6, 165–7.

Durkheim's mythical polarity of egoism-altruism was expanded in a quaint mock-Darwinian way in E. W. Wilson's *Sociobiology,* Harvard University Press, Cambridge, Mass., 1975, with instant success.

73. Ferdinand Toennies had declared psychology to be reducible to biology. He split social life to nature and convention, and declared the natural part, the community aspect of society, *Gemeinschaft,* to be reducible; and the conventional aspect, *Gesellschaft,* irreducible, because arbitrary. Indeed his synonyms for *Gemeinschaft* and *Gesellschaft* are essential will and arbitrary will. All this is tolerably clearly and quite straightforwardly stated in the opening of his "The Nature of Sociology"; see Ferdinand Toennies, *On Sociology: Pure, Applied, and Empirical,* selected writings, edited and with an introduction by Werner J. Cahnman and Rudolf Heberle, University of Chicago Press, Chicago and London, 1971, pp. 87–91.

Peculiar to Toennies is not the idea that collectivism allows for only one ideal social order — this is already in Plato; rather, it is peculiar that he considers collectivism to be reducible to psychology but not conventionalism. Anyway, I think the popularity of Toennies' distinction between community and society is mainly due its usefulness for the promulgation of reactionary romanticism. See p. ix of that volume and references there to Ralf Dahrendorf's *Gesellschaft und Demokratie in Deutschland,* pp. 151ff.

The romantic-irrationalist aspect of the ideas of Toennies is the same as the one endorsed by functionalists, functionalist-structuralists, et al.:

"all irrational and less rational forms of thought" [he said, were to him]
". . . never simply unreasonable but that they had their peculair meaning which finally was a derivation from human will."

Quoted by Rudolf Heberle, in his "The Sociological System of Ferdinand Toennies", *Amer. Soc. Rev.* Vol. 2, 1937, reprinted in H. E. Barnes, ed., *An Introduction to History of Sociology,* University of Chicago Press, 1948, p. 145 of the abridged edition; see reference to Toennies' statement there.

One hardly need say that a theory of partial rationality renders the functionalist view innocuous by ascribing to the "less rational forms of thought", as Toennies himself puts it, a low but not zero degree of rationality; clearly the rationalist traditional ascription of zero value to them was nearer the mark than the romantic ascription of full value to the same "less rational forms" yet the rationalists were led to ignore all folk wisdom and folkways, whereas the romantics could study it. See also notes 20 to Section XI, 32 to Section XII, 46 to Section XIV and 18 to Section XVI above.

74. The new collectivism is expressed in the literature on the global village, which is nonexistent, on spaceship earth, which does exist, though much of the writings on which is hysterical ecology, and on ethology, of the Lorenz-Ardrey-Tiger-Desmond Morris style. Each of these literatures is quite enormous, and I am not able to sift the grain from the chaff.

75. The reason that the reductionist character of collectivism is not stressed is, of course, the fact that it is oppressive and reactionary. It "was introduced into the stream of French social thought by Louis De Bonald and Joseph De Maistre, who maintained that the social group precedes and constitutes the individual; that it is the source of culture and of all the higher values; and that social states and changes are not produced by, and cannot be directly affected or modified by, the desire and volition of individuals." So says Emile Benoit-Smullyan, in "The Sociologism of Emile Durkheim and His School", in H. E. Barness, ed., *An Introduction to the History of Sociology*, Chicago University Press, 1948, 1966, first paragraph. Obviously, this statement reflects the reaction to the French Revolution which assesses it not as a modification but as a mere destruction.

76. See Reinhard Bendix, *Embattled Reason, Essays in Social Knowledge,* Oxford University Press, 1970, where Freud and Durkheim are rightly put on a par as two reductionists who each came to his own *cul-de-sac* (pp. 11ff.).

XX A NON-REDUCTIONIST DEMARCATION BETWEEN PSYCHOLOGY AND SOCIOLOGY

To be more precise, the philosophies which accept the present society as it is may be used, or applied, to bring the deviant and the alienated back to the fold. It is no accident that social psychology is inherently in favor of conformism, regardless of the fact that its ancestry is largely McDougall's theory which is his attempt, as he explains, to implement psychologism, and partly Durkheim's social psychology, intended to illustrate now much seeming free choice is dictated by society, how much the level of adjustment to, or integration with, society dictates the individual's behavior.[77]

Here we see, again, that for psychologism social psychology equals both sociology and psychology; whereas for collectivism it is small group psychology. Even infant psychology is traditionally the same as social psychology of the smallest social cell — the small family. The question they all ask is merely, is sociology a part of psychology or the other way around; they are all reductionists, whether they reduce society to the individual or vice versa.

Let us reject all this, let us ignore all reductionism, and see how different things look then. Or, for those who insist on essences[78] and on some reduction, however tentative, and who view valid explanation as a reasonable example of reduction — for these we should say the following. If you admit both space and particles as different essences, why not accept both society and individuals in this way? If one objects that unlike particles, individuals are parts of society, we need not tell him that his physics is old-fashioned, but rather deny his claim that the whole and the part must share their essence. We can easily show that this is so, that though geometry gives structures of houses, say, houses need not share the essence of geometry, that though we have words making sentences the essence of words differs from the essence of sentences. Let us use the traditional invalid terminology for a while, and call the rules pertaining to words "grammar" and the rules pertaining to sentences "syntax".[79] We can then make the analogy between grammar and syntax and individuals and societies. We can even compare *pointillistic* pictures to societies and say that the essence of the picture is quite irreducible to the specks though the structure of the picture is, no doubt, conveyed by specks. No doubt, the word has a structure and the sentence has a structure, and the point and the line do. This is why a word retains its identity through diversities of locations and pronunciation and spellings and mis-spellings, just as the sentence does and a tune and a symphony does. But interrelated as the word and the sentence are, as the theme and the symphony are, they need not be reducible to each other.[80] And so even on the assumption of some theories of reduction, some modern variants of them that is, we need not insist that either society is reducible to the individual or vice versa.

When comparing social science with linguistics I may give the impression that psychology deals with the individual and sociology with society.[81] I do not wish to give this impression. It is, again, a very deep-seated intuition that it must be so, and the existence of this deep-seated intuition is a tribute to Max Weber. For it was Weber, as J. W. N. Watkins has shown in a classic paper of his, who made this division part and parcel of social philosophy.[82] When we have an archetype to which a society conforms it becomes sociological; other-wise it is psychological. As Watkins shows, the model of the British policeman is sociological, as one British policeman is, *qua* policeman, much akin to another; but not so with Julius Caesar.

The intuitive force of this division is a tribute to Weber. For, in fact, this division is quite obviously false. We have a few simple and reasonable models of schizophrenia — archetypes of schizophrenia. How many people conform to any particular archetype of schizo-phrenia in western countries is not known, but their number is known to be substantial, even if we ignore cases of schizophrenia not in need of medical care (which we often and erroneously dismiss). We feel, quite intuitively, that no matter how frequent schizophrenia may be, or how infrequent, is totally irrelevant to the fact that the archetype is psychological, not sociological. There is such a thing as the sociology of schizophrenia, where the sociology of the incarcerated schizophrenic is especially different from that of the outpatient, no matter how similar they may be psychologically; and, according to Goffman, it is more similar to that of a cell inmate or of a small rural college professor or a kibbutz member, as all exhibit the sociological pattern of trapped populations.[83]

Intuitive as the difference between the psychology and the sociology of schizophrenia is, not only Max Weber does not allow for it — I do not know who does; nor how it was thus far demarcated, if at all.[84] So let me offer here a demarcation between sociology and psychology.

I propose that psychology studies the adjustment of the individual to society, and the problems involved in this, and including problems of maladjustment of the individual such as schizophrenia.[85] Sociology, symmetrically with this, studies the adjustment of society to the individual, and the problems involved, and including problems of maladjustment of society such as caste system and other rigidities.[86]

Let us take classical economic theory as an example. The theory concerns itself with the allocation of resources, or rather their reallocation. The changes of individual consumers' tastes are exogenous, or given without further ado; their causes are of no interest to the economist. But the way the market adjusts to changes like changes of taste, and the resultant reallocation of resources, in particular, is what classical economic theory is largely concerned with. Hence, economics is a part of sociology and concerns itself with the market, free or not-so-free, and not with economical man, who is a redundant fiction. And so, economics is a part of sociology rather than psychology, as it should be.

To be more precise, psychology should contain not only the adjustment of the individual to his institutions, but also the adjustment of one individual to his companion. This is more obvious when the companion is institutionally an adjunct, for example, a spouse or a co-worker, but we should, by extension, include the individual's adjustment to a friend. In each of these cases, obviously, the adjustment is made via institutions, via the given institutional means of adjustment. Similarly, sociology should include the adjustment of one institution to another, for example, the effect of political changes on the market — and, again, the adjustment must be made with the mediation of the individual. This should be so because it is not in the least reasonable to assume that institutions care enough about their adjustment to other institutions, but people may, and sometimes do. To the extent that they do, their society becomes more functional, in the sense in which functionalists (falsely) declare all societies to be totally functional. The deviations from functionalism, then, might be a matter of the individual's high ability to adapt to a non-functional society and low requirement from society to be functional. Thus, we can see that the present demarcation makes excellent sense of the fact that gang sociology is in no-man's land between sociology and psychology, since a gang is a social whole of sorts, but with no institutions and so very fluid and so very taxing on the psychology of its individual members.[87]

This also resolves the old dispute about primitive or preliterate man: is he adept and clever or is he rather lethargic and gullible? He is both, but in different ways. He lives in a more highly and rigidly institutional, and so in a less functional, society than we live, and so he has to show more ingenuity in so doing; but alas! his great patience with his social circumstance is not so laudable as the functionalists would have us believe.[88] And so, ideally, tribes and gangs are opposite poles.

Of course, this is not to blame the preliterate man or his society any more than the metropolitan anomie-stricken teenager for his society. Rather, it is to show that education has one foot in psychology and one foot in sociology — again as we should expect — and that education may indeed be conservative or progressive in the sense hinted at in the last paragraph, making either man or society better integrated.

It is really a trivial point, and a trivial corollary to the above,[89] that, paradoxically, in the better society (rather than in the worse society) one may frequently find individuals less willing to accept society as they find it. I say trivial, though many of my colleagues call this state alienation and use its existence as an argument proving that certain very primitive societies — most rigid though not exactly preliterate — are the better ones. For example, communist China.[90] But I consider these colleagues victims rather than serious thinkers and so I will not criticize them severely.[91]

What can be done when an argument is hardly possible, is to explain the phenomenon rather than argue against those whose positions are not open to argument. This is, of course, only reasonable after hope for argument is given up: explanation is a bad substitute for argument. Now, to explain the wide spread of a phony theory of alienation today, I feel, one must consider the wide spread of its very opposite, whether King and Country, or motherhood and apple pie. That is to

say, few people look at society wholly in terms of alienation or of
motherhood and apple pie; most people simply vacillate between the
two. It is only when one gives up the apple pie view of society that
one also gives up its opposite. Then one can see that though apple pies
do not grow on trees it is no calamity and no cause for declaring a
state of anomie or alienation.[92] In other words, sociologists today
still operate with two polar and intuitive conceptions of society, the
individualistic or atomistic and the collectivistic or holistic. And seeing
that society does not fit the one they conclude that it fits the other,
judging it a boon or a calamity from the one or the other point of
view. Hence the great division into optimists and pessimists in either
camp. The mixture of optimism and pessimism in each camp is a
Lévi-Strauss type of mitigating extremes.

Let us assume, contrary to both the traditional schools, that man is
neither integrated or socialized, nor alienated or atomized; let us
rather assume that he tries to adjust himself to his society and his
society to himself. This, in a sense, does away completely with the
very concern with integration or socialization, as well as with
alienation or atomization, both of which are so prevalent in the current literature. Yet, it is important to notice that only the specific
senses are excluded, of total alienation and of atomization, or of total
integration or socialization; we do indeed wish to have a discussion of
partial alienation, of partial atomization, of partial integration, of
partial socialization.

I contend that it is plain common sense to debate the partiality of
such processes, and that it is healthy to hold debates about the
desirable and acceptable degrees of anomie and of socialization, or
degrees of autonomy and of integration, whether of individuals or of
subgroups. Here the political, sociological, and psychological studies
of quite a few scholars have broken away from old demarcations and
old frameworks of philosophical anthropology. And, indeed, the very
first test of any demarcation such as the one here introduced, is to see
whether it makes good sense of the intuitive concept we already have,
especially in the more advanced parts of the sciences of man, of a
more integrated and less integrated society, of a more integrated sub-
group and individual and a more alienated one, as well as of their
modes of interdependence and interaction.[93] (As Bertrand Russell has
observed, the modern man is morally more autonomous but economically less autonomous than his ancestors. The Romantics preached
economic autonomy so as to conceal the fact that they opposed moral
autonomy.)[94]

Notes to Section XX

77. See Notes 65 and 72 to the previous section.

78. The suggestion to reduce neither individual nor society was made by Harold D. Lasswell in 1930. See Heinz Eulaw, "Maddening Methods of Harold D. Lasswell", in Arnold A. Rogow, ed., *Politics, Personality, and Social Science in the Twentieth Century, Essays in Honor of Harold D. Lasswell,* University of Chicago Press, Chicago and London, 1969, pp. 15–40, esp. pp. 20ff. Incidentally, the suggestion came from the background of the philosophy of A. N. Whitehead, which rejects the ideas of essence and of substance altogether. I do not, however, find it possible to go into details of either Whitehead's philosophy or any logic of emergence. Also, let me observe, it is possible to contend that Lasswell's work itself is an attempt to reduce society. See Bruce Lannes Smith, "The Mystifying Intellectual History of Harold D. Lasswell", *op. cit.,* pp. 41–106, esp. pp. 79–80. Nevertheless, Lasswell made a methodological contribution in the direction of the interaction of the individual and society in a few ways. See, in particular, Allan R. Holmberg, "Dynamic Functionalism", *op. cit.,* pp. 261–296, esp. p. 265. That paper relates to methodological aspects of the epoch-making Cornell-Peru study, so-called, of the Vicos Hacienda, conducted by Holmberg, presumably in part under Lasswell's influence.

79. The comparison between sociology and syntax belongs to Georg Simmel, who seems to be here as on many other issues, the first to suggest the new view, denying that either society or the individual is reducible. See his 1908 work *Conflict and the Web of Group Affiliations,* translated by Kurt H. Wolff, Free Press, Glencoe, 1955, p. 14, reprinted in his *On Individuality and Social Forms,* ed. Donald N. Levine, University of Chicago Press, Chicago and London, p. 71:

> "At one time it appeared as if there were only two consistent subject matters of the science of man: the individual unit and the unit of individuals (society); any third seemed logically excluded. In this conception, conflict . . . found no place for study."

He adds that harmony exists neither in the individual nor in society. In other words, both psychologism and collectivism explain conflict away or ignore it or see in it only the positive. So all studies of conflict which take it seriously (to exclude functionalist and psychologist elimination or reduction of it) break away from the classic dichotomies!

80. For the newest view of the primacy of sentences see David McNeill, *The Acquisition of Language,* Harper, New York, 1970, p. 2: "Children everywhere begin with exactly the same initial hypothesis: sentences consist of single words . . ." This is a theory — I suppose empirically testable — of primariness in an ontogenetic sense. But there is also the phylogenetic sense, and — the one I am presenting here — the abstract sense. It seems that in Chomsky's view ontogeny recapitulates phylogeny — the child's history recapitulates the race's history, since both exhibit the universal deep structure of language. But is deep structure able to settle the question of abstract primariness? I do not know.

W. V. Quine holds that the sentence rather than the word is primary. And when he postulates the primariness of the sentence over the word — "the unit of communication is the sentence and not the word" — he naturally falls into a description of the process of acquisition of meaning:

"We can allow the sentences a full monopoly of 'meaning' in some sense without denying that the meaning must be worked out — by one who understands the words but hears the sentence for the first time. [But, he goes on to say,] Dictionary definitions are mere clauses in a recursive definition of the meaning of sentences".

From this it follows that some primitive sentences are understood prior to the understanding of some of its constituent words — or phrases — perhaps those learned at the earliest childhood.

If so, then it follows from my theory that what makes a second language (in adults) inferior to the mother tongue is the use of the mother tongue as a tool to acquire the second language; that it is better to learn sentences in a second language *without first knowing how to break it down to words.* Every native speaker knows how to break a sentence to words and this is not trivial at all. If so, it is understandable that novices want to be told how to break a sentence to words; but, perhaps, this only expresses their (rational but erroneous) desire to use the crutch of the mother tongue.

See Quine's "Russell's Ontological Development" in R. Schoenman, ed., *Bertrand Russell, Philosopher of the Century,* London, 1967, p. 306, quoted in David Wiggins' "On Sentence-sense, Word-sense, and Difference of Word-sense" in D. D. Steinberg and L. A. Jakobovitz, eds., *Semantics, An Interdisciplinary Reader in Philosophy, Linguistics, and Psychology,* Cambridge, 1971, p. 21. See also Edward Sapir, *Language, An Introduction to the Study of Speech,* Harcourt, Brace and Co., New York, 1921, 1949, pp. 32–3, 35–7, 109–10, for a similar view. See also my "Can Adults Become Genuinely Bilingual?" in Asa Kasher, *Language in Focus,* Bar Hillel memorial volume, *Boston Studies in the Philosophy of Science* Vol. 43, 1976, pp. 473–484.

81. In fact, as Alex Inkeles observes, "Sociology and Psychology", in S. Koch, ed., *Psychology: A Study of a Science,* Vol. 6, McGraw-Hill, New York, 1963, pp. 317–387, the prevalence of psychologism amongst psychologists and of sociologism amongst sociologists, is what creates such a division. Sociologism, he says, is responsible for "the relative exclusion of psychology from sociological analysis" (p. 321), and, he says, this is quite erroneous: "It is more difficult to affirm, however, as Durkheim seems at various points to do, that he needed no psychology of the individual to explain . . . " (p. 323). Inkeles also offers an exactly analogous analysis of psychologism (pp. 333–4).

What Inkeles himself preaches is precisely that the two sciences cooperate. Thus, he says (p. 370):

"So long as the personal system and the social system are kept clearly in mind as the distinct foci of psychological and sociological research, the two disciplines seem to "share" few concepts or methods other than those common to all analyses of systems. Exception must, however, be made with regard to at least four foci of interest which seem to involve considerable overlap or sharing of concepts and methods: small-group research, choice patterns (sociometrics), attitude and opinion study, and the study of values and ideologies. . . . Some people are dismayed by this, feeling it threatens the purity and distinctiveness of their discipline. Others are greatly heartened by the same fact. They see in it evidence that ultimately psychology and sociology "are the same thing" and the promise of a unified science of man which is yet to come. Both judgments seem to be overreactive."

Inkeles suggests (p. 373) to keep the two sciences distinct but not separate. I must leave him at that, perhaps adding the obvious that I fully agree.

82. J. W. N. Watkins, "Ideal Types and Historical Explanation", *Brit. J. Phil. Sci.*, Vol. 13, 1952, pp. 22—43. Revised and expanded edition, in H. Feigl and M. Brodbeck, eds., *Readings in the Philosophy of Science*, Appleton-Century-Croft, New York, 1953, pp. 723—743.

83. Ervin Goffman, *Asylum, Essays on the Social Situation of Mental Patients and Other Inmates*, Garden City, N.Y., 1961. It has been repeatedly noted that Goffman's works, as a body of knowledge, offer an extremely different impression when viewed as a specific philosophy than when viewed as a picture of a specific corner of life. And, in my opinion, the latter is the truth, yet Goffman does seem to be philosophically relevant — precisely because he mixes sociology and psychology, or works on their common ground.

Even this should not be exaggerated, since one can accept the common ground unphilosophically and take, on the basis of common sense, both sciences as given. And so the view offered there may be accepted unphilosophically, or on the basis of a shallow philosophy that distrusts all reductionism as "too abstract".

What this amounts to is the claim that we have an intuitive and significant distinction between psychopathology and sociopathology (deviant psychology and deviant sociology) and reductionists plan to explain away this very distinction.

84. George Herbert Mead, *Mind, Self, and Society from the Standpoint of a Social Behaviorist*, Chicago, 1934, 1962. See, e.g. pp. 211, 322—3: the critique of (Cooley's) psychologism, p. 224n, and of (Watson's) mechanistic behaviorism, e.g. p. 101n, and his critique of extreme sociologism, e.g. p. 74n, and pp. 238ff. on the difference between human and animal society as rooted in man's ability to reflect. See also his critique of the Rousseavian utopia on pp. 286ff. Significantly, in his conclusion Mead states that he has two concepts of consciousness, both of which are necessary for the making of our theory comprehensive enough, the one social the other psychological — but I am not very clear about this. See also Mead's classic "Cooley's contribution to American Social Thought," *Amer. J. Soc.*, Vol. 135, 1930, pp. 693—706, reprinted in his *On Social Psychology*, ed. A. Strauss,

University of Chicago Press, Chicago, 1956, pp. 293–307, esp. pp. 303 and 307.

Ralf Dahrendorf has a similar view. In his well-known "Homo Sociologicus", *Essays in the Theory of Society,* Standford University Press, 1968, he defines roles as rights and privileges associated with a social position and these as sets or patterns of expected expectations – all very much in accord with the role literature. It seems to me clear that this theory is thus an attempt to move towards a reductionist theory of society. Dahrendorf counters this move by two arguments, one that we have latent expectations here, determined by all sorts of laws or rules that may become explicit and active when challenged, when the statute-book is consulted, etc., and one that society as a whole determines roles, that there is a social space which defines which instant could be allotted which roles. He thus comes to the view that roles are intermediary or interface between sociology and psychology – reflecting or concretizing institutions on one side. And so, "for the sociologist roles are irreducible elements of analysis". The psychologist, by contrast, is concerned with their other, inner side, the side facing the individual, and he is accordingly led to resolve roles into their psychologically relevant components. "A systematic delimitation of the two disciples in these terms would be conceivable, but like other such delimitations it would be of doubtful utility" (p. 56n).

Now the utility I expect from a delimitation is the avoidance of all attempts at reduction and the resultant neglect of the interaction of society with the individual in both psychological and sociological literature. For example, Dahrendorf speaks of the roles for the psychologist as internalized, as psychological mirrors of social sets. This is often so, but it need not be so. A person may aspire to a role, or suffer its burdens, or feel trapped in a dual role. Dahrendorf also speaks, in the text to the note quoted above, about socialization and internalization – both having to do with the individual's adjustment to his society. The parallel phenomena, of the flexibility or accomodation of a society (say to eccentrics like Nelson), and of its institutionalization of certain individual qualities (such as Stalin's love to work by night) there is not much discussion, except perhaps in the theory of charisma.

Dahrendorf himself is, of course, fully cognizant of the fact that psychological man who is not sociological does not exist (pp. 43–4), and sociological man who is not a psychological man is a product of *Brave New World, 1984,* etc. What I think is still missing in this instructive celebrated essay, is not the complementariness but the interaction of the two fields. I think this is best illustrated in an error of his, itself minor, of identifying (pp. 54–58n, 59ff.) position (= rights and duties) with status, where in status psychological motive to attain position is gratified or frustrated.

85. Lawrence S. Kubie has repeatedly claimed, in opposition to most of his psychoanalytic colleagues, that
the essence of normality is flexibility . . .
The essence of illness is the freezing of behaviour
into unalterable and insatiable pattern . . .

(*Neurotic Distortion of the Creative Process,* New York, 1958, 1961, paper edition, pp. 20–21). This raises the intriguing question, the frozen but satiable, or the unfrozen but unsatiable, is it neurotic or not? Kubie does not distinguish sufficiently between adjustment and flexibility, but does so enough to make room for creativity (since adjustment is uncreative, of course).

86. The idea that society and the individual interact via mutual adjustment is not in the least new. However, it willy nilly clashes with the two traditional philosophies, psychologism and collectivism. I cannot put my finger on it, but have the general feeling that Claude Lévi-Strauss spoke of this, however vaguely, in his inaugural lecture, *The Scope of Anthropology*, translated by S. O. Paul and R. A. Paul, Cape, London, 1967. I think he credits Mauss with the proposal to retain the idea of the autonomy of sociology while paying more attention to the integration of sociology and psychology (p. 13), and he praises Ferdinand de Saussure for his invention of the science of semiology for the same reason. For, when he defines anthropology as semiology minus linguistics (p. 17), he offers no definition (in the traditional sense of the word "definition"; tradition anyway forbids reference to residues) but tries to view all social institutions and acts as interpersonal means of communication and coordination. I fully symphathize with this view (see final sections of my "Methodological Individualism", mentioned in note 8 to Introduction above), and feel that perhaps here lie both the fascination of Lévi-Strauss, and his failure as a failure to keep to this (e.g. his acceptance of the Durkheimian group spirit so strongly rejected by Leach; see note 18 to Section XI above).

Furthermore, Lévi-Strauss himself wonders (p. 18) whether anthropology, apart from semiotics, does not study beliefs and social organization. I think he answers by saying that organization has meaning, and its meaning is semiotic. For my part, I would say, where belief comes in is no small problem.

Amer. Soc. Review, Vol. 39, No. 3, June 1974 contains responses of Raymond L. Schmitt, Gregory Stone, and others, to Joan Huber, pp. 453–466. On p. 453 Schmitt says (italics mine) explicitly enough (SI stands for Symbolic Interactionism):

> "The fact that SI is not a theory is regarded by its critics as a major deficiency, but ironically, that SI is a sociological social psychological orientation or perspective, i.e., a broad set of interrelated concepts, ideas, findings, and *assumptions about the two-way relationship between man and the socio-cultural system,* rather than a theory, enables it to withstand internal and external criticism and makes it amenable to broad usage and extension."

Yet, this, too, is too vague. Apart from the fuzzy wording and irrationalist escape from criticism, the whole debate is so confused and confusing that I cannot say. Huber, for her part, complains that symbolic interactionists confuse their views with Merton's (p. 463), and she considers symbolic interactionism as Hegelian. She herself follows R. B. Braithwaite in matters methodological, she says. Now, to me she seems to be too establishment and I find her zeal somewhat excessive.

87. The classic study is Frederick M. Thrasher, *The Gang,* University of Chicago

Press, 1927; the emphasis on the amorphism of the gang and the resultant hardship on its members has been made by William F. Whyte, *Street Corner Society*, University of Chicago Press, enlarged edition, 1955.

See Francis E. Merril, *Society and Culture, an Introduction to Sociology*, Prentice Hall, Englewood Cliffs, 1961, 1969, Chapter 2; Primary Groups; The Delinquent Gang; The Corner Boys; The Dysfunction of the Primary Groups; and more references there. To these I should like to add a reference to one thoughtful recent paper on the rationality of members of large crowds which operated for surprisingly long stretches, as new phenomena of student revolts and their likes illustrated in recent years — Richard A. Berk, "A Gaming Approach to Crowd Behavior", *Amer. Soc. Rev.*; Vol. 39, 1974, pp. 355—372.

88. Doubtless, the organicist aspect of collectivism was fostered by romanticism and made a century later for bucolic utopianism of the kind that makes Margaret Mead's *Coming of Age in Samoa* such a work of fiction. The contrast between her text and her appendix shows she was not unaware of what she was doing. On the whole, no doubt, social anthropology includes a lot of propaganda, good, bad, and indifferent, and the reader is better equipped if he is sensitive to this fact. It is amazing to me that anthropologists who are so allergic to parochialism in their own society are so often quite receptive to it in the remote tribal societies in which they spend years.

Of course, there is also a vast secondary literature discussing this fact, such as the comments on Malinowski's posthumous *Diary in a True Sense*, where he allowed himself to express his true contempt for the natives he so extolled in his publications.

89. The literature on education and its aim was traditionally directed at socialization, since Plato is the major influence in the history of the philosophy of education. Plato's theory is that of character building by molding it. The Enlightenment tended to change the idea into that of character building in and of itself, i.e., letting nature come out. In modern times Martin Buber is one who emphasized that this idea — which he fostered — makes the teacher a cautious artist who must observe the pupil and trim his education to fit the individual pupil. Yet, Buber stressed, an educated man who has found himself is also one who has found his way to integrate into the community.

Rather than criticize this, let me say that most practicing educators feel that this is a fine ideal but in fact we must help a pupil socialize even before he feels the need.

Rather than criticize this, let me say that in modern democratic society, socializing is at best democratizing, and so the best school is the democratically run school.

The criticism of this view is always the argument that in a democratic school pupils will make study noncompulsory and then they will not study at all.

This argument is poor. It runs in the face of the fact that everybody agrees that character building or socialization is more important than building the stock of knowledge. (If you have character you will learn if you want to; it not, your knowledge from your school days will be of no avail.) It runs in the face of the fact that in most schools there is practically no learning anyway, as has been repeatedly attested on strictly empirical grounds and by diverse criteria of learning or knowledge. It runs in the face of the fact, finally, that humans learn at any given opportunity. But, as Daniel A. Greenberg of the famed Sudbury Valley School observes, in a democratic school pupils learn what they want, not what their elders and betters think is good for them.

In brief, schools are undemocratic because in our democratic society there is a high distrust of and dislike for democracy.

It is curious to notice the following historical facts. The question of motivation — how can we make young people want to study? — is the most pervasive in education theory. The Jewish tradition solved it by respecting learning; the vocational training tradition solved it by offering young people opportunities to acquire skills respected and rewarded in the community. These two solutions are identical, in that they offer motivations, but ones that are worthwhile and so credible and so accepted by the young. All other motivations fail, since they are meant to fool. Both the Montessori and the progressive systems of education impose on the young people by rationing love, thus putting enormous pressures on them, at times leading to scholarly success but at the cost of destroying character. Rousseau thought that motivation will sort itself out by itself, and Kant concluded from this that motivation is useless since young people have no will-power to try and achieve what they want anyway so that school has to impose character on them.

The movement towards free education, from Homer Lane to Bertrand Russell, assumed that there is no problem of motivation to begin with. As Russell says in his "Freedom versus Authority in Education", *Skeptical Essays*, Allen and Unwin, London, 1928, 1934, pp. 184–201, p. 193 — children love to invest effort in study. Not only did Skinner show this with the aid of his teaching machines; animal psychologists illustrated this in experiments with apes. Also, free education is based on the idea, polarly opposed to Kant's, that even a baby has full human rights, including the right to his own opinion — to the extent that he can voice it, whatever this be; see Russell, *Education and the Good Life*, Boni and Liveright, New York, 1926, p. 100. This implies, among other things, that we should abolish the idea of minimum voting age. The movement of children's rights works on such principles. It is interesting to notice that even Buber, who, as mentioned above, does not belong to the school of free education, accepts as empirical their conclusion that all compulsion misses its educational target. See his *Between Man and Man*, trans. R. G. Smith, Beacon Press, Boston, 1947, 1955, III, Education, p. 91, p. 95; also IV, The Education of Character.

The strange fact is that all educationists who advocate character building admit that we should prepare our pupils, and yet they offer their pupils only weapons in the form of processed knowledge, and not any training. Indeed, they have no time for training since they are busy absorbing knowledge. Even conservative writers complain about this. See, for example, A. Koestler's complaint, *Insight and Outlook*, London and New York, 1949, p. 272:

"The current method of presenting to the student not the problem, but only the finished solution, is to deprive the solution of all interest and stimulus value for the exploratory drive, to shut off the creative impulse, to reduce the adventure of mankind to a dusty heap of theorems."

Caleb Gattegno rightly says this of the new idea of education in *What We Owe Children, The Subordination of Teaching to Learning*, Outerbridge and Dienstfrey, New York, distributed by E. P. Dutton, 1970, p. 101:

"The obviousness of all this is reminiscent of what occurred in the Renaissance; when Europeans looked at the universe with new eyes and found so much to see and report. Still, the Establishment burnt some of the seers, jailed others, exiled others, prevented some from making a living. Today, we may be less ready to burn but as ready to ignore."

"The task is so simple" he says further, p. 19, "that today we can say that *the problem of reading* is solved."

90. A remarkable work on Communist China is Robert S. Elegant's *Center of the World, Communism and the Mind of China,* Doubleday, Garden City, 1964. It is a work that has been dismissed by academic experts (Elegant is a journalist) as muddled because it is neither a conservative study which proves that Mao is a pure Confucian nor a radicalist study which proves that Mao is a pure Marxist but, lo and behold, in between.

91. I cannot begin to survey the cheap pseudo-intellectual pro-Mao reportage on China. And, looking at its predecessor, regarding Russia of the heydays of Stalin, I suppose there is no need to: it will all soon boil down to the standard mention of a few titles and a couple of anecdotes. Let me mention now, however, that if *Observer's* Far Eastern correspondent, Dennis Bloodworth, *Chinese Looking Glass*, Secker and Warburg, London, 1967, Penguin, London, 1969, and Cambridge doyen economist Joan Robinson, *The Cultural Revolution in China*, Penguin, London, 1969, 1970, are indicative of a trend, then the pro-Mao literature has departed from the style of the pro-Stalin literature (emulated by the classic mock-journalist Ehrenburgesque of Jan Myrdal, *Report From a Chinese Village*, Heinemann, London, Signet, New York, 1963, 1965, 1966): whereas the pro-Stalin literature represented the power of positive thinking, the pro-Mao literature presents an enormous titanic struggle against the pervasive evils that should have been eliminated once and for all but with all the power of evil cling and prolong the battle indefinitely. See Judith Buber Agassi, "The Significance of Mao's Fourth Volume", Abstract, in E. F. Szczepanik, ed., *Symposium on Economic and Social Problems of the Far East*, Hong Kong University Press, Hong Kong, 1962, p. 238.

We are often told that suffering pain with fortitude is a virtue — some say a great virtue indeed — especially if it is suffered for a higher cause. I think it is a vice, and I think it is a vice tolerated because of self-deception, rooted in the simple fact that impotence may easily be mistaken for resignation and resignation for stubbornness and stubbornness for single-mindedness. Be this as it may, the vice of tolerating pain is the vice of accepting it even though it may perchance be overthrown. Unless you try, you never know. John Donne has noticed all this, in his typically bitter and ruthless self-criticism:

"For mee (if there be such a thing as I)
Fortune (if ther be such a thing as shee)
Spies that I beare so well her tyranny,
That shee thinks nothing else so fit for mee."

92. Let me repeat here, that it is not the interaction between the sociological and psychological that breaks new grounds, but the conflicts and adjustments between them. See also Inkeles' survey mentioned in note 81 above. The general feel of the new approach is, also, quite commonsense. See the almost rhetoric expression of the same sentiment in the passage quoted in the next note.

93."How to reconcile group freedom to individual freedom is one of the most important challenges facing the world in the second half of this century . . . Group freedom is a primitive, robust, massive thing; it hardly needs any special protection [from the individual]. It is individual freedom that is relatively new and fragile, and that therefore requires every possible tender care. . . . The ultimate problem with which we have to wrestle is whether under the pressure of group, nation, culture, and the machine, some remnants of man, the individual human person, can still be saved . . ."
Charles Malik, Lebanese Ambassador to U.S. and UN, in *New Frontiers of Knowledge, A Symposium by Distinguished Writers, Notable Scholars, and Public Figures,* Public Affairs Press, Washington, D.C., 1957, p. 3.

94. See Bertrand Russell, *The Impact of Science on Society,* Simon and Schuster, New York, 1953, Chapter 1.

Chapter Five

Man in the Image of God

Traditionally, man was viewed as divine, or as a mixture of the divine and the devil, or as devilish; in conformity with my anti-all-or-nothing attitude I shall attempt to present man as nothing of the sort, but rather as something neither devilish nor divine, yet which struggles to come nearer to the divine than he is.[1]

Thus far we saw that whether man is a machine (an animal) may be left open on the understanding that he is, at least, a special kind of machine (animal) — a moral one. Now, man's morality is conditioned, first of all, on his rationality, particular and defective because it is particular and defective. And his rationality is conditioned on his gregariousness. This does not mean that man is merely confined to his social setting, but that he may also conflict and thereby interact with it. Already the Romantics allowed man to conflict and interact with society — they conceded that much of individualism to the Rationalists — but on the condition, they added, that he be a hero. This is obfuscation; the individual and society both limit each other, and so both sociology and psychology have room within the social sciences.

This seems a compromise between psychologism and sociologism and I am anxious to argue that it is, rather, a rejection of their very disjunction, i.e. of the assumption common to both, i.e. the all-or-nothing attitude. And the best way to illustrate this is by showing that both have the same ideal of man, the same view of man in the image of God — one which must be rejected — of perfect harmony between ideal society and ideal individual. This divine ideal is beyond our reach; which fact forces the philosophers to add a devilish ingredient to the makeup of human nature. I think we need now a better image of man, that we are in a position to mold an image not mixed of polar opposites, and striving not to a polar ideal position but to something more reasonable and humane.

Notes

1. The sentiment expressed in this chapter is anything but new. Indeed, even Lessing, child of the Enlightenment, admitted that the search is better than the final finding. This is one of his most often quoted passages, which conflicts with almost everything else he and his peers stood for. I often wondered how this is possible, but Lévi-Strauss has made it clear that when we must employ a consistent but incorrect philosophy, we also want an extreme opposite to temper it with.

The idea that the search matters more than the find comes out more strongly when pessimistic suggestions of failure to find are clearer. Thus, the punch line in Karel Čapek's pessimistic *R.U.R.* is, "It was a great thing to be a man. There was something great about it."

See also my "On Pursuing the Unattainable," in R. S. Cohen and M. W. Wartofsky, eds., *Boston Studies for the Philosophy of Science*, Reidel, Dordrecht and Boston, Vol. 11, 1974, pp. 249–257.

George Santayana, *The German Mind: Philosophical Diagnosis*, with an introduction by A. L. Rowse, Ths. Crowell Co., 1968, complains, on p. 129, that Lessing is insincere in his preference of the search for the truth over the finding of it. I must agree with his logic, except to say that he was taking too literally an aphorism. The question is not, would Lessing draw the consequence from his aphorism and sabotage the search once its chance for success is high enough? Rather, he asked, is the world more interesting if its secret can be revealed once and for all or not? And here, of course, Lessing was not true to character.

XXI UTOPIAS OF PSYCHOLOGISM AND COLLECTIVISM ARE IDENTICAL[2]

Psychologism and collectivism are at variance with any intuitive idea we have about education for integration. For psychologism there is no society to intergrate into, only people to befriend. For collectivism there is nothing oppressive in a society which fully engulfs the individual.[3] And so for collectivists there is merit in conservative education — socialization, it is called — a means of social cohesion and integration.[4] The collectivists will see in individualistic critical education a cause of alienation.[5] In a very impressive essay Dennis Wrong has argued that diverse sociologists of the functionalist persuasion study socialization in a manner which is nothing short of conservatism.[6] Psychologism, of course, will go the other way and declare the freedom from superstition and myth, the growth of enlightenment and science, to be the sole way to integration, and to the resolution of conflict between individual and society.[7] The classical economists, especially Adam Smith, saw in the free market nothing but an expression of such a society, or a commonwealth of totally free and rational individuals. Keynes, the great revolutionary, likewise adopted the idea of a free individual in a perfect market. He thought he only added to the classical profit motive a new motive: liquidity preference: when the stock market is very bleak, he felt, it is reasonable that people would prefer cash to shares regardless of the low price of shares.[8] I do not mean to say that Keynes — or Smith for that matter — consistently stuck to psychologism. It is still very interesting that Keynes did not think of himself as much of a rebel. He dismissed his predecessors whose prescriptions he rejected as lightly as Smith rejected his. For, under the view that society is nothing but the rational conduct of anyone, the social scientist who disagrees with me becomes less rational than the man in the street! Consequently, all economic policy based on my predecessors' recommendations is to be explained away as mere prejudice. On this Smith and Keynes were agreed.

I stress this point not in order to dismiss either Smith or Keynes. For, rejecting their dismissal of their predecessors, I am bound not to dismiss them. Nor do I stress this on account of its quaintness or peculiarity. Rather, I have a point to make, and one which easily evades inspection. It is the prevalence of utopianism.

The more the adherents of either psychologism or functionalism offer theories which claim to be explanatory, the less obvious is their polarization; and the less obvious is their utopianism. The utopianism is of perfect freedom of the individual or of perfect socialization and integration. But being utopian, both visions tend to merge.[9]

Perhaps the merger of both utopias is the subtlest aspect to them; it is certainly the most important one. For, in either utopia man is absolutely natural.[10] Whether he is so perfectly adjusted as to have perfectly internalized his society, or whether he is so perfectly rational that his society is but a projection of his own rational self — in the last resort, this matters not. Indeed, we may claim that the final product must be amenable to both analyses so that the dispute between them regarding the final product is purely metaphysical. For, the final product will have no conflict and this may be either perfect internalization or perfect projection — or both! As we shall see, the new biologism[11] of the Lorenz and Ardrey school, which is the final nightmare where the rational and the beastly in man operate in perfect harmony, has just the fascination of merging the internalization and the projection aspects.[12]

I do not mean to deny the significance — especially for educational practices — of the metaphysical disagreement: for the adherent of psychologism the utopia is one in which (through the elimination of all indoctrination in the process of education) society has finally been utterly eliminated; whereas to his collectivist opponents (through an ideal system of effective education) society has been utterly internalized and so reigns unchallenged. But common to the two is the ideal of harmony[13] — an ideal which I wish to reject: *man is inherently a struggler* (and should be trained to struggle well).[14] And so I suggest, again, that, of necessity, any society, any social institution, is in part natural in part conventional. And I propose pluralism rather than either pole — nature in its purity or mere convention — as the ideal to strive for. I shall propose that in pluralism, in pluralistic practice, we may achieve a greater measure of liberation of the individual from the fetters of the society to which he happens to have been born.

My educational ideal is not really new. It is the liberal ideal of seeking from the earliest stages the maximal options to choose from. I think the critique of conventionalism offered by Hume and Smith — namely that a convention is one which we may contract out of but we cannot contract out of society any more than out of a boat in the middle of the ocean — need not be so valid: it depends on the availability of other boats in the middle of the ocean and how easy it is to move from one to the other. (It is clear that, by definition, we cannot trade our nature, and man by nature is a social animal; so we can only trade one convention for another.) I claim, then, that an individual is more free and more natural the more familiar he is with the local conventions of diverse societies and the more able he is to adjust to any of them.[15] This can be argued without entering the vexing question, what part of a society is natural? And, it is the general tenor of the present study that when such questions can be avoided, some effort should be made to avoid them and some effort should be invested in the opposite direction.

The most important pragmatic aspect (psychological as well as educational) of my proposal seems to me to be this. When a person feels comfortable in a society he need not declare it natural (for himself) and he need not endorse its customs. On the contrary, he may feel at home in a society precisely because it is expanding, because he may use one of its customs to destroy another. That is to say, the very polarization between the integrated and the alienated has to be thrown overboard as a part of the polarization which leaves little or no room for the sense of integration that the reformer may feel.[16]

To backtrack. Since time immemorial and until fairly recently it was taken for granted that people believe in their own customs, in the society which bred them, in the superiority of that society, etc. We saw this illustrated by both Herodotus and Bertrand Russell. The distinction between nature and convention, we remember, came both to shake the belief in custom and to destroy custom itself. This is radicalism; it is impossible; it is disastrous.[17] Thus, in ancient Greece, as social anthropologists tell us, ordinary daily life went on not much disturbed, with primitive tribal ways of life, primitive religion, and such.[18] Political historians, however, tell us of the disintegration of customary Greek frameworks, the destruction of the foundations of Greek society due to the rise of philosophy — to the extent that civil war was unavoidable and was fought not along geographic lines but in accord with philosophic principles, with Athens standing for radicalism and Sparta for reaction.[19] The vacillation and clash between the two poles seem to me to be characteristic of the West; but they need not be.

The saddest fact about the reaction is, to my mind, the degree to which it shares with radicalsim rigidity and indoctrination. Reaction seems an extreme response to the extreme radicalism, but it concedes much too much to its bitterest opponent.[20] Perhaps the very semblance of extreme reaction is precisely what makes reaction hardly extreme. Perhaps its very ardent defense of the old, in spirit as well as in practice, is a concession to the radicalists's kind of extremism, his polarization. This concession to radicalism, this readiness to debate with radicalists on their own extremist grounds and in their own extremist manner, makes the reactionary defend wholeheartedly any existing society, any existing religion, etc. And this makes the reactionary, sophisticated and worldly wise as often as he is, a muddlehead of a philosophical relativist and epistemological relativist, who advocates every local religion, every local system as the best — suggesting to believers that any belief in a doctrine makes it true. The reactionary then ends up as a scoundrel of a moral relativist. I need not discuss here the relativist's idealism or his nihilism. Both were illustrated to be one in George Orwell's horror fable *1984*. If any better proof is necessary, it is enough to point out that the most relativist reactionaries, namely the Communist governments, take pride in their radicalist ancestry, boast of their own relativism, yet declare the relativism of any of their opponents, alleged or real, to be idealistic and reactionary and decadent.[21]

The nihilist can, of course, call his opponents nihilists and prove his own distance from nihilism by the fact that he insists on a strict and rigid adherence to his own traditional norms. Of course, this is not to endorse the nihilist's claim that he is orthodox[22] — it is merely to point out that once you give up the standards of decent and rational debate, then anything goes and so the reactionary in his nihilism is utterly orthodox at times and utterly reformist at other times yet he can claim to be orthodox all the way. I think it is a thought-provoking fact that this mock-orthodoxy is shared by both the Communist governments and the leadership of the National Religious Party in Israel.[23] They exhibit the same logic, the same polarization between radicalist and reactionary, which makes it hard to distinguish the one from the other; the polarization, that is, between believing in, while adhering to, one's society, as one pole, and disbelieving in it while rejecting it as another. This polarization is the target of my critique, and I shall show how the deviation from the polarization will open up new possibilities, how we can educate a new type of liberal man not susceptible to polarization and not so muddled either.

With this I shall have turned the tables. Radicalist and reactionary together congratulate themselves as extremists, as clear-sighted.[24] In one league they see the non-extremist reformist as a muddle-headed fellow who mixes and blends parts of one extreme with parts of the other, they consider his national and economic policy a muddling through and his educational policy a disaster to both character and logic. I think things are the other way around, but I think we cannot justly blame either extremist: the whole philosophical tradition on which we build goes their way. It is a wonder[25] that nonetheless our culture is pluralist and tolerant. It is time, however, to clear up the mess and show the classical polarization and pluralism to be mutually exclusive.

Notes to Section XXI

2. The odd fact about the identity of the individualist and collectivist utopias is that it raises profound problems on all fronts, from metaphysics to biology. The metaphysical problem of individuation is obvious (see my "Methodological Individualism", mentioned in note 8 to the Introduction above, final section). The biological problem is fascinating. The opening paragraph of Edward O. Wilson's review of Richard S. Boardman, Alan H. Cheethan and William A. Oliver Jr., eds., *Animal Colonies, Developments and Function Through Time*, Dowden, Hutchison, and Ross, Stroudsburg, Pa., 1973, entitled "Perfect Societies", in *Science*, Vol. 184, 5 April, 1974, pp. 54—5, puts it very aptly:

"The study of sponges, corals, and other colony-forming invertebrate animals is circumscribed by a paradox. These organisms are for the most part anatomically simple, and in some cases they are phylogenetically very primitive, yet by most intuitive criteria their societies are the most advanced among living organisms. In fact some are just about perfect. In zoology the very word colony implies that the members of the society are physically united, or differentiated into reproductive and sterile castes, or both. When both conditions exist to an advanced degree, as they do in many of these animals, the society can equally well be viewed as a super-organism or even as an organism. The dilemma can therefore be expressed as follows: At what point does a society become so well integrated that it is no longer a society? On what basis do we distinguish the extremely modified members of an invertebrate colony from the organs of a metazoan animal?

These are not trivial questions. They address a theoretical issue seldom made explicit in biology: the conception of all possible ways by which a complex organism can be created in evolution. The coelenterate order Siphonophora, which includes the familiar Portuguese man-of-war, is a case in point. A swimming siphonophore superficially resembles a jellyfish but is actually a complex assemblage of highly reduced individuals variously specialized to provide locomotion, protection, reproduction, and other functions on behalf of the colony as a whole. So complete are the dual processes of differentiation and integration that the colony cannot be regarded as functionally distinct from a scyphozoan jellyfish or some other complex coelenterate individual. As G. O. Mackie has pointed out, the signal achievement of the Siphonophora has been to reach the organ grade of body construction by converting individuals into organs. If other Precambrian invertebrate lines had not invented mesoderm, modern higher animals might well be designed as diploblastic superorganisms in the siphonophore manner."

3. Alastaire MacIntyre, *Marcuse,* Fontana, London, 1970, p. 26, presents the collectivist utopia thus:
"Hegel in some of his most youthful writings saw in the Greek *polis* a form of human community in which the individual found his identity within the political community and did not think of the state as an alien power set over him, but rather as his true home. . . . In the modern world the individual and the state were at odds . . . partly because of . . . the Judeo-Christian tradition. . . ."
Herbert Marcuse, *Counterrevolution and Revolt*, Beacon, Boston, 1972, pp. 70–71, presents the collectivism of the mature Hegel of the *Phenomenology* rather differently:
". . . For *Hegel*: Reflection on the content and mode of *my* immediate sense certainly reveals the 'We' in the 'I' of intuition and perception. When the still unreflected consciousness has reached the point where it becomes conscious of itself and its relation to its objects, where it has experienced a 'trans-sensible' world 'behind' the sensuous appearance of things, it discovers that *we* ourselves are behind the curtain of appearance. And this 'we' unfolds as social reality in the struggle between Master and Servant for 'mutual recognition'."
Marcuse represents Hegel's view correctly, but he plays down the idea of Hegel that in Hegelian philosophy the conflict comes to rest. For this side of Hegel

we must apply Lévi-Strauss here and see the master-slave struggle and the Hegelian reactionary utopia as two extremes of one myth. Robert C. Tucker, *Philosophy and the Myth in Karl Marx,* Cambridge University Press, 1961, 2nd ed., 1972, offers an excellent reading of Hegel's metaphysics. He says Hegel identifies himself as God's consciousness and he sees God as self-alienated or, in Horney's sense (see note 44 to Section XXIII below), neurotic; but one who comes to reconcile himself with himself in the process of self-recognition and in the sense of unifying the whole world (in a process where learning the external world equals consuming it) and thus becoming truly infinite and all-in-all.

To return to Marcuse, he goes on, *op. cit.* (pp. 73–4), to contrast *"Kant"* and *"Hegel"* with "the *Marxian*" — why not "Marx"? — attributing to "the *Marxian* conception" nothing less than "the reconciliation of human freedom [individualism?] and natural necessity [collectivism?] subjective [individualism?] and objective [collectivism?] freedom [?]". This, of course, is plain distortion: every philosopher worth his salt tried to do the same thing. Yet for Marcuse "This union presupposes liberation: the revolutionary *praxis* which is to abolish the institutions of capitalism and to replace it by socialist institutions and relationship." I do not know what to do with such a hodge-podge except to say it is very remote from Marx.

4. Peter Berger, *The Precarious Vision,* Doubleday, New York, 1961, p. 50, says, "socialization is now seen not just as the process by which the self becomes integrated into society but rather the process in which the self is actually produced". Quoted in Joseph H. Fichter, "The Concept of Man in Social Science: Freedom, Values and Second Nature", in the *Journal for the Scientific Study of Religion,* Vol. 11, 1972, pp. 109–121, p. 113. See also next note.

5. Peter L. Berger and Richard J. Neuhaus, *Movement and Revolution, On American Radicalism,* Anchor, New York, 1970, p. 30., where Berger says, "Accept "alienation" — it is the price of freedom. *Learn how to stand apart.*" See also previous note.

6. Dennis H. Wrong, "The Oversocialized Conception of Man in Modern Sociology" *Am. Soc. Rev.,* Vol. 26, 1961, pp. 183–193. This paper is reprinted in a number of anthologies.

It is only fair to mention that Wrong has Freudian leanings, but I do not think he endorses psychologism.

7. G. W. Allport, "Religion and Prejudice", *Crane Review,* 1959, 2, pp. 1–10, notices the evil of bigotry and intellectual arrogance in the form of intolerance towards disagreement. There is little doubt in my mind that our intellectual heritage constantly attempted to exclude such attitudes as non-intellectual, no matter how learned and technically competent. But on this we have failed. And, I propose, this still is the first item on the agenda of any sociology of science that aims at scientific humanism.

Also, taking seriously M. Rokeach's view, *The Open and Closed Mind: Investigations into the Nature of Belief Systems and Personality Systems,* Basic Books, New York, 1960, that the believer is more anxiety-ridden than the heretic, then, surely, the same should apply to the scientific bigot. Students of professors who are scientific bigots may be greatly relieved of enormous pressures by merely noticing this fact. See also Appendix B. to M. Rokeach, *Beliefs, Attitudes, and Values,* San Francisco, 1968.

8. That Keynes has offered his new idea of liquidity preference as a psychological one has been noticed by Watkins, in a paper mentioned in note 82 to Section XX above, p. 737, where liquidity preference is declared "psychological"; see Keynes' own expression in his classical *General Theory of Employment, Interest, and Money*, London, 1936, pp. 246–7. Nevertheless, it should also be noticed that the last chapter of Keynes' *General Theory* is claimed to be an outline of a new social philosophy. Keynes observes there that moneymaking is a relatively harmless activity to which "dangerous human proclivities can be canalized", especially if the rich are encouraged to spend, by means of high death duties, and the lowering of interest rates. This, of course, may make saving no longer worthwhile, and then it will be replaced by "communal saving through the agency of the State" so as to "allow the growth of capital up to the point where it ceases to be scarce". He adds that he sees the disappearance of the rentier capitalist as a gradual peaceful process. Since all this can be regulated by the State, it will depend on "the common will". All this, he comments, is "moderately conservative in its implications". He is at pains to exclude "State Socialism" as too embracing, especially since state ownership of the means of production is quite redundant. Rather, he aims at "decentralization and the play of self-interest": "individualism, if it can be purged of its defects and its abuses, is the best safeguard of personal liberty in the sense that, compared with any other system, it greatly widens the field for the exercise of personal choice".

The new social philosophy, thus, is no innovation of an ideal, but a refinement of an older liberal technique, where intervention is used as means for overcoming obstacles towards increased personal liberty; except that with Bentham intervention was legal and Keynes recommended fiscal intervention as well. What was new, I suppose, is the idea of a smooth and "moderately conservative" transition to socialism while retaining an ever increased range of individual liberty.

9. The utopian streak of the Enlightenment is seldom discussed, even though, say, Adam Smith's *Wealth of Nations* has a Commonwealth which is clearly a laissez-faire Utopia as possible. See Fred Polak, *The Image of the Future*, translated and abridged by Elise Boulding, Jossey Bass, Inc., San Francisco, Washington, 1973, pp. 100ff.

H. G. Wells, whose utopianism was far from anarchistic or democratic, nonetheless presents his Utopia (*Men Like Gods,* Chapter The Fifth, §3) as both anarchistic and collectivistic; indeed as there is no coercion it is hard to say whether there is government (as decisions are made by experts that bind the public) or not (since people voluntarily comply with them, or else have reason not to or else are mentally deranged).

Olaf Stapledon, the philosopher science fiction writer, evidently had the same idea in mind when he described an individualist-*cum*-collectivist Utopia in his *First and Last Man* (p. 228 of Dover, New York, edition):

". . . this society of ours, in which citizens live in perfect . . . accord without the aid of armies or even a police force . . . our much prized social organization assigns a unique function to each citizen, controls the procreation of new citizens of every type in relation to social need, and yet provides an endless supply of originality. We have no government and no laws, if by law is meant a stereotyped convention supported by force, and not to be altered without the aid of cumbersome machinery. Yet, though our society is in this sense an anarchy, it lives by means of a very intricate system of customs, some of which are so ancient as to have become spontaneous taboos, rather than deliberate conventions even as mere individuals, we are learning to trust more and more to the judgment and dictates of our own super-individual experience."

The idea that individualist and collectivist utopias are the same – and suffer from the same shallowness – has been explored at some length in the works of Karel Čapek. He did not explore in depth but went into the diverse projections and ramifications of ideas. See Alexander Matuska, *Karel Čapek, Man Against Destruction, An Essay,* trans. by Carthoryn Alan, Artia, Prague, 1964, especially p. 244. The author refers to Z. G. Mintz and O. M. Malevich, *K. Čapek i A. N. Tolstoi* which I cannot check.

Of course, Čapek had a philosophy, and one that does not stand up to criticism very well. But he was a marvellous critic and a great humanist who had a feel for (and knowledge of) natural science and so could not take refuge in the split into two cultures. The most moving thing about all his utopian or anti-utopian works is his addition to the Wellesian universalism a genuine concern for humanity and for the travails of the common man – something which Welles lacked partly because of his bitter memories of his own struggling youth.

The religious aspect of utopianism, and thereby of science fiction, is treated in Section 17, De-eschatologizing, of Fred Polak, *op. cit.*

10.   The claim that the utopian society is absolutely natural equals the claim that it is unalienated. Usually discussions of alienation include complaints which imply, but not assert explicitly, that there can be unalienated society. This is why Karl Popper has criticized alienation theory, in his *Objective Knowledge*, Clarendon Press, Oxford, 1972, p. 285, by saying we are all alienated, men, animals, and even plants. This is powerful stuff! It shows how utopianism is an offshoot of Nature worship. For Nature worship as radicalist see my "Unity and Diversity in Science", mentioned above, note 9 to Section I, and E. Gellner, "French 18th Century Materialist", reprinted in his *The Devil in Modern Philosophy,* Routledge, London and Boston, 1974.

Here, clearly Marx comes up as a run-of-the-mill utopian, who had no blueprints for utopia not because he thought we should cross the bridges when we come to them but because he rejected all blueprint utopianism as not utopian enough. This is the thesis of Tucker's *Philosophy and Myth in Karl Marx,* mentioned above, note 3. (Still, no doubt Fourier had an influence on Marx's utopianism, as Tucker notices, and as also Kaufmann notices in his *Without Guilt and Justice,* Wyden, New York, 1973, pp. 246–7.) As Tucker argues, Marx accepted much of Hegel's critique of classical radicalism, yet felt that Hegel offered his own version of resolution of the difficulties he mentions, and that in a correct reading Hegel's Utopia is the same in the last analysis as the radicalist one.

11. What seems to me to be erroneous with the contemporary biological approach to philosophical anthropology – the continental school, so-called – is not its mixture of Darwinism, Marxism, Freudianism, and Lorenzism – in spite of the admittedly Fascist (Haekelian) element in the concoction (I view it as rather innocuous). Rather, I will push the biological approach a bit further, to include the hackneyed pragmatist (Deweyite) idea that thinking has high survival value. An infant clings – to mother, to primary group, to herd. The clinging mechanism is obviously the more innate, the earlier; it is deeply modified in puberty (in those animals which undergo puberty: without puberty there is no infancy of course). The mechanism then develops into that of the isolated primary group, the collection or colony of primary groups, or the herd, as the case may be. The very fact that even on the most primitive level humans have diverse groupings (social and political organizations) (even the small family is different in different societies) is instructive of the fact that in humans by the time of puberty even the most elementary biological processes are drastically interfered with. (Even the fact that deviation, such as homosexuality, is different in different societies, is indicative here.) What seems most common to what Popper calls closed societies (and erroneously identifies with tribes, and their ideology with tribalism) is the tendency to create mechanisms which prolong the tendency to cling beyong puberty. And clinging is, intellectually, dogmatism. Indeed, as Gellner observes, dogmatism may be required as an expression of loyalty, and preferably the dogmatic acceptance of an absurd doctrine: only if the king is naked it is loyalty that makes you see him clothed. Dogmatism is thus detrimental to survival in a manner much more significant and advanced than the primitive manner in which it is conducive to survival. Hence the concern with acceptance and with security which traditional societies quite erroneously encourage. Hence, the real revolution seems to me to be educational: under influences of Darwin, Marx, and Freud, we are – or should try to be – building a society without mechanisms for the perpetuation of infancy.

It is hard for me to take the Continental schools seriously. Ever so often what they say looks trite and bombast – at times intentionally unclear. I tried American expositions – the best seems, still, Marjorie Grene – and they do not help much. An essay on "Plessner's Philosophical Anthropology" by Freud R. Dallmayer, *Inquiry,* Vol. 17, 1974, pp. 49–77, seems easy enough, but I failed to connect. I quote here a footnote (no. 2) from his essay, on the definition of philosophical anthropology, since the topic has been discussed at length here, so that my incomprehension of what I quote should not be discussed as the incomprehension of one who is alien to the topic. Here it is (p. 73):

"In the words of Jurgen Habermas, philosophical anthropology 'integrates and digests the findings of all those sciences which — like psychology, sociology, archeology or linguistics — deal with man and his works; but it is not in turn a specialized discipline'. Perched 'between empiricism and theory', the task of philosophical anthropology is 'to interpret scientific findings in a philosophical manner'."

See his article "Anthropologie," in Alwin Diemer and Ivo Frenzel, eds., *Fischer-Lexikon: Philosophie,* Fischer Verlag, Frankfurt-Main, 1958, pp. 18 and 20.

12. An amusing example of the new collectivism is of Konrad Lorenz, 1950:

"Whereas the old atomic analytical approach aimed at deriving the nature of total entities exclusively from the sums of their elements, in complete igno-rance of the characteristics of organic systemic entities, the pendulum of scien-tific 'public opinion' has nowadays swung to the opposite extreme. Now there is an almost exclusive search for the influence exerted by society, by virtue of its specific structure, upon the personality structure of the individual growing within the social framework. There is scarcely ever an enquiry after the pres-ence of individually invariable species-specific structures in human behaviour as determinants of certain species-typical characteristics common to *all* human societies. The focus of analysis is almost always the structural *differences* between different types of human society, and scarcely ever the structural *similarities* arising fron invariable individual response patterns.

   The exclusive treatment of the causal chains extending from the society to the individual, this complete neglect of causal effects in the opposite direction, represents a breach of scientific methodological rules . . ."

Konrad Lorenz, *Studies in Animal and Human Behaviour,* translated by Robert Martin, Harvard University Press, Cambridge, Mass., Vol. 2, 1971, p. 115. (Equating atomic and analytical is a myth, of course.)

Lorenz does not really require that psychology become autonomous; rather, in line with Toennies' philosophy he believes that the common to all societies is the communal kernel. See note 73 to Section XIX above.

13. Metaphysics is a unifying element, and so, any metaphysical system should be contestable. It seems as if this broadens the scope of debate beyond limit, and so Polanyi and Kuhn both recommend the dogmatic acceptance of some meta-physics which should (temporarily) serve as an intellectual framework. See notes 5–9 to the Introduction above.

   Now, no doubt, some intellectual framework is necessary. Consider the fact that each question has at least two possible answers, that each country has on its political agenda at least five to ten major questions at any time, and you can see that there exist between thirty and one thousand different views on major matters, and if at least one of the five questions has three or four possible answers, for example one question on which three of four major political groups differ, then we have to start with at least fifty possible views, and more likely ten to one hundred thousand. Yet, from the start, all these collapse to no more than two or three debates, with strongly interrelated answers which keep the number of political groupings manageable almost in all operative democracies.

This is done by the adoption of a small number of intellectual frameworks, and these are debateable and should, indeed, be debated at quite some length. What is rather disappointing is that the accepted views which are most prevalent are individualism and collectivism, and these share quite a lot.

"All utopias from Plato's Republic to George Orwell's brave new world of 1984 have one element in common: they are all societies from which change is absent." Ralf Dahrendorf's Popperian "Out of Utopia", first sentence: his *Essays in the Theory of Society,* Stanford University Press, 1968, pp. 107–128, p. 107. In explaining this he adds (pp. 108–9):

"... Consensus can be enforced, as it is for Orwell; or it can be spontaneous, a kind of *contrat social,* as it is for some eighteenth century utopian writers ... One might suspect, on closer inspection, that from the point of view of political organization the results in the two cases would turn out to be rather similar ...

Universal consensus means, by implication, the absence of structurally generated conflict ... Utopias are perfect — be it perfectly agreeable or disagreeable ... social harmony ..."

Raymond Aron expresses the same sentiment in his *The Opium of the Intellectuals*, W. W. Norton, New York, 1962, end of Foreword:

"The fanatic, animated by hate, seems to me terrifying. A self-satisfied humanity fills me with horror."

Harmony, then, or self-satisfaction, is what characterizes all (past) utopias. It is this harmony, let me add, that makes it hard to say whether society is perfectly internalized by its members or whether members are utterly free to project all their internal life onto society, i.e. whether it is an entirely collectivist or an entirely individualist utopia.

14. See previous note.

Ralf Dahrendorf, *op. cit.*, p. 126, contrasts utopianism which is an "equilibrium model" with a "conflict model of society". It is a 1958 paper, and he says there *(loc. cit.)*, "Only in the last year or two has there been some indication that [it] ... is gaining ground in sociological analysis", even though it, too, "has a long tradition" (p. 125).

The idea, we remember, not 21 to Section XVII above, belongs to Georg Simmel.

15. The idea that it is in man's nature to have conventions has been used throughout history, but never to collapse the dichotomy between nature and convention. On the contrary, naturalists repeatedly used this idea as the last refuge when their naturalism was hard pressed. And conventionalists used it either to refute naturalism and support conventionalism or to collapse the two polar views into one. And Burke and Hegel did both.

What is specific to the view advocated here is first the suggestion to accept convention without internalizing it and second the claim that this suggestion breaks away from the classic dichotomy. I think the first point here, but not the second, namely the suggestion that we participate without internalizing, is the one advocated by most game theory enthusiasts, role reversal and simulation theoreticians, and their like.

See, for example Charles D. Elder's review of Clark C. Abt, *Serious Games* and Richard F. Barton, "A Primer of Simulation and Gaming", *Am. Pol. Sci. Rev.,* Vol. 65, December 1971, No. 4, pp. 1158–9:

"Games promote a sense of detachment and objectivity, while at the same time engaging the emotions of the participants and fostering the intense involvement with the problems being gamed . . . [Abt also points out that] . . . the designing of a game can be a potent educational experience and an illuminating analytic exercise."

Elder complains that these authors do not pay attention to "the large and growing body of research and literature on simulation and gaming" which is ripe for a survey.

See also note 58 to Section XV above on Cornford's view that detachment is what myth lacks and science has. See also next two notes.

16. Man is born free, yet everywhere he is in chains, says J. J. Rousseau. And his chief problem was, how come this is so. E. M. Forster reversed this (*Two Cheers for Democracy*, Edward Arnold, New York, Harcourt, Brace, London, 1951, p. 21): "For politics are based on human nature; even a tyrant is a man, and our freedom is really menaced to-day [1935] because a million years ago Man was born in chains". This view, that freedom is from nature and not in nature, was adopted by Popper.

"To the best minds of the eighteenth and nineteenth centuries [continues Forster (p. 22),] freedom appeared as a blessing which had to be recovered. They believed that a little energy and intelligence would accomplish this. The chains had only to be broken violently, the conventions patently unloosed . . .The twentieth century knows more history than that and more psychology, and has suffered more . . . The tyrant no longer appears as a freak from the pit, he is becoming the norm . . ."

17. "No society and no harmony without doublethink", says E. Gellner in his review of R. E. Money Kyrle, "Man's Picture of the World", in *Inquiry*, Vol. 4, 1961, pp. 209–214, p. 209. See also Erazim V. Kohak, "Russia: The Fire Next Time? " *Dissent,* October 1971, pp. 478–484, p. 482.

I have discussed this point at some length in my "Conventions of Knowledge in Talmudic Law", mentioned in note 6 to Chapter Two above.

The most amusing case is that of a Catholic reformer of a doctrine which he is obliged to believe in but permitted to argue against in the hope of repealing it nonetheless; a point that causes much confusion among rationalists who find this unconceivable since it is cheap hypocrisy at best. See my "On Explaining The Trial of Galileo", mentioned in note 81 to Section V above.

I have later on found that the idea is quite prevalent in the literature, indeed even in works I should know better, such as Heine's *Religion and Philosophy in Germany,* where Heine presents Pope Leo X as an old sinner and hypocrite and confesses he prefers him to the fanatic trouble-maker Luther — pp. 38—40 of the edition quoted in note 101 to Section IX above — and such as Bertrand Russell's 1899 study of German Socialism, which he deemed cruel and which he conjectured would soon take over, and he hoped the socialists be rather kindly inconsistent than cruelly consistent.

In a similar vein Samuel Butler advocated hypocricy in the end of his *Erewhon Revisited*, and so did Bernard Shaw and Somerset Maugham in many of their works.

The logic of the situation is odd. The polarization

nature : convention :: truth : lies

makes many people liars, and whether one approves of their lies or not depends on whether one is a conventionalist or not. Now the conventionalist who admits he lies is cynical and the one who denies it is a hypocrite; there is no other alternative. This is why hypocrisy is allegedly a flattery to truth: cynicism is an insult to truth. And this is why only naturalists hated hypocrites, whereas conventionalists, skeptics, and those who rejected the dichotomy, were more tolerant towards hypocrisy or even actually advocated it.

18. I have in mind, in particular, M. I. Finley's *The Ancient Greeks,* Chatto and Windus, Pelican, London, 1963, 1966; and his *The Ancient Economy*, Chatto and Windus, 1974. See also the somewhat intentionally idealizing H. D. F. Kitto, *The Greeks*, Penguin, 1951, which is very readable, clear, and vivid.

19. There is a dual role radicalism played in Greece: the destruction of Greek religion, and the destruction of Greek politics. This, of course, also raises the question how interdependent the two were, but this is a subsidiary question.

The traditional view is that Greek politics did not suffer from the collapse of Greek religion, and that the collapse of the Greek political system is not in the least intellectual. This view was expressed by Gilbert Murray in his *Four Stages of Greek Religion,* New York, 1912, opening of Chapter III, pp. 107—8. His view is clearly inconsistent, as he views the Alexandrean regime non-*polis,* yet Rome as a *polis* to the last. But we can easily alter or ignore the background, and anyway Murray's view of what is a *polis* and which city was a *polis* has been rejected. And so we come to the leading modern authority Martin P. Nilsson, who says, *Greek Folk Religion*, 1940, Harper Torch, New York, 1961, pp. 86—7,

"After the great victory over the Persians, Athens took the lead in commerce and in culture . . . Patriotic and even chauvinistic feelings sprang up, and in this age they could find expression only in religion . . . The Athenians gloried in being the most pious of all people and in celebrating the most numerous and magnificent festivals in honor of the gods . . .

In the long run this kind of religion was no boon for the great gods. Religion was to a certain degree secularized . . ."

And on p. 94,

"The masses were perhaps materialistic in this age. Sophists had begun to criticise belief in the gods and to prove its irrationality by arguments. Aristophanes and other comic poets mocked the gods in an incredible manner. The general public laughed at their jests and were somewhat impressed by the criticism of the Sophists, but the old belief lurked in the background . . . on certain occasions a real religious hysteria broke out. The most outstanding examples are the trials for . . . Certainly these trials had a political background . . . The good Athenians believed that they believed in the gods . . ."

It is not clear from all this whether the Sophists' assault on religion was successful enough to enable politicians to pervert religion or so unsuccessful that religion was still a powerful political weapon.

No matter. The debate is really pushed aside by Alof Gigon in his review of Martin P. Nilsson, *Geschichte der griechischen Religion, Diogenes,* Vol. 1, No. 3, Summer, 1953, pp. 114–118, p. 118: "Never in any civilization did religion find itself from the beginning and all through its history in as precarious a situation as it did in Greece". And so, the collapse of Greece cannot be put on the collapse of Greek religion. Consistent with this Gigon says in his "Ancient Philosophy, New Tasks" in the same volume, pp. 101–11, last page, ". . . the victory of Christianity is not extraneous accident. Ancient philosophy of itself was ready to go down."

E. R. Dodds, *The Greeks and The Irrational,* California University Press, Los Angeles, 1951, final chapter, asserts a similar view of the decline of Greece as its inability to cope with its own — too liberal and rationalistic — individualism.

W. K. C. Guthrie, *The Beginning, Some Greek Views on the Origins of Life and the Early State of Man,* Methuen, London, 1957, p. 104, admits very grudgingly that Greek philosophy led to the collapse of Greek society, but he, too, blames the Sophists for having "seized on the mechanistic Ionian theories of the origins of all things in support of their view that moral standards have no basis in nature but are purely relative and temporary" [and so not binding].

Without being able to quote a single piece of evidence I have the impression nonetheless that the view of the Greek philosophers as the creators of ideas that led to the collapse of Greece and of Greek society seems to be present in W. Windelband, *History of Ancient Philosophy,* especially Chapter IV, The Greek Enlightenment. I overlook, of course, the reactionary romantic literature on ancient Greek political history; but, no doubt, the idea is of romantic origins: I only center here on its counterpart in intellectual history of some rationalistic bent.

20. The views of the Enlightenment's radicalism and the Romantic reaction here offered are fairly similar to those expressed by Ernest Gellner in his "French Eighteenth Century Materialism", in D. J. O'Connor, ed., *A Critical History of Western Philosophy,* New York, 1964, reprinted in his *The Devil in Modern Philosophy,* Routledge, London and Boston, 1974, esp. pp. 119–20. For more details see my "Genius in Science", *Phil. Soc. Sci.,* Vol. 5, 1975, pp. 145–161. The sophistication and wisdom of the reactionary has by now been conceded even by the radicalists; see, for a conspicuous and important example, C. P. Snow, *The*

Two Cultures: And a Second Look, Cambridge, 1964, for his friendly comments on Dostoevsky the confirmed reactionary.

21. Zbigniew Brzezinski, *Between Two Ages, America's Role in the Techno-tronic Era,* New York, 1970, p. 138:
> *"The Bureaucratization of Boredom*
> The Communist Party of the Soviet Union has a unique achievement to its credit: it has succeeded in transforming the most important revolutionary doctrine of our age into dull social and political orthodoxy."

Also, on p. 152,
> "Shocking though it may sound to their acolytes, by the year 2000, it will be accepted that Robespierre and Lenin were mild reformers."

And, on p. 222, Brzezinski speaks of "infantile ideology."

I think this judgment is utterly false. I do prefer Russell's opposite view, as expressed in his "Zahatopolk" (*Nightmares of Eminent Persons and other Stories,* 1954, Penguin, 1962, pp. 81–127), according to which this process is the by-product of all institutionalized ideology. The corollary from Russell's view is indeed, that one should learn to transcend one's institutionalized beliefs and start thinking for oneself as soon as possible. The process, then, is the result of identifying with one's institutions, and the identification — or is it internalization — is created — the process of internalizing is a significant part of all known educational systems — in order to ensure stability. But, I say, stability can well be ensured by hypocrisy and so identification is wasteful.

It is customary among left-wingers of all sorts to be extremely harsh on Stalin. (It is no accident that the perceptive Solzhenitsyn prefers to poke fun at him and even empathize with him in his *First Circle.*) In truth, the evils of Stalinist practices are to be found in Lenin's theory and practice as Solzhenitsyn argues — and he argues very forcefully, with the aid of many quotations — in *Gulag Archipelago,* Part I, Chapter 2. And indeed, all his life Lenin got along well with reactionaries, whom he liked best next to none but his revolutionaries. He felt the two extremes understood each other very well, though from the opposite side of the barricade. That is to say, he knew that the two extremes are all the more in factual agreement the more they differed on matters of preference. And he explained this by the claim that thinking requires courage and courage leads to extremism in trying times — when extremism is called for.

This is Lenin's standard ploy in politics and economics as well as in the theory of knowledge. The thesis of his *Materialism and Empiriocriticism* of 1908 is just this: either you are a materialist or you sink into the extreme solipsism which allows only for the sensations I have just now. Even dialectics was secondary, in his view, to this polarization, since dialectics can be adduced from the facts of the real world once the real world is admitted.

22. Lenin's view that reformism is worse than reaction was restated in recent times by Herbert Marcuse: the reformist, in his improvement of the existing order, buttresses it against the revolution and is so the worst enemy of the revolution.

This criticism is valid and can even be improved upon: the best reformist is the one who improves the system so well that he makes it better than any system that any revolution might bring about. And so the best reformist is one who makes the revolution utterly redundant and so he is the greatest enemy of the revolution.

In other words, the reason that Marcuse's criticism is valid is in his taking the revolution to be more important than its goals. This is more violent than even the philosophy of Sorel.

Marx, we remember, and at times even Lenin, advocated collaboration with all reformists amongst the workers since when the reformists will be disillusioned they may join the extremists and become revolutionaries. The logic of this argument seems to me impeccable: try to improve things by peaceful means and rebel only when reform fails. The logic of Marcuse is the reverse: reformism is evil because reform succeeds!

23. I am alluding, in particular, to Thomas More's view that religion, or even the law, cannot be bent every time in a different direction to suit the rulers or the ruling party's short-term interest. If one thing is clear about the Jewish religious leadership in Israel it is that almost to a man they are willing, in order to strengthen their own political power, to violate everything that is sacred in Jewish religion. See Shulamit Aloni, *The Arrangement,* in Hebrew, and Gershon Weiler, *Jewish Theocracy,* forthcoming.

24. See, for example, Neil Harris, review of *The Irony of Early School Reform: Educational Innovation in Mid-19th Century Massachusetts* by Michael B. Katz, *Harvard Educational Review,* Vol. 39, No. 2, Spring 1969, p. 383:
"What do we do with reformers? As a group they have proven to be both fascinating and maddeningly elusive. Their stance towards the social order tends to be complex and ambivalent. Lacking the clarity [sic] of reactionaries and revolutionaries, they are totally committed to neither the old way of doing things, nor to a new order which is meant to overturn and purify. Their intentions generally outstrip their achievements, and their reputations are often more imposing than their actual accomplishments. Yet in almost every period of American history . . . some variety of reform temperament has exerted a primary force on the political, social, and intellectual life of the nation."

25. I have discussed the wonder of a pluralist society with polarized philosophies in my "Conventions of Knowledge in Talmudic Law", mentioned in note 6 to Chapter Two above.

I should add here that were our society so deeply seeped in mythical thinking as Lévi-Strauss says all preliterate societies are, then there would be no wonder here. But, clearly, even though his view applies to a surprisingly broad spectrum of literate societies, indeed even to the world of science, see Section XIII above, nonetheless literate societies as wholes are certainly not as deeply Lévi-Straussian as preliterate societies seem to be.

XXII SKEPTICISM REHABILITATED

Pluralism, let me argue, is skeptical. And it is not easy to be skeptical.[26] To begin with, historically, pluralism was skeptical. Even Lessing, the child of the Age of Reason, supported pluralism by a skeptical fable: a father gives his three sons three rings, only one of which is genuine, but they know not which it is. Yet Lessing was a radicalist. Kant tried but failed to reconcile radicalism and skepticism. Robespierre combined radicalism with logic and bred intolerance.

The myth illustrating the impossibility of skepticism is related as an anecdote concerning the father of skepticism, the Greek philosopher Pyrrho. The anecdote relates to his attitude towards his teacher in skepticism. Here we see, incidentally, the true mythical moment: the father of skepticism has a teacher in skepticism, just as the father of the Gods, Zeus, has a father, Kronos. Well, then, Pyrrho's teacher fell into a ditch; Pyrrho was taking his constitutional when he saw him in his predicament, contemplated the case for and against pulling him out, came to no conclusion, and continued with his daily walk. The end of the story is that others, who saved Pyrrho's teacher, blamed Pyrrho for his heartlessness, but his teacher praised his consistency. Here we see that skeptical inaction is praised as consistency; this praise is but the false doctrine which says, doubt paralyzes. Indeed there is another anecdote, which Pierre Bayle calls a bad joke, which says that Pyrrho could not even take his constitutional, that he was utterly paralyzed by his skepticism. God knows how often this folly has been mustered as the final blow to skepticism.[27]

The practical corollary to the theory, doubt paralyzes, is that it is evil to take a man's faith away from him without replacing it. That is to say, destructive criticism is always evil but constructive criticism is at times beneficial. Now, how am I going to find a new theory unless I am dissatisfied with the old one, and how am I going to find a new one if doubt paralyzes? But we need not cling to this argument (which only comes to explain, anyway, why the demand for constructive criticism and against destructive criticism leads to dogmatism).[28] We have as much empirical evidence as we wish to refute the classic anti-skeptical contention.[29] We can also illustrate that often we follow advice which we doubt most profoundly, given by a colleague or by mother-in-law, by a doctor or by a clergyman, by the gang in the club or by the expert.[30] Often we do things out of sheer despair, hoping for nothing and believing in less. If doubt paralyzes then all this would be very different from what it is.[31]

But the theory, doubt paralyzes, has its hold on us, even while we act in a manner which illustrates its falsity. We impose on ourselves in these cases a form of controlled schizophrenia – in Koestler's sense – and try to numb our feeling. True to schizophrenia, we treat our own selves in these cases as if we were mere robots – robots who act indifferently in accord with strict specifications. I think we all have had such experiences, I think these experiences are harmful, because too taxing emotionally, and I think they are utterly unnecessary and re- placeable by the rejection of, or the disbelief in, the doctrine that doubt paralyzes. [32] I think, finally, that when the emotional burden due to such experiences is too heavy – for example when a researcher who has come to an utterly blind alley concerning a practically im- portant topic tries a wild idea and stays with it longer than he had anticipated – then something snaps, and we commit ourselves to be- lieve in the idea we explore. This produces cranks. The existence of cranks proves to us the danger of exploring outlandish ideas, however tentatively, and this reinforces the idea that science should be re- sponsible and stick to fact and suspend judgement [33] on unproven theory, i.e. not test or examine a theory for long. This, in turn, is the good old polarization between scientific belief – which is in nature – and all else as mere appearance, lies, superstition, etc.

The true radicalist tries to stay aloof from all emotional attach- ments which he cannot rationalize. The collectivist feels the need to feel loyal even to what is beneath him and to feel no sympathy with foreign societies and customs which seem to him more civilized. In particular, if he is sophisticated, he fears being uprooted and alienated, but he fears submersion no less. He feels the need to feel loyal to his habitat and that loyalty goes beyond criticism and reason; but reason does not always allow us to transcend it. Doubts gnaw and paralyze because they are supposed to paralyze – not quite, but enough to ruin self-confidence and reinforce the view that doubt is evil. The way one tries to overcome reasonable doubts is to preach the doubted doctrine in the hope of being infected with one's audience's enthusiasm. The doubter will bully his audience and tell them they must believe in something with an insistence which betrays a personal motive – the hope to have faith and thereby find salvation. This is reinforced by the unhappiness of the radicalist – just as the unhappiness of the collec- tivist reinforces the radicalist. Myths, in their polarities, think for us, says Lévi-Strauss.

I am not speaking of mere demagogues or of village priests and school masters. Even when we speak of scientific method, which is tra- ditionally radicalist, and we take the least radicalist methodologists, the celebrated Karl Popper and the popular Thomas S. Kuhn, we can find that the one thing they both agree about is the loyalty to science and the need for some dogmatism even in science. I find this most impressive and most frightening.[34]

There is no need, *a priori,* to ask, what do these thinkers want a scientist to be dogmatic for? Let us assume that for some purpose a certain measure of dogmatism is required. Why then can the person of whom dogmatism is required, why then can he not simply act as a dogmatist? Why will feigning dogmatism not do and why is faith, dogmatic commitment, required? The answer one might offer is, one cannot act as a dogmatist unless one is. It is an empirical fact that such a theory is refuted. And hence, there is no need to inquire into the reason for the readiness Popper and Kuhn show to support dogmatism: it is misplaced.

It is not that I am picking on Popper and on Kuhn. Nor is it that I merely wish to illustrate the trapping of the ancient polarization on thinkers today: I hope that my illustration is very characteristic. I think that in political science and in politics the advocacy of the thesis, we need a measure of dogmatism, led to much evil and corruption. Julien Benda and George Orwell have exposed this corruption. Benda did not explain it, except perhaps as a manifestation of original sin. George Orwell is only slightly more sophisticated. He said that the corruption is due to the snobbism of the intellectuals, their power worship.[35] For my part, I think Sorel's perversity[36] is characteristic of some intellectuals' insane effort to be sincere:[37] not so much that they worship power, as that they see in violence the best protestation of sincerity.[38] I see in the oddest conduct of the intellectuals a desperate effort to practice what they preach, to be sincere, to believe what they practice, etc. Like Sorel they see in acts of violence the supreme expression of sincere commitment.

Let me quote a few sentences from Karl W. Deutsch's most modernistic, game theoretical, cybernetistic, sophisticated *The Nerves of Government, Models of Political Communication and Control* of 1963.[39] I am quoting from page 69.

"Any premature application of these ideas [brinkmanship] would be an irresponsible use of a brilliant and responsible book [of Thomas C. Schelling, which advocates brinkmanship]. Theorists must be free to make certain experiments in their minds, precisely in order to save us all the disastrous costs of making them in reality. The crucial point is that Professor Schelling's intellectual experiments, as well as his analysis of them, are quite unfinished . . . little or no empirical evidence . . . has been used . . ."

Let me stress, that eminently reasonable as Deutsch's paragraph is, it is unfortunately not going to convince people who wish to be consistent in their beliefs in a peculiar way. The passage condones an author's belief in his idea since he has to think it out, but forbids the public believing it since it is still uncertain. But uncertainty is either the fate of all ideas, or else, when the public thinks about it seriously for some time then the same style of sincerity which made the author believe it will make the public believe the same.[40]

I confess that when thought experiments such as Herman Kahn's were published, I was a bit puzzled by the outcry by some intellectuals. I now understand: Following the logic just discussed, they rightly feel that if they worry long enough and hard enough about thermonuclear war they may learn to love it. And when the movie — science fiction, I hope — with the subtitle, *How I Learned to Stop Worrying and Love the Bomb,* appeared, regardless of how slapstick the movie was, they incredibly identified with Dr. Strangelove, the most strange ex-Nazi scientist in it, and then they were (rightly) insulted. I could not believe that people could make such a mental exercise and identify with such an absurd caricature only to feel insulted. (It is allright to be bored, but to be hurt of course betrays a greater weakness.) I underestimated the impact which the fundamental polarizations of Greek philosophy have on social scientists who, with love for neither Greece nor philosophy, manage to apply the fundamental polarization even when they are invited to enjoy a light-hearted satire on a serious matter. Perhaps, then, I should also talk against the polarization between seriousness and levity. But as Shakespeare and Cervantes have failed here I do not aspire to do any better.

Notes to Section XXII

26.   If the Sun and Moon should doubt,
       They'd immediately go out
             William Blake, The Tiger, Stanza 6

   The faculty of doubting is rare among men. A few choice spirits
   carry the germ of it in them, but these do not develop without training.
             Anatole France, *Penguin Island,* Bk. VI. Ch. 2

   We are divided in our faith and united in our doubt.
             Peter Ustinov

   The first two quotes are taken from Bartlett's *Book of Quotations.*

27.   Pierre Bayle, *Dictionary*, Art. Pyrrho.
   The latest application I found of this brilliant idea is in D. M. Armstrong,

"Epistemological Foundations for a Materialistic Theory of the Mind", *Philosophy of Science,* Vol. 40, June 1973, pp. 178–193, p. 185, italics in the original:

"It must be admitted that there are certain *philosophers*, at the present times, in particular, some of those influenced by the thought of Karl Popper [meaning myself, no doubt] who are inclined to deny that science does yield knowledge. They cannot be accused of not being conversant with the scientific enterprise, and it would be impolite to urge that their judgment is hopelessly impared on the matter."

So much for the unpleasant existence of skeptics. They are then dismissed in one paragraph:

"If, however, we turn from their explicit pronouncements to what they implicitly assume in the same page or lecture, there is reason to assert that, although they say these things about scientific knowledge, they do not really believe them. Their scientific references make it quite clear that there is a huge body of scientific fact which they do not seriously doubt. They are like the lady who wondered why more people were not convinced by the arguments for solipsism."

Mrs. Ladd-Franklin, who wrote to Bertrand Russell "I am a solipsist; why isn't everybody?", is supposed to have refuted herself both by writing to Russell and by mentioning everyone else. I cannot consider this a straight matter. I often meet old friends who once were very much alive, and thus open to criticism, but who are now no longer capable of accepting criticism. Even though I know this, I naturally slip into debates with them – out of habit, out of friendship, and willing to grant them the benefit of doubt. Now just as I argue with opponents who are not really there, so Mrs. Ladd-Franklin may write to and talk about people who do not really exist; after all, being a solipsist she doesn't even think she really writes. Talking back to a television commercial is another prevalent example.

Solipsism is, thus, quite consistent with normal social behavior. Of course, solipsists may be unable to explain things – but then they may not care much for explanation. It is here that behaviorism is quite weaker than solipsims: as it claims scientific status it is obviously incumbent on it to explain, but in its insistence on reporting experiences only, it is solipsistic, as Russell has noted.

As to the view that since I accept much scientific information as true my skepticism is insincere or else my "judgment is hopelessly impaired on the matter", I have discussed this in logical detail, I think, in my "The Standard Misinterpretation of Skepticism", *Philosophical Studies,* Vol. 22, 1971, pp. 49–50, reprinted in my *Science in Flux,* Reidel, Dordrecht and Boston, 1975. Briefly, the dogmatists insist that action bespeaks conviction instead of seeing in hesitant actions the refutation of their dogmatism.

28. The demand for constructive criticism is only an excuse to silence the critic – even in cases where, quite obviously, one cannot throw away the dirty water before procuring clean water. The desire to silence critics seems to me easier to gratify by frankly declaring one's intention. For my part I do not quite understand the fear of criticism that makes one refuse to listen even to interesting or useful criticism.

29. The view that beliefs influence action has been amply refuted in empirical tests. See, for example, Milton Rokeach, *Beliefs, Attitudes, and Values,* Jossey Bass, Inc., San Francisco, 1968, p. 80:

"Our three experiments and some of the others referred to in this chapter suggest that the importance of racial attitude *per se* as determinants of racial discrimination have been greatly overestimated and the importance of similarity of beliefs correspondingly underestimated. . . . Reinforcing these findings is Malof and Lott's findings (1962) that highly prejudiced white subjects significantly reduced their conformity behavior in an Asch-type experiment when they receive support . . ."

Asch-type experiments are those where the subject has the exclusive choice between speaking his mind and expressing agreement with his peers.

All this experimental material merely illustrates Michael Banton's point (*White and Coloured. The Behaviour of British People Towards Coloured Immigrants,* Rutgers University Press, 1960) that whether people behave well or not may depend solely on the fact that the leading voice of the company is a clergyman or a thug. Rokeach does not refer to Banton, but research can show his impact on race and prejudice studies in this direction.

One may always rescue the theory that people act on their beliefs by *ad hoc* hypotheses, especially regarding an actor's meta-beliefs. For example, I believe one thing and the doctor believes another, but I also believe the doctor's belief superior. For people not familiar with the literature on rational belief, whether eighteenth-century or modern, this sounds eminently convincing. In fact, however, this is giving up the doctrine altogether. We may, of course, reinstate a variant of it by developing a new — there is none yet in evidence — theory of rational (as opposed to authoritarian) meta-beliefs and discuss the question, if belief and meta-belief clash, under which conditions which one wins? (How far do I listen to the doctor and disregard my own opinions in spite of empirical evidence?) When this be done it will be found necessary, in due course, to take recourse to the meta-meta-level. Oh, this is ancient knowledge, discovered and rediscovered in each generation the hard way.

And, of course, there is no end in sight. If you trust your doctor more than you trust yourself, whom does your doctor trust? The answer is simple: he has a blind faith because he too believes the dogma that doubt paralyzes. See Eliot Friedson, *Profession of Medicine, A Study of the Sociology of Applied Knowledge,* New York, 1970, pp. 168–9.

"Given a commitment to action and a practical solution, in the face of ambiguity the practitioner is more likely to manifest a certain will to believe in the value of his actions than to manifest a skeptical detachment. (How could a present day psychiatrist work if he really believed studies which emphasize the unreliability of diagnosis and the undemonstrability of success of psychotherapy? And how could physicians work . . .?)
. . . One whose work requires practical application to concrete cases simply cannot maintain the same frame of mind as the scholar or scientist: he cannot suspend action in the absence of incontrovertible evidence or be skeptical of

himself, his experience, his work and its fruit. In emergencies he cannot wait
for the discoveries of the future . . ."

30. See Michael Banton, *White and Coloured, The Behaviour of British People
Towards Coloured Immigrants,* Rutgers University Press, 1960, Chapter VI, When
Custom Fails. See also Appendix I, Ten Commandments of Inter-Group Relations,
Propositions 5 and 6 (p. 191), about the importance of initiative in leading people
to act.

31. For a detailed discussion of the content of this paragraph see my "Imperfect
Knowledge", *Philosophy and Phenomenological Research,* Vol. 32, 1972, pp. 465—
477; "Positive Evidence as a Social Institution", *Philosophia,* Vol. 1, 1970,
pp. 143—157, and "Positive Evidence in Science and Technology", *Philosophy of
Science,* Vol. 37, 1970, pp. 261—270, reprinted in my *Science in Flux,* Reidel,
Dordrecht and Boston, 1975.

32. For the term "controlled schizophrenia" see Arthur Koestler, *The Sleepwalkers, A History of Man's Changing View of the Universe,* Hutchinson, London,
1959, pp. 73 and 518; see also pp. 100—103 there, and his *The Ghost in the
Machine,* Macmillan, New York, 1968, pp. 259—265 and references to his other
works there.

33. The idea that mental illness is a sort of privilege is, of course, ancient, and
"holy madness" is its widespread expression. In modern times it was first advocated by C. G. Jung, who repeatedly claimed that in a psychotic delusion the
patient reports things he has not personally acquired, but rather drew up from the
depth of the collective subconscience. Already Freud has encountered phenomena
of extremely clear and vivid memory of events not accessible to their reporters;
yet he insisted on explaining them away.

   In modern political terms we can say, mental illness is a political privilege, an
exemption — justified (by Jung) or not (by Freud) — from social responsibility.
This is Thomas S. Szasz's starting point. And I find his liberalism magnificent. For
a criticism of his view see Y. Fried and J. Agassi, *Paranoia, a Study in Diagnosis,*
Reidel, Dordrecht and Boston, 1976.

34. See notes 5—8 to Introduction above.

35. For Orwell's view of the attraction that left-wing politics exerts on certain
intellectuals see note 103 to Section IX above, where Orwell's view is compared
with that of Silone and Koestler.

36. The perversity of Sorel is amply illustrated in his celebrated "Letter to Daniel
Halevy" which serves as the introduction to his *Reflections on Violence* (1908),
trans. T. E. Hulme and J. Roth, new edition with an introduction by E. A. Shils,
Free Press, Glencoe, 1950, reproduced in Carl Cohen, ed., *Communism, Fascism,*

Democracy, The Theoretical Foundations, Random House, New York, 1962, pp. 321–6. The following excerpt should quite suffice; notice the accent on sincerity in the middle passage.

"In employing the term myth I believed that I made a happy choice, because I thus put myself in a position to refuse any discussion whatever with the people who wish to submit the idea of a general strike to general criticism . . .

. . . a myth which gives to socialism such high moral value and such great sincerity. It is because the theory of myths tends to produce such fine results that so many seek to dispute it.

No failure proves anything against socialism since the latter has become a work of preparation (for revolution); if they are checked it merely proves that the apprenticeship has been insufficient; they must set to work again with more courage, persistence, and confidence than before . . ."

So much for quotations from Sorel. A valiant attempt to present his views in an orderly and reasonable fashion can be found in Preston King, *Fear of Power, An Analysis of Anti-Statism in Three French Writers*, Frank Cass, London, 1967, pp. 68–91, especially pp. 75 and 83. According to King, p. 90, it was a "typically liberal contractual assumption" of possible harmony without conversion. This assumption leads to explaining the existence of disharmony and conversion as due to a mere conspiracy. (The conspiracy theory of society, incidentally, is quite generally an explanation schema taken as explanation, and so half-way between explaining and explaining away. I have discussed the error of taking an explanation schema for an explanation as the mark of pseudo-science in my "The Nature of Scientific Problems and Their Roots in Metaphysics" mentioned in note 8 to Section I.)

J. L. Talmon says in the conclusion of his "The Legacy of Georges Sorel", *Encounter*, Vol. 34, No. 2, February 1970, pp. 47–60, "The revulsion from 'hypocrisy' and the resulting quest for 'authenticity' very easily evolve into a glorification of instinct and direct action. The condemnation of arbitrariness and the craving for certainty can so rapidly take the form of an apologia for an élite and its cult of violence. The emphasis upon the existential situation or collective myth has as its corollary the denial of individual judgment and personal decision . . . Finally the Manichean confrontation between the forces of darkness and of light . . . easily becomes a warrant for violence without end."

37. The idea that the advocacy of violence is an expression of sincerity, and that it is quite unconvincing, has been expressed by Karl Popper, in his "Utopia and Violence", *The Hibbert Journal*, Vol. 46, 1948, reprinted in *Conjectures and Refutations, The Growth of Scientific Knowledge*, Basic Books, New York, 1963, 1965, pp. 355–363, p. 357, note, where he quotes Jaspers to say genuine love must be cruel and adds: "This attitude, to my mind, reveals weakness rather than the strength it wishes to show; it is not so much plain barbarism as an hysterical attempt to play the Barbarian". Later in life, incidentally, Jaspers' barbarian sadism turned into a humanistic masochism: *The Question of German Guilt*, trans. E. B. Ashton, Dial Press, 1947, Capricorn Books, New York, 1961, p. 32, "Metaphysical Guilt" ". . . If I was present at the murder of others without risking my life to prevent it, I feel guilty in a way not adequately conceivable either legally, politically or morally . . ."

38. It is a fact, known to criminologists and even to viewers of old movies of the 'thirties like "Little Caesar" and "Enemy of the People", that one is not trusted in criminal society unless one is wanted by the police for more than questioning. It is this sense of being committed to the life of crime, namely the sense of having one's bridges burned, that is extremely common in professional life as well. Thus, the reason for the requirement of high and seemingly pointless standards of scholarship, discussed in the Introduction above, is to demand that a scholar is committed, to impose specialization on scholars; similarly educators destroy talents and more so independence of mind. See George Santayana, *The German Mind,* originally *Egotism in German Philosophy,* Thomas Corwell Co., New York, 1968, Chapter VII, p. 80, "An ideal education" à la Fichte, he says, "must make men over so that they shall be incapable of willing anything but what the education wills them to will. The statesmen then rely upon its subjects, 'for whoever has a well-grounded will, wills what he wills for all eternity'."

The view that freedom of thought, once exercized, becomes uncontrollable, belongs to Robert Boyle and Spinoza. See note 72, Section V above. See also my "Rationality and the *Tu Quoque* Argument", *Inquiry,* Vol. 16, 1973, pp. 395–406.

39. Peter H. Merkl, " 'Behavioristic' Tendencies in American Political Science", in Heinz Eulan, ed., *Behavioralism in Political Science,* Atherton Press, New York, 1969, pp. 141–152, ends by saying that "theory has to be derived from induction" and praising his school for its inductivism. He appends to this a final note:

"This absence of a sound foundation in the philosophy of science is often the weakest aspect of the new research methods. But now, see Abraham Kaplan, *The Conduct of Inquiry: Methodology for Behavioral Sciences* (San Francisco, Chandler Publishing Company, 1964); and Karl W. Deutsch, *The Nerves of Government: Models of Political Communication and Control* (New York: The Free Press, 1963), Chapter 1."

Jokes apart, I am afraid Deutsch cannot assure us that brinkmanship has not won by the logic of the situation of all sides in the nuclear armament race.

40. See Sir Karl Popper, "On the Sources of Our Knowledge and Ignorance" in his *Conjectures and Refutations,* pp. 3–30, especially Section IX, for the Greek origins of these ideas discussed here: the view that we should purge the mind of all error and that dialectics rinses the mind as a preparation for science seems to be Aristotle's. Yet it was Sir Francis Bacon who made the most of it in his *Novum Organum,* thus reviving radicalism; and it was he who stressed that dwelling on an erroneous view causes a commitment to it. Yet Bacon's radicalism is also more radical than Greek radicalism in that he explicitly said we could give up all errors without even bothering to argue about them. (I have discussed Bacon's radicalism at length in my doctoral dissertation, University of London, 1956, unpublished.)

XXIII CULTURE IS NO BURDEN

Back from popular intellectual responses and a slapstick science fiction movie to Sir Karl Popper. He has offered us a new philosophical anthropology in his imposing *The Open Society and Its Enemies* of 1945, where he speaks of the strain of civilization and the cross of civilization.[41]

Popper sees in us a natural tendency towards the concrete, towards a concrete society which tends to be face-to-face and so closed and so tribal. He thinks our aspirations for freedom, however, push us towards an open society and so an abstract one. We are all doomed, then, to suffer alienation as it is now called, or the strain of civilization as he calls it (the alienation philosophers dislike civilization and he approves of it, and this is reflected in their difference of terminology).

Here,[42] Popper is in error on a few counts. Tribal society need not be closed and closed societies are not all tribal even by his own admission. And we can easily create face-to-face subsocieties which thrive on the openness of the societies in which they are fruitfully embedded. And he errs while, if not because, he endorses the old Protestant maxim: work and suffer with a stiff upper lip. First he says, he offers no philosophical anthropology, not knowing what the nature of man is. Then he expounds a theory of an inherent strain which we should bear as our cross. Popper says explicitly, we do not know what of our conduct is inherent, what is learned; he says it is hard to know even what a young ape learns. Yet, he says we are inherently concretists and, so, tribal, and he therefore advocates tribalistic modes of education: teachers may and perhaps even should exploit the sense of loyalty of their pupils — although of course strictly and solely in order to make them morally autonomous, intellectually independent, and socially and politically quite anti-tribalist.[43]

Let me say at once that I find this point to be the most harmful part of Popper's teaching — potentially and even in practice. I do not object to tribalism, and I think one can belong to a tribe without committing oneself to exploiting a student's loyalty to his teacher. And I think such exploitation is abhorrent, event if it is done for the best purpose and for the student's own good. In particular, I say, the teacher does not know what he is doing. He may offer his student a "good" ideal self-image and thus cause him much self-disappointment due to inability to live up to his self-image, and thus cause him much harm.[44] Also, in his mere attempt to appeal to his student's sense of loyalty he may reinforce that sense of loyalty and dependence to an extent that does more harm than all the good which the teacher may credit himself for. And the teacher may even be in no position to observe the damage, which becomes manifest only in his absence.[45]

This is not an idle speculation; it tallies all too well with Lorenz's theory of learning as trigger action of something inbuilt.[46] Let us take an example which is interesting as an illustration of one's ignorance of what one does. Chicks, says Lorenz, have an inbuilt mechanism for pecking the ground. The mechanism is released by seeing an act of pecking — usually performed by the chicken who is the mother. Without such a release, says Lorenz, a chick may starve to death. This raises a simple question: how do chicks in a hatchery learn to peck? There is no mother there. Well, the release may be the sight of a simulation of a pecking, such as knocking on the ground with a pencil. But there is no mother and no pencil in the hatchery. It seems, then, that the person in charge of the hatchery has some idea about the situation, since he can be regularly seen attempting to induce the chicks to eat. He talks to them, he imitates a chicken flapping her wings, he rubs his hands, and so forth. From Lorenz's study we learn that *inter alia*, from here to there, sooner or later, he makes the right move; namely, hits the board with his finger and releases at least one chick's pecking mechanism. This is not to say that he knows what he is doing, since a task of one move takes him a few minutes; but this is not to say that he has no knowledge at all, or else he would not be bothering himself in the first place.

The person just described seems to me the best model of the educator, on one condition. I would expect him, after reading this page, to try to release the chick's pecking mechanism the easy way and if it works stick to it. If he refuses, then he is just about a perfect example of our modern educators.

This is not just a simile. Whether education releases Lorenzian mechanisms is not known, but their existence in man is there allright. Let me describe an event which takes a split second, i.e. one or two tenths of a second, a near accident. One driver is negligent, the other looks hard at him, praying. Query: did the prayer help avert the accident at the very last split second? Some twenty years ago I would have said with no hesitation, no; of course not. Today, under the impact of Lorenz, I would be hesitant. Possibly an intense praying stare releases an alarm mechanism. This may be an empirically testable hypothesis. For example, after witnessing the near accident the negligent driver will be filled with fear. Yet, he may also feel a general sense of friendship, of strange camaraderie, an abstract sense of brotherhood. This may be attributed to the sense of love of life, awakened by the sense of near-death; perhaps it was awakened, released, by the intense stare — quite unknowingly.

This may be so, and tests to examine it are not difficult to design. Lorenz has compared man to any aggressive animal, in a manner complimentary to neither. I think my example, if it be true, or if any other one like it be found, may illustrate that some innate qualities we have may show man to be a social animal[47] who is not tribal or parochial, and who is not half as acquisitive as Lorenz would have us believe.

The difficulty we have to find out what is natural, instinctive if you will, stems in part from our education for tribalistic loyalty which is not natural. In this way convention enters our lives at an early stage, and most naturally, so-to-speak. This is not to advocate the return to nature, let me remind you, but to argue that the natural, when and to the extent that it is discovered, may turn out to be abstract, strange. Yet educationally it may turn out to be more useful than the plain old tribalist loyalty still advocated in Popper's educational theory as a tool for educational uses.

Lorenz's theory of the release of inborn mechanisms was used by later studies of child psychology, mainly of Piaget and Chomsky. Both think that a child learns by himself, but unlike Rousseau's *Emile,* they say, the child must live in a social milieu, not in the bosom of Nature. Thus the question how come a child learns this language rather than that is reconciled with the view of language as inborn mechanism. The mechanism is here, as abstract as language can be, which is neither English nor Bantu nor any other concrete language.

The question is, can this be exploited? [48] Perhaps as it stands it cannot. For, society is here much too passive — it is merely there to be imitated in some release mechanism. Now, no doubt, many parents think they teach their children language by ostensive definitions: this is an eye, this is a nose, this is a chair. No doubt they are mistaken. Yet it does not follow that teaching in an active manner and a more efficient manner than this games does not go on: indeed parents do take an active part in the process of language acquisition;[49] remember the farmer who both imitates the chicken flapping her wings and taps a board with his finger, one act being useless and the other essential.

Indeed, a number of followers of Chomsky have already criticized him[50] on the point of the social setting of language acquisition.[51] I will not enter their criticism. Also, quite intuitively, whatever happens to a learner of the mother tongue may be transferred perhaps by a teacher of a foreign language.[52] Recent discoveries of the importance of sentence intonation and of certain aspects of accent were used by foreign language teachers, especially by Gattegno, who taught students to manipulate creatively a stock of no more than 100 words, and who eliminated all memorizing from learning.[53]

This great success can, I suppose, be much increased. Here is a proposal which may be tested, and perhaps used perhaps refuted; in any case, it is of interest for the present discussion as an example of how what seems natural may instead be an impediment.

It seems to me obvious[54] that babies learn language by using certain sounds known onomatopoetically in American English as kuchi-koo or in Yiddish as putsiniu mutsiniu. It is a known significant fact that kuchikoo differs in different parts of the world, much depending on local language and even on local dialect and local musical idiom. These differences can be studied and taught, and, I should think, teaching them should much accelerate learning. Learning of a language is better unimpeded by orthography.[55] It seems to me obviously advantageous to learn a language not only purely orally, but also as closely to the way babies do as possible.[56] But there is a snag here. Experiments show that the use of kuchikoo amongst adults creates very strong embarassment.[57] The explanation may be Freudian. The Freudian explanation of a mother's excessive outrage at her child's play with excrement, we remember, is the mother's own repressed wish or desire to do the same. We know that some men forbid their wives saying kuchikoo to their children. We know that the mothers at times have a strong urge to do so nonetheless, and if they are liberated educated women they are at times themselves most embarassed about it – because, I suppose, they have very strongly internalized the repressing ideas. Yet, I suppose it is not too utopian to hope that such repressions may be overcome almost totally for all practical purposes.[58]

Notes to Section XXII

41. The cross of civilization is for Popper no mere metaphor. "Of course, every student is fallible", he says in his "Moral Responsibility of the Scientist", *Encounter*, Vol. 32, No. 3, March 1969, pp. 52–57, p. 53.

   ". . . everybody is bound to make mistakes, even the greatest thinkers. Though this fact should encourage us not to take our mistakes over-seriously, we must resist the temptation to look upon our mistakes leniently: the establishment of high standards to judge our work by, and the duty constantly to raise these standards by hard work, are indispensable."

I find the hortatory tone, the moral view, the anthropological view, the empirical generalization, of this passage, quite beyond reasonable debate: they reflect not a thinker but a bag of relics or survivals – some old-fashioned misanthropic dangerous paraphernalia that have managed to stay along in the mind of a great humanist and a great thinker.

Worse remarks are present in the same work, such as, 'The student . . . owes loyalty to all his teachers who freely and generously share with him their knowledge and enthusiasm." This is licence for professors of the old European school, including Sir Karl himself, to treat their students, at least those to whom they show great devotion, as mere extensions of .themselves. Of course, Popper would also have them listen attentively to their students' criticisms and work hard on it; but this does not release the student from the bond of loyalty.

I therefore withdrew my criticism of E. Gellner's characterization of Popper's moral philosophy in his "On Being Wrong" (*Rationalist Annual*, 1955, pp. 74–81 and his *The Devil in Modern Philosophy*, Routledge, London and Boston, 1974, pp. 45–51) as presented in my *Towards an Historiography of Science*, note 149, p. 109 and I declare my view as expressed there more Popperian than Popper's. See also my "The Last Refuge of the Scoundrel", *Philosophia*, Vol. 4, 1974, pp. 315–317, where all loyalty is criticized as opposed to individual responsibility.

42.   There is a perennial confusion among individualists who all contrast the individual's responsibility which is the pillar of the open society with the herd instinct which is the pillar of primitive tribalism. For the herd instinct is primitive, indeed, but it operates in a mob better than in a tribal organization. Any organization can be endorsed by responsible individuals, including tribal ones. So tribal open societies are at least logically possible, and, Berek Gross argues, such was the ideal of Moses and perhaps also of Solon. The closed society, as characterized by Popper, is one where individuals are deprived of any sense of responsibility or the need to make decisions. In this Popper follows all sorts of thinkers from Plato to Aldous Huxley (*Brave New World*); yet the idea that the lack of a sense of responsibility has to be supplemented, that in itself it is alienation, as well as the idea that it can be supplemented by a revamped herd instinct, this idea belongs to Hegel et co. and though Popper is critical of it he is still under its spell. E. Gellner has argued that any modern state needs a system of education that provides what is reliably taken later on as public knowledge. Now the means to impose such a common background that comes very handy is, indeed, the herd instinct. One can see it operate even among groups of intellectuals such as physicists, Oxford philosophers, etc., who respond like a herd when their common knowledge is challenged – intentionally or not – by declaring the challenger to be an outcast, ignoramus, and such, without allowing him to state his case. This is why I view even men of science as tribalist (see notes 5 to 8 to the Introduction); but I thereby fall into the common confusion, since I do not quite mean that they are a herd. Now, no doubt, the herd mentality of such a diverse and scattered group as

men of a given discipline must have some conspicuous weather vanes. It is even easy to assume a hierarchy of weather vanes, and the confusion of herds and tribes will lead to view these as a hierarchy of a tribal leadership or of a church like the Catholic Church of Rome (a triple or quadruple confusion, that of lack of decision with herd mentality with a tribal and a quasi-tribal hierarchy). John von Neumann admitted to the existence of the hierarchy — which I think is very nice, even though confused, since he was not proud of being a kind of bishop.

Popper, to conclude, speaks of tribalism only in the sense of the return to tribalism. This is a bit hard on the primitive tribesman who never left his way of life. Yet, no doubt, on this point Popper is right: irrationalism is an attempt to revive prerational innocence, which is obviously impossible, unless we destroy civilization so thoroughly that it will be forgotten. Science fiction is full of both super-modern tribes and newly primitive ones.

43. See Popper, *Open Society,* Chapter 25, final section, p. 276.

Popper's theory rests on the assumption that children cannot be autonomous, though educators should try to make them so. All I can concede is that children can more easily be robbed of their autonomy than adults, and even this only on the whole and only in a certain way: It is easy to fool a child to prefer love to respect, and the trappings of love to the real thing (Shaw, *Getting Married*). This, no doubt, is an archaism, and by no means confined to children. In particular, it is easy to fool an adult to perfer suspicion to respect, and the trappings of suspicion to the real thing.

Almost every theory of education is wrong chiefly because it does not take account of children's autonomy. And, experience shows, prejudice is very strong here. I suppose the only way to make serious progress is to make suffrage utterly universal, and if anyone is too young or weak to go to the polls, then they will be physically unable to exercize the right to vote. The main argument, then, against universal suffrage is that children will not know how to use their right to vote. This argument is valid, and was used by Plato against democracy as such. Think of the educational value of kindergartens going to the polls!

44. The (really Adlerian) view of all neurosis (and, *a fortiori,* psychoses) as rooted in too violent a polarization between an individual's ideal self-image and (allegedly) realistic one is ascribed to Karen Horney by Robert C. Tucker, who, in the beginning of Chapter I, on p. 32, of his *Philosophy and Myth in Karl Marx,* Cambridge University Press, 2nd edition, 1972, sums up her view in a forceful note (Chapter I is on "the self as God in German philosophy", and is one of the earliest applications of Freudianism to Romanticism):

"A noted psychiatrist, the late Dr. Karen Horney, considers that self-deifying pride is the nucleus of the neurotic type of personality. A person who has been able to find a sense of identity only through pride transfers his energies into the drive to actualize his idealized image of himself, this is what self-realization comes to mean to him. He develops a set of coercive inner dictates by which he seeks to mould himself into the absolute self. Since he is only human, however, the effort necessarily falls short of its goal. A rift opens up in the personality, for the person is conscious of himself as two discordant beings: the god-like being of perfection on the one hand, and the imperfect actual being on the other. He regards the actual or empirical self as an alien being and starts to despise it. The rift in the personality becomes a raging inner conflict: 'And this indeed is the essential characteristic of every neurotic: he is at war with himself' (*Neurosis and Human Growth*, p. 112). Horney uses the phrase 'neurotic process' to describe this entire pattern of self-development growing out of the quest to actualize the superhuman self."

45. In his *Childhood and Society*, in the essay on the legend of Hitler's youth, Erikson contrasts the German's insecurity, his lack of a sense of ontological security, which makes him so sensitive and inflexible, with the Jew's alleged deep sense of ontological security which made him so adaptable. Here identity and national identity merge, partly because Erikson expounds a nationalist myth, partly because he has not worked things out. Yet the very force of his description indicates the need to work it out — on lines suggested here, need I say. I think that Erikson here takes autonomy to be rooted in strong identity, a thesis empirically refutable by known cases. But I do agree that a lack of autonomy may easily — and at times in truth — be blamed on ontological insecurity. Yet the opposite of insecurity is not security, just as courage is not fearlessness but the ability to overcome and control fear. I suppose this is obviously true. See also note 42 to Section III above.

46. What I discuss in the text above is an attempt to apply Lorenz's theory of imprinting to education. One obvious corollary to Lorenz's theory is that what an animal can learn easily at a given stage it will not learn at any cost at an earlier stage. Indeed, this corollary has been observed on all sorts of animals, avian and mammal — and it surely holds for humans too, though it has not been tried yet.

But what can also be argued is that undesirable results of faulty imprinting can be eliminated; and, I think, all too easily. I have experimented with people who can't concentrate under given conditions (usually noise), who get severe headaches under given conditions (usually inability to concentrate) and such; I have found that a clear discussion of the situation and a controlled attempt to do things right overcomes the imprinting. And, though Lorenz does not discuss it, I suggest that at times an imprinting which is once overruled is entirely destroyed: any obsession, for example, can be destroyed by one single voluntary overruling.

47. See L. Eisenberg, "The *Human* Nature of Human Nature", *Science*, Vol. 176, 14 April 1972, pp. 123–128, p. 127:
"There may be much to be gained from comparative studies of animal learning — to be sure, we are primates ourselves, but primates of a very special sort . . . We have done least well at the task of encouraging the development of humane values based upon the recognition that we are a single species. The idea of brotherhood is not new, but . . ."

See also Darwin's Notebooks on Man, Mind and Materialism, p. 84, in Howard
E. Gruber, *Darwin on Man*, together with *Darwin's Early and Unpublished Note-
books*, transcribed and annotated by Paul H. Barrett, foreword by Jean Piaget,
Dutton, New York, 1974, p. 281.

"Origin of man now proved. — Metaphysics must flourish. — He who understands
baboon would do more toward metaphysics than Locke."

48. The question whether the advancements in linguistics and in anthropology
can be applied to language teaching is discussed in Sol Tax, Loren Eiseley, Irving
Rouse, Carl F. Voegelin, eds., *An Appraisal of Anthropology Today*, Chicago
University Press, Chicago, 1953, pp. 189—190. Speakers refer to the unusually
high degree of conservatism of foreign language teachers. I think that willy-nilly
conservatism gives way to spectacular success, just as witch doctors learn to use
antibiotics. Indeed, the discussants admit that the only serious alternative they
have is the total immersion program such as those developed by the US Army.
Language teachers have no objection to such programs, and indeed regret that
they cannot bully their students all day long but merely a few hours a week.

Chomsky's view of language acquisition as the triggering of an inborn mechanism explains, he says, *Aspects of the Theory of Syntax*, MIT Press, Cambridge,
Mass., 1965, p. 58, how an infant can acquire a whole language from a very small
and very faulty sample. True or false, this draws attention to the fact that language teachers unnecessarily and pedantically invest great efforts in maintaining
correctness of performance, their own as well as their charges'. And a very useful
immediate corollary to this is that they better train themselves to be much less
sensitive to errors. The same goes, of course, for violin teachers and their likes.

But there is more to that. The things that upset language teachers most is that
their charges transfer knowledge of one language to another, including grammar
and what sophisticated linguists would view as metaphysical presuppositions. And
this raises the question, how much of one language's metaphysical presuppositions
may be transferred to another. On this the literature is in its infancy.

This is surprising, since already Whorf noticed the situation, and even anticipated much of what Chomsky says. See *Language, Thought, and Reality*, Selected
Writings of Benjamin Lee Whorf, edited with introduction by John B. Carrol,
Foreword by Stuart Chase, MIT Press, Cambridge, Mass., 1956, paperback ed.
1964, p. 238:

"To rid ourselves of this [mechanistic] way of thinking is exceedingly difficult
when we have no linguistic experience of any other . . . For the mechanistic
way of thinking is perhaps just a type of syntax natural to . . . Western Indo-
European languages, rigidified.

. . . the effortless speech and the subconscious way we picked up the activity in
early childhood lead us to regard talking and thinking as wholly straightforward and transparent . . . There are here no laws of thought. Yet the
structural regularities of our sentences enable us to sense that laws are SOME-
WHERE in the background. . . .

. . . It is the grammatical background of our mother tongue . . . This fact is important for science, because it means that science CAN have a rational or logical basis even though it be a relativistic one and not Mr. Everyman's natural logic. Although it may vary with each tongue, and a planetary mapping of the dimensions of each variation may be necessitated, it is, nevertheless, a basis of logic with discoverable laws. Science is not compelled to see its thinking and reasoning procedures turned into processes merely subservient to social adjustments of emotional drives."

49. Gina R. Ortar, of the Hebrew University of Jerusalem, has examined the thesis that mothers' verbal behavior towards their infants improves their understanding in general even though they are too young to comprehend what their mothers say to them. She trained mothers to talk more to children, and younger children consequently showed, in a follow-up study, more intelligence as compared with their older siblings, and perhaps also with the control group.

Ortar's training of the mothers is interesting, and contains two important components; first, she explained the importance of it all; second, she discouraged naming in favor of more sophisticated exercizes such at teaching antonyms and clauses. For my part, I think any liberating program might have succeeded more: the best is to let mother and child interact any old way, but frequently. And, I suppose, but am not sure, Ortar herself seems to agree: she cites S. Tulkin and J. Kagan ("Mother-Child Interaction in the First Year of Life", *Child Development*, Vol. 43, 1972, pp. 31—41) to say the main difference between lower class and upper class verbal behavior is quantitative, and J. Fodor ("How We Learn to Talk: Some Simple Ways", in F. Smith and G. A. Miller, eds., *The Genesis of Language*, MIT Press, Cambridge, Mass., 1966, pp. 105—122) to say there is an enormous variety of ways to teach a language.

Of course, at a later stage of an infant's development, intellectual encouragement of all sorts matters more and more and mother's inhibitions — shame at low level of education and such — matter more and are harder to overcome. More so is father's hostility to brightness of child, learning of poetry in kindergarten, sex education in high school, etc.

I am grateful to Gina Ortar for mimeo copies of her as yet unpublished papers.

50. Chomsky tends to ignore the social — as opposed to the psychological — context both of verbal learning and of verbal conduct. Of course, the verbal ambiguities discovered by Chomsky were left unnoticed beforehand because usually the correct variant of all possible variants of an expression or a statement is chosen by the speaker and his audience so quickly that the incorrect variant is ignored. Correctness of the correct variant depends on context. The context may be accidental — when speaking, say, of the shooting of the hunter we know whether we speak of a person suffering from a gunshot or not — or psychological, or social, or even epistemic. Thus, in a Ray Bradbury classic science fiction novel, the fire-squad, of course, sets houses on fire and no one thinks it even necessary to extinguish an accidental fire, as such do not happen. Thus, when liking her cooking we do not mean that we like to watch her boiling inside the soup pot: we simply exhibit our not being cannibals. Yet Chomsky, as well as Fodor and Katz, declared that they wanted such factors out of language as they wanted language to be universal to its native speakers. See Judith Greene, *Psycholinguistics*, Penguin, London, 1972, pp. 73–4.

It is no doubt the case that some misunderstandings are rooted in verbal ambiguities caused by a change of context (quoting out of context, so-called) where context can be epistemic. That is, speakers assume they share an item of information on which, in fact, they differ. For the latest sociologically oriented reform of Chomskianism, see George Lakoff, "Interview with Herman Parret", to appear in *Discussing Language*, Mouton, The Hague. Lakoff discusses the import of "comparative semantics as a research strategy where sentences are related to meaning in a limited sorts of context" (p. 3). Likewise (p. 5), "Chomsky [too] speaks of particular languages . . . specific language-particular rules . . . Where can we reasonably draw the line? . . . Very strange indeed."

Particularly important is a generalized Whorfian hypothesis (p. 12): "A great many types of participants' assumptions in a conversation interact with the rules of grammar." Lakoff rightly suggests (p. 23) that his view may be a major departure from Chomsky. See also next note.

51. The significance of the social setting in language acquisition is not in what we call instruction, but in correction, which is the best form of coaching. For the importance of correction and for the problems involved, see Dan I. Slobin, *Psycholinguistics*, Glenview, Illinois, and London, 1971, which is, anyway, one of the better, though still not sufficiently critical, expositions of Chomsky's transformational grammar, Chapter III, "Language Developmet in the Child", particularly the section; "Theories of Language Acquisition", pp. 55–61, and references there. The most important difference a child has to learn is between the grammatical and the true. It seems to me that due to heavy doses of miseducation most adults forget or deliberately ignore or block out (cause themselves to have a mental block against) this distinction. I propose that utilizing this distinction and correcting, rather than imparting knowledge, will certainly help langauge acquisition in adults, especially when correctness will be a matter of levels, i.e. in imitating infant and child locutions.

Incidentally, I think there is a mystery here in some philosophers' concern regarding the distinction between the ungrammatical and the untrue. The distinction is not only one which every child has to learn in the process of language acquisition; it was made explicit by philosophers, ancient, medieval, and modern. It received an honorific place when, early in the century, Bertrand Russell used it to overcome his own antinomy and when Ludwig Wittgenstein soon after offered the pronouncement that all philosophical pronouncements are ungrammatical. Wittgenstein's philosophy made it impossible to assert or deny any philosophical thesis, such as, man is a mere machine, or a mere animal, etc. This, however, did not stop his disciples from holding or rejecting mechanistic views.

In the forties and fifties the term "nonsense" covered at time obviously false statements (the ordinary sense of "nonsense"); at times, the ungrammatical (technical sense of "nonsense"); so that the center of the Wittgensteinians' philosophy was the greatest crime they said a philosopher can commit, i.e. a confusion of the ordinary and the technical sense. I think the widespread of all this verbal nonsense for so long is a puzzle well worthy of further examination, perhaps even a psycholinguistic one, or an anthropological one: what does the confusion of the meaningless and the false signify? Is it only a matter of unanswered questions? (See note 7 to Section I above; see also note 68 to Section II above; see also my "The Future of Berkeley's Instrumentalism" mentioned in note 54 to Section IV.

52.   The difference between the acquisition of the mother tongue and a second or third language is discussed by Otto Jespersen, *Language, Its Nature, Development and Origin,* George Allen and Unwin, London, 1922, 10th impression, 1954, Chapter VII, 1, "Why is the Native Language Learnt So Well? "Jespersen refutes current views and offers one of his own. He assumes that people's minds are best at birth. This is at best a wild speculation, probably it is refuted in many ways. Second, a child has ample opportunity to hear his mother tongue and to have private lessons in it all day. This is refuted by so many cases of immigrants that I gasp at the poverty of the discussion. And yet, it precedes the real nugget: "There is a Slavonic proverb, 'If you wish to talk well, you must murder the language first.' But this is very often overlooked by teachers of language, who demand faultless accuracy from the beginning . . ." and he goes on attacking the teacher and observing that children often have their private languages (pp. 143–144). Jespersen goes even further and notes that babbling is a child's earliest verbal exercise. And this is even before Piaget and Norbert Wiener – which is quite a feat. Anyway, it is high time to apply all this to language training. See also *op. cit.*, Chapter VIII, 4 and 5, on playing at languages and on secret languages.

The formation of all sorts of quasi-languages, including jargons, pidgins, and creoles, has, of course, many social and psychological and technical causes. I cannot help notice, however, that certain phenomena of this sort come from surprisingly uninhibited people who may be uninhibited because their culture is so primitive (whatever this means) or even quite degenerate (as that of slum folks), or because they encounter conditions that require unusually high adjustability. In any case, they can start conversing in an utterly foreign tongue after learning a few words and hardly any grammar. This corroborates Jespersen's view of the obstacles created by teachers and so there may be a ray of hope here.

Eric H. Lenneberg expresses the view – the received one, I should think – that the cause of adults' inability to acquire a language by absorption like infants is rooted in brain physiology. See Eric H. Lenneberg, "How Babies Learn to Talk", *Parents Magazine,* Summer 1964, p. 71, reprinted in Hermann K. Bleibtreu and James F. Downs, ed., *Human Variation, Readings in Physical Anthropology,* Glencoe Press, Beverly Hills, 1971, pp. 83–90, p. 88.

Of course, this theory may be true: yet the arguments offered in its support seem to me flimsy to the extreme. We have no rudiments of explanation of how language is acquired in the child or in the adult. Even phenomenologically, the difference between illiterate immigrants who acquire a second language reasonably well and their bilingual children, is barely studied; and, what we know already is not explained. *Adults transfer knowledge from one language to another; bilingual children do not, even when they are accomplished speakers of one language before they encounter another language.*

I think this quality can be simulated and then monolingual adults can become bilingual. See my "Can Adults Become Genuinely Bilingual?" in Asa Kasher, *Language in Focus,* Bar Hillel Memorial Volume, *Boston Studies in the Philosophy of Science,* Vol. 43, 1976, pp. 473–484.

53. Caleb Gattegno, *Teaching Foreign Languages in Schools,* Educational Explorers, Reading, England, 1963. *The Silent Way in Spanish, French, English,* Educational Explorers, Reading, England, 1964–66. See also note 89 to Section XX above.

54. I should note that going to kindergartens to learn the local language requires no special sophistication or depth of understanding and many a simple immigrant as well as a poet – such as the Hebrew poetess Rachel – have found going to kindergarten the naturally right and easy thing to do.

55. "The fact that almost anyone except a professed student of language explains matters of speech [especially "incorrect" speech] by statements which really apply only to writing, is of great psychological interest" says Leonard Bloomfield, *American Speech,* Columbia University Press, 1927, Vol. 2, p. 433, reprinted in Dell Hymes, ed., *Language in Culture and Society, A Reader in Linguistics and Anthropology,* Harper and Row, New York, 1964, p. 392. Preliterate speech is unconscious, and conscious speech is derivative of conscious writing. See also note 72 to Section VII above.

This raises a very important question – both theoretically and practically important: can we learn to read and write "unconsciously", namely, incidentally to other activities and without teachers' pressures? Rousseau said we could and should; but hardly anything has ever happened in this direction. If we could – and Gattegno says we can, see quotation, note 89 to Section XX above – succeed in this, we would evidently learn to be conscious of speech and of writing in another way. For, preliterate poetic forms prove that we can be conscious of speech without writing, as Bloomfield himself records a couple of pages later.

56. The superiority of children's learning is proverbial already in ancient literature. And the proverb, you can't teach an old dog new tricks, may even define senescence. We know that most people are senescent almost as soon as puberty is over; we know that very few people retain their ability to stay young to the last. In my opinion, for what it is worth, senescence is due to two, usually interconnected factors, the traumas (learning or otherwise) which helped determine one's personality, and one's sense of identity or need for ontological security. I think we can learn to make light of identity and teach plasticity as openness to criticism and modification of one's personality or character or habits. See note 42 to Section III.

57. An interesting fact about babbling is that it is still *terra incognita*. Let me quote the *Fybeta Lecture Notes, Introduction to Linguistic Anthropology* (Anthropology 4) Berkeley, California, 1970, p. 49:

"Can you tell from a baby's babbling what language he is learning? Until recently, it was thought that we could (see Ruth Weir's *Language in the Crib*). However, several years ago Kay Atkinson recorded the babbling of six Chinese, six Russian and six English babies at six, ten, and sixteen months, and then presented the tapes to a group of laymen and linguists to see whether they could tell which language each child was being exposed to. No one got more than 60–70% correct, and the linguists did worse than the laymen."

Without debating the reliability of this information I should say it is evidently possible to train people to do much better, at least for the 16-months age group — on the basis of really elementary theorizing.

58. See note 49 above.

In Robert Borger and Frank Cioffi, eds., *Explanation in the Behavioural Sciences*, Cambridge, 1970, pp. 459–60, Max Black argues against the claim that children's facility in learning languages is an argument in favor of Chomsky's nativism. He mentions as counter-example children's ability to learn to swim, and offers the counter-hypothesis that "external facilitating conditions, such as the obvious advantage of learning the first language, the influence of adults, etc., suffice to account for the imputed difference in learning rates" between child and adult.

This argument is too poor. First the imputed difference applies to second languages no less than to first, and often a second language is learned only from children and yet becomes more like a first language than the mother's. There remains, however, the etc. which will, I suppose, be refuted if children can be emulated in detail by adults who would learn a foreign tongue in language labs equipped with tapes of baby talk, in the experiment advocated above.

The strange fact is that nativists are unable to explain the decline of the child's language acquisition facility. My explanation, that the decline is caused by teachers and the tradition they follow is consistent with nativism and is easily refuted by the failure of the experiment advocated above. Also, of course, as Chomsky observes in his comments on Black (*op. cit.*, p. 469), empiricists are unable to explain the same fact (if it is a fact, he says), and this is nearer to a refutation of empiricism.

XXIV AN IMAGE OF THE DEMOCRATIC MAN

This returns me to my suggestion about adjustability. Most societies, at present, I propose, still secure an individual's adjustment to his society by making him highly dependent on his society, to the extent that it is deeply internalized and feels natural to him. The process is that of joint conditioning and trauma (both behaviorism and Freudianism are crude theories). The result is that the individual cannot adjust to other societies; he has no access to other societies which speak unmasterable languages and have disgusting habits such as eating peas. [59]

We do not need all that; much of the rigidity of our educational system stems from the fact that it is run by individuals who have the urge to destroy free spirits "for their own good". We can try to see what will happen with education in an utterly democratic school, where the individual is not forced by bullies into molds.[60] We can see the character of resultant individuals in certain science fiction[61] works. These are highly adjustable — some of them have machines called universal translators, some of them pick up languages the way we pick up table manners. They are not shocked by people who eat peas. They are still shocked by displays of cruelty and the like, but not by the diversity of customs.

I do not wish to declare this picture true. I wish to declare that this picture may be subject to much empirical study, and this I recommend. Also, I say, this picture breaks the dichotomy, the polarization, between nature and convention. For, it is the picture of a person who can move from one convention to another, who can see convention both from the outside, as the naturalist does, and from the inside, as the conventionalist does, though in both cases with more detachment and thus with more ability to criticize. In particular, he does not think that his beliefs must accord with the conventions he practices while he practices them, and he does not despise himself as a hypocrite because of this, especially if he is ready to do something in order to improve these conventions.[62] And so he is better able to be at peace with himself.

What kind of a man is conveyed by this composite picture, the picture drawn by Isaac Asimov, Arthur C. Clarke, Fred Hoyle, and myriads of hack T.V. science fiction writers? It is hard to say because up till now the individual internalized his society by traumas and by obviously false social theories, and so he could be described only by reference to his institutions, especially his customs, particularly his more intimate ones. The science fiction man is a bit different. He can easily switch customs, even those which are rather intimate. This is surprising, since the best science fiction presents societies that are more technologically advanced than socially advanced.[63] Yet they represent the best that we aspire to.[64]

And so the man of the composite picture of science fiction is more abstract. He is, to be sure, a democratic man.[65] He can be, and at times he is, a tribalist; but his tribal life is not linked to the ideology of the closed society. Whether tribalist or not, he carries his culture or civilization lightly — he bears no cross of civilization and treats its discontents as best he knows how but he does not feel torn between nature and convention. He is tolerant and understanding though his patience is short on inhumanity. How much this image is of the man of the future I cannot possibly guess — it takes too much imagination even to conceive this man, let alone conceive his plausibility or otherwise. But there is always the future which is obscure and yet to come, and the future which is present,[66] dim but forceful, in people's mind. This future, the one expected, aspired, hoped for, is our image of our better selves, the seed of our future philosophy of man.

Notes to Section XXIV

59. The description of "Consciousness III" in Charles A. Reich's best-selling *The Greening of America*, New York, 1970, though very old-fashioned and sentimental, has in it an inkling of the idea of the new character which emerges. " 'I felt lonesome, so I came looking for some people,' a III will say." But I confess that these are only glimmerings. On the whole Reich's idea is tribalism *cum* individualism nourished by the slow experimenting with small communities with the hope of building societies without conflicts between individual ("Consciousness I") and society ("Consciousness II"). I find this to be the central idea of all utopians (see Section XXI and notes 13–15 above). Reich recommends psychedelic drugs, and adds (p. 328) that throughout the book "we have argued that consciousness plays a key role in the shaping of society." This, after the dissipation of the New Left (regardless of its possible rejuvenation), should seem simply a bitter aftertaste to those who had pinned hopes on it as a cultural revolution of sorts, while looking for vigor in the very naive unself-consciousness, not to say sheer ignorance and irrationalism, of the young rebels. The fact that the same intellectuals who adored the New Left also were impressed with Reich's volume I suppose it should be viewed, on the whole, as a quietist expression of the denial of failure.

Charles Reich observes, as a matter of fact, that most Americans are either individualists or collectivists. I think this is a gross exaggeration, even though most (American) social philosophers (and many social scientists) are. This distinction was made already by Malinowski who noted, in *Crime and Custom in Savage Society*, Routledge, London, 1926. "The savage", he says, Part I, Chapter XI, second paragraph, "is neither an extreme 'collectivist' nor an intransigent 'individualist' — he is, like men in general, a mixture of both."

60. The idea of democratizing schools goes to Homer Lane, Janusz Korczak, and Anton Makarenko; that of democratizing hospitals, including psychiatric ones, goes to Maxwell Jones (*The Therapeutic Community: A New Testament Method in Psychiatry*, Basic Books, New York, 1953) and to Robert Robenstein and Harrold D. Lasswell (*The Sharing of Power in a Psychiatric Hospital*, Yale University Press, 1966). The idea of industrial democracy and of neighborhood democracy are both earlier than the above-mentioned ones, yet their applications through job reforms and community centers with local political power are new enough. There is no doubt that to be effective each of these reform movements should bring about far-reaching structural changes. In a sense, these should be mainly matters of decentralization of power; in a sense, they should introduce variety and thus more organicity. Yet, organicity should not mean closed societies, but, on the contrary, may strive to obtain such rules as, anyone can vote in any meeting he actively participates in, regardless of any qualifications, including how long he is in the place [school, plant, hospital, neighborhood], or how old or sane he is, etc. Of course, some meetings will always remain closed or semi-closed.

See Louis E. Davis and James C. Taylor, *Design of Jobs,* Selected Readings, Penguin Books, 1972, which contains both a history and an excellent bibliography. See, in particular, the concluding essay by Einar Thorsrud (1972), "Job Design in the Wider Context", pp. 451–459. I would love to quote it, but it is already extremely condensed and should be read in full.

61.The idea that free society is the society with no wants – and so one which has no use for human robots, for slaves of any kind whatever, is probably ancient, and shared by stoics and cynics alike. That it was part and parcel of the Enlightenment ideology was noted by Marx in *The Holy Family.*

See discussion in H. B. Acton's superb "Moral Futurism and Ethics of Marxism" in P. A. Schilpp, ed., *The Philosophy of Karl Popper,* La Salle, Ill., 1974, pp. 867–888, especially p. 884. See also J. W. N. Watkins' moving essay, "The Strange Face of Evil", *The Listener,* Vol. 52, 1954, September 30, pp. 522–3.

Carl L. Becker, says, in his *Modern Democracy,* Yale University Press, New Haven and London, 1941, p. 12:

"It is not altogether fanciful to suppose that, but for the railroad and the telegraph, the United States would today be divided into many small republics maneuvering for advantage and employing war and diplomacy for maintaining an unstable balance of power . . . the conditions essential to the success of democratic government are mobility, ease of communication . . . [and] a certain measure of economic security . . ."

62. Is the hypocrisy of a law-abiding citizen who dissents from the law increased by his fight for a legal reform while scrupulously going on to keep the law, or is it decreased by his sincere attempt to act on his dissent? I submit that after all the discussions on sincerity and hypocrisy, this question has hardly been noticed, and individual examples were judged and misjudged one way and another quite arbitrarily.

63. The reason that science fiction stories usually depict societies not better than ours is I feel, the fear that the outcome would be a utopia rather than a science fiction. Of course, there are exceptions, such as the best-selling fantasy by Robert Heinlein where earthlings can learn from a Martian all sorts of ideas that Heinlein

considers revolutionary and I consider derivative of vulgar Spinozism. Yet, on the whole, science fiction writers do not describe socially advanced societies, but only technologically advanced on us, for fear of becoming utopians. Consequently they may try to become devoid of social relevance and then they qualify as space operas. Alternatively they can become either anti-utopias or social criticisms or social experiments — and thus not socially advanced.

In consequence there is some confusion about what is anti-utopia and what not, just as much as whether all anti-utopia can qualify as science fiction. This is reflected in the literature as the debate on what was the first anti-utopia. Some say Swift's *Voyage to Laputa*, others that it is Butler's *Erewhon*, and still others insist it is only E. M. Forster's "The Machine Stops" of 1909. Clearly what they want to see is a utopian blueprint plus a nightmare like in Zamyatin, Orwell, or Huxley, and so they disqualify even H. G. Wells's "Time Machine". But then Wells's *When Sleepers Wake* and *First Man on the Moon* should also qualify, and they precede Forster's "The Machine Stops" by a few years. See Fred Polak, *The Image of the Future*, translated and abridged by Elise Boulding, Jossey-Bass, San Francisco, Washington, 1973, pp. 188ff.

And so, I think, all this is a bit overblown, and much science fiction expresses the pleasurable fantasy of the ease with which reason can expose current prejudices such as race prejudices. And it expresses this by describing societies devoid of these prejudices, or by describing societies just like ours except that they discriminate against whites. It sounds silly but it is tremendously gripping to millions of readers who evidently dig it. Abram Tertz [Andrei Sinyavsky], "On Socialist Realism" (translated by George Dennis, Vintage Russian Library, New York, 1968) ends with a very similar idea:

"Right now I put my hope in a phantasmagoric art, with hypotheses instead of a Purpose . . . Such an act would correspond best to the spirit of our time. May the fantastic imagery . . . of . . . realists and nonrealists teach us how to be truthful with the aid of the absurd and the fantastic . . . We don't know where to go . . . we start to think, to set riddles, to make assumptions. May we thus invent something marvellous? Perhaps; but it will no longer be socialist realism."

In this respect, then, science fiction as mild social thought experiment (see Isaac Asimov, "Social Science Fiction", in R. Breknor, ed., *Modern Science Fiction, Its Meaning and Its Future*, New York, 1953, pp. 157–176) comes to replace utopias proper. This view seems to me the one advocated by Fred Polak, *op. cit.*, pp. 100ff.

64. There is no doubt that some science fiction is thinly veiled fascist propaganda, some thinly veiled democratic and egalitarian propaganda. I do not speak of the science fiction literature as a whole but observe that it does contain a remarkable expression of some of our best aspirations. Now it is not that these aspirations are in any way original with science fiction. But whereas elsewhere they occur in spurts, and in high quality at that, in science fiction they appear in a more prosaic way. I wish to quote one example, namely skepticism, which in many a science fiction story has the right tone, yet which elsewhere comes in high prose even if presented as fairly common sense. I should like to quote a passage I like from Gilbert Murry, *Four Stages of Greek Religion*, pp. 152–3:

"There is no royal road in these matters. I confess it seems strange to me as I write here, to reflect that at this moment many of my friends and most of my fellow creatures are, as far as one can judge, quite confident that they possess supernatural knowledge. As a rule, each individual belongs to some body which has received in writing the results of a divine revelation. I cannot share in any such feeling. The uncharted surrounds us on every side and we must needs have some relation towards it, a relation which will depend on the general discipline of a man's mind and the bias of his whole character. As far as knowledge and conscious reason will go, we should follow resolutely their austere guidance. When they cease, as cease they must, we must use as best we can those fainter powers of apprehension and surmise and sensitiveness by which, after all, most high truth has been reached as well as most high art and poetry: careful always really to seek for truth and not for our own emotional satisfaction, careful not to neglect the real needs of men and women through basing our life on dreams; and remembering above all to walk gently in a world where the lights are dim and the very stars wander."

65. The term "democratic man" is from Plato's *Republic*, Bks. VIII and IX.

66. The view that the classical ideal of man — utopianism — must be rejected has been hailed as the end of ideology. This is like the adolescent who, rejecting his own parochial morality, rejects morality as such, thereby showing not enough freedom from parochialism. There is more to morality and to ideology than what we have considered thus far. This is, in brief, the content of the famous and extensive debate on the end of ideology, started by Dennis Wrong.

I must, in fairness to Daniel Bell, quote a passage from his *The End of Ideology, On the Exhaustion of Political Ideas in the Fifties,* revised edition, Free Press, New York, and MacMillan, London, 1962, p. 405:

"The end of ideology is not — should not be — the end of utopia as well. If anything, one can begin anew the discussion of utopia only by being aware of the trap of ideology. The point is that ideologists are "terrible simplifiers." Ideology makes it unnecessary for people to confront individual issues on their individual merits. One simply turns to the ideological vending machine, and out comes the prepared formulae. And when these beliefs are suffused by apocalyptic fervor, ideas become weapons, and with dreadful results.

There is now, more than ever, some need for utopia, in the sense that men need — as they have always needed — some vision of their potential, some manner of fusing passion with intelligence. Yet the ladder to the City of Heaven can no longer be a "faith ladder," but an empirical one: a utopia has to specify *where* one wants to go, *how* to get there, the costs of the enterprise, and some realization of, and justification for, the determination of *who* is to pay."

XXV TOWARDS A RATIONAL PHILOSOPHICAL ANTHROPOLOGY

The question at hand is, what is man? Now, in a preliminary exploration of this question we may ask, what is required of an answer to such a question, and what constraints should we put on it?

I think we must realize first that our conditions — both requirements and constraints — should not be too demanding. What is easier to say than achieve, our answer should be true; the answer should explain as much as possible of the known facts and conflict with none; perhaps even that it explain all known facts and entail new ones. This is but a dream, or a very long-term project.

Whereas all theoreticians engaged in such activities agree that total explanation is not required, they often insist that some explanation must be performed by the new theory. I find this an error: scientific theories of man should; philosophical anthropology only need offer some general ideas. It is felt that Newtonianism, for example, explained at least the movement of the heavenly bodies. This is an error. Newtonian mechanics did, Newtonian metaphysics did not. It only offered interpretations of the facts which could, and at times did, lead to the generation of scientific Newtonian hypotheses. But the metaphysics remained unexplanatory to the last. I. B. Cohen discussed this history at great length, and I discussed the methodology of it, however cursorily, in other places. I do not think I need go into this further now.[67]

Also, most philosophers agree, a theory of man should, at the very least, not conflict with any known facts. Let us consider this slowly. Does the theory, all men are good, contradict the existence of human evil and human malice? I think it does not. If it conflicts with observed evil and malice, then it also explains observed goodness; but in reality it does neither: it does not refer to phenomena but to reality.

And so, it seems, in the case of philosophical anthropology, theory can scarcely conflict with facts, anyway. I do not know if this is true, and at the very least I should say that seeming conflicts abound, and when a seeming conflict is declared real enough then the theory must go. But what I should recommend at first is some measure of tolerance. Examples exist both in the natural sciences and in the social sciences where conflict between theory and observation could be beneficially tolerated for a while.[68]

Hence, a metaphysical theory need not be related to facts one way or another, at least in the first instance. This led almost all thinkers to the hasty conclusion that metaphysical theories gain their validity from *a priori* thinking and that they have a position superior to empirical science. This, of course, is an error too, at the very least because there are competing alternative metaphysical theories and they cannot all be true.

What is required of a metaphysical theory is that it open an interpretation of the facts in a manner suggestive of new scientific hypotheses. For example, when Durkheim says that society is integrated and every member of society does contribute to it somehow, this makes one wonder how criminals contribute to the stability of society. Durkheim said they do so by reminding people of the illegality of crime. Taken to be the whole idea, we may regret that no one ever engages in lynching anymore so as to remind the world that lynching is illegal. But taken as a suggestion, it enabled people to explain the institution of prostitution as one which is both the outcome and the buttress of the institution of wedlock − a theory which may be viewed as scientific in being both explanatory and testable. Perhaps even it is testable enough to have been refuted by the relaxation of marital standards in some communities not accompanied by the reduction of numbers of members of the oldest profession; I cannot judge. Likewise, it was suggested that the black market is essential to a rationing planned economy since the penalty for a planning error may be so high as to make the black market a reduced penalty and so a benefit. Now it is hard to say, how Durkheimian this is (as perhaps Durkheim will deny the existence of defects). But discussions such as those alluded to here may illustrate the desirability of thinking on different levels, metaphysical and scientific, while looking for interactions between the two levels. (Perhaps Robert Merton's addition of dysfunctions to functionalism should be such an example.)

Thus far we studied peculiarities of metaphysical theories, such as meta-sociology and meta-economics. Also we noted at once that Durkheim's ideas pertained to both: they belonged to philosophical anthropology proper. And so, perhaps, we should try to operate simultaneously on diverse levels, scientific, narrow metaphysical, broad metaphysical, and even the broadest level where mechanism and its alternatives may play significant roles.

Thus much for requirements. I now come to discuss constraints, such as the constraint on assumptions regarding morality.

It is not inconsistent with all that has thus far been said in this present and final section, to erect a metaphysical theory which declares man amoral and lacking all freedom and dignity. The trouble with such a metaphysical theory is that it is rooted rather in a moralistic than a scientific concern; and so, not surprisingly, it barely offers an interesting interpretation of the relevant phenomena. As a consequence of this kind of metaphysics, the relevant phenomena were traditionally all too easily disregarded rather than studied.

I should therefore propose that we might now operate with a philosophical anthropology that assumes man to be a moral and rational and a social animal, first and foremost. I also suggest that philosophical anthropology should take at least the rationality of science for granted as a group activity, and should deem the world of science as fairly democratic.[69]

In accord with this, I suggest that the autonomy of both sociology and psychology should be assumed; so that the individual is consequently limited by his society and vice versa. And I suggest that we should view society as natural to the Humean-Smithian extent that the individual has the choice only between society and the deep blue sea, but also as conventional to the Socratic extent that the individual has Socrates' choice to stay in it or to leave it and stay elsewhere – in another society, at least. This may inspire the preference of convention over nature when, and to the extent that, it is at all possible.

It seems to me that these ideas, sparse as they are, offer quite easily a number of interpretations of a number of facts. Some of these have already been developed into scientific theories, explanatory and testable, refuted or not, as the case may be. I speak, in particular, of such studies, theoretical and practical, which pertain to social and legal reform: reform is neither going back to nature, nor the replacement of one arbitrary convention with another equally arbitrary one. Also, I should mention studies pertaining to the individual's problems of adjustment to individuals, such as Szasz's in psychology and the whole literature on penal reform.[70] Other examples would follow suit, and, I presume, with relative ease.

I cannot leave this matter, however, without a final comment on original sin, protestantism, work ethic, and all that. Far as our society is from these in its pluralism, utilitarianism, and competitive character, our society still imposes these curses on us in the oppressive pain and agony of boredom in schools and in factories. That these are nowadays less and less justified by practical argument makes their curse of boredom and conformism only more blatantly the curse of Adam.[71] The sooner we realize that we do not need to reinforce the curse, that human beings suffer enough without our reinforcing their suffering, the better.

It is a fact, I think, that most of the existing social sciences have a moral bias, and a bias in favor of the work ethic, either as an expression of original-sin-theory – we must work in order to expiate for it – or in the utilitarian[72] denial of the same doctrine – we must work because we choose to enjoy the fruit of our labor — or, worst, in a mixture of both doctrines of original sin and hedonism. It is easy to see that all studies of society have moral implication, and almost always in the same circle of ideas.[73]

By and large, social science began as hedonistic. The factual study of ethics in action started with the Romantic reaction to hedonism, especially Hegel's theory of great men as moved by and consumed by great passions which passions in the last resort serve society at large (the cunning of reason, so called). Its peak is Marx's theory of the "Jewish" ethos of capitalism, and Max Weber's theory of the Calvinist ethos of capitalism; all these writers were caught in the dichotomy between collectivist and individualist ethics:[74] which has moral priority, they all asked, the individual or this society? Is the one more irreplaceable than the other? Will we sacrifice the one to save the other? Now, both individualism and collectivism are reductionist, and so answer the question, which is replaceable, in the same way: that which is reducible is replaceable, and so, should be sacrificed first, if need be. But neither is reducible, and, at times, we do sacrifice individual lives so as to protect society — at times lives of innocent bystanders, hostages, etc. There is a limit, and we feel that a time comes when we say, unless we prefer to risk society and try to save individuals, this society is no better than any old dictatorship. These are facts, and facts of the kind that is barely studied, yet of the kind open to empirical studies as well as to vast and far-reaching social-moral reforms.

We have, then, the collectivists who oppose hedonism and the hedonists who oppose collectivism. The controversy is raging in two distinct spheres of moral debate now. The extreme, where sacrifice may be required, and the everyday, stable, ordinary problems. Here, again, we see that the traditional and radical views go together — to the extent of making the very same recommendations: in ordinary circumstances the two doctrines assume no conflict between individual and society but in extreme conditions that which can be reduced should be sacrificed. But what makes it possible to have such a great similarity between the two parties is the mediating pole, the view that the individual can and normally does make allowance. For the collectivist the allowance is obvious: we must make allowance for man's imperfection, for the weakness of his flesh. And for the hedonist it is the idea of deferred gratification, the idea that we must first earn what we later consume and/or enjoy. This makes children work hard even though their adult life is not guaranteed; students prepare for college even though most of them will not make it in college, etc. All this is cock-and-bull. We are adult enough to change it all. The slogan, I believe, is not, pay now and enjoy later; the slogan has to be, the polarization of all conduct into enjoy and pay is obviously false. Even the Marxist utopia is based on giving and taking as separate entities. Yet, life gets exciting in cases not classifiable as more work than play or as vice versa. Life is neither giving nor taking: Nor can one conclude from this denial of the individualistic idea of life as give and take, the affirmation of the collectivist idea that life is sharing: all of these categories are antedeluvian: Living is exchange and transformation; man is, by nature, a progressive animal. [75]

Notes to Section XXV

67. I. B. Cohen, *Franklin and Newton: An Inquiry into Speculative Newtonian Experimental Science and Franklin's Work in Electricity as a Example There of,* American Philosophical Society, Philadelphia, 1956. For my own works see reference in note 66 to Section IV.

68. For details of my recommended toleration of seeming refutations see my "When Should We Ignore Evidence in Favor of a Hypothesis? " *Ratio,* Vol. 15, 1973, pp. 183–205, reprinted in my *Science in Flux,* Reidel, Dordrecht and Boston, 1975.

69. Charles Morgan, *The Writer and His World,* Madrilla, London, 1961, p. 2, expresses this sentiment:
> "We, in our turn, are called upon to regather our strength from Athens and the Renaissance that, after the terrible retrogression which our lives have witnessed, we may prepare a way for what our children or our grandchildren, if they survive, may dare to call the Re-enligthtenment."

70. Leon Radzinowicz, *Ideology and Crime, A Study of Crime in its Social and Historical Context,* London, 1966, clearly outlines (pp. 9–14) the Enlightenment's attitude to criminal law as follows. There should be as little of it as possible; the administration of it should be constrained by the scrupulous protection of the rights of the individual; it should be clear and certain; and so on. He then describes the determinists, whom I shall skip as having no place in my present study. He describes Durkheim's collectivist position (pp. 72–3) stressing only it functionalist aspect. Though Durkheim was a positivist, and though Radzinowicz prefaces his discussion of Durkheim with the endorsement of the charge that Marxists and positivists alike were simplifiers, he believes Durkheim was the man who showed how complex is the pattern of crime (p. 74). Radzinowicz seems then to suggest (pp. 75–7) that the rise of interest in juvenile delinquency was due to the fact that there we cannot avoid notice the natural and the conventional factors intermingle, or rather "interplay", thereby breaking away from traditional naturalism.

Of course, once naturalism is abandoned, the natural disposition is towards conventionalism. Let me quote Radzinowicz here, to show why I consider him (together with Hart) a pioneer in the breaking away from the polarization. He says (p. 81), in regard to E. H. Sutherland's theory of crime as developed through contacts with criminals,

"It is hardly disputable that professional criminals have to learn their techniques or that criminal attitudes and methods are passed on in delinquency areas and groups. Those facts were recognized and profusely illustrated by Mayhew and elevated into the theory of imitation by Tarde. It is the jump from this to the proposition that all crime is necessarily learned that is difficult to accept. The complementary tenet of the theory, which implies that crime also results from inadequate learning to be law abiding, may well be of wider application. Yet this aspect has been neglected by most exponents of the theory and ignored in attempt to test it."

Radzinowicz then discusses Tarde, Poletti, and Arthur Cleveland Hall, all in a Durkheimian manner. He quotes Hall to say that the individual's adjustability to new laws is a significant factor in the determination of crime rate, views this as corroborating Poletti's views, yet he admits it is not quite identical with Durkheim's (pp. 86–7). He seems to view Durkheim's idea of anomie – of crime which is dysfunctional – as a break from functionalism. For my part, I view it as an escape clause against conceivable empirical criticism.

Radzinowicz offers then a few theories of anomie, as malintegration, disintegration, etc. He goes back to juvenile delinquency, ending up (p. 98) with the theory that high crime rate in affluent societies much depends on

"the sheer frequency with which situations present themselves which make crime both tempting and easy . . . This, you will remember, is what Poletti said, and you will remember that Poletti was largely brushed aside."

What, again, seems to fascinate Radzinowicz, is the case of a rapidly moving society – where it is hard to say whether nature or convention is acting.

I cannot sum up Radzinowicz's position; it seems to me that he is looking for a new approach, but that rather than look at the nature *versus* convention dichotomy which he illustrates throughout his volume, he tries to attack the retribution *versus* protection *versus* reform trichotomy (all three alternatives, as he shows, are naturalistic of sorts), and he views the breakaway from them all as the new pragmatism. For my part I can only see in pragmatism the thin edge of the wedge of nihilism and so something which will force us back into naturalism in due course.

71. *Work in America,* Report of a Special Task Force to the Secretary of HEW, Foreword by Elliot L. Richardson, MIT Press, Cambridge, Mass., and London, 1973, claims, p. 79, that "job satisfaction [is] perhaps one of the best ways of extending the length of life", e.g. that coronary heart disease due to known causes, such as cholesterol, blood pressure, smoking, etc. amount to no more than 25% of the cases examined. See also note 60 to Section XXIV above.

72. The work ethic can be used to justify inequality in the name of egalitarian-

ism thus: all men are born equal and all their subsequent inequality of station is the outcome of unequal efforts invested in long-term goal attainment. (That is, great effort plus postponed gratification equal high station.) The popularity of this silly view can be judged from such facts as that Jack London had to contest it in his novels, especially *Martin Eden*, where he explicitly states and repudiates it; the whole novel, indeed, is the tragic story of one who invested too much and postponed gratification too much (not out of conviction, though, but out of brute necessity!). For the historical force of the silly view of all inequality as justified by invested effort, see Reinhard Bendix, *Embattled Reason, Essays in Social Knowledge,* Oxford University Press, New York, 1970, Chapter VIII, opening of the chapter and notes; see also his *Work and Authority in Industry*, John Wiley and Sons, New York, 1956.

73. The old idea that productive work is in the essence of man was offered as new by Feuerbach, and explicitly by Moses Hess, as a means of converting Feuerbach's philosophy to a version of communism, which he (Hess) later transmitted to Engels and Marx. The statement is repeated, for example, in Engels' *Anti-Duhring.* See Robt. C. Tucker, *Philosophy and Myth in Karl Marx,* Cambridge University Press, Cambridge, 2nd edition, 1972, pp. 107–8.

The first to challenge this idea seem to me to be Robert Louis Stevenson, in his "An Apology for Idlers", and Bertrand Russell, e.g. in his "In Praise of Idleness", or *Conquest of Happiness.*

Yet the best and most forceful critic of the classical work ethic is George Bernard Shaw, e.g. preface to his *Too True to be Good.* What he says is, laziness is too easy to practice as far as normal circumstances permit and too difficult from a psychological viewpoint. What the work ethic succeeds to do is to destroy and debase work, just as puritanical ethics destroys the joy of life that it is incumbent of us to cherish, appreciate, enjoy, and be grateful for.

Now, there is obviously an important difference between work, play, and study. It is obvious that Western − puritanical − tradition divides the three more than any other, whereas that the ideal goes the opposite way − of creating conditions under which the three are not separate activities but aspects of one and the same activity. This, I think, was Marx's lofty ideal expressed in a clumsy sentence in *German Ideology* that has gained fame since it is his sole expression of his utopian dream. Utopian, surely, this is; but it need not be so removed from reality as our puritanical organizers contrive to make it: there is a wide scope between the ideal of misanthropy and that of humanism.

74. R. H. Tawney, *Religion and the Rise of Capitalism,* Mentor, New York, 1926, 1954, p. 176, says

"There was in Puritanism an element which was conservative and traditionalist, and an element which was revolutionary; a collectivism . . . and individualism . . .; a sober prudence . . . and a divine recklessness . . ."

Quoted in Charles K. Wilber, "The 'New' Economic History Re-examined: R. H. Tawney on the Origins of Capitalism", *Am. J. Econ. and Soc.*, Vol. 33, 1974, pp. 249–258, p. 254.

It is quite clear, I think, that the inner conflicts of the puritans are both intellectual and emotional, and their projection is therefore so pernicious: it must be attacked on both levels at once.

75. As J. Herman Blake, "After the Ethnic Experience", *The Center Magazine,* Vol. 7 (4), July—August 1974, pp. 44—50, p. 50, puts it
   " . . . I do not recommend an ethos of work, but an ethos of struggle — philosophical struggle, moral struggle, political struggle, ideological struggle."
Yet Blake also says there "we must develop a collective ethic" which I strongly reject.

   L. Eisenberg, "The *Human* Nature of Human Nature", *Science,* Vol. 176, 14 April 1972, pp. 123—8, p. 127, says,
   "The state of man takes its meaning from involvement in the struggle for human betterment. Struggle it is and will be . . ."
The work which adequately expresses the view endorsed here is Robert Louis Stevenson's essay "Pulvis et Umbra", see his *Essays,* Scribner, New York, 1909, pp. 173—181, esp. pp. 176—7
   ". . . . filled with imperfect virtues . . . rising up to do battle for an egg or die for an idea . . . we find in him one thought, strange to the point of lunacy: the thought of duty . . . an ideal of decency. . . . The design of most men is one of conformity; here and there . . . soars . . ."

INDEX OF NAMES

INDEX OF SUBJECTS